D1378406

Spanish Rare Books
of the
Golden Age

guide to the microfilm collection

rp
research publications ®
Woodbridge, CT Reading, England

Research Publications
12 Lunar Drive
Woodbridge, CT 06525
(203) 397-2600

P.O. Box 45
Reading RG1 8HF, England
0734-583247

International Standard Book Number 0-89235-103-9

Printed on acid-free paper

TABLE OF CONTENTS

FOREWORD

It is my pleasure to provide a foreword for this guide to the
microfilm edition of **Spanish Rare Books of the Golden Age.** The
guide details the holdings of the Spanish Golden Age found in the
University of Illinois Library at Urbana-Champaign and
microfilmed by Research Publications. It is based on **The Spanish
Golden Age (1472-1700), A Catalog of Rare Books ...** by Joseph L.
Laurenti and Alberto Porqueras-Mayo (Boston, G.K. Hall, 1979).

In general, the collections of the University of Illinois' Rare
Book and Special Collections Library are strong in holdings of
sixteenth-and seventeenth-century history and literature. The
Spanish holdings can be considered complementary to the notable
British holdings for the same period, and together they are
cultural manifestations of two major political rivals of that
time.

The earliest books represented in the guide and microfilmed for
the collection are medieval works in Latin, written by Spanish
authors or printed in Spain. Although the main arrangement is not
chronological, the next period represented is that of the rise of
vernacular literature in Western Europe during the fifteenth and
sixteenth centuries -- whether translations of Greek and Latin
(and medieval) classics into Spanish, or original works by such
authors as Boscan (died 1542), Antonio de Guevara (died ca.
1545), or Luis de Leon (died 1591). These works show the
development of Spanish prose and poetical styles. Moreover, the
works, particularly those of Antonio de Guevara, were regarded
highly enough outside of Spain to be translated into other
vernacular literatures, including English. A number of Spanish
emblem books, written at a somewhat later date by Saavedra
Fajardo, Horozco y Covarrubias, and Borja, have found their way
into the University of Illinois Library over the past several
decades. The faculty of the Department of Spanish, Italian, and
and Portuguese was most enthusiastic about acquiring books of
this genre in Spanish to augment the already strong emblem book
collections. At the same time rare editions of picaresque novels
by Cervantes, Aleman, and Quevedo were also acquired. I should
mention that as far as bibliographic control of North American
copies of Spanish literature of the Golden Age is concerned, this

guide contains a number of works noted neither by the **National Union Catalog** nor by the on-line data bases OCLC or RLIN as being held by the University of Illinois at Urbana-Champaign. In this Library the originals are only partially cataloged and hence not recorded, but are as accessible to the public as are any cataloged items.

Additional partially cataloged items at Illinois, now part of the microfilm collection, include numerous works by such authors as Ramon Lull, Juan Luis Vives, Pedro Mexia, Luis de Gongora, and Baltasar Gracian, as well as many classics translated into Spanish.

This guide to the microfilm collection lists in excess of one thousand items from the glorious Spanish Golden Age -- works written by Spanish authors, works in classical languages printed in Spain, and works in the Spanish language printed outside of Spain. This is indeed a rich collection.

N. Frederick Nash
Curator of Rare Books
University of Illinois Library
Urbana-Champaign

USAGE AND ACKNOWLEDGMENTS

Spanish Rare Books of the Golden Age: Guide to the Microfilm Collection is arranged alphabetically by main entry. The first word of each entry is underlined for ease of use. Title wording is taken as it appears on the title-page of each work. Notes detail the physical condition of the works, describe other items bound with the works, and provide bibliographic references.

To locate an item in the microfilm collection, note the italicized reel and location number information at the end of the entry. There are 204 35mm microfilm reels in the collection with 1301 consecutively numbered items.

An "Index of Printers" at the end of the guide is arranged alphabetically by printer. The city of printing is listed next to the printer's name. A chronological list by imprint date of the authors printed, abbreviated title, and reel and location information is located beneath each entry.

Our thanks to Mr. Frederick Nash for his invaluable bibliographic assistance throughout the project and for his foreword to this guide. Thanks also to the authors on whose original catalog this guide is based -- Mr. Joseph Laurenti and Mr. Alberto Porqueras-Mayo. Our deepest gratitude to the University of Illinois Library at Urbana-Champaign.

A

ABRABANEL, LEÓN, d. 1535.
Dialoghi di amore, composti per Leone medico, di natione hebreo, et dipoi fatto christiano. [Colophon: In Vinegia: In casa de' figlivoli di Aldo], 1545.
[3], 2-261 (i.e. 241), [1] l.; 16cm.

Third ed.
Nos. 135-154 omitted in paging.
Palau, 420; Short-Title, I, p. 5.
Reel 1, No. 1

ABRABANEL, LEÓN, d. 1535.
Dialoghi di amore, composti per Leone medico, di natione hebreo, et dipoi fatto christiano. Vinegia: In casa di Figlivoli di Aldo, 1549.
228 l.; 16cm.

Palau, 421; Short-Title, I, p. 5.
Reel 1, No. 2

ABRABANEL, LEÓN, d. 1535.
Dialoghi di amore, composti per Leone medico, di natione hebreo, et dipoi fatto christiano. Aldi Filli in Vinegia, 1552.
228 l.; 16cm.

Palau, 422; Short-Title, I, p. 5.
Reel 1, No. 3

ABRAHAM BEN MOSES BEN MAIMON see MOSES BEN MAIMON.

ABRAVANEL, ISAAC.
Liber De Capite Fidei, In quo continentur radices & capita vel principia religionis. Avtore Isaaco Abravanele. Et in latinum sermonem translata per Gvilielmvm Vorstivm C.F. Amstelodami: Apud Gviliel. & Iohannem Blaev., 1638.
118, [9] p.; 20cm.

Bound in: Moses ben Maimon. Constitvtiones De Fvndamentis Legis Rabbi Mosis F. Mailemon..., 1638.
Reel 115, No. 731

ABRIL, PEDRO SIMÓN (translator) see CICERO, MARCUS TULLIUS.

ACHILLES, TATIUS.
Amorosi Ragionamenti. Dialogo Nel Qvale si Racconta Vn Compassionevole Amore Di Dve Amanti... Vinegia: Appresso Gariel Giolito de Ferrari, 1546.
56, [1] l.

Colophon: "Stampato in Venetia per Bernardino de Viano, de Lexona Vercellese: nel anno del nostro Signore Miser Iesu Christo M.D. XXI, Adi vintido de zugno."
Bound in: San Pedro, Diego de: Carcel de amor, n.d.
Reel 164, No. 1074

ACOSTA, CRISTÓBAL DE, ca. 1540-1599.
Tratado en loor de las mugeres. Venetia: Giacomo Cornetti, 1592.
133, [15] l; 21cm.

Jerez, p. 1; Penney, p. 5; Salvá, I, 1619; Simon Díaz, IV, 1415; Short-Title, I, p. 11.
Reel 1, No. 4

ACOSTA, JOSÉ DE, ca. 1539-1600.
Historia natvral y moral de las Indias, en qve se tratan las cosas notables del cielo, y elementos, metales, plantas, y animales dellas: y los ritos, y ceremonias, leyes, y gouierno, y guerras de los Indios. Compuesta por el padre Joseph de Acosta religioso de la Compañia de Jesus. Dirigida a la serenissima infanta Doña Isabella Clara Eugenia de Austria. Seuilla: Impr. en casa de Iuan de Leon, 1590.
535, [36] p.; 21cm.

Imperfect: lacks t.-p. and pp. 529-530.
Escudero, 772; Graesse, p. 15; Palau, 1918; Simón Díaz, IV, 1464.
Reel 1, No. 5

ACOSTA, JOSÉ DE, ca. 1539-1600.
Iosephi Acosta ... De natvra novi orbis libri dvo. et de promvlgatione evangelii apvd barbaros, siue De procvranda Indorvm salute, libri sex. Coloniae Agrippinae, in officina Birckmannica: sumptibus Arnoldi Mylij, 1596.
[16], 581 p.; 21cm.

Title vignette; tail-pieces; initials.
Bartlett, 492; Graesse, p. 15; HC, 346 / 768; Palau, 1979; Penney, p. 5; Simón Díaz, IV, 1481.
Reel 1, No. 6

ACOSTA, JOSÉ DE, ca. 1539-1600.
Historia natvrale, e morale delle Indie; scritta dal R. P. Gioseffo di Acosta della Compagnia del Giesù; nella quale si trattano le cose notabili del cielo, et de gli elementi, metalli, piante, et animali di quelle: i suoi riti, et cerimonie: leggi, et gouerni, et guerre degli Indiani. Nouamente tradotta della lingua spagnuola nella italiana da Gio. Paolo Galvcci ... Venetia: Presso Bernardo Basa, 1596.
[24], 173 l.; 22cm.

Italian translation by Gio. Paolo Galucci.
Graesse, p. 15; Palau, 1991; Penney, p. 6; Simón Díaz, IV, 1512; Toda y Güell, 21; Short-Title, I, p. 11.
Reel 2, No. 7

ACOSTA, JOSÉ DE, ca. 1539-1600.
Histoire natvrelle et morale des Indes, tant Orientalles qu'Occidentalles. Où il est traitté des choses remarquables du ciel, des elemens, metaux, plantes & animaux que sont propres de ce païs. Ensemble des moeurs, ceremonies, loix, gouuernemens, & guerres des mesmes Indiens. Composée en castillan par Ioseph Acosta. & traduite en François par Robert Regnault Cauxois. Paris: Marc Orry, 1598.
[8], 375, [16] l.; 18cm.

French translation by Robert Regnault Cauxois.
Bartlett, 519; Graesse, p. 15; HC:327 / 368; Palau, 1996; Penney, p. 6; Simón Díaz, IV, 1502.
Reel 2, No. 8

ACOSTA, JOSÉ DE, ca. 1539-1600.
Histoire natvrelle et moralle des Indes, tant Orientalles qu'Occidentalles. Où il est traitté des choses remarquables du ciel, des elemens, metaux, plantes & animaux que sont propres de ce païs. Ensemble des moeurs, ceremonies, loix, gouuernemens, & guerres des mesmes Indiens. Composée en castillan par Ioseph Acosta. & traduite en François par Robert Regnault Cauxois. 2. ed. Paris. M. Orry, 1606.
8, 352, 19 l.; 18cm.

Bartlett, 2/43; Palau, 1988; Simón Díaz, IV, 1504.
Reel 2, No. 9

ACOSTA, JOSÉ, DE, ca. 1539-1600.
The natvrall and morall historie of the East and
West Indies. Intreating of the remarkeable things of
heauen, of the elements, mettalls, plants and beasts
which are proper to that country: together with the
manners, ceremonies, laws, governements, and warres
of the Indians. Written in Spanish by Joseph Acosta,
and translated into English by E. G. London: Printed
by Val Sims for E. Blount and W. Aspley, 1604.
[22], 590 p.; 19.5cm.

English translation by E. G. i.e. Edward Grimeston.
Allison, 1; Palau, 1996; Graesse, p. 15; Pollard and
Redgrave, 94; Simón Díaz, IV, 1509.
Reel 2, No. 10

ACOSTA, JOSÉ DE, ca. 1539-1600.
America, oder wie mans zu teutsch nennt die neuwe
welt, oder West India ... In sieben buchern, eins
theils in lateinischer, und eins theils in hispanischer
sprach, beschrieben ... Ursel, 1605.
[74] p.: maps.

German translator unknown.
Palau, 56; Simón Díaz. IV, 1500.
Reel 2, No. 11

ACOSTA, JOSÉ DE, ca. 1539-1600.
Historie naturael en morael van de Westersche
Indien ... Door Ian Huyghen van Linschoten. De
tweede editie. Amsterdam: By Broer Jansz, 1624.
5 p., 177, [4] l: ill., (13 Woodcuts).; 20cm.

Dutch translation by Jan Huyghen van Linschoten.
Graesse. p. 15; Palau, p. 56.
Reel 2, No. 12

ADVERTENCIAS para saberse portar una persona provecta
en un Gobierno de Indias.
6 manuscript l.
Bound with: HERRERA Y SOTOMAYOR, JACINTO DE, fl.
1644. Iornada que su Magestad hizo a la Andalvzia.
[Madrid: En la Imprenta Real, 1624].
Palau, 114276 (List only printed folios 1-6).
Reel 77, No. 484.22

AGRIPPA VON NETTESHEIM, HEINRICH CORNELIUS, 1486?-
1535.
Henrici Agrippes Ab Nettesheym De incertitudine
& Vanitate scientiarum declamatio inuectiua, denuo
ab autore recognita & marginalibus aucta. Capita
tractandorum totius operis, sequens indicabit
pagella. [s.l.: s.n.] 1536.
[5], 410 p.; 16cm.

Bound in: Vives, Juan Luis: Ioannis Lvdovici Viuis
Valentini, de Disciplinis Libri XX ..., 1536.
Reel 195, No. 1257

AGUSTÍN, ANTONIO, abp. of Tarragona, 1517-1586.
...Amendationum et opinionum, libri quatuor ...
Lugduni: Apud. Seb. Griphicum, 1544
372, [43] p.; 18cm.

Palau, v. I, p. 116; Simón Díaz, IV, 2442.
Reel 3, No. 13

AGUSTÍN, ANTONIO, abp. of Tarragona, 1517-1586.
Antonii Avgvstini archiepiscopi Tarraconensis De legibvs
et senatvs consvltis liber. Adiunctis legum antiquarum et
senatusconsultorum fragmentis, cum notis Fvlvi Vrsini.
Romae: ex typographia Dominici Basae, 1583.
[16], 339 p.; [70], 54 p.; 20cm.

Graesse, p. 252; Palau, 4075; Simón Díaz, IV, 2463;
Toda y Guël, I, 64.
Reel 3, No. 17

AGUSTÍN, ANTONIO, abp. of Tarragona, 1517-1586.
Antonii Avgvstini ... Antiqvitatvm romanarvm
hispanarvmqve in nvmmis vetervm dialogi XI. Latinè
redditi ab Andrea Schotto ... cuius accessit duodecimus,
De prisca religione, diisque gentium. Seorsim editae
numismatvm icones, a Iacob Biaeo, aeri graphicè
incisae. Antverpiae: apud Henricum Aertssium, 1617.
[18], 182, [22] p., 68 l.; 20cm.

Device of printer on t.-p.; head and tailpieces;
initials.
Errors in paging: no. 78 repeated, 79 omitted, p. 125
numbered 119.
"Vita Antonii Avgvstini ex oratione ... And Schotti":
7th-9th prelim. leaves.
"Qvi de nomismatis scripserint et icones hibverint":
p. 181-182.
HC 327/1312; Penney, p. 11; Palau, 4108; Simón
Díaz, IV, 2480.
Reel 4, No. 18

AGUSTÍN, ANTONIO, abp. of Tarragona, 1517-1586.
Antonii Avgvstini ... Antiqvitatvm romanarvm
hispanarvmqve in nvmmis vetervm dialogi XI. Latinè
redditi ab Andrea Schotto ... cuius accessit duodecimus,
De prisca religione, diisque gentium. Seorsim editae
numismatvm icones, a Iacob Biaeo, aeri graphicè incisae.
Antverpiae: Apud Henricvm Aertssens, 1653.
[17], 202, [19] p.; 37cm.

Palau, V.I, p. 118; Simón Díaz, IV, 2481.
Reel 4, No. 19

AGUSTÍN, ANTONIO, abp. of Tarragona, 1517-1586.
Dialoghi di don Antonio Agostini, arcivescovo di
Tarracona, intorno alle medaglie, inscrittioni, et
altre antichità. Tradotti di lingua spagnuola in
italiana da Dionigi Ottaviano Sada, e di nvovo
accrescivti con diverse annotationi, e illustrati
con disegni di molte medaglie, e d'altre figure ...
In Roma: Appresso Andrea Fei à spese di Pompilio
Totti, et Andrea Montano, 1625.
6 p. l., 300, [32] p. ill.; 33cm.

Title vignette; initials; head and tail-pieces.
Colophon: "In Roma, appresso Gulielmo Faciotto.
CIƆIƆXCII."
Italian translation by Dionigi Ottaviano Sada.
Palau, 4103; Simón Díaz, IV, 2475.
Reel 4, No. 22

AGUSTÍN, ANTONIO, abp. of Tarragona, 1517-1586.
Familiae Romanae In Antiqvis Nvmismatibvs, Ab Vrbe
Condita, Ad Tempora Divi Avgvsti. Ex Bibliotheca
Fvlvii Vrsini, Cum adiunctis Antonij Augustini, Episc.
Ilerdensis. Carolvs Patin, Doctor Medicvs Parisiensis,
Restitvit, Recognovit, Avxit. [Printer's device]
Parisiis: Apud Ioannem Dv Bray, via Iacobaea, sub
signo Craticulae, prope S. Benedictum. Et Robertvm de
Ninville, in via dicta de la Vieille Bouclerie, sub
signo Scuti Franciae & Nauarrae. [n.d.] [1663].
41, 429, [1] p.: ill., 2 port.; 38cm.

Simón Díaz, IV, 2454.
Reel 5, No. 23

AGUSTÍN, ANTONIO, abp. of Tarragona, 1517-1586.
[Verrius Flaccus, Marcus.] M. Verri Flacci Qvae
extant. Et Sex. Pompei Festi De Verborvm significatione,
lib. XX. In eundem Festum annotationes. Index rerum
obiter dictarum. Ex. bibliotheca Antonij Augustini.
Cum priuilegijs. Venetiis: ex officina Stelle Iordani
Zilleti, 1560.
[29], DVII, [177], p.; 18cm.

The notes are by Antonio Agustín.
Simón Díaz, IV, 2446.
Reel 3, No. 14

AGUSTÍN, ANTONIO, abp. of Tarragona, 1517-1586.
[Verrius Flaccus, Marcus.] M. Verri Flacci Qvae
extant. Et Sex. Pompei Festi De Verborvm significatione,
lib. XX. In eundem Festum annotationes. Index rerum
obiter dictarum. Ex. bibliotheca Antonij Augustini.
Cum priuilegijs. Parisiis: apud Arnoldum Sittart,
sub Scuto coloniensi monte diui Hilarij, 1584.
[28], cccix, [26], LXXV, CCXVI, [23], 84 p.; 17cm.

Simón Díaz, IV, 2446.
Reel 3, No. 15

AGUSTÍN, ANTONIO, abp. of Tarragona, 1517-1586.
[Verrius Flaccus, Marcus.] M. Verri Flacci Qvae
extant. Et Sex. Pompei Festi De Verborvm significatione,
lib. XX. In eundem Festum annotationes. Index rerum
obiter dictarum. Ex. bibliotheca Antonij Augustini.
Cum priuilegijs. [Heidelbergae]: apud Petrum
Santandreanum, 1593.
[30], cccix, [26], lxxv, [11], ccxvi, [26],
84 p.; 17cm.

Many errors in numbering of pages.
Device of printer on t.-p.
A reprint of the 1584 Paris edition, with the
addition of 84 (i.e. 80) pages of notes at the end.
In manuscript on t.-p.: Christiani Rheineri;
annotations in margins and inside back cover.
Reel 3, No. 16

AGUSTÍN, ANTONIO, abp. of Tarragona, 1517-1586.
Varro, Marcus Terentius. M. Terentii Varronis Opera
omnia qvae extant. Cum notis Iosephi Scaligeri, Adriani
Turnebi, Petri Victorii, et Antonii Augustini. His
accedunt tabvlae navfragii, seu fragmenta ejusdem
auctiora et meliora, additis ad singula loca, autorum
nominibus unde haec petita sunt. Durdrechti: ex
officinâ Ioannis Berevvout, 1619.
[5], 48, 77, 129, [18], [3] - 143, [76], 255, [22],
242, [2] p.; 19cm.

Device of printer on t.-p. and on verso of last
leaf; head-pieces; initials.
A re-issue of the edition of Esteinne first
published in 1573.
Simón Díaz, IV, 2444.
Reel 4, No. 20

AGUSTÍN, ANTONIO, abp. of Tarragona, 1517-1586.
Varro, Marcus Terentius. M. Terentii Varronis Opera
omnia qvae extant. Cum notis Iosephi Scaligeri, Adriani
Turnebi, Petri Victorii, et Antonii Augustini. His
accedunt tabvlae navfragii, seu fragmenta ejusdem
auctiora et meliora, additis ad singula loca, autorum
nominibus unde haec petita sunt. Amstelodami: apud
Ioannem Iansonium, 1623.
2 p. l., 129, [18], 77, 48, 143, [74], 224, 242
(i.e. 240), [20] p.; 19.5cm.

AGUSTÍN (Cont'd)
Closely related to the above 1619 edition of
Dordrecht, which in turn is based upon the edition
of 1573 edited by H. Estienne.
Imperfect: p. 99-114 and p. 163-178 (last group of
numbered pages): 9-11 omitted; 12 repeated.
Illus. t.-p., engr. Head-pieces; initials.
Simón Díaz, IV, 2444.
Reel 4, No. 21

ALAMOS, BALDASSARE see ALMOS DE BARRIENTOS, BALTASAR.

ALAMOS DE BARRIENTOS, BALTASAR, 1550-1640.
[Opera. Italian]
Opere Di G. Cornelio Tacito, Annali, Historie,
Costumi de' Germani, E Vita Di Agricola, Illvstrate
Con Notabilissimi Aforismi Del Signor D. Baldassar'
Alamo Varienti, Trasportati dalla lingua Castigliana
nella Toscana Da D. Girolamo Canini D'Anghiari
Aggiuntoui dal Medesimo il Modo di Cauar profitto
dalla Lectura di questo Autore, E la vita di Tacito,
le Testimonianze fatte di lui dagli Antichi Scrittori,
l'Arbore della Famiglia di Avgvsto, le Postille in
margine del Lipsio, la Cronologia dell'Avberto, Et in
questa seconda Impressione molti Confronti di cinque
Traduttioni, col Testo Latino ne' luoghi piu scabrosi,
& il Disegno in rame dell'Imperio Romano. Arrichite
di tre copiosissimi, & ordinatissimi Indici; l'vno
delle voci, e delle materie Historiali, e Politiche
del Testo, il secondo delgi Aforismi, & il terzo de'
nomi antichi piu oscuri de' luoghi della Germania,
e di altre Prouincie. Il tutto migliorato, e di nuouo
corretto, abbellito, & accomodato alla Traduttione
del Sig. Adriano Politi. In Venetia: Appresso I.
Givnti, 1620.
77, 554 (i.e. 550), [58], 83, [296] p.: incl.
double map.; 27cm.

Italian translation by Girolamo Canini
d'Anghiari.
Half-title: G. Cornel Tacito Illvstrato Sec.
Impres.
"Aforismi" in smaller type in margin of text.
Errors in paging: no. 281-282 omitted; no. 483-490
repeated.
Ex-libris: Cecilia Isabella Finch.
Simón Díaz, V, 60.
Reel 5, No. 24

ALBORNOZ, DIEGO FELIPE DE.
Cartilla politica, y christiana. Ofrecela a los
pies del Rey Nvestro Señor: y para que llegue
decentemente à ellos, la pone ... Diego Felipe de
Albornoz. Madrid: por M. Sánchez, A costa de M. de
la Bastida, 1666.
[8], 90, [24] l.; 21cm.

Simón Díaz, V, 239.
Reel 5, No. 25

ALBURQUERQUE, BELTRÁN DE CUEVAS, duque de, d. 1492.
Maiorazgo che fece l'illvstriss. sign. Duca
d'Alburcherche de gli suoi stati, con quella facultà,
che per farlo hebbe dalla Maesta del Rè di Castiglia.
Milano: I.B. Ponte [n.d.].
[52] p.: fold. general table; 20cm.

Reel 5, No. 26

ALBURQUERQUE, DIEGO DE.
Sermon, que predicó el Padre ..., en el Cóvéto de S.
Antonio de Sevilla, a las onras, que hizo el insigne
Colegio de San Buenaventura, en la muerte del
Reverendissimo P. General Frai Iuan del Hierro.
Sevilla: Alonso Rodriguez Gamarra, 1613.
16 *l*.; 21cm.

Simón Díaz, V, 255.
Reel 5, No. 27

ALCIATI, ANDREA, 1492-1550.
Andreae Alciati Emblemata cvm commentariis Clavdii
Minois i.c. Francisci Sanctii Brocensis, & notis
Lavrentii Pignorii Patavini. Nouissima hac editione
in continuam vnius commentarij seriem congestis, in
certas quasdam quasi classes dispositis, & plusquam
dimidia parte auctis, opera et bigiliis Ioannis Thyilii
Mariae montani Tirol ... Opus copiosa sententiarum,
apophthegmatum, adagiorum, fabularum, mythologiarum,
hieroglyphicorum, nummorum, picturarum & linguarum
varietate instructum & exornatum ... Accesserunt in
fine Federici Morelli ... Corollaria & monita, ad
eadem Emblemata Cvm indice triplici. Patauij: typis
Pauli Frambotti bibliopolae, 1661.
LXXX, 905 p. ill.; 24cm.

Added illus. title-page, engraving.
Device of printer on title-page; initials; head and
tail-pieces.
212 emblems, including the tree series (nos. CXCIX -
CCXII) each emblem followed by commentary in double
columns.
Book-plate of Giacomo de Toma.
Not in Palau's ...
Reel 5, No. 28

ALCIATI, ANDREA, 1492-1550.
Declaracion Magistral Sobre Los Emblemas De Andres
Alciato. Con Todas Las Historias, Antigvedades,
Moralidad, Y Doctrina, Tocante A Las Bvenas Costvmbres.
Dedicadas A La Mvy Noble Insigne, Leal, Y Coronada
Civdad De Valencia. [Printer's mark]. En Valencia:
por Geronimo Vilagrasa, A costa de Geronimo Sanchiz,
Mercader de libros, à la placa de la Seo, enfrente
de la puerta de los Apostoles, 1670.
[9], 706 (i.e. 716), 15 p.: ill.; 21cm.

Spanish translation with commentary by Diego López.
HC419/3; Penney, p. 15.
Reel 6, No. 30

ALCIATI, ANDREA, 1492-1550.
Los emblemas de Alciato, traducidos en rhimas españolas
[por Bernardino Daza Pincinano (i.e. Pinciano)], añadidos
de figuras y de nuevos emblemas en la tercera parte de
la obra. En Lyon: M. Bonhome, Gvilielmo Rovillio, 1549.
256 p. Ill.; 19cm.

Spanish translation by Bernardino Daza Pinciano.
[In his Emblemata, 1548].
Gallardo, 1992; Quaritch. Cat. 148/85; Salvá, 2044;
Penney, p. 15.
Reel 6, No. 29

ALDOVERA Y MONSALVE, JERÓNIMO DE, 1564-1630.
Discvrsos En Las Fiestas De Los Santos, Qve La Iglesia
Celebra sobre los Euangelios que en ellas dize. Compvestos
Por El P. Maestro F. Geronimo de Aldouera y Monsalue, de la
Orden de N. P. S. Agustin, Catedratico de Visperas jubilado
en la Vniuersidad de Caragoca, Calificador del S. Oficio
de la Inquisicion, y dos vezes Prouincial en la Prouincia de
la Corona de Aragon. A la Imperial Ciudad de Caragoca. Tomo
Primero. [Printer's device]. Con Licencia. En Caragoca:
Por Pedro Cabarte, Impresor del Reyno de Aragon, 1625.
[32], 820, [60] p.; 21cm.

ALDOVERA Y MONSALVE (Cont'd)
Colophon: "En Caragoca. Por Pedro Cabarte, Impressor de
Reyno de Aragon, año M.DC. XXV."
Palau, 6392; Penney, p. 15; Simón Díaz, V, no. 617;
Toda y Güell, Italia, no. 119.
Reel 6, No. 31

ALDRETE, BERNARDO JOSÉ, 1565-1645.
Del Origen, Y Principio De La Lengva Castellana O
Romáce que oi se usa en España Por el Doctor Bernardo
Aldrete Canonigo en la Sancta Iglesia de Cordoua [Coat
of arms] Dirigido Al Rei Catholico De Las Españas Don
Philippe III - Deste Nombre Nestro Señor. En Roma:
acerca de Carlo Wllietto (sic), en el año del Señor
1606.
[9], 371, [19] p.; 22cm.

Engraved t.-p.
Colophon: "En Roma, Por Carlo Vulliet, MDCVI."
Palau, 6392; Penney, p. 15; Simón Díaz, V, no. 617;
Toda y Güell, Italia, no. 119.
Reel 6, No. 32

ALDRETE, BERNARDO JOSE, 1565-1645.
Del Origen Y Principio De La Lengva Castellana ò
Romance que oy se vsa en España. Compvesto Por El Doctor
Bernardo Aldrete, Canonigo En La Santa Iglesia de Cordova.
Al Señor Don Gregorio Altamirano Portocarrero, Cauallero
de la Orden de Santiago, del Consejo de su Magestad
en el de Hazienda, y su Contaduria mayor, Contador mayor
de la Orden, y Cavalleria de Alcantara, &c. [Printer's
device]. Con Privilegio. En Madrid: por Melchor
Sanchez. A costa de Gabriel de Leon, Mercader de
Libros, vendese enfrente de la calle de la Paz, 1674.
[4], 89 *l*.; 31cm.

Bound with: Covarrubias Orozco, Sebastian de. Parte
primera (and Parte segunda) del tesoro de la lengva
Castellana; o Española.
Reel 6, No. 33

ALDRETE, BERNARDO JOSÉ, 1565-1645.
Varias Antigvedades De España Africa Y Otras Provincias
Por el Doctor Bernardo Aldrete Canonigo en la Sancta
Iglesia de Cordoua. En Amberes: a costa de Iuan Hasrey,
1614.
[24], 640, [73] p.; 23.5cm.

Engr. title-page: Domine tu nouisti omnia nouissima
et antiqua. (At center:) TE ducente nouos HISPANIA
detegit orbes.
Colophon: Antverpiae, Typis Gerardi Wolsschatii,
Et Henrici Aertsii. Anno cIↃ. IↃc.XV.
Cosens, no. 64; Peeters-Fontainas, I, no. 30; Simón
Díaz, V, no. 620.
Reel 7, No. 35

ALEMÁN, MATEO, 1547-1616?
Primera Parte De La Vida Del Picaro Gvzman De
Alfarache. Compvesto Por Matheo Aleman, criado del Rey
Don Phelipe. III nuestro Señor, y natural vezino de
Seuilla. Dirigido a Don Francisco de Roxas Marques
de Poza, Señor de la casa de Moncon. Presidente del
Consejo de la hazienda de su Magestad, y tribunales
della. [Printer's device]. Con licencia. En
Caragoca: Por Angelo Tauanno, 1603.
[8], 207 *l*.; 15cm.

Bookplate of Antonio Almunia de Proxita y de León.
Binding signed by P. López - Valencia.
Doublet, p. 23; Jerez, p. 3; Jiménez-Catalán, no.
21; Laurenti, no. 1131; Salvá, II, 1697; Simón Díaz,
V, 718.
Reel 7, No. 36

ALEMÁN, MATEO, 1547-1616?
Vida Y Hechos Del Picaro Gvzman De Alfarache. Atalaya De La Vida Humana. Por Mateo Aleman Criado del Rey nuestro Señor, y natural Vezino de Sevilla. Nueva Impression, corregida de muchas erratas, y enriquescida con muy lindas Estampas. Parte Primera. [Printer's device]. En Amberes: Por Geronymo Verdussen, Impressor y Mercader de Libros, en el Leon dorado, 1681.
2 v. ([15], 299, [4] p.; [17], 396, [5] p.); 20cm.

Imperfect: plates and illus. half-title wanting.
Jerez, p. 3; Laurenti, no. 1150; Peeters-Fontainas, I, no. 35; Simón Díaz, V, 735.
Reel 7, No. 37

ALEMÁN, MATEO, 1547-1616?.
The Rogve: Or The Life of Gvzman De Alfarache, Written in Spanish by Matheo Aleman, Seruant to his Catholike Maiestie, and borne in Sevill. [Printer's device]. London: Printed for Edward Blount, 1622.
[25], 267 p.; 29cm.

[Pt. 2:]. The Rogve: Or The Second Part Of The Life Of Gvzman De Alfarache. Written In Spanish by Matheo Aleman, Seruant to his Catholike Maiestie, and borne in Sevill. [Pinter's mark]. London: Printed by G. E. for Edward Blovnt, 1623.
[17], 357 p.

Pts. 1-2 in 1 vol.
English translation by James Mabbe.
Allison, p. 18, no. 6; Pollard and Redgrave, no. 288; Simón Díaz, V, 876; Laurenti, no. 1281.
Reel 7, No. 39

ALEMÁN, MATEO, 1547-1616?
The Rogve: Or The Life Of Gvzman De Alfarache. Written In Spanish by Matheo Aleman, Seruant to his Catholike Maiestie, and borne in Sevill. [Printer's device]. London: Printed for Edward Blount, 1623.
[24], 267 p.; 29cm.

[Pt. 2:] The Rogve: Or The Second Part Of The Life Of Gvzman De Alfarache. Written In Spanish by Matheo Aleman, Seruant to his Catholike Maiestie, and borne in Sevill. [Printer's device]. London: Printed by G. E. for Edward Blovnt, 1623.
[17], 357 p.

Pts. 1-2 in 1 vol.
English translation by James Mabbe.
Allison, p. 18, no. 6.1; Laurenti, no. 1282; Pollard and Redgrave, no. 289; Simón Díaz, V, 877.
Reel 8, No. 40

ALEMÁN, MATEO, 1547-1616?.
The Rogve: Or, The Life Of Gvzman De Alfarache. Written In Spanish by Matheo Aleman, Servant to his Catholike Majestie, and borne in Sevill. [Printer's device]. Oxford: Printed by William Tvrner, for Robert Allot, and are to be sold in Pauls Church-yard, Ann. Dom. 1630.
[37], 267 p.; 29cm.

[Pt. 2:]. The Rogve Or, The Second Part Of The Life Of Gvzman De Alfarache. Written In Spanish by Matheo Aleman, Servant to his Catholike Majestie, and borne in Sevill. [Printer's mark]. Printed by W.T. for Robert Allott. Ann. Dom. 1630.
[17], 357 p.

Pts. 1-2 in 1 vol.
English translation by James Mabbe.
Allison, p. 18, no. 6.2; Graesse, p. 66; Laurenti, no. 1283; Pollard and Redgrave, no. 290; Simón Díaz, V, 878.
Reel 8, No. 41

ALEMÁN, MATEO, 1547-1616?.
The Rogve: or, The life of Gvzman De Alfarache. Written in Spanish by Meteo Aleman... To which is added, the Tragi-Comedy of Calisto and Melibea, represented in Celestina. The third edition corrected. [Printer's device]. London: Printed by R.B. for Robert Allot, and are to be sold at his Shop in Pauls Church-yard, at the Signe of the blacke Beare. An. Dom. 1634.
[37], 267 p.; 29cm.

[Pt. 2:]. The Rogve Or, The Second Part Of The Life Of Gvzman De Alfarache. Written in Spanish by Matheo Aleman, Servant to his Catholike Majestie, and borne in Sevill. [Printer's device]. London: Printed by R. B. for Robert Allott, Anno Dom. 1633.
[17], 357 p.

Pts. 1-2 in 1 vol.
English translation by James Mabbe.
Allison, p. 18, 6.3; Graesse, p. 66; Laurenti, no. 1284; Pollard and Redgrave, no. 291; Simón Díaz, V, 879.
Reel 8, No. 42

ALEMÁN, MATEO, 1547-1616?
The Rogue, Or The Life of Gvzman De Alfarache: In two Parts. Written In Spanish By Matheo Aleman, Servant to his Catholick Majesty, and born in Sevil. The fourth Edition corrected. [Printer's device]. London: Printed by W. B. for Phillip Chetwind, 1656.
[19], 207 p.; 29cm.

[Pt. 2. book I:]. The Rogue Or, The Second Part Of The Life Of Guzman De Alfarache. The first Book.
63 p.
[Pt. 2. book II:]. The Rogue Or, The Second Part Of The Life of Guzman De Alfarache. The second Book.
101 p.
[Pt. 2. book III:]. The Rogue: Or, The Second Part Of The Life Of Guzman De Alfarache. The third Book.
116 p.

Pts. 1-2.
English translation by James Mabbe.
Allison, p. 18, 6.5; Graesse, p. 66; Laurenti, no. 1286; Palau, 6785; Simón Díaz, V, 881; Ticknor, p. 8; Wing A.903a.
Part 2, Books 2 & 3: Not Available
Reel 8, No. 43

ALEMÁN, MATEO, 1547-1616?
Le Gvevx Ov La Vie De Gvzman D'Alfarache, Image de la vie humaine. En laquelle toutes les fourbes & toutes les meschancetez qui se pratiquent dans le monde. sont plaisamment & vtilement descouuertes. Divise En Trois Livres. [Printer's device]. A Roven: Chez Iean De La Mare, au haut des degrez du Palais, 1632.
[17], 389, [42] p.; 16cm.

[Pt. 2:] Le Volevr Ov La Vie De Gvzman D'Alfarache. Povrtraict Dv Temps, & Miroir de la Vie Humaine. Seconde Partie. Où toutes les fourbes & meschancetez qui se font dans le monde sont vtilement & plaisamment descouuertes. Piece non encore veuë, & renduë fidelement de l'original Espagnol de son premier & veritable autheur, Mateo Alleman. Derniere Edition. [Printer's device]. A Roven: Chez Iean De La Mare, au haut des degrez du Palais. [Line], 1633.
[24], 549, [4] p.

Pt. 1-2 in 1 vol.
French translator unknown.
Laurenti, no. 1208; Simón Díaz, V, 807.
Reel 7, No. 38

ALFARO, GREGORIO DE, tr.
   Govierno ecclesiastico y seglar qve contiene el pastoral del gloriosissimo Padre S. Gregorio el magno papa y monge de la Orden de S. Benito, traduzido de Latin en romance, cō vn Tratado de Republica compvesto por el P. Fr. Gregorio de Alfaro ... Alcalá: Por Justo Sánchez Crespo, 1604.
   [23], 494, [47] p.; 20cm.

   Title page and following 3 leaves mutilated, affecting imprint and text.
   Catalina, no. 779; HC: 387/908; Palau, 6988; Penney, p. 244; Simón Díaz, V, 1006.
Reel 8, No. 44

ALFONSO X, el Sabio, King of Castilla and Leon.
   Tabulae astronomicae. Tabule Astronomice Alfonsi Regis. Exhortatoria in impressionē tabularū Astronomicarū Alfonsi Regis. [Venice: Johannes Hammam, Oct. 31, 1492].
   114 l. 5ª: 43 lines, 154 x 108 mm. Woodcut capitals, also spaces. Diagrams: woodcut border-pieces in quires g and h.; 29.5cm.

   Colophon: Expliciunt Tabule tabularum Astronomice Diui Alfonsi Romanorum Castelle reg illustrissimi: Opera arte mirifica viri solertis Iohānis Hamman de Landoia dictus Hertzog Curaq sua nō mediocri: impressiōe complete existunt Felicibus astris. Anno a Prima Re etherea circuitione. 8476. Sole in parte. 18. gradiente Scorpij Sub celo Veneto. Anno Salutis. 1492. currente: Pridie Caleñ. Nouembr̄. Venetijs.
   Edited by Johannes Lucilius Santritter and preceded by his Canones in Tabulas Alphonsi.
   Goff, A-535; Hain, no. 869; Simon Díaz, III, vol. I, 1295.
Reel 10, No. 46

ALFONSO X, 1221-1284 also see CASTILLE.
   Laws, Statutes, etc.

ALFONSO de Zamora, d. 1531 (also known as ALPHONSUS of Zamora).
   Fons erat hebreus siccus nec clarus abunde: Presulis Alfonsi tempore ad vso grauis. Cum fonseca suo venit cum sydere quino: fulgens pinqueq fecit opus: [Coat of arms, with five stars]. Introductiones Artis grammatice hebraice nunc recenter edite. Impresse in Academia complutensi in Edibus Michaelis de Eguia. [Alcalá de Henares, Miguel de Eguia, 1526].
   223 unumb. l.; 19cm.

   Colophon: Excussum est atq absolutum praesens opus in Academia Cōplutensi expensis Egregii viri Michaelis de Eguia Typice Artis solertissimi. Anno. 1526. kalēdis Maij, die Martis.
   Adams, I, no. 800; Salvá, II, 2452.
Reel 10, No. 47

ALMANSA Y MENDOZA, ANDRÉS DE.
   The Ioyfull Returne, Of The Most Illvstrious Prince, Charles, Prince of great Brittaine, from the Court of Spaine. Together, With a Relation of his Magnificent Entertainment in Madrid, and on his way to St. Anderas, by the King of Spaine. The Royall and Princely Gifts interchangeably giuen. Translated out of the Spanish Copie. His wonderfull dangers on the Seas, after his parting from thence: Miraculous deliuery, and most happy-safe Landing at Portsmovth on the 5. of October Stil. veteri, to the vnspeakable Ioy of both Nations. Testified no lesse by Triumphall Expressions of the Spanish Ambassadours, (here now residing) as by the lowd Acclamations of our owne People. London: Printed by Edward All-de for Nathaniell Butter and Henry Seile, 1623.
   46 p., 1 l.; 19cm.

ALMANSA Y MENDOZA (Cont'd)
   The account of the "magnificent entertainment" is a translation of Almansa y Mendoza's Relación de la partida del Serenissimo Principe de Walia; the rest of the account is "from the report of some of His Highnesse traine."
   Bound with A Trve Relation and Iovrnall and other works. See PEÑA, Juan Antonio de la, fl. 1623-1638. 17th cent. news-letter writer.
   Allison, p. 20, no. 9; HC 380/105; Penney, p. 19; Pollard and Redgrave, no. 5025.
Reel 10, No. 48

ALONSO DE MADRID see MADRID, ALONSO DE.

Alphabetum diuini amoris (1500-1520).
   [30] l.

   Bound with: Cassianus, Joannes. Joānis' Cassiani collationes patrū abbrete [sic] ...
   Lacks T.-p.
Reel 36, No. 186A

ALPHONSUS, ZAMORENSIS see ALFONSO de Zamora.

ALVAREZ, FRANCISCO.
   Historia De Las Cosas De Etiopia, En La Qval Se Cventa muy copiosamente, el estado y potēcia del Emperador della, (que es el que muchos an pensado ser el Preste Ivan) con otras infinitas particularidades, assi dela religion de aquella gente, como de sus cerimonias: Segun que todo ello fue testigo de vista Francisco Aluarez, Capellan del Rey Don Manuel de Portugal. Agora nueuamente traduzido de Portugues en Castellano, por el Padre Fray Thomas Padilla. [Printer's device]. En Anvers: En casa de Iuan Steelsio, 1557. Con Gracia y Priuilegio.
   21, 207, 1 l.; 15cm.

   Colophon: "En casa de Iuan Latio. 1557."
   Adams, I, no. 848; Antonio, III, p. 399; HC:327/1363; Heredia, no. 7684; Palau, 9249; La Serna, IV, no. 5665; Peeters-Fontainas, I, no. 43; Salvá, II, 3266.
Reel 10, No. 49

AMADIS DE GUALA [author unknown]. Bk. 7.
   Le Septiesme Livre D'Amadis De Gavle, Mis En Francoys Par Le Seigneur des Essars Nicolas de Herberay, Commissaire ordinaire de l'artillerie du Roy, & Lieutenant en icelle, es pais & gouuernement de Picardie, monsieur Brissac, Cheualier de l'ordre, grand maistre & Capitaine general d'icelle artillerie. Acuerdo Oluido: [Printer's device]. Auec priuilege du Roy. A Paris: Pour Vincent Sertenas, Libraire tenant sa boutique au Palays, en la Gallerie par ou lon va à la Chancellerie: & au mont S. Hylaire en l'hostel d'Albert, 1555.
   [7], CXCII l.: ill.; 16.5cm.

   Simon Diaz, III, vol. II, 6737
Books 1 - 6: Not Available
Reel 10, No. 50, Book 7

AMADIS DE GAULA [author unknown]. Bk. 8.
   Le Hvitiesme Livre D'Amadis De Gavle, Mis En Francoys, Par Le Seigneur des Essars Niclas de Herberay, Commissaire ordinaire de l'artillerie du Roy, & Lieutenant en icelle, es pais & gouuernement de Picafdie, monsieur Brissac, Cheualier de l'ordre, gran maistre & Capitaine general d'icelle artillerie. Acuerdo Oluido: [Printer's device: Vincenti Non Victo Gloria].
   [11], CCCII l.

   Simon Diaz, III, vol. II, 6737
Reel 10, No. 50, Bk. 8

AMADIS DE GAULA [author unknown]. Bks. 11-12.
L'onzieme livre d'Amadis de Gayle: continuant les entreprises cheualereuses, et auentures estranges, tant de luv que des princes de son sang: ou reluisent principalement les hauts faitz d'armes de Rogel de Grece, ceux Agesilan de Colchos, au long pour chas de l'amour de Diane, la plus belle princesse du monde ... Anvers: Guillaume Silvius, 1573.
4 l., 219 p.; 22cm.

French translation: Book 11 translated by Jacques Gohory, book 12 by Guillaume Aubert.
Bound with: Le Dovzieme Livre D'Amadis De Gavle, Traduit Novvellement D'Espagnol En Francois, ... En Anvers: Guillaume Silvius, 1573.
[8], 355, [6].
Simón Díaz, III, vol. II, 6776.
Reel 11, No. 50, Bks. 11-12

AMADIS DE GAULA [author unknown]. Bks. 12-13.
Le dovzieme livre d'Amadis de Gavle, tradvit novvellement d'espagnol en francois, contenant quelle fin prindrent les loyalles amours d'Angesilan de Colchos, et de la princesse Diane et par quel moven la royne Sidonie se rapaisa, apres auoir longuement pourchassé la mort de dom Florisel de niquee, auec plusieurs estranges auentures non moins recreatiues que singulieres, et ingenieuses sur toutes celles que ont esté traitees es liures precedents. Traduit d'espaignol en françois par ... En Avers: Par Guillaume Silvius, imprimeur du roy, 1573.
[8], 355, [6] p.; 20cm.

Bound with: Le trezieme livre d'Amadis de Gavle, tradvit novvellement d'espagnol en francois par I. G. P. Traittant les hauts faits d'armes du gentil cheualier Sylves de la Selue fils de l'empereur Amadis de Grece, et de la royne de Thebes Finistee ... En Anvers: par Guillaume Silvius, imprimeur du roy, 1572.
[8], 159, [4] p.; cm.
French translation: Book 12 translated by G. Aubert de Poitiers, book 13 by Jacques Gohory.
Titles within ornamental border; device of printer on title-pages.
Errors in paging: p. 81-155 numbered 85-159.
Dedicatory letter signed: Iaques Gohry Parisien, le solitaire.
Simón Díaz, III, vol. II, 6783. Adams, I, no. 894; Simon Díaz, vol. II, 6800.
Reel 11, No. 50, Bks. 12-13

AMADIS DE GAULA [author unknown]. Bk. 13.
Le Tresiesme Livre D'Amadis de Gavle: Traduit nouuvellement d'Espagnol en François, par I.G.P. Traittant les hauts faits d'armes du gétil Cheualier Sylves de la Selue, filz de l'Empereur Amadis de Grece, & de la royen de Thebes Finistee: auec les auentures estranges d'armes & d'amours de Rogel de Grece, Angesilan de Colcos & auentures sur l'entreprise & cours de la guerre du grand Roy Balthasar de Russie, contre les Chrestiens. Et apres, les mariages de Diane, Leonide & autres. Adressé a ma Dame la Contesse de Retz. A Montlvel: Par Bartholemy Pro, 1576.
507, [15] p.; 11cm.

French translation by I.G.P.
Simón Díaz, III, vol. II, 6803.
Reel 11, No. 50, Bk. 13

AMADIS DE GAULA [author unknown]. Bk. 14.
Le Qvatorziesme Livre d'Amadis de Gavle. Traittant les hauts faicts d'armes & amours de Prince Sylu es de la Selue, & les estranges auentures mises à fin tant par luy que par autres magnanimes Princes de la Grece. Dedié a la tres-illustre & magnifique Princesse Henriette de Cleues Duchesse de Neurs. A Paris: Par Nicolas Bonfons, ruë neuue nostre Dame à l'enseigne S. Nicolas, 1577.
[16], 352 l.; 11cm.

AMADIS DE GAULA (Cont'd)
Simón Díaz, III, vol. II, 6809.
Reel 11, No. 50, Bk. 14

AMADIS DE GAULA [author unknown]. Bk. 15.
Le Qvinziesme Livre d'Amadis de Gavle, Continuant les hauts faits d'armes & amours de dom Silues de la Selue & de maints autres notables cheualiers, par vn discours autāt beau & plaisant comme il est grandement profitable: qu'auec plusieurs belles sentences, lon y peu parfaictement remarquer l'example d'vn bon vertueux & secourable Prince. Mis en François par Gabriel Chappuys Tourangeau. A Lyon: Benoist Rigavd, 1578. Auec priuilege du Roy.
526, [17] p.; 11cm.

French translation by Gabriel Chappuys Tourangeau.
Palau, 10514.
Reel 11, No. 50, Bk. 15

AMADIS DE GAULA [author unknown]. Bk. 16.
Le Seiziesme Livre d'Amadis de Gavle. Traictant les plusque humaines & admirables prouësses & amours des inuincibles & incōparables Princes Spheramōde & Amadis d'Astre: auec la deliurance du Roy Amadis de Gaule, d'Espladian, de Don Rogel, & de Fortune. Mis en Lumiere Françoise par Nicolas de Moutreux, Gentilhomme du Mans. A Paris: Chez Iean Parant, ruë sainct Iaques, M.D.LXXVII (1577).
[16], 249, [7] l.; 11cm.

French translation by Nicolas de Moutreux, Gentilhomme du Mans.
Palau, 10514.
Reel 11, No. 50, Bk. 16A

AMADIS DE GAULA [author unknown]. Bk. 16.
Le seiziesme livre d'Amadis de Gavle, traitant des amours, gestes et faicts heroiques des illustres et vertueux princes Sferamond & Amadis d'Astre: ensemble de plusieurs autres grands seigneurs y denommez, par le plaisant et profitable discours d'vne histoire belle entre les plus belles que ont procedé, cōme chucun pourra facilement iuger par la lecture d'icelle. A Lyon: par Francoys Didier, 1578.
845 p.; 13cm.

Device of printer on t.-p.
Dedicatory letter signed: Gabriel Chappuys Tourangeau.
Palau, 10514.
Reel 11, No. 50, Bk. 16B

AMADIS DE GAULA [author unknown]. Bk. 17.
Le Dixseptieme Livre d'Amadis de Gavle. Continuant à traiter des amours, gestes & faicts heroiques des illustres & vertuex Princes Sferamond & Amadis d'Astre: ensemble de plusieurs autres grāds Seigneurs y denōmez, ... (Traduict d'Italien en Francois par Gabriel Chappuys Tourangeau.) A Lyon: Par Estienne Michel [1578?].
[16], 432, [17] l.

T.-p. wanting.
French translation by Gabriel Chappuys Tourangeau.
Palau 10514.
Reel 12, No. 50, Bk. 17

AMADIS DE GAULA [author unknown]. Bk. 18.
Le dixhvictiesme Livre d'Amadis de Gavle, Continuant les amours, gestes & faits heroiques des illustres & vertueux princes Sferamond & Amadis d'Astre, ensemble de plusieurs autres grands Seigneurs y denommez, par le plaisant & profitable discours d'vne histoire en inuention subtile & emerueillable, autan & plus que les precedentes. Traduict d'Espagnol en Francois. A Lyon: Pour Loys Cloquemin, 1579.
999, [18] p.; 12cm.

French translation by Gabriel Chappuys.
Palau, 10514.
Reel 12, No. 50, Bk. 18

AMADIS DE GAULA [author unknown]. Bk. 19.
Le Dixnevsiesme Livre d'Amadis de Gavle. Traittant des amours, gestes, & faicts heroiques, de plusieurs illustres & magnanimes princes nepueux d'Amadis de Gavle, & faisant mention de plusieurs autres grands Seigneurs, par le plaisant & profitable discours, d'vne hystoire belle & agreeable, sur toutes les precedentes. Traduit d'Espagnol en langue Francoyse, Par Gabriel Chappuis Tourangeau. A Lyon: Par Iean Beravd, M.D. LXXXII (1582).
[15], 447 l.; 12cm.

French translation by Gabriel Chappuys.
Palau, 10514.
Reel 12, No. 50, Bk. 19

AMADIS DE GAULA [author unknown]. Bk. 20.
Le Vingtiesme Et Penvltime livre d'Amadis de Gavle, Traittant des amours, gestes & faicts heroïques de plusieurs illustres & vertueux princes de la race & souche dudict Amadis, ensemble de plusieurs autres grands Seigneurs, par l'agreable & utile discours d'vne histoire aussi belle & plaisante que l'on scauroit voir. Mis d'Hespagnol en Francois par Gabriel Chappvys Tourangeau. A Lyon: Povr Loys Cloqvemin, 1581. Auec priuilege de Roy.
[16], 539 l; 12cm.

French translation by Gabriel Chappuys.
Palau, 10514.
Reel 12, No. 50, Bk. 20

AMADIS DE GAULA [author unknown]. Bk. 21.
Le Vingt Vniesme Et Dernier Livre d'Amadis de Gavle, Contenant la fin & mort d'iceluy, les merueilleux faicts d'armes & amours de plusieurs grands & notables Princes de son sang, & les diuers & estranges effects d'vn amour chaste & honneste: d'ou, en fin, l'on peut recueillir grand fruict, plaisir & contentement. Traduict d'Hespagnol en Francois. A Lyon: Povr Loys Cloqvemin, 1581.
[16], 448 l.; 12cm.

Palau, 10514.
Reel 12, No. 50, Bk. 21

AMADIS DE GAULA [author unknown]. Bk. 22.
Le Vingt Et Devxiesme Livre d'Amadis de Gavle. Traitant Les Havts Faits d'Armes, Amours & vertus nompareilles, auec les estranges Auantures mises à fin tant par les Princes illustres yssus de la noble maison D'Amadis, qu'autres vaillans Cheualiers, en la queste & pourchas de la deliurance des deuxiemes Princes Safiraman & Hercules d'Astre. Histoire non encores veuë en nostre langue, mais au reste belle entre les plus belles qui ont precedé, & d'vn discours non moins plaisant que profitable: comme chacun pourra facilement iuger par la lecture d'icelle, faict d'Espagnol Francois. A Paris: Chez Gilles Robinot ruë vielle Drapperie au plat d'estain, Et au Pallais en la petite Gallerie, M.D.C.X.V. (1615).
[26], 857, [9] p.; 17cm.

Palau, 10515.
Reel 13, No. 50, Bk. 22

AMADIS DE GAULA [author unknown]. Bk. 23.
Le Vingt Et Troisiesme Livre d'Amadis de Gavle. Continvant a Traiter des Amours, gestes & faicts Heroiques de plusieurs illustres & vertueux Princes descendus de la race du grand Amadis: & notamment du vaillant Fulgoran, fils de Rogel de Grece & de la Roine Florelle: Discours non moins plaisant que profitable, comme chacun pourra facilement iuger par la lecture, fait d'Espagnol Francois. A Paris: Chez Clavde Rigavd, ruë sainct Iacques ... M.D.C.XV (1615). Auec priuilege du Roy.
920 (i.e. 922) p.; 17cm.

AMADIS DE GAULA (Cont'd)
Dedicatory letter to: "A la Royne" instead of "Au Roy".
Graesse, p. 94; Palau, 10515.
Reel 13, No. 50, Bk. 23

AMADIS DE GAULA [author unknown]. Bk. 24.
Le Vingt Qvatrieme et Dernier Livre D'Amadis De Gavle. Continvant A Traiter des Amours, gestes & faicts Heroiques de plusieurs illustres & vertuez Princes descendus de la race du grand Amadis: & notamment du vaillant Fulgoran, fils de Rogel de Grece, & de la Roine Florelle, Discours non moins plaisant que profitable, comme chacun pourra facilement iuger par la lecture, fait d'Espagnol Francois. A Paris: Chez Gilles Robinot, ruë de la vielle Drapperie au plat d'estaing, & au Palais en la petite Gallerie, M.DC.XV (1615).
[6], 853, [17] p.; 17cm.

Graesse, p. 94; Palau, 10515.
Reel 13, No. 50, Bk. 24

AMADIS DE GAULA [author unknown].
Splandiano, E Le Sve Prodezze, Le Qvali Segvono I quattro libri di Amadis di Gaula suo padre, Scritte Fidelmente Dal maestro Helisabatte, che si ritrouò nella maggior parte presente, Et Recate Hora dalla Lingva Spagnuola à questa nostra volgare. His Dvcibvs. In Venetia: Per Francesco Lorenzini da Turino, M.D.LX (1560).
[7], 270 l.; 16cm.

Italian translation by Mambino Roseo da Fabriano.
Palau, 10550.
Reel 13, No. 51

AMADIS DE GAULA [author unknown].
The Ancient, Famovs And Honourable History of Amadis de Gaule. Discovrsing The Adventvres, Loues and Fortunes of many Princes, Knights and Ladies, as well of Great Brittaine, as of many other Kingdomes beside, &c. Written in French by the Lord of Essars, Nicholas de Herberay, Ordinairie Commissarie of the King Artillerie, and his Lietenant thereof, in the Countrie and gouernment of Picardie, &c. Printed in London by Nicholas Okes, 1619.
4 v. in 1; 29cm.

1st. t.-p. in facsimile.
Books 3 and 4 dated 1618. Ex - libris: P.R. Lyell
English translation by Anthony Munday.
Each part has separate t.-p. and own pagination.
Title pages of books 2, 3 and 4 have the following note: "Translated into English by A. M. (i.e. Anthony Munday) and all four books are dedicated separately by him to Philip, Earl of Montgomery. In the dedication of the Fourth Book, Munday promises the fifth and sixth to be shortly forthcoming, but it was not until 1562 that the Sixth Book was translated by J. J. [ohnson] First edition of all four books of the Amadis and extremely rare."
Allison, p. 23, 15; Pollard and Redgrave, 543, 544; Simón Díaz, III, vol. II, 6823.
Reels 13 & 14, No. 52

AMADIS DE GAULA [author unknown].
The most excellent and famous history of the most renowed knight, Amadis of Greece, Surnam'd, The Knight of the Burning Sword. Son to Lisvart of Greece, and the Fair Onoloria of Trebisond. ... London: Printed for J. Deacon and J. Blare, 1694.
[7], 220 p.; ill, front; 20.5cm.

The 7th book of the English version of Amadis de Gaula, corresponding to the 9th book of the Spanish version. It is a reprint of the first edition of 1693, which had the following title: ... By a Person of Quality.
Allison, p. 24, 18.1; Wing, 2877.
Reel 14, No. 53

AMBROSIO BAUTISTA, father, fl. 1635.
Discvrso Breve De Las Miserias De La Vida Y
Calamidades De La Religion Catolica / por el Padre
Ambrosio Bautista, Canonigo Premostense. Madrid:
En la Imprenta Real, 1635.
30 p.

Bound in: Cespedes y Meneses, Gonzalo de: Francia
Engañada Francia Respondida ... Empresso en Caller,
1635.
Reel 41, No. 221

AMOROSI Ragionamenti. Dialogo, Nel Qvale Si Racconta
Vn Compassionevole Amore Di Dve Amanti, Tradotto
Per M. Lodovico Dolce, Dai Fragmenti D'Vno Antico
Scrittor Greco. Con Gratia & Priuilegio. In
Vinegia: Appresso Gabriel Giolito de Ferrari,
1546.
56 *l.*; 16cm.
Reel 54, No. 314

ANDRÉS, JUAN, a Moor, 16th century.
Confvsio sectae Mahometanae. Liber à Iohanne Andrea
... lingua hispanica conscriptus; ac per Dominicum de
Gaselu ... italicè redditus; nunc autem interpretatione
latina expositus à Iohanne Lauterbach ... [Lipsiae],
1595.
Pp. 85-268.

Reel 14, No. 54

ANDRÉS DE UZTARROZ, JUAN FRANCISCO.
Defensa de la patria del invencible martyr san
Lavrencio. Escrivela el Doctor Juan Francisco Andres
de Vztarroz ... Zaragoca: En el Hospital Real, i
General de N. Señora de Gracia, 1638.
[13], 248, [9] p.; 21cm.

HC 384/1478; Jiménez Catalán, 375; Penney, p. 25;
Simón Díaz, V, 2654.
Reel 14, No. 55

ANDRÉS DE UZTARROZ, JUAN FRANCISCO.
Monvmento De Los Santos Martyres Ivato, I Pastor,
En La Civdad De Hvesca. Con Las Antiguedades, que se
hallaron, fabricando una Capilla, para transladar sus
Santos cuerpos. Escribelo El Doctor Ivan Francisco
Andres, Cesar-Augustano. I Lo Dedica Al Doctor D. Ivan
Orencio De Lastanosa. Canonigo de la santa Iglesia
de Huesca. Con licencia, impresso en Huesca, por Ivan
Nogves, Año 1644.
[42], 272, [12] p., ill., 3 fold., plates.; 15cm.

Arco, p. 32; Jerez, p. 7; Penney, p. 25; Simón
Díaz, V, 2669.
Reel 14, No. 56

ANDRÉS DE UZTARROZ, JUAN FRANCISCO.
Progressos De La Historia En El Reyno De Aragon, Y
Elogios De Geronimo Zvrita, Sv Primer Coronista.
Contienen Varios Svcessos Desde El Año De M.D.XII.
Hasta el de M.D.LXXX. Con Licencia: En Zaragoca:
por los Herederos de Diego Dormer, Año 1680.
[41], 608, [16] p.; 31cm.

Jiménez Catalán, no. 957; Penney, p. 26; Simón
Díaz, V, 2687.
Reel 14, No. 58

ANDRÉS DE UZTARROZ, JUAN FRANCISCO.
Relacion Del Jvramento De Los Fueros de Aragon, que
hizo el Serenissimo Principe D. Baltasar Carlos, en la
iglesia Metropolitana de la ciudad de Zaragoza, en 20.
de Agosto de 1645. Con licencia. En Madrid: Alonso
de Paredes, [n.d.]
3 *l.*; 28cm.

Caption title.
Reel 14, No. 57

ANTONIO, NICOLÁS [1617-1684].
Bibliotheca Hispana Sive Hispanorvm, Qvi Vsqvam
Vnqvamve sive Latinâ sive populari sive aliâ quavis
lingua scripto aliquid consignaverunt Notitia, His
Qvae Praecesservnt Locvpletior Et Certior brevia elogia,
editorum atque ineditorum operum catalogum Dvabvs
Partibvs Continens, Qvarvm Haec Ordine Qvidem Rei
posterior, conceptu verô prior duobus tomis agit, Qvi
Post Annym Secvlarem MD. usque ad praesentom diem
floruere. Tomvs. Primvs. [y Secundo] Avthore D.
Nicolao Antonio Hispalensi, I.C. Ordinis S. Iacobi
Eqvite, Patriae Ecclesiae Canonico, Regiorum negotiorum
in Vrbe & Romana Curia Procuratore generali. Romae:
ex Officina Nicolai Angeli Tinassii, MDCLXXII (1672).
Svperiorvm Permissv.
2 v. ([39], 633 p.; 690 p.); 33cm.

Simón Díaz, V, 3103.
Reels 14 & 15, No. 60

ANTONIO, NICOLÁS, 1617-1684.
De Exilio Sive De Exilii Poena Antiqva Et Nova,
Exvlvmqve Conditione Et Ivribvs Libri Tres Avctore D.
Nicolao Antonio Hispalensi, I.C. Et Ordinis S. Iacobi
Eqvite. [Printer's device]. Antverpiae: Apud Iacobvm
Mevrsivm, Anno M.DC.LIX. (1659). Cum Gratia & Priuilegio.
16, 300, [26] p.; 31cm.

Simón Díaz, V, 3101.
Reel 14, No. 59

ANTONIO DE CÓRDOBA see CÓRDOBA, ANTONIO DE.

ANTONIO DE LEBRIJA [i.e. Elio Antonio Martinez de Cala
y Jarava].
Aelii Antonii Nebriss. Ex grammatico rhetoris in
Conplutēsi Gymnasio: ato proinde Historici Regn. APOLOGIA
earum nerum quae illi obijciuntur. Eivsdem Antonii
Nebriss. in Quinquaginta sacrae scripturae locos non
vulgariter enarratos. Tertia Quinquagerna Eivsdem
Antonii De Digitorvm Compvtatione. Cum priuilegio.
Apvd Inclytam Garnatam Mense Febrvario, D.XXXV. (1535).
xliii, [3] *l.*; 20cm.

Palau, 189323; Simón Díaz, III, vol. II, 5900.
Reel 15, No. 61

ANTONIO DE LEBRIJA [i.e. Elio Antonio Martinez de Cala
y Jarava].
Aelii Antonii Nebrisseñ. introductiones in latinam
grammaticen per eundem recognite atq exactissime correcte
glossematis cum antiquo exemplari collatis. Cum
priuilegio Imperiali. [Compluti, 1533].
cxlvi *l.*; 21cm.

Colophon [f. 146:] Aelii Antonii Nebrisseñ.
grāmatici: viri disertissimi commentaria: introductionum
suarum in grammaticam latinam nunc denuo Impressa:
diligenter o ad exemplare prototypū redacta. Multis
locis repositis & restitutis, o ex superioribus
aeditionibus erant deprauata. In Aedibus Michaelīs de
Eguia Compluti. Anno domini: Millesimo quingentesimo
Trigesimo tertio. Pridie Kalendas Octobris.
Title-page imperfect, affecting text, also A².
Palau, 188936; Simón Díaz, III, vol. II, 5937.
Reel 15, No. 62

ANTONIO DE LEBRIJA [i.e. Elio Antonio Martinez de Cala
y Jarava].
Dictionarivm Ex Hispaniensi in Latinvm Sermonem,
Aelio Antonio Nebrissensi interprete, per multis nunc
demum vocibus, locutionumque formulis locupletatum.
[Portrait of Nebrija]. Antverpiae: In Aedibus Ioan.
Steelsij, M.D.LIII (1553). Cum Priuilegio Caesareo.
[84] *l.*; 21cm.

Colophon: Antverpiae, Typis Ioannis Latij. M.D.LIII.
Volume II.
Palau, 189187; Peeters-Fontainas, II, no. 826;
Penney, p. 24; Simón Díaz, III, vol. II, 5910.
Reel 15, No. 63

ANTONIO DE LEBRIJA [i.e. Elio Antonio Martinez de Cala y Jarava].
  Dictionarivm Latinohispanicvm, Et Vice Versa Hispanicolatinvm, Aelio Antonio Nebrissensi Interprete, Nvnc Denvo Ingenti vocum accessione locupletatum, pristinoc nitori sublata mendarum colluuie restitutum. Ad Haec. Dictionarium propriorum nominum, ex probatissimis Graecae & Latinae linguae autoribus, addita ad calcem neoterica locorum appellatione concinnatum. [Coat of arms]. [Mark]. Antverpiae: In Aedibus viduae & haeredum Ioannis Steelsij, M.D.LXX. (1570). Cum Priuilegio Regis.
  [216] l.; 21cm.

  Three volumes; each with separate t.-p. and pagination:
  Vol. II-: Dictionarivm Ex Hispaniensi In Latinvm Sermonem, Aelio Antonio Nebrissensi interprete, permmultis nunc demum vocibus, locutionumq; formulis locupletatum. [Coat of arms].
  [88] l.; 21cm.
  Vol. III-: Dictionarivm Propriorvm Nominvm, ex probatis. Graecae & Latinae linguae authoribus, solerti cura ac studio concinnatum. Additae sunt ad calcem vulgares locorum appellationes, alphabetica serie vice versa digestae. [Coat of arms].
  [128] l.; 21cm.
  Adams, II, no. 122; Palau, 189190; Peeters-Fontainas, II, no. 828; Simón Díaz, III, vol. II, 5910.
Reel 15, No. 64

ANTONIO DE LEBRIJA [i.e. Elio Antonio Martinez de Cala y Jarava].
  Dictionarivm Aelii Antonii Nebrissensis Grammatici, Chronographi Regii, Imo Recens Accessio facta quadruplex eiusdem antiqui dictionarij supplementum. Quorum primum continet dictiones Latinas in sermonem Hispanum versas. Secundum nomina propria regionum, vrbium, montium, fluuiorum, & Tertium autem neotericas, ac vulgares regionum, & vrbium appellationes viceversa complectitur. Quartum, & vltimum voces Hispanas Latinitate donatas. Praeter Ioannis Lopez Serrani Malacitani Labores, Ex Ciceronis Lexicis, & historicis, multa, quae desiderabantur addita. Index insuper vtilissimus in quo opposita, emendataque quotidiani sermonis barbaries, opera M. Ioannis Alvarez Sagredo Burgensis. Accesservnt Permvltae Icciones, Tvm Ex Sacrarvm litterarum, tùm ex vtriusque iuris voluminibus. Index verborum veterum, & vsitatorum apud Terentium. Dictionarium Arabicum positum in calce Dictionarij Hispani. Omnium penè syllabaroum quantitas annotatur. Posita Svnt, Etiam Omnia Recognita, Et Ab Innvmeris quibus scatebant mendis vindicata, & pristinae integritati restituta vocabula, à R.P.M.Fr. Petro Ortiz de Luiando ad calcem addita. Insuper sexmillia pene vocabula addita per M.D. Guillielmum de Ocahasa. Tandem hac vltima editione prodeunt plusquam quatuormillia vocabula, quae hos signo notantur studio, & diligentia I.D. Ioannis Gonzalez Manriqve Praesbyteri, non sine cura, & labore. ... Matriti; Ex Typographia Ioannis Garcia Infazon, [1699?].
  [14], 776 p.; 31cm. 639 p.; 31cm.

  Title in red and black.
  Part II: Diccionario De Romance En Latin Por El Maestro Antonio De Nobrisa, Gramatico Cronologo De Los Reyes Catolicos. Se han impresso en este Vocabulario; y hase enmendado de infinitos vicios, y errores que tenia de la Imprenta, y que mudavan totalmente el propio sentido de los vocablos: Por el Maestro Don Guillelmo Ocahasa, Notario de la Santa Sede Apostolica en toda la Christiandad, natural, y Vicario perpetuo de la muy antigua, noble, y leal Ciudad de Clonmelia en Irlanda, y Cura propio de la Villa de Ornos, Diocesis de Cartagena en España, Averiguase en el de Latin, si es el vocablo de Ciceron, Ò no; y tambien de su acento. Pvsose Assimismo En El Fin De Este Vocabulario Vn Compendio De Los vocablos. En Madrid: En la Imprenta de Juan Garcia Infacon, [1681?].
  Several errors in paging.
  Continuously paginated.
  Palau, 189205.
Reel 15, No. 65

ANTONIO DE LEBRIJA [i.e. Elio Antonio Martinez de Cala y Jarava].
  Grāmatica Antonij Nebrissensis cū cōmento. En opus tibi oādidissime lector post quarta editione auctius adeo elimatiius Aelij Antonij Nebrissensis. Additis sparsim nōnullis nullibi antea (vt. videre est) excusis: q̄ studiosus asq & optabat & expectabat. Uerte si videtur hao pagelle facie: liquido videbis in elencho que in hoc principe opere cōtenta: q adiectitia: si prius fueris cospicatus eorum nōmēclatura quoru sunt vel opera: vel scholia: idque erit volume tibi - Praestantiu virorū noia quorum diligēntia hoc opus amendatius atque copiosius redditum est: heo sunt frater Babtista Mantuanus Car., Franciscus Ryzius a Ualle Oletana, Raymundus Palasinus Albigeñ., Lucius Christophorus Scobar, Andreas Laurentinus Serranus, Hieronymus Saguinus Uindocinus. Hilari Bertulphus Lodi Cādau: q̄ nuperrime post diligentissimā castigatione huic operi cōplures adnotationes adiecit hac nota ab alijs secretas. Lvgdvni, 1522.
  [8], ccviii l.; 26cm.

  Colophon: Veneunt he per ep docti grāmatici Aelij Antonij Nebrissensis latine introductiones Lagduni in edib honesti viri Simonis Uincentij in vico mercuriali moram trahentis.
  Title in red and black within architectural border.
  Device of printer on title-page and on verso of last leaf.
  Gothic type; headpieces.
  Errors in foliation: cxxxvii-ccxxxviii duplicated in numbering; cliii-cliv omitted.
  Bound in wooden boards covered with pigskin.
  Stamped on front cover the words: Christ's Hospital, and its seal.
Reel 15, No. 66

ANTONIO DE LEBRIJA [i.e. Elio Antonio Martinez de Cala y Jarava].
  Lexicon Iyris Civilis Antonio Nebrissensi viro non vulgariter erudito autore. Ipsumo, infinitis propemodum mendis bona fide emaculatum, scholiis passim in marginibus illustrius, & quam ante hac locupletius factum. Francisci Iametij Iurisconsulti, singulari diligētia: non minus meliorū literarum studiosis, quàm iuris ciuilis cadidatis vtile. Ad Senatum Parisiensem. Cvm Privilegio Regio, ad decennium. Parisiis: Apud Audoenum Paruum, sub insigni Lilij aurei, in via Iācobaea, 1549.
  [8], 304 p.; 12cm.

  Palau, 189276; Simón Díaz, III, vol. II, 5939.
Reel 16, No. 67

ANTONIO DE LEBRIJA [i.e. Elio Antonio Martinez de Cala y Jarava].
  Sapientvm Dicta Vafre Et Acytissime Cvm Glosemate Aelij Antonij Nebrissensis nunc denuo recognita & emendata. [Coat of arms]. [LEBRIJA]: In aedibus Aelij Antonij Nebrissensis, 1577.
  90 l.; 15cm.

  Simón Díaz, III, vol. II, 5977.
Reel 16, No. 68

ANTONIO DE LEBRIJA [i.e. Elio Antonio Martinez de Cala y Jarava].
  Vocabvlarivm Vtriusqve Ivris, nuperrimè summa cura summoque iudicio recognitum ac emendatum: atque ex confusa vocum serie in rectum ordinem redactum multisq̄ue multarum vocum significationibus, cuae hactenus à Juris studiosis maiorem in modum deside rabantur, locupletatum: Cum tractatu ad modum vtili de ratione studij. Accesit praeterea Lexicon Ivris Civilis: in quo vrij & insignes errores Accursij notantur: Antonio Nebrissensi viro doctissimo autore. [Printer's device]. Venetiis: Apvd Michaelem Bonellvm, M D L X X V (1575).
  481 l.; 12cm.

  Colophon: Venetiis Apvd Michaelem Bonellvm. M D L X X V.
  Palau, 189280.
Reel 16, No. 69

ANTONIO DE LEBRIJA see also PERSIUS FLACCUS, AULUS;
PRUDENTIUS CLEMENS, AURELIUS.

ANUNCIACIÓN, JUAN DE LA UNSHOD CARMELITE see JUAN DE
LA AÑUNCIACION.

APHTHONIUS, SOPHISTES.
Aphthonii Sophistae Progymnasmata rhetorica. Rodolpho
Agricola Phrisio interprete. Salmanticae: excudebat
Andreas de Portonariis, 1550.
27 𝑙.; 19cm.

Title vignette; initials.
"Avthor innominatvs De rhetoricis": leaves 23-25.
Reel 16, No. 71

APHTHONIUS, SOPHISTES.
Aphthonii Sophistae Progymnasmata Rhetorica. Rodolpho
Agricola Phrisio interprete. Cum scholijs nuper additis
per Franciscum Sanctium Brocensem Rhetorices professorem.
[Printer's device]. Salmanticae: Excudebat Andreas à
Portonarijs. S.C.M. Typographus, M.D.L.V.I. (1556).
32 𝑙.; 19cm.

Adams, I, no. 1262 (Paris' edition only).
Reel 16, No. 72

APPENDIX NOTARVM MISCELLANEA, 1654 see MOSES BEN MAIMON.
Porta Mosis Sive, Dissertationes Aliqvot ..., 1655.

APPIANUS, of Alexandria, Gr.
[De Bellis Civilbus Romanorum. Spanish]
Historia de todas las guerras ciuiles que vbo entre los
romanos; segũ que lo escriuio el muy eloquẽte historiador
App. Alex. Agora nueuamẽte trad. de latin en nr̄o vulgar
castellano. [Alcalá de Henares, M. Eguía, 1536].
[3], cxlix 𝑙.; 29cm.

Spanish translation by Diego de
Salazar.
Lacking t.-p.; title supplied from Graesse, J.G.T.
Trésor de livres rares et précieux; imprint taken from
colophon.
Text in double columns.
Colophon: "Imprimiose esta historia del muy eloquente
Appiano Alexandrino en la nobel villa insigne
uniuersidad de Alcala de Benares: [sic] en casa de
Miguel Eguía. Y vuo fin la impression saluador Jesu
Christo de MDXXXVI."
Catalina, no. 158; HC 346/1162; Penney, p. 31.
Reel 16, No. 73

ARAGON. Laws, statutes, etc.
Fveros y Observancias Del Reyno De Aragon. En
Caragoca: por Pedro Cabarte, impressor y librero de
dicho de Aragon, 1624, 1627, 1647.
1 v.; 37cm.

Each section has separate t.-p.
Arranged chronologically by date of publication.
(A) Fveros y Observancios Del Reyno De Aragon,
1624. [27] 𝑙., 𝑙. 1-188.
(B) Fveros Del Reyno De Aragon Del Año De Mil
Qvinientos Y Cincventa Y Tres, 1624.
𝑙. 189-216.
(C) Fveros Del Reyno De Aragon, Del Año De Mil
Qvinientos Y Ochenta Y Cinco, 1624.
𝑙. 217-227.
(D) Fveros, Y Actos De Corte Del Reyno De Aragon.
Hechos En Las Cortes, Por La Catholica, Y
Real Magestad del Rey Don Phelipe nuestro
Señor: celebradas en la Ciudad de Taracona,
el Ano MDXCII, 1624.
(E) Observantias, Consvetvdines Qve Regni Aragonvm
In Vsv Commvniter Habitas, 1624.
[2], 50 𝑙.

ARAGON (Cont'd)
(F) Fori, Qvibvs. In Ivdiciis Nec Extra Ad Praesens
non vtimvr: Propter illorum correctionem, &
aliquorum temporis lapsu extinctionem, aliorunq̃
à cessante causa deficientium non vsum, ne'
quid antiquitatis occultetur, in ordine priorum
descripti sequuntur, 1624.
53 𝑙.
T.-p. lacking.
(G) Fveros, Y Actos De Corte Del Reyno De Aragon,
Hechos Por La S.C. y R. Magestad Del Rey Don
Felipe Nvestro Señor, En las Cortes conuocadas
en la Ciudad de Barbastro, y fenecidas en la
de Calatayud, en el Año de MDCXXVI, 1627.
[8], 68p.
(H) Fveros, Y Actos De Corte Del Reyno De Aragon,
Hechos Por La S.C. y R. Magestad Del Rey Don
Felipe Nvestro Señor, En Las Cortes conuocadas
y fenecidas en la Ciudad de Caragoca en los
años MDCXLV y MDCLXVI, 1647.
[8], 28p.
HC 411/515/3; Jiménez Catalan, no. 925; Penney, p. 34.
Reel 16, No. 74

ARAGON. Laws, etc. see also SARAGOSSA. Laws, etc.

ARGAIZ, GREGORIO DE, 17th century.
Corona Real de España Fvndada en el credito de los
muertos y Vida de San Hyeroteo, Obispo de Atenas y
Segovia. Madrid: Por Melchor Alegre, 1668.
[28], 290, [3], 291-368, [15] p.; 31cm.

Imperfect: pages 121-132 wanting; front. wanting.
HC 384/768; Palau, 16068; Penney, p. 37; Simón Díaz,
V, 4154.
Reel 17, No. 75

ARGENSOLA, LEONARDO DE see LEONARDO Y ARGENSOLA,
BARTOLOME [JUAN], 1562-1631.

ARIAS, FRANCISCO, S. J., 1533-1605.
[Del buen uso de los Sacramentos. English]
The Little Memorial Concerning the Good and Frvittfvll
Vse of the Sacraments. Wherein Be handled such defects as
some persons commit in the vse of them, and the remedies
therein to be practised. Composed in Spanish, by the R.
Father Francis Arias of the Society of Iesus, and newlie
translated into our English tongue. Printed at Roan, 1602.
[22], 253; 12cm.

English translator unknown.
Title within rules.
Stained; title page and other leaves mended;
Some margins shaved.
Bound in contemporary calf.
Reel 17, No. 76

ARIAS, FRANCISCO, S. J. 1533-1605.
Thesaurus Inexhaustus Bonorum. Quae in Christo habemus.
Unerschöpffter Schatz deren Güttern so wir in Christo
haben Durch dessen unterschiedliche Ehren-Namen, Tugend-
Zeugnussen, und Byspiele auf neue weyss, sowol zu eines
jedem Rechtglaubinges besonderem Auffnehmen, als zu
offentlichem Gebrauch der Prediger erkläret, und in
dreyfächtiges Buchband abgeteilet; Mit jedem Band,
beygelegtem Register deren Haubstücken; zum Ende aber
aller dreyen, Für die Prediger beygeschlossener
lateinischer Anleitung. In Spanischer Sprach beschrieben,
Von P. Francisco Arias: Ins Latein ubersetzet, Von P.
Leonardo Creder; Nun aber verdeutschet Von P. Bartholomaeo
Christelio. Gesambten Priestern der Societät Jesu. Mit
guttsprechen des Obern. Glatz: Gedruckt bey Andreas
Pegen, Anno 1685.
3 v. ([26], 668 p.; [10], 671 p.; [8], 587, [44] p.);
34cm.

A reprint of the 1685 edition cit. by Simón Díaz, VI,
166.
Reel 17, No. 77

ARISTOTLE.
[De Animalibus Historia. Spanish]
   Historia general de aves, y animales de Aristoteles
Estagerita. Tradvzida de latin en romance, y añadida de
otros muchos autores griegos, y latinos, que trataron
deste mesmo argumento, por Diego de Funes y Mendoca.
Valencia: Por Pedro Patricio Mey, junto a S. Martin.
A costa de Iuan Bautista Marcal, 1621.
   [16], 441, [7] p. 21cm.

   De Animalibus Historia ... Spanish translation by
Diego de Funes Mendoza.
   Title vignette; initials.
   Palau, 16716
Reel 17, No. 78

ARTHUR, KING (Romances, etc.) see DEMANDA DEL SANCTO GRIAL.

ARTÍCULO de la renovación de las treguas entre los
   muy altas, y poderolos senores Estados Generales,
   por sus Camislarios y el Reynado de la Ciudad de
   Argel. [Argel], 1662. 1 printed l.

   Bound with: HERRERA Y SOTOMAYOR, JACINTO DE, fl.
1644. Iornada que su Magestad hizo a la Andalvzia.
[Madrid: En la Imprenta Real, 1624].
   Palau, 114276 (List only printed folios 1-6).
Reel 77, No. 484.4

AUGURELLO, GIOVANNI AURELIO, 1454?-1537?
   Ioannis Avrelii Avgvrelli P. Ariminensis Chrysopoeiae
Libri III. Et Geronticon Liber I. Anterpiae: Ex
officina Christophori Plantini, 1582.
   99 p.

   Bound in: Sánchez De Las Brozas, Francisco:
Paradoxa ..., 1582.
Reel 167, No. 1087

AUGUSTINUS, AURELIUS, SAINT, bp. of Hippo.
   D. Avrelii Avgvstini hipponensis episcopi, De civitate
Dei. Libri XXII. Veterum exemplarium collatione nunc demum
castigatissimi facti, eruditissimisque doctiss. Lodovici
Vivis commentariis illustrati. Quorum XII. priores, hac
omnium illius operum tomi quinti parte prima continentur:
cum indice, hac postrema editione castigatissimo
ditissimóque facto. Lvgdvni: apud Sebastianum
Honoratum, 1570.
   [26], 739, [51] p.

   Printer's device on title-page.
Reel 18, No. 79

AUGUSTINUS, AURELIUS, Saint, bp. of Hippo.
   D. Avrelii Avgvstini hipponensis episcopi. De civitate
Dei, libri XXII, cum doctissimis commentariis Ioannis
Lodouici Viuis. Ex vetustissimis manuscriptis exemplaribus
per theologos lovanienses ab innumeris mendis repurgati.
Quorum diligentiam attestatur sub fines tomi.
castigationum ratio, & lectionum varietas, maiori ex
parte annotata. [Parisiis, 1586].
   432, [26] p. 38cm.

Colophon: Parisiis excudebat Dionvsius Duvallius,
impensis Societatis parisiensis, anno Domini M.D. LXXXV.
   Device of printer on title-page; title in red and
black.
   In double columns.
   Adams, I, no. 2196
Reel 18, No. 80

AUGUSTINUS, AURELIUS, Saint, bp. of Hippo.
   D. Avrelii Avgvstini Hipponensis episcopi. De ciutate
Dei libri XXII. Veterum exemplarium collatione nunc demum
castigatissimi facti, eruditissimísque doctissimi Lodovici
Vivis commentariis illustrati ... Cum indice, hac postrema
editione castigatissimo ditissimóque facto. [Genevae]:
excvdebat Iacobvs Stoer, 1622.
   2 v. in 1, (32, [25], 739, [49] p.)

AUGUSTINUS (Cont'd)
   Title within ornamental border; head and tail-pieces;
initials.
   Book - plate with crest and motto: "Vive ut vivas" of
"H.I."
   Continuously paged.
Reel 18, No. 81

AUGUSTINUS, AURELIUS, Saint, bp. of Hippo.
[De ciutate Dei. Spanish]
   La Cividad de Dios del glorioso Doctor de la Iglesia S.
Agustin, Obispo Hiponense en veynte y dos libros.
Contienen los principios, y progressos desta Ciudad con
vna defensa de la Religion Christiana contra los errores
y calunias de los Gentiles. Tradvzidos de Latin en Romance
por ..., natural de la villa de Vergara. Dirigidos a don
Pedro Manrique Arcobispo de Zaragoca del Consejo de su
Magestad. Con privilegio. En Madrid: por Iuan de la
Cuesta. Vendese en casa de Francisco de Robles, Librero
del Rey N.S., 1614.
   [9], 783 p.; 29cm.

   Spanish translation by Antonio de Roys y Rozas.
   Device of printer on t.-p.
   Palau, 289384; Penney, p. 43; Pérez Pastor, 1262.
Reel 18, No. 82

AUGUSTINUS, AURELIUS, Saint, bp. of Hippo.
[De ciutate Dei. English]
   St. Avgvstine, Of the citie of God: with the learned
comments of Io. Lod. Vives. Englished by J. H. [London]:
Printed by George Eld, 1610.
   19, 921, [8] p.; 30cm.

   English translation by John Healey.
Reel 19, No. 83

AUISOS que se embian desta Corte, de algunas cosas notables,
   que sucedieron en la enfermedad y muerte del ... Duque de
   Osuna ... [Madrid: n.p.-n.d., 1624?].
   3 l.

   Imperfect: numerous pages missing.
   Bookplate: William Stirling.
   Caption title.
Reel 19, No. 84

AVILA, JUAN DE, 1500-1569.
[Audi filia. English]
   The Avdi Filia, Or A Rich Cabinet Fvll Of Spiritvall
Ievvells. Composed by the Reuerend Father, Doctovr Avila,
Translated out of Spanish into English . [Printer's mark
of the English College at St. Omer]. . . Permissu
Superiorum, M.DC. XX (1620).
   [25], 584, [16] p.; 18cm.

   English translation by Sir Tobie Matthew.
   "The Dedicatory to all English Catholics, by L. T.
[i.e. Sir Tobie Matthew].
   Allison, p. 31, 31; Pollard and Redgrave, 983. Vid.
also: A.F. Allison and D. M. Rogers. A Catalogue of
Catholic Books in English Printed abroad or Secretly in
England, 1558-1640. Bognor Regis, Arundel Press, 1956,
no. 53.
Reel 19, No. 85

AVILA Y ZÚÑIGA, LUIS DE, 1500-1564.
   Comentario ... de la Guerra de Alemaña hecha de Carlo
(sic) V. Maximo Emperador Romano, Rey de España. En el
año de M.D. XLVI y M.D. XLVII. (Carta del Serenissimo Rey
de Romanos ... sobre el sucesso de Boemia.) Anvers: En
casa de Iuan Steelsio, [1549].
   83 l; 15cm.

   Almirante, p. 43; Gallardo, I, no. 309; Peeters-
Fontainas, I, no. 87.
Reel 19, No. 86

AZPILCUETA, MARTIN DE, 1492?-1586.
Capitvlo veynte y ocho de las Addiciones del Manual
de Confessores, del Doctor Martin de Azpilcueta Nauarro,
anadido por el mismo Author ... Con su tabla. Valladolid:
Por Adrian Ghemart ... Vendese en la libreria casa de
Antonio Suchet, 1570.
[2], 86, [12] *l.*; 20cm.

Palau. 21296; Simon Diaz, VI, 2069.
Reel 19, No. 88

AZPILCUETA, MARTÍN DE, 1492?-1586.
Manval de Confessores y Penitentes, que contiene quasi
todas las dudas que en las Confessiones suelen occurrir
de los peccados, absoluciones, restituciones, censuras, &
irregularidades. Con cinco Comentarios de Vsuras Cambios,
Symonia mental, Defensiõ del proximo, de Hurto notable, &
Irregularidad. Compvesto por el doctor Martín de Azpilcueta.
Nueuamente reuisto, emendado, y añadido [!] el capitulo
veynte y ocho, por el mesmo author. Con su repertorio
copiosissimo. Impresso en Valladolid: por Fernández de
Cordoua, 1570.
[17], 799 p.; 20cm.

Chapter 28, The Commentary and the Index each have
special t.-p.
Simón Díaz, VI, 2042.
Reel 19, No. 87

AZPILCUETA, MARTÍN DE, 1492?-1586.
Repertorio general, y muy copioso del Manual de
Confessores, y de los cinco Comentarios para su declaracion,
cõpuestos ... [Valladolid], 1570.
[32] *l.*; 21cm.

Simón Díaz, VI, 2063.
Reel 19, No. 89

AZPILCUETA, MARTÍN DE, 1492?-1586.
Enchiridion: sive, Manvale confessariorvm et
poenitentivm ... Antuerpiae: Ex officina Christophori
Plantini, 1575.
[16], 827, [43] p.; 23cm.

Simón Díaz, VI. 2092; Palau, 21315.
Reel 20, No. 90

AZPILCUETA, MARTÍN DE, 1492?-1586.
Compendivm omnivm opervm ... Vna cum allegationibus et
attestationibus theologorum, philosophorum, atque vtriusque
iuris interpretum. Collectum R. D. Iacobvm Castellanvm,
Tarvisinum ... Venetiis: apud Robertum Mejettum, 1598.
[14], 283 *l.*; 21cm.

Simón Díaz, VI, 2114.
Reel 20, No. 91

B

BALBUENA, BERNARDO see VALBUENA, BERNARDO DE, bp.
   of Puerto Rico, 1568-1627.

BALLESTEROS Y SAAVEDRA, FERNANDO DE, abbot of the Church
   of San Justo.
   Vida de San Carlos Borromeo, Cardenal de la Santa
Iglesia de Roma, y Arzobispo de Milan. En Alcala: Por
Antonio Vazquez, 1642.
   [16], 189 p.; 15cm.

   Colophon: "En Alcala. Por Antonio Vazquez Impresor
de la Vniversidad Año de 1642."
   Palau 23074; Simón Díaz, VI, 2460.
Reel 20, No. 93

BANDELLO, MATTEO, 1480-1561.
   Il Primo [-terza] Volume Delle Novelle Del Bandello
novamente corretto, et illustrato dal sig. Alfonso Vlloa.
Con una aggiunta d'alcuni sensi morali del sig. Ascanio
Centorio degli Hortensi a ciascuna nouella fatti. Alla
Magnifica, & nobilis. signora; la signora Pichebella
Ragazzoni Paiarina. Con Privilegio. In Venetia: Appresso
Camillo Franceschini, 1566.
   3 v. ([4], 158 l.; [4], 154 l.; [3], 128 l.)

   Device of printer on title-pages; initials.
   First published in three volumes in 1554. A fourth vol.
appeared in 1573 at Lyons.
   All three volumes bound in one.
   Graesse I, p. 286.
Reel 20, No. 94

BAÑOS DE VELASCO Y AZEBEDO, JUAN, d. 1682.
   El Ayo, y Maestro de Principes, Seneca en sv vida. A
don Carlos Segundo ... Con Licencia. En Madrid: Por
Francisco Sanz, en la Imprenta del Reyno, Año 1674.
   [25], 506 (i.e. 500), A-D, 507-665 p.: front; 20cm.

   Numerous errors in paging incl. 283-284 and 475, 476
repeated and 371-380 omitted.
   Palau 23448; Simón Díaz VI, 2670.
Reel 21, No. 97

BAÑOS DE VELASCO Y AZEBEDO, JUAN, d. 1682.
   El hijo de David, Salomon Coronado, y acciones de su
minoridad. Premio de la obediencia, y castigo a la
ambición, y tirania de svs hermanos. Politica de principes,
historiada con morales advertencias para escarmiento
exemplar a los vasallos. Por Don Iuan Baños de Velasco y
Azevedo. Madrid: Francisco Sanz, 1672.
   [16], 325, [14] p.; 19.5cm.

   End papers are part of legal ms. dated 1657.
   Limp vellum with four thongs.
   Simon Díaz VI, 2667.
Reel 21, No. 96

BAÑOS DE VELASCO Y AZEBEDO, JUAN, d. 1682.
   El sabio en la pobreza, comentarios estoycos, y
historicos a Seneca. En Madrid: Por Francisco Sanz. En
la Imprenta del Reyno. Vendese en casa de la viuda de
Bernardo de Sierra, 1671.
   [16], 304 p.; 21cm.

   Gallardo II, 1303; Palau 23443; Simón Díaz, 2666.
Reel 20, No. 95

BAPTISTA, MANTUANUS.
   Bap. Mantuani Carmelitae Theologi Adolescentia
seu Bucolica, breuibus Iodoci Badij commentariis
illustrata. His accesserunt Ioannis Murmellij
in singulas eclogas argumenta, cum annotatiuncu-
lis eiusdem in loca aliquot obscuriora Accessit &
Index, non ille vetus & indigestus, sed nouus
omnino ac locupletior multo, opera Barthol.
Laurentis. Antverpiae : In aedibus Ioannis
Steelsii, 1546.
   [8], 104 l.

   Bound in: Vives, Juan Luis: Lingvae Latinae
Exercitatio, 1544.
Reel 197, No. 1270

BARBA, ALVARO ALONSO, b. 1569.
   [Arte de los metales. English]
   The First Book of the Art of Mettals, In which is
Declared the manner of their Generation; and the
Concomitants of Them. Written in Spanish by Albaro Alonso
Barba, Master of Art, born in the Town of Lepe in
Andaluzia, and Curate of St. Bernards Parish in the
Imperial City of Potosi, in the Kingdom of Peru in the
West - Indies, in the Year 1640. Translated into English
in the Year 1669. London: Printed for S. Mearne,
Bookbinder to the Kings most Excellent Majesty, 1670.
   156 p.; 16cm.

   English translation by Edward Montagu, 1st Earl
of Sandwich.
   With this is bound the author's second book of the
Art of Mettals (London, 1670).
   Allison, p. 33, no. 2; Goldsmith, no. 33; Graesse,
I, p. 288; Simón Díaz, V, 1283; Wing B nos. 679 & 681.
Reel 21, No. 98

BARBARANUS, JULIUS.
   Officinae Ivlii Barbarani Tomi Tress: Promptvarivm
Rervm Electarvm, In re praesertim Romana. Index
Titvlorvm Omnivm. Cum Licentia Superiorum, ac
Priuilegio Summi Pontificis, & Illustriss. Senatus
Veneti. Venetiis: Apud Ioannem Andream Valuassorem,
cognomine Guadagninum, 1569.
   3 pts. ([8], 404 p.; 156 p.; [3], 288, [5] p.); 23cm.

   Bound in: Simancas, Jacobus: De Repvblica Libri
IX. ..., 1569.
   Adams, I, no. 167.
Reel 171, No. 1111

BARCELONA. CONSELL DE CENT JURATS.
   Proclamación Catolica A La Magestad Piadosa De Felipe
El Grande Rey De Las Españas, Y Emperador De Las Indias
Nvestro Señor. Los Conselleres, y Consejo de Ciento de la
Ciudad de Barcelona. [s.l. : s.n.], 1640.
   266, [4] p; 20cm.

   Important historical document concerning the uprising
in Catalonia during the reign of Philip IV (1605-1665).
   Palau (1st ed.), vol. VI, p. 167.
Reel 21, No. 99

BARCLAY, JOHN, 1582-1621 see PELLICER DO OSSAU Y TOVAR,
   JOSÉ.

BARRIOS, MIGUEL DE, 1635-1701. [i.e. DAVID LEVI DE BARRIOS]
Las Poësias Famosas, Y Comedias, De Don Migvel De
Barrios. Segunda Impression enriquescida con lindissimas
Estampas. [Printer's device]. En Amberes: En Casa de
Geronymo y Iuanb. Verdussen, Impressores y Mercaderes de
Libros, 1674.
[25], 256, 55, [9], 107 p.; 22cm.

Colophon: "En Bruselas, De La Imprenta De Baltasar
Vivien, Impressor Y Mercader De Libros En El Buen Pastor."
Imperfect: title-page mutilated and repaired, with loss
of the first four words of the title.
First published under title: Flor de Apolo.
Ex-libris: Luis Bardón.
Gallardo II, 1329; Goldsmith, no. 96; Jerez p. 17;
Peeters-Fontainas 86; Penney p. 53; Simón Díaz VI, 3179.
Reel 21, No. 100

BARROS, ALONSO DE, d. 1640?
Provebios (sic) Morales, Heraclito De Alonso de Varros,
Concordados por el Maestro Bartolome Ximenez Paton. Al
Retor, Y Maestros Del Colegio Imperial de la Compañia de
I E S V de la Villa de Madrid. [Device of printer]. Con
Previlegio. En Baeca: por Pedro de la Cuesta. Vendense
en Villanueua de los Infantes, en casa de Francisco de
Valuerde mercader de libros, 1615.
[11], 78, [2] l.; 21cm.

Spanish and Latin on opposite pages.
Gallardo II, 1332; Goldsmith, no. 107; Graesse I, 298;
Jerez p. 121; Penney p. 53; Salvá II, 2050; Simón Díaz
VI, 3257.
Reel 21, No. 101

BARROS, ALONSO DE, d. 1640?
Proverbios Morales, Heraclito De Alonso de Varros,
Concordados por el Maestro Bartolome Ximenez Paton. Al
Retor, Y Maestros Del Colegio Imperial de la Compañia de
I E S V de la Villa de Madrid. Lisboa: Pedro Craesbeeck
[for] A costa de Tomás de Valle, 1617.
[10], 80, [2] l; 19cm.

Gallardo II, 1334; Penney p. 53; Quaritch Cat.
148/163; Simón Díaz VI, 3258.
Reel 21, No. 102

BASTA, GIORGIO, 1550-1607?
[Il Governo della Cavalleria. Spanish]
Govierno della cavalleria ligera. Compvesto por George
Basta, Conde del Sacro Imperio Romano. Gouernador y
Capitan General en Vngria, y Transiluania por el
inuictissimo Emperador Rodolfo II. de gloriosa memoria,
y su Lugarteniente General de Alemania. Traducido del
Lengvage Toscano en Español por Pedro Pardo Ribadeneyra,
Entretenido por su Magestad en los Estados de Flandes,
y Dirigido Al Excelentissimo Señor Don Gaspar de Gvzman,
Conde de Oliuares, y Duque de San-Lucar la Mayor, &c.
Con Licencia. En Madrid: En la Imprenta de Francisco
Martinez, 1642.
[24], 142 p.

Spanish translation by Pedro Pardo
Ribadeneyra.
Jerez p. 83; Palau 25366; Penney p. 54; Serís,
Nuevo 53.
Reel 21, No. 103

BATHE, WILLIAM, 1564-1614.
Ianva lingvarvm, sive modvs maxime accommodatvs, qvo
patefit aditvs ad omnes lingvas intelligendas, industria
patrum Hibernorum Societatis Iesu ... totiva lingvae
vocabvla, qvae frequentiora, et fundamentalia sunt
continentur: cum indice in lucem edita: et nunc ad
linguam Latinam ... accomodata ... Salmanticae: Apud
Franciscvm de Cea Tesa, 1611.
[9], 215 p.; 16cm.

First edition.
In Spanish and Latin.
Palau 123032; Vindel 2, 554.
Reel 21, No. 104

BENAVENTE Y BENAVIDES, CRISTÓBAL, b. 1582.
Advertencias Para Reyes, Principes Y Embajadores,
Dedicadas Al Sereniss. mo Principe De Las Españas Don
Balthasar Carlos D'Austria N.S. Por Don Christoval
De Benavente Y Benavides ... Madrid: Juan de Noort,
por Francisco Martinez, 1643.
[11], 700, [34] p; 21cm.

Gallardo II, 1361; Knapp p.90;
Penney p.57; Simon Diaz VI, 3872.
Reel 21, No. 105

BENTIVOGLIO, ANTONIO GALEAZZO, 1390 ca. - 1435.
Oratio ad Alexandrum VI nomine Bononiensium habita.
[Rome: Stephan Plannck, not before Sept. 1492].
[2] l., recto of first leaf blank; 21cm.

Gesamtkat. der Wiegendr. 3853.
Edited by Fernandus de Salazar.
Modern decorated stiff wrappers.
Reel 21, No. 106

BENTIVOGLIO, GUIDO, CARDINAL, 1579-1644.
[Della guerra di Fiandre.]
Gverra De Flandes, escrita por el eminentissimo Cardenal
Bentivollo. Tomos I. II. III. Traduxola de la lengua
toscana en la española el P. Basilio Varen. Madrid: Por
Francisco Martínez, a costa de Manuel López, 1643.
[11], 540, [19] p.; 29cm.

Spanish translation by Basilio Varen de los
Clerigos Menores.
Double columns.
Reel 22, No. 107

BERART, SERAPIO DE, Deacon of Gerona, 1677-1697.
Manifestacion, en qve se pvblican mvchos, y relevantes
servicios, y nobles hechos, con qve ha servido à sus
señores reyes la excelentissima ciudad de Barcelona;
singularmente en el sitio horroroso, que acaba de padecer
este presente año de 1697. Barcelona: En Casa de
Cormellas, por T. Loriente, [1697].
247 (i.e. 251) p.; 19cm.

Four unnumbered pages are inserted between p. 212 and
213.
Simón Díaz VI, 3995.
Reel 22, No. 108

BERMÚDEZ DE PEDRAZA, FRANCISCO, 1585-1655.
Antigvedad y excelencias de Granada. Por el licenciado
... Madrid: L. Sanchez, impressor del Rey N. S., 1608.
[12], 190, [7] l; 20cm.

Title vignette: Arms of Granada, inscribed Fundamenta
eius in montibus sacris.
Paging irregular: nos. 103-108 omitted; signatures:
Cc and Dd consist of one leaf each (101, 102); Ee begins
with leaf 109.
In four books; the fourth has special t.-p. (leaf 149):
Libro qvarto del santo mõte Ilipulitano, y sus excelencias
[title vignette]. En Madrid, Por Luis Sãchez, impressor
del Rey N. S. año M.DC. VII (date on last page: En Madrid,
Por Luis Sánchez, 1608).
Doublet, p. 33; Gallardo II, 1370; Penney p. 58;
Perez Pastor 992; Simón Díaz VI, 4080; Salvá II, 2834.
Reel 22, No. 109

BERMÚDEZ DE PEDRAZA, FRANCISCO, 1585-1655.
El Secretario del Rey, A Felipe Tercero, Monarca
Segundo de España ... [Madrid: Por Luis Sãchez, 1620]
[4], 86 l.; 20cm.

Bookplate of Juan M. Sánchez.
Pérez Pastor II, 1648; Simón Díaz VI, 4088.
Reel 22, No. 110

BERNARDO DE QUIRÓS, FRANCISCO, fl. 1629-1656.
La lvna de la sagra, vida y mverte de Santa Juana de
la Cruz [n.p.-n.d.]
40 p.; 21cm.

Bound with: CARDONA Y ALAGÓN, ANTONIO FOLCH DE: El
mas heroyco silencio. Comedia famosa. Valencia ...
1688.
Reel 33, No. 150

BEUTER, PEDRO ANTONIO, fl. 1510.
[Coronica general de toda España. Italian]
Cronica generale d'Hispagna, et del regno di Valenza.
Nella qvale si trattano gli avenimenti, & guerre, che dal
diluuio di Noe insino al tempo del re Don Giaime d'Aragona,
che acquistò Valenza in Spagna si seguitarono: insieme con
l'origine delle città, terre & luoghi piu notabili di
quella, & di tutte le nationi, & popoli del mondo: opera
ueramente molto curiosa, & diletteuole. Composta dall'
eccellente M. Anton Beuter ... & nuouamente tradotta in
lingua italiana dal S. Alfonso d'Vlloa. Con dve tavole,
la prima de' capitoli. & la seconda delle cose piu
notabili ... In Vinegia: Appresso G. Giolito de'
Ferrari, 1556.
[76], 533 p.: map; 16cm.

Italian translation by Alfonso de Ulloa.
Güell 686.
Reel 22, No. 111

BIBLE. LATIN. 1492. VULGATE.
[Biblia latina cum postillis Nicolai de Lyra]
[Strassburg: Johann Grüninger] 3 Nov. (III Nõn. Nov.)
1492.
4v. (468 l.; 370 l.; 348 l.; 364 l.); 32cm.

Vol. I title-leaf: Prima pars venerabilis fratris
Nicolai de lvra ordinis seraphici francisci (in
testamentũ vetus) tractãs super toto corpore biblie
cum suis additionibus, decz replicis, et figuris
sculptis.
Vol. II text: Incipit prefatio beati. Hieronymi
presbyteri in librum Esdre.

BIBLE (Cont'd)
Vol. III title leaf lacking: [Secunda pars Nicolai
de Lira tractãs super todo corpore biblie. cũ additionibus Replicas. z Figuris sculptis]
Vol. IV title leaf: Quarta pars dñi Nicolai de
Lira cum suis additõibus. deq replicas
tractans super todo corpore biblie.
A complete illustrated Bible. Of the ten copies
in the Stillwell Census, six are single volumes or
fragments of volumes only. The British Museum set is
made up of four odd volumes, different in size from
this copy. Five of the six copies reported by Polain
are incomplete, as are four of the seven in Pellechet.
All of the woodcuts are present in this copy.
Pages missing at end of Vol. IV.
Goff, B-617; Hain, 3161.
Reels 136 & 137, No. 853

BIBLE. N.T. 1 JOHN. Syriac. 1652.
Epistola D. Johannis, Apostoli. & Evangelistae,
Catholica Prima, Syriace, Juxta exemplar Cotheniense,
qvodest B. Mart. TrostI, Adjuncto è regione charactere
Ebraeo, etemq Versione Latinã, In Usum Philo-Syrorum
tyronum, seorsum excusa. Editore Andrea Sennerto,
P.P. in Academiã VVittenberg: Typis & Sumptibus Jobi
VVilhelmi Fingelii, 1652.
[2], 21 p.

Paged from left to right.
John I, 1-14 and the Lord's Prayer, Matt. VI,
9-13, in Syriac and Latin at end, p. 19-21.
Bound with Buxtorf, Johann.Lexicon Chaldaicum et
Syriacum. Basileae. 1622.
Reel 116, No. 734

BIBLE. POLYGLOT. 1514-17. In Academia Complytensi.
[Biblia polyglotta] [Alcala de Henares, industria
Arnaldi Guillelmi de Brocario in Academia complutensi,
1415-17]
6 v; 36cm.

Vol. I. Vetus testamentũ multiplici lingua nũc primo
impressum. Et imprimis Pentateuchus Hebraico
Greco atoz Chaldaico idio-mate. Adiũcta vnicuioz
sua latina interpretatione. 1517. (Genesis-
Deuteronomius).
Vol. II. Secũda pars Vet. Test. (Josua-Paralipomena et
Oratio Manasse en latin).
Vol.III. Tertia pars Vet. Test. (Esra-Ecclesiasticus).
Vol. IV. Quarta pars Vet. Test. (Jesaias-Maccab.) 1517.
Vol. V. Nouum testamentum grece & latine. 1514.
Vol. VI. Vocabularium hebraicum atoz chaldaicu totius
veteris testamenti ... 1516.

Titles, with Cardinal Jiménez' coat of arms, are within
woodcut borders.
Initials; tail-pieces.
Vol. I. has Hebrew, Greek and Latin in parallel columns,
with Chaldaic text at foot of page; vols. 2-4 are without
Chaldaic; vol. 6 has Greek and Latin only.
Vols. 1 and 2-4 have colophon (vol. 4) dated, 10 July
1517; vol. 6 has two colophons dated, respectively, 17
March 1515 and 31 May 1515.
The New Testamente (vol. 5) has colophon dated, 10
January 1514.
The first polyglot Bible, edited by eminent scholars,
headed by Diego López de Zúñiga, and printed, in an edition
of 600 copies, at the expense of Cardinal Jiménez.
For full description of this work, see British and
Foreign Bible Society. Historical Catalogue, vol. 2, no.
1412.
Catalina 19; Doublet, p. 34; Palau 28930; Penney
p. 61; Thomas p. 12.
Reels 22, 23 & 24, No. 112

BIBLE. SPANISH. 1602. Valera.
La Biblia, que es, Los Sacros Libros Del Vieio y Nvevo Testamento. Segunda Edicion. Revista y conferida con los textos Hebreos y Griegos y con diversas translaciones. Por Cypriano de Valera. [Device of printer on title page, with motto: "La palabra de Dios permanece para siempre"]. En Amsterdam: En casa de Lorenco Iacobi, 1602.
[12], 268, 67, 88 l.: double columns.

Amsterdam. Spanish translation by Casiodoro de Reina, brought out by Cipriano de Valera.
Reel 24, No. 113

BIVERO, PEDRO DE, 1575-1656.
Sacrvm oratorivm imaginvm Immacvlate Mariae et animae creatae ac baptismo, poenitentia et evcharistia innovatae, ars nova bene vivendi et moriendi ... Avctore R.P.P. Petro Bivero ... Antverpiae: ex officina Plantiniana Balthasaris Moreti, 1634.
[17], 769, [10] p.: ill; 21cm.

Graesse I, p. 433; Simón Díaz VI, 4458.
Reel 25, No. 115

BIVERO, PEDRO DE, 1575-1656.
Sacrvm Sanctvarivm Crvcis et Patientiae crvcifixorvm et crvciferorvm, emblematicis imaginibvs laborantivm et aegrotantivm ornatvm; artifices gloriosi novae artis bene vivendi et moriendi secvndvm rationem regvlae et circini, avctore ... Antverpiae: ex officina Plantiniana Balthasaris Moreti, 1634.
[24], 678, [19] p.: ill. plates; 21cm., in 4s.

Graesse 1, p. 433; Palau 30028; Simón Díaz VI, 4459.
Reel 25, No. 114

BLANCAS Y TOMÁS, GERONIMO DE, d. 1590.
[Ad regum aragonum. Spanish]
Inscripciones latinas a los retratos de los Reyes de Sobrarbe, Condes antiguos, y Reyes de Aragon, puestos en la Sala Real de la Diputacion de la Ciudad de Zaragoca. Contiene vna breve noticia de las heroycas acciones de cada vno, tiempo en que florecieron, y cosas tocantes a sus Reynados ... Se añadieron las inscripciones a los retratos de los reyes D. Felipe Primero, Segundo, y Tercero. Tradvcidas en vvlgar, y escoliadas, las de los Reyes de Sobrarbe, y Condes antiguos de Aragon, por ... Martin Carrillo ... Las de los Reyes de Aragon, con la descripcion de la Sala, y otras noticias, señaladamente la de averse colocado en la misma el Retrato del Rey nuestro Señor Don Carlos II que es lo que ocasiona este escrito, por ... Diego Iosef Dormer ... Zaragoca: Herederos de Diego Dormer, 1680.
[35], 532 p. ill.; 20cm.

Ad regum aragonum. Spanish translation by Martín Carrillo continued by Diego Dormer.
Half-title: Explicacion historica de las inscripciones de los reyes de Sobrarbe ...
Goldsmith, no. 247; Jiménez Catalán 958; Palau 30148; Penney p. 65; Salvá II, 2839; Simón Díaz VI, 4492.
Reel 25, No. 117

BLANCAS Y TOMÁS, GERÓNIMO DE, d. 1590.
Aragonensivm rervm commentarii ... Omnia S. R. E. animadversioni subjiecta sunto. Caesaravgvstae: Apud Laurentium Robles, et Didacum fratres, 1588.
[21], 519, [60] p.: ill; 32cm.

Adams, no. 2097; Penney p. 65; Salvá II, 2837; Sánchez 680; Simón Díaz VI, 4489; Thomas p. 14.
Reel 25, No. 116

BLANCAS Y TOMÁS, GERONIMO DE, d. 1590.
Coronaciones de los Serenisimos Reyes de Aragon. Escritas por ... Con dos Tratados del Modo de tener Cortes del mismo Autor, y de Geronimo Martel ... Publícalo el Doctor Iuan Francisco Andres de Vztarroz ... Caragoca: por Diego Dormer. A costa de Pedro y Tomás Alfay, 1641.
[25], 261, [33] p.; 20cm.

Bound with: Martel, Jerónimo, Forma De Celebrar Cortes en Aragon ... En Caragoca, Por Diego Dormer, 1641.
Palau, 152700.
Reel 26, No. 119

BLANCAS Y TOMÁS, GERONIMO DE, d. 1590.
Modo de proceder en Cortes de Aragon. Escrito por Geronimo de Blancas Chronista del Reyno. A los Qvatro Brazos del Reyno Ivuntos en Cortes Generales. Pvblicalo el Doctor Iuan Francisco Andres Vztarroz, con algunas notas [Tail-piece] Con Licencia, y Privilegio. En Caragoca: por Diego Dormer, 1641.
[4], 111, [7], l.; 20cm.

Cosens 540; Jiménez Catalán 418; Penney p. 66.
Reel 26, No. 118

BLÁZQUEZ MAYORALGO, JUAN.
Perfecta racon de Estado. Dedvcida de los hechos de el Señor Rey Don Fernando el Catholico ... Contra los politicos atheistas. México: Por Francisco Robledo, 1646.
[65], 194, [34] l.; 20cm.

Gallardo II, 1400; Heredia IV, 4287; Medina, México, II, 620; Palau 30917; Simón Díaz VI, 4600.
Reel 26, No. 121

BLEDA, JAIME. ca. 1550-1622.
Coronica de los moros de España dividida en ocho libros ... Valencia: Felipe Mey, 1618.
[33], 1072, [11] p.; 29cm.

Lacks t.-p. and leaf at end.
Title within ornamental border; head and tail pieces; initials.
Gallardo II, 1402; Goldsmith, no. 250; Graesse I, p. 439; Penney p. 66; Quaritch Cat. 148/192; Simón Díaz VI, 4606.
Reel 26, No. 122

BOCANGEL Y UNZULETA, GABRIEL, ca. 1608-1658.
Rimas y Prosas, ivnto con la fabvla de Leandro y Ero ... Madrid: Por Iuan Goncalez. A costa de Alonso Perez, 1627.
[16], 136 l.; 15cm.

Graesse I, p. 445; Jerez p. 17; Penney p. 67; Salvá I, 1120; Simón Díaz VI, 4655.
Reel 26, No. 123

BOCCALINI, TRAIANO, 1556-1613.
[Delli avvisi di Parnaso. Spanish]
Discvrsos politicos, y avisos del Parnasso ... Tradvxolos de la lengua Toscana en la Española ... Hvesca: Por Iuan Francisco Larumbe, A costa de Pedro Escuer, 1640.
[12], 133 l.; 21cm.

Delli avvisi di Parnaso. Spanish translation by Fernando Pérez de Sousa.
Reel 26, No. 124

BOCCALINI, TRAIANO, 1556-1613.
[Delli avvisi di Parnaso. Spanish]
Aviso del Parnaso ... Primera y Segvnda Centvria.
Tradvcidos De Lengva Toscana en Espanola por Fernando
Perez de Souza ... Madrid: por Diego Diaz de la
Carrera, A costa Fernando de Mateo de la Bastida, 1653.
2 v. ([14], 177 *l*.; [8], 144 *l*); 21cm.

Palau I, p. 293, 31182.
Reels 26 & 27, No. 125

BORJA, FRANCISCO DE, príncipe de Esquilache, 1582-1658.
Las obras en verso De Don Francisco De Borja, Principe
de Esquilache, Gentilhombre de la Camara de Su Magestad.
Dedicadas Al Rey Nvestro Señor Don Phelipe. Qvarto de este
nombre. Madrid: por Diego Diaz de la Carrera, 1648.
[13], 684, [22] p.; 20cm.

Jerez, p. 18; Palau, 33122; Penney, p. 71; Salvá,
I, 592; Simón Díaz, VI, 4989.
Reel 27, No. 126

BORJA, FRANCISCO DE, príncipe de Esquilache, 1582-1658.
Las Obras En Verso De Don Francisco De Borja, Principe
de Esquilache, Gentilhombre de la Camara de Su Magestad;
Dedicadas Al Rey Nvestro Señor Don Philipe IV. Edition
Segunda, reuista y muy añadida. A Amberes: En La
Emprenta Plantiniana De Blathasar Moreto, 1654.
[17], 692, [23] p.; 23cm.

Colophon: [1 Vvvv³: Printer's device] "En Amberes
En La Emprenta Plantiniana. M.DC. LIII."
Engr. title-page.
Antonio, III, p. 110; Gallardo, 1435; Heredia, 2032;
Jerez, p. 18; Palau, 33124; Peeters-Fontainas, I, 140;
Penney, p. 71; Salvá, 594; Simón Díaz mentions only the
1653 edition.
Reel 27, No. 127

BORJA, FRANCISCO DE, principe de Esquilache, 1582-1658.
Poema heroico, Napoles recvperada por el rey don Alonso,
qve dedica ... Francisco de Boria.. Caragoca: En el Real
y General Hospital de Nuestra Señora de Gracia, 1651.
[32], 398 p.; 20cm.

Gallardo, II, no. 1437; Goldsmith, no. 286; HC:NS4/20;
Jerez, p. 18; Jiménez Catalán, no. 566; Palau, 33126;
Penney, p. 71; Salvá, I, 598; Simón Díaz, VI, 4998.
Reel 27, No. 128

BORJA, JUAN DE b. 1553.
Empresas Morales, Compuestas Por El Excellentissimo
Señor, Don Juan De Borja, Conde de Mayalde, y de Ficallo,
Treze, y Comendador de la Orden de S. Jago, Embaxador
por el Señor Rey PHELIPE II. à la Corona de Portugal,
y, à la Magestad Cesarea, Mayordomo Mayor de la Serenissima
Señora Emperatriz Maria; de los Consejos de Estado, y
Guerra del Señor Rey PHELIPE III. Presidente en el Real
de Portugal; y Mayordomo Mayor de la Serenissima Señora
Reyna Doña Margarita. Sacalas A Lvz El Doctor Don Francisco
De Borja su Nieto, Arcediano Mayor de la S. Metropolitana
Iglesia de Valencia, y Capellan mayor que fue de su
Magestad en su Real Capilla, y Monasterio de las Reales
Descalcas Franciscas de Madrid. Dedicals A La S.C.R. M.
Del Rey Don Carlos II. Nvestro Señor. En Brvsaelas: Por
Francisco Foppens, Mercader de Libros, 1680.
[11], 455, [6] p.: ill; 20cm.

Added title-page, engraved, mended along outer edge;
title-page and several leaves mended, affecting date on
title-page but not text.
Gallardo, no. 1445; Heredia, 1111; Jerez, p. 20; La
Serna, no. 3442; Morante, Cat., 749; Palau, 33113;
Peeters-Fontainas, I, no. 143; Penney, p. 71; Simón Díaz,
VI, 5039.
Reel 27, No. 129

BOSCÁN ALMOGAVER, JUAN. d. 1542.
Las obras de Boscan y algunas de Garcilasso de la Vega
repartidas en qvatro libros. [Barcelona]: en la Officina
de Garles Amoros [sic for Carles] A los XX del mes de
Marzo, 1543.
[8], CCXXXVII *l*; 21cm.

Adams, I, no. 2526; Keniston, I; Palau, 33376; Penney,
p. 72; Simón Díaz, VI, 5077.
Reel 27, No. 130

BOSCÁN ALMOGAVER, JUAN. d. 1542.
Las obras de Boscan y Algunas de Garcilasso de la Vega,
Repartidas en quatro libros. Barcelona: [en la officina
de la Viuda Carles Amorosa], 1554.
[8], cclxviii, [23] *l*; 15cm.

Gallardo II, 1457; Keniston 13; Penney p. 72;
Palau 33385; Salvá I, 478; Simón Díaz VI, 5093.
Reel 27, No. 131

BOVERIO, ZACCARIA, 1568-1638.
[Annalium. Spanish]
Las chronicas de los frailes menores capvchinos.
Madrid: Por Carlos Sanchez, 1644-46.
v. 1-2 of 5 ([32], 582 p; p. 99-107, 23 *l*): ill.

Annalium. Spanish translation by Francisco Antonio
de Madrid.
Engraved t.-p. of vol. 2 appears to be dated 1649.
Leaves 1-3, of vol. 1 (t.-p. and 2 following leaves)
msg; also pp. 1-98 of next series of pagination
following p. 582.
Palau 34206.
Reel 28, No. 132

BOVERIUS, ZACHARIAS see BOVERIO, ZACCARIA.

BRAONES, ALONSO MARTÍN DE.
Epitome de los trivnfos de Jesvs, y finezas de su amor
en la redempcion del hombre. En cuya meditacion dessea
el espiritu conocer la Suprema y Divina Magestad por medio
de su Humanidad Santissima, y á su amor adoracion, y
alabanca combida á las criaturas. Escrivialo en qvinientas
octavas ... Lleva añadida al fin las aspiraciones
Jaculatorias del mismo Autor para los siete dias de la
semana. Sevilla: Lucas Martin de Hermosilla, vendese
en casa de P. Ponce, 1686.
[5], 89 *l*.; 21cm.

Escudero 1814; Jerez p. 19; Palau 34499; Penney p.
75; Simón Díaz VI, 5280.
Reel 28, No. 133

BRAVO, BARTOLOMÉ, d. 1607.
Thexavrvs verborvm, ac phrasivm, ad orationem ex
Hispana Latinam efficiendam, et locuplentadam. ... Hac
postrema editione, non modica verborum, ac phrasium
accessione, atq; ortographiae auctus ... Matriti: Ex
officina viduae Illephonsi Martini à Balboa. Sumptibus
Sebastiani Perez Bybliopolae, 1619.
[135] *l*; 20cm.

Palau 34629.
Reel 28, No. 134

BREVE relacion del horroroso incendio que ha padecido la
Ciudad de Londres, desde Domingo 12. de Septiembre,
hasta Iueves 16. del mesmo mes, de este Año de 1666.
Sevilla: por Iuan Gomez de Blas, 1666.
4 l.

Colophon: "Con licencia, impresso en Sevilla, por Iuan
Gomez de Blas, su Impressor mayor - Año de 1666.
Reel 28, No. 135

EL BROCENSE see SÁNCHEZ DE LAS BROZAS, FRANCISCO.

BRUSANTINI, PAOLO, CONTE, (translator) see DAZA, ANTONIO,
Brother.

BUSBECQ, OGIER GHISLAIN DE, 1522-1592.
Itinera Constantinopolitanvm Et Amasianvm Ab
Augerio Gislenio Busbequio ad Solimannum Turearum
Imperatorem C. M. Oratore confecta. Eiusdem Bvsbeqvii
de re militari contra Turcam instituenda consilium.
Altera Editio. Antverpiae: Ex officina Christophori
Plantini, 1582.
127 p.; 17cm.

Bound in: Sánchez De Las Brozas, Francisco. De
Avtoribvs Interpretandis ..., 1582.
Adams, I, no. 3330.
Reel 166, No. 1083

BUSTAMANTE DE LA CÁMARA, JEAN, 16th cent.
De reptilibvs vere animantibus S. Scripturae libri
sex, duobus tomis comprehensi ... Cvm triplici indice;
primo capitum, altero locorum S. Scripturae; tertio
rerum & verborum. Lvgdvni, Semptibus A. Pillehotte,
1620.
2 v. in 1 ([17], 1382, [62] p.) 18cm.

Engraved title page.
Title of the first edition (1595): De Animantibus
Scripturae Sacrae ... Tomus primus. Books 3, 5 and 6
have separate titles.
Doublet, p. 38; Palau p. 481; Thomas, p. 16.
Reel 28, No. 136

BUXTORF, JOHANN, 1564-1629.
Lexicon Chaldaicum Et Syriacum; Quo Voces Omnes Tam
Primitivae, Quotquot In Sacrorum Vet. Testamenti
librorum Targumim seu Paraphrasibus Chaldaicis, Onkeli
in Mosen, Johathanis in Prophetas, & aliorum authorum
in Hagiographa: Item In Targum Hierosolymitano,
Jonathane altero in Legem, & Targum secundo in librum
Esther: Denique In Novi Testamenti Translatione
Syriaca reperiuntur. Accurate Et Methodice Dispositae,
& fideliter explicatae, copiosē absolutéq; describuntur.
Collectum, & ingratiam harum linguarum studiosorum: in
lucem editum. A M. Johanne Buxtorfio Jun.
[Basilea: Ludovici Regis,] 1622.
[21], 640 p.; 22cm.

Reel 116, No. 735

C

CABREGA, PEDRO DE NAVARRA Y DE LA, MARQUES DE.
Logros De La Monarqvia En Aciertos De Vn Valido.
Al Rey nuestro señor Don Carlos Segvndo. Por Don
Pedro de Nauarra y de la Cueua, Cauallero de la Orden
de Sant Iago, Marques de Cabrèga, Mayordomo de la
Reina Nuestra Señora. Madrid: Por Iulian de Paredes,
1669.
[20], 83 l.; 21cm.

Palau, 187993.
Reel 119, No. 750

CABRERA DE CORDOBA, LUIS, 1559-1623.
De Historia, Para Entenderla Y Escrivirla. A Don
Francisco De Sandoval Duque de Lerma, y Cea mayor de
Castilla, del Consejo de Estado, Cauallerizo mayor, y
Soumillier de Corps, del Rey don Felipe IIII. N.S. Ayo,
y Mayordomo mayor del Principe D. Felipe IIII. &c. LVIS
CABRERA DE CORDOVA, criado de su Magestad. Con priuilegio,
En Madrid: Por Luis Sanchez, 1611.
[3], 110, [2] l.; 21cm.

Goldsmith, p. 26, no. 14; Palau 38915; Penney,
p. 81; Pérez Pastor, 1125; Simón Díaz, VII, 231;
Ticknor, p. 47.
Reel 28, No. 137

CABRERA DE CORDOBA, LUIS, 1559-1623.
Felipe Segvndo rey de España. Al serenissimo principe
sv nieto esclaracido don Felipe de Austria ... En Madrid:
Por Luis Sanchez, impressor del Rey, 1619.
[9], 1176, [60] p.; 32cm.

Engraved t.-p.
This edition includes only the first part (1527-1583).
The Second part was published for the first time in the
edition of 1876, from a manuscript in the Bibliothèque
Nationale, Paris.
Goldsmith, p. 26, no. 15; HC384/76; Palau, 38917;
Penney p. 81; Pérez Pastor, 1586; Simón Díaz, VII, 233.
Reel 29, No. 138

CAESAR, CAIUS JULIUS.
Los comentarios de Gayo Ivlio Cesar. Contienen las
gverras de Africa, España, Francia, Alexandria, y las
ciuiles de los ciudadanos romanos, con el libro otauo de
Aulo Hircio añadido ... Vn. Argvmento de las gverras de
Francia, y vna declaracion de su diuision para concordar
a Cesar con otros autores. Madrid: Por la Viuda de A.
Martin, A costa de D. Goncalez, 1621.
244, [13] l.; 21cm.

Spanish translation by Diego López de Toledo.
Title page and several other pages mutilated, with some
loss of text.
Goldsmith, p. 26, no. 41; Graesse, II, p. 10.
Reel 29, No. 139

CAESARIUS, JOANNES.
Rhetorica Ioannis Caesarii, In Septem Libros Sive
tractatus digesta, uniuersam ferè eius artis uim
compendio complectens, tertiò iam per authorem
diligenter recognita, & castigata, locpletáq.
Coloniae: Ad intersignium Monocerotis, 1565.
[76] l.; 16cm.

Bound in: Soarez, Cypriano: De Arte Rhetorica
Libri Tres ..., 1570.
Adams, I, no. 102 (Rhetorica ..., only)
Reel 173, No. 1139

CALDERÓN DE LA BARCA, PEDRO. 1600-1681.
Primera Parte De Comedias del Celebre Poeta Español,
Don Pedro Calderon De La Barca, Cavallero Del Orden De
Santiago, Capellan de Honor de su Magestad, y de los
señores Reyes Nueuos en la Santa Iglesia de Toledo, Qve
Nvevamente Corregidas Pvblica Don Ivan De Vera Tassis Y
Villarroel, Sv Mayor Amigo, Y Las Ofrece Al Excelentissimo
Señor Don Iñigo Melchor Fernandez de Velasco y Touar,
Condestable de Castilla, y de Leon, Camarero Mayor del
Rey nuestro Señor, su Copero Mayor, su Cazador Mayor,
y su Mayordomo Mayor, de los Consejos de Estado, y Guerra,
Comendador de Vsagre en la Orden, y Caualleria de
Santiago, y Treze della, Duque de la Ciudad de Frias, &c.
Con Privilegio. En Madrid: Por Francisco Sanz, Impressor
del Reino, y Portero de Camara de su Magestad, 1685.
[29], 543 p.; 21cm.

Goldsmith, p. 27, no. 58; Graesse, II, p. 14; Palau,
39765; Ticknor, p. 49. Simón Díaz, VII, no. 994,
cites a fake edition of 1685. His title page reads
'Juan ... Su Mayor Amigo', where our genuine title
page reads 'Ivan De Vera Tassis ... Sv Mayor Amigo'.
Reel 29, No. 140, Part 1 (A)

CALDERÓN DE LA BARCA, PEDRO. 1600-1681.
Primera Parte De Comedias Del Celebre Poeta Español
Don Pedro Calderon De La Barca, Cavallero Del Orden De
Santiago, Capellan de Honor de su Magestad, y de los
señores Reyes Nuevos en la Santa Iglesia de Toledo, Que
Nvevamente Corregidas Don Juan De Vera Tassis Y
Villarroel, Su Mayor Amigo. Y Las Ofrece Al Excelentissimo
Señor Don Iñigo Melchor Fernandez de Velasco y Tovar,
Condestable de Castilla, y de Leon, Camarero Mayor del Rey
nuestro Señor, de los Consejos de Estado, y Guerra,
Comendador de Vsagre en la Orden, y Cavalleria de Santiago,
y Treze della, Duque de la Ciudad de Frias, &c. Con
Privilegio. En Madrid: Por Francisco Sanz, Impressor del
Reino y Portero de Camara de su Magestad, 1685.
[9], 18, 18, 20, 18, 20, [21], 18, [41], 20, [24],
18. l.; 21cm.

Text with no continuous page-numbers to which one can
refer.
Simón Díaz, VII, no. 994, cites the same fake edition
as ours.
Reel 31, No. 140, Part 1 (B)

CALDERÓN DE LA BARCA, PEDRO. 1600-1681.
Parte Segunda De Comedias Del Celebre Poeta Español,
Don Pedro Calderon De La Barca, Cavallero De La Orden De
Santiago, Capellan de Honor de su Magestad, y de los
señores Reyes Nueuos en la Santa Iglesia de Toledo, Qve
Nvevamente Corregidas Pvblica Don Ivan De Vera Tassis Y
Villarroel Sv Mayor Amigo: Y Las Ofrece Al Excelentissimo
Señor Don Iñigo Melchor Fernandez de Velasco y Touar,
Condestable de Castilla, y de Leon, Camarero Mayor del
Rey nuestro Señor, su Copero Mayor, su Cazador Mayor, y
su Mayordomo Mayor, de los Consejos de Estado, y Guerra,
Comendador de Vsagre en la Orden, y Caualleria de Santiago,
y Treze della, Duque de la Ciudad de Frias, &c. Con
Privilegio. En Madrid: Por Francisco Sanz, Impressor
del Reyno, y Portero de Camara de su Magestad, 1686.
[17], 572, [5] p.; 21cm.

Graesse, II, p. 14; Palau, 39765, Salvá, I, 1126;
Simón Díaz, VI, 996 (fake); Ticknor, p. 49.
Reel 29, No. 140, Part 2

CALDERÓN DE LA BARCA, PEDRO. 1600-1681.
Tercera Parte De Comedias Del Celebre Poeta Español
Don Pedro Calderon De La Barca, Cavallero Del Orden De
Santiago, Capellan de Honor de su Magestad, y de los
señores Reyes Nueuos en la Santa Iglesia de Toledo; Qve
Nvevamente Corregias Pvblica Don Ivan De Vera Tassis Y
Villarroel, Sv Mayor Amigo, Y Las Ofrece Al Excelentissimo
Señor Don Iñigo Melchor Fernandez de Velasco y Tovar,
Condestable de Castilla, Y de Leon, Camarero Mayor del
Rey nuestro señor, su Copero Mayor, su Cazador Mayor,
y su Mayordomo Mayor, de los Consejos de Estado, y Guerra,
Comendador de Vsagre en la Orden, y Cavalleria de Santiago,
y Treze della, Duque de la Ciudad de Frias, &c. Con
Privilegio. En Madrid: Por Francisco Sanz, Impressor
del Reino, y Portero de Camara de su Magestad, 1687.
[17], 586, [5] p.; 21cm.

The fake edition of 1687 has four preliminary leaves
instead of eight.
Graesse, II, p. 14; Palau 39765; Simón Díaz, VII,
997, cites three copies, only two of the three are
genuine. Salvá, I, no. 1126; Ticknor, p. 49.
Reel 29, No. 140, Part 3

CALDERÓN DE LA BARCA, PEDRO. 1600-1681.
Quarta Parte De Comedias Del celebre Poeta Español,
D. Pedro Calderon De La Barca, Cavellero Del Orden De
Santiago, Capellan de Honor de su Magestad, y de los
Señores Reyes Nuevos en la Santa Iglesia de la Ciudad
de Toledo ... Madrid: Por los Herederos de Juan Garzia
Infanzon, 1731.
[17], 606 p.
Reel 30, No. 140, Part 4

CALDERÓN DE LA BARCA, PEDRO. 1600-1681.
Verdadera Qvinta Parte De Comedias De Don Pedro
Calderon De La Barca, Cavallero Del Orden De Santiago,
Capellan de Honor de su Magestad, y de los señores Reyes
Nueuos de la Santa Iglesia de la Ciudad de Toledo,
Celebre Poeta Español: Qve Publica Don Ivan De Vera
Tassis Y Villarroel, Sv Mayor Amigo, Debaxo De La
Proteccion Del Excelentissimo Señor Don Francisco
Antonio Casimiro Alfonso Pimentel de Herrera Ponce
de Leon Velasco Quiñones y Benauides, Conde-Duque de
Benauente, Conde de Luna, Marquès de Xaualquinto y
Villarreal, &c. Con Privilegio. En Madrid: Por
Francisco Sanz, Impressor del Reyno, y Portero de
Camara de su Magestad, 1682.
[84], 542 p.; 21cm.

Graesse, II, p. 14; Palau, 39765; Simón Díaz, VII,
999, has only 4 preliminary leaves; Ticknor, p. 49.
Reel 30, No. 140, Part 5

CALDERÓN DE LA BARCA, PEDRO. 1600-1681.
Sexta Parte De Comedias Del Celebre Poeta Español Don
Pedro Calderon De La Barca, Cavallero Del Orden de
Santiago, Capellan de Honor de su Magestad, y de los
señores Reyes Nueuos de la Santa Iglesia de Toledo. Sacadas
De Svs Originales Qve Pvblica La Amistad De Don Ivan De
Vera Tassis Y Villarroel, Debaxo De La Proteccion Del
Excelentissimo Señor Don Francisco Antonio Casimiro Alfonso
Pimentel de Herrera Ponce de Leon Valasco Quiñones y
Benauides, Conde-Duque de Benauente, Conde de Luna,
Marquès de Xaualquinto, y Villa-Real, &c. Con Privilegio,
En Madrid: Por Francisco Sanz, Impressor del Reyno, y
Portero de Camara de su Magestad, 1683.
[67], 579 p.; 21cm.

Graesse, II, p. 14; Palau, 39765; Simón Díaz, VII.
1000 (fake); Ticknor, p. 49.
Reel 30, No. 140, Part 6

CALDERÓN DE LA BARCA, PEDRO. 1600-1681.
Septima Parte De Comedias Del Celebre Poeta Español
Don Pedro Calderon De La Barca, Cavallero Del Orden De
Santiago, Capellan de Honor de su Magestad, y de los
señores Reyes Nueuos de Toledo, Qve Corregidas Por Svs
Originales, Pvblica Don Ivan De Vera Tassis Y Villarroel,
Sv Mayor Amigo, Y las Ofrece Al Muy Ilvstre Señor Doctor
Don Alonso Brauo de Buiza, Gentilombre de Camara, Y
Compañero del Eminentissimo señor Cardenal Brancacho,
En el Conclaue en que se eligiò à N.S. Padre Alexandro
VII. Canonigo de Zamora, Arcediano de Palencia,
Comendador Mayor de la Orden de San Antonio Abad de
Castro-Xeriz, Canonigo de la Santa Apostolica, y
Metropolitana Iglesia de Santiago, Arcediano de Nendos,
&c. Con Privilegio. En Madrid: Por Francisco Sanz,
Impressor del Reyno, y Portero de Camara de su Magestad,
1683.
[17], 562, [5] p.; 21cm.

Graesse, II, p. 14; Palau, 39765; Simón Díaz, VII,
1001 (fake); Ticknor, p. 49.
Reel 30, No. 140, Part 7

CALDERÓN DE LA BARCA, PEDRO. 1600-1681.
Octava Parte De Comedias Del Celebre Poeta Español
Don Pedro Calderon De La Barca, Cavallero Del Orden De
Santiago, Capellan de Honor de su Magestad, y de los
señores Reyes Nueuos de Toledo, Qve Corregidas Por Svs
Originales, Pvblica Don Ivan De Vera Tassis Y Villarroel,
Sv Mayor Amigo, Y Las Ofrece Al Mvy Ilvstre Señor Don Ivan
Francisco Perez de Saauedra Ponce de Leon y Guzman,
Marquès del Villar, Señor de las Guadamelenas,
Veintiquatro de la Ciudad de Cordoua, Patrono del Colegio
de los Escriuanos del Numero della, y Patrono del Conuento
de Santa Iusta, y Rufina de la Ciudad de Seuilla, &c.
En Madrid: Por Francisco Sanz, Impressor del Reino, y
Portero de Camara de su Magestad, 1684.
[17], 570, [5] p.; 21cm.

Graesse, II, p. 14; Palau, 39765; Simón Díaz, VII,
1002, cites a fake edition also of 1684, Ticknor, p. 49.
Reel 30, No. 140, Part 8

CALDERÓN DE LA BARCA, PEDRO. 1600-1681.
Novena Parte De Comedias Del Celebre Poeta Español,
Don Pedro Calderon De La Barca, Cavallero Del Orden De
Santiago, Capellan de Honor de su Magestad, y de los
señores Reyes Nuevos en la Santa Iglesia de Toledo; Que
Nuevamente Corregidas, Publica Don De Vera Tassis Y
Villarroel; Fiscal de las Comedias destos Reynos, por
su Mag. Y Las Ofrece Al Excelentissimo Señor Don Iñigo
Melchor Fernandez de Velasco y Tovar, Condestable de
Castilla, y de Leon, Camarero Mayor del Rey nuestro
señor, su Copero Mayor, su Cazador Mayor, y su
Mayordomo Mayor, de los Consejos de Estado, y Guerra,
Comendador de Vsagre en la Orden, y Cavalleria de Santiago,
y Treze della, Duque de la Ciudad de Frias, &c. Con
Privilegio. En Madrid: Por Juan Garcia Infazon, 1698.
[15], 566, [2] p; 21cm.

Graesse, II, p. 14; Palau, III, p. 45; Simón Díaz,
VII, 1012.
Reel 30, No. 140, Part 9

CALDERÓN DE LA BARCA, PEDRO. 1600-1681.
Avtos Sacramentales, Alegoricos, Y Historiales.
Dedicados Al Patriarca San Jvan De Dios. Compvestos Por
Don Pedro Calderon de la Barca, Cavallero de la Orden
de Sãtiago, Capellan de Honor de su Magestad, y de los
Señores Reyes Nuevos de la Santa Iglesia de Toledo.
Con Licencia. En Madrid: Por Jvan Garcia Infazon, 1690.
[9], 398 p.; 22cm.

Palau, 39830; Ticknor, p. 52.
Reel 31, No. 141

CALDERÓN DE LA BARCA, PEDRO. 1600-1681.
Comedia Famosa: Los Tres Afectos De Amor: Piedad,
Desmayo, Y Valor. De Don Pedro Calderon de la Barca.
[n. p., 17--?]
[21] l; 21cm.

Caption title.
Palau, 40131; Simón Díaz, VI, 2022; Ticknor, p. 50.
Reel 31, No. 142

CALENDARIVM perpetuum & Generale breuiarii romani. Ex
decreto Sacrosancticoncilii Tridentini nuper editi
Triginta sex Tabulis constans, protota Hispania cum
festis que generaliter in Hispaniarum Regnis auctoritate
Apostolica celebrantur. In quo de concurrentia, &
ocurrentia officiorum singulis cuius q; Anni diebus,
dèq; alijs dubijs copio sius, ac euidentius quam alias,
Petro Rvyssio presbytero Toletano annotatur auctore.
Cvm Licentia Maiestatis Regiae. Escvdebat Toleti
Ioannes A Plaza. Typographus, 1578.
[63], 992, 104 p.; 15cm.

Palau, 40355; Pérez Pastor, Toledo, no. 355.
Reel 31, No. 143

CAMÕES, LUIS DE, 1524?-1580.
[Lvsiades. Spanish]
Los Lvsiadas de Lvys de Camoes, traduzidos en octaua
rima castellana por Benito Caldera, residente en Corte.
Impresso en Alcalá de Henares por Iuã Gracian, 1580.
[388] p.; 20cm.

Lusiades. Spanish translation by Benito Caldera.
Catalina, 552; Gallardo, II, 1525; Graesse, II,
p. 27; HC:NS4/1206; Palha, 1754; Penney, p. 86; Palau,
41051; Simón Díaz, VII, 448; Salvá, I, 448; Thomas,
p. 18.
Reel 31, No. 144

CAMÕES, LUIS DE, 1524?-1580.
[Lvsiades. Spanish]
Los Lvsiadas de Lvys de Camoes, traduzidos de portugues
en castellano por Henrique Garces ... En Madrid:
Impresso con licencia en casa de Guillermo Drouy Impressor
de libros, 1591.
[4], 185 l.; 20cm.

Title vignette (royal arms of Spain).
Numerous errors in foliation.
Spanish translation by Enrique Garces.
Graesse, II, p. 27; Palha, 1755; Palau, 41052;
Pérez Pastor, 352; Penney, p. 86; Simon Díaz, VII,
3705; Thomas, p. 18.
Reel 31, No. 145

CAMÕES, LUIS DE, 1524?-1580.
[Lvsiades. Spanish]
Lvsiades de Luis de Camoes, principe de los poetas
de España. Al Rey N. Señor Felipe Qvarto el Grande ...
Madrid: Ivan Sanchez, a costa de Pedro Coello, 1639.
4 v. in 2 (25 p., 552 double columns on 276 p.; 652
double columns on 326 p.; 528 double columns on 264 p.;
670 double columns on 335 p.)

Colophon, Vol. II: En Madrid: por Antonio Duplastre,
1639
Canto, 25; Goldsmith, p. 29, no. 128; Palha, 1632-
Westermann, 163; Palau, 41053; Simón Díaz, VII, 3706.
Reels 31 & 32, No. 146

CAMOS, MARCO ANTONIO DE, 1543-1606.
Microcosmia, y govierno vniversal del hombre Christiano,
para todos los estados y qvalquiera de ellos ... Con
quatro indices necessarios y copiosos. En Barcelona:
en el Monasterio del Sancto Augustin por Pablo Malo, 1592.
3 pts. ([17], 211; 236; 192, [80] p.): 30cm.

CAMOS (Cont'd)
In three separately paginated parts.
Adams, I, no. 460; Graesse, II, p. 27; Palau, 41077;
Simón Díaz, VII, 3758; Thomas, p. 18.
Reel 32, No. 147

CARAMUEL LOBKOWITZ, JUAN, bp. of Vigevano, 1606-1682.
Caramuelis Praecursor Logicvs. Complectens Grammaticam
Audacem, Cuius partes sunt tres, Methodica, Metrica,
Critica Quarum. Prima Ab Omnibus Linguis Parescindens
Disputat Philosophice De Artificio et Secvndis Intentionibus
Artis Grammaticae: de Partibus Orationis: de earumdem
numero: de singularum qualitatibus, causis & usu. [Hic.
corrigitur & reformatur veteris Scholae dialectus; &
instituitur nova, disputationibus Philosophicis &
Theologicis appositissima, subsistens brevibus &
clarissimis regulis.] Secunda Disserit Etiam Philophice De
Syllabarvm Natvra Et Ingenio: de Principis & Causis
intrinsecis & extrinsecis: de Accentu & loco: de
Magditudine, Compositione, & Propositione, de Quantitate
verâ & secundum dici, de Motu, & primo Motore, seu Deo.
[Hic clauditur tota Philosophia Naturalis, & multae
controversiae curiosae & difficiles summâ claritate
explicantur & dilucidantur: & praeparatur animus, ut
sequentia omnia utiliter legere possit.] Tertia Ausu
generoso Et Felici In Omnes Scientias Nobiliores Se
Insinuat, Et ideis Grammaticarum affertionum praeventa,
examinat & tradit Logicam, Physicam, Metaphysicam, &
Theologiam Scholasticam Moralemque: & illas pure
Grammaticis (adeoque certis, & cuivis puero notis)
fundamentis subcollat, & merè litterariis exemplis &
notitiis dilucidat. [Et hic ingenioso Lectori facillima
& securissima clavis potrigitur, ut possit inire omnes
scientias, & in singulis intricatissimas difficultates
solvere, & caecas quaestiones anerire.] Est Opvs Breve,
Et Omnino Necessarivm Discipvlis, Qvi A Rhetorica, Avt
forte à Grammatica immediatè se conferunt ad Philosophiam:
in quo obscuras & graves controversias, tam de creaturis
quàm de creatore, clarè & dilucidè evolutas invenies, quae
implicantur interdum, ubi altiùs de rebus supremis tractatur
Cum gratia & Privileg. S. Caesarea Maiestatis. Et Regis
Hispaniarum. Francofurti: Sumptibus Iohan. Godofredi
Schönwetteri, 1654.
3 pts. in 1 (503 p.; 88, [18] p.; 452, 258 p.) 32cm.

Last three pages of part 3 numbered 156, 157, 158.
Reel 32, No. 148

CARDONA Y ALAGÓN, ANTONIO FOLCH DE, 1623-1694.
El mas heroyco silencio. Comedia famosa. Valencia:
en la Imprenta de Iayme de Bordazar ... Vendese en casa
de Luis la Marca, 1688.
48 p.; 21cm.

Title page missing.
Colophon: "A costa de Luys de la Marca, Mercader de
Libros."
Bound with:
(A) Bernardo de Quirós, Francisco: La luna de la
sagra. [n.p.-n.d.]
40 p.
(B) Rojas Zorrilla, Francisco de: La gran comedia de
los aspides de Cleopatra, Valencia [n.d.]
48 p.
(C) Mira de Amescua, Antonio: El negro del mejor amo
[n.p.-n.d.]
44 p.
(D) Pérez de Montalván, Juan: Teagenes, Madrid [n.d.]
48 p.
(E) Vega, Lope de: Dineros son calidad, [n.p.-n.d.]
34 p.
(F) Pérez de Montalbán, Juan: Don Florisel de Niqvea,
[n.p.-n.d.]
40 p.
Reel 33, No. 149

CARLO BORROMEO, SAINT see BALLESTEROS Y SAAVEDRA, FERNANDO
DE.

CARLOS II, King of Spain, 1661-1700.
    Last will and codicil of Charles II, King of Spain
made the 2nd of October, 1700 ... London: Printed for
H. Rhodes, A. Bell and E. Castle, 1700.
    27 p.; 23cm.

    Palau, 44371; Wing C593.
Reel 33, No. 156

CARNERO, ANTONIO.
    Historia de las gverras civiles qve ha avido en los
Estados de Flandes desdel año 1559 hasta el de 1609 y
las cavsas de la rebelion de dichos Estados. Bruselas:
Iuan de Meerbeque, 1625.
    [9], 565, [6] p.; 31cm.

    Goldsmith, p. 31, no. 204; HC:NS4/329; Graesse, II,
p. 50; Peeters-Fontainas, I, no. 190; Penney, p. 92;
Salvá, II, 2858; Simón Díaz, VII, 4977; Vaganay, 1006;
Palau, 44764.
Reel 33, No. 157

CARRILLO, ALONSO, fl. 1650.
    Origen de la Dignidad de Grande de Castilla.
Preeminencias de qve goza en los actos publicos, y palacios
de los reyes de España... Madrid: Imprenta Real, 1657.
    [3], 52 l; 30cm.

    2nd. edition.
    Bound with: SALAZAR DE MENDOZA, PEDRO. Origen de las
dignidades seglares de Castilla y Leon, 1657.
    Goldsmith, p. 32, no. 226; Navas, 2063; Penney p. 93;
Simón Díaz, VII, 5307.
Reel 33, No. 158

CARRILLO, MARTÍN, 1561-1630.
    Annales y memorias cronologicas. Contienen las cossas
mas notables assi Ecclesiasticas como Seculares succedidas
en el Mundo señaladamente en España desde su principio y
poblacion hasta el año M.DC.XX... Impresso en Huesca:
por Pedro Bluson: En la impreta de la Viuda de Iuan Perez
Valdiuielso, 1622.
    [10], 452 l: ill,; 29cm.

    Arco, p. 20; Goldsmith, p. 32, no. 232; Graesse, II,
p. 55; Palau, 45513; Penney, p. 94; Simón Díaz, VII,
5363.
Reel 33, No. 162

CARRILLO, MARTÍN, 1561-1630.
    Anales cronologicos del mvndo, del abad de Monte-Aragón
el dotor don Martin Carrillo. Añadese en esta segunda
impression en diuersas partes adiciones, las quales
comiencan con esta señal y acaban con esta *. Mas se añaden
los años 1621. hasta 1630. que son diez años de historia,
las quales tenia el autor para imprimir, y sacadas licencias
del ordinario antes que muriera ... En Zaragoca: en el
Hospital real y general de Nuestra Señora de Gracia, a
costa de Pedro Escuer, mercader de libros, 1634.
    [11], 525 l.; 30cm.

    2nd. ed.
    Errors in foliation and signatures.
    Coat of arms, with motto: D. L. Escveres, on title
page.
    Goldsmith, p. 32, no. 223; HC:380/92; HC:NS4/330;
Jiménez Catalán, 332; Penney, p. 94; Palau, III, p. 203;
Simón Díaz, VII, 5426.
Reel 34, No. 163

CARRILLO, MARTÍN, 1561-1630.
    Apologia De La Bvlla De Los Diffvntos. Por el D. Martin
Carrillo Presbitero. Saltim vos amici mei. Iob. 19.
Miseremini mei, miseremini mei. Con Licencia Y Privilegio.
En Caragoca: Por Angelo Tauanno, 1602.
    [61] p.; 21cm.

    Palau, III, p. 203.
Reel 33, No. 161

CARRILLO, MARTÍN, 1561-1630.
    Explicacion De La Bvlla De Los Difvntos. En la qual
se trata de las penas y lugar del Purgatorio; y como
puedan ser ayudadas las Animas de los difuntos con las
oraciones y sufragios de los viuos. Por el Doctor Martin
Carrillo Presbytero, Cathedratico del Decreto de la
Vniuersidad de Caragoca. Va en esta segunda impression
corregida y enmendada, y añadida a la postre vna Apologia
por el mismo Autor. Saltim vos amici mei Iob. 19.
Miseremini mei, miseremini mei. Con Licencia Y Privilegio.
En Caragoca: Por Angelo Tauanno, 1602.
    [17], 308, [17] p.; 20cm.

    Imperfect: title-page wanting, replaced by hand-
written title-page; p. 63-66 wanting; many errors in
numb. of pages.
    In double columns.
    Palau, III, p. 203; Simón Díaz, VII, 5358.
Reel 33, No. 160

CARRILLO LASO DE LA VEGA, ALONSO, 1582-1647?
    Sagrada Eratos, Y Meditaciones Davidicas De D. Alonso
Carrillo Laso De La Vega mi Señor, Maiordomo del Sereniss.
Señor el Señor Cardenal Infante D. Fernando De Avstria
Cauallerico Maior de las Reales Cauallericas de Cordoua
Alcaide de Hucles del Orden de Santiago. Libro Terzero.
Sobre Los Vltimos Cinqventa Psalmos. Dedicado A Mi
Señora Sor Francisca Maria De Iesvs Mi Señora, Y Mi
Hermana. Por D. Fernando Carrillo, Y Manvel Gentilombre
De La Camera Del Serenissimo Señor El Señor D. Ivan.
Señor de la Casa del Maestre de Santiago D. Pedro Muñiz
de Godoi, y de la Villa de Alua de Tajo. Comendador del
Almendralejo del Orden de Santiago, y Cuatraluo de las
Galeras de Napoles. Napoles: Por los Herederos de
Roberto Molo, 1657.
    [9], 169 p.; 24cm.

    Psalms, 101-145.
    Gallardo, II, 1619; Graesse, II, p. 55; Palau,
45593; Penney, p. 94; Salvá, I, 943; Ticknor, p. 34;
Toda y Güell, Italia, I, no. 982.
Reel 34, No. 164

CARRILLO Y SOTOMAYOR, LUIS, ca. 1583-1610.
    Obras de Don Lvys Carrillo y Sotomayor, Cavallero
de la Orden de Santiago ... natural de la ciudad de
Cordoua. En Madrid: Por Iuan de la Cuesta, 1611.
    [24], 272 l.; 21cm.

    Gallardo, II, 1621; Graesse, II, p. 56; Jerez, p.
23; Penney, p. 94; Palau, 45607; Simón Díaz, VII,
5451; Ticknor, p. 61.
Reel 34, No. 165

CARRILLO Y SOTOMAYOR, LUIS, ca. 1583-1610.
    Obras De Don Lvys Carrillo Y Soto Mayor, Comendador
de la Fuente del Maestre, Quatraluo de las Oaleras
(sic) Natural de Cordova. A Don Manvel Alonso
Perez de Guzman el bueno, Conde de Niebla, Capitan
general de la Costa de Andaluzia. Con privilegio. En
Madrid: por Luys Sanchez, 1613.
    [24], 239 l.; 21cm.

    Gallardo, II, 1622; Jerez, p. 23; Penney, p. 94;
Pérez Pastor, 1216; Salvá, I, 516; Simón Díaz, VII,
5452.
Reel 34, 166

CARVAJAL, LUIS DE, O.F.M.
   Theologicarvm Sententiarum liber vnus Lôisio Carbaialo Baethico ordinis Minorum authore. Dilutio quorumdam argumentorum, cum approbatione libri ad generosum Do. Lodouicum Carbaialum Osorium. Typographus. En damus tibi candide Lector egregium hoc opus ab Authore iam denuò illustratum: in quo adnititur Theologiam ud suos ueros & uiuidos fontes restistuere & à Sophistica & barbarie pro uirili repurgare, cum nouo Indice. Oratio eiusdem Authoris habita in Cocilio Triden. [engraving] Antverpiae, Imprimebat Ioannes Grauius Typographus iuratus Caes. Maiest. Anno, 1548. Cum gratia & priuilegio.
   4 l., 385 p., 45 l.; 15cm.

   Separate title-page for the Oratio ...
   Palau, 46580. Not in Peeters-Fontainas, not in Simon Díaz.
No. 167: Not Available

CASA, GIOVANNI DELLA, abp. of Benevento, 1503-1556.
   [Il Galateo. French, German, Spanish and Latin]
   Le Galatee, premierement compose en Italien ... et depuis mis en François, Latin, Allemand et Espagnol ... [Lyon]: par Iean de Tovrnes, 1598.
   [4], 459 p.; 12cm.

   Il Galateo, with French translation by Nathan Chytrée, as well as German, Spanish and Latin ranslations.
   Graesse, II, p. 59; Palau, 46661; Ticknor, p. 62.
Reel 35, No. 168

CASA, GIOVANNI DELLA, abp. of Benevento, 1503-1556.
   [Il Galateo. French, German, Spanish and Latin]
   Le Galatee, premierement compose en Italien ... et depuis mis en François, Latin, Allemand et Espagnol ... [Lyon]: Jean de Tovrnes, 1609.
   [19], 619 p.; 13cm.

   Graesse, II, p. 59; Heredia, 4235; Penney, p. 96; Thomas, p. 19; Ticknor, p. 62.
Reel 35, No. 169

CASAS, BARTOLOME DE LAS, bp. of Chiapa, 1474-1566.
   [Aquí se contiene vna disputa, o controversia: entre el Obispo don Fray Bartholome de las Casas ... Italian]
   Conqvista Dell'Indie Occidentali di Monsignor Fra Bartolomeo Dalle Case, ò Casaus, Siuigliano, Vescouo di Chiapa. Tradotta in Italiano per opera di Marco Ginammi. All' Illmo. & Ecc.^{mo} Sig.^{re} Sig.^{or} & mio Padron Col.^{mo} Il Sig.^{or} Pietro Sagredo Procvratore Di S. Marco. [engraving with motto: Spes Mea In Deo Est] Venetia: Presso Marco Ginammi, Con Licenza de' Superiori, & Priuilegio, 1645.
   [12], XVII, 31-184 p.; 20cm.

   Aquí se contiene vna disputa, o controversia: entre el Obispo don Fray Bartholome de las Casas ... Italian translation by Marco Ginammi.
   Spanish and Italian in parallel columns.
   Bound with his: Istoria ... (1643), see below.
   Goldsmith, p. 33, no. 264; Graesse, II, p. 61; Palau, 46958; Simón Díaz, VII, 5868; Toda y Güell, Italia, I, 1005.
Reel 35, No. 170

CASAS, BARTOLOMÉ DE LAS, bp. of Chiapa, 1474-1566.
   [Breuissima relacion de la destruycion de las Indias. Italian].
   Istoria ò Breuissima Relatione della Distrvttione dell'Indie Occidentali di Monsig. reverendiss. don Bartolomeo dalle Case, ò Casaus, Siuigliano dell' Ordine de' Predicatori; et Vescovo di Chiappa Città Regale nell'Indie. Conforme Al Svo Vero Originale Spagnuolo, già stampato in Siuiglia. Tradotta (sic) in Italiano dal eccell. sig. Giacomo Castellani, già sotto nome di Francesco Bersabita ... Venetia: Presso Marco Ginammi, 1630.
   [17], 150, [2] p.; 21cm.

CASAS (Cont'd)
   Spanish and Italian in parallel columns.
   Graesse, II, p. 61; Palau, III, p. 246; Simón Díaz, VII, 5863; Ticknor, p. 63.
Reel 35, No. 172

CASAS, BARTOLOMÉ DE LAS, bp. of Chiapa, 1474-1566.
   [Breuissima relacion de la destruycion de las Indias. Italian]
   Istoria ò Breuissima Relatione della Distrvttione dell'Indie Occidentali di Monsig. reverendiss. don Bartolomeo dalle Case, ò Casaus, Siuigliano dell'Ordine de' Predicatori; et Vescovo di Chiappa Città Regale· nell'Indie. Conforme Al Svo Vero Originale Spagnuolo, già stampato in Siuiglia. Tradotta (sic) in Italiano dal eccell. sig. Giacomo Castellani, già sotto nome di Francesco Bersabita ... In Venetia: Presso Marco Ginammi, 1643.
   [8], 150, [2] p.; 20cm.

   Breuissima relacion de la destruycion de las Indias. Italian translation by Francesco Bersabita, pseud. of Giacomo Castellani.
   Bartlett, 2/514; Goldsmith, p. 34, no. 267; Graesse, II, p. 61; Palau, III, p. 246; Penney, p. 97; Simón Díaz, VII, 5866.
Reel 35, No. 171

CASAS, BARTOLOMÉ DE LAS, bp. of Chiapa, 1474-1566.
   [Breuissima relacion de la destruycion de las Indias. Latin]
   Regionvm Indicarum per Hispanos olim devastatarum accuratissima descriptio, insertis Figuris aeneis ad vivum fabrefactis, authore Bartholomaeo de las Casas ... Editio nova priori longè correctior. Heidelbergae: typis Gvilielmi VValteri, 1664.
   [9],112 p.: ill; 20cm.

   Latin translator unknown.
   Bartlett, 2/944; Penney, p. 97; Palau, III, p. 246; Simón Díaz, VII, 5876.
Reel 35, No. 175

CASAS, BARTOLOMÉ DE LAS, bp. of Chiapa, 1474-1566.
   [Breuissima relacion de la destruycion de las Indias. French]
   La découverte des Indes Occidentales, par les Espagnols. Ecrite par Dom Balthazar de Las-Casas, evêque de Chiapa. Dedié à Monseigneur le comte de Toulouse. A Paris: Chez Andrè Pralard, 1697.
   [11], 382, [2] p.; 17cm.

   French translation by Jean Baptiste Morvan de Bellegarde.
   Title vignette. Added t.-p., engraving.
   Doublet, p. 41; Palau, 46966; Simón Díaz, VII, 5847.
Reel 35, No. 173

CASAS, BARTOLOMÉ DE LAS, bp. of Chiapa, 1474-1566.
   [Breuissima relacion de la destruycion de las Indias. French].
   Relations des Voyages et des Découvertes que les Espagnols ont fait dans les Indes Occidentales; Ecrite par Dom Balthazar de Las-Casas, evêque de Chiapa. Avec la Relation curieuse des voyages des du Sieur de Montauban, capitaine des filbustiers, en Guinée l'an 1695. Amsterdam: Chez J. Louis de Lorme, 1698.
   [11], 402 p.: front.; 17cm.

   French translation by Jean Baptiste Morvan de Bellegarde.
   Bound with L'art de voyager utilement ....
   Bartlett, 2/1527; Graesse, II, p. 60; Palau, III, p. 247; Simón Díaz, VI, 5848.
Reel 35, No. 174

CASAS, BARTOLOMÉ DE LAS, bp. of Chiapa, 1474-1566.
[Breuissima relacion de la destruycion de las Indias. English].

An Account Of the First Voyages and Discoveries Made by the Spaniards in America. Containing The most Exact Relation hitherto publish'd, of their unparallel'd Cruelties on the Indians, in the destruction of above Forty Millions of people. With the Propositions offer'd to the King of Spain, to prevent the further Ruin of the West-Indies. By Don Bartholomew de las Casas ... Illustrated with cuts. To which is added, The Art of Travelling, shewing how a Man may dispose his Travels to the best advantage. London: Printed by J. Darby for D. Brown, 1699.
[10]., 248, 40 p. 2 double plates.; 20cm.

A translation from the French, apparently from the Relation des voyages et des de'couvertes que les Espagnols ont fait dans les Indes Occidentales. Amsterdam, 1698 [Cfr. above]. The English work, following the French, contains abridged translations of the following tracts of Las Casas: Breuissima relacion de la destruycion de las Indias (p. 1-104); Lo que se sigues em pedaco de vna carta (p. 104-114); Entre los remédios (p. 114-138); Aquí se cõtiene treynta proposiciones (p. 138-149); Aquí se contiene vna disputa, o controuersia (p. 150-160); Este es vn tratado ... sobre materia de los yndios (p. 160-184); Entre los remedios [apparently another version]
The Art of Travelling to Advantage: 40 p. at end, is also a translation from the French by Joseph Stennett, the Seventh Day Baptist.
Allison, p. 42, 11.1; Palau, 46971; Ticknor, p. 63; Simón Díaz, VII, 5858; Wing C.798a.
Reel 35, No. 176

CASAS, CRISTÓBAL DE LAS, d. 1576.
Vocabulario de las dos lengvas toscana y castellana de Christoval de las Casas. En qve se contiene la declaracion de Toscano en Castellano, y de Castellano en Toscano. En dos partes con vna introdvcion para leer, y pronunciar bien entrambas lenguas. Sevilla: vendese en casa de Francisco de Aguilar, impresso en casa de Alonso Escriuano, 1570.
247 l.; 20cm.

Doublet, p. 41; Escudero, 637; Palau, 47000; Simón Díaz, VII, 6069; Thomas, p. 20, Viñaza, no. 722; Penney, p. 98.
Reel 35, No. 177

CASAS, CRISTÓBAL DE LAS, d. 1576.
Vocabulario de las dos lengvas toscana y castellana de Christoval de las Casas. En qve se contiene la declaracion de Toscano en Castellano, y de Castellano en Toscano. En dos partes con vna introdvcion para leer, y pronunciar bien entrambas lenguas. Venetia: Damian Zenaro, 1576.
[49], 437 p.; 16cm.

Colophon: "Impresso en Venetia, en casa di Egidio Regazola, a instantia di Damiano Zenaro, Mercader de Libros, 1576".
Adams, I, no. 820; Palau, 47001; Short-Title, p. 366; Simon Díaz, VII, 6070; Thomas, p. 20.
Reel 35, No. 178

CASAS, CRISTÓBAL DE LAS, d. 1576.
Vocabulario de las dos lengvas toscana y castellana de Christoval de las Casas. En qve se contiene la declaracion de Toscano en Castellano, y de Castellano en Toscano. En dos partes con vna introdvcion para leer, y pronunciar bien entrambas lenguas. Venetia: Paulo Zanfretti. Vendese en casa de Damian Zenaro, 1582.
[49], 437 p.; 16cm.

Palau, 47003; Penney, p. 98; Simón Díaz, VII, 6071; Short-Title, p. 367; Toda y Güell, Italia, no. 1007.
Reel 36, No. 179

CASAS, CRISTÓBAL DE LAS, d. 1576.
Vocabulario de las dos lengvas toscana y castellana de Christoval de las Casas. En qve se contiene la declaracion de Toscano en Castellano, y de Castellano en Toscano. En dos partes con vna introdvcion para leer, y pronunciar bien entrambas lenguas. Venetia: [Gio. Antonio Bertano]. Vendese en casa de Damian Zenaro, 1587.
[49], 437 p.; 16cm.

HC: NS4/32; Palau, 47005; Penney, p. 98; Short-Title, p. 367; Simón Díaz, VII, 6073; Viñaza, no. 722.
Reel 36, No. 180

CASAS, CRISTÓBAL DE LAS, d. 1576.
Vocabulario de las dos lengvas toscana y castellana de Christoval de las Casas. En qve se contiene la declaracion de Toscano en Castellano, y de Castellano en Toscano. En dos partes con vna introdvcion para leer, y pronunciar bien entrambas lenguas. Venetia: Olivier Alberti, 1600.
[48], 413 (i.e. 435) p.; 16cm.

Many errors in paging.
Palau, 47007; Short-Title, p. 367; Simón Díaz, VII, 6076; Toda y Güell, Italia, IV, no. 5718.
Reel 36, No. 181

CASAS, CRISTÓBAL DE LAS, d. 1576.
Vocabulario de las dos lengvas toscana y castellana de Christoval de las Casas. En qve se contiene la declaracion de Toscano en Castellano, y de Castellano en Toscano. En dos partes con vna introdvcion para leer, y pronunciar bien entrambas lenguas. Venecia: Vendese en casa de Pedro Miloco, 1622.
[49], 437 p.; 16cm.

Printer's device on t.-p. and at end.
Palau, 47011; Simón Díaz, VII, 6081; Toda y Güell, Italia, no. 1010.
Reel 36, No. 182

CASAS, CRISTOFORO DE LAS see CASAS, CRISTÓBAL DE LAS.

CASCALES, FRANCISCO DE, 1564?-1642.
Al Bven Genio encomienda svs Discvrsos historicos de la mvi noble i mvi leal civdad de Murcia, el Licenciado Francisco Cascales. Mvrcia: Por Luys Beros, 1621.
[9], 458, [9] l.; 27cm.

Colophon: "En MVrcia, Por Luys Beros".
Doublet, p. 41; Goldsmith, p. 41, no. 272; Palau, 47158; Salvá, II, 2864; Simón Díaz, VII, 6117.
Reel 36, No. 184

CASCALES, FRANCISCO DE, 1564?-1642.
Tablas Poeticas Del Licenciado Francisco Cascales. Dirigidas al Excelentissimo Señor Don Francisco de Castro, Conde de Castro, Duque de Taurisano, Virrey, y Capitan general del Reyno de Sicilia Vt ex columba pax ita ex arte perfectio. Con Privilegio. Murcia: Por Luis Beros, 1617.
[16], 448 p.; 14cm.

Eight of sixteen preliminary leaves missing.
Goldsmith, p. 34, no. 274; Graesse, II, p. 61; Jerez, p. 23; Knapp, p. 130; Palau, 47157; Penney, p. 98; Simón Díaz, VII, 6115; Tejera y Moncada, vol. 1, pp. 128-29; Viñaza, no. 422.
Reel 36, No. 183

CASES, GABRIEL.
    Interrogatori de tots los pecats, pera fer Confessiõs
llargues, y generals, ab molta facilitat, y breu espay
de terms. Recopilat, ara novament, dels que han cõpost,
los Pares Antoni de Torres, Antoni Fernãdez. Frãcisco
Veron, y altres Doctors de la Cõpañia de I E S V S.
Per lo Doctor Gabriel Cases Vicari perpetuo d la Iglesia
Perrochial de Sãta Creu, de la Ciutat d Mallorca.
[engraving]. En casa dls Here⁹ de Gabriel Guasp. 1635.
    32 l.; 11cm.

    A perfect copy of this rarissimum. Not in Palau,
not in Simón Díaz.
Reel 36, No. 185

CASSIANUS, JOANNES, ca. 370-ca. 435.
    Joãnis' Cassiani collationes patrũ abbrete [sic!]: et
Speculum religiosorũ diui Hieronymi epistolis excerptum.
G. L. Cesarauguste, Arte et Impẽsis Georgius Coci, 1510.
    lxxv l.; 14cm.

    With this is: Alphabetum diuini amoris (1500-1520).
    Thomas, p. 20.
Reel 36, No. 186

CASTAÑIZA, JUAN DE, d. 1598.
    [Historia de San Romvaldo. Italian]
    Historia della vita di S. Romvaldo, padre, a fondatore
dell'Ordine camaldolese, ch'è vna idea, e forma perfetta
della vita solitaria. Composta dal reverendo padre don
Giovanni da Castagnizza, monaco dell'Ordine di san
Benedetto. Trasportata dalla lingua spagnola nella
italiana da don Timotheo de Bagno, monaco della
Congregatione camaldolese. Di ordine del reu.ᵐᵒ p. d.
Gio. Lodovico Pasolini da Faenza ... Venetia: Appresso
Domenico Imberti, 1605.
    [8], 392 p.: fold. front.; 23cm.

    Device of printer on title page.
    Historia de San Romvaldo. Italian translation by
Timotheo de Bagno.
    Palau, 47530; Simón Díaz, VII, 6225; Toda y Güell,
Italia, I, no. 1016.
Reel 37, No. 187

CASTELLÁ FERRER Y LUZÓN, MAURO.
    Historia del apostol de Jesus Christo Sanctiago
Zebedeo, patron y capitan general de las Españas.
Dedicasela Don Mauro Castella Ferrer. Madrid: Alonso
Martin de Balboa, A costa del Autor, [1610-17].
    [19], 486, [29] l.; 28cm.

    1st ed.
    Goldsmith, p. 34, no. 282; Palau, 47746; Simón
Díaz, VII, 6289.
Reel 37, No. 188

CASTIGLIONE, BALDASSARE, CONTE, 1478-1529.
    [Il Cortegiano. Spanish]
    El Cortesano, Traduzido de Italiano en nuestro vulgar
Castellano, por Boscan. Con licencia de los Señores del
muy alto Consejo de la C.R. M. Salamanca: En casa de
Pedro Lasso, 1581.
    296 l.; 14cm.

    Il Cortegiano. Spanish translation by Juan Boscán.
    Graesse, II, p. 66; Simón Díaz, VI, 5124; Ticknor,
p. 64.
Reel 37, No. 189

CASTILLE. LAWS, STATUTES, ETC.
    Ordenanças reales de Castilla, por las quales
primeramente se han de librar, y juzgar todos los
pleytos ciuiles y criminales, nueuamẽte glossadas, y
enmẽdadas en el texto, con las aplicaciones de los
fueros de Aragon, y ordenanças de Portugal: por el
doctor Diego Perez de Salamanca ... Con su repertorio

CASTILLE (Cont'd)
muy copioso, assi del texto, como de la glossa ...
Salmanticae: excudebat Ioannes Maria à Terranoua,
1560.
    [6], [2] l., 3-1572 cols., [30] l.; 28cm.

    At head of title: Sub Philippo. II. hisp. reg.
    Colophon dated 1559.
    Two columns to the page.
    Title vignette (coat of arms).
    Commentary in Latin.
    "Recopiladas, y cõpuestos por el doctor Alphonso
Diaz de Montaluo." - p. 1.
    "Index copiosisimvs ac sententiarvm maxime notabilivm,
qvae in prioribvs quattuor libris Ordinationum regiarum
contentur" (with special title page): [30] l.
    Gil Ayuso, 236; HC: 384/3398; Penney, p. 101.
Reel 37, No. 190

CASTILLE. LAWS, STATUTES, etc., 1252-1284 (ALFONSO X,
    1221-1284).
    Las Siete Partidas Del Sabio Rey y don Alonso el
Nono, nueuamente Glosadas, por el Licenciado Greggorio
Lopez, del Consejo Real de Indias de su Magestad.
Con su Reportorio muy copioso, assi del Testo como
de la Glosa. [Coat of Arms]. En Salamanca: En casa
de Andrea de Portonarijs, Impressor de su Catholica
Magestad, 1565.
    7 parts in 3 v.

    Each part has separate t.-p., repeated imprint,
part number and coat of arms.
    Pagination is distinct for each part:
        Vol. I, pt. 1: 151 l, pt. 2: 116 l; 39cm.
        Vol. II, pt. 3: 186 l, pt. 4: 73 l, pt. 5:
        112 l; 39cm.
        Vol. III, pt. 6: 116 l, pt. 7: 112 l; 39cm.
    The Repertorio has a special t.-p.: Index Sev
Repertorivm materiarum ac vtriusque iuris decisionum
quae in singulis Septem Partitarum glossis continentur:
Copiosissimè atque luculentissime concinnatum, per
Iacobum Bossaeum. [Coat of arms]. Salmanticae, In
aedibus Andreae à Portonarijs, Sacrae Catholicae
Maiestatis, Typógraphi, 1565.
    29 l.

Adams, I, no.736; Simon Diaz, III, vol. I, 1264.
Reels 9 & 10, No. 45

CASTILLO, ANTONIO DEL, d. 1699.
    El devoto peregrino. Viage de Tierra Santa. Madrid:
Imprenta Real, 1656.
    [25], 511, [18] p.: ill., maps, plates (part fold.);
24cm.

    Gallardo, II, 1700; Goldsmith, p. 35, no. 310;
Graesse, II, p. 66; HC: 387/1841; Palha, 2364-Westermann,
349; Penney, p. 102; Simón Díaz, VII, 6552.
Reel 37, No. 191

CASTILLO, FRANCISCO DEL, 17th cent.
    Migaias caydas de la mesa de los santos, y doctores
de la iglesia. Colegidas, y aplicadas à todos los
Euangelios de los santos. Pamplona: Por Nicolas
de Assiayn, A costa de Iuan de Bonilla, 1620.
    [8], 347, [3] l., 34 p.; 15cm.

    Simón Díaz, VII, 6445.
Reel 38, No. 192

CASTILLO, HERNANDO DEL, 1529-1595.
    [Historia general de Santo Domingo. Italian]
    Dell'Historia Generale Di S. Domenico Et Dell'Ordine
Svo De' Predicatori, Composta Per Il Molto Rever. Padre
M.F. Ferdinando Del Castiglio, In Lingva Castigliana;
E poi tradotta nella nostra Italiana lingua dal
Reuerendo Padre F. Timoteo Bottoni. Parte Prima. Con

CASTILLO (Cont'd)
Dve Tavole Copiosissime, vna de' Capitoli, & l'altra
delle cose notabili. Con Privilegio. Venetia:
Appresso Damiano Zenaro, 1589.
2 pts. in 1 v. ([36], 486 p.; 256 p. [i.e. 268])

Italian translation by F. Timoteo Bottoni. Part 2
translation by Filippo Pigafetta.
Imperfect: Part II missing.
Adams, I, no. 955; Simon Díaz, VII, 6660; Toda y
Güell, Italia, no. 1028.
Part 2: Not Available
Reel 38, No. 193

CASTILLO MANTILLA Y COSSÍO, GABRIEL DE.
Laverintho poetico, texido de noticias natvrales,
historicas, y gentilicas, ajvstadas a consonantes para
el exercicio de la Poesía. Madrid: En la officina
de Melchor Alvarez, 1691.
[50], 765, [2] p.; 21cm.

Coat of arms.
Penney, p. 104; Salvá, I, 527; Simón Díaz, VII,
6738.
Reel 38, No. 194

CASTILLO SOLÓRZANO, ALONSO DE, 1584-1647?
Los alivios de Casandra ... Barcelona: En la
emprenta de Iayme Romeu, delante Santiago ... en casa
de Iuan Capera, 1640.
3, 191 l.; 16cm.

Title page mended; letters supplied from Simón Díaz.
Gallardo, II, no. 1697; Goldsmith, p. 35, no. 329;
Graesse, II, p. 67; Jerez, p. 24; Palau, 48405; Penney,
p. 104; Simón Díaz, VII, 6808.
Reel 38, No. 195

CASTILLO SOLÓRZANO, ALONSO DE, 1584-1647?.
[La Garduña de Sevilla. French]
La fouyne de Sevilla ov l'hamecon des bovrses.
Traduit de l'Espagnol de Alonco: de Castillo Sonorcano.
A Paris: chez Lovys Bilaine, au second pilier de la
grande Salle du Palais, au Grand Cesar, 1661.
[4], 592, [2] p.; 16cm.

French translation by Antoine Le Metal, sieur
d'Ouville or Francois Le Metal de Boisrobert, abbé
de Chastillon.

Foulché-Delbosc, Bibliographie, no. 1582; Graesse,
II, p. 67; Laurenti, no. 1964; Palau, 48415; Penney,
p. 104; Simón Díaz, VII, 6850.
Reel 38, No. 196

CASTRILLO, HERNANDO, 1586-1667.
Historia y magia natural, o Ciencia de filosofia
ocvlta, con nvevas noticias de los mas profundos
mysterios, y secretos del vniverso visible, en que se
trata de animales, pezes, aves, plantas, flores,
yervas, metales, piedras, aguas, semillas, Parayso,
montes, y valles. Por el padre Hernando Castrillo ...
Donde trata de los secretos que pertenecen à las partes
dela tierra ... Madrid: Por Jvan Garcia Infazon,
1692. A costa de Francisco Sazedon.
[12], 342, [16] p.; 21cm.

Title within border of type ornaments.
Printed in double columns with marginal references.
Bound in vellum.
Goldsmith, p. 36, no. 345; Simón Díaz, VII, 6921.
Reel 39, No. 197

CASTRO, ALFONSO DE, 1495-1558.
Fr. Alfonsi De Castro Zamorensis, ordínis Mínorum,
aduersus omnes hereses Líb. XIIII. In quíbus recésentur
& reuíncútur omnes hereses quarum memoría extat, que

CASTRO (Cont'd)
ab Apostolorum tempore ad hoc vsq seculum ín Ecclesia
ortae sunt. [Paris]: Venundantur Iod. Badío, &
Ioanní Roígny, sub Basilísco, 1534.
[10], CCXI l.; 32cm.

Adams, I, no. 963.
Reel 39, No. 198

CASTRO, FRANCISCO DE, d. 1632.
De Arte Rhetorica. Dialogi qvatvor. Hispali: In
typographia Frãcisci de Lyra, 1625.
[18], 247, [44] p.; 14cm.

Palau, 48672; Simón Díaz, VII, 7091.
Reel 39, No. 199

CATHOLIC CHURCH.
Aurea expositio hymnorum vna cum textu. [Toledo:
Press of Pedro Hagenbach, 28 August 1504]
46 l.; 21cm.

Edited by Jacobus Alora.
Fine woodcut of Last Supper on title-page and
decorative woodcut initial at beginning of text.
Colophon: "Aurea hymnorũ expositío vna cũ textu
accuratissime correcta felici numine est explicita.
Impressa Toleti: Anno dñice natiuitatis Millesimo
quingentesimo q̃rto: Die vero XXVIII. mensis Augusti".
Not in Palau, not in Pérez Pastor, not in Simón
Díaz, not in British Museum, not in Bibliothèque
Nationale, not in Hispanic Society.
Reel 39, No. 200

CATHOLIC CHURCH. Diocese of Caracas, Venezuela.
Constituciones synodales del Obispado de Venecuela
y Santiago de Leon de Caracas. Madrid: L. A. de
Bedmar, 1698.
[16], 474 p.; 32cm.

Added t.-p. engraved.
Imperfect: lacks preliminary pages [1-8] and pp.
127-130 and 467-74; wormeaten.
The Synod met in 1687 with Diego de Baños y Sotomayor,
bishop of Caracas, presiding.
Reel 39, No. 201

CEBALLOS, JERÓNIMO DE see CEVALLOS, GERÓNIMO DE.

CÉDULA de S. M. dando la forma con que el Consejo
de la Cámara ha de obrar en lo que le toca.

Bound with: HERRERA Y SOTOMAYOR, JACINTO DE, fl.
1644. Iornada que su Magestad hizo a la Andalvzia.
[Madrid: En la Imprenta Real, 1624].
Palau, 114276 (List only printed folios 1-6).
Reel 77, No. 484.25

CERDA, JUAN LUIS DE LA, 1560-1643.
[Paedia religiosorum. German]
Paedia religiosorum: oder Der religiosen mans und
weibspersonen schulzucht. Begreifft drey theyl: im
ersten wird gehandlet wie die lehrmeisterin der
nouitzen oder jungen closterpersonen beschaffen sein
vnd in was für tugenten vnd sitten sie dieselben
vnterweisen vnd abrichten sollen. Im andern wird
von den praelaten vnd abtissin geredt vnd beynebens
vier vnd zwaintzig sehr schõne ermahnungen eingeführt
welche den closterpersonen zur zeit ihrer profession
fürzuhalten. Im dritten werden die religiosen in
gemein ihres ampts vnd pflicht erinnert. Anfangs durch
den ehrwürdigen Ioannen de la Cerda, Franciscaner
ordens, in hispanischer sprachen beschrieben. Vnd
anjetzo durch AEgidivm Albertinvm mit fleiss verteutscht
... Gedruckt zu München: Durch Nicolaum Henricum, 1605.
[4], 164, 16 l.; 20cm.

CERDA (Cont'd)
German translation by Aegidius Albertinus.
Title in red and black.
Errors in foliation: no. 6 repeated, 100 omitted (1st group of paging).
"Dess heiligen algemeinen Jungst zu Triendt gehalten Concilij Decret von den ordenspersonen closterfrawen": 16 leaves at end.
Reel 39, No. 203

CERDA, MELCHOR DE LA, 1550-1615.
Consolatio Ad Hispanos Propter Classem In Angliam Profectam Subita Tempestate submersam, Autore Jesuita: Melchiore De La Cerda, Primario Professore Hispali Eloquentiae Anno M.D.LXXXVIII. His calamitosis temporibus lectu nec infrugifera nec injucunda. 1621.
24 p.; 19cm.
Reel 39, No. 204

CERONE, PIETRO, 1560 (ca.) - 1625.
El melopeo y maestro. Tractado de mvsica theorica y pratica: en que se pone por extenso, lo que vno para hazerse perfecto musico ha menester saber: y por mayor facilidad, comodidad, y claridad del Lector, esta repartido en XXII. libros ... Compuesto por el ... Napoles: Por Iuan Bautista Gargano, y Lucrecio Nucci, impressores, 1613.
[16], 1160, [1] p., ill., diagrs.; 31cm.

Title in red and black within line borders; title vignette.
On verso of second leaf a picture of the Virgin and Child; on verso of third leaf, coat of arms of Philip III of Spain; on verso of fourth leaf, portrait of Cerone.
Paging irregular; no. 294-295, 375-376 repated; no. 371-372, 1157-1158 omitted.
HC: 380/820; Penney, p. 124; Simón Díaz, VII, 7873; Toda y Güell, Italia, no. 1095.
Reel 39, No. 205

CERTAMEN Poetico, Que En La Solenne Festividad de la Assumpcion gloriosa De Maria SS^ma Dedico A Su Maravillosa Imagen De Gracia la generosa Hermandad de Recetores del Numero de la Real Chancilleria de Granada el dia 4. del mes de Setiembre de este año de 1690. En El Real Convento de la Santissima Trinidad de Redentores Descalcos. Siendo sus Mayordomos D. Estevan Lopez Maldonado, Y D. Luis Andres Bermudo. Que Segunda Vez, Estampado, le consagran à su sacratissimo Simulacro. Granada: en la Imprenta de la SS Trinidad, por Antonio Torrubia, Impressor de la S. Iglesia Cathedral de dicha Ciudad, 1690.
42 l.; 21cm.

Colophon: "q Imprimiòse à costa de D. Estevan Lopez Maldonado, y D. Luis Andres Bermudo. Y para ayuda de la obra del Templo del Hospital de Corpus Christi permitieron se imprimiessen por la Hermandad de la Caridad los tomos que quisiessen".
Palau, 51835.
Reel 40, No. 206

CERVANTES DE SALAZAR, FRANCISCO, ca. 1514-1575.
Obras q̃ Francisco Ceruantes de Salasar, ha hecho, glosado, y traduzido. La primera es vn Dialogo dela dignidad del hombre ... comẽcado por el maestro Oliua, y acabado por Frãcisco Ceruãtes de Salazar. La segunda es el Appologo de la ociosidad y el trabajo, intitulado Labricio portundo ... Compuesto por el protonotario Luys Mexia, glosado y moralizado por

CERVANTES DE SALAZAR (Cont'd)
Francisco Ceruantes de Salazar. La tercera es la Introducion y camino para la sabiduria ... compuesta en latin por Luys Viues ... con muchas adiciones que al proposito hazian por ... [Alcalá de Henares: Juan de Brocar, 1546].
3 v. in 1 (190 p.; 162 p.; 108 p.); 21cm.

Colophon: "Esta obra ... imprimiose en esta casa de Alcala a. XVIIJ. de junio año de nuestra saluacion de M.D.XlVJ".
Device of printer, Juan de Brocar, on last verso of first and third part, and on last recto of second part.
Catalina, Tip. compl., no. 209; Gallardo, II, no. 1758; Penney, p. 125; Salvá, II, no. 3869; Simón Díaz, VIII, 3769; Thomas, p. 23.
Reel 40, No. 207

CERVANTES SAAVEDRA, MIGUEL DE, 1547-1616.
[El Ingenioso Hidalgo Don Quijote de la Mancha. Italian]
Dell'ingegnoso Cittadino Don Chisciotte Della Mancia. Composta da Michel di Cervantes Saavedra. Et hora nuouamente tradotta con fedeltà e chiarezza, di Spagnuolo in Italiano, Da Lorenzo Franciosini. Fiorentino. Parte Prima. Opera doue accopiato l'vtile, - il diletto, con dolcezza di stile, e con leggiadissima inuenzione si dimostra, quanto infruttuosa, e vana sia la lettura de libri di Caualleria, e con intrecciatura di fauole, e d'altri gentilissimi accidenti, si spiegano dicersi nobili, succesi marauigliosi, sentenze graui, & altre cose belle, e degne di qual si voglia giudizioso lettore. In questa Seconda Impressione corretta, e migliorata con la Traduzione de i versi Spagnuoli, non tradotti nella prima edizione. Ventia: Appresso Andrea Baba, 1625.
xi, [14], 662 (i.e. 694) p.; 17cm.

Italian translation by Lorenzo Franciosini, Fiorentino.
A list of Cervantes' works and a biography in manuscript are inserted in the front of the book.
Title-page lacking.
Ford-Lansing, p. 78; Givanel, I, no. 65; Graesse, II, p. 107; Grismer, p. 64; Palau, 53136; Plaza, I, no. 1423; Rius, I, no. 781; Rodríguez, no. 250; Simón Díaz, VIII, no. 1480; Toda y Güell, Italia, no. 1100.
Reel 40, No. 210

CERVANTES SAAVEDRA, MIGUEL DE, 1547-1616.
[El Ingenioso Hidalgo Don Quijote de la Mancha. English]
The History Of The Valorous and Witty-Knight-Errant, Don-Quixote, Of the Mancha. Translated out of the Spanish; now newly Corrected and Amended. London: Printed by Richard Hodgkinsonne for Andrew Crooke, 1652.
[8], 274 l.; 28cm.

English translation by Thomas Shelton.
Head and tail-pieces; initials.
Continuously paginated, second part has special t.-p.
Armorial book-plate bearing name: Munden.
Aguilera, p. 31; Allison, p. 48, no. 25.3; Ford-Lansing, p. 44; Givanel, I, no. 95; Graesse, II, p. 107; Mateu, no. 20; Plaza, I, no. 1152; Penney, p. 127; Río y Rico, no. 440; Rius, I, 608; Simón Díaz, VIII, 1406; Wing C. 1777.
Reel 40, No. 211

CERVANTES SAAVEDRA, MIGUEL DE, 1574-1616.
[El Ingenioso Hidalgo Don Quijote de la Mancha.
English].
The History Of the most Renowned Don Quixote Of
Mancha; And his Trusty Squire Sancho Pancha, Now made
English according to the Humour of our Modern Language.
And Adorned with several Copper Plates. By J. P.,
London: Printed by Tho. Hodgkin, and are to be sold
by John Newton, at the three Pigeons over against the
Inner-Temple Gate in Fleet street, 1687.
    10 p. l., 616 p. l., [16].

    English translation by John Phillips.
    First edition of Phillips' translation.
    Title-page lacking.
    Allison, p. 48, no. 26; Givanel, I, no. 129;
Graesse, II, p. 107; Linn, no. 24; Plaza, I, nos. 1156-
57; Río y Rico, no. 442; Rius, I, no. 619; Simón
Díaz, VIII, 1409; Ticknor, p. 74; Wing C. 1774, 1774a.
Reel 40, No. 212

CERVANTES SAAVEDRA, MIGUEL DE, 1547-1616.
[Novelas ejemplares. Italian]
    Il Novelliere Castigliano Di Michiel Di Cervantes
Saavedra; Nel quale, mescolandosi lo stile graue co'l
faceto, si narrano auuenimenti curiosi, casi strani, e
successi degni d'ammiratione: E si dà ad ogni sorte di
persona occasione d'apprendere e precetti Politici,
e documenti Morali, e concetti Scientifichi, e fruttuosi:
Tradotto dalla lingua Spagnuola nell'Italiana Dal Sig.
Gvglielmo Alessandro de Nouilieri, Clauelli: E da lui
fattiui Argomenti, e dichiarate nelli margini le cose
piu difficili. Venetia: Presso il Barezzi, 1629.
Con Licenza de' Superiori, et Priuilegio.
    [16], 720 p.; 16cm.

    Italian translation by Guglielmo Alessandro de
Novilieri Clavelli.
    Ford-Lansing, p. 93; Givanel, I, no. 76; Graesse,
II, p. 108; Grismer, p. 112; Palau, III, p. 454;
Rius, I, no. 971; Simón Díaz, VIII, 1530; Ticknor, p. 97.
Reel 40, No. 209

CERVANTES SAAVEDRA, MIGUEL DE, 1547-1616.
    Relatione Di Qvanto E' Svccesso Nella Città Di
Vagliadolid. Dopò il felicissimo nascimento del
Principe Di Spagna Don Filipo Dominico Vittorio Nostro
Sig. Fin che si finirono le dimostrazi ni d'allegrezza,
che per quel si fecero; Tradotta di lingua Castigliana
da Cesare Parona. Ad instanza di Girolamo Bordoni.
Con Priuilegio, & licenza de' Superiori. Milano: Per
Girolamo Bordoni & Pietro Martire Locarni, 1608.
    [13], 116 p.; 23cm.

    Work attributed to Cervantes. Italian translation
by Cesare Parona.
Reel 40, No. 208

CÉSPEDES Y MENESES, GONZALO DE, 1585?-1638.
    Francia Engañada. Francia Respondida, Por Gerardo
Hispano [pseud.], Al Grande Primogenito de la siempre
grande y esclarecida casa de Gvzman. El Conde De
Niebla. Empresso en Caller: [n.p.], 1635.
    [3], 153 p.; 21cm.

    Ex libris: Luis Bardón.
    Page 25 misnumbered 21; numbers 77-8 repated in the
paging.
    Simón Díaz, VIII, 4004.
    Bound with:
(A) Quevedo y Villegas, Francisco Gómez de, 1580-
1645: Carta Al Serenissimo, Mvy Alto, Y Mvy Poderoso
Lvis XIII. Rey Christianissimo De Francia. En Caragoca,
[1635]. 50 p.;

CÉSPEDES Y MENESES (Cont'd)
    (B) Respuesta Al Manifiesto De Francia. En Madrid,
Año 1635. 54p.;
    (C) Declaracion De Sv Alteza, del Señor Cardenal
Infante ... [n.p.-n.d.] 8p.;
    (D) Ambrosio Bautista, father, fl. 1635: Discvrso
Breve De Las Miserias De La Vida Y Calamidades De La
Religion. Catolica ... En Madrid, 1635. 30p.;
    (E) Ivstificacion de las acciones de España.
Manifestaciones de las violencias de Francia [n.p.-
n.d.], 1635. 51 p.;
    (F) Respvesta De Vn Vassallo De Sv Magestad, De los
Estados de Flandes, a los manifiestos del Rey de
Francia ... Año 1635. pp. 53-63.
Reel 41, No. 217

CÉSPEDES Y MENESES, GONZALO DE, 1585?-1638.
    Historia apologetica en los svcessos del Reyno de
Aragon y su Ciudad de Caragoca, Años de 91 y 92 y
relaciones fieles de la verdad, que hasta aora
manzillaron diuersos Escritores ... Zaragoca: Por
Iuan de Lanaja y Quartanet, 1622.
    [5], 236 p.; 29cm.

    Errors in numbering of pages.
    Title vignette (coat of arms).
    Gallardo, II, 1800; Goldsmith, p. 40, no. 501;
Graesse, II, p. 109; Jiménez Catalán, 215; Palha,
3950-Westermann, 535; Penney, p. 129; Salvá, II,
2870; Simón Díaz, VIII, 3979.
Reel 41, No. 213

CÉSPEDES Y MENESES, GONZALO DE, 1585?-1638.
    Primera parte. Historias peregrinas, y exemplares.
Con el origen, fvndamentos y excelencias de España,
y Ciudades adonde sucedieron [Pt. I]. Caragoca:
Iuan de Larumbe. A costa de Pedro Ferriz, 1623.
    [6], 191, [5] l.; 19cm.

    Title page and following leaf badly damaged,
affecting imprint, title and some text.
    Gallardo, II, no. 1801; Jiménez Catalán, 220;
Jerez, p. 27; Penney, p. 129; Salvá, II, 1763; Simón
Díaz, VIII, 3984.
Reel 41, No. 214

CÉSPEDES Y MENESES, GONZALO DE, 1585?-1638.
    Primera Parte De La Historia De D. Felipe El IIII.
Rey De Las Españas Por Don Goncalo de Cespedes, y
Meneses. Al Excel.mo Señor Don Iorie De Gardenas
Manrrique (sic), duque de Najara, y Maqueda. Lisboa:
con licencia la imprimio Pedro Graesbeeck, 1631.
    [9], 607 p.; 27cm.

    Goldsmith, p. 40, no. 508; Graesse, II, p. 109;
Palau, 54200; Simón Díaz, VIII, 4001; Ticknor, p. 79.
Reel 41, No. 215

CÉSPEDES Y MENESES, GONZALO DE, 1585?-1638.
    Historia De Don Felipe IIII. Rey De Las Españas.
Por Don Goncalo De Cespedes y Meneses. Barcelona:
Por Sebastian de Cormellas, 1634.
    [4], 281 l.; 30cm.

    Covers the first four years of the King's reign.
    Goldsmith, p. 40, no. 509; Graesse, II, p. 109;
Navas, 2541; Penney, p. 129; Salvá, II, 2871; Simón
Díaz, VIII, 4002; Ticknor, p. 79.
Reel 41, No. 216

CEVALLOS, GERONIMO DE, b. 1560.
Arte Real Para El Bven Govierno De los Reyes, y
Principes, y de sus vassallos. En el qual se refieren
las obligaciones de cada vno, con los principales
documentos para el buen gouierno. Con Vna Tabla De
Las Materias, reduzida a trezientos Aforismo de Latin
y Romance. Dirigido A La Catolica Magestad del Rey
don Felipe IIII. N.S. Monarca y Emperador de las
Españas, no reconciente superior en lo temporal. Por
el licenciado Geronimo de Zevallos Regidor de la
Imperial ciudad de Toledo, en el vanco y assiento de
los caualleros, y unico Patron del Monasterio de los
Descalzos Franciscos de la dicha ciudad. Toledo: A
costa de su autor, 1623.
[8], 190, [16] l.; 20cm.

Title-page mutilated affecting imprint.
Colophon: "En Toledo, en casa de Diego Rodriguez,
Impressor del Rey nuestro señor. Año de M.DC. XXIII".
Goldsmith, p. 40; Pérez Pastor, no. 515; Simón
Díaz, VII, 7597.
Reel 39, No. 202

CHACÓN, ALFONSO, 1540-1599.
Historia Vtrivsqve Belli Dacici A Traiano Caesare
Gesti, Ex Simvlachris Qvae In Colvmna Eivsdem Romae
Visvntvr Collecta. Avctore F. Alfonso Ciacono Hispano
Doctore Theologo Praedicatorvm, & Romani Pontificis
Poenitentiario. Romae: Ex Typographia Iacobi
Mascardi, 1616.
[5], 42, [6] p.: ill., 2 fold. p. l., 130 plates,
plan.; 46cm.

A series of engravings by Francesco Villamene.
Each leaf of the text has been mounted on heavy
paper uniform in size with the plates.
Colophon: "Romae, Typis Iacobi Mascardi, MDCXVI".
Reel 41, No. 224

CHACÓN, ALFONSO, 1540-1599.
Vitae et Res Gestae Pontificvm Romanorvm Et S.
R. E. Cardinalivm Ab initio nascentis Ecclesiae,
vsque ad Vrbanvm VIII ... Avctoribvs M. Alphonso
Ciaconio ..., Francisco Cabrera Morali, Andrea
Victorello ... Alia plvra Victorellvs, et Ferdinandvs
Vghellys florent, abbas ord. cisterciencis theol.
ex mss. praesertim monumentis addiderent. Hieronymus
Aleander ... & alij Ciaconianum opus recensuerunt.
Romae: Typis Vaticanis, 1630.
2 v. ([13] p., 1034 cols.; [3] p.; cols. 1035-2030).
Title vignettes; arms of Pope Urbanus VIII.
In double columns.
Reel 42, No. 225

CHACÓN, ALFONSO, 1540-1599.
Vitae, Et Res Gestae Pontificvm Romanorvm Et S. R. E.
Cardinalvm Ab initio nascentis Ecclesiae vsque
Clementem IX. P.O.M. Alphonsi Ciaconii Ordinis
Praedicatorvm. & aliorum operâ descriptae: Cum
vberrimis Notis. Ab Augustino Oldoino Societatis Iesv
recognitae, & ad quatuor Tomus ingenti vdique rerum
accessione productae. Addiis pontificum recentiorum
Imaginabus, & Cardinalium insignibus, plurimisque
aenis Figuris, cum Indicibus locupletissimis. Tomvs
Primus. [et Tomvs Secundvs]. Romae: Cvra, Et Svmp.
Philippi, Et Ant. De Rvbeis, 1677.
2 v. ([12] p., 1166 cols.; [5] p., 1118 cols.);
42cm.

Half-title: Historiae pontificvm Romanorvm et S.R.E.
cardinalivm.
In Double columns.
Tome I contains the introduction to the second
edition of 1630 by Andrea Vittorelli.
Palau, 66743.
Reel 43, No. 226

CHACÓN, PEDRO, ca. 1527-1581.
Petrvs Ciacconivs Toletanvs De Triclinio siue, de
modo convivandi apvd priscos Romanos, & de conviviorvm
apparav. Accedit Fvlvi Vrsini appendix. In his
scriptores veteres quamplurimi explicantur & emandantur.
[Romae]: in officina Sanctandreana, 1590.
[5], 192, [11] p.; 17cm.

Errors in paging: p. 81-96 numbered 80-85, 98,
87-95.
Palau, 66773; Short-Title, I, p. 401.
Reel 43, No. 227

CHACÓN, PEDRO, ca. 1527-1581.
Petri Ciaconii Toletani Opuscula. In Columnae
inscriptionem De Ponderibus. De Mensuris. De Nummis.
Romae: Ex Typographia Vaticana, 1608.
[9], 189, [10] p.; 18cm.

Text in Latin and Spanish.
Includes index.
Palau, 66774.
Reel 44, No. 229

CHACÓN, PEDRO, ca. 1527-1581.
Petrus Ciacconius Toletanus De Triclinio, Sive De
Modo Convivandi Apud priscos Romanos, & de conviviorum
apparatu. Accedit Fulvii Ursini Appendix. & Hier.
Mercurialis De accubitus in coena Antiquorum origine,
Dissertatio. Amstelaedami: Apud Henricum Wetstenium,
1689.
[13], 445, [23] p.; 14cm.

Half-title: Petrvs Ciacconivs Toletanvs de Triclinio
sive de modo convivandi apud priscos Romanos.
Amstelaedami: Apud. Henr. Wetstenium (1689).
Palau, 66773.
Reel 43, No. 228

CHACÓN, PEDRO, ca. 1527-1581 see also FLORUS, LUCIUS
ANNAEUS.

CHARLEMAGNE, 742-814.
Opus Inlvstrissimi & Excellentissimi seu spectabilis
viri, Caroli Magni, nutu Dei, regis Francorum, Gallias,
Germaniam, Italiamque, siue harum finitimas provincias
domino opitulante regentis, contra Synodum quae in
partibus Graeciae, pro adorandis imaginibus stolide
sive arroganter gesta est. Item, Pavlini Aqvileiensis
Episcopi adversus Felicem Vrgelitanum, & Eliphandum
Toletanum Episcopos libellus. Quae nunc primum in lucem
restituuntur. [Paris], Anno salutis M.DXLIX (1549).
[568] p.; 18cm.

"Eli. Phili. [pseud. of editor] Christiano lectori
s.":p. [3].
Text lacks Caput XXIX. Cf. Migne. Patrologia. Ser.
Latina, vol. 98, pp. 990-1248.
The first part known as the Libri Carolini, is a
manifesto condemning the second Council of Nicaea in
783.
The second part is an attack against the heresy of
the archbishop of Toledo, Elipandus, and the Bishop
Felix of Urdel, who claimed that Jesus Christ in only
the adoptive son of God.
Part I and part II edited by Jean du Tillet, from a
manuscript of the Bibliothèque de l'Arsenal of Paris.
Extremely rare. See British Museum Catalogue of
French Book, p. 103 and British Museum Catalogue of
German Books, p. 674.
Reel 44, No. 230

CHARLES I, Emperor see CHARLEMAGNE, 742-814

CHUMACERO Y CARRILLO, JUAN see PIMENTEL, DOMINGO, joint author.

CIACONO, ALFONSO see CHACÓN, ALFONSO.

CICERO, MARCUS TULLIUS, b. B.C. 106, d. B.C. 43.
[De Amicitia. Spanish]
Libros De Marco Tvlio Ciceron, En Qve Tracta Delos (sic) Officios, Dela Amicicia, y Dela Senectud. Cõ la Economica de Xenophon, traduzidos de Latin en Romãce Castellano. Anadieronse Agora Nveuamente los Paradoxos, y el Sueño de Scipion, traduzidos por Iuan Iaraua. Anvers: En casa de Iuan Steelsio, 1549.
[26], 400 l.; 14cm.

Spanish translation by Francisco Thamar.
Palau, 54346; Peeters - Fontainas, I, no. 250; Penney, p. 134; Thomas, p. 24.
Reel 44, No. 231

CICERO, MARCUS TULLIUS, b. B.C. 106, d. B.C. 43.
[Epistularum ad familiares libri sedecim. Spanish]
Los Dezeseis Libros De Las Epistolas, ò cartas de M. Tulio Ciceron, vulgarmēte llamadas familiares: traduzidas de lengua Latina en Castellana por el Dotor Pedro Simon Abril, natural de Alcaraz. Con v̄na Cronologia de veyntiun Consulados, y las cosas mas graues que en ellos sucedieron, en cuyo tiempo se escriuieron estas cartas. Dirigidas à Mateo Vazquez de Leca Colona, del Consejo del Rey nuestro señor, y su secretario. Madrid: en casa de Pedro Madrigal, 1589.
[8], 471 l.; 15cm.

Spanish translation by Pedro Simón Abril.
Thomas, p. 24.
Reel 44, No. 232

CICERO, MARCUS TULLIUS, b. B.C. 106, d. B.C. 43.
[Orationes. Spanish]
Qvatro Elegantissimas Y Gravissimas Orationes De M. T. Ciceron, contra Catalina, trasladadas en lengua Española, Por el Doctor Andres de Laguna, Medico de Iulio III. Pontifice Maximo. Anvers: En casa de Christoual Plantin en el Vnicornio Dorado, 1557.
[8] , 88 l.; 15cm.

Spanish translation by Andrés de Laguna.
Gallardo, no. 2602; Palau, 54394; Peeters-Fontainas, I, no. 253; Thomas, p. 24.
Reel 44, No. 233

EL CID CAMPEADOR.
Chronica Del Famoso Cavallero Cid Rvy Diez Campeador. Bvrgos: En la Imprimeria de Philippe de Iunta y Iuan Baptista Varesio, 1593.
[45], 317 p.: ill.; 27cm.
Adams, I, 398; Penney, p. 134; Salvá, II, 2891; Ticknor, p. 83.
Reel 44, No. 234

CIRUELO, PEDRO see SACRO BOSCO, JOANNES DE.

COHEN DE LARA, DAVID, 1602-1674.
Sive De Convenientia Vocabvlorv̄m Rabbinicorv̄m Cum Graecis, & quibusdam aliis linguis Europeis, Auctore David Cohen De Lara. [Amstelodami: typis N. Ravestenii, 1638].
92 p.; 20cm.

COHEN DE LARA (Cont'd)
Imperfect: title-page mutilated.
Doublet, p. 45.
Bound with: FABRICIUS, JOHANN. Specimen Arabicum Quo exhibentur Aliquot scripta Arabica ..., 1638.
Reel 87, No. 559

COLLENUCCIO, PANDOLFO, 1444-1504.
[Del Compendio dell'Istoria. Spanish].
Historia Del Reyno De Napoles, Auctor Pandolfo Colenucio de Pesaro Iurisconsulto. Traduzida De lengua Toscana por Iuan Vazquez del Marmol, Corrector general por su Magestad. Dirigida al Illustrissimo Señor Don Agustin de Herrera y Rojas Marques, Conde de las yslas de Fuerte ventura, y Lancarote del Consejo de su Magestad. Seuilla: por Fernando Diaz, 1584.
[2], 167 l.

Wood engraving precedes title.
Spanish translation by Juan Vázquez del Mármol.
Adams, I, no. 2347; Escudero, no. 734 (for Diego Montoya); HC:346/1215; Graesse, II, p. 222; Palau, 56780; Penney, p. 139.
Reel 44, No. 235

COMINES, PHILIPPE DE, SIEUR D´ARGENTON, 1445?-1509.
[Chronique. Spanish]
Las Memorias De Felipe De Comines Señor De Argenton De Los Hechos Y Empresas De Lvis Vndecimo Y Carlos Octavo Reyes de Francia Tradvcidas De Frances Con Escolios Propios Por Don Ivan Vitrian Prior Y Provisor De Calatayvd Asesor Del Sancto Officio Y Capellan Del Rey Nvestro Señor Dirigidas A Sv Sobrino El Señor Don Ivan Vitrian Presidente De La Española Cavallero Del Orden De Calatrava. Dedicatoria, que es Proemio; y dos Tablas, que son Sumario de la Historia y Escolios; y una breve Annotacion. Tomo Primero [Y Secundo]. Amberes: En La Emprenta de Ivan Mevrsio, 1643.
2 v. ([28], 429, [29] p.; [8], 477, [34] p.); 32cm.

Spanish translation by Juan Vitrián.
Goldsmith, p. 44, no. 632; Graesse, II, p. 239; Morante, 1667; Peeters-Fontainas, I, no. 266; Penney, p. 141; Palau, 58239.
Reel 45, No. 236

CONSEJO Real de las Indias.
Ordenanzas Del Consejo Real De Las Indias. Nvevamente Recopiladas, Y Por El Rey Don Felipe Qvarto N. S. Para Sv Govierno, Establecidas Año de M.DC.XXXVI. Madrid: Por Ivlian De Paredes, 1681.
206, [14] p.; 30cm.

Vignette with Spanish Royal Coat of Arms.
"Avtos acverdos y decretos de govierno del Consejo Real y svpremo de las Indias": p. 113-206.
The Council was founded in 1511 or 1524.
Palau, 202820.
Reel 172, No. 1124

CONSTITUCIONES, Reglas Y Instrucciones, Para Las Hermanas Donzellas del nuevo Retiro del Hospital de Nuestra Señora de Misericordia: Baxo La Tercera, Y Venerable Regla De Penitencia Del Serafico, y Patriarca P.S. Francisco. Dedicadas A Los Excelentissimos Señores Concelleres de la Excelentissima Ciudad de Barcelona. Con licencia: Barcelona: en la Imprenta de Cormellas, por Thomas Loriente Impressor, Año 1699.
258, [38] p.; 21cm.

Palau, 59968.
Reel 45, No. 237

A CONTINUATION Of a former Relation Concerning The
   Entertainment given to the Prince His Highnesse by
   the King of Spaine in his Court at Madrid.
   London: Printed by John Haviland for William
   Barret, 1623.
   [3], 18p.

   Bound in: Peña, Juan Antonio de la. [Relación
y juego de cañas que la Magestad Católica-...]
   Allison, p. 139, no. 6; Graesse, p. 190; Palau,
217386; Pollard and Redgrave, no. 19594.
Reel 138, No. 875

COPIA de consulta hecha por la Junta de Medios, año
   1694.
   10 manuscript *l.*
   Bound with: HERRERA Y SOTOMAYOR, JACINTO DE, fl.
1644. Iornada que su Magestad hizo a la Andalvzia.
[Madrid: En la Imprenta Real, 1624].
   Palau, 114276 (List only printed folios 1-6).
Reel 77, No. 484.23

COPIA de papel que el Obispo de Solsona formó el año
   1634 en cumplimento de el Rey en la forma de
   remediar dos desordenes de la Monarchia y conseguir
   su remedio.
   20 manuscript *l.*
   Bound with: HERRERA Y SOTOMAYOR, JACINTO DE, fl.
1644. Iornada que su Magestad hizo a la Andalvzia.
[Madrid: En la Imprenta Real, 1624].
   Palau, 114276 (List only printed folios 1-6).
Reel 77, No. 484.9

COPIA de tres cartas escritas por la Junta de Gobierno
   de la Monarchia de España al Serenissimo Rey de
   Francia Luis XIV.
   8 manuscript *l.*
   Deals with the death of Charles II and the succession
   of his nephew to the throne of Spain.
   Bound with: HERRERA Y SOTOMAYOR, JACINTO DE, fl.
1644. Iornada que su Magestad hizo a la Andalvzia.
[Madrid: En la Imprenta Real, 1624].
   Palau, 114276 (List only printed folios 1-6).
Reel 77, No. 484.17

COPIA de un papel francés que se halló entre otros
   reservados de la Reyna Doña María Luisa de Borbón,
   dándole documentos del modo de gobernarse con su
   marido el rey Catolico D. Carlos II ...
   10 manuscript *l.*

   Bound with: HERRERA Y SOTOMAYOR, JACINTO DE, fl.
1644. Iornada que su Magestad hizo a la Andalvzia.
[Madrid: En la Imprenta Real, 1624].
   Palau, 114276 (List only printed folios 1-6).
Reel 77, No. 484.8

COPIA de una carta del Rey de Francia escrita a su
   Embajador para que manifestara al Cardenal
   Portocarrero la estimacion con quedaba de lo obrado
   en la elección de su nieto.
   1 manuscript *l.*
   Bound with: HERRERA Y SOTOMAYOR, JACINTO DE, fl.
1644. Iornada que su Magestad hizo a la Andalvzia.
[Madrid: En la Imprenta Real, 1624].
   Palau, 114276 (List only printed folios 1-6).
Reel 77, No. 484.19

COPIA de una carta en que se refieren las circunstancias
   que concurrieron en la exaltación de Clemente XI.
   2 manuscript *l.*

   Bound with: HERRERA Y SOTOMAYOR, JACINTO DE, fl.
1644. Iornada que su Magestad hizo a la Andalvzia.
[Madrid: En la Imprenta Real, 1624].
   Palau, 114276 (List only printed folios 1-6).
Reel 77, No. 484.18

COPIA de vna carta, que escrivio vn señor desta Corte
   a vn su amigo. [Valladolid: Dated: 13 de abril de
   1621].
   [4] p.; 29cm.

   Lacks title-page.
   Published by Andrés y Almansa de Mendoza.
   Narrates the death of Philip III.
   Palau, 61122; Simon Díaz, V, 1113-14 and vol.
VIII, 5511.
Reel 45, No. 239

COPIA de vna carta qve ha embiado el Rey don Phillipe
   nuestro señor, al illustrissimo señor el Duque de
   Maqueda, visorey y capitan general del reyno de
   Valencia: En la qual le haze saber como ha hecho
   paz con Enrique rey d'Francia. Va juntamente con
   esta, las capitulaciones de la dicha paz. Impresso
   en Cuenca: [n.p.], 1559.
   [7] p.; 21cm.

   Palau, 61089.
Reel 45, No. 238

CÓRDOBA, ANTONIO DE, 1485-1578.
   Libellvs de detractione et famae restitvtione
fratris Antonii Cordubensis de sacro ordine Minorum
observãtiae, guardiani sancti Francisci Complutensis.
Et Annotationes eiusdem in tractatum De secreto
magistri Soto de ordine Praedicatorum. Complvti:
ex officina Ioannis Brocarij, 1553.
   [2], 99-152 (i.e. 155), 16 *l.*; 19cm.

   Colophon: "Compluti excussum, in aedibus Ionnis
Brocarii die, xxviij, decembris, anno domini. 1553."
   Device of printer on title-page and on verso of
last leaf.
   Catalina, no. 260; Simón Díaz, V, 3172.
Reel 45, No. 240

CORREAS, GONZALO, d. 1630?
   Trilingve De Tres Artes De Las Tres Lengvas
Castellana, Latina, I Griega, Todas En Romanze. Por
el Maestro Gonzalo Correas Catredatico propietario
de la Catreda de lẽguas Hebrea i Caldea, i de la maior
de Griego en la Vniuersidad de Salamanca: Dedicado al
Catolico Rey Don Felipe IIII: nuestro Señor.
Salamanca: en la Oficina de Antonia Ramirez, 1627.
   [16], 138 (i.e. 336), 143 p.; 14cm.

   Gallardo, II, 1916; Graesse, II, p. 275; Salvá, II,
2233; Simón Díaz, IX, 480; Viñaza, no. 134.
Reel 45, No. 241

CORRO, ANTONIO DEL, 1527-1591.
   Dialogvs Theologicvs. Qvo Epistola Divi Pavli
Apostolia Ad Romanos Explanatvr. Ex prelectionibus
Antonij Corrani Hispalensis, sacrae theologiae
professoris, collectus, & concinnatus. Psal. 122.
Ichoua, libera animam meam à labijs falsitatis, à
lingua doli. Quid dabit tibi, aut quid addet tibi
lingua doli? saggitta robusti viri acutae cum
carbonibus iuniperorum. Londini: Pridie calendas
Iunij, excudebat prelum Thomae Purfoetij ad Lucretiae
symbolum, 1574.
   [14], 108 *l.*; 17cm.

   Engraving on last leaf, followed by Colophon:
"Excusum Londini apud Thomam Purfoetum. Anno.
M.D.LXXIIII".
   8vo. old calf, slightly rubbed, slight marginal
restorations to lower margin of B^4 and D^4, a few
leaves dust-soiled, slightly stained.
   Palau, 62858; Simón Díaz, IX, 518.
Reel 45, No. 242

CORRO, ANTONIO DEL, 1527-1591.
Reglas gramaticales para aprender la lengua Española y Francesa, confiriendo la vna con la otra, segun el orden de las partes de la oration Latinas. Oxford: Por Ioseph Barnes, 1586.
[14], 126 p.; 17cm.

Dedication signed A.D.C. (i.e. A.de Corro).
Aguilar, no. 408; Palau, 62865; Simón Díaz, IX, 509.
Reel 45, No. 243

CORRO, ANTONIO DEL, 1527-1591.
[Reglas gramaticales. English]
The Spanish Grammer: vvith certeine Rules teaching both the Spanish and French tongues. By which they that haue some knowledge in the French tongue, may the easier attaine to the Spanish, and likewise they that haue the Spanish, with more facilitie learne the French: and they that are acquainted with neither of them, learne either or both. Made in Spanish, by M. Anthonie de Corro. With a Dictionarie adioyned vnto it, of all the Spanish wordes / most necessarie for all such as desire the knowledge of the same tongue. By Iohn Thorius, graduate in Oxenford. London: Imprinted by Iohn VVolfe, 1590.
[6], 119, [14] p.; 19cm.

English translation by John Thorius.
A translation of the 1586 edition (vid. supra) printed at Oxford, where Corro was lecturer in divinity.
Aguilar, no. 416; Allison, p. 58, no. 46; Palau, 62866; Penney, p. 150; Pollard and Redgrave, 5790; Simón Díaz, IX, 516; Thomas, p. 26.
Reel 45, No. 244

COSTA, CRISTÓVÃO DA see ACOSTA, CRISTÓBAL DE.

COVARRUBIAS, PEDRO DE, d. 1530.
[Remedio de jugadores. Italian]
Rimedio De' Givocatori, Composto Per Lo R.P.M. Pietro Di Cobarvbias, dell'ordine de' Predicatori. Nel Qvale Con L'Avtorita de' Sacri Dottori s'insegna a giuocare senza offesa di Dio. E Si Reprobano I Cattivi Givochi dimostrando quanto sieno dannosi alla Repvblica, Nuouamente di lingua Spagnuola tradotto Dal S. Alfonso Vlloa Con Priuilegio. Venetia: Appresso Vincenzo Valgrisi, 1561.
[16], 195, [3] p.; 17cm.

Italian translation by Alfonso Ulloa.
Colophon: "In Venetia Appresso Vincenzo Valgrisi. M D L X I."
Simón Díaz, IX, 1082; Toda y Güell, Italia, I, no. 1218.
Reel 45, No. 245

COVARRUBIAS HOROZCO, SEBASTIÁN DE, fl., 1611.
Emblemas Morales De Don Sebastian De Couarrubias Orozco, Capellan del Rey N. S. Maestrescuela, y Canonigo de Cuenca, Consultor del santo Oficio. Dirigidas A Don Francisco Gomez de Sandoual y Roxas, Duque de Lerma, Marq̃s de Denia, Sumiller de Corps Cauallerizo mayor del Rey N.S. Comendador mayor de Castilla, Capitan General de la caualleria de España. En Madrid: Por Luis Sanchez, 1610.
[4], 300, [7] l., ill.; 21cm.

COVARRUBIAS HOROZCO
Goldsmith, p. 47, no. 719; Pérez Pastor, Madrid, II, no. 1088; Jerez, p. 29; Penney, p. 155; Simón Díaz, IX, 1106.
Reel 45, No. 246

COVARRUBIAS HOROZCO, SEBASTIAN DE, fl., 1611.
Tesoro De La Lengva Castellana, O Española. Compvesto Por El Licenciado Don Sebastian de Cobarruuias Orozco, Capellan de su Magestad, Mastrescuela y Canonigo de la santa Yglesia de Cuenca, y Consultor del santo Oficio de la Inquisicion. Dirigido A La Magestad Catolica del Rey Don Felipe III. nuestro señor. Madrid: por Luis Sanchez, impressor del Rey N.S. Año del Señor, 1611.
[10], 602, 79, [1] l.; 30cm.

Colophon: "En Madrid, Por Luis Sanchez. Año M.DC.XI."
Goldsmith, p. 47, no. 720; Graesse, II, p. 291; Knapp, p. 23; Penney, p. 155; Pérez Pastor, Madrid, II, no. 1130; Simón Díaz, IX, 1102; Viñaza, no. 726.
Reel 46, No. 247

COVARRUBIAS HOROZCO, SEBASTIÁN DE, fl., 1611.
Parte Primera Del Tesoro De La Lengva Castellana; o Española. Testo Por El Licenciado Don Sebastián De Covarruuias Orozco, Capellan de su Magestad, Maestrescuela, y Canonigo de la Santa Iglesia de Cuenca, y Consultor del Santo Oficio de la Inquisicion. Añadido Por El Padre Benito Remigio Noydens Religioso de la Sagrada Religion de los PP. Clerigos Regulares Menores. Al Señor Don Gregorio Altamirano Portocarrero Cauallero de la Orden de Santiago, del Consejo de su Magestad en el de Hazienda y su Contaduria mayor, Contador mayor de la Orden, y Cavallero de Alcantara, &c. [Printer's device]. Con Privilegio. En Madrid: por Melchor Sanchez. A costa de Gabriel de Leon, Mercader de Libros, vendese enfrente de la calle de la Paz, 1674.
6, 274, [1], l.

[Part II:] Parte Segvnda Del Tesoro De La Lengva Castellana, O Española. Compvesto Por El Licenciado Don Sebastian De Covarrvvias Orozco, Capellan De Sv Magestad, Maestrescvela, y Canonigo de la Santa Iglesia de Cuenca, y Consultor del Santo Oficio de la Inquisicion. Añadido Por El Padre Benito Remigio, de los Clerigos Menores. [Printer's device]. Con Privilegio. En Madrid: por Melchor Sanchez. A costa de Gabriel de Leon, Mercader de Libros, vendese enfrente de la calle de la Paz, 1673.
213, [3] l.

Colophon: "En Madrid Por Melchor Sanchez Año M.DC.LXXIV."
Doublet, p. 23; Morante, 119-20; Simón Díaz, V, no. 618.
Reel 6, No. 34

CRUZ, JUANA INES DE LA see JUANA INÉS DE LA CRUZ, Sister.

D

DÁVILA, JUAN BAUTISTA, 1598-1664.
Passion del Hombre-Dios referida y ponderada En Decimas Españolas. Por el Maestro Ivan Davila. ... En Leon de Francia: A Costa de Horacio Boissat y George Remevs. Clavdio Bovrgeat y Migvel Lietard, 1661.
[8], 72, 57 (i.e. 59), 82, 44, 55, 81 p., 14 plates; 27cm.

Three unsigned leaves (engraved title-page; title-page dedication).
Error in pagination: p. 57-59 in second group numbered 55-57.
The added title-page vignette and plates are engraved.
Goldsmith, p. 49, no. 14, dated 1611 (i.e. 1661); Graesse, II, p. 342; Jerez, p. 33; Palau, 68875; Penney, p. 164; Salvá, I, 560; Ticknor, p. 24.
Reel 46, No. 250

DÁVILA PADILLA, AGUSTÍN, abp. of Santo Domingo, 1562-1604.
Historia De La Fvndacion Y Discvrso De La Provincia, De Santiago De Mexico, De La Orden De Predicadores Por las vidas de sus varones insignes y casos Notables de Nueua España. Por el Maestro Fray Avgvstin Davila Padilla Al Principe de España Don Felipe nuestro Señor. Edicion Segvnda. En Brvsselas: En casa de Ivan De Meerbeqve, 1625.
[8], 654, [6] p.; 31cm.

Title in red and black within double lines. Title vignette: Device of Dominican order.
Goldsmith, p. 49, no. 16; HC:339/559; Penney, p. 164; Peeters-Fontainas, I, no. 286.
Reel 46, No. 251

DAZA, ANTONIO, Brother.
[Historia, vida, milagros de la Santa Juana de la Cruz. Italian]
Historia, Vita, Miracoli, Estasi, E Revelationi Della bene auuenturata Vergine Svor Giovanna Della Croce Del Terzo Ordine del nostro Serafico Padre S. Francesco. Composta, e di nuouo corretta, & emendata per Frà Antonio Dazza Frate Min. Diffinitore della S. Prouincia della Concettione, e Cronista dell'Ordine. Indirizzata alla Catt. Maestà del Rè D. Filippo III. Tradotta di Spagnuolo in Italiano da Paolo Brusantini Conte di Nismozza, & Aqua Buona. In Pavia: Appresso Gio. Battista Rossi, 1618.
[48], 269, [5] p.; 13cm.

Ex-libris: From the library of Conte Antonio Cavagna Sangiuliani Di Gvaldana Lazelada di Beregvardo. 1921.
Imperfect: all after p. [274] wanting.
Italian translation by Paolo Brusantini.
Palau, vol. IV, p. 313.
Reel 47, No. 252

DECLARACIÓN De Sv Alteza, del Señor Cardenal Infante, acerca de la guerra, contra la Corona de Francia. Madrid: Por los herederos de la viuda de Pedro de Madrigal. A costa de Pedro Coello, Mercader de libros, 1635.
8 p.; 21cm.

DECLARACIÓN (Cont'd)
Ex-libris: Luis Bardon.
Caption title.
Original French title unknown. Spanish translation by Martin Goblet.
Bound in: Cespedes y Maneses, Gonzalo de: Francia Engañada Francia Respondida, ... Empresso en Caller, Año 1635.
Palau, 69406.
Reel 41, No. 220

DEIPHIRA Di messer Leon Battista Alberto Firentino, ne la quale ne insegna amare temperatamente, & ne fa Diuenire, o piu prudenti a fuggir amore, nouamente stápata (sic). [Vinegia: Bindoni & Pasiníl, 1534.
[1], 10-23, [1] l.; 16cm.

Colophon: "Stampata in Vinegia a Santo Moyse per Francesco Bindoni, & Mapheo Pasini compagni. Del mese di Genaro. Nelli anni del Signore. M. D. XXXIIII."
Palau, 95502; Short-Title, I, p. 644.
Reel 54, No. 321

DEIPHIRA Di Messer Leon Battista Alberto Firentino, Ne La Qvale Ne insegna amare tēperatamente, & ne fa diuenire, o piu dotte ad amare, o piu prudenti à fuggir amore, nouamēte stampata. In Venetia: [n.p.], 1545.
[1], 10-23 l.; 16cm.

Reel 54, No. 320

DEL RIO, MARTIN ANTOINE, 1551-1608.
Ad Cl. Clavdiani V. C. Opera Martini Antonii Del-Rio Notae. Antverpiae: Ex officina Christophori Plantini, 1572.
80, [4] p.; 13cm.

Error in binding: F^2 misbound before A^1.
"Errata & omissa": p. [84].
Bound with: Poelmann, Theodor. Cl. Clavdianvs, Theod. Pvlmanni Cranebvrgii Diligentia, & fide summa, è vetustis codicibus restitutus, 1571.
Adams, I, no. 240; Palau, 268242; Simón Díaz, Jesuitas, no. 1447.
Reel 153, No. 1008

DEL RIO, MARTIN ANTOINE, 1551-1608.
Ad Cl. Clavdiani V. C. Opera Martini Antonii Del-Rio Notae. Antverpiae: Ex officina Christophori Plantini, 1585.
80, [3] p.; 13cm.

Bound with: A) Poelmann, Theodor: Cl. Clavdianvs, Theod. Pvlmanni Cranebvrgii Diligentia, & fide summa, è vetustis codicibus restitutus. 1585.
B) Poelmann, Theodor: Aviani Aesopicarvm Fabvlarvm Liber. A Theod. Pvlmanno Cranebvrgio Ex Membranis In Lvcem Editvs. 1585.
Adams, I, no. 241; Palau, 268243; Simón Díaz, Jesuitas, no. 1448.
Reel 153, No. 1010

DEL RIO, MARTIN ANTOINE, 1551-1608.
Ad Cl. Clavdiani V. C. Opera Martini Antonii Del-Rio Notae. Antverpiae: Apud Ioannem Moretum, 1607.
90, [3] p.; 13cm.

Bound with: A) Poelmann, Theodor: Cl. Clavdianvs, Theod. Pvlmanni Cranebvrgii Diligentia, & fide summa, è vetustis codicibus restitutus. Vnâ cum M. Ant. Del-rio Notis. 1607.
B) Poelmann, Theodor: Aviani Aesopicarvm Fabvlarvm Liber, A Theod. Pvlmanno Cranebvrgio Ex Membranis In Lvcem Editvs. 1607.
Contains the complete works of Claudian, the last great Latin poet, who was born in Greece, spent his childhood in Alexandria and ca. 400 A.D. onwards lived in Rome.
Palau, 268249; Simón Díaz, Jesuitas, no. 1449.
Reel 153, No. 1013

DEL RIO, MARTIN ANTOINE, 1551-1608.
Adagialia Sacra Veteris Et Novi Testamenti: Collectore Ac Interprete, Martino Del Rio Antverpiensi, Societatis Iesv Sacerdote, & S. Sripturae publico Salmanticae Professore. Editio secunda & accurata. Cum Indicibus necessariis. Lvgdvni: Sumptibus Horatij Cardon, 1614.
[40], 609, [54] p.; 26cm.

Palau, 268306; Simón Díaz, Jesuitas, no. 1474.
Reel 153, No. 1016

DEL RIO, MARTIN ANTOINE, 1551-1608.
Commentarivs Litteralis In Threnos, id est, Lamentationes Ieremiae Prophetae. Auctore Martino Del - Rio Presbytero Societatis Iesv Doctore Theologo & publico S.S. in Salmanticensi Academia Professore. Nunc primùm in lucem editum. Accesserunt duo Indices, vnus locorum S. Scripturae, alter verò rerum & verborum. Lvgdvni: Sumptibvs Horatii Cardon, 1608.
[11], 250, [15] p.; 25cm.

Engraved title-page.
Doublet, p. 112; Palau, 268302; Simón Díaz, Jesuitas, no. 1470.
Reel 153, No. 1017

DEL RIO, MARTIN ANTOINE, 1551-1608.
Disqvititionvm Magicarvm Libri Sex, In Tres Tomos Partiti. Auctore Martino Del Rio Societatis Iesv Presbitero, Sacrae Theologiae Doctore, & in Academiâ Graetiensi S.S. Professore Tomus Primus. Nvnc Secvndis Cvris Avctior longê, additionibus multis passim insertis: correctior quoq mendis sublatis. Mogvntiae: Apud Ioannem Albinvm, 1603.
3v. in 1 ([24], 276, [15] p.; [5], 268, [18] p.; [5], 250, [11] p.); 31cm.

Engraved title-page.
Vol. II has separate t.-p.: Magicarvm Disqvisitionvm Tomvs Secvndvs, Secundâ curâ correctior & auctior. In Qvo Agitvr De Maleficio, Vana Observatione, Divinatione, Et Con. Iectatione. Avctore Martino Del Rio Societatis Iesv Presbytero, Sacrae Theologiae Doctore, & in Academiâ Graetiensi S. S. Professore.
Vol. III has separate t.-p.: Disqvisitionvm Magicarvm Tomvs Tertivs. Sev Methodvs Vndicvm Et Confessariorvm Directioni Commoda. Hac vltimâ curâ emendatior, âuctiorq; Avctore Martino Delrio, Societatis Iesv Presbytero, S. Theologiae Doctore, & in Academia Graetiensi S.S. Professore.
Palau, 268269; Simón Díaz, Jesuitas, no. 1456.
Reels 153 & 154, No. 1018

DEL RIO, MARTIN ANTOINE, 1551-1608.
Disqvisitionvm Magicarvm Liùri Sex: Quibus continetur accurata curiosarum artium, & vanarum superstitionum confutatio, vtilis Theologis Jurisconsultis Medicis Philologis. Auctore Martino Del Rio Societatis Iesv Presbytero. L L. Licentiato, & Theologia Doctore, olim in Academia Gratzensi, nunc in Salmáticensi publico Sacrae Scripturae. Professore Editio Postrema Quae vt auctior castigatiorque coeteris, sic & Indicibvs pernecessariis prodit hodie illustrior. Lvgdvni: Apvd Horativm Cardon, 1612.
[52], 468, [20] p.; 34cm.

Engraved title-page.
Palau, 268274; Simón Diaz, Jesuitas, no. 1460.
Reel 154, No. 1020

DEL RIO, MARTIN ANTOINE, 1551-1608.
Disqvisitionum Magicarvm Libri Sex, In Tres Tomos Partiti. Auctore Martino Delrio Societatis Iesv Presbytero sacrae Theologiae Doctore, & in Academia Gretiensi, S. S. professore. Tomvs Primvs. Nunc tertiis curis ab ipso Auctore auctior longe, Additionibus multis passim insertis, correctior quoque mendis sublatis. S. Caes. Maiest. ad annos sex Prodit Ex Archiepiscopatus Moguntinensis Officina Vrsellana: Impensis Iacobi Köning, 1606.
3v. ([46], 773, [43] p.; [28], 724, [55] p.; [25], 687, [33] p.); 20cm.

Engraved title-page.
Vol. II has separate t.-p.: Disqvisitionum Magicarvm Libri Sex, In Tres Tomos Partiti. Auctore Martino Delrio Societatis Iesv Presbytero sacrae Theologiae Doctore, & in Academiae Gretiensi, S.S. professore. Tomvs Secvndvs. Nunc tertiis curis ab ipso Auctore auctior longe, Additionibus multis passim insertis, correctior quoque mendis sublatis.
Vol. III has separate t.-p.: Disqvisitionum Magicarvm Libri Sex, In Tres Tomos Partiti, Auctore Martino Delrio Societatis Iesv Presbytero sacrae Theologiae Doctore, &. in Academiae Gretiensi, S.S. Professore. Tomvs Tertivs. Nunc tertiis curis ab ipso Auctore auctior longe, Additionibus multis passim insertis, correctior quoque mendis sublatis.
Palau, 268271; Simón Díaz, Jesuitas, no. 1457.
Reel 154, No. 1019

DEL RIO, MARTIN ANTOINE, 1551-1608.
Disqvisitionvm Magicarvm Libri Sex, Quibus continetur accurata curiosarum artium, & vanarum superstitionum confutatio; Apprime vtilis, & pernecessaria Theologis, Iurisconsultis, Medicis, Philosophis, ac praesertim Verbi Dei Concionatoribus, & vtriusque Fori Iudicibus, quibus in primis aurea praecepta traduntur. Auctore Martino Del Rio Societatis Iesu Presbytero. LL. Licentiato, & Theol. Doct. olim in Academia Gretzensi, ac dein Salmatic. publico S.S. Profesore. Hac Veneta, & Postrema Editione omnium maxime elaborata, suaque pristinae integritati restituta ac praeterea Auctoris Vita, Et quattuor Locupletissimis Indicibus aucta. Admodum Reuer. Patri D. Ioanni Avgvstino Ex Comitibus Linguillie Congregationis Somaschae Theologo ac Concionatori praecellentissimo. Venetiis: Apud Iuntas, 1652.
[20], 768, [89] p.; 23cm.

Palau, 268282.
Reel 155, No. 1021

DEL RIO, MARTIN ANTOINE, 1551-1608.
Ex Miscellaneorvm Scriptoribv₃ Digestorvm Sive
Pandectarvm Iuris Ciuilis Interpretatio. Opus antehac
à M. Antonio Delrio Regio in Brabantiae Cancellaria
Consiliario editum. Nunc verô multô feliciùs quàm
antea renatum, & à mendis propemodum innumeris quae in
priori editione resederant, studio ac diligentia Petri
Brossaei I.C. quàm accuratissimê repurgatum, multisq̃
Scriptoribus cum veteribus tum neotericis auctum atque
locupletatum. His accesserunt Indices duo: Prior
Authorum atque Scriptorum Miscellaneorum, ex quorum
libris has notas excerpsimus: Posterior Titulorum
Pandectarum in hoc libro explicatorum Secvnda Editio
priore duplo auctior. Lvgdvni: Apud Franciscum
Fabrum, 1590.
2 pts. ([9] l. 972 cols.; [17] l., 820 cols.); 25cm.

Adams, I, no. 244; Palau, 268261; Simón Díaz,
Jesuitas, no. 1452.
Reel 155, No. 1022

DEL RIO, MARTIN ANTOINE, 1551-1608.
Martini Antonii Delrii Ex Societate Iesv Syntagma
Tragoediae Latinae. In tr₃s partes distinctum. Quib
in ijsdem contineatur, sequens pagina indicabit.
Antverpiae: Apud Viduam, & Ioannem Moretum, 1593.
3v. ([17], 188 p.; 315 p.; 559, 174 p.); 25cm.

Vol. II has separate title-page: Martini Antonii
Delrii Ex Societate Iesv Syntagmatis Tragoediae Latinae.
Pars secunda. In qua L. Annaei Senecae Tragoedia
(sic) cum Aduersariis recognitis, &c. vti sequens
pagina indicabit. Antverpiae: Apud Viduam, & Ioannem
Moretum, 1593.
Vol. III has separate title-page: Martini Antonii
Delrii Ex Societate Iesv Syntagmatis Tragici Pars
vltima, sev Nouus Commentarius in decem Tragoedias,
quae vulgô Senecae ascribuntur. Cum Indicibus.
Antverpiae: Apud Viduam, & Ioannem Moretum, 1594.
Adams, I, no. 248; Simón Díaz, Jesuitas, no. 1453.
Reels 155 & 156, No. 1023

DEL RIO, MARTIN ANTOINE, 1551-1608.
Martini Antonii Delrii Ex Societate Iesv Syntagma
Tragoediae Latinae In tres partes distinctum. Qvid
In I₃sdem Contineatvr, Seqvens Pagina Indicabit.
Lvtetiae Parisiorvm: Sumptibus Petri Billaine, viâ
Iacobaeâ sub signo Boane Fidei, & in Palatio iuxta
D. Michaëlis Sacellum, 1620.
3 v. in 1 ([18], 188 p.; 315 p.; 559, [164] p.);
25cm.

Vol. II has separate title-page: Martini Antonii
Delrii Ex Societate Iesv Syntagmatis Tragoediae Latinae
Pars secunda. In qua L. Annaei Senecae Tragoediae
cum Aduersariis recognitis, &c. vti sequens pagina
indicabit. (1619)
Vol. III has separate title page: Martini Antonii
Delrii Ex Societate Iesv Syntagmatis Tragici Pars
vltima. Sev Nouus Commentarius in decem Tragoedias,
quae vulgô Senecae ascribuntur.
Title in red and black. Title vignette. Vol. I
lacks special title page.
Palau, 268256.
Reel 156, No. 1024

DEMANDA DEL SANCTO GRIAL.
La demànda del sancto Grial: Con los
marauillosos fechos de Lâcarote y de Galaz
su hijo 1535 [Seuilla].
[8], cxciiij l., ;28cm.

DEMANDA DEL SANCTO GRIAL (Cont'd)
Error in foliation: nos. xciii-xcvi omitted;
other pagination errors.
"Las profecias del subio Merlin", leaves
lxxxviij-xcvij (i.e. xcvii).
Graesse, II, p. 355; Palau, IV, p. 352.
Reel 47, No. 253

DEVEREUX, ROBERT, 2nd earl of Essex see ESSEX, ROBERT
DEVEREUX, earl of, 1566-1601.

DIALOGO Dove Si Ragiona Della Bella Creanza Delle
Donne. In Vinegia: appresso Domenico Farri,
[n.d.].
46 l.; 16cm.
Foliation errors throughout.
Reel 54, No. 315

DIAMANTE, JUAN BAUTISTA, 1625-1687.
Comedias De F. Don Ivan Bavtista Diamante, Del
Abito De San Ivan Prior, Y Comendador De Moron.
Dedicadas Al Excelentisimo Señor D. Ivan Bavtista
Ludouisio, por la gracia de Dios Principe de Pomblin.
Con Privilegio. En Madrid: por Andres Garcia de la
Iglesia. A costa de Iuan Martin Merinero, Mercader
de libros en la Puerta del Sol, 1670.
[4], 288, 158 p.; 20cm.

Gallardo, II, no. 2004; Graesse, II, p. 381; Palau,
71749; Penney, p. 169; Salvá, I, 1219; Simón Díaz,
IX, 2807.
Reel 47, No. 255

DÍAZ DE MONTALVO, ALONSO, 1405-1499? see CASTILLE. Laws,
Statutes, etc.

DÍAZ DE MONTALVO, ALONSO, 1405-1499? see also NICCOLO
DE TUDESCHI.

DÍAZ DE VARGAS, FRANCISCO, b. in Trujillo.
Francisci Vargas, Catholicae Maiestatis Rervm
Statvs A Consiliis, & eiusdem apud sanctiss. D. N.
Pivm IIII. Oratoris, De Episcoporum iurisdictione,
Et Pontificis Max. auctoritate, Responsvm. Romae:
Apud Paulum Manutium Aldi F. In Aedibvs Popvli
Romani, 1563.
[16], 160 p.; 20cm.

Not in Simón Díaz; not in Palau's ...
Reel 47, No. 259

DÍAZ DEL CASTILLO, BERNAL, 1496-1584.
Historia verdadera de la Conquista de la Nueva-
España. Escrita Por el Capitan Bernal Diaz del Castillo,
uno de sus Conquistadores. Sacada á lvz Por el P.M.
Fr. Alonso Remon, Predicador, y Coronista General
del Orden de Nuestra Señora de la Merced, Redempcion
de Cautivos. A la catholica magestad del mayor monarca
Don Felipe Quarto ... Madrid: Imp. del Reyno, 1632.
[6], 254, [6] l.; 30cm.

First ed.
Binding signed: A. Palomino. Red morocco, gold tooled.
Bartlett, 2/387; Palau, 72354; Penney, p. 171; Salva,
II, 3308; Simón Díaz, IX, 3105; Ticknor, p. 118.
Reel 47, No. 256

DÍAZ RENGIFO, JUAN, fl. 1592.
Arte Poetica Española, Con Vna Fertilissima Sylua de Consonantes Comunes, Propios, Esdruxulos, y Reflexos, y vn diuino Estimulo del Amor de Dios. Por Ivan Diaz Rengifo, natural de Auila. Dedicada A Don Gaspar De Zuñiga y Azeuedo, Conde de Monterey, y señor de la casa de Viezma y Vlloa, &c. Madrid: por Iuan de la Cuesta, 1606.
[12], 364 p.; 20cm.

Goldsmith, p. 51; Palau, 72825; Simón Díaz, IX, 3348.
Reel 47, No. 257

DÍAZ RENGIFO, JUAN, fl. 1592.
Arte Poetica Española, Con Vna Fertilissima Sylua de Consonantes Comunes, Propios, Esdruxulos, y Reflexos, y vn diuino Estimulo del Amor de Dios. Por Ivan Diaz Rengifo, natural de Auila. Dedicada A Don Gaspar De Zuñiga y Azeuedo, Conde de Monterey, y señor de la casa de Viezma y Vlloa. Con Licencia. En Madrid: Por la viuda de Alonso Martin, 1628. A costa de Domingo Goncalez, mercader de libros.
[12], 324, 40, [5] p., ill.; 20cm.

Manuscript index.
Title-page and first few leaves mended not affecting text.
Goldsmith, p. 51, no. 78; Palau, IV, p. 431; Simón Díaz, IX, 3349.
Reel 47, No. 258

DIEGO DE ESTELLA see ESTELLA, DIEGO DE.

DIEGO DE SAN PEDRO.
Carcer d'amore traduto (sic) dal magnifico miser Lelio de Manfredi Ferrarese: de Idioma Spagnolo in lingua materna. Nouamente Stampato. [n.p., n.d.].
48 *l.*; 16cm.

Reel 54, No. 318

DISCURSO en que se representa a el Rey Christianissimo de Francia de romper la guerra con España, 1630?
4 manuscript *l.*

Bound with: HERRERA Y SOTOMAYOR, JACINTO DE, fl. 1644. Iornada que su Magestad hizo a la Andalvzia. [Madrid: En la Imprenta Real, 1624].
Palau, 114276 (List only printed folios 1-6).
Reel 77, No. 484.6

DISCURSO político de un gentilhombre veneciano sobre la sucesión de la Monarchia de España y de la Justicia y conveniencias que concurren en que sea preferido al Principe Fernando de Baviera.
14 manuscript *l.*

Bound with: HERRERA Y SOTOMAYOR, JACINTO DE, fl. 1644. Iornada que su Magestad hizo a la Andalvzia. [Madrid: En la Imprenta Real, 1624].
Palau, 114276 (List only printed folios 1-6).
Reel 77, No. 484.11

DISCURSO y Plática entre cierto Ministro favorecido y un veinte y cuatro sobre la concesión de millones.
14 manuscript *l.*

Bound with: HERRERA Y SOTOMAYOR, JACINTO DE, fl. 1644. Iornada que su Magestad hizo a la Andalvzia. [Madrid: En la Imprenta Real, 1624].
Palau, 114276 (List only printed folios 1-6).
Reel 77, No. 484.27

DIVISIÓN de las facciones de los Cardenales en el Conclave de 1700 en que fue exaltado a la Tiara Clemente XI.
4 manuscript *l.*
Bound with: HERRERA Y SOTOMAYOR, JACINTO DE, fl. 1644. Iornada que su Magestad hizo a la Andalvzia. [Madrid: En la Imprenta Real, 1624].
Palau, 114276 (List only printed folios 1-6).
Reel 77, No. 484.20

DONATI, L. see FERNÁNDEZ, MARCUS, joint author.

DORMER, DIEGO JOSÉ, d. 1705.
Discvrsos varios de historia; con mvchas escritvras reales antigvas, y notas a algvnas dellas. Recogidos, y compvestos por el Doctor Diego Iosef Dormer, ... Zaragoza: por los herederos de Diego Dormer, 1683.
[12], 472 p.; 21cm.

P. 425 misnumbered 254.
Doublet, p. 53; Graesse, II, p. 428; HC:384/187; Jiménez Catalán, 999; Palau, 75750; Penney, p. 177; Salvá, II, 2923; Simón Díaz, IX, 3994.
Reel 47, No. 260

DORMER, DIEGO JOSÉ see BLANCAS Y TOMAS, GERÓNIMO DE, d. 1590.

DOZE Comedias las mas grandiosas qve hasta ahora han salido, De los mejores, y más insignes Poetas. Aora de nuevo impressas. Lisboa: Pablo Craesbeeck, 1653.
[4], 498 p.; 21cm.

Contains:
(A) Francisco de Rojas: El Caín de Cataluña;
(B) Agustín Moreto: El Príncipe Perseguido;
(C) Juan Mátos Fragoso: El Príncipe prodigioso;
(D) Calderón de la Barca: El garrote más bien dado;
(E) Luis Vélez de Guevara: La luna de la sierra;
(F) Jerónimo de Villaizan: A gran daño gran remedio;
(G) Francisco Antonio de Monteser: El caballero de Olmedo. Burlesca;
(H) Tres Ingenios: El pleito que puso al diablo el cura de Madrilejos;
(I) Luis Vélez de Guevara: El privado perseguido;
(J) Antonio Enriquez Gómez: Zelos no ofenden al sol;
(K) Antonio de Huerta: Competidores y amigos;
(L) Pedro Calderón de la Barca: El guardarse a sí mismo.

Title page lacking.
Pagination errors through.
Palau, 76096; Salvá, I, 1226.
Reel 47, No. 261

DU CHOUL, GUILLAUME, 16th cent.
[Discours... Spanish]
Los discvrsos de la religion, castramentacion, assiento del Campo, Baños y exercicios de los Antiguos Romanos y Griegos, Del Illustre Guillermo de Choul. Traduzido en Castellano de la lengua Francesa por el Maestro Balthasar Perez del Castillo ... Leon de Francia: Gvillelmo Rovillio, 1579.
[8], 488, [42] p.; 24cm.

Spanish translation by Baltasar Pérez del Castillo. The "Discurso del assiento del campo ..." has special title.
Adams, I, no. 1034; Graesse, II, p. 441; HC:387/2320; Penney, p. 178; Salvá, II, 3547; Thomas, p. 30.
Reel 48, No. 262

E

ELIPANDUS, Archbishop of Toledo, ca. 718-802 see
CHARLEMAGNE [CHARLES I. Emperor].

ELOGIO a la Provincia de Guipúzcoa por Miguel de
Avendaño.
11 manuscript *l*.
Bound with: HERRERA Y SOTOMAYOR, JACINTO DE, fl.
1644. Iornada que su Magestad hizo a la Andalvzia.
[Madrid: En la Imprenta Real, 1624].
Palau, 114276 (List only printed folios 1-6).
Reel 77, No. 484.32

ENRÍQUEZ GÓMEZ, ANTONIO, 1602-1662?
Sanson Nazareno. Pòema heroico. Por Antonio
Henriqvez Gomez. Rvan: En la emprenta de Lavrenco
Mavrry, 1656. Con Licencia.
[12], 338 p.; 23cm.

Doublet, p. 54; Goldsmith, p. 54, no. 52; Jerez, p.
36; Miró, 284; Penney, p. 184; Simón Díaz, IX, 4561.
Reel 48, No. 263

EPICTETUS.
[Enchiridion. Spanish]
Dotrina Del Estoico Filosofo Epicteto, que se
llama communmente Enchiridion, traduzido de Griego.
Por El Maestro Francisco Sanchez Catedratico de
Retorica, y Griego en la Vniuersidad de Salamanca
Madrid: Por Iuan de la Cuesta, 1612.
8, 76 l.; 16cm.

Spanish translation by Francisco Sánchez de las
Brozas.
P. 46 misnumbered 49.
Goldsmith, p. 55, no. 61; Palau, 80174; Salvá,
Reel 48, No. 264

ERASMUS, DESIDERIUS, d. 1536.
De Conscribendis Epistolis Des. Erasmi Roterdami
Opvs. Ioannis Lvdovici Vivis Valentini Libellus
uerè aureus. Conradi Celtis Methodus. Christophori
Hegen dorphini Epitome. Omnia nunc demum in studiosorum
gratiam & utilitatem uno libello comprehensa, &
longe quàm antea emendatius excusa. Basileae: Per
Nicolavm Brylingerum, 1555.
[4], 550 (i.e. 552) p.; 16cm.

Errors in paging: 467 and 470 repeated.
Reel 48, No. 265

ESCALONA Y AGÜERO, GASPAR DE, d. 1659.
Gazophilativm Regivm Pervbicvm. Opvs Sane Pvlcrvm,
A Plerisqve Petitvm, Et ab omnibus, in vniuersum,
desideratum, non sine magno labore, & experientia
digestum, provideque, & accurate illustratum. In
Qvo Omnes Materiae Spectantes, Ad Administrationem
calculationem, & conservationem, iurium regalium
Regni Peruani latissimè discutiuntur, & plene manu per
tractantur. Editvm A D. Gaspare De Escalona Agvero.
I.C. Argentino Peruano, ex Correctore Provintiae de
Xuaxa, ex Gubernatore Ciuitatis Castro-Virreynae,
ex Visitatore Arcarum Regaliu, ex Generali Procuratore
Ciuitatis Cusquensis, omnium Peruano tractus primarias,
& Senatore Chilensi. Dicatvm Illmo D. D. Petro Egidio
de Alpharo, Equiti Iacobeo, in Regio Castellae Senatu
Consiliario, & Rei Dominicae Supremo Presidi, &c.
Cvm Facvltate Matriti. Ex Typographia Antonij Gonzalez
Reyes, 1675. Sumptibus Gabrielis de Leon Bibliopolae.
[20], 199, [1], 302, [57] p.; 30cm.

ESCALONA Y AGÜERO (Cont'd)
Title in red and black, with mark of "Gabriel de
Leon". All except the first part in Spanish.
Bartlett, 2/1114; HC: 418/319; Palau, 80776; Penney,
p. 187; Wilkinson, 232.
Reel 48, No. 266

ESCOBAR, ANDRÉS DE, bp. d. ca. 1431.
Casus Papales Confessorum. Interrogationes et
doctrinae. [Ulm: Johann Zainer, ca. 1490]
[8] *l*.; 20cm.

Leaf [1ª]: Half-title: Casus papales confessorum.
Gesamtkat. d. Wiegendr. 7310; Goff, C830; Hain,
no. 4674. Not in Proctor or Stillwell. Although
Stillwell lists a number of editions, all rare,
printed in Italy, there is no other copy in the United
States of the edition printed in Germany.
Title page lacking.
Reel 48, no. 267

ESCOBAR, ANDRÉS DE, bp. d. ca. 1431.
Interrogationes et doctrinae. [Rome: Eucharius
Silber, ca. 1490-95]
[8] *l*.; 14cm.

Leaf [1ª]: Interrogationes siue doctrine quibus
quilibet sacerdos debet interrogare suum confitentem.
Palau, 80963.
Reel 48, No. 269

ESCOBAR, ANDRÉS DE, bp. d. ca. 1431.
Interrogationes et doctrinae quibus quilibet
sacerdos debet interrogare suum confitentem. [Venice:
Manfredus de Bonellis, ca. 1495]
[8] *l*.; 15cm.

Gesamtkat. d. Wiegendr., 7239; Stillwell, C737.
Reel 48, No. 268

ESCOBAR, ANDRÉS DE, bp. d. ca. 1431.
Modus confitendi compositus per R.P.D. Epm Andream
Hispanum sancte Roman ecclesie Penitentiariū. [Romae:
Eucharius Silber, ca. 1500].
[12] *l*.; 14cm.

Leaf [1ª]: Half-title: Modus confitendi, got. char.
Engraving showing a confessor and a penitent, with
an angel and a devil.
Colophon: Leaf 12: "Deo gratias".
Goff, A685; Hain, no. 1009; Palau, 80964.
Reel 48, No. 270

ESCOBAR, ANDRÉS DE, bp. d. ca. 1431.
Cōtēta hoc libello Modus confitendi Compostitus
per Re. epm Andream Hispanuz Sancte Romane ecclesie
Pe. Interrogationes et doctrine quibus quiliber
sacerdos debet interrogare suum confitentem. Canones
penitentiales per Episcopum Ciuitateñ summa cū
diligentia Cōpositi et correcti. Casus Papales et
Episcopales. [Argentine: Mathias Hupfuff, 1507].
[20] *l*.; 21cm.

Colophon: "Impressum Argentine. Anno domini
millesimo quingentesimo septimo, per Honorabilē virum
Mathiaz Hupfuff."
Palau, 80968.
Reel 48, No. 271

ESCOBAR, ANDRÉS DE, bp. d. ca. 1431.
Contenta hoc libello. Modus confitendi compositus
per Reuerendum episcopum Andream Hispanum sancte
Romane ecclesie Penitentionarium (sic). Interrogationes
et doctrine quibus quiliber sacerdos debet interrogare
suum confitentem. Canones penitentiales per episcopum
Ciuitateñ. compositi. Casus Papales et Episcopales.
[Auguste: per Johannē Froschauer, 1508].
[26] l.; 19cm.

Colophon: "Impressum Auguste per Johannē Froschauer.
Anno dm. M D.VIII."
Not in Palau's ...
Reel 48, No. 272

ESCOBAR, ANDRÉS DE, bp. d. ca. 1431.
Contenta hoc libello: Modus confitendi, compositus
per reverendum episcopum Andream Hispanum sancte
romane Ecclesie Penitentionarium [sic]. Interrogationes
et doctrine quibus quiliber sacerdos debet interrogare
suū cōfitentē. Canones penitentiales, per episcopum
Ciuitateñ. compositi. Casus papales et episcopales.
[Argentinae: 1515].
22 l.; 19cm.

Colophon: "Impressum et recognitum Argentine VI.
kalendas novembris anno MDXV."
HC: NSI / 772; Palau, 80974; Penney, p. 25.
Reel 48, No. 273

ESCOBAR DEL CORRO, Juan, fl. 1637-1642.
Tractatvs Bipartitvs De Pvritate Et Nobilitate
Probanda, Secvndvm Statvta S. Officii Inqvisitionis
Regii Ordinum Senatus, sanctae Ecclesiae Toletanae,
Collegiorum, aliarúmque communitatum Hispaniae.
Ad Explicationem Regiae Pragmaticae Sanctionis S. 20
incipit, Y porque el odio, à Domino nostro Rege
Philippo IV. latae Matriti 10. Februarij Anno Domini
1623. In Cvivs Parte I. Agitur de natura, vtilitate,
fine & intelligentia statutorum puritatis: recensentúrque
omnes species probationum, ex quibus praedictae
qualitates possunt & debent probari, ex mente ipsorum
statutorum, secundum ius commune. II. Explicatur
praedicta Pragmatica per singulos SS. in calcéque
adduntur vtilissimae Questiones de Officio Promotoris
Piscalis, & de officio Iudicum circa iudicandas
Puritatis & Nobilitatis Probationes. Et tandem
Instructio sermone vulgari edita, ministris, qui
versantur, in conficiendo informationes Puritatis, &
Nobilitatis, vtilissima. Authore D D. Ioanne Escobar
à Corro, I.V.D. Fidei causarum Censore, tune in
Llerenensi Praetorio, nunc in Cordubensi, ac quondam
apud Hispalenses S. Mariae de Iesv maximi Collegij
rogato, & in ejus Vniuersitate Decreti Cathedrae
Antecessore. ... Editio vltima, ab ipsōmet Avthore
aucta, & à mendis expurgata. Genevae: Escvdebat
Philippvs Gamonetvs, 1664.
[12], 359, [1], 156, [72] p.; 35cm.

Printed in double columns. A reprint of the 1637 ed.
Book plate of the "Bibliotheca Lindesiana."
Pp. 215, 227, and 275 misnumbered 216, 219, and
276 respectively.
Palau, 81090.
Reel 48, No. 274

ESCRITURA otorgada el año de 1625 entre S. M. y el
Rector del Colegio Imperial de la Compañia de
Jesus de esta Corte, en razon de la fundacion
Patronazgo Real y Dotacion perpetua de los
estudios generales, 1625.
5 printed l.
Bound with: HERRERA Y SOTOMAYOR, JACINTO DE, fl.
1644. Iornada que su Magestad hizo a la Andalvzia.
[Madrid: En la Imprenta Real, 1624].
Palau, 114276 (List only printed folios 1-6).
Reel 77, No. 484.1

ESCRIVÁ, P. FRANCISCO, 1539-1617.
Discvrsos sobre los qvatro novissimos, Muerte,
Iuyzio, Infierno, y Gloria. [Valencia: En el Colegio
de San Pablo de la Compañia de Iesus, por Pedro
Patricio Mey, 1604-9].
Vol. I: [16], 671, [81] p.; 21cm.

Colophon, vol. I: "En Valencia, Impresso en el
Colegio de S. Pablo de la Compañia de Iesus, por Pedro
Patricio Mey, 1604."
Vol. 2 not available.
Errata mutilated causing loss of print.
Doublet, p. 55; Goldsmith, p. 56, no. 89; Palau,
81573; Simon Diaz, IX, 5247.
Reel 49, No. 275

ESPINOSA, PEDRO, 1578-1650.
Primera Parte De Las Flores De Poetas Ilvstres De
España, Diuidida en dos Libros. Ordenada Por Pedro
Espinosa: natural de la ciudad de Antequera. Dirigida
Al Señor Duque de Bejar. Van escritas diez y seis
Odas de Horacio, traduzidas por diferentes y graues
Autores, admirablemente. Con Privilegio. En Valladolid:
Por Luys Sanchez, 1605.
[8], 204 (i.e. 192), [4] l.; 19cm.

Errors in foliation. Omission of 53-54 and 183-192.
Imperfect title page (monted) mutilated, affecting
beginning of title and imprint.
Goldsmith, p. 56, no. 107; Graesse, II, p. 503;
Palau, 82752; Simón Díaz, IV, 51 and IX, 5705; Ticknor,
p. 130.
Reel 49, No. 276

ESSEX, ROBERT DEVEREUX, earl of, 1566-1601.
A Trve Coppie of a Discourse written by a Gentleman
employed in the late Voyage of Spaine and Portingale:
Sent to his particular friend, and by him published,
for the better satisfaction of all such, as hauing
been seduced by particular report, have entred into
conceipts tending to the discredit of the enterprise,
and Actors of the same. [Anthony Wingfield]. London:
Printed for Thomas Woodcock dwelling in Paules
Churchyard, at the signe of the blacke Beare, 1589.
[4], 58 p.; 14cm.

HC:346/1337; Palau, 71330; Penney, p. 169; Pollard
and Redgrave, no. 6790.
Reel 47, No. 254

ESTELLA, DIEGO DE, 1524-1578.
Primera [y Segvnda] Parte Del Libro De La Vanidad
Del Mvndo. Hecho por el R.P.F. Diego de Estella, de la
orden de Sant Francisco. Quanto (sic) este libro sea
mayor que el passado, y la ventaja q̄ haze al de
hasta aqui, en la buelta desta hoja lo vera el Lector.
Con licencia y aprobacion del Consejo general dela
sancta Inquisicion [Lisbon: Antonio Ribero] 1576.
2 v. ([4], 246, [2] l.; 249, [3] l.); 14cm.

Part 1, Colophon: "Fve Impresso en la Officina de
Antonio Ribero. 1576."
Palau, 83912; Simón Díaz, IX, 3505-3515.
Reel 49, No. 277

ESTELLA, DIEGO DE, 1524-1578.
Primera [y Tercera] Parte Del Libro ... lo vera el
Lector. Salamanca: En casa de Iuan Fernandez, 1581.
2 v. ([8], 273, [3] l.; 277, [3] l.); 16cm.

Part 3, Colophon: "En Salamanca En casa de Iuan
Fernandez M.D.LXXXI."
Palau, 83914; Simón Díaz, IX, 3507, 3515, 3526.
Part II: Not Available
Reel 49, No. 278

ESTELLA

ESTELLA, DIEGO DE, 1524-1578.
    Tercera Parte Del Libro De La Vanidad Del Mvndo.
Hecho por el R. P. F. Diego de Estella, de la Orden
de S. Francisco. Impresso con licencia del supremo
Consejo de la Sancta y General Inquisicion, por
Manuel de Lyra. [n.p. Lisbon], 1584.
    277, [3] l.; 15cm.

    Colophon: "Emmanuel de Lyra Typog. Escudebat."
    P. 89 misnumbered 80.
    Bound with another work by the same author: Tabvla
Rervm Omnivm. Qvae Continentur in tribus libris.
R. P. F. Didaci Stellae, Ordinis Minorum, de Vanitate
seculi, Euãgelijs Dominicarum totius anni, & Sanctorum
accõmodata.
    Palau, 83917; Simón Díaz, IX, 3529.
Reel 49, No. 279

ESTELLA, DIEGO DE, 1524-1578.
    Tabvla Rervm Omnivm. Qvae Continentur in tribus
libris. R.P.F. Didaci Stellae, Ordinis Minorum, de
Vanitate seculi, Euãgelijs Dominicarum totius anni,
- Sanctorum accomodata. Excudebat Emmanuel de Lyra
Topographus. Cum facultate Supremi Consilij Generalis
Inquisitionis, 1583.
    Palau, 83917; Simón Díaz, IX, 3529.
Reel 50, No. 280

ESTELLA, DIEGO DE, 1524-1578.
    [Tratado de la vanidad del mundo. English]
    A Methode Vnto Mortification: Called heretofore,
The contempt of the world, and the vanitie thereof.
Written at first in the Spanish, afterward translated
into the Italian, English, and Latine tongues: now
last of all perused at the request of some of his
godly friends, and as may bee most for the benefite
of the Church, reformed and published by Thomas
Rogers. Allowed by authoritie. I. Iohn. 2.15. If
any man loue the world, the loue of the Father is not
in him. Imprinted at London: by Iohn Windet, 1608.
    [20], 499 (i.e. 500), [2] p.; 13cm.

    English translation by Thomas Rogers.
    Device of printer (McKerrow 243a) on verso of
last leaf.
    Error in paging: 328 repeated in numbering.
    Allison, p. 66, no. 11.1; Palau, 83974; Pollard
and Redgrave, no. 10543.
Reel 50, No. 281

EUCLIDES.
    [Elements of Geometry. The First Six Books. Spanish]
    Elementos Geometricos De Evclides, Los Seis Primeros
Libros De Los Planos; Y Los Onzeno, Y Dozeno De Los
Solidos: Con Algvnos Selectos Theoremas De Archimedes.
Tradvcidos Y Explicados Por El P. Jacobo Kresa De
La Compañia De Jesvs, Cathedratico de Mathematicas
en los Estudios Reales del Colegio Imperial de Madrid;
y en interim en la Armada Real en Cadiz. En Brvsselas:
Por Francisco Foppens, año de 1689.
    [8], 459, [1] p., 7 plates; 21cm.

    Spanish translation by Jacob Kresa.
    Palau, 84725; Peeters-Fontainas, I, no. 406.
Reel 50, No. 282

F

FABRICIUS, JOHANN, 1608-1653.
Specimen Arabicum Quo exhibentur Aliquot Scripta
Arabica Partim in Prosâ, partim Ligatâ oratione
composita Jam primum in Germania edita, Versione
Latina donata, Analysi Grammatica expedita, Notisque
necessariis illustrata. Quibus accessit Judicium De
Soluto dicendi genere Arabum proprio. Ut Et Coronis
De Poësi Arabica hactenus â nemine in Germania
traditae. Adjectus in fine est Index Latinus Verborum,
Nominum & Particularum Iocupletissimus, qui instar
Lexici esse potest. Omnia e curâ M. Johannis Fabrici
Dantiscani. Rostochi Aeredum Richelianorum typis
expressa. Impensis Johannis Hallervordij Bibliop,
1638.
[8], 235 p.; 20cm.

Bound with: Cohen De Lara, David, 1602-1674.
Sive De Convenientia Vocabulorum Rabbinicorum
Cum Graecis, & quibusdam aliis linguis Europeis, Auctore
David Cohen De Lara [Amstelodami: N. Ravestenii,
1638.]
Doublet, p. 45.
Reel 87, No. 560

FARIA E SOUSA, MANUEL DE, 1590-1649.
Africa Portvgvesa Por Sv Avtor Manvel De Faria,
Y Sovsa Cavallero de la Orden de Christo, y de la
Casa Real. Tomo Unico Dedicala Antonio Craesbeeck de
Mello Al Serenissimo Principe Don Pedro Regente Y
Gobernador De Portvgal &c. Lisboa: Con las
licencias necessarias, y Privilegio Real. A costa
d'Antonio Craesbeeck de Mello Impressor de Su Alteza.
Año 1681. Vendese en su Casa en la Calle de los
Espingarderos en Valverde.
[6], 207 (i.e. 205), [11] p.; 30cm.

Error in paging: 87-88 omitted in numbering.
Goldsmith, p. 58, no. 23; Graesse, III, 552; Simón
Díaz, X, 272.
Reel 50, No. 283

FARIA E SOUSA, MANUEL DE, 1590-1649.
Asia Portuguesa Tomo I. ... Lisboa: En la Officina
de Antonio Craesbeeck de mello Impressor de sua (sic)
Alteza Ano 1674 (?)
Volume not available.
No. 284, v. I.

FARIA E SOUSA, MANUEL DE, 1590-1649.
Asia Portuguesa Tomo II. De Manuel De Faria, Y Sousa
Cavallero de la Orden de Christo, y de la Casa Real.
Dedicala Su Hijo El Capitan Pedro de Faria, y Sousa
Al Princepe (sic) N.S. D. Pedro Regente, Y Gobernador
Destos Reynos de Portugal, &c. Lisboa: En la Officina
de Antonio Craesbeeck de mello Impressor de sua (sic)
Alteza Año 1674.
[4], 969, [1] p.; 30cm.

Fold. plates, ports., fold plans, illus., t.-p.
engraved.
Goldsmith, p. 58, no. 24; Graesse, p. 552; Palau,
V, 86692; Simón Díaz, X, 269.
Volume I not available.
Reel 50, No 284, Vol.1

FARIA E SOUSA, MANUEL DE, 1590-1649.
Asia Portuguesa Tomo III. De Manuel De Faria, Y
Sousa Cavellero (sic) de la Orden de Christo, y de
la Casa Real. Dedicala Su Hijo El Capitan Pedro de
Faria, y Sousa. Al Principe N.S. D. Pedro Regente,
Y Gobernador Destos Reynos de Portugal, &c. Año 1675.
Lisboa: En la Officina de Antonio Craesbeeck de
mello Impressor de sua (sic) Alteza Año 1675.
[8], 564, [6] p.; 30cm.

Fold. plates, port., fold plans, illus., t.-p.
engraved. [Vol. I, 1703. Lisboa. B. da Costa Carvalho].
Goldsmith, p. 58, no. 24; Graesse, p. 552; Palau,
V, 86692; Simón Díaz, X, 269.
Reel 50, No. 284, Vol. 3

FARIA E SOUSA, MANUEL DE, 1590-1649.
Epitome De Las Historias Portvguesas. Primero i
Segundo Tomo. Divididos en quatro Partes. Por Manvel
De Faria i Sovsa. Al Excel^mo Señor Don Manvel De
Movra Corte-Real Marqves De Castel-Rodrigo, Conde de
Lumiares, Comendador Mayor de la Orden de Christo,
Capitan i Governador de las islas Terceras, San Iorge,
Fayal i Pico, Grande de España, Gentilhombre de la
Camara de su Magestad, de su Consejo de Estado, i
Veedor de su hazienda. Con Privilegio. En Madrid:
Por Francisco Martinez. A costa de Pedro Coello,
Mercader de Libros, 1628.
2 v. in 1 ([12], 696, [24] p.); 21cm.

Paged continuously.
Goldsmith, p. 58, no. 25; Penney, p. 197; Palau,
V, 86682; Salvá, II, 2934; Simón Díaz, X, 254.
Reel 51, No. 289

FARIA E SOUSA, MANUEL DE, 1590-1649.
Epitome De Las Historias Portvguesas Tomo Primero
[y Segundo] Dividido en dos partes Oferecido Ao Excell^mo
Senhor D. Francisco De Sovsa, Conde do Prado, Marques
das Minas, Presidente do Conselho Vltramarino,
Governador das Armas do exercito, & Provincia d'Entre
Douro, & Minho, dos Cõselhos d'Estado, & Guerra do
serenissimo Princepe D. Pedro, seo Embaixador
extraordinario de obediencia as Sātidades dos Papas
Clemēte IX. & X. Autor Manoel De Faria, Y Sovsa,
Lisboa: Na Officina de Francisco Villela, 1673.
2 v. in 1 ([18], 391, [5] p.; [16], 416, [24] p.);
22cm.

Pagination errors throughout.
Doublet, p. 57; Goldsmith, p. 58, no. 26; Graesse,
III, p. 552; Palau, V, 86684; Simón Díaz, X, 255.
Reel 51, No. 290

FARIA E SOUSA, MANUEL DE, 1590-1649.
Epitome De Las Historias Portvguesas, Dividido En
Quatro Partes: Por Manuel De Faria Y Sousa. Adornado
de los retratos de sus Reyes con sus principales
hazañas. Brusselas: Por Francisco Foppens, Impressor
y Mercader de Libros, 1677.
[10], 398 p.; 31cm.

Almirante, no. 282; Goldsmith, p. 58, no. 28;
Graesse, III, p. 552; Jerez, p. 43; Palau, V, 86685;
Peeters-Fontainas, I, no. 415; Penney, p. 197; Simón
Díaz, X, 256.
Reel 52, No. 291

FARIA E SOUSA, MANUEL DE, 1590-1649.
Evropa Portuguesa. Segvnda Edicion Correta, (sic)
Ilvstrada, Y Añadida En tantos lugares, y con tales
ventajas que es labor nueva. Por Su Autor Manvel De
Faria, Y Sovsa Cavallero de la Orden de Christo,
y de la Casa Real. Tomo I. [y Tomo II-III]. Dedicala
Antonio Craesbeeck De Mello Al Serenissimo Principe
Don Pedro Regente, Y Gobernador De Portugal, &c.
Lisboa: Con las licencias necessarias. A costa
d'Antonio Craesbeeck de Mello Impressor de S. Alteza,
1678-1680.
    3 v. ([8], 492 p.; [8], 624 p.; [14], 442 p.);
29cm.

    Pagination errors throughout.
    Vol. III: Two of the dedications of this Vol.
are dated 1681.
    Graesse, III, p. 552; HC: 346/1249; Palha, 2771;
Palau, 86681; Penney, p. 197; Salvá, II, 2935; Simón
Díaz, X, 271; Ticknor, p. 133.
Reels 50 & 51, No. 285

FARIA E SOUSA, MANUEL DE, 1590-1649.
El Gran Iusticia de Aragõ Don Martin Batista De
Lanuza. A Dõ Miguel Batista De LaNuza Cav.º d̃la Orden
de Santiago del Consejo del Rei N.º Señor i su Protonoto,
en los Reynos de la Corona de Aragon Por Manuel de
Faria i Sousa Cav.º d̃la Ordẽ d̃ Christo i de la Casa
Real. [Madrid: Diego Diaz de la Carrera], [1650].
    [16], 194, [8] l.; 22cm.

    Bound with: MORENO PORCEL: F. Retrato de Manuel
Faria y Sovsa, Cauallero del Orden Militar de Christo,
y de la Casa Real.
    Gallardo, II, no. 2167; Goldsmith, p. 58, no. 31;
Palau, V, 86691; Penney, p. 197; Simón Díaz, X, 268.
Reel 51, No. 286

FARIA E SOUSA, MANUEL DE, 1590-1649.
Noches Claras, Divinas, Y Humanas Flores. Compuestas
Por Manuel De Fària, Y Sosa Cavallero De La Orden De
Christo, Y Casa Real, y por el mismo añadidas, y
emendadas en esta Impression. Lisboa: Con las licencias
necessarias. En La Officina De Antonio Craesbeeck
De Mello Impressor De S. Alteza, 1674.
    [4], 417 (i.e. 437), [3] p.; 15cm.

    Pagination errors throughout.
    Goldsmith, p. 58, no. 34; Jerez, p. 40; Palha,
1315; Palau, V, 86676; Penney, p. 197; Salvá, II,
1799; Simón Díaz, X, 253.
Reel 51, No. 288

FELICES DE CÁCERES, JUAN BAUTISTA, 1601-1630.
El Cavallero De Avila. Por La Santa Madre Teresa de
Iesvs; En Fiestas, y Torneos de la Imperial Ciudad
de Caragoca. Pohema Heroico. Por Ivan Batista Felizes
de Caceres, natural de la Ciudad de Calatayud. Con vn
Certamẽ Poetico por la Cofradia de la Sangre de Christo,
accion del mismo Cavallero. En Caragoca: por Diego
Latorre, 1623.
    [24], 512 (i.e. 528) p.; 14cm.

    Pagination errors throughout.
    Palau, V, 87224; Simón Díaz, X, 344.
Reel 52, No. 292

FELIPE II, King of Spain, 1527-1598.
Relacion Svmaria Cierta, Y Verdadera, Del Processo
Actitado en la Corte del señor Iusticia de Aragon: a
instancia de la Magestad del Rey don Phelipe nuestro
señor, contra los Diputados, y Vniuersidad del Reyno
de Aragon, acerca del poder y facultad que su Magestad
tiene en el dicho Reyno de Aragon de nombrar
Lugarteniente general suyo, natural, o estrangero: como
mas de su Real seruicio sea, y le pareciere mas
conueniente para el bien publico, vtilidad, y buen
gouierno del dicho Reyno de Aragon, &c. Impressa
con licencia en Caragoca: en el Real Palacio de la
Aljaferia, por Lorenco de Robles Impressor del
Reyno de Aragon, y de la vniuersidad, 1590.
    132 p.; 33cm.

    Palau, XVI, 257246.
Reel 52, No. 293

FELIPE IV, King of Spain, 1605-1665.
Executoria en el pleyto de reivindicacion de la
baronia y casal de la Placa entre D. Antonio Statela,
marqués de Spaccafurno con D.ª Mariana M. Quintana
Dueñas, baronesa de Flores y su padre el marqués
D. Antonio de Quintana Dueñas. [Madrid, 1623].
    103 p.; 29cm.

    Lacks t.-p.
    Pagination errors throughout.
    Text begins: "Don Felipe, por la gracia de Dios, rey
de Castilla, de Aragon ..."
Reel 52, No. 294

FELIPE IV, King of Spain see also MILAN. LAWS, STATUTES,
    ETC.

FENIX DE CANALES, FRANCISCO.
Sermon De El Mandato. Y Sanctissimo Sacramento.
Hecho el Iueues Sancto de 1620. à instancia de la
nacion Española en Alexandria, Por el muy Reuerendo
Padre Maestro Fr. Francisco Fenix de Canales Religioso
Seruita natural de la Villa de Talauera de la Reyna,
y Couentual de S. Dionisio de Milan. Dirigido, y
dedicado A Los Ex.ᵐᵒˢ Señores Dvqves De Feria, y
Gouernadores de Milan, por el mismo auctor. En Milan:
En El Real, Y Dvc. Palacio. Por Marco Tulio Malatesta,
Impressor Regio, 1620.
    [16], 43 p.; 22cm.

    Palau, V, 87654; Simón Díaz, X, 455; Toda y Güell,
Italia, II, no. 1698.
Reel 52, No. 296

FENTON, SIR GEOFFREY.
    Golden Epistles ... London, 1575.
    [16], 201 p.

    Bound with: Guevara Antonio de: Epistolas
Familiares, London, 1575.
Reel 70, No. 425A

FENTON, SIR GEOFFREY.
    Golden Epistles ... London, 1582.
    [4], 347, [3] p.

    Bound with: Guevara, Antonio de. Epistolas
Familiares, London, 1577.
Reel 70, No. 426A

FERDINAND OF AUSTRIA, SON OF PHILIP III, Infant of
Spain, 1609-1641.
Manifiesto Del Serenissimo Infante Cardenal, [Don
Fernando] Pvblicado En Mons en el Pais de Henao a
los cinco de Iulio de mil y seiscientos y treinta y
seis: con la entrada que hizieron las armas Catolicas
en Francia, y presa de la Capela. Con Licencia, En
Madrid: por Maria de Quiñones, 1636. Vendese en
la Calle mayor en casa de Pedro Coello, enfrente de
San Felipe.
4 *l*.; 29cm.

Colophon: "Está tassado à seis marauedis cada
pliego. Con prohibicion que ninguna persona lo pueda
imprimir."
Reel 52, No. 297

FERNANDES VILLA REAL, MANUEL, 1611?-1652.
[Político cristianísimo ... French]
Le Politique Tres-Chrestien Ou Discours Politiques
Sur les actions principales de la vie de feu Monsr
l'Eminentissime Cardinal Duc De Richelieu. A Paris:
[i.e. Leyde, B. et A Elzevier], 1645.
[28], 308 p.; 13cm.

French translation by Francois de Grenaille, sieur
de Chatonnières.
Imperfect: p. 297-300 wanting; replaced by zerox
copy.
Doublet, p. 57; Simón Díaz, X, 1361.
Reel 53, No. 305

FERNÁNDEZ, GERÓNIMO, fl. 1570.
[Libro primero del valeroso e invincible Principe
don Belianis de Grecia ... English]
The Honour Of Chivalry. Or the famous and delectable
History of Don Bellianis of Greece, Containing, The
Valiant Exploits of that magnanimous and Heroick
Prince; Son unto the Emperonr (sic) Dòn Bellaneo of
Greece. Wherein are described, the strange and
dangerous adventures that befell him: with his love
toward the Princess Florisbella, daughter to the
Soldan of Babylon. Translated out of the Italian.
Sed tamen est tristissima janua nostrae, Et labor
est unus tempora prima pati. London: Printed by
E. A. and T. F. for F. Coles, W. Gilberson, and C.
Tyus, 1663.
[6], 254 (i.e. 244) p.; 18cm.

English translation from the Italian version of
Oratio Rinaldi by unknown.
Very rare. Not in Allison's English Translations
from the Spanish ... Graesse, I, p. 324: "Le véritable
auteur de ce roman fut le licencié Jerónimo Fernández,
avocat de profession et né à Burgos et non pas Toribio
Fernández, son père, como dit Antonio, Bibl. Hisp.
N. Il à été publié après la mort de Geronimo par son
frère, Andrés Fernández. Vid. Don Belianis, partie
III, cap. 28."
Reel 53, No. 298

FERNÁNDEZ, GERÓNIMO, fl. 1570.
[Libro primero del valeroso e invincible Principe
don Belianis de Grecia ... English]
The Honour Of Chivalry: or, The Famous and Delectable
History of Don Bellianis of Greece. Continuing As
well the valiant Exploits of that Magnanimous and
Heroick Prince, ... London: Tho. Johnson, for Fran.
Kirkman, 1671.
[4], 244 (i. e. 246) p. ; 18cm.

English translation by Francis Kirkman.
Pagination errors throughout.
Allison, p. 69; Not in Palau's Manual ...
Reel 53, No. 299

FERNÁNDEZ, GERÓNIMO, fl. 1570.
[Libro primero del valeroso e invincible Principe
don Belianis de Grecia ... English]
The Honour Of Chivalry. Or The Famous and Delectable
History of Don Bellianis of Greece. Containing The
Valiant Exploits of that Magnanimous and Heroick
Prince; Son unto the Emperour Don Bellaneo of Greece.
Wherein are described, the Strange and Dangerous
Adventures that befel him: with his Love toward the
Princess Florisbella, Daughther [sic] to the Soldan
of Babylon. Translated out of Italian. Sed tamen est
tristissima janua nostrae, Et labor est unus tempora
prima pati. London: Printed for Tho. Passinger, at
the Three Bibles on London Bridge, 1683.
2 vols. in 1. Vol. I: [4], 242 p.; 18cm.

English translation from the Italian by J. Shirley.
Pagination errors throughout.
Vol. II: The Honour of Chivalry: The Second and
Third Part: Being A Continuation Of the First Part
of the History Of the Renowned Prince Don Bellianis
of Greece. Containing his many strange and wonderful
Adventures; as Fights with Monsters and Gyants,
Dissolving Inchantments, Rescuing Distressed Ladies,
overthrowing Tyrants, and obtaining the fair Princess
Florisbella in Marriage. Together, with the rare
Adventures of many other Heroick Emperours, Kings,
Princes, and Knights, with their Amorous Intreagues
and fortunate success in their Undertakings. Being
worthy the perusal of all Persons, as well for its
pleasantness as the profit that may accrue thereby.
Written by J. S. Gent. London: Printed for T.
Passinger, at the Sign of Three Bibles, on London-
Bridge, 1683.
[4], 167 p.; 18cm.
Pp. 118-119 misnumbered 119-118.
Allison, p. 69, no. 4.2. Not in Palau's Manual ...
Reel 53, No. 300

FERNÁNDEZ, GERÓNIMO, fl. 1570.
[Libro primero del valeroso e invincible Principe
don Belianis de Grecia ... English]
The Honour of Chivalry: Or, The Renowned and Famous
History of Don Bellianis of Greece: Giving an Account
of all his Valiant and Wonderful Exploits and Adventures;
as, Fighting Battles, single Combates, finishing
Enchantments, rescuing distressed Ladies, destroying
Monsters, &c. ... London Printed by W. O. and sold
by the Bookseller of Pye-Corner and London-bridge.
[ca. 1700].
[12] *l*.; 18cm.

Another ed. of the English translation by Francis
Kirkman.
A very free adaptation.
Reel 53, No. 301

FERNÁNDEZ, MARCUS, fl. 1655; GARNIER, PHILIPPE, d.
ca. 1655, and DONATI, L., joint authors.
Dialogues En Quatre Langues, Francoise, Espagnole,
Italienne, & Allemande. Par P. Garnier, Francois. M.
Fernandez, Español. & L. Donati, Italien. Gemein
Gesprach In vier Spraachen Frantzösisch / Spanisch /
Italiänisch / und Hoochdeutsch. Durch P. Garnier,
in Frantzösisch. M. Fernandez, in Spanisch vnd L.
Donati, in Italiänisch / verdolmetscht. [Vignette]
A Amsterdam: Chez Louys & Daniel Elzevier, 1656.
231 p.; 15cm.
Reel 53, No. 302

FERNÁNDEZ DE CÓRDOVA Y AGUILAR, GONZALVO, called EL
GRAN CAPITAN, 1453-1515.
Chronica del Gran Capitan Goncalo Hernandez de
Cordova y Agvilar. En la qual se contienen las dos
conquistas del Reyno de Napoles, con las esclarescidas
victorias que en ellas alcanco, y los hechos Illustres
de don Diego de Mendoca, don Hugo de Cardona, el
Conde Pedro Nauarro, y otros Caualleros y Capitanes
de aquel tiempo. Con la vida del famoso cavallero
Diego García de Paredes. Nueuamente añadida a esta
historia ... Alcala de Henares: En casa de Hernán
Ramirez, a su costa. 1584.
Fol. Fragment: ff.II-LXXVIII, 29cm.

Lacks ff. LXXIX-CLXV and the first two preliminary
leaves.
Catalina, Tip. complutense, no. 610; Palau, IV,
no. 64957; Salvá, II, pág. 462; Simón Díaz, IX, 1280.
Reel 53, No. 303

FERNÁNDEZ DE OVIEDO Y VALDÉS, GONZALO see OVIEDO Y
VALDÉS, GONZALO FERNÁNDEZ DE.

FERNÁNDEZ DE VILLAREAL, MANUEL see FERNANDES VILLA
REAL, MANUEL.

FERNÁNDEZ NAVARRETE, PEDRO, fl. 1621.
Conservacion De Monarqvias Y Discvrsos Politicos
sobre la gran Consulta que el Consejo hizo al Señor
Rey don Felipe Tercero Al Presidente, Y Consejo Supremo
de Castilla. Por El Licenciado Pedro Fernandez
Nauarrete Canonigo de la Iglesia Apostolica de Señor
Santiago Capellan S.º de sus Mag.des y Alt.as Consultor
del S.to Of. de la Inquisicion Stemate Religione Et
Charitate Conivnti. Madrid: en la Imprenta Real,
1626. F. Agus. Leonardo Inuen. Alardo de Popma Sculp.
[10], 344 p.; 29cm.

Doublet, p. 58; HC384/3389; Heredia, IV, no. 7223;
Palha, 410; Palau, V, 89491; Salvá, II, 3667; Simón
Díaz, X, 1036.
Reel 53, No. 306

FERNANDO see FERDINAND.

FERRER, P. JUAN GASPAR, 1538-1636.
Platica o lección de las mascaras, en la qval se
trata si es pecado mortal, o no, el emascararse ...
Hecha por el muy reuerendo padre Diego Perez de
Valdiuia ... Barcelona: Por Geronymo Margarit,
1618.
49 (i.e. 48) l.; 16cm.

L. 48 misnumbered 49.
Gallardo, no. 1397; Simón Díaz, VI 4410 and X,
1463; Ticknor, p. 136.
Reel 53, No. 308

FERRER, P. JUAN GASPAR, 1538-1636.
Tratado De Las Comedias En El Qval Se Declara Si
Son Licitas. Y Si Hablando En Todo rigor sera pecado
mortal el representarlas, el verlas, y el consentirlas.
Por Frvctvoso Bisbe Y Vidal Doctor en entrambos
Derechos. Al Mvy Illvstre Y Reverendissimo Señor Don
Luys Sans Obispo de Barcelona, y del Consejo de su
Magestad. Va Añadido Vn Sermon De las mascaras,
y otros entretenimientos, predicado en S. Maria de la
mar por el venerable P. Diego Perez de piadosa memoria
Predicador Apostolico. Barcelona: Por Geronymo
Margarit, y a su costa, 1618.
[16], 113 (i.e. 112) l.; 16cm.

Pp. 87 and 89 misnumbered 70 and 98 respectively.
Bound with his: Platica olección de las mascaras,
en la qval se trata si es pecado mortal, o no, el
emascararse ..., 1618.
Gallardo, no. 1397; Simon Diaz. VI 4410 and X,
1463; Ticknor, p.136.
Reel 53, No. 307

FERRER DE VALDECEBRO, ANDRÉS, 1620-1680.
Govierno General. Moral, Y Politico. Hallado En
Las Aves Mas Generosas, Y Nobles. Sacado De Svs
Natvrales Virtvdes, Y propiedades. Añadido En Esta
Vltima Impression En diferentes partes; y el Libro
diez y nueve de las Aves Monstruosas. Corregido, Y
Enmendado Por El Santo Oficio de la Inquisición.
Le Escrive El Padre Fray Andres Ferrer De Valdecebro,
Calificador de la Suprema Inquisicion, del Orden de
Predicadores. Se Consagra Al Glorioso Patriarcha San
Ioseph. Con Qvatro Tablas Diferentes; Es La Vna para
Sermones varios de tiempo, y de Santos. Barcelona:
en Casa de Cormellas, por Thomàs Loriente Impressor,
Año 1696.
[16], 432, [32] p.: ill.; 20cm.

Jerez, p. 43; Palau, 90590; Penney, p. 204; Salvá,
II, no. 2701; Simón Díaz, X, 1552.
Reel 53, No. 310

FERRER DE VALDECEBRO, ANDRES, 1620-1680.
El Templo De La Fama Con Instrvcciones Politicas,
Y Morales. Lo Escrivia El M.R.P.M. Fr. Andres Ferrer
De Valdecebro, Calificador de la Suprema, del Orden
de Predicadores. Le Da A La Estampa Don Avsias
Antonio Ferrer De Valdecebro, Dignidad de la Santa
Iglesia de Tarragona. Y Consagra Al Reverendissimo
P. M. Fr. Francisco Nuñez de la Vega, Prouincial,
Inquisidor, y Visitador, que basido del Nueuo Reyno
de Santa Fé, y Santa Martha, &c. Madrid: en la
Imprenta Imperial; Por la Viuda de Ioseph Fernandez
de Buendia, Año 1680.
[14], 270 (i.e. 272), [8] p.; 20cm.

Pp. 145-end of book misnumbered 143-etc.
Half title: El Templo De La Fama Instrvcciones
Politicas, y Morales.
Jerez, p. 126; Palau, 90613; Penney, p. 204; Salvá,
II, 1809; Simón Díaz, X. 1560.
Reel 53, No. 311

FERRER MALDONADO, LORENZO, d. 1625.
Imagen Del Mvndo, Sobre La Esfera, Cosmografia,
y Geografia, Teorica de Planetas, y arte de nauegar.
Dirigido Al Ilvstrissimo, y reuerendissimo señor don
Iuan de la Serna, del Consejo de su Magestad, y
Arcobispo de Mexico. Por El Capitan Lorenço Ferrer
Maldonado. Alcala: Por Iuan Garcia, y Antonio
Duplastre, 1626.
[8], 276, [4] p.: ill., diagrs., tables; 20cm.

P. 99 misnumbered 66.
Catalina, Tip. complutense, no. 920; HC380/122;
Medina, II, no. 812; Palau, 90542; Penney, p. 204;
Sabin, no. 44108; Simón Díaz, X, 1523.
Reel 53, No. 309

FLÉCHIER, ESPRIT, bp. of Nimes, 1632-1710.
　　[Histoire du Cardinal Ximénez. Spanish]
　　Historia De El Señor Cardenal Don Francisco
Ximenez De Cisneros, Escrita Por El ILL.mo Y Rmo
Señor Esprit Flechier, Obispo De Nimes. Tradvcida
De Orden De El Exc.mo Y R.mo Señor Don Antonio
Ybañez De La Riva Herrera, Arcobispo de Zaragoca,
de el Consejo de su Magestad, &c. Por El D. D.
Migvel Franco De Villalba, su Vicario General. En
Zaragoza: Por Pasqval Bveno, Impressor del Reyno
de Aragon, 1696.
　　[24], XVJ. 496 p.　: port.; 18cm.

　　Spanish translation by Miguel Franco de Villalba.
HC384/3228; Jiménez Catalán, no. 1228; Penney, p.
206; Palau, 92127.
Reel 54, No. 312

FLORES, JUAN DE.
　　[Historia de Aurelio e Isabel, hija del Rey de
Escocia.　Italian.]
　　Historia Di Isabella Et Avrelio, Composta da Giovanni
di Fiori in Castigliano, tradotta in lingua volgare
Italica p. M Lelio Aletiphilo, & da lui dedicata al
molto gentile & vertuoso [sic] L. Scipione Atellano.
Oue se disputa chi piu dia occasione di peccare,
l'huomo alla donna, o la donna à l'huomo.　Nuouamēte
cõ somma diligenza reuista & correta.
　　[Vinegia : n.p.], 1534. [39] l., 16cm.

　　Italian translation by Lelio Aletiphilo, pseud.
　　Bound with the following works:
　　1. Amorose Ragionamenti. Dialogo, Nel Qvale Si Racconta
Vn Compassionevole Amore Di Dve Amanti, Tradotto Per M.
Lodovico Dolce, Dai Fragmenti D'Vno Antico Scrittor Greco.
In Vinegia = Appresso G briel Giolito de Ferrari, 1546.
56 l.; 16cm.
　　2. Dialogo Dove Si Ragiona Della Bella Creanza Delle
Donne.　In Vinegia: appresso Domenico Farri, [n.d.].
46 l.; 16cm.
　　3. Regole Bellissime D'Amore In Mode Di Dialogo Di M.
Giovanni Boccaccio.　Interlocvtori.　Il Signor Alcibiade,
& Filaterio giouane. Tradotte Di Latino in volgare, da M.
Angelo Ambrosini.　Opera Degna, E Bella.　Doue s'insegna
che cosa sia amore.　Qual siano i nobili affetti, &
saporiti frutti di quello.　Qual siano le persone che non
sono buone all'amore.　In che mode s'aquisiti.　Come
s'accresca.　Come si possi mantenere.　Come mancha (sic).
Con altre bellissime regole d'amore.　[n.p., n.d.]　31 l.;
16cm.
　　4. Lettere Amorose Di Madonna Celia Gentildonna Romana,
scritte al suo Amante.　In Venetia:　Appresso Francesco
Lorenzini, da Turino, 1563.　70 l.; 16cm.
　　5. Diego de San Pedro. Carcer d'amore traduto [sic] dal
magnifico miser Lelio de Manfredi Ferraresa: de Idioma
Spagnolo in lingua materna.　Nouamente Stampato.
[n.p., n.d.].　48 l.; 16cm.
　　6. Hecatom Phila Di Messer Leon Battista Alberto
Firentino (sic) ne la quale ne insegna l'ingeniosa arte
d'Amore, Mostrandona il perito modo d'amare, oue di
sempij, et rozzi, saggi, et gentili ne fa divenire.　In
Venetia: n.p., 1545. 16 l., 16cm.
　　7. Deiphira Di Messer Leon Battista Alberto Firentino, Ne
La Qvale Ne insegna amare tēperatamente, & ne fa diuenire,o
piu dotte ad amare, o piu prudenti à fuggir amore, nouamēte
stampata. In Venetia: [n.p.], 1545 [1], 10-23 l.; 16cm.
　　8. Deiphira Di messer Leon Battista Alberto Firentino, ne
la quale ne insegna amare tēmperatamente, & ne fa
Diuenire, o piu prudenti a fuggir amore, nouamēte stápata
(sic) [Vinegia: Bindoni & Pasini], 1534.　[1], 10-23, [1]
l., 16cm.
　　Heredia, II, no. 2549; Short-Title, I, p. 644; Simon
Diaz, III, 5624; Palau, 95502; Toda y Guell, Italia, II,
no. 1764.
Reel 54, No. 313

FLORES, JUAN DE.
　　[Historia de Avrelio e Isabel. Italian]
　　Historia Di Avrelio Et Isabella, Nella quale si
disputa: chi dia occasione di peccare, ho l'huomo
alla donna, ho la donna a l'huomo, Di Lingva Spagnvola
in Italiana tradotta da M. Lelio Aletiphilo.　In
Venetia:　Appresso Gabriel Gioli di Ferrarij, 1543.
　　38, [1] l.; 14cm.

　　Colophon: "In Venetia Appresso Gabriel Gioli
Di Ferrarii Da Trino Di Monferra 1543."
L. 24 misnumbered 44.
　　Adams, I, no. 626; Palau, 92503; Short-Title, I,
p. 645; Simón Díaz, III, 5625.
Reel 54, No. 322

FLORES, JUAN DE.
　　[Historia de Aurelio e Isabel. Italian]
　　Seconda Editione De L'Historia di Aurelio e
Issabella [sic], figliuola del Re di Scotia, meglio
che inanzi corretta. Seconde edition de l'histoire
d'Aurélie & d'Isabelle, fille du Roy d'Escosse mieulx
corrigée que parcy deuant.　A Paris:　Par Arnoul
l'Angelier, tenāt sa boutique au second pillier
de la grand' salle du Palais, 1547.
　　128 l.; 12cm.

　　Printer's device on verso of last leaf.
　　Text in Italian and French. The French translation
is by Gilles Corrozet.
　　Palau, V, p. 427; Simón Díaz, III, 5636.
Reel 54, No. 323

FLORES, JUAN DE.
　　[Historia De Avrelio E Isabel. French]
　　Histoire De Avrelio Et Isabelle, fille du Roy
d'Escoce, nouuellement traduict en quattre langues,
Italien, español, Francois, & Anglois. Historia Di
Avrelio E Issabella, Figliuola del Re di Scotia,
nuouamente tradotta in quatro lengue [sic], Italiano,
Spagnuolo, Francese, & Inglese. Historia De Avrelio,
Y De Ysabela, hija del Rey Descocia, nueuamente
traduzida en quatro lenguas, Frances, Italiano,
Español, & Yngles. The Historie Of Avrelio And Of
Isabell, doughter of the kinge of Schotlande, nyeuly
translated In foure langagies, Frenche, Italien,
Spanishe, and Inglishe.　Cum gratia & priuilegio.
[Anuers:　en casa de Iuan Steelsio, 1556.]
　　[246] p., port.; 14cm.

　　French translation by Gilles Corrozet.
　　Colophon:　"Fue Impressa en la muy noble villa
de Anuers, en casa de Iuan Steelsio, Año de M. D. LVI."
　　Adams, I, no. 627; Gallardo, no. 248; Palau, 92515;
Peeters-Fontainas, I, no. 466; Simón Díaz, III, 5651.
Reel 54, No. 324

FLORES, PEDRO.
　　Petri Flores Hispani Episcopi Castellimaris Iu.
vtriusque doctoris, oratio habita Romae in basilica
principis Apostolor ad sacrum Collegiū Sacrosancte
Roma. Ecclesie Card. de summo pont. eligendo Iulij.
II. Pontific. Maxi. successore. Lector eme, & gaudebis.
[Argentorati: Ex Aedibus Schürerianis, Mense Maio,
1513.]
　　9 l.; 19cm.

　　Palau, V, p. 428.
Reel 54, No. 325

FLORUS, LUCIUS ANNAEUS.
L. Annaeus Florus Recensitus & illustratus A
Joanne Georgio Graevio. Trajecti Batavorum: Apud
Joannem Ribbium, 1680.
[36], 210 (i.e. 202), 179, [123] p.: ill.; 20cm.

"Columna rostrata a Ciacconio suppleta, explicata":
p. [143]-[180] third group of paging.
Bound in vellum.
Half-Title: L. Annaei Flori Res Romane Cum Notis
Joan. Georg. Graevii. apud J. Ribbium M.DC. LXXX.
1680.
Graesse, III, p. 605.
Reel 54, No. 326

FONSECA, CRISTÓBAL DE, 1550?-1621.
[Discvrsos para todos los Evangelios de la Quaresma.
English]
Devovt Contemplations Expressed In two and Fortie
Sermons vpon all ȳ Quadragesimall Gospells. Written
in Spanish by Fr. Ch. de Fonseca. Englished by J. M.
of Magdalen Colledge in Oxford. London: Printed
by Adam Islip, 1629.
[6], 648, [18] p.; 29cm.

English translation by James Mabbe.
Allison, p. 73, no. 11; Palau, 93188; Pollard and
Redgrave, 11126; Simón Díaz, X, 2259.
Reel 54, No. 327

FONSECA, CRISTÓBAL DE, 1550?-1621.
[Tratado del amor de Dios. English]
Theion Enōtikon, A Discourse Of Holy Love, By which
the Soul is united unto God. Containing the various
Acts of Love, the proper Motives, and the Exercise
of it in order of Duty and Perfection. Written In
Spanish By the learned Christopher de Fonseca. Done
into English with some Variation and much Addition
By Sr. George Strode Knight. London: Printed by
J. Flesher, for Richard Royston, at the Angel in Ivy-
lane, 1652.
[10], 268 p., front.; 15cm.

English translation by George Strode.
Half-title: A Discourse of Holy Love Written in
Spanish by Christopher de Fonseca And done into
English by Sr. George Strode - Knight.
Added title-page, engraved, with portrait of Strode
signed by G. Glover; Strode's coat of arms in engraved
frontispiece.
"Bound by R. Larkins."
Allison, p. 73, no. 12; Wing F. 1405.
Reel 54, No. 328

FONSECA, DAMIAN, 1573-1640.
Ivsta Expvlsion De Los Moriscos De España: Con La
Instrvccion, Apostasia, Y Traycion Dellos: y respuesta
à las dudas que se ofrecieron acerca desta materia.
Del M. F. Damian Fonseca de la Orden de Predicadores
de la Prouincia de Aragon, Compañero del R.ᵐᵒ P.
Maestro del sacro Palacio. Al Illustr. ᵐᵒ y Excel.ᵐᵒ
Señor Don Francisco De Castro Conde de Castro, y
Embaxador en Roma de la Magestad Catholica. En Roma:
Por Iacomo Mascardo, 1612.
[30], 478, [20] p.; 17cm.

Imperfect: title-page (possible from another copy)
mounted; leaf following title-page wanting.
Doublet, p. 59; Graesse, III, p. 610; Jerez, p.
43; Palau, 93190; Penney, p. 210; Simón Díaz, X,
2271; Toda y Güell, Italia, II, 1775.
Reel 55, No. 329

FONSECA, PEDRO DE, 1528-1599.
Institvtionvm Dialecticarvm Libri Octo. Avtore
Petro Afonseca Ex Societate Iesv. Cum priuilegio
Regio ad quinquennium, & cum facultate ordinarij,
& Inquisitoris. Olyssippone: Apud haeredes Ioannis
Blauij, 1564.
[4], 255 (i.e. 253), [1] l.; 19cm.

Errors in foliation.
Reel 55, No. 330

FONSECA, PEDRO DE, 1528-1599.
Institvtionvm Dialecticarvm Libri Octo. Auctore
Petro Fonseca Doctore Theologo Societatis Iesu.
Postrema hac nunc aeditione ab ipso recogniti. Cum
Indice locuplentissimo. Coloniae: Apud Maternum
Cholinum, 1586.
[16], 557, [26] p.; 16cm.

Reel 55, No. 331

FONSECA, PEDRO DE, 1528-1599.
Institvtionvm Dialecticarvm Libri Octo Auctore
Petro A' Fonseca ex Societate Iesv. Nunc quidem
pluribus purgata mendis. Venetiis: Apud Nicolaum
Morettum, 1592.
390 (i.e. 392), 8 p.; 15cm.

Error in paging: nos. 127-128 repeated.
Reel 55, No. 332

FONSECA, PEDRO DE, 1528-1599.
Institvtionvm Dialecticarvm Libri Octo, Auctore
Petro A Fonseca ex Societate Iesv: Amendis quae
postrema editione irrepserant, diligenter purgati.
Tvrnoni: Apud Clavdivm Michaelem Tipographum
Vniuersitatis, 1597.
357, [15] p.; 17cm.

Lacks all after Aa (Index).
Reel 55, No. 333

FONSECA, PEDRO DE, 1528-1599.
Petri Fonsecae Societatis Iesv. Institvtionvm
Dialecticarvm Libri Octo. Emendatiùs quàm ante
hac editi. Qvibvs Accessit Eivsdem Avthoris Isagoge
Philosophica, nunc demum in Germania Cum librorum
argumentis. Indice copiosisssimo & capitum & rerunt.
Coloniae: Apud Gosuinum Cholinum, Cum gratia &
priuilegio Cas. Maiest, 1605.
[2], 689, [35] p.; 15cm.

Separate title-page for his Isagoge Philosophica.
Reel 55, No. 334

FRANCIOSINI, LORENZO, (translator) see CERVANTES
SAAVEDRA, MIGUEL DE.

FRANCISCO DE LOS SANTOS see SANTOS, FRANCISCO DE.

FRANCISCO DE SALES, Saint see FRANCOIS DE SALES,
Saint, Bp. of Geneva, 1567-1622.

FRANCISCO XAVIER, SAINT, 1506-1552.
S. P. Francisci Xaverii E Soc. Iesv, Epistolarvm
Libri IV. Ex Hispano in Latinum conuersi ab Horatio
Tvraellino, eiusdem Societatis Iesv Sacerdote. Editio
nouissima, recensita, & Epistolarum Summariis aucta.
Antverpiae: Ex Officina Plantiniana Balthasaris
Moreti, 1657.
[8], 474, [6] p.; 11cm.

Reel 55, No. 335

FRANCOIS DE SALES, Saint, Bp. of Geneva, 1567-1622.
[Lettres ... Spanish]
Cartas Espiritvales De S. Francisco De Sales,
Obispo, Y Principe De Geneva, Fundador del Orden de
Religiosas de la Visitacion de Santa Maria. Traducida
del Idioma Frances Al Castellano Divididas en siete
libros. Por El Lic. D. Francisco De Cvbillas Donyagve,
Presbytero, y Abogado de los Reales Consejos. Primera
[y segvnda] Parte. Va Al Fin de La Segunda Parte
Una Carta Pastoral de advertencias, à los Curas, y
Confessores. Con Licencia En Barcelona: A costa
de Antonio Ferrer, Balthasar Ferrer, Miguel Planella,
Iuan Casañas, Miguel Badia, y Pedro Pau, Libreros,
1686.
2 v. ([6], 464 p.; [4], 408 p.); 20cm.

Spanish translation by Francisco de Cubillas.
Palau, XIX, 290784.
Reels 55 & 56, No. 336

FRANCOIS DE SALES, Saint, bp. of Geneva, 1567-1622.
[Tractvs amoris divini. Spanish]
Practica Del Amor De Dios. Qve En Frances Escrivio
San Francisco De Sales, Obispo, Y Principe de Geneva,
Fundador de la Orden de la Visitacion de Santa Maria.
Y Traduxo Al Castellano, El Licenciado Don Francisco
Cuvillas Donyague, Presbytero, Abogado de los Reales
Consejos. Con Vn Epithome De La Vida Del mismo Santo.
Barcelona: A costa de Antonio Ferrer, Baltazar Ferrer,
Miguel Planella, Iuan Cassañas, Miguel Badia, y Pedro
Pau, Libreros, 1684.
[67], 472, [12] p.; 20cm.

Spanish translation by Francisco Cubillas.
Colophon: "Con Licencia En Barcelona, en la Placa
de Sant Jayme, en la Imprenta de Antonio Ferrer, y
Balthazar Ferrer, Libreros."
Palau, XIX, 290756.
Reel 56, No. 337

FRAY Juan de la Anunciacion ... 4 manuscript *l.*
4 manuscript *l*
Bound with: HERRERA Y SOTOMAYOR, JACINTO DE, fl.
1644. Iornada que su Magestad hizo a la Andalvzia.
[Madrid: En la Imprenta Real, 1624].
Palau, 114276 (List only printed folios 1-6).
Reel 77, No. 484.33

FUENTES, ALFONSO DE.
[Summa de philosophia natvral ... Italian]
Somma Della Natvral Filosofia Di Alfonso Di Fonte
Divisa In Dialoghi Sei, Ne' Qvali, Oltra (sic) Le
Cose Fisiche, S'Ha Piena Cognitione Delle Scienze,
Astronomia, Et Astrologia, Dell'Anima, Et Della
Notomia Del Corpo Humano, Novellamente Tradotta Di
Spagnvolo In Volgare Da Alfonso Di Vlloa. Con la
tauola delle cose piu degne, che in essa si leggono.
Venetia: Per Plinio Pietrasanta, 1557.
[9], 161, [14] p.; 21cm.

Italian translation by Alfonso de Ulloa.
Palau, 95384; Simon Diaz, X, 3429; Toda y Güell,
Italia, 1867.
Reel 56, No. 338

FUENTES, ALFONSO DE.
Le Sei Giornate Del S. Alfonso Di Fonte. Nelle
Qvali Oltre Le Materie di Filosofia, s'ha piena
cognitione delle sciēze, Astronomia, & Astrologia:
dell' Anima, & della Notomia del corpo humano.
Nvovamente Di Lingva Spagnuola tradotte dal S.
Alfonso Vlloa. Con Privilegio. Vinegia: appresso
Domenico Farri, 1567.
[7], 128 *l.*; 16cm.

Translation by Alfonso de Ulloa.
Palau, V, p. 518; Simón Díaz, X, 3430; Toda y
Güell, Italia, 1868.
Reel 56, No. 339

FURIÓ CERIOL, Fabrique, d. 1592.
Specvli Avlicarvm Atqve Politicarum obseruationum
Libelli quatuor, nimirum I. De Concilijs & consiliarijs
Principum Fridericvs Fvrivs, &c. 2. Consiliarius
Hyppoliti à Collibvs. 3. Aulicus Politicus, Dvri de
Pascolo. 4. Hypomneses Politicae Francisci Gvicciardini.
Denvo Ob Penvriam Exemplarium omnes coniunctem,
correctius in vsum Aulicorum atq̄; Politicorum omniam
continnati atq̄: aediti. Procurante Lazaro Zetznero
Bibliopola Argentinensi, 1599.
[27], 416 p.; 13cm.

De Concilijs & consiliarijs Principum Fridericvs
Fvrivs translation by Simon Schard.
Includes folded table.
Reel 56, No. 340

G

GARAY, BLACO DE see OUDIN, CÉSAR DE, Refranes o
    proverbios.

GARCÍA, CARLOS.
    [La desordenada codicia de los bienes ajenos.
English]
    The Sonne Of The Rogve, Or, The Politick Theefe.
With The Antiqvitie Of Theeves. A worke no lesse
Curious then delectable: first written in Spanish by
Don Garcia. Afterwards translated into Dutch, and
then into French by S.D. Now Englished by W. M.
London: Printed by I.D. and are to be sold by Bernard
Langford at the Bybell on Holborn-Bridge, 1638.
    [11], 254 p.; 14cm.

    English translation by W. Melvin.
    Colophon: Imprimatur Thomas Weekes Februarie
5. 1637."
    Allison, p. 77, no. 2; Laurenti, no. 1609; Palau,
VI, 97793; Pollard and Redgrave, no. 11550.
Reel 56, No. 341

GARCÍA DE CÉSPEDES, ANDRÉS.
    Regimiento De Navegacion Q' Mando Hazer El Rei
Nvestro Señor Por Orden De Sv Conseio Real De Las
Indias A Andres Garcia De Cespedes Sv Cosmografo
Maior siendo Presidente en el dicho consejo el conde
de Lemos. Madrid: En casa de Iuan de la Cuesta,
1606.
    [5], 184 l.: ill., diagrs., map.; 28cm.

    At head of title: PLVS VLTRA.
    Engraved title-page.
    In two parts. Part II has title: Segvnda parte,
en qve se pone vna hydorgrafía que mando hazer su
Magestad a Andres Garcia ... Madrid: En casa de
J. de la Cuesta, 1606. l. 115-184.
    Goldsmith, p. 70, no. 61; Penney, p. 223; Pérez
Pastor, no. 936; Salvá, II, 3774; Simón Díaz, VIII,
3845; Ticknor, p. 496.
Reel 56, No. 342

GARCÍA DE ZURITA, ANDRES.
    Discvrso De Las Missas Conventvales Qve Sv Magestad
Manda Se Digan En Las Iglesias De Las Indias. A Don
Ivan De Palafox Y Mendoza, Capellan y Limosnero de
los señores Reyes de Vngria y Bohemia, del Consejo
del Rei nuestro señor, en el Real de las Indias.
Escrivialo El Dotor Andres Garcia de Zurita, Canonigo
Teologal de Lima, para votar en su Cabildo. Madrid:
En la Imprenta de Francisco Martinez, 1636.
    22 l.; 21cm.

    Palau, 10059.
Reel 56, No. 343

GARCILASO DE LA VEGA, el Inca, 1539-1616.
    [Comentarios reales. English]
    The Royal Commentaries Of Peru, In Two Parts. The
First Part Treating of the Original of their Incas
or Kings: Of their Idolatry: Of their Laws and
Government both in Peace and War: Of the Reigns and
Conquests of the Incas. With many other Particulars
relating to their Empire and Policies before such
time as the Spaniards invaded their Countries. The
Second Part Describing the manner by which that new
World was conquered by the Spaniards. Also the Civil
Wars between the Picarrists and the Almagrians,
occasioned by Quarrels arising about the Division
of that Land. Of the Rise and Fall of Rebels; and
other Particulars contained in that History. Written
originally in Spanish By the Inca Garcilasso De La
Vega, And rendred (sic) into English By Sir Pavl

GARCILASO DE LA VEGA (Cont'd)
Rycavt, Knight. London; Printed by Miles Flesher,
for Christopher Wilkinson, 1688.
    [9], 1019, [10] p.: ill.; 33cm.

    English translation by Paul Rycaut.
    Title in red and in black.
    Number 23-26 omitted in paging; 48 and 535
misnumbered 84 and 527.
    Allison, p. 180, no. 9; Palau, 354798; Simón
Díaz, X, 4789; Wing G 214-217.
Reel 57, No. 347

GARCILASO DE LA VEGA, el Inca, 1539-1616.
    La Florida Del Ynca. Historia Del Adelantado
Hernando de Soto, Gouernador y capitan general del
Reyno de la Florida, y de otros heroicos caualleros
Españoles è Indios; escrita por el Ynca Garcilasso
de la Vega, capitan de su Magestad natural de la
gran ciudad del Gozco, (sic) cabeca de los Reynos y
prouincias del Peru. Dirigida al serenissimo Principe
Duque de Braganca &c. Con licencia de la santa
Inquisicion. Lisbona: Impresso por Pedro Crasbeeck,
1605.
    [10], 351, [7] l.; 19cm.

    Privilege dated: i de marco de 1605.
    Numerous errors in paging.
    Church, 329; HC 325/338; Palau, 354790; Simón
Díaz, X, 4729.
Reel 57, No. 345

GARCILASO DE LA VEGA, el Inca, 1539-1616.
    [La Florida del Inca. French]
    Histoire De La Floride Ov Relation De Qvi S'est
Passe' au voyage de Ferdinand de Soto, pour la
conqueste de ce pays; Composée en Espagnol par l'Inca
Garcilasso de la Vega, Et traduite en Francois par
P. Richelet. Tome Premier. [y Tome Second]. Paris:
Chez Gervais Clovzier, au Palais, sur les degrez
en montant à la sainte Chappelle, à la seconde Boutique,
à l'Enseigne du Voyageur, 1670.
    2 v. ([13], 452 p.; [12], 414 p.); 15cm.

    French translation by P. Richelet.
    Palau, 354837; Simón Díaz, X, 4783.
Reel 57, No. 346, Vol. 1-2

GARCILASO DE LA VEGA, 1503-1536.
    Obras De Garcilasso De La Vega Con Anotaciones De
Fernando De Herrera, Al Ilvstrissimo I Ecelentissimo
Señor Don Antonio de Guzman, Marques de Ayamonte,
Governador del Estado de Milan, i Capitan General
de Italia. Sevilla: Por Alonso De La Barrera, 1580.
    [12], 691, [5] p.; 19cm.

    Escudero, 700; Graesse, II, p. 25; Jerez, p. 56;
Keniston, C 5; Penney, p. 225; Salvá, I, 706; Simón
Díaz, 4436; Ticknor, p. 388.
Reel 56, No. 344

GARIBAY Y ZAMALLOA, ESTEBAN, 1525-1599.
    Los Qvarenta Libros Del Compendio Historial De
Las Chronicas Y Vniversal Historia de todos los
Reynos de España, Compvestos Por Estevan De Garibay
y Camalloa, de nacion Cantabro, vezino de la villa
de Mondragon, de la Prouincia de Guipuzcoa, diuidido
en quatro tomos. Dirigidos Al Dotor Monserrate Ramon,
y del Consejo de su Magestad, en el Principado de
Cathaluña. Tomo Primero [Y Tomos Segvndo, Tercero,
Qvarto]. Barcellona: Por Sebastian de Cormellas,
1628.

GARIBAY Y ZAMALLOA (Cont'd)
4 v. ([15], 466, [16] p.; [4], 808, [19] p.;
[5], 568, [12] p.; [5], 430, [11] p.); 31cm.

Vol. 2: Compendio Historial De Las Chronicas Y
Universal Historia De Todos Los Reynos de España,
donde se escriuen las vidas de los Reyes de Castilla,
y Leon. Prosigvese Tambien La Svcession de los
Emperadores Occidentales y Orientales. Tomo Segvndo.
Vol. 3: Compendio Historial De Las Chronicas Y
Vniversal Historia De Todos Los Reynos de España,
donde se escriuen las vidas de los Reyes de Nauarra.
Escrivese Tambien La Svcession De todos los Reyes
de Francia, y Obispos de la S. Iglesia de Pamplona.
Tomo Tercero.
Vol. 4: Compendio Historial De Las Chronicas Y
Vniversal Historia De Todos Los Reynos de España,
donde se ponen en suma los Condes, señores de Aragon,
con los Reyes del mesmo Reyno: y Condes de Barcelona,
y Reyes de Napoles y Sicilia. A La Fin Destos Principes
Se Escrive Vn breue tratado de las insignias y duisas
de los escudos de armas, materia digna de saber todo
hombre discreto, especialmente Noble... Tomo Qvarto.
Goldsmith, p. 70, no. 77; Palau, 100102; Penney,
p. 226; Salvá, II, 2954; Ticknor, p. 150.
Reels 57 & 58, No. 348

GARNIER, PHILIPPE see FERNÁNDEZ, MARCUS, joint author.

GIL POLO, GASPAR see POLO, GASPAR GIL, 1516?-1591?

GIOVIO, PAOLO, bp. of Nocera, the Elder, 1483-1552.
[Elogia doctorvm vivorum. Spanish]
Elogios O Vidas Breues, de los Cavalleros antiguos
y modernos, Illustres en valor de guerra, q̃ estan al
biuo pintados en el Museo de Paulo Iouio. Es autor
el mismo Pavlo Iovio. Y traduxolo de Latin en
Castellano, el Licenciado Gaspar de Baeca. Dirigido
A La Catholica Y Real Magestad del Rey don Philippe.
II nuestro señor. Granada: En casa de Hugo de
Mena, 1568.
[4], 222 *l.*; 27cm.

Spanish translation by Gaspar de Baeza.
Autograph: Manuel Ponde de León y Zunita.
Palau, 125422.
Reel 58, No. 350

GÓMARA, FRANCISCO, LOPEZ DE, 1510-1560?
[Historia de México. Italian]
Historia Di Mexico Et Qvando Si Discoperse La
Nvova Hispagna, Conqvistata Per L'Illvstriss. Et
ualoroso Principe. Don Ferdinando Cortes Marchese
del Valle. Scritta Per Francesco Lopez de Gomara
in lingua Spagnuola, & Tradotta nel Volgare
Italiano per Avgvstino De Cravaliz. In Roma: Appresso
Valerio & Luigi Dorici fratelli, 1555.
240 *l.*

Italian translation by Augustino de Cravaliz.
Colophon: "In Roma per Valerio Dorico, & Luigi
fratello Bresciani, nel M. D. L V I."
Foliation errors throughout.
Palau, 141165; Short-Title, II, p. 276.
Reel 91, No. 588

GÓMARA, FRANCISCO, LOPEZ DE, 1510-1560?
La Historia General De Las Indias, con todos los
descubrimientos, y cosas notables que han acaescido
enellas, dende (sic) que se ganaron hasta agora,
escrita por Francisco Lopez de Gomara, clerigo.
Añadiose de nueuo la descripcion y traca de las
Indias, con vna Tabla alphabetica delas Prouincias,
Islas, Puercos, (sic) Ciudades, y nombres de
conquistadores y varones principales que alla han
passado. En Anvers: Por Iuan Bellero, ala enseña
del Halcon, 1554.
2 v. ([16], 287 *l.*; 349, [12] *l.*)

GÓMARA (Cont'd)
Vol. 1: Prelim. leaves 3, 4, 7, 8 are numbered.
Errors in pagination: leaves 5, 17, 19, 21, 24,
41-49, 51, 53, 55 numbered respectively, 6, 16, 18,
20, 22, 23, 28-36, 38, 40, 41.
"Impresso en Anuers por Iuan Lacio. M.D. L.IIII"
verso of p. 116.
The "traca delas Indias" entitled "Brevis exactaq.
totius Novi orbis eiusq. insularum descriptio recens
a Ioan Bellero edita" is wanting in the present
copy of the IU.
Reprint of the first part of the author's Historia
general de las Indias, Zaragoza, 1553.
Volume II has special title page: Vol. II: Historia
De Mexico, Con El Descvbrimiento de la nueua España,
conquistada por el muy illustre y valeroso Principe
don Fernando Cortes, Marques del Valle, Escrita
por Francisco Lopez de Gomara, clerigo. Añadiose
de la nueuo (sic) descripcion y traca de todas las
Indias, con vna Tabla Alphabetica de las materias,
y hazañas memorables enella contenidas.
Errors in numbering: 73 omitted, 97 duplicated;
leaves 23, 111, 315, 316 numbered, respectively,
13, 101, 215, 216.
Colophon: "Impresso en Anuers por Iuan Lacio. 1554."
The "traca de todas la Indias" is wanting.
Reprint of the second parte of the author's Historia
general de las Indias, Zaragoza, 1552.
Adams, I, no. 1480; Bartlet, 189 (vol. II); Jerez,
p. 129 (vol. II); Palau, 141144; Penney, p. 314 (vol.
II); Peeters-Fontainas, Impressions, I, no. 715;
Thomas, p. 52.
Reel 91, No. 587, Vol. 1-2

GÓMEZ, VICENTE.
Govierno De Principes, Y De Svs Consejos Para el
bien de la Republica. Con vn Tratado de los Pontifices,
y Prelados de España, y de los Grandes, y Titulos, y
linages Nobles della. Compvesto Por Vn Devoto Religioso,
que por su hmildad (sic) no se nombra. Corregido y
emendado en esta vltima impresion, por el P. Maestro
Fray Vicente Gomez Prior del Real Conuento de
Predicadores de Valencia. A Don Luys Ferrer Cardona
Portavezes de general Gouernador en la Ciudad y Reyno
de Valencia, &c. Valencia: por Iuan Bautista Marcal,
1626.
[17], 532 p.; 20cm.

Goldsmith, p. 73, no. 161; Simón Díaz, X, 5697.
Reel 58, No. 351

GÓMEZ MIEDES, BERNARDINO, bp. of Albaracín, 1521-1589.
[De vita gestis Iacoby I Regis Aragonum. Spanish]
La Historia Del Mvy Alto E Invencible Rey Don Iayme
De Aragon, Primero Deste Nombre Llamado El Conquistador.
Compvesta Primero En Lengva Latina por el maestro
Bernardino Gomez Miedes Arcediano de Muruiedro, y
Canonigo de Valencia, agora nueuamente traduzida por
el mismo autor en lengua Castellana. Dirigida Al Mvy
Alto Y Mvy Poderoso Señor Don Phelippe de Austria
Principe de las Españas, &c. Valencia: en casa de
la viuda de Pedro de Huete, 1584.
[13], 461 p.; 29cm.

Spanish translation by the author.
Palau, 104102; Penney, p. 234; Salvá, II, 2966;
Simón Díaz, X, 5863.
Reel 59, No. 352

GÓMEZ MIEDES, BERNARDINO, bp. of Albaracín, 1521-1589.
Siue Diascepseon De Sale Libri Qvatvor. Quorũ
1. 2. 3. 4. est de Sale Physico seu Philosophico.
Medico siue Empirico. Geniali seu Iocoso. Mystico. à
Bernardino Gomesio Miede, prim1em summa cum diligentia
conscripti & publicati. Nunc vero denuo revisi, in
certa quaedam capita distincti, duplicique indice
locupletati. Per Petrvm Vffenbachivm Reip.

GÓMEZ MIEDES (Cont'd)
Francofurtensis Medicum ordinarium. Ursellis: Ex Officina Tupographica Cornelij Sutorij, Sumptibus Ioan. Berneri Francofurtens. Bibliop, 1605.
  [39], 679, [17] p.; 17cm.

  Not in Simón Díaz.
Reel 59, No. 353

GÓNGORA Y ARGOTE, LUIS DE, 1561-1627.
  Obras En Verso Del Homero Español, que recogio Iuan Lopez de Vicuña. Al Ilvstris.^mo Y Reverend.^mo Señor don Antonio Zapata, Cardenal de la santa Iglesia de Roma, Inquisidor general en todos los Reynos de España, y del Consejo de Estado del Rey nuestro señor. Madrid: Por la viudad de Luis Sanchez, Impressora del Reyno. A costa de Alonso Perez, mercader de libros, 1627.
  [6], 160 *l*.; 19cm.

  Imperfect: leaves 155-158 wanting; many leaves slightly mutilated and repaired; loss of part of imprint on title-page; copy 2 lacks title-page (replaced by facsimile), leaves [2]-[4], 73, 100, 112-113, and 148; leaves 111 and 160 badly mutilated with much loss of text.
  Goldsmith, p. 75, no. 230; Jerez, p. 46; Palau, 104626; Salvá, I, 640; Ticknor, p. 155; Penney, p. 235.
Reel 59, No. 354

GÓNGORA Y ARGOTE, LUIS DE, 1561-1627.
  [Las obras comentadas por Garcia de Salzedo Coronel.] Madrid: Imprenta Real [for] Domingo Gonzalez, 1636-48.
  2v. in 3. ([12], 312, [8], [7] *l*.; *l* 313-420, [4] *l*.; [20], 784, [18] p.; [11], 574, [37] p.); 21 cm.

  Each part has special title-page: Vol.I, Bk. 1, Pt.1: Soledades De D. Lvis De Gongora. Comentadas por D. Garcia De Salzedo Coronel. Cauallerizo del Ser^mo. Infante Car^l. y Capitan de la Guarda del Exmo Duque de Alcala Virrey de Napoles. Dedicadas Al Illmo. y Nobilisimo Sor D. Ivan De Chaves Y Mendoza. Cauallero del Abito de Santiago Marques de Santa Cruz de la Sierra Conde de la Calzada de los Consejos Real y de la Camara y Presidente del de Ordenes.
  Vol. I, Bk. 1, Pt. 2: El Polifemo De Don Lvis De Gongora Comentado Por Don Garcia De Salzedo Coronel. Cauallerizo del Serenisimo Infante Cardenal Dedicado Al Exmo Sor D. Fernando Afan de Ribera Enriquez Duque de Alcala Adelantado Mayor del Andaluzia del Consejo de Estado del Rey Nro. S.^or y su Virrey y Capitan general del Reino de Napoles. I. de Courbes F.
  Vol. II, Bk. 2, Pt. 1: [Full-title:] Obras De Don Lvis De Gongora Comentadas Dedicalas Al Excelentissimo Señor Don Luis Mendez de Haro Conde de Morente. Cauallero de la Orden de Santiago Gentilhombre de la Camara de su Mag.^d y Cauallerico mayor del Seren.^mo Principe de España Nuestro Señor. Don Garcia de Salcedo Coronel Cauallero de la Orden de Santiago. Tomo Segvndo.
  Vol. III, Bk. 2, Pt. 2: [First title-page:] Obras De Don Lvis De Gongora Comentadas. Dedicalas Al Excelentissimo Señor Don Luis Mendez de Haro Marqués del Carpio. Conde Duque de Olivares Comendador may.^or de Alcátara.
  Pagination errors throughout.
  Goldsmith, p. 75, no. 233; Jerez, p. 46; Palau, 104628; Penney, p. 235; Salvá, I, 642.
Reel 59, No. 355

GÓNGORA Y ARGOTE, LUIS DE, 1561-1627.
  Obras De Don Lvis De Gongora. Dedicadas Al Excellent^mo Señor Don Luis De Benevides, Carillo, Y Toledo, &c. Marques De Caracena, &c. Brusselas: De la Imprenta de Francisco Foppens, Impressor y Mercader de libros, 1659.
  [16], 650, [21] p.; 23cm.

GÓNGORA Y ARGOTE (Cont'd)
  Six leaves initialed Y between signatures Y and Z, pages 175-185.
  Doublet, p. 65; Goldsmith, p. 75, no. 236; Jerez, p. 46; Foulché-Delbosc, Bib. de Góngora, 109; Heredia, no. 1988; Palau, 104633; Peeters-Fontainas, I, no. 507; Penney, p. 235; Salvá, I, 645.
Reel 60, No. 356

GÓNGORA Y ARGOTE, LUIS DE, 1561-1627.
  Obras De Don Lvis De Gongora, Primera Parte. Sacadas a luz de nuevo, y enmendadas en esta vltima Impression. Lisboa: En la Officina de Ivan Da Costa. Con todas las licencias, 1667.
  2 v. in 1. ([4], 390 p.; 425 p.); 11cm.

  Vol. II: Obras De Don Luis de Gongora. Dezjmas amorosas.
  Jerez, p. 46; Palau, 104634; Penney, p. 235.
Reel 60, No. 357

GÓNGORA Y ARGOTE, LUIS DE, 1561-1627.
  El Polifemo De Don Lvis De Gongora Comentado Por Don Garcia De Salzedo Coronel Cauallerizo del Serenisimo Infante Cardenal. Dedicado Al Exmo Sor D. Fernando Afan de Ribera Enriquez Duque de Alcala Adelantado Mayor del Andaluzia del Consejo de Estado del Rey Nro S^or y su Virrey y Capitan general del Reino de Napoles. Madrid: Por Iuan Goncalez, Año 1629.
  [12], 124 *l*.: ill.; 20cm.

  Engraved title-page.
  First edition.
  Goldsmith, p. 75, no. 238; Jerez, p. 46; Penney, p. 235; Salvá, I, no. 647.
Reel 60, No. 361

GÓNGORA Y ARGOTE, LUIS DE, 1561-1627.
  Todas Las Obras De Don Lvis De Gongora En Varios Poemas. Recogidos Por Don Gonzalo de Hozes y Cordoua, natural de la Ciudad de Cordoua. Dirigidas A Don Francisco Antonio Fernandez De Cordova, Marques de Gvadalcazar, &c. Madrid: en la Imprenta del Reino, 1633.
  [16], 234 *l*.: ill., port.; 21cm.

  Errors in foliation.
  Goldsmith, p. 75, no. 231; Jerez, p. 46; Palau, 104627; Penney, p. 235.
Reel 60, No. 358

GÓNGORA Y ARGOTE, LUIS DE, 1561-1627.
  Todas Las Obras De Don Lvis De Gongora En Varios Poemas. Recogidos Por Don Gonzalo de Hozes y Cordoua, natural de la Ciudad de Cordoua. Dirigidas A Don Francisco Antonio Fernandez De Cordova, Marques De Guadalcazar, &c. En Madrid: En la Imprenta del Reyno, 1634.
  [14], 232 *l*.: illus. (port.); 21cm.

  Goldsmith, p. 75, no. 232; Jerez, p. 46; Palau, vol. 6, p. 262; Salvá, I, 641.
Reel 60, No. 359

GÓNGORA Y ARGOTE, LUIS DE, 1561-1627.
  Todas Las Obras De Don Lvis De Gongora, En Varios Poemas. Recogidos Por Don Gonzalo De Hozes y Cordova, natural de la Ciudad de Cordoua. Dedicadas A Don Lvis Mvriel Salcedo y Valdiuiesso, Cauallero de la Orden de Alcantara, &c. Madrid: En la Imprenta Real, 1654.
  [10], 234 *l*.; 21cm.

  Pirated edition printed at Zaragoza.
  Gallardo, IV, no. 4431; Heredia, no. 5471; Quaritch, no. 662-3; Salvá, I, no. 643; Vindel, no. 3243.
Reel 60, No. 360

GONGORA Y ARGOTE, LUIS DE, 1561-1627 see also PELLICER
DE OSSAU Y TOVAR, JOSÉ, 1602-1679; SALAZAR
MARDONES, CRISTÓBAL.

GONZÁLEZ DÁVILA, GIL, 1578-1658.
    Compendio Historico De Las Vidas De Los Gloriosos
San Ivan De Mata I S. Felix De Valois, Patriarcas I
Fvndadores De La Ilvstrissima Orden De La Santissima
Trinidad, Redencion De Cavtivos. Por El Maestro Gil
Gonzalez Davila Coronista De La Magestad Catelica.
Al Ilvst.mo Irev.mo Señor Don Francisco Barberino,
Cardenal De La Santa Iglesia. Madrid: Por Francisco
Martinez, 1630.
    [5], 86 l.: ill.; 22cm.

    Title within ornamental border; text within double
line border.
    Colophon: "En Madrid Por Francisco Martinez. Año
1629."
    Goldsmith, p. 76, no. 253.
Reel 60, No. 362

GONZÁLEZ DÁVILA, GIL, 1578-1658.
    Historia de la vida y hechos del rey Don Henriqve
tercero de Castilla, inclito en Religion y Ivsticia.
Al mvi catolico y poderoso, señor don Felipe Qvarto
... El Maestro Gil Gonzalez Davila. Madrid:
Francisco Martinez, 1638.
    [10], 223, [8] p.; 22cm.

    Goldsmith, p. 76, no. 255; Palau, 105288; Penney,
p. 236; Salvá, II, 2970.
Reel 60, No. 363

GONZÁLEZ DE MENDOZA, JUAN, Bp., 1545-1618.
    [Historia de las cosas más notables de la China.
English]
    The Historie of the great and mightie kingdome of
China, and the situation thereof: Togither (sic)
with the great riches, huge Citties (sic) politike
gouernement, and rare inuentions in the same.
Translated out of Spanish by R. Parke. London:
Printed by I. Wolfe for Edward White, and are to be
sold at the little North doore of Paules, at the
signe of the gun, 1588.
    [8], 410 p.; 20cm.

    English translation by Robert Parke.
    "A commentarie or short discourse of all such
notable thinges as be twtwixte Spaine till you come
vnto the kingdome of China, and from China vnto
Spaine, returning by the orientall or east Indias,
after that they had almost compassed the whole world
... Made and set forth by the author of this booke
as well by that which he hath seene, as also by true
relation that he had of the religious and barefoot
fryers of the order of Saint Francis, who trauailed
the same the yeare 1584", pp. 395-410 (Based chiefly
on oral account of fray Martín Ignacio de Loyola.
cf. chap. V; Navarrete, Biblioteca Marítima Española,
t. II, p. 471: Pardo de Tavera, Bibl. fil. no. 1199).
    First English edition.
    Imperfect: pp. 119-122 wanting. Title - page
mutilated with loss of text.
    Not in Allison's English Translations ...
Reel 61, No. 364

GONZÁLEZ DE ROSENDE, ANTONIO DE, 17th cent.
    Vida I Virtvdes Del Ill.mo I Exc.mo Señor D. Ivan
De Palafox I Mendoza De Los Consejos De Sv Magestad
En El Real De Las Indias, I Svpremo De Aragon. Obispo
De La Pvebla De Los Angeles, I Arzobispo Electo de
Mexico. Virrey que fue, Lugar-Teniente del Rey nuestro
señor, Su Governador, i Capitan General de la Nueva-
España, Presidente de la Audiencia, i Chancilleria
Real que en ella reside, Visitador General de sus
Tribunales, I Iuez de Residencia de Tres Virreyes. I·

GONZÁLEZ DE ROSENDE (Cont'd)
ultimamente Obispo de la Santa Iglesia De Osma. Qve
Ofrece A la Magestad Catolica de la Reina nuestra
señora Doña Mariana de Avstria, Primera deste Nombre.
El Padre Antonio Gonzalez De Rosende, de los Clerigos
Menores. Madrid: Por Iulian de Paredes, 1666.
    [61], 534 (i.e. 532), [23] p.: port; 31cm.

    HC 336/602; Medina, Bib. his. amer. no. 1413;
Penney, p. 237.
Reel 61, No. 365

GONZÁLEZ DE ROSENDE, ANTONIO DE, 17th cent.
    Vida Del Il.mo I Exc.mo Señor Don Ivan De Palafox
Y Mendoza; De los Consejos De Su Magestad, En El Real
De Las Indias, I Supremo De Aragon, Obispo De La
Puebla De Los Angeles, Y Arzobispo Electo De Mexico.
... En Madrid: En la Oficina de Lucas de Bedmar,
1671.
    [40], 646, [29] p.: port.; 31cm.

    First. edition published under title: Vida i
virtudes del...
    Pages 371-372 torn, with some loss of text.
    Bartlett 2 / 1063; Palau, vol. 6, p. 300; Penney,
p. 238.
Reel 61, No. 366

GONZÁLEZ DE SALAS, JUSEPE ANTONIO, 1588-1651.
    Nueva Idea De La Tragedia Antigua; O Ilustracion
Vltima Al Libro Singvlar De Poetica De Aristoteles
Stagirita, Por don Jusepe Antonio Goncalez de Salas.
En Madrid: Lo imprimió Franc. Martinez, 1633.
    [14], 363, [1], 24, [24] p.: port.; 21cm.

    [Half-title:] Ilvstracion Al Libro De Poetica
De Aristotles Stagirita. Por Don Ivsepe Antonio
Gonzalez de Salas.
    Illustrated title-page, engraving.
    Includes: A) Tragedia practica, i observaciones,
que deben preceder a la tragedia española intitulada,
Las Troianas; B) Las Troianas, tragedia latina de
Lvcio Seneca español; C) El theatro scenico a todos
los hombres, exercitacion scholastica; D) Bibliotheca
escripta, o Indice de los avctores, que en la Poetica
de don Ivsepe Antonio Gonzalez de Salas se nombran,
o se ilustran.
    Author's autographed presentation copy to Juan
de Morales Barnuevo.
    Goldsmith, p. 77, no. 292; Palau, 105823; Ticknor,
p. 158.
Reel 61, No. 367

GONZÁLEZ VAQUERO, MIGUEL.
    La Mvger Fverte, Por Otro Titvlo, La Vida De
Doña Maria Vela, Monja de San Bernardo en el Conuento
de Santa Ana de Auila. Escrita Por El Doctor Migvel
Gonzalez Vaquero su Confessor, natural de la misma
Ciudad. Dirigida Al Mvy Ilvstrissimo Señor Don Garcia
de Medrano, del Consejo, y Camara de su Magestad, &c.
En Madrid: En la Imprenta Real, 1674.
    [10], 248, [4] l.; 22cm.

    Numerous errors in pagination; text complete.
    "Del maestro fray Angel Manriqve ... por el libro
de la Mvger fuerte, Doña Maria Vela, respondiendo"
(leaves 198-248) has separate title-page.
    Palau, 106049; Penney, p. 238.
Reel 61, No. 368

GRACIÁN DANTISCO, LUCAS, fl. 1590.
    [Galateo español. English]
    Galateo Espagnol, Or, The Spanish Gallant,
Instrvcting Thee in that which thou must doe, and
take heed of in thy usuall cariage, to be well
esteemed, and loved of the People. Written in
Spanish by Lucas Gracian de Antisco servant to his

GRACIÁN DANTISCO (Cont'd)
Majesty. And done into English by W. S. of the Inner
Temple Esquire. Full of variety, and delight, and
very necessary to be perused, not only of the generous
youth of this Kingdom, but also of all such as are
exercised in their gentile Education. London:
Printed by E. G. for William Lee at the Turkes head
in Fleete-streete, neere to the Mirer Taverne, 1640.
    [22], 209 (i.e. 223), 4 p.; 15cm.

    English translation by William Style.
    With copper plate frontispiece showing a gallant
in full regalia.
    The very rare first English edition of the popular
Spanish book of the courtier, translated by William
Style, the noted 17th century English legalist.
    Slightly worn, but generally in excellent
condition.
    Colophón: "Imprimatur Tho. Wykes."
    Pages 63-72 and 83 repeated in numbering.
    Allison, p. 82, no. 12; Graesse, III, p. 127;
Palau, 106772; Pollard and Redgrave, no. 12145.
Reel 61, No. 369

GRACIÁN Y MORALES, BALTASAR, 1601-1658.
    El Criticon. Primera Parte. En La Primavera De
La Niñez, Y En El Estio De La Ivventvd. Su Autor
Lorenco Gracian. Y Lo Dedica Al Valeroso Cavallero
D. Pablo de Parada, de la Orden de Christo, General
de la Artilleria, y Gouernador de Tortosa. Con
Licencia. En Madrid: Por Pablo de Val, 1658.
    [8], 288 p.; 15cm.

    Pagination errors throughout.
    Gallardo, III, no. 2402; Palau, vol. 6, p. 338;
Simón Díaz, Jesuitas, no. 336.
Reel 62, No. 372

GRACIÁN Y MORALES, BALTASAR, 1601-1658.
    El Criticon. [Tres Partes De] Primera Parte, En
La Primavera De La Niñez, Y En El Estio De La Ivventvd.
Segvnda Parte. Ivyziosa Cortesana Filosofia, En El
Otoño de la Varonil Edad. Tercera Parte. En El
Invierno De La Veiez. Su Autor Lorenco Gracian. Y
Las Dedica. La primera: Al valeroso Cavallero Don
Pablo de Parada: de la orden de Christo, General
de la Artilleria: y Governador de Tortosa. La Segunda:
Al Serenissimo Señor Don Iuan de Austria. La Tecera
[sic]: Al Doctor Don Lorenco Frances de Vrritigoyti,
Dean de la Santa Iglesia de Siguenca. Con Licencia.
En Barcelona: Por Antonio Lacavalleria, 1664.
    [6], 459, [2] p.; 21cm.

    Pp. 211-212 torn causing loss of print.
    Ex Libris: Libreria de Paluzie.
    Palau, 106958, Simón Díaz, Jesuitas, no. 337.
Reel 62, No. 373

GRACIÁN Y MORALES, BALTASAR, 1601-1658.
    [El Criticón. English]
    The Critick. Written Originally in Spanish; By
Lorenzo Gracian One of the Best Wits of Spain, and
Translated into English, By Pavl Rycavt Esq; London:
Printed by T. N. for Henry Brome at the Gun in St.
Paul's Church-Yard, 1681.
    [16], 257 p.: front. port.; 17cm.

    English translation by Paul Rycaut.
    Pagination errors throughout.
    Allison, p. 82, no. 13; Wing, G. 1470.
Reel 62, No. 376

GRACIÁN Y MORALES, BALTASAR, 1601-1658.
    [El Criticón. French]
    L'Homme Détrompé Ou Le Criticon De Baltazar Gracian
Traduit de l'Espagnol en Francois. Paris: Chez
Jacques Collombat, ruë S. Jacques, prés la Fontaine
saint Severin, au Pelican., 1696.
    [12], 282, [10] p.; 17cm.

    French translation by Guillaume de Maunory.
    Translation of the first part of El Criticón.
    Foulché-Delbosc, Bibliographie, V, no. 2004; Palau,
106974; Simón Díaz, Jesuitas, no. 392.
Reel 62, No. 375

GRACIÁN Y MORALES, BALTASAR, 1601-1658.
    [El Criticón. French]
    L'Homme Détrompé Suite De L'Homme De Cour. Traduit
de l'Espagnol en Francois. A Paris: Au Palais,
Chez Augustin Brunet, dans le Grand' Salle, au
quatriême Pillier, devant les Enquestes, au Louis
couronné, 1699.
    [16], 282, [10] p.; 16cm.

    French translation by Guillaume de Maunory.
    Not in Palau's Manual, not in Simón Diaz' Jesuitas
...,not in E. Correa Calderon's Baltasar Gracián
Su vida y su obra, Madrid, Gredos, 1961.
Reel 62, No. 374

GRACIÁN Y MORALES, BALTASAR, 1601-1658.
    El Heroe De Lorenzo Gracian Infazon. Al Illustrissimo,
y Excelentissimo señor D. Francisco Lanier Cauallero
del habito de S. Miguel, Baron de S. Gemma, del Consejo
de estado del Rey Christianissimo Luis XIV. à Deo
dato, y su Embaxador en Portugal, &c. Lisboa: Con
licencia; Por Manuel da Sylua, 1646. A costa de
Vicente de Lemos mercader de libros.
    [8], 72 *l*.; 10cm.

    Loss of print due to poor print.
    Jerez, p. 48; Palau, vol. 6, p. 335; Penney, p.
241; Simon Díaz, Jesuitas, no. 309.
Reel 63, No. 383

GRACIÁN Y MORALES, BALTASAR, 1601-1658.
    El Heroe De Lorenzo Gracian Infazon. En esta
Impression nuevamente corregido. A Amsterdam: En
casa de Juan Blaeu, 1659.
    76 p.; 13cm.

    Goldsmith, p. 78, no. 317; Graesse, III, p. 127;
Palau, 106858; Penney, p. 241; Peeters-Fontainas,
Bibliographie, no. 610; Simón Díaz, Jesuitas, no.
310.
Reel 63, No. 384

GRACIÁN Y MORALES, BALTASAR, 1601-1658.
    Obras De Lorenzo Gracian. Tomo Primero [y segvndo].
Qve Contiene El Criticon, Primera, Segvnda y Tercera
Parte. El Oraculo. Y el Heroe. Al señor Licenciado
Don Gardia de Velasco, Vicario de la Coronada Villa
de Madrid, y su Partido. Vltima impression, mas
corregida, y enrequecida de Tablas. Madrid: Por
Pablo de Val, 1664. A costa de Santiago Martin
Redondo, Mercader de libros. Vendese en su casa en
la calle de Toledo, a la Porteria de la Concepcion
Geronima.
    2 v. ([8], 536, [16] p.; [8], 440, [4] p.); 21cm.

GRACIÁN Y MORALES (Cont'd)
Vol. I: Double columns.
Vol. II: Obras De Lorenzo Gracian Tomo Segvndo. Qve
Contiene, La Agvdeza, Y Arte De Ingenio. El Discreto.
El Politico Don Fernando el Catolico. Meditaciones
varias para antes, y despues de la Sagrada Comunion,
que hasta aora ha corrido con titulo de Comvlgador...
      Includes: Meditaciones Varias para antes, y
despues De La Sagrada comvnion Por el padre Baltasar
Gracian, de la Compañia de Iesus, Lector de escritura,
89 p.
      Goldsmith, p. 77, no. 309; Graesse, III, p. 127;
Palau, 106834; Simón Diáz, Jesuitas, no. 281.
Reels 61 & 62, No. 370

GRACIÁN Y MORALES, BALTASAR, 1601-1658.
      Oracvlo Manval, Y Arte De Prvdencia. Sacada De
los Aforismos que se discurren en las obras de
Lorenco Gracian. Publicala D. Vincencio Ivan De
Lastanosa. Y la dedica Al Excelentissimo Señor D.
Luis Mendez De Haro. Amsterdam: En casa de Ivan
Blaev, 1659.
      200 p.; 14cm.

      Penney, p. 241; Peeters-Fontainas, Bibliographie,
no. 615; Simón Diáz, Jesuitas, no. 328.
Reel 62, No. 377

GRACIÁN Y MORALES, BALTASAR, 1601-1658.
      [Oraculo manual ... English]
The Courtiers Manual Oracle, Or, The Art Of
Prudence. Written Originally in Spanish By Baltazar
Gracian. And now done into English. London:
Printed by M. Flesher, for Abel Swalle, at the
Sign of the Vnicorn, at the West-End of St. Paul's,
1685.
      [28], 272, [4] p.; 19cm.

      Allison, p. 83, no. 14; Palau, 106941; Wing G.
1468.
Reel 63, No. 381

GRACIÁN Y MORALES, BALTASAR, 1601-1658.
      [Oraculo manual ... English]
The Courtiers Oracle, Or, The Art of Prudence.
Written originally in Spanish, By Baltazar Gracian;
And now done into English. London: Printed for
Abel Swalle, and Tim. Childe, at the Sign of the
Vnicorn, at theWest-End of St. Paul's, 1694.
      [32], 256 p.; 18cm.

      The English translation of this edition and the
previous one was made from the French version of
Amelot de la Houssaie, L'Homme de Cour.
      Allison, p. 83, no. 14.1; Graesse, III, p. 127;
Palau, 106942; Wing G. 1496.
Reel 63, No. 382

GRACIÁN Y MORALES, BALTASAR, 1601-1658.
      [Oraculo manual ... French]
L'Homme De Cour Traduit de L'Espagnol, De Baltasar
Gracian, Par le Sieur Amelot De La Houssaie. Avec
des Notes. Paris: Chez la Veuve Martin & Jean
Boudot, Et se vendent A La Haye, Chez Abraham Troyel,
Libraire, dans la Salle du Palais, 1684.
      [70], 311, [10] p.; 16cm.

      French translation by Amelot de la Houssaie.
      Doublet, p. 66; Foulché-Delbosc, Bibliographie, V,
no. 1877; Palau, 106910; Simón Diáz, Jesuitas, no.
374.
Reel 62, No. 378

GRACIÁN Y MORALES, BALTASAR, 1601-1658.
      [Oraculo manual ... French]
L'Homme de Cour De Baltasar Gracian Traduit &
commenté Par le Sieur Amelot De La Houssaie, ci-
devant Secretaire de l'Ambassade de France à Venise.
Troisiéme Edition revûe & corigée. A Paris; Chez la
Veuve-Martin, & Jean Boudot, rûe Saint Jaques, au
Soleil d'or, 1685.
      [66], 373, [2] p.: front.; 16cm.

      French translation by Amelot de la Houssaie.
      Third edition.
      Foulché-Delbosc, Bibliographie, V, no. 1888;
Palau, 106911; Simón Diáz, Jesuitas, no. 375.
Reel 62, No. 379

GRACIÁN Y MORALES, BALTASAR, 1601-1568.
      [Oraculo manual. German]
L'Homme de Cour oder Balthasar Gracians Vollkommenner
Staats und Weltweise, mit Chur = Sächsischer Freyheit.
Leipzig: Verlegts Adam Gottfried Kromayer, 1686.
      [112], 690, [318] p.: front.; 14cm.

      German translation by Johann Leonhard Sauter.
      [At the end:] Index rerum oder Verzeichnuss
derer in der Hoff=Staats = und Welt=Weissheit
gegrundeten Maximen.
      Many errors in paging.
      Includes translation of the French commentary by
Amelot de la Houssaie.
Reel 62, No. 380

GRACIÁN Y MORALES, BALTASAR, 1601-1658.
      El Politico D. Fernando El Catholico De Lorenzo
Gracian. Que publica Don Vincencio Iuan de Lastanosa.
Con licencia en Huesca: Por Iuan Nogues, 1646.
      [2], 222 p.; 11cm.

      Goldsmith, p. 78, no. 320; Palau, 106874; Simón
Diáz, Jesuitas, no. 313.
Reel 62, No. 371

GRANADA, LUIS DE, DOMINICAN see LUIS DE GRANADA.

GRANDE DE TENA, PEDRO, ed.
      Lagrimas panegiricas a la tenprana mverte del gran
Poëta, i Teologo Insigne Doctor Iuan Perez de Montalban.
... Lloradas I vertidas por los mas Ilustres Ingenios
de España. Recogidas i pvblicadas por ... el Licenciado
don Pedro Grande de Tena. Madrid: En la Imprenta
del Reino, 1639.
      [12], 164 l., port. of Montalbán; 20cm.

      Bound with: (1) Niseno, Diego. Elogio evangelico
funeral... Madrid, 1639. and (2) Quintana, Francisco
de. Oración panegirica... Madrid, 1639.
      Gallardo, no. 2404; Goldsmith, p. 78, no. 339;
Penney, p. 242; Salvá, I, 257; Ticknor, p. 162.
Reel 68, No. 409

GRAU, ABRAHAM DE, 1632-1683.
      Specimina philophiae veteris, in qua novae quaedam
ostenduntur. Franekerae Frisiorum: excudit Johannes
Wellens, 1673.
      [16], 399 p.; 16cm.

Reel 68, No. 412

GREGORIUS XV, Pope, 1554-1623.
    The Popes letter to the Prince: in Latine, Spanish,
and English. Done according to the Latine and Spanish
coppies printed at Madrid. A Iesuites oration to the
Prince, in Latine and English. London: Printed for N.
Butter, 1623.
    [2], 34 p.; 19cm.

    Bound with: A trve relation and iovrnall, of the
manner of the arrivall, and magnificent entertainment,
giuen to ... Prince Charles. London, 1623.
    The Pope's letter is to Charles I and the Oration
was made upon his visit to Madrid. The letter is dated
April 20, 1623.
Reel 68, No. 413

GUADALAJARA Y JAVIER, MARCOS DE, ca. 1580-1630.
    Memorable expvlsion y ivstissimo destierro de los
Moriscos de España. Nvevamente compvesta y ordenada
por F. Marco de Guadalajara y Xauierr. Pamplona:
Nicolas de Assiayn, 1613.
    [8], 164 *l*.; 20cm.

    Bound with: Ripoll, Juan: Dialogo de consvelo
por la expvlsion de los moriscos de España. Compvesto
y ordenado por Iuan Ripol. Pamplona: Nicolas de Assiayn,
1613.
    Jerez, p. 49; Penney, p. 245; Pérez Goyena, 286;
Salvá, II, 2972; Ticknor, p. 163.
Reel 68, No. 415

GUARINI, GIOVANNI BATTISTA, 1538-1612.
    [Il Pastor Fido. Spanish]
    El Pastor Fido, Poëma de Baptista Guarino, Traducido
de Italiano en Metro Español, y illustrado con
Reflexiones Por Doña Isabel Correa. Dedicado a don
Manuel de Belmonte, Baron de Belmonte, Conde Palatino
y Regente de su Magestad Catholica. En Amberez: Por
Henrico y Cornelio Verdussen, Mercaderes de Libros,
1694.
    295, [3] p.

    Spanish translation by Isabel Correa.
    Gallardo, II, no. 1918; Heredia, no. 5222; Palau,
109456; Peeters-Fontainas, Impressions, I, no. 541;
Salvá, I, 1276; Ticknor, p. 163.
Reel 68, No. 417

GUERRA Y RIBERA, MANUEL DE, 1638-1692.
    Crisol de la verdad de la cavsa sin cavsa. Dedicada
a la fama, consagrada a la svprema jvsticia. Impression
segunda. Zaragoza, 1684.
    [6], 116 *l*.; 29cm.

    Second edition.
    Concerns the case of Gaspar Téllez Girón, 5th Duke
of Osuna.
Reel 68, No. 418

GUEVARA, ANTONIO DE, bp., d. 1545?
    Libro llamado auiso de priuados y doctrina de
cortesanos. Dirigido al illustre señor don Francisco
de los cobos comendador mayor de Leon y del consejo
de su magestad. &c. Compuesto por el illustre señor
don Antonio de gueuara obispo de Mōdoñedo predicador
y chronista y del cōsejo de su magestad. Es obra muy
digna de leer y muy necessaria de ala memoria se
encomēdar. [Valladdid: J. de Villaquira], 1539.
    [8], xliiii *l*.; 30cm.

    Foulche-Delbosc, no. 18; Heredia, no. 2815 and no.
3743; Laurenti y Porqueras, Guevara, no. 1; Salvá,
II, 2273; Palau, 110072; Ticknor, p. 164.
Reel 74, No. 469

GUEVARA, ANTONIO DE, bp., d. 1545?
    Aviso de privados y doctrina de cortesanos.
Barcelona: Por Hieronymo Margarit, 1612.
    Leaves 81-219. *l*.; 16cm.

    Originally bound with his Menosprecio de corte and
his Arte de marear ... Barcelona, 1613.
    Laurenti y Porqueras, Guevara, no. 15; Palau,
110309.
Reel 73, No. 458

GUEVARA, ANTONIO DE, bp., d. 1545?
    Libro llamado aviso de privados, y doctrina de
    cortesanos. Dirigido al illustre señor Don Francisco
de los Cobos, Comendador mayor de el consejo
de su Magestad, &. Compuesto por el illustre señor
Don Antonio de Gueuara, Obispo de Mondoñedo, predicador
y chronista, y del consejo de su Magestad. Es obra
muy digna de leer, y muy necessaria de a la memoria
se encomendar. Coimbra: En la officina de Manoel
Dias impressor de la Vniuersidad, 1657.
    44, 275 p.; 15cm.

    Foulche-Delbosc, no. 114; Laurenti y Porqueras,
Guevara, no. 12; Palau, no. 110283.
Reel 73, No. 456

GUEVARA, ANTONIO DE, bp., d. 1545?
    [Aviso de privados y doctrina de cortesanos.
German]
    Cortegiano: Das ist: Der rechte wolgezierte Hofmann,
darin viel schöner Regel vnd Anweisungen, wie sich
ein jeder Adelicher Hofmann, Rath, vnd Diener gegen
seinem Herrn, vnd desselben Hofgesind, in allen
seinem Thun vnd Wesen, fleissig, getrew, verschwiegen,
Mannhafft, Sittsam, vnd Ehrsam verhalten solle, damit
er nicht allein seines Herrn Genad erlangen vnd
behalten: Sondern auch mit allen anderen seinen Hofes
Genossen, freundlich, vnd vnverweisslich leben möge.
Erstlichen in Hispanischer Sprach Durch: Herrn
Antonium De Guevara beschrieben. Jetzund aber allen
Hofleuten, vnd denen so sich der Welt gebrauchen vnd
zu einem tugendthafften, Erbarn Leben vnd Wandel,
Lust vnd Neigung haben, nütz, vnd dienlich zu lesen
in Deutsche Sprach versetzet, Durch Aegidium Albertinum,
Fürstl. Durchl. in Bayern Hofraths Secretarium. Bey
Henning Grossen dem Jügern Buchhändlern zu Leipzig,
zu finden. Gedruckt im Jahr, 1619.
    [17], 373 p.; 16cm.

    German translation by Aegidius Albertinus.
    Title in red and black within double line border.
    Errors in paging: numbers 77 and 223 omitted, 192-
193 and 304 repeated; other errors also.
Reel 73, No. 462

GUEVARA, ANTONIO DE, bp., d. 1545?
    [Aviso de privados y doctrina de cortesanos.
Italian]
    Aviso de favoriti et dottrina de cortigiani con
la commendatione de la uilla, opera non meno utile che
deleteuole, tradotta nouamente di spagnolo in in
italiano per ... Venetia: [M. Tramezino], 1544.
    20 *l*., 180 *l*.; 15cm.

    Italian translation by Vincenzo Bondi.
    Errors in foliation: leaves 85 and 87 numb. 79 and
81 respectively.
    Includes translation of the author's Menosprecio
de la corte ... (leaves 122-179) with caption title:
Comincia il libro chiamato Dispregio delle corti, e
laude della uilla.
    Laurenti y Porqueras, Guevara, no. 40; Palau,
110314; Short-Title, II, p. 100.
Reel 73, No. 459

GUEVARA, ANTONIO DE, bp., d. 1545?
[Aviso de privados y doctrina de cortesanos. Italian].
Aviso de favoriti et dottrina di cortigiani con la commendatione de la uilla, opera non meno utile che deleteuole, tradotta nouamente di spagnolo in italiano per ... Venetia: P.G. Giglio, 1559.
205 (i.e. 207)l..; 16cm.

Italian translation by Vincenzo Bondi.
Leaves 143-144 duplicated in numbering. Other errors in foliation.
Includes a translation of the author's Memosprecio de la corte ... (leaves 144-205) with caption title: Comincia il libro chiamato Dispregio delle corti, e lavde della villa.
Laurenti y Porqueras, Guevara, no. 41; Palau, 110316; Short-Title, II, p. 100; Ticknor, p. 164.
Reel 73, No. 460

GUEVARA, ANTONIO DE, bp., d. 1545?
Aviso de favoriti et dottrina di cortigiani con la commendatione de la uilla, opera non meno utile che deleteuole, tradotta nouamente di spagnolo in in italiano per ... Venetia: appresso Bernardo Giunta, 1581.
206 l., 1 l.; 16cm.

Laurenti y Porqueras, Guevara, no. 42; Palau, 110318.
Reel 73, No. 461

GUEVARA, ANTONIO DE, bp. d. 1545?
Epistolas familiares del illustre señor dõ Antonio de gueuara obispo de Mõdoñedo predicador y chronista y del consejo del emperador y rey nuestro señor. Ay en este epistolario cartas muy notables razonamientos muy altos dichos muy curiosos y razones muy naturales. Ay exposiciones de algunas figuras y de algũas auctoridades dela sancta escriptura assaz buenas para p̃dicar y mejores para obrar. Ay muchas declaraciones de medallas antiguas y de letreros de piedras y de epitaphios de supulturas y de leyes y costũbres gẽtiles. Ay doctrinas exemplos y consejos para principes, caulleros plebeyos y ecclesiasticos: muy prouechosas para imitar y muy aplazibles para leer. Va todo el epistolario al estilo y romãce de Marco aurelio, porque el auctor es todo vno. [Valladolid: Juan de Villaquirán, 1539].
127, [1] l.; 28cm.

Stained causing loss of print.
Colophon: "Aqui se acabã las epistolas familiares del illustre señor dõ antonio de gueuara, obispo de mondoñedo, predicador, chronista, y del consejo de su magestad. Obra q̃ es de muy gran doctrina, y de muy alto estilo. Fue impresa enla muy leal y muy noble villa de valladolid: por industria del honrrado varon impressor de libros Juan de villaquiran a veynte y nueue del mes de agosto. Año de mil y quiniẽtos y treynta y nueue."
Ex libris: Luis Bardón.
Alcocer, 101, Foulché-Delbosc, 19; HC: NS4/834; Heredia, no. 2815; Laurenti y Porqueras, Guevara, no. 3; Palau, 110205; Penney, p. 247; Ticknor, p. 164.
Reel 68, No. 419

GUEVARA, ANTONIO DE, bp., d. 1545?
Las epistolas familiares [libro primero de] del illustre señor don Antonio de gueuara obispo de Mondoñedo predicador y chronista y del consejo del Emperador y rey nuestro señor ... Caragoca: George Coci, a expensas de Pedro Bernuz y Bartholome de Nagera, 1543.
107 l.; 31cm.

GUEVARA (Cont'd)
Imperfect copy: Title page-1.II wanting.
Colophon: "Aqui se acan las epistolas familiares del illustre señor don antonio de gueuara obispo de mondoñedo: predicador: chronista: y del consejo de su magestad. Obra q̃ es de muy gran doctrina: y d' muy alto estilo. Fue impressa enla muy leal y muy noble ciudad de caragoca en casa de george coci a espensas de Pedro bernuz y Bartholome de nagera: a veynte de enero. Año de mil y quinientos y quarẽta y tres."
Foulché-Delbosc, 26; Heredia, no. 2803; Laurenti y Porqueras, Guevara, no. 4; Palau, 110209; Salvá, II, 2274; Thomas, p. 41.
Reel 69, No. 420

GUEVARA, ANTONIO DE, bp., d. 1545?
Las Epistolas Familiares [segvnda parte de] del Illustre Señor Dõ Antonio de Gueuara, Obispo de Mondoñedo, Predicador y Chronista: y del Consejo de sus Magestades. Va todo este Epistolario al estilo y Romance de Marco Aurelio: porque el autor es todo vno, y lo que en el se contiene se hallara a la buelta desta hoja. Salamanca: En casa de Pedro Lasso, 1578.
320 l.

Pagination errors throughout.
Foulché-Delbosc, no. 82; Laurenti y Porqueras, Guevara, no. 5; Palau, 110209; Thomas, p. 41.
Reel 69, No. 421

GUEVARA, ANTONIO DE, bp., d. 1545?
Epistolas Familiares De Don Antonio De Gvevara, Obispo de Mondoñedo, Predicador, y Chronista, y del Consejo del Emperador y Rey nuestro señor Y Segunda Parte Dirigido à Don Martin de Saavedra, y Narvaez Pariente mayor, y Cabeca de la de Gueuara, Conde de Tahula, &c.. Vá todo este Epistolario al estilo, y Romance de Marco Aurelio, porque el autor es todo vno, y aora nuevamente se ha añadido su vida. Madrid: Por Matheo de Espinosa y Arteaga, Acosta de Iuan de Calatayud y Montenegro, 1668.
[10], 705 p.; 21cm.

Pagination errors throughout.
Foulché-Delbosc, no. 26; Laurenti y Porqueras, Guevara, no. 6; Palau, 110229.
Reel 69, No. 422

GUEVARA, ANTONIO DE, bp., d. 1545?
[Epistolas familiares. English]
The familiar epistles of Sir Anthony of Guevara, preacher, chronicler, and counceller to the emperour Charles the Fifth. Translated out of the Spanish Toung, by Edward Hellowes, groome of the leashe, and now newly imprinted, corrected, and enlarged with other epistles of the same author. VVherein are contained very notable letters, excellent discourses, curious sayings, and most naturall reasons ... London: Henry Bynneman, 1575.
[8], 412, [4] p.; 20cm.

English translation by Edward Hellowes.
Pagination errors throughout.
With this is bound: Fenton, Sir Geoffrey, Golden epistles ... London, 1575. [16], 210 p.
Allison, p. 85, no. 21.1; Laurenti y Porqueras Guevara, no. 35; Palau, p. 450; Pollard and Redgrave, no. 12433.
Reel 70, No. 425

GUEVARA, ANTONIO DE, bp., d. 1545?
[Epistolas Familiares. English].
The Familiar Epistles of Sir Anthony of Guevara,
Preacher, Chronicler, and Counsellor to the Emperour
Charles the fifth. Translated out of the Spanish tongue,
by Edward Hellowes, Groome of the Leash, and now newly
imprinted, corrected and enlarged ... Imprinted at
London: for Ralph Newberrie, 1577.
[8], 400, [7] p.; 18cm.

Title within ornamental border; initials.
Bound with: Fenton, Sir Geoffrey, Golden epistles
... London, 1582. [4], 347, [3] p.
Allison, p. 86, no. 21.2; Laurenti y Porqueras,
Guevara, no. 36; Palau, 110265; Pollard and Redgrave,
no. 12434.
Reel 70, No. 426

GUEVARA, ANTONIO DE, bp., d. 1545?
[Epistolas Familiares. English]
The Familiar Epistles of Sir Antonie of Guevara,
Preacher, Chronicler, and Counseller to the Emperor
Charles the fifth: Translated out of the Spanish tongue,
by Edward Hellowes, Groome of the Leash, and now
newly imprinted, corrected and enlarged... London:
Printed by Ralph Newberrie, 1584.
[8], 400, [7] p.; 20cm.

Title within border of type ornaments; head and
tail-pieces; initials.
Gothic type.
Allison, p. 86, no. 21.3; Laurenti y Porqueras,
no. 37; Palau, 110266; Pollard and Redgrave, no. 12435.
Reel 70, No. 427

GUEVARA, ANTONIO DE, bp., d. 1545?
[Epistolas Familiares. English]
Spanish letters: historical, satyrical, and moral:
of the famous Don Antonio de Guevara ... Written by
way of Essay on different Subjects, and everywhere
intermixt with both Railleric and Gallantry. Recommended
by Sir R. L'S. and made English from the best Original
by Mr. [John] Savage. London: F. Saunders, 1697.
[8], 183, [8] p.; 19cm.

English translation by John Savage.
Allison, p. 87, no. 24; Laurenti y Porqueras, no.
38; Palau 110268; Wing A. no. 2182.
Reel 70, No. 428

GUEVARA, ANTONIO DE, bp., d. 1545?
[Epistolas familiares. French]
Les epistres dorees, et discours salutaires de
Don Antoine de Gueuarre. Traduites d'espagnol en
francois par le Seigneur de Guterry ... Ensemble
la reuolte que les espaignolz firent contre leur
iene prince, l'an M.D. XX auec vn traitté des
trauaux et priuileges des galeres, le tout du mesme
autheur. Traduit nouuellement d'italien en francois.
Paris: Iehan Ruelle, 1570.
[16], 352, 304, 256 p.; 17cm.

French translation by Seigneur de Guterry.
Title within ornamental border; initials.
Laurenti y Porqueras, Guevara, no. 25; Palau,
110256.
Reel 69, No. 424

GUEVARA, ANTONIO DE, bp., d. 1545?
[Epistolas familiares. Italian]
Libro primo [quarto] delle lettere dell'ill.
sig. don Antonio de Gvevera ... Nuouamente tradotto,
e riformato dal signor Alfonso Vlloa. Doue si leggono
molte lettere, che nella prima tradottione mancauono.
E aggiontoui le postille. Con la tauola de' capitoli,
e delle cose piu notabili ... Venetia: Gli heredi
di Vicenzo Valgrisi, 1565.
4 v. in 1 ([16], 230 p.; [14], 300 p.; [10],
181 p.; [11], 289, [27] p.); 23cm.

Italian translation by Alfonso Ulloa.
Device of printer on title-pages, on verso of last
leaf, and on verso of last leaf of each part; initials.
Laurenti y Porqueras, Guevara, no. 52; Palau, 110244;
Short-Title, vol. II, p. 103; 1575 (i.e. 1565).
Reel 69, No. 423

GUEVARA, ANTONIO DE, bp., d. 1545?
Libro Avreo De Marco Aurelio, emperador, y
eloquentissimo orador, nueuamente impresso. Vendēse en
Enueres: por Iuan Steelsio, en el escudo de Borgoyngna,
1539.
175 l.; 17cm.

Ex-libris: Frederick H. Comstock.
Colophon: Fue impresso en la triunfante villa de
Enueres por Iuan Grapheus. Año del Señor de mill e
quiniētos e XXXIX.
Foulché-Delbosc, no. 21; Laurenti y Porqueras, no.
13; Palau, 110098; Peeters-Fontainas, Impressions, I,
no. 560; Vaganay, no. 125.
Reel 70, No. 429

GUEVARA, ANTONIO DE, bp., d. 1545?
Libro Avreo De La Vida Y Cartas De Marco Avrelio
Emperador, y eloquentissimo Orador, nueuamente
corregido y emendado. Añadiose de nueuo la Tabla de
todas las Sentencias, y buenos dichos que en el se
contienen. En Amberes: En casa de Martin Nucio, à
las dos Cigueñas, 1604.
[24], 381, [9] p.; 13cm.

Foulché-Delbosc, no. 102; Laurenti y Porqueras,
Guevara, no. 14; Palau, 110116; Peeters-Fontainas,
Impressions, I, no. 571.
Reel 70, No. 430

GUEVARA, ANTONIO DE, bp., d. 1545?
[Libro Aureo. English]
The golden Boke of Marcvs Avrelio emperovr and
eloqvent oratovr. Thus endeth the volume of Marke
Aurelie emperour, other wyse called the golden boke
translated out of Frenche into english by John
Bourchier knyghte lorde Barners ... at the instant
desyre neuewe syr Francis Bryan knyghte ended at
Caleys the thenth day of Marche, in the yere of the
reygne of oure Souerayque lorde kynge Henrye the
viii, the XXIII. London: n.p. 1536.
[8], 167, [1], l.; 20cm.

English translation by John Bourchier Berners.
Colophon: "Londini, In aedibus Thomae Bertheleti
regii impressoris. Anno M.D.XXXVII."
Printer's mark on last leaf and on unsigned
leaf 4.
Imperfect: unsigned leaves 1-4 (incl. title-page)
and leaves 153-60 wanting.
Pagination errors throughout.
Allison, p. 87, no. 25.2; Laurenti y Porqueras,
Guevara, no. 28; Pollard and Redgrave, no. 12437.
Reel 70, No. 431

GUEVARA, ANTONIO DE, bp., d. 1545?
  [Libro Aureo. English]
  The Golden Boke of Marcvs Avrelius Emperour and
eloquente oratour. Londini: Thomas Bertheleti, 1546.
  [555 p.]; 14cm.

  English translation by John Bourchier Berners.
  Colophon: "Imprinted at London in Fletestrete, in
the house of Thomas Berthelet ..."
  Black letter.
  Pages unnumbered.
  Allison, p. 87, no. 25.6; Laurenti y Porqueras,
Guevara, no. 29; Pollard and Redgrave, no. 124405.
Reel 70, No. 432

GUEVARA, ANTONIO DE, bp. d. 1545?
  [Libro Aureo. English]
  The Golden Boke of Marcvs Avrelius Emperour and
eloquente oratour. Londini: Thomas Marshe, 1557.
  [568 p.]; 15cm.

  Pages unnumbered.
  Colophon: Imprinted at London, in Fletestreet,
... by Thomas Marshe.
  English translation by John Bourchier Berners.
  Allison, p. 87, no. 25.9; Laurenti y Porqueras,
Guevara, no. 30; Palau, 110139; Pollard and Redgrave,
no. 12443.
Reel 71, No. 433

GUEVARA, ANTONIO DE, bp., d. 1545?
  [Libro Aureo. English]
  The Golden Boke of Marcvs Avrelius Emperour and
eloquente oratour. Imprinted at London by John
Audeley, dwellyng in Litle (sic) Britaine street,
beyonde Aldersgate, 1566.
  [567 p.]; 14cm.

  Pages unnumbered.
  English translation by John Bourchier Berners.
  Allison, p. 87, no. 25.11; Laurenti y Porqueras,
Guevara, no. 31; Palau, 110139; Pollard and Redgrave,
no. 12445.
Reel 71, No. 434

GUEVARA, ANTONIO DE, bp., d. 1545?
  [Libro Avreo. French]
  Liure dore de Marc Aurele empereur et eloquent
orateur: traduict de vulgaire Castillian en frãcoys
par ... Nouellement reueu et corrige. Paris: On
les vend par A. Girault, 1538.
  [222 l.]; 16cm.

  Numerous errors in foliation, pages unnumbered.
  Colophon: "Le present volume ... a este acheue
de imprimer le ix. iour de nouembre mil cinq cens
trête et huyt: par Esteine caueller, imprimeur."
  French translation by René Berthault, sieur de
la Grise.
  Laurenti y Porqueras, Guevara, no. 21.
Reel 71, No. 435

GUEVARA, ANTONIO DE, bp., d. 1545?
  [Libro Avreo. French]
  Le Livre Dore De Marc Avrele Emperevr et Eloqvent
Oratevr... Lyon : Par Iean de Tovrnes, 1550.
  [22], 520 p.

  French translation by R. B[erthault], de la Grise.
  Laurenti y Porqueras, Guevara, no. 22; Palau,
vol. 6, p. 444.
Reel 71, No. 436

GUEVARA, ANTONIO DE, bp., d. 1545?
  [Libro Aureo. Italian]
  Vita, gesti, costvmi, discorsi, lettere di M. Aurelio
imperatore, sapientissimo filosofo, et oratore
eloquentissimo: con la gionta di moltissime cose,
che ne lo spagnuolo no erano, et de le cose spagnuo
Ie che mancauano in la tradottione italiana. Vinegia:
Appresso Vicenzo Vaugris, 1544.
  183, [1] l.; 16cm.

  Italian translation by Sebastiano da Longiano Fausto.
  Adams, I, no. 1499; Laurenti y Porqueras, Guevara,
no. 43; Short-Title, II, p. 101.
Reel 71, No. 437

GUEVARA, ANTONIO DE, bp., d. 1545?
  [Libro Avreo. Italian]
  Vita, Gesti, Costvmi, Discorsi, lettere di Marco
Aurelio imperatore ... con la gionta di molte cose, e
delle cose spagnuole, che macauano [sic] nella
tradottione Italiana. Venezia: 1546.
  148, [5] l.; 16cm.

  Italian translation by Sebastiano da Longiano Fausto.
  Colophon: "In Vinegia, nell'anno. M.D.XXXXVI. In
casa de' figlivoli de Aldo."
  Aldine device on title-page and on verso of last
leaf; spaces with initial indicators.
  Italic type.
  The arms of the Lumley-Saviles of Rufford Abbey
are stamped in gold on back and front covers.
  Adams, I, no. 1500; Laurenti y Porqueras, Guevara,
no. 44; Palau, 110142; Short-Title, II, p. 101.
Reel 71, No. 438

GUEVARA, ANTONIO DE, bp., d. 1545?
  [Libro Avreo. Italian]
  Vita, Gesti, Costvmi, Discorsi, Lettere Di M.
Avrelio Imperatore... Con La Gionta Di Moltissime
cose, che nolo Spagnuolo non crano, & de le cose
Spagnuole, che mancauano in la tradottione italiana.
Vinegia, G. Bucciola a San Luca, 1549.
  182 l.; 15cm.

  Italian translation by Sebastiano da Longiano
Fausto.
  Dedication signed: Fausto da Longiano.
  Colophon: "In Vinegia per Comin de Trino di
Monferrato, l'anno M.D.XLIX."
  Laurenti y Porqueras, Guevara, no. 45; Short-
Title, II, p. 101. Not in Palau's ...
Reel 71, No. 439

GUEVARA, ANTONIO DE, bp., d. 1545?
  [Libro Avreo. Italian]
  Vita, Gesti, Costvmi, Discorsi, Lettere Di Marco
Aurelio... Tradotta dal spagnuolo nella lingua
Toscana, Con l'Agiunta di molte cose, che nello
spagnuolo non erano, e delle cose spagnuolo, che
mancauano nella tradottione Italiana. Vinegia: A.
Bindoni, 1550.
  150 l.; 16cm.

  Italian translation by Sebastiano da Longiano
Fausto.
  Laurenti y Porqueras, Guevara, no. 46.
Reel 71, No. 440

GUEVARA, ANTONIO DE, bp., d. 1545?
　　Vita, Gesti, Costvmi, Discorsi, Lettere Di Marco
Aurelio... Tradotta dal spagnuolo nella lingua
Toscana, Con l'Agiunta di molte cose, che nello
spagnuolo non erano, e delle cose spagnuolo, che
mancauano nella tradottione Italiana. Venetia: F.
Bindoni e M. Pasini, 1551.
　　167 l.; 17cm.

　　Italian translation by Sebastiano da Longiano
Fausto.
　　Laurenti y Porqueras, Guevara, no. 47.
Reel 71, No. 441

GUEVARA, ANTONIO DE, bp., d. 1545?
　　[Libro Avreo. Italian]
　　Vita, Gesti, Costvmi, Discorsi, Et Lettere Di
Marco Avrelio... Con La Givnta Di Moltissime cose,
che nella Spagnuolo non erano, & delle cose Spagnuole,
che mancano nella traduttione Italiana. Vinegia:
Appresso Gabriel Giolito de' Ferrari, 1557.
　　[40], 304 p.; 16cm.

　　Italian translation by Sebastiano da Longiano Fausto.
　　Printer's mark on title-page; head and tail-pieces;
initials; Italic type. Armorial book-plate of Frederick
H. Comstock; labels of Biblioteca Terzi and of the
library of Laurence W. Hodson.
　　Laurenti y Porqueras, Guevara, no. 48; Palau,
110149; Short-Title, II, 101.
Reel 71, No. 442

GUEVARA, ANTONIO DE, bp., d. 1545?
　　[Libro Avreo. Italian]
　　Vita, Gesti, Costvmi, Discorsi, Et Lettere Di
Marco Avrelio... Con La Givnta Di Moltissime cose, che
nella Spagnuolo non erano, & delle cose Spagnuole, che
mancano nella traduttione Italiana. Venetia: Appresso
Francesco Rampazetto, [1564].
　　[60], 345, [1] p.; 14cm.

　　Italian translation by Sebastiana da Longiano
Fausto.
　　Colophon: "In Venetia, Appresso Francesco Rampazetto.
M.DLXIIII."
　　Printer's mark on title-page; head and tail-pieces;
initials; bound in vellum.
　　Laurenti y Porqueras, Guevara, no. 49; Palau,
110156; Short-Title, II, p. 101.
Reel 71, No. 443

GUEVARA, ANTONIO DE, bp., d. 1545?
　　[Libro Avreo. Italian]
　　Vita, Gesti, Costvmi, Discorsi, Et Lettere Di Marco
Avrelio... Con La Givnta Di Moltissime cose, che
nella Spagnuolo non erano, & delle cose Spagnuole,
che mancano nella traduttione Italiana. Venetia:
appresso Domenico & Gio. Battista Guerra, fratelli,
1572.
　　[17], 311 p.; 16cm.

　　Text is that of the Italian translation by Roseo
expanded by Fausto da Longiano.
　　Italian translation by Sebastiana da Longiano
Fausto.
　　Laurenti y Porqueras, Guevara, no. 50; Palau,
110158.
Reel 72, No. 444

GUEVARA, ANTONIO DE, bp., d. 1545?
　　[Libro Avreo. Italian]
　　Vita, Gesti, Costvmi, Discorsi, Et Lettere Di
Marco Avrelio... Con La Givnta Di Moltissime cose,
che nella Spagnuolo non erano, & delle cose Spagnuole,
che mancano nella traduttione Italiana. Vinegia:
Presso Giouanni Antonio Giuliani, 1615.
　　[10], 167 l.; 16cm.

　　Italian translation by Sebastiana da Longiano
Fausto.
　　Laurenti y Porqueras, Guevara, no. 51; Palau,
vol. 6, p. 445.
Reel 72, No. 445

GUEVARA, ANTONIO DE, bp., d. 1545?
　　[Libro aurso de Marco Aurelio con Reloj de
príncipes.]
　　Avreo libro di Marco Avrelio con l'horologio de
principi in tre volvmi. Composto per il molto reuerendo
signor don ... Nel qvale sono comprese molte sententie
notabili, & essempi singulari, appertinenti à i
principi christiani, & à tutti gli huomini generosi ...
Nvovamente tradotto di lingua spagnuola in italiano
dalla copia originale di esso auttore. Con privilegio.
Vinegia: Appresso Francesco Portonaris da Trino, 1556.
　　3v. in 1 ([24], 80 [4] l.; 78 l.; 98 l.); 21cm.

　　Italian translation by Sebastiano da Longiano Fausto.
　　Title vignette: Portonaris' device (also used on
final leaf of parts 1 and 2); initials; Italic type.
　　The second and third books have special title
pages: Il segondo libro di Marco Avrelio ... Novamente
ristampato, et purgato da gli errori da l'istesso
auttore [and] Il terzo libro di Marco Avrelio ...
Novamente corretto con diligentia, dallo istesso
auttore, & ristampato.
　　Leaf 34 in part I numb. 44.
　　Marginal manuscript notes.
　　Laurenti y Porqueras, Guevara, no. 53; Palau,
vol. 6, p. 444; Short-Title, II, p. 102.
Reel 72, No. 446

GUEVARA, ANTONIO DE, bp., d. 1545?
　　[Libro de Marco Aurelio con Reloj de príncipes.
French]
　　L'horloge des princes, avec le tresrenomme livre
de Marc Avrele Tr. en partie de castilan en francois
par feu ... & depuis reueu & corrigé nouuellement
outre les autres precedentes impressions par cy
deuant imprimées. Paris: Iehan Ruelle, 1569.
　　[32], 395 l.; 16cm.

　　French translation by N. de Herberay, seigneur
des Essars.
　　Pagination errors throughout.
　　Laurenti y Porqueras, Guevara, no. 23; Palau,
110179.
Reel 72, No. 448

GUEVARA, ANTONIO DE, bp., d. 1545?
　　[Libro de Marco Aurelio con Reloj de príncipes.
French]
　　L'horloge des princes, avec le tresrenomme livre
de Marc Avrele Tr. en partie de castilan en francois
par feu ... & depuis reueu & corrigé nouuellement
outre les autres precedentes impressions par cy
deuant imprimées. Lyon: B. Rigavd, 1592.
　　[70], 1488 [24] p.; 13cm.

　　French translation by René Berthault, sieur de
la Grise.
　　Laurenti y Porqueras, Guevara, no. 24; Palau,
110184.
Reel 72, No. 449

GUEVARA, ANTONIO DE, bp., d. 1545?
[Libro de Marco Aurelio con Reloj de príncipes.
German]
　　Lustgarten vnd Weckvhr. In welchem die Könige,
Fürsten vnd Herrn, so wol auch die von Adel,
Officier und Beampten, nicht weniger die stattliche
Frawen vnd Jungkfrawen, wie auch menigklich sich
trefflich vnnd nach allem jhrem gefallen recreiren
vnnd erlustigen können. Anfangs durch Hernn Antonium
de Gueuara Bischouen zu Mondonedo, Weilandt Keyser
Carls dess fünfften, rc Rath, Hof-Prediger vndd
Chronisten, in Hispanischer Sprachen beschrieben.
Anjetzo aber durch Der Fürstl: Durchl: Herzog
Maximiliani in Bayern, rc Secretarium Egidium
Albertinum inn die Teutsche Sprach trewlich
verwendt.　Gedruckt zu München, durch Nicolaum
Henricum, 1599.
　　[12], 255 l.; 15cm.

　　German translation by Aegidium Albertinum.
　　Colophon: "Gedruckt zu München durch Nicolaum
Henricum, im Jar. M.D.IC."
　　Laurentis y Porqueras, Guevara, no. 17; Palau,
vol. 6, no. 110193.
Reel 73, No. 450

GUEVARA, ANTONIO DE, bp., d. 1545?
[Libro de Marco Aurelio con Reloj de príncipes.
Italian]
　　Libro di Marco Avrelio Con L'Horologio De' Principi.
Destino In IIII. Volvmi. Composto Per Il MOLTO
Reverendo Signor Don Antonio di Gueuara... Venetia:
Appresso Francesco Portonaris, 1575.
　　4 v. in 1 ([24], 88 l.; [4], 96 l.; [4], 112 l.;
[4], 59 l.); 22cm.

　　Printer's mark on title-page; head-pieces; initials.
　　Pagination errors throughout.
　　Laurenti y Porqueras, Guevara, no. 54; Palau, vol.
6, p. 445.
Reel 72, No. 447

GUEVARA, ANTONIO DE, bp., d. 1545?
　　Libro delos inuentores del arte de marear y de
muchos trabajos que se passan enlas galeras. Copilado
por el illustre señor dõ antonio de gueuara obispo
de mondoñedo predicador y chronista y del consejo
de su maestad. Dirigido al illustre señor dõ franicsco
delos cobos Comendador mayor de leon y del consejo
del estado de su magestad. &c. Tocanse enel muy
excellentes antiguedades y auisos muy notables para
los nauegan en galeras. Valladolid: Juan de
Villaquiran, 1539.
　　[xiv l.]; 30cm.

　　Foulche-Delbosc, no. 18; Heredia, no. 2815 and no.
3743; Laurenti y Porqueras, Guevara, no. 1; Salvá,
II, 2273; Palau, 110072; Ticknor, p. 164.
Reel 74, No. 470

GUEVARA, ANTONIO DE, bp., d. 1545?
　　Libro de los inventores del arte de marear, Y de
muchos trabajos que se passan en las galeras. Copilado
por el illustre señor Don de Gueuara, Obispo de
Mondoñedo, predicador, y chronista, y del consejo de
su Magestad, & Tocanse en el muy excellentes
antiguedades y auisos muy notables para los que
nauegan en galeras.　En Coimbra: En la officina de
Manoel Dias impressor de la Vniuersidad, 1657.
　　[7], 70 p.; 15cm.

　　Foulché-Delbosc, no. 114; Laurenti y Porqueras,
Guevara, no. 12; Palau, no. 110283.

Reel 73, No. 457

GUEVARA, ANTONIO DE, bp., d. 1545?
　　Libro llamado menosprecio de corte y alabanca
de aldeo. Dirigido al muy alto y muy poderoso señor
de portugal dõ Juan tercero deste nombre. Cõpuesto
por el illustre señor dõ Antonio d' gueuara obispo
de Modoñedo predicador y chronista y del cõsejo de
su Magestad... Valladolid, 1539.
　　[4], xxvii l.

　　Foulche-Delbosc, no. 18; Heredia, no. 2815 and
no. 3743; Laurenti y Porqueras, Guevara, no. 1;
Salvá, II, 2273; Palau, 110072; Ticknor, p. 164.
Reel 74, No. 468

GUEVARA, ANTONIO DE, bp., d. 1545?
　　Libro Llamado menosprecio de corte, y alabanca
de Aldea Dirigido al muy alto, y muy poderoso señor
Rey de Portugal, Don Iuan Tercero deste nombre.
Compuesto por el illustre señor Don Antonio de Gueuara,
Obispo de Mondoñedo, predicador, y chronista y del
consejo de su Magestad. Muestra el auctor en este
libro, mas que en ninguno de los otros q̃ ha compuesto,
la grandeza de su eloquencia, y la delicadeza de su
ingenio. Va al estilo de Marco Aurelio, porque el
auctor es todo vno. Con todas las licencias necessarias.
En Coimbra: En la officina de Manoel Dias Impressor
de la Vniuersidad, 1657.
　　[32], 161 p.; 15cm.

　　Bound with two works by the same author:　Libro
llamado aviso de privados, y doctrina de cortesanos.
... Coimbra, 1657. [and] Libro de los inventores del
arte de marear... Coimbra, 1657.
　　Foulché-Delbosc, no. 114; Laurenti y Porqueras,
Guevara, no. 12; Palau, no. 110283.
Reel 73, No. 455

GUEVARA, ANTONIO DE, bp., d. 1545?
[Menosprecio de corte y alabanza de aldea. German]
　　Dv mespris de la covrt: & de la louange de la uie
rusticque. Nouuellement traduict d'Hespaignol en
Francoys. Lyon: E. Dolet, 1543.
　　111 p.; 15cm.

　　French translation by Antoine Allègre.
　　Laurenti y Porqueras, Guevara, no. 26.
Reel 74, No. 465

GUEVARA, ANTONIO DE, bp., d. 1545?
[Menosprecio de corte y alabanza de aldea. German]
　　Libro llamado Menosprecio de corte y alabanca de
aldea, compuesto por el illustre señor don Antonio de
Guevara, Obispo de Mondoñedo, predicador, y chronista,
y del consejo de Su Magestad. De nouueau mis en
francois par L.T. L. ... Pour plus grand enrichissement
de cest oeuure, y ont esté adioustés les vers francois
des euesques de Meaux & de Cambray, & les latins de N.
de Clemèges docteur en theologie, sur la grande disparité
de la vie rustique auec celle de cour. [Lyon]: Par
Iena de Tovrnes, 1591.
　　[9], 551, [1] p.; 12cm.

　　Printer's mark on verso of last leaf.
　　Running title: Mespris de la court.
　　French and Spanish in parallel columns; Italian
version below.
　　Top margins closely trimmed. Bound in mottled calf,
fold trimmed; gilt edges.
　　Adams, I, no. 1496; Foulché-Delbosc, no. 92;
Laurenti y Porqueras, Guevara, no. 11.
Reel 74, No. 464

GUEVARA, ANTONIO DE, bp., d. 1545?
[Menosprecio de corte y alabanza de aldea. German]
Mespris de la covr, et lovange de la vie rustique,
composé premierement en Espagnol par ... et depuis
traduit en Italien, Francois, et Allemand, toutes
lesquelles lángues nous auõn joinctes ensemble en
ceste seconde edition ... A la fin du liure se voyens
les vers francois des euesques de Meaux et de Cambray,
et les Latins de N. Clemenges ... sur la grande
idsparité de la vie rustique avec la vie de cour.
Genève: Le Mignon, 1614.
[17], 743 p. [9] p.; 12cm.

Spanish, Italian, French and German texts in parallel
columns.
The French translation is by Louis Turquet de
Mayerne.
A reprint of De Tourne's 1605 edition.
Laurenti y Porqueras, Guevara, no. 27; Palau,
110298.
Reel 74, No. 466

GUEVARA, ANTONIO DE, bp., d. 1545?
[Menosprecio de corte y alabanza de aldea. German]
Zwey schöne Tractätlein, deren das eine. De
Molestiis Aulae et Ruris Laude, Dariñen die muheseligkeit
des Hofs võ glucksseligkeit des Landlebens angezeiget,
vnd mit denckwürdigen Exempeln erwiesen wird, Wie viel
herrlicher, nützlicher, sicherer, vnd erspriesslicher
das Privatleben vor dem Hofleben sey, vnd was für
gefährligkeiten dieses vor jenem habe. Anfangs durch
Herrn Antonium de Guevara (sic) Bischofn zu Mondonedo,
vnd Weyland Keyser Caroli 5 Historico, in Hispanischer
Sprach beschrieben, Das Andere, De Convivijs &
Compotationibus Von Gastereyen vnd zutrincken, In
welchem beschrieben werden, die antiquiteten, gebräuche,
effect, vnd Wirckungen, der gasterreyen, vnd des
zutrinckens &c. Alles mit schönen lustiges Historien,
vnd kurtzweiligen reden gezieret vnd eingeführet,
Durch: Aegidium Albertinum Fürstl. Durchl. in Beyern
Hofraths (sic) Secretarium verdeutzscht, vnd in Druck
gegeben. Bey Henning Grossen dem Jüngern Buchhändelern
in Leipzig zufinden, Vnd Gedruckt im Jahr, 1619.
2 v. in 1 ([17], 271 p.; 192, [6] p.)

Colophon: "Gedruckt zu Hall in Sachsen. Bey Peter
Schmidt, jn Verlegung Henning Grossen, des Jegern
Buchhändlern in Leiptzig anno M.DC.XIX."
Not in Palau's Manual ...Laurenti y Porqueras,
Guevara, no. 19.
Reel 74, No. 463

GUEVARA, ANTONIO DE, bp., d. 1545?
Las obras del illustre señor don Antonio de
gueuara obispo de Mondoñedo predicador y chronista
y del consejo de su Magestad ... Primeramente: vn
solenne prologo y argumento. En q̃ el auctor toca
muchas hystorias y notables auisos ... Itẽ vna
decada de Cesares: es a saber las vidas de diez
Emperadores Romanos q̃ imperaron enlos tiempos
del buen Marco aurelio ... Item vn libro de Auiso
de priuados y doctrina d' cortesanos. Enel q̃l se
cõtiene de lo q̃ el p̃uado se ha de guardar y el
cortesano ha d' hazer. Itẽ vn libro del Menosprecio
dela corte y alabanca dela aldea. Enel q̃l cõ pocas
palabras se tocã muchas y muy delicadas doctrinas.
Item vn libro delos inuentores del marear y de
sesenta trabajos que ay en las galeras. Obra digna
de saber y graciosa de leer ... Va toda la obra al
estilo y romãce d'Marco aurelio: porque el auctor
es todo vno. Valladolid: Juan de Villaquiran,
1539.
4 pts. in 1 ([5], CXXXIII l.)

Foulche-Delbosc, no. 18; Heredia, no. 2815 and
no. 3743; Laurenti y Porqueras, Guevara, no. 1; Salvá,
II, 2273; Palau, 110072; Ticknor, p. 164.
Reel 74, No. 467

GUEVARA, ANTONIO DE, bp., d. 1545?
Las obras del illustre señor don Antonio de gueuara
obispo de Mondoñedo predicador y chronista y del
consejo de su Magestad ... Primeramente: vn solenne
prologo y argumento. En q̃ el auctor toca muchas
hystorias y notables auisos ... Itẽ vna decada de
Cesares: es a saber las vidas de diez Emperadores
Romanos q̃ imperaron enlos tiempos del buen Marco
aurelio ... Item vn libro de Auiso de priuados y
doctrina d' cortesanos. Enel q̃l se cõtiene de lo q̃
el p̃uado se ha de guardar y el cortesano ha d' hazer.
Itẽ vn libro del Menosprecio dela corte y alabanca
dela aldea. Enel q̃l cõ pocas palabras se tocã muchas
y muy delicadas doctrinas. Item vn libro delos
inuentores del marear y de sesenta trabajos que ay en
las galeras. Obra digna de saber y graciosa de leer ...
Va toda la obra al estilo y romãce d'Marco aurelio:
porque el auctor es todo vno. Valladolid: Juan de
Villaquiran, 1545.
[5], CCXIIII l.; 30cm.

Alcocer, 118; Foulché-Delbosc, no. 37; Laurenti y
Porqueras, Guevara, no. 2; Palau, 110073; Penney, p.
248; Ticknor, p. 164.
Reel 74, No. 471

GUEVARA, ANTONIO DE, bp., d. 1545?
[Las obras del illustre señor don Antonio de
Gueuara... German]
Antonii De Guevara, Barfusser Ordens, Bischoffens
zu Mondonedo, Keysers Caroli V. Hoffpredigers,
Canonisten, Chronisten vnd Raths. Opera Omnia
Historico-Politica. I. Güldene Sendschreiben. 2.
Fürstliche Weckyhr vnd Lüstgarten. 3. Missbrauch
dess = Hoffs vnnd Lob dess LandtsLeben. 4. Der
wolgezierte Hoffmann, oder Hoffschul. 5. Von
Gastereyen vnd Zutrincken. In welchen viel schöne
subtile Politische vnnd Moralische Discursen,
(sonderlich wie sich Fürsten vnd Herren im Regiment,
wie dann auch ihm Ehestandt zuverhalten) auch artliche
Historien, herrliche Antiquitäten, Gebräuch Effecten,
vnd Würckungen des Gastereyen, wie dann auch di
Mühseligkeit dess Hoff=Lebens vnnd Glückseligkeit dess
LandsLeben, neben andern Exemplarischen Sachen, vnd
vortrefflichen Geistlichen vnd Weltlichen Exempeln
begriffen. In Drey Theil abgetheilt. Allen vnd
Jeglichen, hohen vnd niedern, Geistlichen vnd
Weltlichen Standts Personen sehr kurtzweillig,
annehmlich vnd mutzlich zu lesen. Durch Herrn Aegidium
Albertinum. Fürstl: Durchl: in Bayrn Hoffraths
Secretarium, auss der Hispanischen in die Teutsche
Sprach auffs fleissigste versetzt. An jetzo auffs
new vbersehen: zu mehrerm Verstand vnd Nachrichtung
von vnzahlbaren frembden (sic) vnd in gemeiner Sprach
vnannemblichen Worten corrigirt, verbessert, vnd mit
Marginalien, sampt einem vollkömlichen Register
gemehret. Gedruckt zu Franckfurt am Mayn: bey Matthaeo
Kempffern, In Verlegung Johann Gottfried Schönwetter,
1644-1645.
3 pts. in 1 v. ([14], 750 p.; 388 p.; 207); 25cm.

Each part has special title page:
[Pt. II:] Herrn Antonii de Gueuara Bischoffen zu
Mondonedo Fürstlicher Lüstgardten, Weckvher vnd
Dischredt, Ander theill. Durch Aegidium Albertinum
Chür Fürstl: Durchl: in Beyern Hoffraths Secretarium
der Deutscht.
[Pt. III:] Drey schöne Tractätlein, deren Das Eine
De Molestiis Aulae, & Ruris Laude. Das ist: Missbrauch
dess Hoff=lebens. Das Ander: Der rechte wolgezierte
Hoff=Mann, oder Hoff=Schul genannt. Das Dritte: De
Conviviis & Comporationibus, von Gastereyen vnd
Zutrincken. Dritter Theyl. Durch Herrn Antonium De
Guevara In Hispanischer Sprach baschrieben. Jetzund
aber durch Aegidium Albertinum Fürstl. Durchl, in
Bayern Hoffraths Secretarium in Teutsche Spraach
versetzt.

GUEVARA (Cont'd)
  German translation by Aegidium Albertinum.
  [Half-title:] Herrn Antonii de Guevara Bischoffen
zu Mondonedo, Opera Politica et Historica. Darinnen
begriffen, 1. Güldene Sendschreiben, 2. Fürstliche
Weckvhr vnd Lustgarten, 3. Fürstliche Dischredt. 4.
Hoffssmühseligkeit vnd Glücke: dess Landsleben 5.
Der wohlgezierte Hoffmann oder Hoffschül. Alle durch
Aegidium Albertinum verteutscht in Dreytheill abetheilt
Vnd zum Erstenmahl in truck gegeben, Erster theill.
In verlegung Johann Gottfriedt Schönwettere Anno 1644.
  Laurenti y Porqueras, Guevara, no. 20.
Reels 74 & 75, No. 472

GUEVARA, ANTONIO DE, bp., d. 1545?
  Oratorio de religiosos y exercicio de virtuosos:
compuesto por el Illustre señor dõ Antonio de Gueuara
obispo de mondoñedo predicador chronista y del consejo
d' l Emperador y rey nuestro señor... [Valladolid:
J. de Villaquira, 1544]
  [8], cx *l*.; 27cm.

  Colophon: Aquí se acaba el libro llamado Oratorio
de religiosos y exercicio de virtuosos compuesto por
el Illustre señor don Antonio de Guevara obispo de
Mondoñedo predicador chronista y del consejo de su
Magestad: obra que es de muy gran doctrina y de muy
alto estilo. Fue impressa en la muy noble villa de
valladolid: por industria del honrrado varon Juan de
villaquirã impressor de libros: a nueue dias de marco.
Año de mil y quinientos y quarenta y cinco.
  Alcocer, 116; Foulché-Delbosc, no. 35; Laurenti
y Porqueras, Guevara, no. 7, Palau, 110337; Penney,
p. 248; Ticknor, p. 165.
Reel 75, No. 473

GUEVARA, ANTONIO DE, bp., d. 1545?
  Oratorio de religiosos y exercicio de virtuosos:
compuesto por el Illustre señor dõ Antonio de Gueuara
obispo de mondoñedo predicador chronista y del consejo
d' l Emperador y rey nuestro señor... Valladolid:
Por industria del honrrado varon Juan de Villaquiran,
1546.
  [8], cx *l*.; 27cm.

  Title-page wanting; title supplied from Brit. Mus.
Cat. of Print. Books.
  Error in binding: leaves 97-103 duplicated.
  Mutilated: text on leaves 108 and 109 and lower
margins damaged.
  Leaf 110 [colophon] wanting.
  Alcocer, 116; Laurenti y Porqueras, Guevara, no. 8;
Palau, 110338.
Reel 75, No. 474

GUEVARA, ANTONIO DE, bp., d. 1545?
  Oratorio de religiosos y exercicio de virtuosos:
compuesto por el Illustre señor dõ Antonio de Gueuara
obispo de mondoñedo predicador chronista y del consejo
d' l Emperador y rey nuestro señor... [Valladolid:
Sebastian Martinez, criado del auctor, a la parrochia
de Sant Andres. Acabose viernes a veinte y dos de
agosto de M. D. L. 1550].
  cxxviii *l.*; 26cm.

  Lacks leaves 26, 27.
  Adams, I, no. 1497; Foulché-Delbosc, no. 50;
Laurenti y Porqueras, Guevara, no. 9; Palau, 110339.
Reel 75, No. 475

GUEVARA, ANTONIO DE, bp., d. 1545?
  [Relox de principes. English]
  The diall of princes ... Englysshed out of Frenche,
by Thomas North, seconde sonne of the Lorde North.
London: Imprinted by J. Waylande, 1557.
  268 *l.*; 29cm.

  English translation by Thomas North.
  Imperfect: title-page border wanting; title-page
inlaid.
  Allison, p. 88-89, no. 28; Laurenti y Porqueras,
Guevara, no. 32; Palau, 110189.
No. 452: Not Available

GUEVARA, ANTONIO DE, bp., d. 1545?
  [Relox de principes. English]
  The Dial of Princes, Compiled by ... Don Antony of
Guevara now newly reuised with a fourth booke entituled
The fauored courtier. London, R. Tottil and Thomas
Marshe, 1568.
  20 p. *l.*, 165 numb. *l.*, 1 *l.*, 173 numb. *l.*, 24 *l.*;
25.5cm.

  Allison, p. 89, no. 38.1; Laurenti y Porqueras,
Guevara, no. 33; Palau, 110189; Ticknor, p. 164.
No. 453: Not Available

GUEVARA, ANTONIO DE, bp., d. 1545?
  [Relox de Principes. English]
  The Diall of princes: containing the golden and
famovs booke of Marcvs Avrelivs, sometime emperour of
Rome ... Written by the Reuerend Father in God, Don
... , Lord Bishop of Gaudix ... First translated out
of French by Thomas North ... and lately reperused,
and corrected from many grosse imperfections. With
addition of a fourth booke, stiled by the name of
The fauoured courtier. London: Imprinted by Bernard
Alsop, dwelling by Saint Annes church neere Aldersgate,
1619.
  [46], 768 (i.e. 752) p.; 29cm.

  English translation by Thomas North.
  Allison, p. 89, no. 28.3; Laurenti y Porqueras,
Guevara, no. 34; Pollard and Redgrave, no. 12430.
No. 451: Not Available

GUEVARA, ANTONIO DE, bp., d. 1545?
  [Relox de Principes. Latin]
  Horologium principum sive de vita M. Aurelli
imp. libri III ... Editio quarta. Lipsiae, Typis &
sumptibus Henningi grosii Senioris, 1615.
  [72], 695, [27] p.; 34cm.

  Latin translation by John Wanckell.
  Laurenti y Porqueras, Guevara, no. 55; Palau,
vol. 6, p. 447.
Reel 73, No. 454

GUEVARA, ANTONIO DE, bp., d. 1545?
  Vidas De Los Diez Emperadores Romanos, que imperarõ
en los tiempos de Marco Aurelio. Compuestas por el
ilvstris Señor D. Antonio de Gueuara, Obispo de
Mondoñedo, Predicador, y Chronista, y del Consejo de
su Magestad Cesarea. Madrid: Por M. de Espinosa,
a costa de G. Rodriguez, Mercader de libros, 1669.
  [25], [372] p.; 21cm.

  Imperfect: p. 367-372 wanting.
  Original title: Década de las vidas de los diez
Césares.
  Printed in double columns.
  Foulché-Delbosc, no. 120; Laurenti y Porqueras,
Guevara, no. 16; Palau, 110331.
Reel 75, No. 477

GUEVARA, ANTONIO DE, bp., d. 1545?
La Primera parte del libro llamado Mōte caluario. Cōpuesto por ... Trata el auctor en este libro todos los mysterios del monte caluario desde que christo fue a muerte codennado por pilato hasta que por Joseph y nicodemus fue metido en el sepulcro. Trae el auctor en este libro muchas prophecias ... La segūda parte deste libro que tracta delas siete palabras que Christo dixo en la cruz se queda imprimiendo. Valladolid: Sebastian Martinez, 1546.
[8], CXVIII Z.; 26cm.

Printed in double columns.
Foulché-Delbosc, no. 41; Laurenti y Porqueras, Guevara, no. 10; Palau, 110362.
Reel 75, No. 476

GUEVARA, ANTONIO DE, bp., d. 1545?
A chronicle, conteyning the liues of tenne Emperours of Rome. Wherin are discouered, their beginnings, proceedings, and endings, worthie to be read, marked, and remembred (sic). Wherin are also conteyned lawes of speciall profite and policie, sentences of singular shortnesse and sweetenesse, orations of great grauitie and wisedome, letters of rare learning and eloquence examples of vices carefully to be auoyded, and notable paternes of vertue fruitfull to be followed. Compiled by the most famous Syr Anthonie of Gueuara, Bishop of Mondonnedo ... and translated out of Spanish into English, by ... Hereunto is also annexed a table, recapitulating such particularities, as are in this booke mentioned. London: Ralph Newberrie dwelling in Fleetestrete, 1577.
[8], 484, [10] p.

English translation by Edward Hellowes.
Allison, p. 85, no. 19; Laurenti y Porqueras, Guevare, no. 39; Palau, 110335; Pollard and Redgrave, no. 12426.
Reel 75, No. 478

GUICCIARDINI, FRANCESCO see FURIO CERIOL, FADRIQUE.

GULIELMUS, JANUS.
Iani Gvlielmii Verisimilivm Libri Tres. Antverpiae: Ex officina Christophori Plantini, 1582.
[16], 108, [3] p.

Bound in: Sánchez De Las Brozas, Francisco: Paradoxa ..., 1582.
Reel 166, No. 1086

GUTIÉRREZ DE LOS RÍOS, GASPAR, fl. 1600.
Noticia general para la estimacion de las artes, y de la manera en qve se conocen las liberales de las que son mecanicas y seruiles, con vna exortacion a la honra de la virtvd y del trabajo contra los ociosos, y otras particulares para las personas de todos estados. Por el L. ... Dirigido a don Francisco Gomez de Sandoual y Rojas, duque de Lerma ... Madrid: Por Pedro Madrigal, 1600.
[32], 340, [8] p.; 22cm.

Imperfect: last leaf wanting.
Penney, p. 250.
Reel 75, No. 479

GUZMÁN, JUAN DE, 16th cent.
Primera parte de la rhetorica de Ioan de Guzman, diuidida en catorze combites de oradores: donde se trata el modo que se deue guardar en saber seguir vn concepto por sus partes, en qualquiera platica, razonamiento, o sermon, en el genero de liberatiuo, de todo lo qual se pone la theorica y pratica... Alcala de Henares: Impresso en casa de I. Yñiguez de Lequerica, 1589.
[8], 291, [5] Z.; 15cm.

No more published.
Penney, p. 251; Salvá, II, 2281.
Reel 75, No. 480

H

HECATOM. Phila Di Messer Leon Battista Alberto
Firentino (sic) ne la quale ne insegna l'ingeniosa
arte d'Amore, Mostrandone il perito modo d'amare,
oue di sempij, et rozzi, saggi, et gentili ne fa
divenire. In Venetia: n.p., 1545.
16 *l*.; 16cm.

Reel 54, No. 319

HELMESIUS, HENRICUM.
Colymata Sive Impedimenta Christianae Vitae,
Qvibvs Hodie Mvlto Maxima Christifidelium pars
praepeditur, quo minus ad Euangelicae integritatis
apicem peruaeniat. Ex sacris literis per F. Henricum
Helmesium Germipolitanum, accuratissime concinnata.
Horum Elenchum uersa pagella indicabit. Coloniae:
Apud Isapore Gennepaeii, 1554.
[85] *l*.

Bound in: Pérez De Ayala, Martín: Martini
Peresii Aiala. Episcopi Gvidixiensis ..., 1554.
Reel 141, No. 897

HEREDIA, PAULUS DE (translator) see NECHONIAH, BEN
HA-KANAH, Rabbi.

HERNÁNDEZ, FRANCISCO, 1514-1578.
Nova Plantarvm, Animalivm Et Mineralivm Mexicanorvm
Historia A Francisco Hernandez Medico In Indijs
praestantissimo primum compilata, De In A Nardo
Antonio Reccho In Volymen Digesta, A IO Terentio, Io
Fabro, Et Fabio Colvmna Lynceis Notis, & additionibus
longe doctissimis illustrata, Cui demum accessere
Aliqvot Ex Principis Federici Caesii Frontispiciis
Theatri Naturalis Phytosophicae Tabulae Vna cum
quamplurimis Iconibus, ad octigentas, quibus singula
contemplanda graphice exhibentur. Romae: Sumptibus
Blasij Deuersini, & Zanobij Masotti Bibliopolarum,
1651.
[20], 950, [22], 90, [6] p., illus.; 33cm.

Added title-page, engraved: Rervm Medicarvm Novae-
Hispaniae Thesavrvs; sev, Plantarvm Animalivm
Mineralivm Mexicanorvm Historia ...
Imperfect: Added title-page and six(?) prelim.
leaves wanting.
Lacks also the Historiae Animalivm Liber (90, [6]
p. at end).
Eight pages, numbered [457]-464 are inserted after
p. 464 and partially duplicate p. 460-464.
Graesse, III, p. 252; Palau, 113538.
Reel 76, No. 481

HERNÁNDEZ BLASCO, FRANCISCO.
Vniversal Redencion, Passion, Mverte y Resvrreccion
de nuestro Redentor Iesu Christo, y angustias de su
santissima Madre, segun los quatro Euangelistas, con
muy deuotas contemplaciones. Compvesto Por Francisco
Hernandez Blasco clerigo Presbitero, natural del
lugar de Sonseca, jurisdicion de la Imperial Ciudad
de Toledo. Aora Nvevamente Corregido y emendado.
Alcala: En casa de Iuan Gracian que sea en gloria,
1612.
[25], 413, [15] p.; 21cm.

Palau, 113655.
Reel 76, No. 482

HERRERA, FERNANDO DE, 1534-1597.
Versos De Fernando De Herrera. Emendados I
Divididos Por El En Tres Libros. A Don Gaspar De
Gvzman, Conde de Olivares, Gentilombre de la Camara
del Principe nuestro Señor, Alcaide de los Alcacares
Reales de Sevilla, i Comendador de Bivoras en la
Orden de Calatrava. Sevilla: Por Gabriel Ramos
Vejarano, 1619.
[29],`447, [20] p.: port.; 21cm.

Escudero, 1189; Goldsmith, p. 82, no. 35; Jerez,
p. 50; Palau, 114060; Penney, p. 257; Salvá, I, 668;
Ticknor, p. 171.
Reel 76, No. 483

HERRARA Y SOTOMAYOR, JACINTO DE, fl. 1644.
Iornada que su Magestad hizo a la Andalvzia.
[Madrid: En la Imprenta Real, 1624.]
6 *l*.; 33cm.

Bound with the following items:
1. Escritura otorgada el año de 1625 entre S. M.
y el Rector del Colegio Imperial de la Compañia de
Jesus de esta Corte, en razon de la fundacion Patronazgo
Real y Dotacion perpetua de los estudios generales,
1625. 5 printed *l*.
2. Memorial que el Embajador de las Provincias
Unidas del Pais Baxo, sobre unirse la 'Armada Holandesa
y Española contra los corsarios africanos. Madrid,
1661. 7 printed *l*.
3. Memorial que el Embajador de Holanda dió a
S. M. año 1661 sobre lo que contiene el papel
antecedente. Madrid, 1661. 2 printed *l*.
4. Artículo de la renovación de las treguas entre
los muy altas, y poderolos senores Estados Generales,
por sus Camislarios y el Reynado de la Ciudad de
Argel. [Argel], 1662. 1 printed *l*.
5. Tratado de paz entre esta corona y la de Francia
ajustado por el Exe^mo· Sr. D. Luis Mendez de Haro y
Guzman, ... Conde de Olivares ... y por el Sr.
Cardenal Julio Mazarini. Madrid: Domingo Garcia
Morras, 1660. 32 printed *l*.
6. Discurso en que se representa a el Rey
Christianissimo de Francia de romper la guerra con
España. 1630?. 4 manuscript *l*.
7. Memorial que las Santas Iglesias de España
dieron al Sr. Rey D. Carlos II por Junio de 1630,
sobre la distribución del Subsidio y excusado y
demás contribuciones y respuestas de S. M. S. i
principios del siglo XVII. 13 manuscript *l*.
8. Copia de un papel francés que se halló entre
otros reservados de la Reyna Doña María Luisa de
Borbón, dándole documentos del modo de gobernarse
con su marido el rey Catolico D. Carlos II ...
10 manuscript *l*.
9. Copia de papel que el Obispo de Solsona
formó el año 1634 en cumplimiento de el Rey en la
forma de remediar dos desordenes de la Monarchia
y conseguir su remedio. 20 manuscript *l*.
10. Respuesta que un gentilhombre español retirado
de la Corte a un Ministro del Consejo de Estado sobre
la sucesión de la Monarchía de España traducida de
la lengua portuguesa en que se hace presente las
conveniencias y razones que hay para elegir al Rey
de Portugal. 20 manuscript *l*.
11. Discurso político de un gentilhombre veneciano
sobre la sucesión de la Monarchia de España y de la
Justicia y conveniencias que concurren en que sea
preferido al Principe Fernando de Baviera. 14
manuscript *l*.

12. Representación del infeliz estado de la Monarchia de España y medio de que pende su repaso se trata de que conviene elegir para la sucesión al Duque de Anjou. 9 manuscript *l*.

13. Tratado de repartación de la Monarchia de España entre el Rey Cristianissimo y el Rey de Inglaterra y Estados Generales de Holanda. 6 manuscript *l*.

14. Voto del Marques de Fresno sobre la sucession de la Monarchia de España. 13 manuscript *l*.

15. Reflexión al voto del Marqués de Fresno sobre la sucesión a estos reinos de la Francia. 25 manuscript *l*.

16. Revocación que el Rey N. S. D. Carlos II que esta gloria hizo el 2 de Octubre de 1700 al Decreto que dio al Conde de Oropesa el 8 de Septiembre de 1638. 4 manuscript *l*.

17. Copia de tres cartas escritas por la Junta de Gobierno de la Monarchia de España al Serenissimo Rey de Francia Luis XIV. 8 manuscript *l*.

18. Copia de una carta en que se refieren las circunstancias que concurrieron en la exaltación de Clemente XI. 2 manuscript *l*.

19. Copia de una carta del Rey de Francia escrita a su Embajador para que manifestara al Cardenal Portocarrero la estimacion con quedaba de lo obrado en la eleccion de su nieto. 1 manuscript *l*.

20. División de las facciones de los Cardenales en el Conclave de 1700 enque fue exaltado a la Tiara Clemente XI. 4 manuscript *l*.

21. Instrucción de lo que debe saber y cómo ha de obrar un perfecto cortesano. 11 manuscript *l*.

22. Advertencias para saberse portar una persona provecta en un Gobierno de Indias. 6 manuscript *l*.

23. Copia de consulta hecha por la Junta de Medios, año 1694. 10 manuscript *l*.

24. Memorial de D. Juan Duque de Estra sobre Arbitrios. 13 manuscript *l*.

25. Cédula de S. M. dando la forma con que el Consejo de la Cámara ha de obrar en lo que le toca.

26. Papel al Conde Duque sobre la baja de la moneda. - Decreto de remisión al Consejo de Castilla con otro en que pormenor daba la noticia del estado de las cosas de la Monarchia. - Copia de consulta que la Cámara dio el 11 de Octubre de 1623. - Copia de consulta que el Conde Duque hizo a S. M. en el año 1621, excusándose de recibir unos escritos que le presentó el Obispo de Catania. - Consulta que el Conde Duque hizo a S. M. el año 1627 en razon de cómo y cuándo se han de nombrar los tributos a los vasallos cuanto deben y cómo se ha de distribuir. - Receta para agua de canela que inventó un Bachiller de Amor. - Receta de chocolate que se ha de servir despues del agua de canela compuesta por un Indio esclavo de Amor. 48 manuscript *l*.

27. Discurso y Plática entre cierto Ministro favorecido y un veinte y cuatro sobre la concesión de millones. 14 manuscript *l*.

28. Información y plática que el año de 1626 hicieron al Rey algunos veinte y cuatro sobre la contradicción de la venta de vassallos. 12 manuscript *l*.

29. Junta de las aves, en particular del Buho Gallego y el Tordo Vizcaino. 18 manuscript *l*.

30. Tordo Vizcaino. 27 manuscript *l*.

31. Memorial que la provincia de Guipúzcoa dio a S.M. para que se recogiese el Grál dado al Conde Duque de Adelantado Mayor de ella. 11 manuscript *l*.

32. Elogio a la Provincia de Guipúzcoa por Miguel de Avendaño. 11 manuscript *l*.

33. Fray Juan de la Anunciacion ... 4 manuscript *l*.

Palau, 114276 (List only printed folios 1-6).
Reel 77, No. 484

HERRERA Y TORDESILLAS, ANTONIO DE, 1559-1625.
Historia De Antonio De Herrera, Criado De su Magestad, y su Coronista mayor de las Indias, de los sucessos de Francia, desde el año de 1585 que començo la liga Catolica, hasta en fin del año 1594. Dirigida Al Altissimo Y Serenissimo Principe Don Felipe nuestro señor. Madrid: Por Lorenço de Ayala, 1588.
[8], 353, [19] p.; 19cm.

Pagination errors throughout.
Palau, 114284.
Reel 77, No. 485

HERRERA Y TORDESILLAS, ANTONIO DE, 1559-1625.
Tratado, Relación Y Discvrso Historico De Los nouimientos de Aragon. Svcedidos En Los años de mil y quinientos y nouenta y dos: y de su origen y principio, hasta que la Md de D. Felipe II el Prudente Rey nuestro Señor compuso y quieto las cosas de aquel Reyno. Madrid: En la Imprenta Real, 1612.
[4], 140 p.; 19cm.

Palau, 114320; Ticknor, p. 171.
Reel 77, No. 486

HIERONYMUS, Saint.
[Epistolae. Spanish]
Epistolas selectas de S. Jerónimo traducidas de latin en lengua castellana por el Licenciado Francisco López Cuesta dirigidas al Principe don Felipe, nuestro Señor, cvarto deste nombre Año M.DC.XVII. Madrid: Por Ivan de la Cvesta, 1617.
448 p.; 14cm.

Spanish translation by Francisco Lopez Cuesta.
Imperfect: title-page and an unknown number of pages wanting at the beginning and the end.
Title taken from ms. title-page in the volume.
Palau, 292188.
No. 584: Not Available

HIERONYMUS, Saint.
[Epistolae. Spanish]
Epistolas Selectas de San Jerónimo Traducidas de Latin en Lengua Castellana por el Licenciado Francisco López Cuesta. Dirigidas al Principe don Felipe, nuestro Señor, cuarto deste nombre. [n.p.], 1617.
[18], 448 p.; 16cm.

Imperfect: title-page and an unknown number of pages wanting at the beginning and the end; title-taken from ms. title - page in the volume.
Probably published in Madrid by Juan de la Cuesta.
Cf. Palau, vol. 19, no. 292188.
Spanish translation by Francisco López Cuesta.
Reel 77, No. 487

HOLYWOOD, JOHN see SACRO BOSCO, JOANNES.

HOMER
[Odyssey. Spanish]
La Vlyxea de Homero, Repartida en XIII. Libros. Tradvzida de Griego en Romance Qastellano por el Señor ... Imprimióse en Venetia: En casade Gabriel Giolíto de Ferrariis, y svs hermanos, 1553.
209, [1] *l*.; 15cm.

HOMER (Cont'd)
Spanish translation by Gonzalo Pérez.
Printer's device on title-page and a variant
form of the device on last verso above colophon;
initials; head-pieces; Italic type.
Bound in old red morocco; gold tooled.
Ex libris: Jacobi P. R. Lyell.
Adams, I, no. 799; Graesse, III, p. 340; Palau,
115892; Penney, p. 262; Salvá, I, 673; Short-Title,
II, p. 133; Ticknor, p. 174.
Reel 77, No. 488

HOMER
[Odyssey. Spanish]
La Vlyxea De Homero, Tradvzida De Griego en lengua
Castellana por el Secretario Goncalo Perez. Impressa
en la insigne ciudad de Aneurs: en casa de Iuan
Steelsio, 1556.
[8], 440 *l*.; 17cm.

Spanish translation by Gonzalo Pérez.
Pagination errors throughout.
Adams, I, no. 800; Graesse, III, p. 340; Heredia,
no. 1524; Palau, 6, 115893; Peeters-Fontainas,
Impressions, I, no. 604; Salvá, I, 674; Ticknor, p.
174.
Reel 77, No. 489

HORATIUS FLACCUS, QUINTUS.
[Opera. Spanish]
G. Horacio Flacco, Poeta Lyrico latino. Sus
Obras con la Declaracion Magistral en Lengua Castellana.
Por el Doctor ... Granada: Por Sebastian de Mena, A
costa de Iuan Diez, 1599.
[10], 330, [8] *l*.; 29cm.

Spanish translation by Juan Villen de Biedma.
Latin and Spanish.
Pagination errors throughout.
Palau, 116030; Penney, p. 262; Salvá, I, 676.
Reel 78, No. 490

HORATIUS FLACCUS, QUINTUS.
[Opera. Spanish]
Horacio Español, Esto Es, Obras, de Quinto Horacio
Flacco, Tradvcidas en Prosa Española e Illvstradas
con Argumentos, Epitomes, y Notas en el mismo idioma.
Parte Primera. Poesia liricas. Por el R. P. Urbano
Campos. Van al fin la declaracion de las especies
de los Versos, y Odas, y tres Indices, el primero
Alfabetico de las Odas, el segundo Cosmografico,
y el tercero de las cosas notables, que se explican
en las Notas. Barcelona: Por Antonio Lacavalleria,
1699.
[10], 364, [16] p.; 16cm.

Spanish translation by Urbano Campos.
Palau, 116032.
Reel 78, No. 491

HOROZCO SEBASTIÁN DE COVARRUBIUS see COVARRUBIAS
HOROZCO, SEBASTIÁN DE.

HOROZCO Y COVARRUBIAS, JUAN DE, fl. 1589-1608.
Emblemas Morales De Don Ivan Horozco y Couarruuias
Arcediano de Cuellar en la santa Yglesia de Segouia.
Dedicadas A La Bvena memoria del Presidente Don Diego
de Couarruuias y Leyua su tio. Segouia: Impresso por
Iuan de la Cuesta, 1589.
3 v. in 1 ([1], 101, [1]p.; [8], 101 p.; [1], 103-104
(i.e. 204), 271 p.,): ill.; 20cm.

HOROZCO Y COVARRUBIAS (Cont'd)
At end of Book 1: "Fin Del Libro Primero de las
Emblemas Morales."
Each book has special title page:
[Book II:] Libro Segvndo De Las Emblemas Morales.
Hecho por Don Iuan de Horozco y Couarruuias, Arcediano
de Cuellar en la santa Yglesia de Segouia.
At end: "Fin del Libro segundo de las Emblemas
Morales. Hecho por don Iuan Horozco y Couarruuias,
arcediano de Cuellar, en la Yglesia de Segouia."
[Book III:] Libro Tercero de las Emblemas Morales.
Recho por Dõ Iuan de Horozco y Couarruuias, Arcediano
de Cuellar, en la santa Yglesia de Segouia.
Pagination errors throughout.
1st. edition. In three books, the first a general
dissertation, the second and third containing fifty
emblems each.
Illustrations: one hundred and two small woodcuts,
comprising arms (on title-page and elsewhere) and
emblem of the dedicatee (Diego de Covarrubias y
Leyva) and two groups of fifty emblems, each numbered
I - L.
Adams, I, no. 992; Baeza, no. 3; HC:346/1268;
Palau, 116236; Penney, p. 263; Doublet, p. 71;
Graesse, III, p. 372; Salvá, II, 2080.
Reel 78, No. 492

HOROZCO Y COVARRUBIAS, JUAN DE, fl. 1589-1608.
Emblemas Morales De Don Ivan Horozco y Couarruuias
Arcediano de Cuellar en la santa Yglesia de Segouia.
Dedicadas A La Bvena memoria del Presidente Don Diego
de Couarruuias y Leyua su tio. Caragoca: Por Alonso
Rodriguez, 1604.
88, [7], 201, [16] *l*.; 20cm.

Bonilla device with his mark on the title-page and
on verso of the first signature [A⁸] and [Cc⁸]; the
mark in the ornamental borders of all the emblems.
Doublet, p. 71; Graesse, III, p. 372; Jiménez
Catalán, 29; Palau, 116237; Penney, p. 263.
Reel 78, No. 493

HOROZCO Y COVARRUBIAS, JUAN DE, fl. 1589-1608.
Paradoxas Christianas Contra las falsas opiniones
del mundo. Hechas por Don Iuan de Horozco y
Couarruuias Arcediano de Cuellar en la Sancta Yglesia
de Segouia. Segouia: Por Marcos de Ortega, 1592.
[8], 231, [12] *l*.; 20cm.

Errata leaf mounted inside front cover.
"Tassa" (first leaf) inserted at end.
Adams, I, no. 995; Palau, 116240.
Reel 78, No. 494

HOROZCO Y COVARRUBIAS, JUAN DE, fl. 1589-1608.
Tratado De La Verdadera Y Falsa Prophecia. Hecho
por Don Iuan de Horozco y Couarruuias Arcediano de
Cuellar en la santa Yglesia de Segouia. Segouia: Por
Iuan de la Cuesta, 1588.
[8], 183 *l*.; 20cm.

Leaves printed on both sides.
Errors in foliation: Leaves 13, 53, 54, 63, 135,
176 numbered 11, 55, 56, 64, 315, 174 respectively.
Colophon: "En Segovia Por Iuan de la Cuesta Año.
1588."
Graesse, III, p. 372; Palau, 116235; Salvá, II,
3914; Ticknor, p. 175.
Reel 78, No. 495

HUARTE DE SAN JUAN, JUAN, 16th cent.
  Examen De Ingenios Para Las Sciencias. En el
qual el Lector hallara la manera de su ingenio, para
escoger la sciencia en que mas ha de prouechar: y
la diferencia de habilidades que ay en los hombres:
y el genero de letras y artes que a cada vno responde
en particular. Compuesto por el Doctor Iuan Huarte
de san Iuan. Agora neuuamente emendado por el mismo
Autor, y añadidas muchas cosas curiosas, y prouechosas.
Dirigida a la C.R. M. del Rey don Felipe nuestro
señor, cuyo ingenio se declara, exemplificando las
reglas y preceptos desta doctrina. Medina del Cāpo:
Christoual Lasso y Francisco Garcia, 1603.
    [8], 369, [1] ℓ.; 13cm.

    Pagination errors throughout.
    Jerez, p. 53; Palau; 116490; Penney, p. 264;
Pérez Pastor, no. 258.
Reel 79, No. 496

HUARTE DE SAN JUAN, JUAN, 16th cent.
  [Examen De Ingenios. English]
  Examen de Ingenios. The Examination of mens Wits.
In whicch (sic), by discouering the varietie of
natures, is shewed for what profession each one is
apt, and how far he shall profit therein. By John
Huarte. Translated out of the Spanish tongue by M.
Camillo Camilli. Englished out of his Italian by R.C.
Esquire. Il Vostro Malignare Non Giova Nulla. London:
Printed by Adam Islip for Thomas Man, 1594.
    [16], 333, [2] p.; 18cm.

    English translation by Richard Carew.
    Allison, p. 93, no. 5.1; Pollard and Redgrave,
no. 13893.
Reel 79, No. 500

HUARTE DE SAN JUAN, JUAN, 16th cent.
  [Examen De Ingenios. English]
  Examen de Ingenios. The Examination of mens Wits.
In which, by discouering the varietie of natures,
is shewed for what profession each one is apt, and
how far he shall profit therein. By John Huarte.
Translated out of the Spanish tongue by M. Camillo
Camilli. Englished out of his Italian by R.C. Esquire.
Il Vostro Malignare Non Giova Nulla. London: Printed
by Adam Islip, 1596.
    [8], 333, [2] p.; 18cm.

    English translation by Richard Carew.
    Allison, p. 93, no. 5.2; Graesse, III, p. 381; Palau,
116522; Pollard and Redgrave, no. 13893.
Reel 79, No. 501

HUARTE DE SAN JUAN, JUAN, 16th cent.
  [Examen De Ingenios. English]
  Examen de Ingenios. The Examination of mens Wits.
In which, by discouering the varietie of natures,
is shewed for what profession each one is apt, and
how far he shall profit therein. By John Huarte.
Translated out of the Spanish tongue by M. Camillo
Camilli. Englished out of his Italian by R.C. Esquire.
Il Vostro Malignare Non Giova Nulla. London: Printed
by Adam Islip, 1604.
    [16], 333, [2] p.; 18cm.

    English translation by Richard Carew.
    Allison, p. 94, no. 5.3; Graesse, III, p. 381;
Palau, 116523; Pollard and Redgrave, no. 13894;
Ticknor, p. 175.
Reel 79, No. 502

HUARTE DE SAN JUAN, JUAN, 16th cent.
  [Examen De Ingenios. English]
  Examen de Ingenios. The Examination of mens Wits. In
which, by discouering the varietie of natures, is
shewed for what profession each one is apt, and how
far he shall profit therein. By Juan Huarte. Translated
out of the Spanish tongue by M. Camillo Camilli.
Englished out of his Italian by R.C. Esquire. Il
Vostro Malignare Non Giova Nulla. London: Printed
by Adam Islip, for Thomas Adams, 1616.
    [16], 333, [2] p.; 18cm.

    English translation by Richard Carew.
    Pagination errors throughout.
    Allison, p. 94, no. 5.4; Graesse, III, p. 381; Palau,
116523.
Reel 79, No. 503

HUARTE DE SAN JUAN, JUAN, 16th cent.
  [Examen de Ingenios. English]
  Examen de Ingenios: Or, The Tryal of Wits.
Discovering The great Difference of Wits among Men,
and what Sort of Learning suits best with each Genius.
Published Originally in Spanish by Doctor Juan
Huartes (sic). And made English from the most Correct
Edition by Mr. Bellamy. Useful for all Fathers,
Masters, Tutors, &c. London: Printed for Richard
Sare, at Grays-Inn-Gate in Holborn, 1698.
    [40], 502, [2] p.; 20cm.

    English translation by Edward Bellamy.
    Pagination errors throughout.
    Allison, p. 94, no. 6; Graesse, III, p. 381; Palau,
116524; Ticknor, p. 175; Wing. H. no. 3205.
Reel 79, No. 504

HUARTE DE SAN JUAN, JUAN, 16th cent.
  [Examen de Ingenios. French]
  L'Examen Des Esprits Pour les Sciences. Où se
montrent les differences des Esprits, qui se trouvent
parmy les hommes, & à quel genre de science un chacun
est propre en particulier. Composé par Jean Huarte,
Medecin Espagnol. Et augmenté de plusieurs additions
nouvelles par l'Auteur selon la derniere impression
d'Espagne. Le tout traduit de l'Espagnol par Francois
Savinien D'Alquie. A Amsterdam: Chez Jean de
Ravestein, 1672.
    [64], 629 p.; 14cm.

    French translation by Francois Savinien d'Alquie.
    Illustrated title-page engraved: L'Examen Des
Esprits. Amsterdam. Chez Jean de Ravestein.
M.DC. LXXII
Reel 79, No. 505

HUARTE DE SAN JUAN, JUAN, 16th cent.
  [Examen De Ingenios. Italian]
  Essame De Gl'Ingegni De Gli Hvomini, Per apprender
le Scienze: Nel quale, scoprendosi la varietà delle
nature, si mostra, a che professione sia atto ciascuno,
& quanto profitto habbia fatto in essa: Di Gio. Hvarte:
Nuouamente tradotto dalla lingua Spagnuola Da M.
Camillo Camilli. Venetia: [n.p.], 1582.
    [16], 367 p.; 16cm.

    Italian translation by Camillo Camilli.
    Dedication signed by Nicolò Manassi.
    Bound in old vellum.
    Adams, I, no. 1116; Graesse, III, p. 381; Palau,
116517; Short-Title, II, p. 142.
Reel 79, No. 497

HUARTE DE SAN JUAN, JUAN, 16th cent.
[Examen De Ingenios. Italian]
Essame De Gl'Ingegni De Gli Hvomini, Per apprender
le Scienze: Nel quale, scoprendosi la varietà delle
nature, si mostra, a che professione sia atto ciascuno,
& quanto profitto habbia fatto in essa: Di Gio.
Hvarte: Nuouamente tradotto dalla lingua Spagnuola
Da M. Camillo Camilli. Venetia: Presso Aldo, 1586.
   [24], 367 p.; 17cm.

   Italian translation by Camillo Camilli.
   Adams, I, no. 1117; Graesse, III, p. 381; Palau,
116518.
Reel 79, No. 498

HUARTE DE SAN JUAN, JUAN, 16th cent.
[Examen De Ingenios. Italian]
Essame De Gl'Ingegni De Gli Hvomini, Per apprender
le Scienze: Nel quale, scoprendosi la varietà delle
nature, si mostra, a che professione sia atto ciascuno,
& quanto profitto habbia fatto in essa: Di Gio.
Hvarte: Nuouamente tradotto dalla lingua Spagnuola
Da M. Camillo Camilli. Venetia: Presso Aldo, 1590.
   14 *l*., 367 p.; 15.5cm.

   Italian translation by Camillo Camilli.
   Dedication signed: Nicolò Manassi.
   Italic type with some Roman.
   Pages 3-4 wanting.
   Adams, I, no. 1118; Graesse, III, p. 381; Palau,
116519.
No. 499: Not Available

HUARTE NAVARRO, JUAN DE DIOS see HUARTE DE SAN JUAN,
   JUAN, 16th cent.

HUELGA, CIPRIANO DE LA, d. 1560.
Magistri Cypriani Monachi Cisterciensis diuinae
Legis interpretis in Complutensi academia Commentaria
In Librvm Beati Iob & in Cantica canticorum Salomonis
regis. Additi sunt duo locupletissimi indices, alter
rerum & verborum: Sacrae scripturae, quae in cis
explicantur. Complvti: Cvm Privilegio Ex officina
Ioannis Iñiguez à Lequerica, 1582.
   [44], 335, [1], 297 (i.e. 315), [1] p.; 29cm.

   Edited by Ignatius Firminus.
   Pagination errors throughout.
   Colophon: "Complvti Excudebat Ioannes Iñiguez à
Lequerica, 1581."
   Palau, 116618.
Reel 80, No. 506

HUERGA, CIPRIANO DE LA see HUELGA, CIPRIANO DE LA.

HUERTA, JERÓNIMO DE (translator) see PLINIUS SECUNDUS,
CAIUS.

HURTADO DE MENDOZA, DIEGO, 1503-1575.
Gverra De Granada. Hecha Por El Rei De España
don Philippe II. nuestro señor contra los Moriscos
de aquel reino, sus rebeldes. Historia escrita en
quatro libros. Por don Diego de Mendoca, del consejo
del Emperador don Carlos V. su Embaxador en Roma, i
Venecia; su Governador i Capitan General en Toscana.

HURTADO DE MENDOZA (Cont'd)
Publicada por el licenciado Luis Tribaldos de Toledo,
Chronista mayor del Rey nuestro señor por las Indias,
residente en la corte de Madrid, i por el dedicada
A don Vicente Noguera, Referendario de ambas Signaturas
de su Sanctidad, del Consejo de las dos Magestades
Cesarea i Catholica, gentilhombre de la Camara del
Archiduque de Austria Leopoldo. En Lisboa: Por
Giraldo de la Viña: 1627.
   [12], 127 *l*., illus.; 21cm.

   Goldsmith, p. 84, no. 114; Graesse, III, p. 395;
Jerez, p. 53; Palau, 117245; Penney, p. 265; Salvá,
II, 2979; Ticknor, p. 178.   .
Reel 80, No. 508

HURTADO DE MENDOZA, DIEGO, 1503-1575.
Obras Del Insigne Cavallero Don Diego De Mendoza,
Embaxador Del Emperador Carlos Qvinto En Roma.
Recopiladas Por Frey. Ivan Diaz Hidalgo, del Habito
de San Iuan, Capellan, y Musico de Camara de su
Magestad. Dirigidas A Don Iñigo Lopez de Mendoza,
Marques de Mondejar, Conde de Tendilla, Señor de la
Prouincia de Almoguera. Madrid: Por Iuan de la
Cuesta, 1610.
   [8], 155 (i.e. 159), [1] *l*.; 19cm.

   Colophon: En Madrid Por Iuan de la Cuesta Año de
1610."
   Numerous errors in foliation.
   Errata: 2 prelim. *l*.
   Goldsmith, p. 84, no. 112; Jerez, p. 52; Palau,
117240; Penney, p. 265; Pérez Pastor, 1096.
Reel 80, No. 507

HUSEL, JOHAN VAN.
Den Grooten Dictionaris eñ Schat van dry talen, Duytsch,
Spaensch, en Fransch met de namē der Rijcken Steden ende
plaesten der plaesten der wereldt. [Rom.:] El Grande
Dictionario Y Thesoro De las tres lenguas Española,
Francesa y Flamenca, con todos los nombres de los Reynos,
Ciudades y lugares del Mundo. Le Grande Dictionaire Et
Tresor De trois langues Francois, Flameng & Espaignol,
auec tous le noms des Royaumes, villes et lieux du Monde.
Th'Antvverpen: By Caes. Ioachim Trognesius, 1640.
   2 pts. [360 *l*.]

   Pages unnumbered.
   Flemish to Spanish, and French to Spanish only.
   Peeters-Fontainas, Impressions, I, no. 301.
Reel 68, No. 414

HUSEL, JOHAN VAN.
Den grooten Dictionaris eñ Schadt Van dry talen
Duytsch Spaensch ende Fransch met de namen der Rijcken
Steden ende plaetsen der Wreldt. [Spanish:] El Grande
Dictionario De las tres lenguas Española, Francesa
y Flamenca, con todos los nombres de los Reynos,
Ciudades, y lugares del Mundo. [French:] Le Grand
Dictionaire Et Tresor De trois langues Francois,
Flameng, & Espaiñol, auec tous les noms des Royaumes
Villes & lieux du Monde. T'Hantvverpen: By Caes.
Ioachim Trognesius, 1646.
   2 vols. in 1 ([145] *l*.; [205] *l*.)

   Frontispiece portraits of linguists: Caesar
Trogney [sius], Gabriel Meurier, Mathias Sasbout,
Cornelius Kilianus, M. Nicold and C. Oudin.
   Peeters-Fontainas, Impressions, I, no. 302.
Reel 80, No. 509

I

IANUA LINGUARUM see BATHE, WILLIAM.

INDEX Librorum Prohibitorum. 1570. Antwerp.
Philippi II. Regis Catholici Edictvm De Librorum
prohibitorum Catalogo abseruando. Antverpiae: Ex
officina Christophori Plantini, 1570.

Index Librorvm Prohibitorvm: Cvm Regvlis Confectis
Per Patres A Tridentina Synodo delectos, Auctoritate
Sanctiss. D.N.Pij. IIII. Pont. Max. comprobatus. Cvm
Appendice in Belgio, ex mandato Regiae Cathol.
Maiestatis confecta. Antverpiae: Ex officina
Christophori Plantini, 1570.
8 l., 108 p., 2 l.; 17cm.

Second edition.
In Italic type, except the "Appendice in belgio"
(p. 81-96) which is in Gothic; and "Pivs papa IIII,
ad perpetvam rei memoriam" (p. 3-5) and "Ex decreto"
(p. 107-108) in Roman.
Edited by Arias Montanus.
Prefixed: Philipp III ... , in French, Dutch and
Latin. Dated: Bruxelles, le 15 iour de feurier, l'an
de grace mil cincq cens soixante neuf.
Heredia, no. 3542; Peeters-Fontainas, Impressions,
I, no. 622; Penney, p. 269.
No. 510: Not Available

INDEX Librorum Prohibitorum. 1586. Lyon.
Index Expvrgatorivs Librorvm Qvi Hoc Secvlo
Prodiervnt, vel doctrinae non sanae erroribus
insperesis, vel inutilis & offensiuae male dicentiae
fellibus permixtis, iuxta sacri Concilij Tridentini
decretum: Philippi II Regis Catholici iussu &
auctoritate, atque Albani Ducis consilio ac
ministerio in Belgia Concinnatus; anno M.D. LXXI.
Nunc primùm in lucem editus, & praefatione auctus ac
regij diplomatis interpretatione. Lugdunensem: Apud Ioannem
Mareschallum, 1586.
[30], 292 p.; 12cm.

Preliminary leaves contain dedicatory epistle
and preface by Franciscus Junius the elder, edict
of Philipp II of July (in Dutch and Latin, Dutch in
italics), some regulations of the Council of Trent,
and the preface of Benedictus Arias Montanus dated
Antvverpiae, cal. jun. 1571.
Adams, I, no. 100; Penney, p. 270; Reusch, vol.
I, p. 424 / 2.
Reel 80, No. 511

INDEX Librorum Prohibitorum. 1597. Lisbon.
Index Librorvm Prohibitorvm, Cvm Regvlis confectis,
per Patres à Tridentino Synodo delectos. Avctoritate
P. II IIII. Primvm Editus, postea vero a Svxto V.
auctus: Et Nvnc Demvm S. D.N. Clementis PP. VIII.
iussu recognitus, & publicatus. Instrvctione Adiecta.
De exequendae prohibitionis, deq̃. sincerè emédandi, &
imprimendi libros ratione. Impressvs De Mandato
Illustriss. & Reuerendiss. Domini D. Antonij de
Matos de Norogna Episcopi Heluensis, Inquisitoris
generalis Lusitaniae, &c. Olisipone: Apud Petrum
Craesbeeck, 1597.
[27], 73 l.; 19cm.

The edict of publication of Antonio de Matos de
Norogna (prelim. leaves [2 - 3]) subscribed: Obispo
Inquisidro General.
Text within ornamental borders.
Anselmo, no. 515; Penney, p. 271.
Reel 80, No. 512

INDEX Librorum Prohibitorum. 1667. Madrid.
Index Librorvm Prohibitorvm Et Expvrgandorvm
Novissimvs. Pro Catholicis Hispaniarvm Regnis Philippi
IV, Regis Cathol. Ill. AC R. D.D. Antonii A Sotomaior
Supremi Praesidis, & In Regnis Hispaniarum, Siciliae,
& Indiarum Generalis Inquisitoris &c. iussu ac studiis,
luculenter & vigilantissimè recognitus: De Consilio
Svpremi Senatvs Inqvisitionis Generalis. Iuxta
Exemplar excusum. Madriti: Ex Typographaeo Didaci
Diaz, Subsignatum LLᵈᵒ Hverta, 1667.
[6], XXXI, [105], 992 p.; 34cm.

Half-title: Indices Librorvm Prohibitorvm Et
Expvrgandorvm Novissimi, Hispanicvs Et Romanvs Anno
M.DC.LXVII (1667).
Bound with: Index Librorum Prohibitorum Alexandrii
VII. Rome: 1667.
Imprints of both are fictitious, the works probably
having been printed at Lyon or Geneva. Cf. Reusch:
Index der Verbotenen Bücher, II, p. 50.
Cf. Reusch: Index der verbotenen Büchar, II, p. 50,
Palau, 118941; Penney, p. 273; Ticknor, p. 181.
Reel 80, No. 513

INDEX Librorum Prohibitorvm. 1667. Rome.
Index Librorvm Prohibitorvm Alexandri VII,
Pontificis Maximi Ivssv Editvs. Actorum XIX. Mvlti
Avtem Ex Eix Qvi Fverant Curiosa sectati, contulerunt
coram omnibus. Iuxta Exemplar excusum. Romae: Ex
Typographia Rev. Cam. Apost. Cum Priuilegio, 1667.
304 p.; 34cm.

Bound with: Index Libroum Prohibitorum. Madriti:
Ex Typographiaeo Didaci Diaz, 1667.
Imprints of both are fictitious, the works probably
having been printed at Lyon or Geneva. Cf. Reusch:
Index der verbotenen Bücher, II, p. 50.
Palau, 118941; Penney, p. 273; Ticknor, p. 181.
Reel 81, No. 514

INFORMACIÓN y plática que el año de 1626 hicieron
al Rey algunos veinte y cuatro sobre la contradicción
de la venta de vassallos.
12 manuscript l.
Bound with: HERRERA Y SOTOMAYOR, JACINTO DE, fl.
1644. Iornada que su Magestad hizo a la Andalvzia.
[Madrid: En la Imprenta Real, 1624].
Palau, 114276 (List only printed folios 1-6).
Reel 77, No. 484.28

INSTRUCCIÓN de lo que debe saber y cómo ha de obrar
un perfecto cortesano.
11 manuscript l
Bound with: HERRERA Y SOTOMAYOR, JACINTO DE, fl.
1644. Iornada que su Magestad hizo a la Andalvzia.
[Madrid: En la Imprenta Real, 1624].
Palau, 114276 (List only printed folios 1-6).
Reel 77, No. 484.21

ISIDORUS, Saint, bp. of Seville, d. 636.
[De Fide Catholica sive liber contra Judaeos].
B. Isidori Episcopi, Theologi uetustissimi, de
Natiuitate Domini, Passione, & Resurrectione, Regno
atq Iuditio, Libri duo. Eiusdem Tractatulus, de
uita & obitu quorūdam utriusq Testamenti Sanctorum.
Item, Allegoriae quaedam, ex utroq Excerptae, una
cum libro Praemiorum. Omnia haec ex codicibus duobus
antiquissimis sunt excerpta hacte nus prorsus a
nemine uisa. [Haganoae: per Iohannem Secerium, 1529.]
[163] p.; 19cm.

ISIDORUS (Cont'd)
    Colophon: Haganoae, ex officina iohannis secerij
Anno Domini M.D.XXIX Mense Martio.
     Palau, 292099.
Reel 82, No. 525

ISIDORUS, Saint, bp. of Seville, d. 636.
    [De Officiis].
    Beati Isidori Hispalensis Qvondam Archiepiscopi
De Officiis Ecclesiasticis Libri Dvo, Ante Annos
D CCC. Ab Eo Editi, Et Nvnc Ex Vetvsto Codice In
Lvcem Restitvti. Lipsiae: Sub ac Orthodoxo Principe,
Dño Georgio, Saxoniae Duce &c., 1534.
    [48] *l.*; 19cm.

    Colophon: Lipsiae Excvdebat Michael Blvm. Anno
domini, 1534.
    Palau, 292116.

Reel 82, No. 526

ISIDORUS, Saint, bp. of Seville, d. 636.
    De summo bono Libri tres Sancti Isidori hyspalensis
Episcopi. [Leipzig (Lyptzck): Arnoldus de Colonia,
1 Oct. (Kalendas Octobris) 1493].
    [4], lxxvi *l.*; 20cm.

    Colophon: Finis liber Tercius et Vltimus de summo
bono sancti Isidoris hispalensis Episcopi Impressus
Lyptzck p Arnoldum de Colonia anno gratie MCCCC XCIII
Kalendas Octobris.
    Pagination errors throughout.
    Goff, I-196; Palau, 292027.
Reel 82, No. 523

ISIDORUS, Saint, bp. of Seville, d. 636.
    [De Temporibus].
    Opusculum de Temporibus. [Romae: Stephan Plannk,
ca. 1488-91].
    6 *l.*; 20cm.

    Goff, I-190; Hain, no. 9304.
Reel 82, No. 522

ISIDORUS, Saint, bp. of Seville, d. 636.
    Etymologiae. [Augsburg]: Günther Zainer, 19 Nov.
1472.
    [264] *l.*; woodcuts, diagrams, map, geneal. tables;
33cm.

    Rubricates. Some initials in red and blue.
    Table of contents ([4] *l.*). Bound at beginning.
    Bound in contemporary full brown pigskin with blind
stamped ornaments over wooden boards; metal bosses and
clasps; rebacked. Leaf of unidentified vellum manuscripts
used as lining-paper inside front cover.
    Hain, no. 9273; Palau, 292015.
Reel 81, No. 517

ISIDORUS, Saint, bp. of Seville, d. 636.
    [Etymologiarum libri XX].
    Praeclarissimvm opus diui Isidori Hyspalensis
episcopi: quod ethimologiarum intitulat Nec te
fallat opinio studiose lector cū titulū aspicies:
quasi in hocvolumine solū de re grāmatica ato
vocabulorū interpretanionibus mētio fiat. cū i
eo tantarum altissimarum rerum noticia recondita
sit: vt nus q̄ alibi maior dignior īueniatur.
Quicquid enī cognitionis in ceteris scriptorib, cū
grece tum latinae historiae reperitur vniuersis: i
hoc vnico libro vtili quadā breuitate inuenies. Quod
si plegeris cūvarietate historiarum: tum rerum
magnitudine nō minus proficies q̄ oblectaberis.
[Paris]: apud Leonem argenteum, [1509].
    ciii (i.e. ci), [2] *l.*, illus.; 26cm.

ISIDORUS (Cont'd)
    Colophon: Impressum Parrhisii Opa Iohānis barbier
sūptibus Iohannis petit. Anno salutis. Millesimo
quingentesimonono vltim die Mensis Augusti.
    In double columns. Marginal notes in manuscript.
Errors in foliation: XVII numb. XVIII; XXI and LXI
omitted; Cl numb. CL.
    Epistles of Braulius and Isidorus on leaves 2-3a.
    HC384/2803; Palau, 292039; Penney, p. 276.
Reel 81, No. 518

ISIDORUS, Saint, bp. of Seville, d. 636.
    [Etymologiarum libri XX].
    Praeclarissimvm opus diui Isidori Hyspalensis
episcopi: quod ethimologiarum intitulat Nec te
fallat opinio studiose lector cū titulū aspicies:
quasi in hocvolumine solū de re grāmatica ato
vocabulorū interpretanionibus mētio fiat. cū i
eo tantarum altissimarum rerum noticia recondita
sit: vt nus q̄ alibi maior dignior īueniatur.
Quicquid enī cognitionis in ceteris scriptorib, cū
grece tum latinae historiae reperitur vniuersis: i
hoc vnico libro vtili quadā breuitate inuenies.
Quod si plegeris cūvarietate historiarum: tum rerum
magnitudine nō minus proficies q̄ oblectaberis.
[Paris]: sub signo Lilij Aurei, [1520].
    CIII, [3] *l.*, illus.; 28cm.

    Adams, I, no. 204; Palau, 292041.
Reel 82, No. 519

ISIDORUS, Saint, bp. of Seville, d. 636.
    [Etymologiarum libri XX].
    Isidori Hispalensis Episcopi Originum libri
viginti ex antiquitate eruti. Et Martiani Capellae
De nuptijs Philologiae & Mercurij Libri nouem Vterque,
praeter Fulgentium & Veteres Grammaticos, varijs
lectionibus & scholijs illustratus Opera atq Indistria
Bonaventvrae Vvlcanii Brvgensis. Basileae: Per Petrvm
Pernam, [1577]
    2 pts. in 1 ([13] p., 550 double cols, [33] p.;
240 double cols. [4] p.); 32cm.

    Early Swiss imprint.
    Adams, I, no. 206; Palau, 292047.
Reel 82, No. 520

ISIDORUS, Saint, bp. of Seville, d. 636.
    Isidori Hispalensis Episcopi. Sententiarvm Libri
III. Emendati, Et Notis Illvstrati Per Garsiam Loaysa:
Tavrini: Apud Io. Baptistam Beuilaquam, 1593.
    11, 450, [11] p.; 23cm.

    With this is bound his Chronicon D. Isidori Archiep.
Hisp. Emendatum, schollísq; illustratum, Per Garciam
De Loaisa, Sacrae Theologiae D. Archidiaconum de
Guadal Ecclesiae Toletanae Canonicum. Tavrini, Apud
Io. Baptistam Beuilaquam, 1593.
    Adams, I, no. 205; Palau, 292050; Short-Title,
II, p. 160.
Reel 82, No. 521

ISIDORUS, Saint, bp. of Seville, d. 636.
    Sancti Isidori Hispalensis Episcopi, Opera Omnia
Qvae Extant, Partim Aligvando Vivorvm Doctissimorvm
laboribus edita, partim nunc primūm exscripta &
castigata. Per Margarinvm De La Bigne Theologum
Doctorem Parisienem. Indicem Librorum, pagina nona,
Rerum autem & verborum, & authoritatum Scripturae
quae explicantur vel citantur, ad totius Operis
finem habes. Parisiis: Apud Michaëlem Sonnivm, via
Iacobaea, sub Scuto Basiliensi, 1580.
    [12], 124 (i.e. 122), [32] *l.*; 36cm.

    Text in double columns. Errors in pagination.
    Palau, 292001.
Reel 81, No. 515

ISIDORUS, Saint, bp. of Seville, d. 636.
    Sancti Isidori Hispalensis Episcopi, Opera Omnia
Qvae Extant: Partim aliquando virorvm doctissimorum
laboribus edita, partim nunc primùm exscripta, & ad
chirographa exemplaria accuratiùs quàm emendata. Per
Fratrem Iacobvm Dv Brevl Monachum sancti Germani à
Pratis. In Serie Librorum, que sequitur pagina 16.
notantur asterisco ea quae huic, preter ceteras,
editioni accesserunt. Indices autem Auctoritatum
sacrae Sripturae, Rerùmque ac verborum, ad calcem
totius Operis habentur. Parisiis: Apud Michaelem
Sonnivm, via Iacobaea, sub Scuto Basiliensi, 1601.
    [32], 975, [101] p.; 37cm.

    Doublet, p. 73; Palau, 292003.
Reel 81, No. 516

ISIDORUS, Saint, bp. of Seville, d. 636.
    [Synonyma De Homine Et Ratione, seu Soliloquia]
Dialogus siue synonima ysidori de homine et
ratione. [Parisius: in Campo galliard: [sic] per
Guido nem Mercatoris, 1494.]
    [34] p.

    16 *l*. Gothic letter, 27 long lines to a page.
With Marchand's printer's mark (cobbler's shop)
on title.
    Small 8vo, half leather.
    Probably the earliest French-printed edition. Cf.
Hain (Repert. Bibliogr., no. 9298.
    Colophon: Expliciunt synonima ysidori Ispaleñ
Episcopi de Homine et Ratione emēdata et summa cum
diligētia castigata per magistrum Jacobū Lupi Sacre
theologie Bachalarium formatum bene meritum Impressa
Parisius in Campo gallardi per Guidonem Mercatoris
Anno domini M. CCCC. XCIIII. Decimasexta Maij.
    Goff, I-207; Palau, 292066; Stillwell, I - 179.
Reel 82, No. 524

IZQUIERDO, SEBASTIAN, 1601-1681.
    R P. Sebast. Izqvierdo Alcarazensis Soc. Iesv,
Svpremi S. Inqvisitionis Senatvs Censoris Et Olim
Complvti SS. Theologiae Professoris. Pharvs Scientiarvm.
Vbi Qvidqvid Ad Cognitionem Hvmanam humanitùs
acqusibilem pertinet, vbertim iuxtà, atque succincte
petractatur. Scientia De Scientia, Ob Svmmam
Universalitatem vtilissima, Scientificisqve iucundissima,
scientificâ methodo exhibetur. Aristotelis Organvm
Iam Pene Labens Restitvitvr, illustratur, augetur,
atque à defectibus absoluitur. Ars Demvm Legitima,
Ac Prorsvs Mirabilis Sciendi, Omnesqve Scientias
in infinitum propagandi, & methodicè digerendi; a
nonnullis ex Antiquioribus religiosè celata; à multis
studiosè quaesita; à paucis inuenta; à nemine ex
propriis principiis hactenus demonstrata, demonstratiuè,
apertè, & absque inuolucris mysteriorum in lucem
proditur. Quò verae Encyclopediae Orbis facilè a
cunctis circumuoluendus, eximio scientiarum omnium
emolumento, manet expositus. Lvgdvni: Sumptibus
Clavdii Bovrgeat, & Mich. Lietard, 1659.
    2 v. in 1 ([26], 410 p.; 372, [15] p.]; 34cm.

    Pagination errors throughout.
    Palau, 122426. Not in Simón Díaz' Jesuites.
Reel 82, No. 527

J

JANUA LINGUARUM see BATHE, William.

JÁUREGUI Y AGUILAR, JUAN DE, 1583-1641.
  Apologia Por La Verdad. De don Iuan de Iauregui.
Al Excelentissimo Señor Conde Duque de Sanlucar, &c.
Impresso a instancia de Pedro Pablo Bugia mercader
de libros, y a su costa. Con Licencia del Supremo
Consejo. Madrid: Por Iuan Delgado, 1625.
  [4], 44 Z.; 19cm.

    Goldsmith, p. 87, no. 17; Jerez, p. 54; Palau,
123301; Penney, p. 279; Pérez Pastor, no. 2076;
Salvá, II, 2291.
  Reel 83, No. 528

JÁUREGUI Y AGUILAR, JUAN DE, 1583-1641.
  Discvrso Poetico De don Iuan de Iauregui. Al
Excelentissimo Señor Don Gaspar de Guzman, Conde de
Olivares, Sumilier de Corps, Cavallerizo mayor, del
Consejo de Estado y Guerra de su Magestad, gran
Canciller de las Indias, Alcaide perpetuo de los
Alcaçares de Sevilla, Comendador mayor de Alcantara,
&c. Madrid: Por Iuan Goncalez, 1624.
  [2], 40 Z.; 19cm.

    Jerez, p. 54; Palau, 123297; Penney, p. 279; Pérez
Pastor, 2076; Salvá, I, 688.
  Reel 83, No. 529

JÁUREGUI Y AGUILAR, JUAN DE, 1583-1641.
  La Farsalia, Poema Español, Escrito Por Don Ivan
De Iavregvi y Aguilar, Cavallero de la Orden de
Calatrava, Cavallerizo de la Reyna nuestra Señora,
Doña Isabel de Borbon. Sacale A Lvz Sebastian De
Armendariz, Librero de Camara del Rey nuestro Señor...
Madrid: Por Lorenzo Garcia. Acosta de Sebastian de
Armendariz, Mercader de Libros. Vendese en su casa
en la Puerta del sol, [1684].
  2 v. in 1 ([18], 239 Z.; 114 Z.)

    Error in paging.
    Contains also the poem Orfeo.
    Pagination errors throughout.
    Goldsmith, p. 87, no. 20; Jerez, p. 54; Penney,
p. 279; Salvá, I, 753; Ticknor, p. 188.
  Reel 83, No. 530

JÁUREGUI Y AGUILAR, JUAN DE, 1583-1641.
  Orfeo De Don Ivan De Iavregvi. Al Excelentissimo
Señor don Gaspar de Guzman, Conde de Olivares,
Sumilier de Corps, Cavallerizo mayor, del Consejo
de Estado i Guerra de su Magestad, gran Canciller
de las Indias, Alcaide perpetuo de los alcaçares
de Sevilla. Madrid: Por Iuan Goncalez, 1624.
  [4], 34 Z.; 19cm.

    Colophon: En Madrid Por Iuan Goncalez. Año M D C.
XXIIII.
    Goldsmith, p. 87, no. 22; Jerez, p. 54; Palau,
123298; Penney, p. 279; Pérez Pastor, 2075; Salvá,
I, 689; Ticknor, p. 188.
  Reel 83, No. 531

JÁUREGUI Y AGUILAR, JUAN DE, 1583-1641.
  Rimas de Don Ivan de Iavregvi. Sevilla: Por
Francisco de Lyra Varreto, 1618.
  [33], 307, [12] p.; 19cm.

JÁUREGUI Y AGUILAR (Cont'd)
  Includes an Index.
    Escudero, 1138; Graesse, III, p. 455; Jerez, p. 54;
Palau, 123296; Penney, p. 279; Salva, I, 690; Ticknor,
p. 188.
  Reel 83, No. 532

JAVIER, JERÓNIMO, d. 1617.
  ... Historia Christi Persice Conscripta, simulque
multis modis contaminata, A P. Hieronymo Xavier,
Soc. Jesu. Latine Reddita & Animadversionibus notata.
A Ludovico De Dieu. Lvgdvni Batavorvm, Ex Officina
Elseviriana, 1639.
  2 v. in 1 ([25], 636, [4] p.; [8], 144 p.); 21cm.

    Printer's device on title-page.
    Title in Persian characters at head of title-page.
    Bilingual edition: Persion and Latin on opposite
pages.
    Title page of Part II reads: ... Historia S.
Petri Persice Conscripta, simulque multis modis
contaminata. Latine Reddita, & brevibus Animadversionibus
notata, A Ludovico De Dieu.
    Contains: "Narratio brevis rervm a Societate in
regno magni Mogor gestararum trascripta ex literis
p. Hieronymi Xavier Societatis Iesv. anni 1598. &c.
p. Emmanuelis Pignerio, anni 1598": p. 122-44.
    Bound with: Rvdementa Lingve Persice. Authore
Ludovico De Dieu ... Lvgdvni Batavorvm, 1639.
  Reel 83, No. 533, Part 1-2

JESÚS, JOSÉ DE see JOSÉ DE JESÚS.

JIMÉNEZ DE CISNEROS, FRANCISCO, Cardinal see Bible.
  [Polyglot] 1514-17.

JIMÉNEZ PATÓN, BARTOLOMÉ, 1569-1640.
  Epitome De La Ortografia Latina, Y Castellana.
Por El Maestro Bartolome Ximenex Paton. Con
Privilegio. En Baeca: por Pedro de la Cuesta, A
costa de Francisco de Valuer mercader de libros,
que reside en Villanueva de los Infantes, 1614.
  [8], 95 Z.; 13cm.

    Knapp-Huntington, p. 32; Penney, p. 284; Salvá,
II, 2296; Vindel, P.B.g. 281.
  Reel 83, No. 534

JIMÉNEZ PATÓN, BARTOLOMÉ, 1569-1640.
  Mercvrivs Trimegistvs, Sive Detriplici Eloqventia
Sacra., Española Romana. Opvs Conciona-toribvs
Verbisacri poetis vtriusque linguae diuinarum, &
humanarum literarum studiosis vtilissimum. Ad D.
Ihonnem De Tarsis Comitem de Villamediana
Archigrammathophorum Regis. Avthore Magister
Batholomaeo Ximenio Patone Almedinensi, eius publico
Doctore, & Prothogrammatophoro in oppido Villanueua
de los Infantes, Curiae Romanae, & sancti Officijs
Scriba. Pedro de la Cuesta Gallo Typographo Biatiae,
1621.
  286 [24] Z.; ill.; 20cm.

    Texts of the Eloquentia sacra and Eloquentia
romana are in Latin; the Eloquentia española is in
Spanish.
    Colophon: "Este libro está reciuido por la Vniuersidad
de Almagro ante Alonso Rodriguez de Ayollon presbitero
secretario de la dicha Vniuersidad el diez y ocho
de Octubre, de mil y seyscientos y veynte y vno."
    Contains pagination errors.
    Salvá, II, 2297.
  Reel 83, No. 535

JOANNES CLIMACUS, Saint, 6th cent.
  [Scala paradisi. Spanish]
  Libro De San Ivan Climaco, Llamado La Escala
Espiritval, En El qual se descriuen treynta Escalones
por donde pueden subir los hōbres a la cumbre de la
perfeccion. Agora nueuamente Romancado por el Padre
fray Luys de Granada, y con anotaciones suyas en los
primeros cinco Capitulos para inteligencia dellos.
En Madrid: Por Iuan de la Cuesta, 1612.
    239, [1] l.; 16cm.

    Spanish translation by Luis de Granada.
    Palau, 292610.
Reel 84, No. 536

JOHN CLIMACUS, Saint see JOANNES CLIMACUS, Saint, 6th
  cent.

JOHN OF THE CROSS, Saint see JUAN DE LA CRUZ, 1542-1591.

JOSÉ DE JESÚS, 17th cent.
  Cielos De Fiesta Mvsas De Pascva, En Fiestas
Reales, Qve A S. Pascval Coronan. Svs Mas Finos, Y
Cordialissimos Devotos, Los Muy Esclarecidos Hijos
de la muy Ilustre, muy Leal, y Coronada Ciudad de
Valencia, que con la magestad de la mas luzida
pompa, echō su gran devocion el resto, en las Fiestas
de la Canonizacion De San Pascval Baylon. Retratalas
En Mal Formados Rasgos, en el vistoso lienco de los
cielos, el tosco pincel de la menos diestra pluma
del Padre Fray Ioseph De Iesvs, El Menor De Los
Menores Es Hijos De La Santa Madre, de S. Pascual,
la muy reformada Provincia de S. Iuan de Regiosos
Franciscos Descalcos, sita en los Reynos de Valencia,
y Murcia... En Valencia: Por Francisco Mestre,
Impressor del S. Tribunal de la Inquisicion, junto
al Molino de Rovella, 1692.
    [34], 535, [1] p.; 20cm.

    Contains several poems by unknown authors.
    Palau, 123555; Penney, p. 287; Salvá, I, 263.
Reel 85, No. 544

JUAN BAUTISTA DE VIÑONES.
  Espejo De La Conciencia, en donde se trata muy
copiosam.^te de los pecados que se cometen en todos
los estados de vida Y Remedios para el que quiera
aprovecharse de ellos. Medina Del Campo: En la
Imprenta de Francisco del Canto, 1552.
    ccviii, [4] l.; 29cm.

    Title-page in facsimile (ink).
    Thomas, p. 32.
Reel 85, No. 545

JUAN DE LA ANUNCIACION, 1514?-1594.
  La Inocencia Vindicada. Respuesta, Que El Rmo. Padre
Fr. Juan De La Anunciacion, Rector, que ha sido dos
vezes del Colegio de Carmelitas Descalcos de Salamanca,
Ex-Disinidor segunda vez, y al presente General del Orden
de Descalzos, y Descalzas de N.S. del Carmen de la
Primitiva Observancia. Da A Un Papel Contra El Libro
De La Vida Interior del Ilustrissimo, Excelentissimo,
y Venerable señor Don Jvan De Palafox y Mendoza, del
Consejo de su Magestad en los supremos de Guerra, Indias,
y Aragon, Obispo de la Puebla de los Angeles, Arzobispo
electo de Mexico, Virrey, Presidente, Governador, y
Capitan General de la Nueva-España, Visitador de todos
sus Tribunales, Iuez de Residencia de tres Virreyes, y
Obispo de la Santa Iglesia de Osma. Con Licencia.
Madrid: En la Imprenta de Manuel Ruiz Murga, 1698.
    [19], 222, [8] p.; 20cm.

    Palau, I, no. 13503.
Reel 16, No. 70

JUAN DE LA ANUNCIACION see also HERRERA Y SOTOMAYOR,
  JACINTO DE (no. 33).

JUAN DE LA CRUZ, 1542-1591.
  The Catholiqve Ivdge: Or A Moderator Of The
Catholique Moderator. Where in forme or manner of a
Plea or Suite at Law, the differences betvveene
those of the Reformed Church, and them of the Romish
Church are decide; and without partialitie is shewed
which is the true Religion and Catholique Church,
for the istruction of either partie. Together with
eight strong Arguments or Reasons, why the Popes
cannot be competent Iuges in these controversies.
Written in the Dutch and French tongue, by Iohn
of the Crosse, a Catholique Gentleman. Translated
out of French into English, by the Right worshipfull
and learned Knight Sir A. A. Pro. 17. 15. Hee that
iustifieth the wicked, and he that condemneth the
iust, they both are an abhomination to the Lord.
London: Printed by I. D. for Robert Mylbourne; and
are to be sold at his shop, at the great South-doore
of Pauls, 1623.
    [8], 87 p.; 19cm.

    Work attributed to Saint John of the Cross.
    Not in Allison's English Translations from the
Spanish and Portuguese ... 1974.
Reel 84, No. 537

JUAN DE LA CRUZ, 1542-1591.
  Obras Espiritvales que encamina vna alma ala
perfecta vnion con Dios. Por el Venerable P. F. Ivan
De La Crvz, primer Descalzo de la Reforma de N. Señora
del Carmen, Coadjutor de la Bienauturada Virgen. S.
Teresa de Iesus Fundadora de la misma Reforma. Con
vna resunta dela vida del Autor, y unos discursos
por el P. F. Diego de Iesu Carmelita descalzo,
Prior del Conuento de Toledo. Dirigido al Ilustrissimo
Señor Don Gaspar de Borja Cardenal dela Santa Iglesia
de Roma del titulo de Santa crvz en Hierusalen.
Impreso En Alcala: Por La Vivda De Andres Sanches
Ezpeleta, 1618.
    [14], iij-xxxviij p., [2], 682, [46] p.; 20cm.

    Carmelite device on p. [46] at end.
    Errors in paging included repetition of 360 and
511 in numbering.
    Colophon: Lavs Deo Et beatae Virgini, Mariae de
Monte Carmelo.
    Doublet, p. 74; Palau, 292639; Salvá, II, p. 261.
Reel 84, No. 538

JUAN DE LA CRUZ, 1542-1591.
  Obras Espiritvales que encamina vna alma ala
perfecta vnion con Dios. Por el Venerable P. F.
Ivan De La Crvz, primer Descalzo de la Reforma de N.
Señora del Carmen, Coadjutor de la Bienauturada
Virgen. S. Teresa de Iesus Fundadora de la misma
Reforma. Con vna resunta dela vida del Autor, y
unos discursos por el P. F. Diego de Iesu Carmelita
descalzo, Prior del Conuento de Toledo. Dirigido
al Ilustrissimo Señor Don Gaspar de Borja Cardenal
dela Santa Iglesia de Roma del titulo de Santa Crvz
en Hierusalen. [Barcelona: Por Sebastian de Cormellas
al call, 1619]
    [18], 632, [40] p.; 19cm.

    Colophon: Con Licencia, En Barcelona Por Sebastian
de Cormellas al call, Año 1619. Second edition.
    Engraved title - page includes arms of Cardinal
de Borja, the dedicatee, and plate are by Diego de
Astor.
    Imperfect: lacks date and place of publication.
    Goldsmith, p. 90; Jerez, p. 32; Penney, p. 286;
Salvá, II, 2239.
Reel 84, No. 539

JUAN DE LA CRUZ, 1542-1591.
Obras Del Venerable I Mistico Dotor F. Joan De
La Cruz. Primer Descalco, i Padre De la Reforma de
N. S.ª del Carmen Dedicadas Al Serenissimo S.ʳ Infante
Cardenal Arzobispo de Toledo, Don Fernando. Con
Priuilegio En Madrid: In Oratione A. de Poma, fecit.
Et Ieiunio, 1630.
[38], 802, [68] p.; 19cm.

Colophon: "Con Privilegio En Madrid, por los
herederos de la viuda de Pedro de Madrigal, Año de
M.DC. XXX."
Palau, 292641; Salvá, II, p. 261.
Reel 84, No. 540

JUAN DE LA CRUZ, 1542-1591.
Obras Del Venerable Y Mistico Dotor F. Ioan De
La Cruz Primer Descalco Y Padre de la Reforma de
nuestra Señora del Carmen. Dedicadas Al Serenissimo
señor Infante Cardenal, Arcobispo de Toledo, Don
Fernando. Con Licencia, Y Privilegio. En Barcelona:
Por Sebastian de Cormellas, 1635.
[40], 682, [54] p.; 19cm.

Palau, 292642; Salvá, II, p. 261.
Reel 84, No. 541

JUAN DE LA CRUZ, 1542-1591.
Obras Del Venerable Padre Fray Ivan De La Cruz.
Con Privilegio. En Madrid: Por Gregorio Rodriguez,
1649. A costa de Iuan de Valdes, y Esperanca
Francisca.
[58], 802, [108] p.; 19cm.

Pagination errors throughout.
Palau, 292643; Salvá, II, 2240.
Reel 85, No. 542

JUAN DE LA CRUZ, 1542-1591.
Obras Del Beato Padre Fray Juan De La Cruz. Tomo
Primero [y Segundo]. Con Licencia. En Madrid: Por
Iulian de Paredes, Y à su costa, 1694.
2 v. ([54], 432 p.; [2] 433-704, [108] p.); 19cm.

Palau, 292646; Salvá, II, p. 261.
Reel 85, No. 543, Vol. 1-2

JUAN DE LOS ANGELES, FRAY, d. 1609.
Trivmphos Del Amor De Dios; Obra Prouechosissima
para toda suerte de personas, particularmente, para
las que por medio de la contemplacion desseen (sic)
vnirse a Dios. Compuesto por el padre fray Iuan de
los Angeles, Predicador de la prouincia de Sant
Ioseph de los descalcos. Dirigido a Andres de Alua
Secretario del Rey nuestro señor, y del su consejo
de Guerra. Medina del Campo: por Francisco del
Canto, 1590.
[8], 303, [9] l.; 20cm.

En colophon: "En Medina del Cãpo, por Francisco
del Cãto, Año de 1589."
Pagination errors throughout.
Reel 86, No. 546

JUAN DE SANTA MARÍA, brother, d. 1622.
Tratado De Repvblica, y Policia Christiana. Para
Reyes Y Principes: y para los que en el gouierno
tienen sus vezes. Compuesto por Fray Iuan De Santa
Maria, Religioso Descalco, de la Prouincia de San
Joseph, de la Orden de nuestro glorioso Padre San
Francisco. 36. En Barcelona: Por Sebastian de Cormellas,
y a su costa, 1617.
[8], 268, [5] l.; 15cm.

Colophon: "Impresso en la muy insigne y leal
Ciudad de Barcelona, en casa Sebastian de Cormellas
al Call año, 1616."
Pagination errors throughout.
Palau, 298182.
Reel 86, No. 547

JUANA INÉS DE LA CRUZ, Sister, 1651-1695.
Poemas de la unica poetisa americana, musa dezima
soror Juana Ines de la Cruz ... Que en varios metros,
idiomas y estilos, fertiliza varios assumptos: con
elegantes, sutiles, claros, ingeniosos, utiles versos,
para enseñanza, recreo y admiracion.
Dedicalos a la excel.ᵐᵃ señora d. Maria Luisa Goncaga
Manrique de Lara, ... 2. ed. corregida y mejorada
por su authora. Madrid: Por Juan Garcia Infancon,
1690.
[16], 338, [6] p.; 20cm.

First edition, 1689, has title Inundación castalidad
de la única poetisa.
Palau, 65221.
Reel 46, No. 248

JUANA INÉS DE LA CRUZ, Sister, 1651-1695.
Segundo tomo de las obras de soror (sic) Juana
Ines de la Cruz. ... Añadido en esta segvnda impression
por sv avtora. Año 1693. Impresso en Barcelona: Por
Joseph Llopis, y à su costa, 1693.
[8], 470, [5] p.; 21cm.

Palau, 65224, Salvá, I, 1201; Ticknor, p. 192.
Reel 46, No. 249

JUAREZ, RODRIGO, fl. 1555.
Repetitiones Roderici Svarez Ivris Consvlti, In l.
Quoniam in prioribus. C. de in offic. testa. & in l.
Post rem (sic) iudicatam. ff. de re iudic. necnon in
alias fori. ll. & ordinamenti leges, Nvnc Primvm Ab
innumeris, quibus antea scatebant, mendis repurgatae.
Lvgdvni: Apud haeredes Iacobi Iuntae, 1558.
[97], 911 p.; 18cm.

Palau, 323771.
Reel 175, No. 1146

JUNTA de las aves, en particular del Buho Gallego
y el Tordo Vizcaino.
18 manuscript l.
Bound with: HERRERA Y SOTOMAYOR, JACINTO DE, fl.
1644. Iornada que su Magestad hizo a la Andalvzia.
[Madrid: En la Imprenta Real, 1624].
Palau, 114276 (List only printed folios 1-6).
Reel 77, No. 484.29

JUSTIFICACION De Las Acciones De España. Manifestacion
  De Las violencias de Francia. [Madrid: s.n., 1635]
  51 p.

  Caption title.
  Bound in: Cespedes y Meneses, Gonzalo de: Francia
Engañada Francia Respondida, Caller, 1635.
Reel 41, No. 222

JUSTINUS, MARCUS JUNIANUS.
  [Ivstini Historiarum ex Trogo. Spanish]
  Ivstino Clarissimo Abreviador De La Historia general
del famoso y excellente historiador Trogo Pompeyo:
enla qual se contienen todas las cosas notables y
mas dignas de memoria que hasta sus tiempos han
succedido en todo el mundo: agora nueuamente traduzido
en Castellano y dirigido al Illustrissimo señor Don
Pedro Hernandez de Velasco Condestable de Castilla,
&c. Fue impressa y acabada la presente obra en la
fiorentissima villa de Envers: y vendese en la casa
de Iuan Steelsio, en el escudo de Bourgoña, 1542.
  [8], 258, [30] l.; 19cm.

  Spanish translation by J. de Bustamante.
  Heredia, no. 6896; Palau, 126807; Peeters-Fontainas,
Impressions, I, no. 654; Salvá, II, 2767; Thomas,
p. 95; Vaganay, no. 141; Vindel, no. 1363.
Reel 86, No. 548

JUSTINUS, MARCUS JUNIANUS.
  [Ivstini Historiarum ex Trogo. Spanish]
  Ivstino Clarissimo Abreviador De La Historia
General del famoso y excellente historiador Trogo
Pompeyo. En la qual se contienen todas las cosas
notables y mas dignas de memoria que hasta sus tiempos
succedido en todo el mundo. Traduzido en lengua
Castellana. En Anvers: En casa de Martin Nutio, 1586.
  [4], 208 l.; 19cm.

  Spanish translation by Jorge de Bustamante.
  Palau, 126808; Peeters-Fontainas, Impressions, I,
no. 655; Salvá, II, 2768; Thomas, p. 94.
Reel 86, No. 549

JUVENALIS, DECIMUS JUNIUS, ca. 60 - ca. 140.
  [Satirae. Spanish]
  Declaracion Magistral Sobre Las Satiras de Iuuenal,
Principe de los Poetas Satiricos. Por Diego Lopez
Natvral de la villa de Valencia, de la Orden de
Alcantara. Don Fernando Pizarro y Orellana, Cauallero
dela Orden de Calatraua, y Comendador de Betera, del
Consejo de su Magestad en el Real y Supremo de Castilla.
70. Con Privilegio En Madrid: Por Diego Diaz De La
Carrera, 1642. A costa de Pedro Lasso Mercader de
Libros.
  [20], 538, [6] p.; 11cm.

  With commentary by Diego López.
  Bound with: Lopez, Diego. Las Seis Satyras De
Avlo Persio Flacco, con declaracion Magistral en
lengua Castellana.
  Goldsmith, p. 92, no. 181; HC398/1873; Palau,
126852; Penney, p. 291; Salvá, I, 696.
Reel 86, No. 550

L

LABASTIDA, HERNANDO DE.
Antidotto A Las Venenosas Consideraciones De Fr. Pavlo De Venecia, Sobre Las Censvras De N.S^{mo} P^e Pavlo V En el qual se descubren los errores, dislates y engaños deste autor. Compuesto Por el P. Her. De La Bastida, de la Comp^a de Jesvs natural de Valladolid Oua Aspidum ruperunt & teias aranea fexuerunt. Esayae 59. En Leon: Por Nicolas Tvlliety, 1607.
[2], 357 p.; 16cm.

Engraved title-page.
Palau, 128875.
Reel 86, No. 552

LACAVALLERÍA, PEDRO DE.
[Dictionario Castellano.]
Al Excelentissimo Señor Marques de Brezè, Mariscal de Francia, &c. Visorey, y Capitan General por su Magestad Christianissima en en Cataluña, Rossellon, y Cerdaña. / Dictionaire Francois A Tres Excellent Seigneur Marquis de Breze, Mareschal de France, &c. Viceroy, & Capitaine General pour sa Maiesté tres Chrestienne en Catalogne, Rossillon; & Cerdagne. / Dictionari Catala. Al Excellentissim Senyor Marques de Brezè, Mariscal de Franca, &c. Virrey, y Capità General per sa Magestat Christianissima en Catalunyà, Rossello, y Cerdanya. En Barcelona: En casa de Pere Lacavalleria, Any 1642.
[256] p.; 10 x 16cm.

Three languages in parallel columns.
Goldsmith, p. 35, no. 303; Palau, 129317.
Reel 86, No. 553

LA GRAVETTE DE MAYOLAS, f. 1665.
Sentences Latines, Fidellement traduites du Latin en Francois Et en Espagnol, Par Le Sr La Gravete. A Paris, Premiere [y seconde] Partie [n.p.], 1662.
2 parts in 1 ([6], 80 p., [2], 112 p.); 17cm.

Reel 86, No. 554

LAGUNA, ANDRÉS DE (translator) see CICERO, MARCUS TULLIUS.

LAÍNEZ, JOSE see LAYNEZ, JOSÉPH, d. 1667.

LANARIO ARAGON, FRANCISCO, duque-príncipe de Carpiñano, b. 1589.
Las Gverras De Flandes, Desde El año de mil y quinientos y cincuenta y nueue hasta el de seiscientos y nueue. Por Don Francisco Lanario y Aragon, Duque de Carpiñano, Cauallero de la Orden de Calatrava, y del Consejo de Guerra de su Magestad en los Estados de Flandes. Dirigidas A Don Gaspar De Guzman, Comendador de Martos de la Orden de Calatraua, Conde de Oliuares, Sumiller de Corps, Cauallerizo mayor, y de los Consejos de Estado y Guerra de su Magestad, -c. Madrid: por Luis Sanchez, Impressor del Rey N. S., 1623.
[6], 154 *l*.; 19cm.

Goldsmith, p. 93, no. 20; HC:NSI/649; Palau, 130886; Penney, p. 295; Pérez Pastor, 1954; Salvá, II, 2991.
Reel 87, No. 556

LANCINA, JUAN ALFONSO DE, 17th cent.
Historia De Las Rebolvciones (sic) Del Senado De Messina, Qve Ofrece Al Sacro, Catolico, Real Nombre De D. Carlos Segvndo Nuestro Señor, Por Sv Consejo, Y Camara De Castilla, Don Jvan Alfonso De Lancina, Señor de la Villa de las Cuevas de Santiago, Juez de la Gran Corte de la Vicaria en el Reyno de Napoles, Superintendente Delegado en las materias de Estado, Inconfidentes, y Contravandos en las Calabrias por las Reboluciones de Messina, y Auditor General del Exercito que residìa en aquellas Provincias. Madrid: Por Julian de Paredes, Impressor de Libros, en la Placuela del Angel, 1692.
[12], 522, [13] p.: port.; 29cm.

Ex libris: Count Antonio Cavagna.
Palau, 130926.
Reel 87, No. 557

LANUZA, MIGUEL BATISTA.
Vida De La Bendita Madre Isabel De Santo Domingo. Compañera De Santa Teresa De Iesus. Coadjutora De La Santa, En La Nueva Reforma De la Orden de Nuestra Señora dt Monte Carmelo. Fundadora Del Monasterio de S. Iosef de Caragoca. I Relacion De Las Compañeras Que Traxo, I de las Hijas que crio en este Monasterio. Escrita A Las Madres Priora I Religiosas De Por Don Miguel Batista De Lanuza. Madrid: En La Imprēta Del Reino, 1638.
[43], 689, [46] p.; 30cm.

Engraved title-page.
Palau, 13100.
Reel 87, No. 558

LARA, DAVID BEN ISSAC see COHEN DE LARA, DAVID.

LA ROCHE-GUILHEM (translator) see PÉREZ DE HITA, GINÉS, 1544?-1619?

LAUTERBACH, JOHANNES see ANDRÉS, JUAN.

LAVANHA, JOÃO BAPTISTA, 1555-1624.
[Viagem del Rey Felipe III ao reyno de Portugal. Spanish]
Viage De La Catholica Real Magestad Del Rei D. Filipe (sic) III. N. S. Al Reino De Portvgal I relacion del solene recebimiento que en el se le hizo Sv Magestad la mando escriuir Por Ioan Baptista Lavaña Sv Coronista Mayor. Madrid: Por Thomas Iunti Impressor del Rei N. S., 1622.
[3], 76 *l*.: plates (part fold.); 35cm.

Two of the plates are mounted.
Engraved title - page by Joan Schorquens.
Colophon: "En Madrid, Por Tomas Iunti, Impressor del Rey N.S. Año M.DC.XXI."
Numerous errors in pagination after p. 21.
Graesse, IV, p. 126; Jerez, p. 61; Palau, 133207; Penney, p. 297; Pérez Pastor, 1850; Salvá, II, 3781.
Reel 87, No. 561

LAYNEZ, JOSÉPH, d. 1667.
El Privado Christiano Deducido de las Vidas de
Ioseph Y Daniel que fueron Valanzas De Los Validos
en el fiel Contraste del pueblo de Dios: que escriuia
Al Exm.º Don Gaspar De Gvzman Conde Duque de San
Lucar lamayor primer Ministro De Don Phelippe Qvarto
El Grande Rey Catholico De Las Españas Y Emperador
De America. El Maestro Fray Ioseph Laynez Predicador
De sv Magestad de la Orden de san Avgvstin. [Madrid]:
En La Imprenta Del Reyno, [1641].
[16], 72, 316 p.: port.; 30cm.

Half-title: Libro Nvevo El Privado Christiano:
Con los Movimientos De Las Provincias Catalvnía y
Portvgal Por El P. M. F. Ioseph Laynez Predicador
de Sv Magestad.
Vida de Ioseph Patriarcha: p. [47] - 316.
At head of title: Ivstitia De Caelo Prospexit.
Goldsmith, p. 92, no. 9; Palau, 130212.
Reel 87, No. 555

LAZARILLO DE TORMES.
[Vida de Lazarillo de Tormes. English]
The Pleasaunt Historie of Lazarillo de Tormes a
Spaniarde, wherein is conteined his maruelous deedes
and life. With the straunge aduentures happened to
him in the seruice of sundrie Masters. Drawn out of
Spanish by David Rouland of Anglesey. Accuerdo, Oluid.
London: by Abell Ieffes, 1586.
[64] l.; 13cm.

English translation by David Rowland.
Allison, p. 99, no. 2; Graesse, IV, p. 395;
Laurenti, no. 783; Palau, 133501; Pollard and Redgrave,
no. 15336.
Reel 87, No. 562

LAZARILLO DE TORMES.
[Vida de Lazarillo de Tormes. English]
The Pleasant History Of Lazarillo De Tormes a
Spaniyard, wherein is contained his marvellous
deeds and life. With the strange aduentures happened
to him, in the seruice of sundry Masters. Drawn out
of Spanish, by Dauid Rowland of Anglesey. Accuerdo,
Oluido, London: Printed by J. H., 1624.
[85] l.; 13cm.

England translation by David Rowland.
Bound with: LUNA, JUAN DE. The pvrsvit of the
Historie of Lazarillo De Tormes... London, 1631.
Allison, p. 99, no. 2.2; Graesse, vol. IV, p. 395;
Laurenti, no. 786; Palau 133504; Pollard and Redgrave,
no. 15338.
Reel 87, No. 563

LAZARILLO DE TORMES.
[Vida de Lazarillo de Tormes, segunda parte.
English]
The Pvrsvit of the Historie of Lazarillo De
Tormes. Gathered Out of the Ancient Chronicles of
Toledo. By Iean De Lvna, a Castilian. And now
done into English, and set forth by the same Author.
London: Printed by G. P. for Richard Hawkins, 1631.
[15], 195 p.

Juan de Luna, supposed author.
Allison, p. 100, no. 4.1; Laurenti, no. 1086; Pollard
and Redgrave, no. 16928.
Reel 87, No. 564

LAZARILLO DE TORMES.
[Vida de Lazarillo de Tormes. English]
Lazarillo, Or, The Excellent History Of Lazarillo
de Tormes, The witty Spaniard. Both Parts. The first
translated by David Rowland, and the second gather'd
out of the Chronicles of Toledo by Iean de Luna a
Castilian, and done into English by the same Authour.
Accuerdo, Oluido. London: Printed for William
Leake, 1653.
2 v. in 1. ([80] l.; [96] l.)

T.-P. of Part II reads: The Pursuit Of The History
Of Lazarillo De Tormes. Gathered out of the ancient
Chronicles of Toledo. By Jean de Luna, a Castilian.
And now done into English, and set forth by the same
Authour.
English translation by David Rowland.
Allison, p. 101, no. 5.1; Graesse, vol. IV, p. 395;
Laurenti, no. 788; Palau, 133507; Wing, L. 761.
Reel 88, No. 565

LAZARILLO DE TORMES.
[Vida de Lazarillo de Tormes. English]
Lazarillo: Or the Excellent History of Lazarillo
de Tormes, The Witty Spaniard. Both Parts. The first
tranlated by David Rowland, and the second gather'd
out of the Chronicles of Toledo by Jean de Luna, a
Castilian, and done into English by the same Authour.
London: Printed by R. Hodgkinsonne, 1655.
[75] l.; 14cm.

Title page of Part II reads: Juan de Luna: Segunda
parte de la vida de Lazarillo de Tormes 93 l. (1621)
English translation by Thomas Walkley.
English translation by David Rowland.
No record of other copies can be traced. Not in
British Museum Cat., not in Allison's English
Translation ..., not in Pollard and Redgrave's A
Short Title ..., not in Wing's Short-Title ... Palau
(vol. 7, p. 433) and Chandler (Romances of Roguery,
New York, Columbia Univ. Press, 1899, p. 407) mention
only the existence of a London edition of 1655 but
fail to describe it.
Reel 88, No. 566

LAZARILLO DE TORMES.
[Vida de Lazarillo de Tormes. German]
Zwo kurtzweilige, lustige, vnd lächerliche Historien,
die Erste von Lazarillo de Tormes, einem Spanier,
was für Herkommens er gewesen, wo vnd was für
abenthewrliche Possen er in seinen Herrendiensten
getrieben, wie es jme - auch darbey, biss er geheyrat,
ergangen. vnnd wie er letzlichen zu etlichen Teutschen
in Kundschafft gerahten vnd was sich nach Absheid
derselben mit ihne ereignet vnd zugetragen. Auss
Spanischer Sprach ins Teutsche gantz trewlich
transferirt. Die ander, von Isaac Winckelfelder,
vnd Jobst von der Schneid, Wie es disen beyden
Gesellen in der weitberümten Stadt Prag ergangen, was
sie daselbst für win wundersetzame Bruderschafft
angetroffen, vnd sich in dieselbe einverleiben lassen.
Durch Niclas Vlenhart beschriben. Gedruckt zu
Augspurg: durch Andream aperger, In Verlegung Niclas
Hainrichs, 1617.
[7], 389 p.; 18cm.

Title in red and black.
German translation by Niclas Ulenhart.
The History of Isaac Winckelfelder and Jobst der
Schneid is an adoptation of Cervantes' Rinconete y
Cortadillo.
Laurenti, no. 684; Palau, III, no. 133518.
Reel 88, No. 567

LEBRIJA, ANTONIO see ANTONIO DE LEBRIJA.

LEDESMA, GONZALO PEREZ.
    Censvra De La Eloqvencia, Para Calificar Svs Obras, Y Señaladamente Las Del Pvlpito. Dalo A La Estampa El Doctor Don Gonzalo Perez Ledesma, Canonigo Dignidad de la Santa Iglesia de Leon. Al Excelent.ᵐᵒ Señor Conde De Oropesa, &c. Virei de Valencia, &c. Zaragoça: En el Hospital Real, y General de nuestra Señora de Gracia, 1648.
    [13], 128 p.

    Bound in: ORMAZA, Joseph. Sermon En La Assvmpcion De Maria Señora Predicado Por El Padre Ioseph Oromaza..., 1648.
    Palau, 204296; Simón Díaz, Jesuitas, no. 1143.
Reel 126, No. 795

LEO HEBRAEUS see ABRABANEL, LEÓN.

LEÓN, GONZALÉZ DE.
    Por El Señor D. Migvel Batista De Lanvza, Cavallero Del Abito De Santiago ... Zaragoza, 1652.
    31 p.

    Bound in: Moles, Fadrique. In Processv Iesiphi Gviger ...
    Caption title.
Reel 112, No. 704

LEÓN, LUIS PONCE DE, 1528? - 1591.
    De Los Nombres De Christo En Tres Libros, Por El Maestro Fray Luys de Leon. Segunda impression, en que demas de vn libro que de nueuo se añade van otras muchas cosas añadidas y emendadas. Salamanca: Por los Herederos de Mathias Gast, 1585.
    342 l.; 19cm.

    Graesse, vol. IV, p. 165; Palau, 135337.
Reel 88, No. 568

LEÓN, LUIS PONCE DE, 1528? - 1591.
    De Los Nombres De Christo en Tres Libros, por el Maestro Fray Lvys De Leon. Tercera impression, en que demas de vn libro que de nueuo se añade, van otras muchas cosas añadidas. Salamanca: En casa de Guillelmo Foquel, 1587.
    [2], [356] l.; 20cm.

    Palau, 135337.
Reel 88, No. 570

LEÓN, LUIS PONCE DE, 1528? - 1591.
    De Los Nombres De Christo En Tres Libros, por el Maestro Fray Luys de Leon. Quinta impression, en que va añadido el nombre de Cordero, cõ tres tablas, la vna de los nombres de Christo, otra de la perfecta Casada, la tercera de los lugares de la Scriptura. Salamanca: En casa de Antonia Ramirez Viuda, 1603.
    [2], 261 l.; 18cm.

    Coster, 23; HC387/1935; Goldsmith, p. 95, no. 87; Palau, 135341; Penney, p. 303.
Reel 88, No. 571

LEÓN, LUIS PONCE DE, 1528? - 1591.
    La Perfecta Casada, Por El Maestro F. Lvys De Leon. Segunda impression mas añadida y emendada. Salamanca: En casa de Cornelio Bonardo, 1586.
    86 l.; 19cm.

    Graesse, vol. IV, p. 165; Palau, 135337.
Reel 88, No. 569

LEÓN, LUIS PONCE DE, 1528? - 1591.
    La Perfecta Casada, Por El Maestro F. Lvys De Leon. Tercera Impression mas añadida y emendada. Salamanca: En casa de Guillelmo Foquel, 1587.
    89 l.; 20cm.

    Missing leaf 86.
    Palau, 135254.
Reel 88, No. 573

LEÓN, LUIS PONCE DE, 1528? - 1591.
    La Perfecta Casada, Por El Maestro F. Lvys De Leon. Quinta impression mas añadida y emendada. Salamanca: En casa de Antonia Ramirez viuda, 1603.
    64, [21] l.; 18cm.

    Includes index.
    Coster, 23; HC387/1935; Goldsmith, p. 95, no. 87; Palau, 135341; Penney, p. 303.
Reel 88, No. 572

LEÓN, LUIS PONCE DE, 1528? - 1591.
    F. Lvysii Legionensis Avgvstiniani Divinorum librorum primi apud Salmanticenses interpretis, In Cantica Canticorum Salomonis explanatio. Secunda editio ab ipso authore recognita, & purior à mendis quam prima. Salmanticae: Excudebat Lucas à Iunta, 1582.
    2 v. ([8], 293 l. [3] l.; [4], 56, [7] l.); 14cm.

    T.-p. of Pt. II: F. Lvysii Legionensis Avgvstiniani diuinorum librorum Primi apud Salmanticensis interpretis. In Psalmvm Vigesimvm Sextvm Explanatio.
    Gallardo, no. 2979; Palau, 135378; Penney, p. 303.
Reel 89, No. 574

LEÓN HEBREO see ABRABANEL, LEÓN.

LEONARDO Y ARGENSOLA, BARTOLOMÉ [JUAN], 1562-1631.
    Conqvista de las Islas Malvcas al rey Felipe III. n.º S.ᵒʳ Escrita por el Licen.ᵈᵒ Bartolome Leonardo de Argensola ... [Madrid: Alonso Martin, 1609]
    [13], 407 p.; 21cm.

    Goldsmith, p. 95, no. 92; HC:321/1401; Palau, 16089; Penney, p. 304; Salvá, II, 3340; Ticknor, p. 200.
Reel 89, No. 575

LEONARDO Y ARGENSOLA, BARTOLOMÉ [JUAN], 1562-1631.
    Primera Parte De Los Anales De Aragon Que Prosigue Los Del Secretario Geronimo Curita, Desde El Año M.D.XVI Del Nacimiento De N.º Redentor Por El D.ʳ Bartholome Leonardo De Argensola Rector De Villahermosa, Canonigo De La Sᵃ Iglesia Metropolitana da Caragoca, Chronista Del Rey N.º Sʳ De La Corona, Y Reyno De Aragon. Caragoca: Por Ivan de Lanaia Impressor, 1630.
    [29], 1128, [40] p.; 31cm.

    Engraved title-page.
    Goldsmith, p. 95, no. 94; Palau, 16096.
Reel 89, No. 576

LEONARDO Y ARGENSOLA, LUPERCIO, 1559? - 1613.
    Declaracion Svmaria De La Historia De Aragon Para Inteligencia de Sv Mapa. Por Lupercio Leonardo de Argensola, ... Chronista del Rey nuestro Señor, y del Reyno de Aragon. ... Caragoca: Por Ivan De Lanaja Y Qvartanet Impressor del Reyno de Aragon, y desta Vniuersidad, 1621.
    20 p.; 21cm.

    Pagination errors throughout.
    Palau, 16098.
Reel 89, No. 577

LEONARDO Y ARGENSOLA, LUPERCIO, 1559? - 1613.
Rimas De Lvpercio I Del Dotor Bartolome Leonardo
De Argensola. Zaragoza: En el Hospital Real, i
General de nuestra Señora de Gracia, 1634.
[30], 155, [12], 157-501 p.; 19cm.

Goldsmith, p. 95, no. 95; Jiménez Catalán, no.
328; Knapp, p. 41-42; Palau, no. 16101; Penney, p.
304; Salvá, I, 726; Ticknor, p. 200.
Reel 89, No. 578

LEONARDO Y ARGENSOLA, LUPERCIO, 1559? - 1613.
Rimas De Lvpercio I Del Dotor Bartolome Leonardo
De Argensola. Another edition.
[30], 147, [13], 157-502 p.; 19cm.

Some leaves incorrectly arranged in binding.
Edited by Gabriel Leonardo de Albión y Argensola.
Jerez, p. 57; Jiménez Catalán, no. 329; Palau,
16101; Penney, p. 304.
Reel 89, No. 579

LETTERE Amorose Di Madonna Celia Gentildonna Romana,
scritte al suo Amante. In Venetia: Appresso
Francesco Lorenzini, da Turino, 1563.
70 *l*.; 16cm.

L. 68 misnumbered 67.
Reel 54, No. 317

LINDA, LUCAS DE, 1625-1660.
Lucae De Linda Descriptio Orbis & omnium ejus
Rerumpublicarum In Qua Praecipua omnium Regnorum &
Rerumpublicarum. Ordine & methodice pestractantur
quorum seriem versa ostendit Pagina. Amstelodami:
Apud Jacobum De Zetter, 1665.
[16], 1156, [12] p.; 17cm.

First published in Leyden in 1665.
A compilation, taken largely from Les empires,
royaumes, estats ... et principautez du monde of
Pierre d'Avity. Book XII is from the Nieuwe wereldt
of Johannes de Laet.
In manuscript inside front cover: Emptus Francofurti
aõ 1675. Su Iacobi Burckhardi. I.V.D. et pris. Symb.
Virtus laudatur et alget.
Sabin, no. 41288.
Reel 90, No. 580

LINDA, LUCAS DE, 1625-1660.
[Lucae De Linda Descriptio Orbis E & omnium ejus
Rerumpublicarum. Italian]
Le Relationi Et Descrittioni Vniversali, Et
Particolari del Mondo. Di Lvca Di Linda, et Dal
Marchese Maiolino Bisaccioni Tradotte, osservate &
nuouamente molto accresciute, e corrette. Dedicate
all'Illustriss. Sig. e Padron Colendiss. Il Sig.
Francesco Maria Pedori. In Bologna: Per Gioseffo
Longhi, 1674.
[16], 954 p.; 19cm.

Italian translation by Maiolino Bisaccioni.
Reel 90, No. 581

LIPSIUS, JUSTUS, 1547-1606.
Electorvm Liber I. In Qvo, praeter censuras, varij
prisci ritus. Antverpiae: Ex officina Christophori
Plantini, 1580.
191, [8] p.; 17cm.

Bound in: Sánchez De Las Brozas, Francisco. De
Avtoribvs Interpretandis ..., 1582.
Reel 166, No. 1081

LIPSIUS, JUSTUS, 1547-1606.
[Ivsti Lipsi Politicorum siue ciuilis doctrinae
libri sex. Spanish]
Los Seys Libros De Las Politicas O Doctrina
Ciuil de Iusto Lipsio, que siruen para el gouierno
del Reyno, o Principado. Traduzidos de lengua Latina
en Castellana, por don Bernardino de Mendoca. Con
Privilegio. En Madrid: En la Imprenta Real, 1604.
[16], 263, [8] p.; 20cm.

Spanish translation by Bernardino de Mendoza.
Pagination errors throughout.
Colophon: "Por Iuan Flamenco."
Goldsmith, p. 96, no. 146; Palau, 138666.
Reel 90, No. 582

LIVIUS, TITUS.
[Ex XIIII T. Livii Decadibus. Spanish]
Todas Las Decadas De Tito Livio Padvano, Qve Hasta
Al Presente se hallaron, y fueron impressas en latin,
traduzidas en Romance Castellano, agora nueuamente
reconoscidas y emendadas, y añadidas demas libros
sobre la vieja translacion. Vendese la presente
obra en Anuers: en casa de Arnoldo Byreman; à la
enseña de la Gallina gorda. Con Privilegio,
1553.
3 parts: ([1], CCCXVI *l*.; [2], CCCXVIII-DCVII *l*.;
LXXXV-CIII, [1] *l*.); 30cm.

Spanish translation by Francisco de Encinas.
Colophon: "Acabose De Imprimir Esta Historia De
Tito Livio Padvano Principe De La Historia Romana,
en la ciudad Imperial (sic) de Colonia Agrippina,
à costas de Arnoldo Byrckmanno librero, en el año d el
(sic) Señor de M.D. LIII."
Adams, I, no. 1367 (has different signatures than
the IU copy); Palau, 139131.
Reels 90 & 91, No. 583

LIVIUS PATAVINUS, TITUS see LIVIUS, TITUS.

LOCI Commvnes Et Conclvsiones Catholicae, ex diui
Augustini dictis. Quibus ostenduntur Lutheranorum
mendacia. Coloniae: Apud Iasparem Gennepaeum,
1554.
[72] *l*.

Bound in: Pérez De Ayala, Martín: Martini Peresii
Aiala. Episcopi Gvidixiensis ..., 1554.
Reel 141, No. 898

LOPEZ, DIEGO.
Las Seis Satyras De Avlo Persio Flacco, con
declaracion Magistral en lengua Castellana. Por
Diego Lopez, natural de la Villa de Valencia, Orden
de Alcantara. [s.l.:s.n.],[16--].
156, [4] p.; 11cm.

Bound with: Juvenalis, Decimus Junius, ca. 60 - ca.
140. [Satirae. Spanish] Declaracion magistral Sabre Las
Satiras de Ivvenal, Principe de los Poetas Satiricos.
... Madrid: Par Diego Diaz de la Carrera, 1642.
Goldsmith, p. 92, no. 181; HC 398/1873; Palau, 126852;
Penney, p. 291; Salvá, I, 696.
Reel 86, No. 551

LOPEZ CUESTA, FRANCISCO (translator) see HIERONYMUS,
Saint.

LÓPEZ DE ANDRADE, DIEGO, 1569-1628.
   Primera Parte De Los Tratados, Sobre Los Evangelios
Qve Dize La Iglesia En Las Festividades de los Santos.
Compvesto Por El Padre Maestro Fray Diego Lopez
Dandrade, de la Orden san Agustin. Dirigido a la
Excelentissima señora doña Iuana Enriquez de Ribera,
Marquesa de Priego, &c. Con Privilegio. En Madrid:
Por la Viuda de Alonso Martin, 1622.
   [4], 232 (i.e. 322) p.; 22cm.

   Colophon: "Impresso En Madrid por la viuda de
Alfonso Maritin año 1622."
   Many errors in pagination.
   Palau, 140653; Simon Díaz, Jesuitas, no. 1115.
No. 585: Not Available

LÓPEZ DE AYALA, PEDRO, 1332-1407.
   Coronica del serenissimo rey Don Pedro, hijo del
rey don Alonso de Castilla. Nvevamente corregida y
emendada. En Pamplona: Por Pedro Porralis, 1591.
   [2], 222, [12] p.; 30cm.

   Adams, I, no. 1476; Palau, 140778; Penney, p. 157;
Pérez Goyena, 174; Salvá, II, 3003.
Reel 91, No. 586

LÓPEZ DE GOMARA, FRANCISCO see GOMARA, FRANCISCO
   LOPEZ DE, 1510-1560?

LÓPEZ DE HARO, ALONSO, fl. 1525.
   Nobiliario Genealogico De Los Reyes Y Titvlos
De España. Dirigido A La Magestad Del Rey Don Felipe
Quarto nuestro señor. Compvesto Por Alonso Lopez de
Haro, criado de su Magestad, y Ministro en su Real
Consejo de las Ordenes. En Madrid: por Luis Sanchez
Impressor Real, 1622.
   2 parts ([8], 400, [8] p.; 532, [8] p.); 29cm.

   Part II has special t.-p.: Segvnda Parte Del
Nobiliario Genealogico De Los Reyes Y Titvlos De
España. Dirigido A La Magestad Del Rey don Felipe
Quarto deste nombre. Compvesto Por Alonso Lopez
De Haro criado de su Magestad, y ministro en su
Real Consejo de las Ordenes.
   Pagination errors throughout.
   Doublet, p. 80; Goldsmith, p. 99, no. 225; Graesse,
IV, p. 258; Palau, 141238; Pérez Pastor, no. 1857;
Penney, p. 314; Salvá, II, 3570; Sunderland, no. 7576.
Reels 91 & 92, No. 589

LÓPEZ DE MONTOYA, PEDRO, 16th cent.
   Libri Dvo De Concordia Sacrarvm Scriptvrarum,
cum introductorijs quaestionibus ad earum studia, &
noua explicatione plurium locorum difficilium. Opvs
Ipsarvm Scriptvrarum studiosis, verbiq; Dei
concionatoribus valde vtile: nunc denuo recognitum
& auctum. Avctore Petro Lopez de Mõtoya, S. Theologiae
Doctore, & olim in Salmanticensi Academia, Sanctarum
literarum interprete, nunc vero in supremo Sanctae
Inquisitionis Senatu Qualificatore, & Censore.
Madriti: Apud Ludouicum Sanchez, 1600.
   2 parts ([12], 205 p.; [3], 304, [14] p., 5 l.);
19cm.

   Part II has special t.-p.: Liber Secvndvs, De
Concordia sacrarum editionum Hebraice & Graece,
Septuaginta interpretum cum vulgata Latina. Ex Sacri
Tridentini Concilij Decreto iussu sanctiss. Pont.
Six V. & Clementis VIII. Romae nuper edita. Cvm
Explicatione Et Concordia plurium locorum sacrae
Scripturae. Auctore D. Petro Lopez de Montoya. Ipse
Est Pax Nostra, Qvi Fecit Vtraqve Vnvm Reconci
Liansima Svmmis.
   Colophon: "Madriti Apud Ludouicum Sanchez Anno
M.D.XCVI."

LÓPEZ DE MONTOYA (Cont'd)
   Head-pieces; Appendix of 5 numb. leaves at end
of pt. II has, on verso of last leaf: Finis Anno 1600.
   Palau, 141555.
Reel 92, No. 590, Part 1-3

LÓPEZ DE TOLEDO, DIEGO (translator) see CAESAR, CAIUS
   JULIUS.

LÓPEZ DE TOVAR, GREGORIO.
   Repertorio Mvy Copioso del Texto y Leyes De Las
Siete Partidas, agora en esta vltima impresion, hecho
por el Licenciado don Gregorio Lopez de Touar, va
por su Abecedario. En Valladolid: En casa de Diego
Fernandez de Cordoua, Impressor del Rey nuestro
señor, 1588.
   3 v. in 1 ([59] l., [8] l.; 230 l.); 37cm.

   Volumes II and III have special t.-ps.:
   [Vol. II]: Omnes Fere Titvli Tam Ivris Civilis,
Qvam Canonici Leguntur in istis septem Partitarum
legibus, quod sequens tabula demonstrat non sine
magno labore aedita per Licenciatum Gregorium Lopez
à Touar, ipsarum legum glossatoris nepotem, quod
quantae vtilitatis necessitatisque sit omnibus
vtriusque Iuris professo ribus clarissime pater.
   [Vol. III]: Index Sev Repertorivm Materiarum ac
vtriusque iuris decisionum que in singulis Septem
Partitarum glossis continentur: Copiosissime atque
luculentissimò concinnatum, per Licenciatum Gregorium
Lopez à Touar.
   Colophon: Laus Deo, honor & gloria, & cum his
remanet finitum hoc nostrum copiosissimum Repertorium,
Latine compositum. Vallisoleti In officina Didaci
Fernandez à Corduba, Regij Typographi, anno 1588.
   Gil Ayuso, no. 421; HC: NS4/639; Palau, 142084;
Penney, p. 18.
Reel 92, No. 591, Vol. 1-3

LÓPEZ DE VEGA, ANTONIO.
   Heraclito I Democrito De Nvestro Siglo. Descrivese
su legitimo Filosofo. Dialogos Morales, Sobre tres
materias, La Nobleza, La Riqueza, i las Letras.
Dirigidos A Don Manvel Alvarez Pinto i Ribera,
Cavallero del Habito de Santiago, Fidalgo de la Casa
del Rey nuestro señor en la de Portugal, Señor de
la Villa de Chilueches, i de los Lugares de Albolleque,
i la Celada. Por Antonio Lopez de Vega. [Madrid]: Por
Diego Diaz De La Carrera, 1641.
   [24], 429, [1] p.; 19cm.

   Goldsmith, p. 100, no. 251; Palau, 142196.
Reel 92, No. 592

LÓPEZ DE VICUÑA, JUAN, ed. see GÓNGORA Y ARGOTE,
   LUIS DE.

LÓPEZ DE ZÁRATE, FRANCISCO, d. 1658.
   Obras Varias De Francisco Lopez De Zarate. Dedicadas
A Diferentes Personas. Alcala: por Maria Fernandez,
Impressora de la Vniuersidad, 1651.
   [58], 339 (i.e. 343) p.; 20cm.

   Error in paging: no. 103-104 and 205-206 repeated.
   Bound with another work by LOPEZ DE ZARATE: Poema
Heroico De La Invencion De La Crvz, Por El Emperador
Constantino Magno. Dedicalo Al Rey Nvestro Señor
Francisco Lopez de Zarate, natural de la ciudad de
Logroño. Madrid, 1648.

   "Madrigal a la Santissima cruz," l. 268.
   Catalina, no. 1045; Goldsmith, p. 100, nos. 254-255;
Jerez, p. 60; Palau, nos. 142265-142266; Penney, p. 316;
Salvá, I, 745; Ticknor, p. 207.
Reel 93, No. 593

LÓPEZ DE ZÁRATE, FRANCISCO, d. 1658.
Poema Heroico De La Invencion de La Crvz, Por
Francisco Lopez de Zarate, natural de la ciudad de
Logroño. Madrid: Por Francisco Garcia, Impressor
del Reyno, 1648.
[2], 268 l.; 20cm.

Catalina, no. 1045; Goldsmith, p. 100, nos. 254-255;
Jerez, p. 60; Palau, nos. 142265-142266; Penney, p. 316;
Salvá, I, 745; Ticknor, p. 207.
Reel 93, No. 594

LÓPEZ DE ZÁRATE, FRANCISCO, d. 1658.
Varias Poesias De Francisco Lopez De Zarate
natural de la ciudad de Logroño. A don Manvel Alonso
Perez de Guzman el Bueno, Duque de Medina Sidonia,
Conde de Niebla, Marques de Cacaca de la insigne
orden del Tuson, Capitan General del mar Oceano, y
costas del Andaluzia, de la Camara de su Magestad.
[n.p.]: Por la viuda de Alonso Martin de Balboa,
1619.
[4], 99 l.; 12cm.

Date changed in imprint to read 1629.
Foliation errors throughout.
Gallardo, no. 2816; Goldsmith, p. 100, no. 256;
Jerez, p. 60; Palau, 142262; Penney, p. 316; Salvá,
I, 744.
Reel 93, No. 595

LÓPEZ MADERA, GREGORIO.
Discvrsos De La Certidvmbre De Las Reliqvias
Descvbiertas En Granada Desde El Año De 1588. Hasta
El De 1598. Autor el doctor Greg.o lopez Madera
fiscal de su Magestad en la Chancilleria de la dicha
ciudad. Dirigidos Al Illvstrissimo S. Cardenal De
Gvevara Inqvisidor General Destos Reinos Del Conseio
Destado De Sv Magestad. &. Granada: por Sebastian
de Mena Ano [sic], 1601.
[11], 167, [10] l.; 27cm.

Colophon: "Granada por Sebastian de Mena Año de.
1601."
Castello Melhor, no. 1898; Goldsmith, p. 100,
no. 258; HC:384/1446; Palau, 141352; Penney, p. 317.
Reel 93, No. 596

LÓPEZ MADERA, GREGORIO.
Excelencias De La Monarqvia Y Reyno De España.
En Qve De Nvevo Con Grande aumento se trata de su
origen, antiguedad, sucessiones, preeminencias, y
precedencias, nobleza, religion, gouierno, perfecion
de sus leyes, valor, y dotrina de sus naturales;
grandeza, potencia, y riquezas de sus Reynos,
Dignidades, y Titulos de sus vassallos, renombres
de sus Reyes, y conseruacion de su antiquissima
lengua hasta aora. Por el Doctor Gregorio Lopez
Madera, del Consejo supremo de Castilla, &c. A
La Magestad Del Rey Don Filipe IIII Nuestro Señor.
[Madrid]: Por Luis Sanchez impressor de su Magestad,
1625.
[14], 109, [1] l.; 30cm.

Colophon: "En Madrid Por Luis Sanchez Impressor
del Rey nuestro Señor Año M.DC.XXIIII."
Many errors in pagination.
Goldsmith, p. 100, no. 260; Graesse, IV, p. 258;
Jerez, p. 62; Palau, 141350; Penney, p. 317; Pérez
Pastor, no. 141350; Salvá, II, p. 494.
Reel 93, No. 597

LÓPEZ MADERA, GREGORIO.
Excellencias De Sã Ivan Baptista Dirigidas Al
Rey Don Phelippe, III. Nuestro Señor. Y Recopiladas
por el Dor Gregorio Lopez Madera Alcalde de Su Casa,
Y Corte CoRegidor de La Imperial Cibdad de T. [Toledo]:
por bernardino de guzman [sic], 1617.
[13], 305, [30] l.; 21cm.

Engraved title-page with words: Hic Venit In
Testimonivm Vt Omnes Crederent Per Illvm.
Colophon: "Con Privilegio. En Toledo, por Bernardino
de Guzman: Año de 1617."
Many errors in pagination.
Graesse, IV, p. 258; Palau, 141355; Pérez Pastor,
Toledo, no. 490; Vindel, no. 1927.
Reel 93, No. 598

LÓPEZ PINCIANO, ALONSO, fl. 1596-1627.
El Palayo del Pinciano. Madrid: por Luis Sanchez,
1605.
[8], 310 l.; 14cm.

Colophon: "En Madrid. En casa de Luis Sãchez Año
M.DCV."
In verse. Numerous errors in paging.
Goldsmith, p. 100, no. 263; Jerez, p. 59; Palau,
141821; Penney, p. 317; Pérez Pastor, no. 908; Salvá,
I, 738.
Reel 93, No. 599

LOYOLA, IGNACIO DE, Saint, 1491-1556.
Exercitia Spiritualia Sancti Patris Ignatij
Societatis Jesu Fundatoris: Recusa Pragae. Typis
Universitatis Carolo-Ferdinandea in Collegio Societatis
J E S U ad S. Clementem, 1674.
[76] l.; 17cm.
Reel 94, No. 600

LOYOLA, IGNACIO DE, Saint, 1491-1556 see also
RIVADENEIRA, PEDRO DE, S. J., 1527-1611.

LUCANUS, MARCUS ANNAEUS, b. A.D. 39 - d. 65.
Lvcano Tradvzido De Verso Latino En Prosa Castellana,
Por Martin Laso de Oropesa, Secretario del Illustrissimo
Cardenal don Francisco de Mendoca, Obispo de Burgos.
Nuevamente corregido y acabado con la Historia del
Triunuirato. Dirigido al Illustre Señor Antonio
Perez, Secretario del estado de la Magestad Catholica
del Rey don Phelippe Segundo. Bvrgos: En casa de
Phelippe de Iunta, 1588.
[16], 411, [1] p.; 26cm.

Spanish translation by Martín Lasso de Oropesa.
Colophon: "En Burgos. En casa de Phelippe de Iunta
Año 1578."
Date of publication: 1578, not 1588 as stated on
the title-page.
Palau, 143295; Penney, p. 319; Salvá, I, 752.
Reel 94, No. 602

LUCANUS, MARCUS ANNAEUS, b. A.D. 39 - d. 65.
[Pharsalia]
La Historia Qve Escrivio En Latin El poeta Lucano:
trasladada en castellano por Martin Lasso de Oropesa
secretario della excellête señora marquesa del
Zenete condessa de. Nassou. [Antwerp: 1540].
[16], 225 p.; 32cm.

First edition.
Translation into prose by Martín Lasso de Oropesa.
Gallardo, no. 2617; Heredia, no. 1550; Morante,
Cat., 4409; Palau, 143291; Peeters-Fontainas,
Impressions, I, no. 728; Penney, p. 319.
Reel 94, No. 601

LUCANUS, MARCUS ANNAEUS, b. A.D. 39 - d. 65 see also
JÁUREGUI Y AGUILAR, JUAN DE.

LUIS DE GRANADA, 1504-1588.
Conciones Qvae De Praecipvis Sanctorvm Festis In
Ecclesia Habentvr. A Festo Sancti Andrea vsque ad
Festum Beatae Mariae Magdalenae: Auctore R. P. F.
Lvdovico Granatensi, sacrae Theologiae Professore,
Monacho Dominicano. Mirabilis Devs in Sanctis suis
Psalm. 47. Cum viro sancto assiduus esto quemcunque
obseruaueris timentem Dominum Ecclesiastici 37.
Antverpiae: Ex Officina Plantiniana, Apud Ioannem
Moretum, 1588-1600.
2 v. (527 p.; 542 p.); 16cm.

Vol. II: Conciones De Praecipvis Sanctorvm Festis,
A Festo Beatissimae Mariae Magdalenae, vsque ad
finem anni: Auctore R. P. F. Lvdovico Granatensi
sacrae Theologiae Professore, Monacho Dominicano.
Mirabilis Devs in Sanctis suis. Psalm. 47. Cum viro
assiduus esto, quemcumque obseruaueris timentem
Dominum. Ecclesiastici 37.
Colophon: Tam bene quimores Sanctorvm scribit &
acta, Non hunc Sanctorvm Spiritvs intus agit?
Antverpiae Excvdebat Christophorvs Plantinvs,
Architypographvs Regivs. CIƆ. IƆ. L X X X I X.
Adams, I, no. 952-953; Palau, 107820.
Reel 66, No. 398

LUIS DE GRANADA, 1504-1588.
[Conciovm De Tempore]
Primvs Tomvs Concionvm De Tempore, Qvae a prima
Dominica Aduentus vsque ad Quadragesimae initium in
Ecclesia haberi solent. Adiectae sunt in fine quinque
de Poenitentia Conciones, quae diebus Dominicis in
Quadragesima post meridiem habitae sunt. Authore R.
P. F. Ludouico Granatensi, Sacrae Theologiae Professore,
Monacho Dominicano. Antverpiae: Ex officina
Christophori Plantini, Architypographi Regij, 1588.
591 p.; 16cm.

Pagination errors throughout.
Loss of print due to condition of material.
Adams, I, no. 954; Palau, 107820.
Reel 65, No. 394

LUIS DE GRANADA, 1504-1588.
[Conciovm De Tempore]
Secvndvs Tomvs Concionvm De Tempore Quae Quartis,
& diebus Dominicis Quadragesimae in Ecclesia haberi
solent: Authore R. P. F. Ludouico Granatensi, sacrae
Theologiae professore, monacho Dominicano. Matthaei
5. Qui fecerit, & docuerit, hic magnus vocabitur in
regno caelorum. Antverpiae: Ex officina Christophori
Plantini, Architypographi Regij, 1587.
2 pts. in 1 (805, [3] p., 94 p.); 16cm.

Part II: Qvinqve Conciones De Poenitentia, Habitae
In Qvadragesima post meridiem: in quibus primùm
quidem exhortatio ad poenitentiam continetur: deinde
qua ratione vera poenitentia, & peccatorum confessio
agenda sit, traditur. Avctore Eodem R.P. F. Ludouico
Granatensi, monacho Dominicano.
Reel 65, No. 395

LUIS DE GRANADA, 1504-1588.
[Conciovm De Tempore]
Tertivs Tomvs Concionvm De Tempore, Qvae A Pascha
Dominicae resurrectionis ad festum vsque sacratissimi
corporis Christi habentur, nunc primùm in lucem
editus: Authore R. P. F. Lvdovico Granatensi, Sacrae
Theologiae professore, manocho Dominicano. Qui ad
iustitiam erudiunt multos, quasi stellae in perpetuas

LUIS DE GRANADA (Cont'd)
aeternitates. Danielis I.2. Lvgdvni: In off. Q Philippi
Thinghi apud Simphorianum Beraud, Et Stephanum
Michaelem, 1585.
647 p.; 16cm.

Palau, 107788.
Reel 65, No. 396

LUIS DE GRANADA, 1504-1588.
[Conciovm De Tempore]
Qvartvs Tomvs Concionvm De Tempore, Qvae post
festum Sacratissimi Corporis Christi, vsque ad initium
Dominici Aduentus Ecclesia habentur. Avctore R. P. F.
Lvdovico Granatensi, sacrae Theologiae professore,
ordinis sancti Dominici. Adiectae sunt in fine duae
conciones, quarum altera ad mortuorum funera, altera
ad communes, quae in vita accidunt, calamitates,
deseruit. Qui docti fuerint, fulgebunt quasi splendor
firmamenti: & qui ad iustitiam erudiunt multos, quasi
stellae in perpetuas aeternitates. Daniel. 12.
Antverpiae: Ex officina Christophori Plantini, 1583.
725, [1] p.; 16cm.

Loss of print throughout due to condition of
material.
Colophon: Antverpiae, excudebat Christophorvs
Plantinvs, anno CIƆ. IƆ LXXXII.
Palau, 107788.
Reel 66, No. 397

LUIS DE GRANADA, 1504-1588.
Contemptvs Mvndi, Nueuamente romancado y corregido
Añadiose le [sic] vn breue tratado de Oraciones, y
exercicios de deuocion muy prouechosos. Recopilados
de diuersos authores por el Reuerendo Padre Fray
Luys de Granada, de la orden de Sancto Domingo.
Anveres: En casa de Christophoro Plantino
Prototypographo de la Magestad Real, 1572.
2 v. in 1 (538, [10] p.; 124, [1] p.); 17cm.

Translation of De Imitatione Christi of Thomas à
Kempis.
Vol. II: Sigvense Vnas Oraciones Y Exercicios De
deuocion muy prouechosos Recopilados De diuersos y
graues auctores. por el Reuerendo Padre Fray Luys de
Granada, Prouincial de Portugal, de la orden de Sancto
Domingo.
Includes an index in v. 2.
Palau, vol. 6, no. 127402; Peeters-Fontainas, II,
no. 1289.
Reel 65, No. 393, Vol. 1-2

LUIS DE GRANADA, 1504-1588.
Ecclesiasticae Rhetoricae Sive De Ratione
concionandi libri sex, nunc primum in lucem editi.
Authore R. P. F. Ludouico Granateñ. sacrae Theologiae
professore, monacho Dominicano. Fauus mellis composita
verba, dulcedo animae, & sanitas ossium. Qui sapiens
est corde, appellabitur prudens, & qui dulcis eloquio,
maiora reperiet. Prouerb. 16. Olysippone: Excudebat
Antonius Riberius, expensis Ioannis Hispani Bibliopolae,
1576.
[16], 362, [1] p.; 25cm.

Colophon: "Registrvm A B C D E F G H I K L M N
O P Q R S T V X Y Z Olysippone. Excudebat Antonius
Riberius, expensis Ioannis Hispani. Anno Domini 1575."
Doublet, p. 81; Palau, 108132.
Reel 64, No. 390

LUIS DE GRANADA, 1504-1588.
  [Flores. Latin]
  Flores R. P. F. Lodoici Granatensis, Ex Omnibvs
Eivs Opvscvlis spiritualibus iam recens summa fide
excerpti, & in octo partes distributi. Collectore Et
Interprete Michaele ab Isselt Amorfortio. Coloniae:
Apud Geruinum Calenium, & haeredes Ioannis Quentelij,
1588.
  [17], 396 (i.e. 407) l.; 12cm.

  Latin translation by Michael ab Isselt.
  Pagination errors throughout.
  Adams, I, no. 976; Palau, 108237.
Reel 67, No. 404

LUIS DE GRANADA, 1504-1588.
  Introdvccion Del Simbolo De La Fe [Primera Parte
De La] En Ella Se Trata De La Creacion Del Mundo,
para venir por las criaturas al conocimiento del
Criador (sic), y de sus perfecciones. Al Excelentissimo
Señor Don Melchor de Nauarra y Rocaffull, &c. Compvesto
Por El Muy Reverendo Padre Maestro Fray Luis de Granada,
del Orden de Santo Domingo. Delectasti me Domine in
factura tua, & in operibus manu umtuarum exultabo.
Psalm. 91. Ianitor Coeli: Doctor Orbis Pariter:
Ivdices Secli: Vtrivsqve Mvndi Lvmina: En Madrid: En
la Imprenta Real: A costa de la viuda de Iuan Antonio
Bonet, Mercader de Libros, 1672.
  [12], 722, [2] p.; 30cm.

  Half title: Primera Parte Del Simbolo De Fray
Lvis De Granada.
  Palau, 108173.
Reel 66, No. 399

LUIS DE GRANADA, 1504-1588.
  [Introduccion del Symbolo de la Fe]
  Primera [Segvnda, Tercera, y Qvarta] Parte De La
Introdvction [sic] del symbolo de la Fe, en la qual
se trata de la Creacion del mundo para venir por las
criaturas al conocimiento del Craidor, y de sus diuinas
perfectiones. Compuesta por el R. P. Maestro F. Luys
de Granada de la orden de S. Domingo. Delectasti me
Domine in factura tua, & in operibus manuum tuarum
exultabo. Psal. 91. En Salamanca: Por los herederos
de Mathias Gast, 1583.
  4 vols. in 1 ([20], 187, [2] p.; 221, [2] p.; 153,
[2] p.; 215, [3] p.); 30cm.

  Each part has special title-page:
  Vol. II: Segvnda Parte De La Introdvction del
Symbolo de la Fe, y religion Christiana. Compuesta
por el R.P. Maestro F. Luys de Granada de la orden de
Sancto Domingo. Testimonia tua credibilia sancta sunt
nimis. Psal. 92. Deus autem spei repleat vos omni
gaudio & pace in credendo. Rom 15.
  Vol. III: Tercera Parte, De La Introdvction del
Symbolo de la Fe, que trata del mysterio de nuestra
redempcion, en la qual procediendo por lumbre de
razon se declara, quan conueniente medio aya sido
este que la diuina bondad y sabiduria escogio para
salud del linage humano. Compuesta por el R. P. Maestro
F. Luys de Granada de la orden de Sancto Domingo. Va
Esta Parte Tercera Dividida en tres tratados principales.
En el primero, se trata de los fructos del arbol de S.
Cruz. En el segundo, de las figuras del mysterio de
Christo. En la tercera, por via de Dialogo, se responde
a las preguntas que acerca deste mysterio se pueden
hazer.
  Vol. IV: Qvarta Parte, De La Introdvction Del Symbolo
De La Fe: En La qual (procediendo por lumbre de Fe) se
trata del mysterio de nuestra redempcion: Para lo
qual se traen todas las prophecias, que testifican
ser Christo nuestro Saluador el Messias prometido en
la ley, donde tambien se declaran otros mysterios, y
articulos de nuestra sancta Fe, contenidos en el
Symbolo.

LUIS DE GRANADA (Cont'd)
  Colophon: "En Salamanca Por los herederos de
Mathias Gast M.D. LXXXIII."
  Binder's title: Fr. Luis Simbolo de la Fee.
  Contents: Pt. I. De la creacion del mundo; Pt. 2.
De las excelencias de nuestra sanctissima fe, y
religion christiana; Pts. 3, 4. Del mysterio de
nuestra redempcion.
  Palau, 108154.
Reel 66, No. 400

LUIS DE GRANADA, 1504-1588.
  [Introdvccion del symbolo de la Fe. Latin]
  R.P.F. Lvdovici Granaten. Ordinis S. Dominici,
Introdvctionis Ad Symbolvm Fidei, Libri Qvatvor: In
Qvibvs De Admirabili Opere Creationis, Fidei ac
Religionis Christianae praestantijs, Redemptionis
humanae, & alijs Mysterijs ac Articulis, tractatur. A
Ioanne Pavlo Gallvcio Saloensi ex Italico sermone
Latinitate donati. Nunc Partim Ad Italicam Versionem,
Partim Ad ipsos fontes vnde pleraque desumpta sunt,
diligenti facta collatione, ab infinitis, quibus
antea scatebant, & mirum in modum foedati erant,
mendis ac vitijs repurgati, & primum in Germania
editi. Opvs Revera Insigne, Non Tantvm Theologis,
verbique diuini praeconibus, sed & Philosophis, ac
omnibus pietatem amantibus lectu incundissimum &
vtilissimum. Cum Indice Capitum, & Rerum memorabilium
copioso. Coloniae: Apud Geruinum Calenium & haeredes
Ioannis Quentelij, 1588.
  [24], 826, [49] p.; 22cm.

  Translation by Michael ab Isselt.
  Adams, I, no. 977; palau, 108189.
Reel 67, No. 401

LUIS DE GRANADA, 1504-1588.
  [Libro de la Oración y meditación. English]
  Of Prayer, And Meditation. Wherein Are Conteined
Fowertien Deuoute Meditations for the seuen daies of
the weeke, bothe for the morninges, and eueninges.
And in them is treyted of the consideration of the
principall holie Mysteries of our faithe. Written
Firste In The Spanishe tõgue, by the famous Religious
father. F. Lewis de Granada, Prouinciall of the
holie order of peachers [sic] in the Prouince of
Portugall. Imprinted at Roven: by George L'oiselet,
1584.
  692 p.; 14cm.

  English translation by Richard Hopkins.
  Pagination errors throughout.
  Allison, p. 108, no. 19.1; Allison and Rogers,
no. 477; Palau, 107519; Pollard and Redgrave, no.
16908.
Reel 67, No. 402

LUIS DE GRANADA, 1504-1588.
  [Libro de la Oracion y meditación. English]
  Granados [sic] Devotion. Exactly Teaching How A Man
May Trvely Dedicate and deuote himselfe vnto God: and
so become his acceptable Votary. Written in Spanish,
by the learned and reuerend Diuine F. Lewes of Granada.
Since translated into Latine, Italian and French.
And now perused, and englished, by Francis Meres,
Master of Artes, & student in Diuinity. London :
Printed by E. Allde, for Cuthbert Burby, and are to be
sold at his shop vnder the Royall Exchange, 1598.
  [12], 576, [55] p.; 11cm.

  English translation by Francis Meres.
  Allison, p. 108, no. 21; Palau, 107521; Pollard
and Redgrave, no. 16902.
Reel 67, No. 403

LUIS DE GRANADA, 1504-1588.
[Libro llamado Guía de peccadores. English]
The Sinners Gvyde. A Worke Contayning the whole
regiment of a Christian life, deuided into two Bookes:
VVherein Sinners Are Reclaimed From The By-Path Of
Vice And destruction and brought vnto the high-way
of euerlasting happinesse. Compiled In The Spanish
Tongve, By The Learned and reuerend Diuine, F. Lewes
of Granada. Since translated into Latine, Italian,
and French. And nowe perused, and digested into
into English, by Francis Meres, Maister of Artes, and
student of Diuinitie. I. Timothie. 4. verse, 8.
Godlines is profitable vnto all things, which hath
the promise of the life present, and of that is to
come. At London: Printed by Iames Roberts, for
Paule Linley, & Iohn Flasket and are to be sold in
Paules Church-yard, at the signe of the Beare, 1598.
2 pts. in 1 ([8], 528, [28] p.; 18cm.)

English translation by Francis Meres.
Title page of Part II reads: The Seconde Booke, of
the Sinners Guyde. Written in Spanish tongue, by the
learned and reuerend Diuine, F. Lewes of Granada. Since
translated into Latine, Italian, and French, and now
perused, and digested into English, by Francis Meres,
Maister of Arts, and student in Diuinitie.
Paged continuously.
First edition in English.
Pages 36, 186-187, 190-191, 220, 351, 515 incorrectly
numbered 34, 196-197, 200-201, 120, 51, 516, respectively.
Head and tail pieces; initials. Marginal notes.
Allison, p. 108, no. 18, Palau, 107715; Pollard and
Redgrave, no. 16918.
Reel 67, No. 406

LUIS DE GRANADA, 1504-1588.
[Libro llamado Guía de peccadores. Latin]
DVX Peccatorm R. P. F. Lvdovici Granatensis Ordinis
S. Dominici. Opvscvlvm Valde Pivm In duos libros
distributum: quo peccatores a via vitiorum &
perditionis ad regiam virtutum ac salutis eterne viam
perducuntur. Per Michaelem ab Isselt ex lingua Italica
in Latinam antea conuersum, & nunc recognium. Coloniae:
Apud Geriunum Calenium, & haeredes Ionnis Quentelij,
1590.
2 pts. in 1 ([44], 580 p.; 274 p.); 13cm.

Latin translation by Michael ab Isselt.
Part II has special t.-p.: Dvcis Peccatorum Liber
Secvndvs, R. P. F. Lvdovici Granatensis Ordinis S.
Dominici. Per Michaelem ab Isselt ex lingua Italica
in Latinam conuersus & nunc recognitus.
Adams, I, no. 970; Palau, 107706.
Reel 67, No. 405

LUIS DE GRANADA, 1504-1588.
Memorial De La vida Christiana [Segvndo Volvmen
Del]: En el qual se contienen los tres Tratados
postreros que pertenecen a los exercicios de la
deuocion, y el del Amor de Dios, Compuesto por el
R. P. Fray Luys de Granada, de la Orden de Sancto
Domingo. Anveres: En casa de Christophoro Plantino
Prototypographo de la Magestad Real, 1572.
460, [3] p.; 17cm.

Part 2 of vol. I.
Stained throughout causing loss of print.
Antonio, IV, p. 40; Palau, 107909; Peeters-
Fontainas, I, no. 732.
Reel 64, No. 386

LUIS DE GRANADA, 1504-1588.
[Memorial de la vida christiana. English]
A Memoriall Of A Christian Life. Wherin Are Treated
Al Svch things, as appertaine vnto a Christian to
do from the beginning of his cõuersion, vntil the end
of his perfection. Deuided into Seauen [sic] Treatises:
the particulars whereof are noted in the page following.
Written first in the Spanish tongue, by the famous
Religious Father, F. Lewis de Granada, Prouinciall
of the holy order of Preachers, in the Prouince of
Portugall. Imprinted at Rouen: George Lorselet,
1599.
[2], 762 (i.e. 749), [8] p.: illus.; 16cm.

English translation by Richard Hopkins.
Includes four of the seven treatises, the remainder
to be completed in the second volume, were never
published.
Pagination errors throughout.
Allison, p. 110, no. 23.1; Allison and Rogers,
no. 473; Palau, 107983; Pollard and Redgrave, no.
16904.
Reel 64, No. 389

LUIS DE GRANADA, 1504-1588.
[Memorial de la vida christiana. Italian]
Trattato Primo [y Secondo] Dell'Aggivnta Del
Memoriale Della Vita Christiana Del R. P. F. Luigi
di Granata dell'Ordine de' Predicatori. Nel quale
si tratta dell Amor di Dio, nella cui perfettione
consiste la perfettione della vita Christiana.
Nouamente Tradotto dalla lingua Spagnuola per Camillo
Camilli. Con due Tauole; una dei Capitoli, & l'altra
delle cose piu notabili. Con Privilegii. Vinegia:
Presso Giorgio Angelieri, 1581.
2 parts in 1 vol. ([19], 220 l.; [12], 226 l.)

Italian translation by Camillo Camilli.
Part II: Trattato Secondo Dell'Aggivnta Del
Memoriale della vita Christiana Del R. P. F. Luigi di
Granata Dell'Ordine dei Predicatori. Nel quale si
pongono molte deuotissime Meditationi sopra alcuni
Passi, & Misterii principali della Vita del Nostro
Saluatore: & in Particolare della sua santa Pueritia,
Passione, Resurrettione, & gloriosa Ascensione.
Nuouamente Tradotto dalla lingua Spagnuola per
Camillo Camilli. Con due Tauole; una dei Capitoli,
& l'altra delle cose piu notabili.
Pagination errors throughout.
Palau, 107953; not in Short-title ...
Reel 64, No. 387

LUIS DE GRANADA, 1504-1588.
[Memorial de la vida christiana. Latin]
Memoriale Christianae Vitae. Vna cum Adivnctis
duobus, seu Appendicibvs, de eadem materia. Avctore
R. P. F. Lvdovico Granatensi, Ordinis S. Dominici.
Opus valde pium, ex idiomate Italico in Latinum
translatum, opera & studio Michaelis ab Isselt
Amorfortij. Coloniae: Ex officina Arnoldi Quentelij,
1598.
[30], 807 p.; 15cm.

Latin translation by Michael ab Isselt.
Adams, I, no. 982.
Reel 64, No. 388

LUIS DE GRANADA, 1504-1588.
[Obras espirituales. French]
Les Oeuvres Spirituelles Du P. Louis De Grenade
De l'Ordre De S. Dominique; Divisées en quatre Parties.
La Premiere contient la Guide des Pecheurs, où le
Chrestien apprend ce qu'il doit faire depuis sa
conversion jusqu'a la fin de sa vie. La Seconde, le
Traité de l'Oraison & de la Meditation que l'on peut
faire su les principaux Mysteres de nostre Foy & sur
les principales parties de la Penitence, qui son,
la Priere, le Jeusne & l'Aumosne. Troisiéme, le
Memorial de la vie Chrestienne, qui traite de la
Confesion, de la Communion, & de ce que doit faire
une ame nouvellement convertie à Dieu. Et La Quatriéme,
le Traité de l'Amour de Dieu & des principaux Mysteres
de la Vie de nostre Seigneur. Traduites De Nouveau
En Francois Par M. Girard Conseiller du Roy en ses
Conseils. A Paris: Chez Jacques Villery, ruë vielle
Bouclerie, au bas de la ruë de la Harpe, prés le
Pont S. Michel, à l'Estoille d'or, 1690.
[20], 1049, [35] p.; 37cm.

French translation by M. Girard.
Pagination errors throughout.
Stained causing loss of print.
Foulché-Delbosc, Bibliographie, V, no. 1944.
Reel 63, No. 385

LUIS DE GRANADA, 1504-1588.
Paradisvs Precvm, R. P. F. Lvdovici Granatensis
Spiritvalibvs Opvscvlis, aliorumǵue sanctorum Patrum,
Illustrium cùm veterum, tum recentium Scriptorum
concinnatus Per Michaelem ab Isselt. Coloniae: Ex
officina Arnoldi Quentelij, 1596.
[24], 567, [8] p.; 13cm.

Extracts from the works of Luis de Granada. Latin
version by Michael ab Isselt.
Adams, I, no. 985.
Reel 68, No. 407

LUIS DE GRANADA, 1504-1588.
A Paradise of prayers, containing the purity of
deuotion. Gathered out of all the spirituall excercises
of Levves of Granado [sic] And Englished for the
benefit of the Christian Reader. Ascendat oratio,
descendat gratia. London: Printed by R. Field for
Mathew Law, and are to be sold at his shop in Paules
Church-yard neere vnto S. Austines [sic] gate, 1614.
[2], 356 p.; 12cm.

Pagination errors throughout.
A translation of Paradisve Precvm. Probably translated
by Thomas Lodge (cf. Allison, English Translations ...
1974, p. 114).
Not compiled by Thomas Lodge, Bibliographical
Catalogue of the Early Editions, 1973. Allison,
p. 114, no. 31.1; Pollard and Redgrave, 169167.
Reel 68, No. 408

LUIS DE GRANADA, 1504-1588.
R. P. FR. Lvdovici Granatensis, Sacrae Theologiae
Professoris, Ordinis S. Dominici. Ecclesiasticae
Rhetoricae, siue de ratione concionandi, libri sex,
denuò editi, ac diligenter emendati, Fauus mellis
composita verba, dulcedo animae, & sanitas ossium.
Qui sapiens est corde, appellabitur prudens, & qui
dulcis eloquio, maiora reperiet. Prouerb. 16.
Coloniae: In officina Birckmannica, 1582.
[16], 422 p.; 17cm.

Adams, I, no. 973; Palau, 108135.
Reel 64, No. 391

LUIS DE GRANADA, 1504-1588.
R.P. FR. Lvdovici Granatensis, Sacrae Theologiae
Professoris Ordinis Praedicatorum. Rhetoricae
Ecclesiasticae, siue, de ratione concionandi, libri
sex. Item, R. P. FR. Didaci Stellae, Hispani, Ordinis
regularis obseruantiae, De Modo Concionandi Liber.
&, Explanatio in Psalm. CXXXVI. Super flumina
Babylonis. Liber nuncupatus, Directorium Concionatorium
Editio vltima aucta & emendata. Parisiis: Apud
Gvillelmvm Pelé, viâ Iacobeâ, sub signo Crucis
aureae, 1635.
[16], 774 p.; 21cm.

Palau, 108137.
Reel 65, No. 392

LUIS DE GRANADA see also JOANNES CLIMACUS, Saint.

LULL, RAMÓN, d. 1315.
Arbor philosophia amoris. [Paris: Baldio Asensio,
1516].
CIX-CLXXI *l.*; 18cm.

Colophon: In chalcografia Ascensiana: impensis
eius & Ioannis Parui. Ad Idus decembris. M.DXVI.
Bound with: [Liber Proberbiorum]. [Paris: Baldio
Asensio, 1516].
Palau, VII, 143762; Penney, p. 322; Rogent Massó,
p. 360, no. 23.
Reel 94, No. 611

LULL, RAMÓN, d. 1315.
Ars brevis. [Romae: Eucharius Silber, 1485]
[31] *l.*; 21cm.

No signatures. Text in Latin.
Printer identified by the Kommission für den
Gesamtkat. d. wiegendr.
One table and the three diagrams, one with movable
parts, are in manuscript; an additional manuscript
diagram is on the originally blank verso.
Two green and two red initials supplied; paragraph
marks and capital lines supplied in red on leaves
3^r, 9^v - 11^r, 20^v, 21^r.
Bound in a vellum leaf from a Breviary (possible
the Breviarium pragense, printed by Georg Stucks,
Nuremberg, 1502) with the text type and the large
wood-cut initials reproduced in Veröffentlichungen
d. Gesellschaft für Typenkunde d. XV. Jahrhunderts,
respectively plate 941 and plate 944.
Klebs, A. C. (Incunabula Scientifica et Medica
[in Osiris, 1938, vol. IV, p. 1 - 359), item 627.3;
Goff, L-386; Palau, 143701; Stillwell, L-347.
Reel 94, No. 603

LULL, RAMÓN, d. 1315.
[Ars brevis]
Ars Brevis Illvminati Doctoris Magistri Raymvndi
Lvll. Qvae est ad omens scientias pauco & breui
tempore ac sequendas introductorium & breuis via,
vna cum figuris illi materiae deser vientibus, necnon
& illius scientiae approbatione. In cuius castigatione
attendat lector quàm castigatissimè Magister Bernardus
de lavinheta artis illius fidissimus interpres
inudarit. Quia si elementum aut demas, aut addis
(ipsum vel iota) totius rei seummam immutas, & ad
alios artis huiusce libros quae propendiem in eadem
facultate sumus emisuri te reddis inhabilem. Parisiis:
Apud Aegydium Gorbinum, sub insigni Spei, ē regione
Collegi Cameracensis, 1578.
[48] *l.*; 16cm.

Bound with his Opusculum ... de auditu Kabbalistico
(1578), and Liber de Articuli fidei sacrosanctae (1578).
Doublet, p. 83; Graesse, IV, p. 295; Palau, VII,
143708.
Reel 94, No. 604

LULL, RAMÓN, d. 1315.
[Ars Cabbalistica] or [Opusculum de Auditu Cabbalistico.]
Opvscvlvm Raymvndinvm De auditu Kabbalistico siue ad omnes scientias introductorium. Incipit libellus de Kabbalistico auditu in via Raymundi Lullii. Parisiis, Apud Aegidium Gorbinum ē regione Colegii Cameracensis, 1578.
[1], 82 *l*.; 16cm.

Includes diagrams and a table.
Bound with author's: Arvs brevis (1578) and his Liber de Articuli fidei (1578).
Palau, VII, 143864.
Reel 94, No. 606

LULL, RAMÓN, d. 1315.
[De Conceptione B. V. Mariae.] Sevilla : Paulus de Colonia Ct Socii Martinus Almondovar, 12 de Marzo de 1491.
[28] *l*.; 21cm.

Spurious and doubtful work.
Colophon: Ad laudem honorē intemerate virginis marie: liber / de ei' cōceptu ab omi labe originali Imuni: ab egregio vi- / ro magistro Raymundo lull doctore illuminato compita- / tus (qui pro fide catholica laipidū ictibus occubuit apud / tunicem ciuitatem agarenos) felici numine est explicitus. / Impressus hispali impensis religiosi viri fratris martini / almodouar militie de calatraua. opera vero īgenio ma- / gistri pauli & colonia sociorū ei' alemanorū / die martii. Anno ab incarnatione dñi. 1491.
Escudero, no. 23; Goff, L-389; Graesse, IV, p. 296; Haebler, no. 385; Hain, no. 5603-10326; Reichling, no. 1026; Rogent Massó, pp. 11-12, no. 13; Stillwell, no. 1-350; Vindel, no. 22.
Reel 95, No. 616

LULL, RAMÓN, d. 1315.
[Ianua artis magistri Raymundi Lulli.]
Clementissime Devs Cvm Tva Gratia & auxilio: Incipit liber qui uocatur Ianua artis: Magistri Raymundi Lull aeditus a dño Petro degiuille montis Albi presbytero ... [Romae, Eucharius Silber, 1485]
[24] *l*.; 21cm.

Pere de Gui, editore.
Colophon: Finis. Impressum Rome Anno M.CCC LXXXV.
The type is identical with that in the author's Ars brevis (1485), the printer of which has been identified as Eucharius Silber.
Initials and capital strokes supplied in red on Leaves 1^V - 8^r, 20^V - 21^r.
Bound in a vellum leaf from a Breviary (possibly the Breviarium pragense printed by Georg Stuchs, Nuremberg [1502]) with the text type and the large wood-cut initials reproduced in Veröffentlichungen d. Gesellschaft für Typenkunde d. XV. Jahrhunderts, respectively plate 941 and 944.
Goff, G-546; Palau, VII, 143701; Reichling, 606.
Reel 94, No. 608

LULL, RAMÓN, d. 1315.
[Liber de Articuli fidei]
Articvli Fidei Sacrosanctae Ac Salvtiferae legis Christianae cum eorundem perpulchra introductione Quos (cooteras leges omnes improbando) Illuminatus doctor Magister Raymundus Lullius rationibus necessariis demonstratiue probat. Parisiis, Apud Aegidium Gorbinum, sub inisgni spei, ē regione collegij Cameracensis, 1578.
64 *l*.; 16cm.

LULL (Cont'd)
A reprint of the 1509 ed., published in Köln (Cf. E. Rogent Massó and E. Durán Reynals. Bibliografia de les Impressions Lullianes. Barcelona, 1927, p. 104)
Bound with author's: Ars brevis (1578), and Opusculum ... de auditu Kabbalistico (1578).
Doublet, p. 83; Palau, VII, 143782.
Reel 94, No. 605

LULL, RAMÓN, d. 1315.
[Liber de secretis naturae seu de quinta essentia.]
Sacrido ctoris Raymundi Lullii secretis nature sive de quinta essentia libellus. [n.p. : Auguste Vindelicorū, 1518]
[26] *l*.; 21cm.

Colophon: Excusum Auguste Vindelicorū. Anno Sal. M.D. X V III. Die vero prima Iuly.
A Lullian version of the De Consideratione Quintae Essentiae, by Joannes de Rupescissa.
A reprint of the 1514 edition.
Graesse, IV, p. 296; Palau, VII, 143829.
Reel 94, No. 609

LULL, RAMÓN, d. 1315.
[Liber mercuriorum.]
Raymundi Lvlli Doctissisimi Et Celeberrimi Philosophi Mercvriorvm liber iam tandem subsidio manuscripti exemplaris prefecte editus. Item Eiusdem Apertorium, Repertorium, Artis intellectivae Theorica & Practica, Magia naturalis, opuscula plane aurea. Coloniae Agrippinae: Apud Iohannem Birckmannum, 1577.
[16], 381, [1] p.; 15cm.

Colophon [p. 382:] Coloniae Apud Johannem Birckmannum Anno M.D. LXVII (i.e. M.D.LXXVII) Cum gratia & priuilegio Caes. Maiest.
Pages 383-384 blank.
Contains the following works attributed to Ramon Lull: 1) Liber mercuriorum (pp. 1-183); 2) Apertorium (pp. 184-223); 3) Repertorium ad intelligendum Testamentum et Codicillum (pp. 224-239); 4 Ars intellectiva (pp. 240-356) and 5) Magia naturalis (pp. 357-381).
Palau, VII, 143884; Rogent Massó, p. 418, letter D.
Reel 95, No. 614

LULL, RAMÓN, d. 1315.
[Liber proverbiorum]
Prouerbia Raemundi Philosophia amoris eiusdem Iodocii Badii qui impressit tetrastichon. Et cibus hic animi purgati pneumate sacro ... In chalcografia Ascensiana: impensis eius & Ioannis Parui. Ad Idus decembris.,1516.
Bound with: the author's: Arbor philosophiae amoris, written by Lull in October of 1298 in Paris.
Palau, VII, 143762; Penney, p. 322; Rogent Massó, p. 360, no. 23.
Reel 94, No. 610

LULL, RAMÓN, d. 1315.
[Liber proverbiorum.]
Illuminati doctoris: Raymundi Lull. omnium disciplinarum consumatissimi. Qui Deum: z seipsum cognoscere docet. Naturas substantiarum: z e ɔ rum accidentiu demostrat Moralesqz virtutes: z vitia complectitur sententiarum libellus. [Venice: Ioannes Tacuinum, 1507]
75, [1] *l*.; 21cm.

Colophon: Impressum Venetiis per Joannem Tacuinum de Tridino: Anno domini M.D.VII. Die XII, Iulii."
Palau, 143761.
Reel 94, No. 607

LULL, RAMÓN, 1315.
[Logica nova.]
Raymundi Lully Doctoris illuminati de noua logica de correlatiuis necnon de ascensu et descensu intellectus: quibus siquidē tribus libellis p. breui ad facili artificio non solum logicaliuz intētionū req phisicarum: sed theologaliū cotemplationum nō mediocris habetur cognito: opuscula ad Archetypos emēdata feliciter Introspicicto. [Valencia, Jorge Costilla. 1512].
2 v. in 1 (56, 64 (i.e. 62) l.); 16cm.

Colophon: Alphonsus de proaza Asturiecēn ad venerabile virū Joannez suum Martinum Figuerolam z C.
First edition. Not to be confused with two other works by the same author, that is to say: Logica brevis e nova and Logica brevis.
Adams, I, no. 1701; Palau, VII, 143737; Thomas, p. 55.
Reel 95, No. 615, Vol. 1-2

LULL, RAMÓN, d. 1315.
[Opera.]
Raymvndi Lvlii Opera Ea Qvae Ad Adinventam Ab Ipso Arten Vniversalem, Scientiarvm omnium breui compendio, firmaque memoria apprenhendendarum, locupletissimaque vel oratione ex tempore pertractandarum, pertinent. Vt Et In Eandem Qvordvndam Interpretum scripti commentarij: quae omnia Sequens indicabit pagina: & demum tempore coniunctim emendatiora locupletioraqz non nihil edita sunt. Accesit Index Cvm Capitvm tum rerum ac verborum locupletissimus. Argentinae: Sumptibus Lazari Zetzneri, 1598.
[24], 992, [31] p.; 19cm.

Contains the following works: 1) Ars brevis; 2) Ars cabbalistica; (attributed); 3) Liber lamentationis philosophiae; 4) Logica brevis et nova; 5) Tractatus de venatione medie inter subjectum et praedicatum (attributed); 6) Tractatus de conversione subjecti et praedicati per medium; 7) In Rhetoricam isagoge (attributed); 8) Oratio exemplaris (attributed); 9) Ars generalis ultima; 10) Liber de articuli fidei; 11) Remigius Rufus: Antonio Bohero Epistola; 12) Giordano Bruno: a) De lulliano specierum scrutinio; b) De lampade combinatoria lulliana; c) De progessu logicae venationis; d) De progressu et lampade venatoria logicorum; 13) Heinrich Cornelius Agrippa von Nettesheim: a) Commentaria in artem brevem Raymundi Lulli; b) Joanni Laurencino Ludgunsensi Epistola.
Reel 94, No. 612

LULL, RAMÓN, d. 1315.
[Opera.]
Raymundi Lulli Opera Ea Quae Ad Adinventam Ab Ipso Aretem Universalem Scientiarum Artiumque Omnium Brevi compendio firmaqz memoria apprehendendarum, locupletissimaque vel oratione ex tempore pertractandarum, pertinent. Ut Et In Eandem Qvorvmdam Interpretum scripti commentarii: quae omnia sequens indicabit pagina: & hoc demum tempore conjunctim emendatiora locupletioraqz non nihil edita sunt. Accessit Valerii de Valeriis, Patricii Veneti aureum in artem Lvllii generalem opus: Adiuncto Indice Cvm Capitv, tùm rerum ac verborum locupletissimo. Editio Postrema. Argentorati: Sumptibus Haeredum Lazari Zetzneri, 1651.
2 v. in 1 ([16], 734 p.; 735-1109, [41] p.); 18cm.

Graesse, IV, p. 296; Palau, VII, 143678; Rogent Massó, p. 338; no. 33.
Reel 95, No. 613, Vol. 1-2

LUMBIER, RAYMUNDO.
Josephina Carmelitana, De Varios Sermones Del Santissimo Patriarca San Joseph Esposo De Nvestra Señora, y Padre de Jesvs. Pvblicala Sv Avtor. El Rmo. P. M. Fr. Raymvndo Lvmbier, del Orden de nuestra Señora del Carmen Observante, Cathedratico de Prima en la Vniversidad de Zaragoza, Examinador Synodal de su Arzobispado, Calificador de la Suprema, Predicador de su Magestad, y segunda vez Provincial de su Provincia de Aragon, &c. Zaragoza: por Agustin Verges, 1676.
[4], 174, [1] p.; 20cm.

Palau, 143954.
Reel 95, No. 617

LUNA, JUAN DE, fl. 1620. for the spurious second part of Lazarillo de Tormes, by Juan de Luna, see LAZARILLO DE TORMES.

LUNA, MIGUEL.
La Verdadera Hystoria Del Rey Don Rodrigo, en la qual se trata la causa principal dela perdida de España y la cōquista que della hizo Miramolin Almācor Rey que fue del Africa, y de las Arabias. Cōpuesta por el sabio Alcayde Abulcacim Tarif Abentariq, de nacion Arabe, y natural de la Arabia Petrea. Nvevamente Tradvzida De La Lengua Arabiga, por Miguel de Luna vezino de Granada, interprete del Rey don Phelippe nuestro señor. [Granada]: Impressa por Rene Rabut, 1592.
[8], 112, [4] l.; 21cm.

Foliation errors throughout.
Colophon: "Impresso en Granada en casa de Rene Rabut año de. 1592."
Jerez, p. 129; Graesse, I, p. 7; Penney, p. 322; Salvá, II, p. 437; Toda y Güell, 13.
Reel 95, No. 618

LYRA, NICOLAUS DE see Bible. Latin. 1492. Vulgate.

M

MACROPEDIUS, GEORGIUS, 1475?-1558.
Epistolarvm Artificiose Conscribendarvm Methodvs,
Auctore Georgio Macropedio. Eivsdem Epitome
praeceptionum de paranda Copia verborum & rerum, per
Quaestiones: Item de nouem speciebus argumentationum
Rhetoricarum, rem omnem breuiter explicans. Accesait
Christophori Hagendorphini Epistolas conscribendi
Methodus Hac aeditione longè quam anteâ emendatior.
Antverpiae: Excudebat Ioannes VVithagius, 1582.
200 p.; 16cm.

Bound in Vives, Juan Luis: De Conscribendis
Epistolis ..., 1536.
Reel 195, No. 1253

MADARIAGA, JUAN DE.
Del Senado, Y De Sv Principe. Por Fray Iuan de
Madariaga, Monge de la Cartuxa de Porta caeli.
Posuit Deus oculum ipsorum super corda illorum.
Eccli. 17. Valencia: en la Impresion de Felipe Mey,
1617.
[24], 532 p.; 21cm.

Graesse, IV, p. 331; Palau, 146205; Salvá, II, 3938.
Reel 95, No. 619

MADRID, ALONSO DE, 16th cent.
[Arte para servir a Dios (and) Espejo de ilustres
personas. Latin]
Libellvs Avreu De vera Deo Apte Inserviendi
methodo, iam olim Hispanicè editus à F. Alfonso
Madiliensi: nunc autem in Latinum traductus per F.
Iohan. Hentneium, S. Theologiae professorem, &
conuentus Dominicanorum in Louanio Prioratufungentem.
Adiectum est, vice Coronidis, Speculum illustriũ
personarum, eorũdem authoris & interpretis. Lovanii:
Apud Petrum Zangriũ Tiletanum, 1560.
[4], 160 (i.e. 170) *l*.; 13cm.

Latin translation by John Hentenio.
Foliation errors throughout.
Cancelled stamp and armorial book-plate of the
Library of Christ College, Cambridge.
Adams, I, no. 778.
Reel 96, No. 620

MAIMONIDES, MOSES see MOSES BEN MAIMON.

MALDONADO, ALONSO.
Chronica Vniuersal de todas Las naciones y tiempos
compuesta por fray Alonso Maldonado de La Orden de
Santo Domingo. Con diez y seys tratados de los puntos
mas importantes de la chronologia. Dirigida Al Illmo.
Y R^{mo}. Señor don Melchor de Moscoso Y. Sandoual.
Obispo de Segouia del Consejo de su Mag.^{d} Dies Seculi
quis dinumerauit ? ecclesiastici I Solus Deus qui
et perseurtanti Sacram scripturam diligenter: Luculenter
manifestabit. Sapientiam non Vincit malitia, neq.
ignorantia. Madrid: Luis Sanchez impressor del Rey
N. S., 1624.
[4], 218 *l*.; 29cm.

MALDONADO (Cont'd)
Pagination errors throughout.
Goldsmith, p. 103, no. 33; Graesse, IV, p. 350;
HC:384 / 407; Palau, 147638; Penney, p. 328; Pérez
Pastor, no. 2080; Ticknor, p. 212.
Reel 96, No. 621

MALDONADO, JUAN DE, 1533-1583.
Ioannis Maldonati Societatis Iesv Theologi
Commentarii In Qvattvor Evangelistas Nunc primùm
in lucem editi, & in duos Tomos diuisi. Quorum prior
eos, qui in Matthaevm, & Marcvm; posterior eos, qui
in Lvcam, & Ioannem, complectitur. Ad Serenissimvm
Lotharingiae Dvcem. Mvssiponti: Ex Typographia
Stephani Mercatori eiusdem Ducis Typographi, 1596-97.
2 v. in 1 ([6] *l*., 952 cols.; [4] *l*., 1195 cols.);
36cm.

Pagination errors throughout.
Vol. II title: Ioannis Maldonati Andalvsii Theologi
Commentariorvm In Qvattvor Evangelistas. Tomvs II.
In Lvcam, Et Ioannem, Ad Serenissimvm Lotharingiae
Dvcem.
Adams, I, no. 283; Graesse, IV, p. 350; Palau,
147699.
Reel 96, No. 622, Vol. 1-2

MALDONADO, JUAN DE, 1533-1583.
Ioannis Maldonati Sapharensis, Societatis Iesv
Theologi, Commentarii In Qvatvor Evangelistas: Ad
Serenissimvm Lotharingiae Dvcem. Hac vltima editione
quatuor indicibus aucti: primus, vberior Sacrae
Scripturae locorum: secundus, Hebraismorum, &
Hebraicarum, Chaldaicarum, & Syriacarum dictionum:
tertius, errorum, & haeresum: quartus, est rerum, &
Sententiarum, verborumque, tum Graecorum, tium
Latinorum. Quae praeterea addita sunt, ad lectorem
Bibliopolae Epistola indicabit. Lvgdvni: Sumptibus
Horatij Cardon, 1607
2 v. ([6] *l*., 864 cols.; 865-1974 cols., [36] *l*.);
36cm.

No separate title for vol. II.
Colophon, vol. II: Excvdebat Guichardus Iullieronus,
Typographus Regius, Lugduni, 1607.
Graesse, IV, p. 350; Palau, 147706.
Reel 97, No. 623, 2 vols.

MALDONADO, JUAN DE, 1533-1583.
Ioannis Maldonati Sapharensis Societatis Iesv
Theologi Commentarii in quatuor Euangelistas. Cvm
Qvatvor Indicibvs: Primò locorum sacrae Scripturae:
Secundò, Habraïsmorum, & Hebraïcarum, Chaldaïcarum
& Syriacarum dictionum: Tertio, errorum, & haeresum:
Quartò. rerum & sententiarum, verborúmque tum Graecorum,
tum Latinorum. Nunc demum accuratè reuisi, scholiis
illustrati, & mendis quamplurimis repurgati. Editio
Postrema. Lvtetiae Parisiorvm: Sumptibus Ioannis
Billaine, 1651.
[4] *l*., 1904 cols., [34] *l*.; 36cm.

Pagination errors throughout.
Graesse, IV, p. 350; Palau, 147709.
Reel 98, No. 624

MALLORCA, FRANCISCO DE.
El Sol De La Iglesia S. Thomas De Aqvino, Cvyas
Lvzes Brillan En Las Qvatro Partes Del Mvndo. Aplavdido
En El Real Convento De Santo Domingo de Mallorca, en
la Ereccion de su Milicia Angelica, y Solemnidad de
40. horas. Orador El M.R.P. Fr. Francisco De Mallorca,
Religioso Capuchino. Sale A Lvz A Expensas De Vn
Afecto Devoto, y se Consagra al mismo Angelico Dotor.
Barcelona: Por Rafael Figvero, 1697.
[16], 20 p.; 19cm.

Palau, 148178.
Reel 98, No. 625

MALVEZZI, VIRGILIO, MARCHESE, 1599-1654.
La Libra De Grivilio Vezzalmi Tradvcida De Italiano
En Lengva Castellana. Pesanse Las Ganancias, Y Las
Perdidas De La Monarqvia De Espana En El Felicissimo
Reynado De Filipe IV El Grande. Mirabiles Elationes
Maris. Pamplona: [Iacomo Gafaro, 1639-40].
[4], 188 p.; 20cm.

Spanish translation by Alvaro de Toledo.
Engraved title-page: Aeqvator.
Original title unknown.
Jerez, p. 72; Palau, 148060; Penney, P. 329; Salvá,
II, 3218; Toda y Güell, Italia, 3032.
Reel 98, No. 626

MALVEZZI, VIRGILIO, Marchese, 1599-1654.
[Opere. Spanish]
Las Obras Del Marqves Virgilio Malvezzi. Dauid
perseguido, Romulo, y Tarquino. Tradvzido De
Italiano, por Don Francisco de Quevedo Villegas.
Cauallero del Abito de Santiago, Señor de la Villa
de Iuã Abad. Dedicados. A Antonio de Saldaña
Cauallero professo del habito de Christo, y Capitan
de cauallos, de las coracas, en las fronteras de
Alentejo. Lisboa: Paulo Craesbeeck, 1648.
[4], 140 *l.*; 15cm.

Spanish translation by Francisco Gómez de
Quevedo Villegas.
HC:NS4 / 139; Palau, 148044; Palha, no. 414;
Penney, p. 329.
Reel 98, No. 627

MANERO, PEDRO, fl. 1654.
Vida De La Serenissima Señora Doña Ivana
Valois, Reina Christianissima de Francia.
Fvndadora De La Religion de la Anunciata de la
Virgen N. S. sugeta à la Obediencia de la Orden
de san Francisco de la Regular Observancia.
Dedicada A La Serenissima Señora Doña Maria Teresa
de Austria, Infanta de España. Escrita Por Fray
Pedro Manero, Ministro General de toda la Orden
de los Frayles Menores de San Francisco. Madrid:
En la Impreta Real, 1654.
[8], 121, [1] *l.*; 21cm.

Leaves 22 and 91 misnumbered 21 and 92
respectively.
Graesse, IV, p. 362; Palau, 148431; Salva, II,
3468.
Reel 98, No. 628

MANESCAL, ONOFROE.
Apologetica Dispvta, Donde Se Prveva, Qve
La Llaga Del costado de Christo N. Señor fue
obra de nuestra redencion. Por El D. Honofre
Manescal natural de Barcelona, y catedratico
que fue de prima de Theologia en la Vniuersidad
della. Van anadidos tantos discursos en esta
segunda impression, que parescera [sic] otro
libro. Dirigida Al Illvstrissimo Y Excell. Ọ
Señor Don Gaston de Moncada, Marques de Itona,
Conde de Osona, Bisconde de Bas, y Cabrera, gran
Senescal, Capitan General y Virrey en el Reyno de
Aragon, del Consejo de su Magestad. Barcelo
[sic]: Acosta de Miguel Manescal, Merca. de
Libros, 1611.
[56], 321, [38] p.; 14cm.

Colophon: "Impresso en la insigne y muy leal
Ciudad de Barcelona en casa de Sebastian Matheuad,
al Call. Año M.DC.XI"
Error in binding: pp. 273-278 bound between
pp. 304 and 305.
Goldsmith, p. 104, no. 61; Palau, 148448;
Simón Díaz, Impresos no. 112.
Reel 99, No. 629

MANESCAL, ONOFRE.
Miscellanea De Tres Tratados, de Las
Apariciones De Los Espiritvs El Vno, Donde
Se Trata como Dios habla à los hombres, y si
las almas del Purgatorio bueluen: De Antichristo
el segundo, y de Sermones predicados en lugares
señalados el tercero. Es El Avtor El Maestro
Honofre Manescal Doctor en Theologia, y
Catedratico que fue della de Prima en la
insigne Vniuersidad de Barcelona. Hallaran
todos cosas de prouecho, en particulares los
predicadores. Dirigida Al Illustris. Y
Reverendis. Señor Don Ioan de Moncada Obispo de
Barcelona, del consejo de su Magestad. Barcelona:
A costa de Geronymo Genoues mercader de Libros.
En la Emprenta de Sebastian Matheuad, en la calle
del Call, 1611.

3 pts. ([16], 182 p.; 187 p.; 227, [54] p.);
22cm.
Goldsmith, p. 104 no. 62; Graesse, IV, p. 362;
Palau, 148449.
Reel 99, No. 630

MANTUANO, PEDRO, d. 1656.
Advertencias A La Historia De Ivan De Mariana
De La Compañia De Iesvs. Impressa en Toledo en
latin año 1592. y en Romance el de 1601. En Qve
Se Enmienda Gran Parte de la Historia de España.
Por Pedro Mantuano Secretario del Condestable de
Castilla; y Leon, &c. Con Privilegio. Milan: Por
Hieronimo Bordon, 1611.
[12], 216 p.; 23cm.

Graesse, IV, p. 369; Goldsmith, p. 104, no. 72;
Palau, 149611; Salvá, II, 3010
Reel 99, No. 631

MANTUANO, PEDRO, d. 1656.
Advertencias A La Historia Del Padre Ivan
De Mariana De La Compañia De Iesvs. Impressa
En Toledo En Latin ano de 1592 y en Romance el de
1601. en Qve Se Enmienda Gran parte de la Historia
de España. En Esta Segvnda Impression va añadida
la respuesta à todas las dificultades que puso el
Padre Iuan de Mariana, a los Discursos que prueuan
la venida de Santiago à España, sacados de la
libreria del Condestable de Castilla. Y también
se responde al Padre Iuan de Pineda, en lo que
escriuio en su libro de Rebus Salomonis, de la
venida de Nabuchodonosor. A Don Bernardino
Fernandez de Velasco Condestable de Castilla, y
Leon, &c. Por Pedro Mantvano su Secretario.
Madrid: En la Imprenta Real, 1613.
[20], 322, [1]p.; 20cm.

Manuscript note on title page: Ex. lib. Sancty
Hurtado de la Puente quẽ mihi donauit D. Gasp.
Vrachams.
Goldsmith, p. 104, no. 71; HC384/430; Palau,
149612; Penney, p. 333; Pérez Pastor, 1552; Salvá,
II, 3011; Ticknor, p. 215.
Reel 99, No. 632

MANZANARES, JERÓNIMO PAULO DE.
Estilo Y Formvlario De Carta Familiares, segun
el gouierno de Prelados, y Señores temporales. Do
Se Ponen Otras Cartas con sus respuestas, y algunas
de oficios de Republica. Dirigido Al Ilvst͞m͞o Señor
Don Bernardo de Rojas y Sandoual, Arcobispo de Toledo,
Cardenal de la S͞a͞ta Iglesia de Roma, del Consejo de
Estado del Rey N.S. Por El Maestro Geronimo Pavlo de
Mancanares, Arcipreste de Vzeda. Madrid: Alonso
Martin, 1607.
[12], 293, [15] *l.*; 22cm.

MANZANARES (Cont'd)

Colophon: "En Madrid Por Iuan De La Cuesta Año de M.DC.VII.

Imperfect: leaves 228 and 229 wanting.

Doublet, p. 87; HC:NSI/571; Palau, 150224; Penney, p. 334; Pérez Pastor, no. 970; Salvá, II, no. 4053.

Reel 99, No. 633

MARCH MOSEN, AUSÍAS, 1397?-1459.

Las Obras Del Poeta Mosen Ausias March, corregidas delos errores q̃ tenian. Sale con ellas el vocabulario delos vocablos enellas contenidos. Diragidas al Illustrissimo señor Goncalo Fernandez de Cordoua, Duque de sesa, y de Terra noua,, Conde de Cabra, Señor dela casa de Vaena. &c. Tassado en treinta y cinco marauedis. Valladolid: [Sebastien Martinez], 1555.

276 l.; 16 cm.

[Engraved title-page].

Colophon: "Fue impresso el presente tractado en la muy noble villa de Valladolid, Iũto a sant Andrés. En casa de Sebastiã Martinez impressor. Acabose de Imprimir a veynte dias d'Febrero Año. De. 1555."

Adams, I, no. 535; Graesse, IV, p. 382; Jerez, p. 64; Palau, 151297; Penney, p. 334; Salvá, I, 769; Thomas, p. 56.

Reel 99, No. 634

MARCH MOSEN, AUSÍAS, 1397?-1459.

Les Obres Del Valeros Cavaller, Y Elegantissim Poeta Ausias March: Ara nouament ab molta diligẽcia reuistes y ordenades, y de molts cãts aumẽtades. Barcelona : en casa de Claudi Bornat, 1560.

[4], 207, [5] l.; 16cm.

Adams, I, no. 536; Graesse, IV, p. 382; Palau, 151298; Penney, p. 334; Salvá, I, no. 770; Thomas, p. 56; Ticknor, p. 214.

Reel 99, No. 635

MARCILLO, Manuel.

Crisi De Cataluña, Hecha Por Las Naciones Estrangeras, Compvesta Por El P. Manvel Marcillo De La Compañia De Iesvs, Natural De La Villa De Olot. Barcelona : en la Imprenta de Mathevat delante la Retoria del Pino, 1685.

[24], 407, [29] p.; 21cm.

Lacking pages 386-387.

Backer, I; HC:NSI/ 657; Palau, 151149; Penney, p. 334.

Reel 100, No. 636

MARCOS DA LISBOA, Bp., 1511-1591.

[Chronicas de los frayles menores. Italian].

Chroniche Degli Ordini Instivti Dal P.S. Francesco Prima Parte Divisa In Dieci Libri. Che Contiene La Sva Vita, La Sva Morte. Ed i suoi miracoli; composta dal R.P. Fra Marco da Lisbona in lingua Portughese. Poi ridotta in Castigliana dal R.P.F. Diego Nauarro: E tradotta nella nostra Italiana dal S. Oratio Diola Bolognese. Ed hora solamente vscita assieme coll'altre sotto d'vn Torchio migliorata, e corretta, per diligenza, e somma vigilanza del P. Leonardo Da Napoli, Padre dell'Ordine Serafico. Da chi si dedica alla Purissima, e sempre Immacolata Regina de Cieli; e s'aopoggia con tutto'l rimanente dell'Opera alla protettione Dell' Eminentiss. Principe Sig. Cardinal Cibo Protettore Di Tvtto L'Ordine Serafico. In Napoli: per Nouello de Bonis, Stampatore Arciu, 1680.

4v. ([112], 640 p.; [83], 612 p.; [143], 710 p.; [88], 512 p.); 22cm.

MARCOS DA LISBOA (Cont'd)

Italian translation by Orazio Diola and Barezzo Barezzi.

Each volume has a special title page:

Vol. II: Chroniche Degli Ordini Instivti Dal P.S. Francesco Seconda Parte Divisa in Dieci Libri. Nelle quale si contiene quello, che accorse nella Religione del Padre San Francesco, nel tempo di ventiquattro Ministri Generali, per lo spatio d'anni centocinquanta. Composta dal R.P.F. Marco da Lisbona, in Lingua Portughese. Poi ridotta nella Castigliana dal Padre Fra Filippo de Sosa. E tradotta nella nostra Italiana dal Signor Horatio Diola Bolognese.

Vol III: Croniche Degli Ordini Instivti Dal P.S. Francesco Terza Parte Divisa In Dieci Libri. Ne' quali si descrivono le Vite, e Miracoli di trecento, e piu Serui, e Serue di Dio; e si racconta la Riforma, ed Osseruanza dell'Ordine, e suo accrescimento. Composta dal R.P.F. Marco da Lisbona in lingua Portughese: E tradotta di lingua Spagnuola nella nostra Italiana dal Signor Oratio Diola Bolognese:

Vol. IV: Croniche Degli Ordini Instivti Dal P.S. Francesco Parte Qvarta. Tomo Primo. Diviso In Sei Libri, Ne' Qvali Copiosamente si descriuono le Vite i Martirij, le Morti, i Miracoli, e gli Esercitij santi di vari Religiosi, Serui, e Serue di Dio della stessa Religione Serafica. E ne' quali parimente si narra la nuoua Riforma, e la continua Osseruanza nell'Ordine; come anco il grand' accrescimento della Fede Cattolica, fatta da essi, si ne' Regni di Spagna, di Portogallo, e nell'Indie Orientali, ed Occidentali; come in diuerse altre parti del Mondo...

Reel 100, No. 637

MARIANA, JUAN DE, 1536-1624.

[Historiae de rebus hispaniae. Spanish]

Historia General De España, Compvesta, Emendada, Y Añadida Por El Padre Ivan De Mariana De La Compañia De Iesvs, Con El Svmario, Y Tablas. Y Aora Nvevamente Añadida En Esta Vltima Impression Todo Lo Svcedido desde el año de mil y seiscientos y cincuenta, hasta el de sesenta y nueue. Dedicada Al Eminentissimo Señor Don Pasqval De Aragon, Cardenal De La Santa Iglesia de Roma, del Titulo de Santa Balbina, Arcobispo de Toledo, Primado de las Españas, gran Canciller de Castilla, del Consejo de Estado, y de la Iunta de Gouierno Vniuersal, &c.. Tomo Primero. Madrid: Por Andres Garcia de la Iglesia, 1669.

2v. ([29], 618, [23] p.; [5], 830, [20] p.); 29cm.

Spanish translation by the author.

Vol. II, half title: Historia General De España. Tomo Segundo.

Palau, 151674; Penney, p. 336.

Reel 102, No. 648, Vol. 2

MARIANA, JUAN DE, 1536-1624.

Iõ. Marianae Hispani. E Socie. Iesv, Historiae De Rebvs Hispaniae Libri XX. Toleti: Typis Petri Roderici, 1592.

[7], 959, [12] p.; 30cm.

Missing pages 717-719.

Adams, I, no. 580c.; Graesse, IV, p. 395; Palau, 151660; Salvá, II, 3016; Thomas, p. 56; Pérez Pastor, Toledo, no. 402; Simón Díaz, Jesuitas, no. 705.

Reel 101, No. 643

MARIANA, JUAN DE, 1536-1624.
Ioannis Hispani E Societate Iesu Historiae De Rebus
Hispaniae Libri XXX. Cum Indice copioso, & explicatione
vocum obscuriorum. Mogvntiae: Typis Balthasaris
Lipii, impensis heredum Andreae Wecheli, 1605.
2 pts. in 1 ([17], 619 p.; 638, [37] p.); 22cm.

Caption title of second part: Ioannis Marianae
Historiae De Rebvs Hispaniae. Tomvs II. Liber XV.
Noui in Castella motus.
Includes cumulative index at end of volume.
Bound with the author's: Svmmarivm ad historiam
hispaniae eorum quae accidervnt annis seqventibvs,
1619.
Du Fay, no. 3607; Graesse, IV, p. 395; Palau,
151662; Penney, p. 335; Simón Díaz, Jesuitas, no. 709.
Reel 102, No. 644

MARIANA, JUAN DE, 1536-1624.
Ioannis Marianae E Societate Iesv Historiae De Rebus
Hispaniae Libri XXX. Editio noua, ab Auctore
recensita, & aucta Svmario rerum quae superiore
saeculo gesta sunt, perducta ad hanc aetatem historia.
Cum Indice copioso, & explicatione vocum obscuriorum.
Impensis Aubrianorum fratrum, & Clementis Schleichii,
1619.
2 pts. in 1 ([16], 619 p.; 638, [37]p); 22cm.

Caption title of second part: Ioannis Marianae
Historiae De Rebvs Hispaniae. Tomvs II. Liber XV.
Bound with the author's: Svmmarivm Ad Historiam
Hispaniae Eorvm Qvae Accidervnt Annis Seqventibvs,
1619.
Reel 102, No. 646

MARIANA, JUAN DE, 1536-1624.
Ioannis Marianae Hispani, E Societate Iesv, De Rege
Et Regis Institvtione Libri III. Ad Philippum III.
Hispaniae Regem Catholicum. Eiusdem de Ponderibus &
Mensuris Liber. Mogvntiae: Typis Balthasaris Lippii,
Impensis Heredum Andreae VVechelis, 1605.
[9], 372, [15] p.; 16cm.

Bound with the author's: Ioannis Marianae Hispani,
E Socie. Iesv, De Ponderibvs Et Mensvris. Mogvntiae:
Typis Balthasaris Lippij, 1605.
Doublet, p. 87; Graesse, IV, p. 394; La Serna, no.
1570; Penney, p. 335; Simon Díaz, Jesuitas, no. 712.
Reel 101, No. 639

MARIANA, JUAN DE, 1536-1624.
Ioannis Marianae Hispani, E Societate Iesv, De Rege
Et Regis Institvtione Libri III. Ad Philippum III.
Hispaniae Regem Catholicum. Eiusdem de ponderibus &
mensuris Liber. Editio secunda. Typis Wechelianis,
apud haeredes Ioannis Aubrii, 1611.
[9], 372, [15] p.; 18cm.

Bound with the author's: Ioannis Marianae Hispani,
E Socie. Iesv, De Ponderibvs Et Mensvris. Typis
Wechelianis, 1611.
Graesse, IV, p. 394; Palau, 151725.
Reel 101, No. 641

MARIANA, JUAN DE, 1536-1624.
Ioannis Marianae Hispani, E Socie Iesv, De
Ponderibvs Et mensuris. [Toleti: Apud Thomam Gusmanium],
1599.
[9], 192 p.; 21cm.

Adams, I, no. 580A; Graesse, IV, p. 395; HC:NS⁴/1033;
Palau, 151724; Penney, p. 335; Pérez Pastor, no. 436;
Salvá, II, 2584; Simón Díaz, Jesuitas, no. 711; Thomas,
p. 56; Ticknor, p. 215
Reel 101, No. 638

MARIANA, JUAN DE, 1536-1624.
Ioannis Marianae Hispani, E Socie. Iesv, De
Ponderibvs et Mensvris. Mogvntiae: Typis Balthasaris
Lippij, 1605.
160, [8] p.; 16cm.

Doublet, p. 87; Graesse, IV, p. 394; La Serna, no.
1570; Penney, p. 335; Simon Díaz, Jesuitas, no. 712.
Reel 101, No. 640

MARIANA, JUAN DE, 1536-1624.
Ioannis Marianae Hispani, E Socie. Iesv, De
Ponderibvs Et Mensvris. Typis Wechelianis, 1611.
160, [7] p.; 16cm.

Bound with the author's: Ioannis Marianae Hispani,
E Societate Iesv, De Rege Et Regis Institvtione
Libri III ..., 1611.
Graesse, IV, p. 394; Palau, 151725
Reel 101, No. 642

MARIANA, JUAN DE, 1536-1624.
Svmmarivm ad historiam hispaniae eorvm quae
accidervnt annis seqventibvs. Mogvntiae: Impensis
Danielis ac Dauidis Aubriorum & Clementis
Schleichii, 1619.
41, [12] p.

Bound with the author's: Ioannis Hispani E
Societate Iesu Historiae De Rebvs Hispaniae Libri XXX
..., 1605.
No. 645: Not Available

MARIANA, JUAN DE, 1536-1624.
Svmmarivm Ad Historiam Hispaniae Eorvm Qvae
Accidervnt Annis Seqventibvs. Mogvntiae: Impensis
Danielis ac Dauidis Aubriorum & Clementis Schleichii,
1619.
41, [12] p.

Bound with the author's: Ioannis Marianae E
Societate Iesv Historiae De Rebus Hispaniae
Libri XXX, 1619.
Reel 102, No. 647

MARIANA, JUAN DE see also TAMAYO DE VARGAS, TOMÁS.

MARMOL CARVAJAL, LUIS DEL, fl. 1575.
Historia Del Rebelion Y Castigo De Los Moriscos
Del Reyno de Granada. Dirigida a don Iuan de Cardenas
y quñiga Conde de Miranda, Marques de la Bañeza, del
consejo de estado del Rey nuestro señor, y su presidente
en los dos Reales consejos de Castilla, y de Italia.
Hecha por Luys del Marmol Caruajal, andante en corte
de su Magestad. Malaga: por Iuan Rene a costa del
auctor, 1600.
[4], 245, [5] l.; 26cm.

Pages 181-182 missing.
Cosens, no. 2938; Graesse, IV, p. 406; Palau,
152437; Penney, p. 337; Salvá, II, 3028; Soubise,
no. 7552; Thomas, p. 56; Ticknor, p. 216.
Reel 103, No. 649

MARQUÉS DE CAREAGA, GUTIERRE.
Desengaño De Fortvna Mvy Provechoso Y Necessario Para Todo genero de gentes y estados. Por El Doctor Don Gvtierre Marques de Careaga, natural de la ciudad de Almeria costa del Reyno de Granada, tiniente de corregidor de Madrid corte de su Magestad, por el Rey nuestro Señor. Dirigido A Don Rodrigo Calderon señor de las Villas de la Olyba, Placencuela, y siete Yglesias &c Y de la camara de su Magestad. Alguacil mayor perpetuo de la Real Chancilleria de Valladolid, y Regidor perpetuo de la dicha ciudad. Veritati Cedit Invidia. Vnguento & varijs adoribus delectatur cor: & bonis amici concilijs anima dulcoratur. Proue. 27. Barcelona: en la Emprēta de Frācisco Dotil, 1611.
[24], 211, [4] l.; 15cm.

Colophon: "En Barcelona en la Emprenta de Francisco Dotil delante la Retoria del Pino Año 1611."
Goldsmith, p. 105, no. 100; Palau, 152578.
Reel 103, No. 650

MÁRQUEZ, JUAN, 1564-1621.
Los Dos Estados. De La Espiritval Hiervsalem, Sobre Los Psalmos CXXV Y CXXXVI. Por El Maestro Fray Ioan Marquez, de la Orden de San Augustin Dirigidos A Don Christoval Gomez de Sandoual, Marques de Cea, Gentil hombre de la Camara del Rey. Barcelona: En la Emprenta de Iayme Cendrat, 1603.
[4], 304, [20] l.; 21cm.

Index pages missing.
Reel 103, No. 653

MÁRQUEZ, JUAN, 1564-1621.
El Governador Christiano. Dedvcido De Las Vidas De Moysen, Y Iosve, Principes Del Pveblo De Dios. Por El Maestro Fr. Ivan Marqvez, de la Orden de san Agustin, Predicador de la Magestad del Rey don Felipe III Catedratico de Visperas de Teologia de la Vniuersidad de Salamanca. Dirigido A Don Ivan De Isasi Idiaqvez Cauallero del Abito de Santiago, Maestro del Principe nuestro Señor, Señor de los Palacios, Casas y Torrefuerte de Ysasi y Orbea, y de las villas de Ameyuco, Turo, Barcena y Covejo, de la Provincia de Guipuzqua. Tercera Impression, Avmentada En diferentes partes, con extension de la doctrina, y nueuas Questiones. Con Qvatro Tablas Mvy Copiosas. La Primera de los Capitulos. La segunda de las Questiones. La tercera de las cosas notalbes. Y la quarta de los lugares de Escritura. Alcala: Por Antonio Vazquez, Impressor de la Vniuersidad, 1634.
[2], 227 p.; 29cm.

Bound with the author's: La Vida De Iosve Libro Segvndo. 227 p. 38 l (Index).
Lacks t.-p. and leaves after qq⁸
Palau, 152689; Salvá, II, p. 797.
Reel 103, No. 651

MÁRQUEZ, JUAN, 1564-1621.
[Origen de los frayles ermitaños de la orden de San Augustín. Italian]
Origine Delli Frati Eremitani Dell'Ordine Di S. Agostino, E la sua vera Institutione auanti al gran Concilio Lateranese. Raccolta Dal M. R. P. Maestro F. Giovanni Marqvez, Predicatore della Maestà Catolica di Filippo III. Rè delle Spagne, e delle Indie, Catedratico di Teologia Scolastica dopò il Vespero nelli studij di Salamanca. Tradotta dalla lingua Spagnuola nella nostra Italiana dal R. P. Fra Innocentio Rampini da Tortona Baccilliero in Sacra Teologia del medesimo Ordine. Tortona: Appresso Nicolò Viola.
[9], 364, [7] p.; 31cm.

MÁRQUEZ (Cont'd)
Italian translation by Innocenzo Rampini Da Tortona.
Ex-libris: Count Antonio Cavagna.
Colophon: "In Tortona, Appresso Nicolò, L'anno del Signore M.DC.XX. Con Licenza de' Signori Superiori."
Palau, 152700.
Reel 104, No. 654

MÁRQUEZ, JUAN, 1564-1621.
La Vida De Iosve Segvndo. [Madrid: Por Francisco de Ocampo, 1634.]
227, [53] p.

Caption title.
Lacks t.-p.
Bound in the author's: El Governador Christiano, 1634.
Includes index.
Reel 103, No. 652

MARTEL, JERÓNIMO.
Forma De Celebrar Cortes En Aragon. Escrita Por Geronimo Martel Chronista Del Reyno. Dedicada A Los Ilvstrissimo Señores Dipvtados Del Reyno. Pvblicala El Doctor Iuan Francisco Andres de Vztarroz, con algunas notas. [Tail-piece] Con Licencia, y Privilegio. En Caragoca: Por Diego Dormer, 1641.
[21], 108, [7] p.; 20cm.

Bound with: Blancas, Jerónimo de, Coronaciones De Los Serenissimo Reyes De Aragon ... En Caragoca, Por Diego Dormer. Año M.DC. XLI (1641) and Modo De Proceder En Cortes De Aragon. Escrito Por Geronimo De Blancas Chronista Del Reyno ... En Caragoca: por Diego Dormer, 1641.
Palau, 153132.
Reel 26, No. 120

MARTINEZ, MARTÍN.
Libri Decem Hypotyposeon Theologicarvm, Sive Regvlarvm ad intelligendum scripturas diuinas, in duas partes distribuiti. Quarum prior, quae octo libros complectitur, locos aliquot communes ad scripturarum exactam intelligentiam spectantes satis enucleatè tractat. Posterior, quae duobus voluminibus clauditur, duas Regularum Quinquagenas continet: quas non inutiles fore illis Theologis, qui sacris Bibliorum mysterijs initiantur, re ipsa cognosces. Hac Secvnda Editione Svmma Cvra Ac Diligentia elaborati, & multorum locorum noua interpretatione, qui nonnullos hactenus fefellerant, insigniti, A Martino Martini Cantapetrensi, sacrae Theologiae Magistro, ac primo post. C C C annos a Salmanticensi Academia condita, sacrorum Bibliorum in tribus Primario ac perpetuo interprete, I O A N N E B R A C A M O N T I O Auilensi viro admodum Illustri Academiae praefecto, ad id munus obeundum cooptato, elucubrati. Salmanticae: Ex officina Ildefonsi à Terranoua, & Neyla, 1582.
2 pts. in 1 ([6], 10 l., cols. 10-661; 40, [33] l.); 27cm.

Part II has special title page: Martinvs Martini Cantapetrensis, Sacrae Theologiae magister, ac diuinarum scripturarum, in tribus linguis, Salmanticae, primarius professor, Illustrissi. ac Reuerendissi. D. D. Petro Pontio Legionensi, Episcopo Placentino, Salutem. P.D.
Colophon: "Salmanticae, Ex Officina Ildefonsi à Terranova & Neyla. M D L X X X II"
In double columns.
Includes index.
Adams, I, no. 726.
Reel 104, No. 655

MARTÍNEZ DE AMILETA, ANDRÉS.
    Discvrsos Politicos Y Cessareos A La Magestad
Catolica De Don Felipe IV. nuestro Señor, y Rey
de las Españas. En Qve Se Da Forma, Y Cventa De
Las Conveniencias, Y Avmento, que tendran los
reales Tesoros de su Magestad, y el que gozaran
tambien sus vassallos, con el acrecentamiento
del valor de la plata, y oro. Siruiendose de
mandar se ponga en execucion lo que este papel
contiene, y a suplicado varias vezes el Reyno
por sus Procuradores en Corte. Por Andres
Martinez De Amileta, natural de la villa de
Vergara, en la Prouincia de Guipuzcoa, residente
en la ciudad de los Reyes del Pirù, 1632.
    [2], 24 ℓ.; 28cm.

    Palau, 154694
Reel 104, No. 656

MARTÍNEZ DE GRIMALDO, JOSÉ.
    Fvndacion. Y Fiestas De La Congregacion De Los
Indignos Esclavos Del SS. Sacramento, Qve Esta EnEl
Religioso Convento De Santa Maria Magdalena, De La
Orden De S. Agvstin De Esta Corte. Celebradas En
Los Primeros Cinqventa Años De Sv Edad Felice:
Descripcion De Los Excelentes Adornos, Qve para
ellas se han dispuesto y de los sumptuosos Altares,
que se han erigido. Recopilanse Los Svtiles
Conceptos, Y Admirables motetes, que al assumpto
glorioso de estas Festiuidades han escrito los mayores
Ingenios desta Corte. Presentalo Al Exc. Señor
Marques De Aytona, Protector De La Congregacion.
D. Ioseph Martinez De Grimaldo, Indigno Esclauo del
SS. Sacramento. Madrid: por Diego Diaz De La
Carrera, Impressor del Reyno, 1657.
    [6], 250 ℓ.; 20cm.

    Colophon: "Con Licencia En Madrid, Por Diego Diaz
De La Carrera, Impressor Del Reyno. Año De M.DC.LVII."
Title-page stained and torn affecting print.
Missing leaves 181-185, 188-193, 213-217.
    Palau, 155098
Reel 104, No. 657

MARTÍNEZ DE LA PUENTE, JOSÉ, fl. 1681.
    Epitome De La Cronica Del Rey Don Ivan El Segvndo
De Castilla Hecho Por Don Ioseph Martinez De La
Pvente. Añadidas Varias Noticias, Pertenecientes à
esta Historia, y declarados muchos vocablos de la
Lengua Antigua Castellana, que toda vã incluso estas
dos señales + . y *. Dedicado Al Señor Don
Ambrosio de Onis, Cavallero de la Orden de Santiago,
Señor de la Villa de Olivares, Casa, y Bosque Real de
la Quemada, del Consejo de su Magestad, en su
Tribunal de la Contaduria mayor de Cuentas, y su
Alguacil mayor del de la santa Cruzada. Madrid: Por
Antonio Gonzalez de Reyes, 1678.
    [11], 342, [29]; 21cm.

    Palau, 155604; Salvá, II, 3033
Reel 104, No. 658

MATEO DEL CASTELLAR, BERNARDO.
    Memorial De La Practica De Los Concvrsos De las
dos Iglesias de Zaragoca, cuyas diferencias estan
comprometidas en el Rey nuestro señor, y en su
sacro, y Real Consejo de Aragon. Escrito Por El
Doctor Bernardo Matheo del castellar, Canonigo de
la Santa Iglesia dei (sic) Pilar, primera Cathedral
de Zaragoca. En doze de Marco, n.p., 1657.
    22 ℓ.; 28cm.

    Palau, 157917
Reel 104, No. 659

MEDICIS, GIROLAMO DE.
    Svmmae Theologiae S. Thomae Aqvinatis Doctoris
Angelici Formalis Explicatio. Qvo Omnia Argvmenta, Et
Rationes, quae in singulis Articulis tractantur, non
modica claritate formantur, & explicantur,
Argumentorumque Responsiones explicatae ad ipsorum
partes aptè accommodantur. Cvm Variis Indicibvs.
Auctore F. Hieronimo De Medicis A Camerino Sacrae
Theologiae Magistro, Ordinis Praedicatorum, et Mantuae
contra Haeriticam prauitatem Generali Inquisitore.
Tertia Pars. Parisiis: Sumptibus Simeonis Piget,
Viã Iacobaea ad insigne Prudentiae. M.DC.LVII. Cvm
Privilegio Regis.
    3 pts. in 2 [?] ([17], 463 p.; 319, [148] p.);
37cm.

    Second part has t.-p.: Formalis Explicatio
Svpplementi Tertiae partis Svmmae Theologiae Sancti
Thomae Aquinatis ...
Reels 145 & 146, No. 939

MEDINA, BARTOLOMÉ DE, 1526?-1580?
    Breve Instrvccion De Como Se Ha De Administrar el
Sacramento de la penitencia, diuidida en dos libros,
compuesta por el padre Maestro F. Bartolome de Medina
Cathedratico de prima de Theologia en la vniuersidad
de Salamanca de la orden de S. Domingo. En la qual se
contiene todo lo que ha de saber y hazer el sabio
confessor para curar almas, y todo lo que deue hazer
el penitente para conseguir el fruto de tan admirable
medicina. Con vn indice copiosissimo y prouechoso.
Alcala: en casa de Iuan Iñiguez de Lequerica, 1593.
    [8], 334, [22] ℓ.; 15cm.

    Leaf 332 incorrectly numbered 330.
    Palau, 159418
Reel 104, No. 660

MEDINA, PEDRO DE, 1493?-1567?
    Libro De La Verdad Donde Se Contienan, Dozientos
Dialogos, que entre la Verdad y el Hombre se tratan,
sobre la conuersion del pacador. Compvesto Por El
Maestro Pedro de Medina, vezino de la ciudad de
Seuilla. Alcala: De Henares En casa de Iuan
Gracian, 1576.
    176, [10] ℓ.; 28cm.

    Palau, 159696.
Reel 104, No. 662

MEDINA, PEDRO DE, 1493?-1567?
    [Regimiento de navegación. French].
    L'Art De Navigver De M. Pierre De Medine, Espagnol
Contenant toutes les reigles, secrets & enseignemens
necessaires à la bonne nauigation, Tradvict De
Castillan En François, auec augmentation &
illustration de plusieurs figures & annotations, par
Nicolas de Nicolai, du Dauphiner Geographe du Tres-
chrestien Roy Henry II. de ce nom: & dedié à sa
tres-Auguste Maiesté. Lyon: Par Gvillavme
Roville, 1569.
    [9], 225, [6] p.; 22cm.

    French translation by Nicolas de Nicolini.
    Graesse, IV, p. 462; Palau, 159671.
Reel 104, No. 661

MEDRANO, DIEGO DE.
    De Consensv Connvbiali Tractatvs. Autore D.
Didaco De Medrano, Jurisconsulto Hispano. Nvnc
Primvm In Lvcem emissus, & suis Indicibvs
pernecessariis insignitus. Lvgdvni: Sumptibus
Horatij Cardon, 1609.
    [17], 91, [14] p.; 21cm.
Reel 105, No. 663

MEJÍA, PEDRO see MEXIA, PEDRO, 1496-1552.

MELLO, FRANCISCO MANUEL DE, 1608-1666.
Demostracion Que Por el Reyno de Portugal Agora Offrece (sic) El Dotor Geronimo De Sancta Cruz a todos Los Reynos y Provincias de Europa en prueba de la Declaracion Por el mesmo Autor, y por el mesmo Reyno atodos Los Reynos, y Provincias de Europa ya offrecida Contra las Calunias publicadas de sus Emulos y en favor de las Verdades por el Tiempo Manifestadas. Lisboa: n.-p., 1644.
54 p.; 19cm.

Palau, 160447.
Reel 110, No. 688

MELLO, FRANCISCO MANUEL DE, 1608-1666.
Epanaphoras De Varia Historia Portvgveza. Ao Excellentissimo Senhor Domioað Da Sylva Marquez De Gouvea, Conde De Portalegre, Presidête do Dezembargo do Paço do Cõselho de Estado, & Guerra, Mordomo Mõr da Casa Real, &c. Em Cinco Relao, oens De sucessos pertencentes a este Reyno. Que Contem Negocios Publicos, Politicos, Tragicos, Amorosos, Belicos, Triunfantes. Por Dom Francisco Manvel. Lisboa: A despesa d'Antonio Craesbeeck de Mello, Impressor de S. Alteza, 1676.
[5], 624, [1] p.; 21cm.

Pagination errors throughout.
Doublet, p. 90; Palau, 160459.
Reel 110, No. 690

MELLO, FRANCISCO MANUEL DE, 1608-1666.
El Mayor Peqveño. Vida, Y Mverte del Serafin humano Francisco De Assis Recverdalas A La piedad vniuersal D. Francisco Manvel, Ofrecido A La Muy Venerable Prouincia de la Arrabida. Qui autem est in regno caelorum, maior est illo. Math. 6. 11. Lisboa: Por Manuel da Sylua, 1647.
[16], 164, [1] l.; 16cm.

Half-title: H. El Mayor Pequeño Por D. Francisco Manuel A La muy venerable Provincia De la Arabide.
Palau, 160451.
Reel 110, No. 689

MELO, FRANCISCO MANUEL DE see MELLO, FRANCISCO MANUEL DE

MEMORIAL de D. Juan Duque de Estra sobre Arbitrios.
13 manuscript l.

Bound with: HERRERA Y SOTOMAYOR, JACINTO DE, fl. 1644. Iornada que su Magestad hizo a la Andalvzia. [Madrid: En la Imprenta Real, 1624].
Palau, 114276 (List only printed folios 1-6).
Reel 77, No. 484.24

MEMORIAL que el Embajador de Holanda dió a S. M. año 1661 sobre lo que contiene el papel antecedente. Madrid, 1661.
2 printed l.
Bound with: HERRERA Y SOTOMAYOR, JACINTO DE, fl. 1644. Iornada que su Magestad hizo a la Andalvzia. [Madrid: En la Imprenta Real, 1624].
Palau, 114276 (List only printed folios 1-6).
Reel 77, No. 484.3

MEMORIAL que el Embajador de las Provincias Unidas del Pais Baxo, sobre unirse la 'Armada Holandesa y Española contra los corsarios africanos. Madrid, 1661.
7 printed l.
Bound with: HERRERA Y SOTOMAYOR, JACINTO DE, fl. 1644. Iornada que su Magestad hizo a la Andalvzia. [Madrid: En la Imprenta Real, 1624].
Palau, 114276 (List only printed folios 1-6).
Reel 77, No. 484.2

MEMORIAL que la provincia de Guipúzcoa dio a S.M. para que se recogiese el Grál dado al Conde Duque de Adelantado Mayor de ella.
11 manuscript l.
Bound with: HERRERA Y SOTOMAYOR, JACINTO DE, fl. 1644. Iornada que su Magestad hizo a la Andalvzia. [Madrid: En la Imprenta Real, 1624].
Palau, 114276 (List only printed folios 1-6).
Reel 77, No. 484.31

MEMORIAL que las Santas Iglesias de España dieron al Sr. Rey D. Carlos II por Junio de 1630, sobre la distribución del Subsidio y excusado y demás contribuciones y respuestas de S. M. S. i principios del siglo XVII.
13 manuscript l.
Bound with: HERRERA Y SOTOMAYOR, JACINTO DE, fl. 1644. Iornada que su Magestad hizo a la Andalvzia. [Madrid: En la Imprenta Real, 1624].
Palau, 114276 (List only printed folios 1-6).
Reel 77, No. 484.7

MEMORIAL Qve Se Presento Al Rey Catolico Por El Embaxador De La Fidelissima villa de Perpiñan en el Octubre 1640. Barcelona: en casa de Iaume Matevat Impresor de la Ciut. y Vniuer, 1641.
10 l.; 19cm.

Colophon: "31. Maij 1641 Imprimatur Cum prohibitione ne alius ha typis mandet sub paena quinquaginta librarum. Vidal Assesor."
Palau, 161830.
Reel 111, No. 691

MÉNDEZ DE HARO SOTOMAYOR Y GUZMÁN, LUIS, MARQUIS DEL CARPIO, 1598-1661.
A Translate of a letter from Don Lewis de Harro, Chief Counsellor and Minister of State to His Majesty of Spaine, sent unto the King of Scots at Brussels concerning the affaires in England, publication of the articles of Peace and marriage with France, &c. London: 1659.
1 p.; 33cm.

The translator is unknown.
A letter on behalf of the King of Spain (Philip IV) for the restoration of Charles II to the English throne.
Allison, p. 122, no. 11; Palau, 163138; Wing M.no. 803.
Reel 111, No. 692

MENDO, ANDRÉS, 1608-1684.
Epitome Opinionvm Moralivm, Tum earum, quae certae
sunt; tum quae certò probabiles, & in praxi tutò
teneri possunt. Cum Discursu circa opiniones
probabiles, &c. Appendice Casuum valde Notabilium.
Avthore R. P. Andrea Mendo, Locruniensi, è Societate
Iesv In Prouincia Castellana: Regum Catholicorum
Philippi IV, & Caroli II. Concionatore; Supremi
Hispaniarum Senatus Fidei Censore; olim Salmanticae
Theologiae Professore, ac Sacrae Scripturae
Interprete, & inibi Examinatore, Synodali. Eitio
Tertia. Venetiis: Apud Benedictum Milochum. 1682.
[25], 734, [1] p.; 16cm.

Palau, 163616.
Reel 111, No. 693

MENDO, ANDRÉS, 1608-1684.
Principe Perfecto Y Ministros Aivstados, Docvmentos
Politicos, Y Morales. En Emblemas. Por el R. P.
Andrés Mendo, de la Compañia de Iesvs, Calificador
del Consejo de la Inquisicion Suprema, Lector de
Theologia, y de Sagrada Escritura en Salamanca.
Leon De Francia: A Costa de Horacio Boissat Y
George Remevs, 1662.
4 pts. ([45], 184 p.; 56 p.; 56 p.; 111 p.);
23 cm.

Pagination errors throughout.
Palau, 163591; Simón Díaz, Jesuitas, no. 784.
Reel 111, No. 694

MENDOZA, BERNARDINO DE, [1540]-1604.
Comentarios De Don Bernardino de Mendoça, de lo
sucedido en las Guerras de los Payses baxos, desde el
Año de. 1567. hasta el de 1577. Madrid: Por Pedro
Madrigal, 1592.
[8], 336, [12] l.; 19cm.

Palau, 163695; Salvá, II, 3052.
Reel 111, No. 695

MERCADO, LUIS, 1520-1606.
De Pvlsibvs Libri Dvo In Qvibvs Tota Ars
Cognoscendi Morbos, Et Prognosticandi Disertissime
Tractatvr, Avtore Ludouico Mercato Medico et
primario professore In Academia Soletana, Cvm Indice
Gemino Altero Capitvm, altero rerum magis memorabilium.
Patatauii: Apud Paulum Meiettum, 1592.
[10], 184, [1] l.; 20cm.

Ex-libris: Skene Library.
Palau, 165013.
Reel 111, No. 696

MERCADO, THOMAS DE, d. 1575.
Svmma De Tratos, Y Contratos. Compvesta Por el
muy Reuerendo Padre Fray Thomas de Mercado de la Orden
de los Predicadores, Maestro en sancta Theologia.
Diuidida en seys libros. Añadidas A La Primera
addicion, muchas nueuas resoluciones. Y dos libros
enteros, como paresce en la pagina siguiente.
Sevilla: En casa de Hernando Diaz Impressor de
Libros, en la calle dela Sierpe, 1571.
([12], 162 l.; 228, [13] l.); 20cm.

Pagination errors throughout.
Ex-libris: Diego Gonzalez Olgado.
Escudero, no. 652; HC:NS5/27; Palau, 165052;
Penney, p. 356; Salvá, II, 3704.
Reel 111, No. 697

MEXÍA, PEDRO, 1496-1552.
Dialogos eruditos compuestos por Pedro Mexia
Cronista de la Magestad Cesarea del Señor Carlos V.
Savilla (sic): en la imprenta de Hernando Diaz, 1570.
[16], 269 p.; 16cm.

Palau, 167374; Porqueras-Laurenti, no. 4.
Reel 105, No. 664

MEXÍA, PEDRO, 1496-1552.
[Dialoges eruditos. French].
Discovrs des septs sages de Grèce avec plusieurs
sentences notables qu'ils ont laissées par escrit.
Ensemble vn Traitté singulier des septs merueilles
du monde ... Paris: Chez Federic Morel, 1579.
[1], 56, [1] p.; 16cm.

Palau, 167384; Porqueras-Laurenti, no. 16.
Reel 105, No. 665

MEXÍA, PEDRO, 1496-1552.
Historia imperial y Cesarea: el la qval se
contienen las vidas y hechos de todos los Cesares
Emperadores de Roma: desde Iulio Cesar hasta el
Emperador Maximiliano: dirigida al muy alto y muy
poderoroso Principe y señor nuestro don Philippe,
Principe de España y de las dos Sicilias, &c. la qual
compuso y ordenò el Manifico cauallero Pero Mexia,
vezino de la ciudad de Sevilla. Con gracia y
privilegio Cesareo por cinco annos. Sevilla:
Sebastian Trugillo, 1545.
[5], 334, [1] l.; 32cm.

Colophon: "Haze fin la presente obra initolada
Hystoria imperial. Fue impressa en Sevilla, en casa
de Sebastian Trugillo. Acabose a veynte y ciaco
dias del mes de agosto. Año de M.D.LXIIIJ A costa
del impressor."
In Double column First Edition, Seville, 1545.
Pagination errors throughout.
Adams, I, no. 1383; Escudero, no. 452; Gallardo,
no. 2996; Palau, 167345; Porqueras-Laurenti, no. 2.
Reel 105, No. 667

MEXÍA, PEDRO, 1496-1552.
Historia imperial y Cesarea: en la qval se contienen
las vidas y hechos de todos los Cesares Emperadores de
Roma: desde Iulio Cesar hasta el Emperador Maximiliano:
dirigida al muy alto y muy poderoroso Principe y
señor nuestro don Philippe, Principe de España y de
las dos Sicilias, &c. la qual compuso y ordenò el
Manifico cauallero Pero Mexia, vezino de la ciudad
de Seuilla. Con gracia y priuilegio Cesareo por
cinco annos. Basilea: En casa de Ioan Oporino, 1547.
[8], 717 p.; 32cm.

Colophon: "Acabose de imprimir esta obra en
Basilea en casa de Iohan Oporino, con gracia y
Priuilegio Cesareo concedido al mismo Iohan Oporino
por cinco annos."
Missing pages 676-678.
Graesse, IV, p. 512; Palau, 167342; Porqueras-
Laurenti, no. 1; Salvá, II, 3473; Thomas, p. 60.
Reel 105, No. 666

MEXÍA, PEDRO, 1496-1552.
Historia imperial y Cesarea. En qve svmariamente
se contienen las vidas, y hechos de todos los
Emperadores, desde Iulio Cesar, hasta Maximiliano
Primero. Compvesta por el Magnifico Cavallero Pedro
Mexia, vezino de la Ciudad de Seuilla. Prosigvela
el Padre Basilio Varen, Assistente Prouincial de
los Clerigos Reglares Menores, enriqueziendola con
las proezas de los vltimos siete Cesares Austriacos,
desde Carlos Quinto à Ferdinando Tercero. Dirigida
al señor don Lorenzo Ramirez de Prado, Cauallero
del Orden de Santiago, del Consejo Real de Castilla,
y de Cruzada, &c. Madrid: Por Melchor Sanchez, 1655.
[13], 725, [32] p.; 30cm.

Pages 557-560 missing.
Bustamante, no. 2408; HC384/480; Graesse, IV,
p. 512; Palau, 167347; Penney, p. 347; Porqueras-
Laurenti, no. 3.
Reel 105, No. 668

MEXÍA, PEDRO, 1496-1552.
The Imperiall historie: or The lives of the
emperovrs, from Ivlivs Caesar, the first fovnder of
the Roman monarchy, vnto this present veere:
containing their liues and action, with the rising
and declining of that empire; the originall, and
successee, of all those barbarous nations that haue
inuaded it, and ruined it by peece-meale with an
ample relation of all the memorable accidents that
haue happened during these last combustions. First
written in Spanish by Pedro Mexia: and since
continued by some others, to the death of Maximilian
the Second; translated into English by W. T. : and
now corrected, amplified and continued to these
times by Edvvard Grimeston ... London: Printed by
H. L. for Mathevv Lovvnes, 1623.
[10], 867 p.; 34cm.

Allison, p. 124, no. 16.1; Palau, 167362; Pollard
and Redgrave, no. 17852; Porqueras-Laurenti, no. 19.
Reel 107, No. 673

MEXÍA, PEDRO, 1496-1552.
[Historia imperial y cesarea. Italian].
Le Vite de tvtti gl'imperadori (sic) da Givlio Cesare
insino a Massimiliano, tratte per M. Lodovico Dolce dal
libro spagnvolo del nobile cavaliere Pietro Messia,
con alcvne vtili cose in diversi lvoghi aggivnte.
Con vna tavola compiosissima de' fatti piv
notabili in esse vite contenvti ... Vinegia:
Appresso Gabriel Giolito de' Ferrari, 1558.
[69], 1054, [3] p.; 24cm.

Italian translation by Lodovico Dolce.
Device of printer on title - page and different
form on verso of leaf; head pieces; intalic type.
Palau, 167384; Porqueras-Laurenti, no. 6;
Short-title, II, p. 389.
Reel 106, No. 669

MEXÍA, PEDRO, 1496-1552.
[Historia imperial y cesarea. Italian]
Vite di tutti gli Imperadori (sic), nelle quali si
contengono tutti le cose piu degne di memoria
vniuersalmente auenute nel mondo, cominciando da
Giulio Cesare fino à Massimiliano. Composte in
lingva spagnvola da Pietro Messia, et nuouamente in
lingua italiana tradotte dal signor Alfonso Vlloa.
Venetia: Appresso Vincentio Valgrisio, 1561.
[37], 1119, [2] p.; 22cm.

Italian translation by Alfonso Ulloa.
Palau, 167351; Porqueras-Laurenti, no. 7;
Short-title, II, p. 389.
Reel 106, No. 670

MEXÍA, PEDRO, 1496-1552.
[Historia imperial y cesarea. Italian]
The Historie of all the Romane emperors, beginning
with Caivs Ivlivs Caesar, and Successiuely ending
with Rodvlph the Second now raigning ... First
collected in Spanish by Pedro Mexia, since enlarged
in Italian by Lodovico Dvlce and Girolomo Bardi, and
now Englished by W. T. London. Printed for M.
Lovvnes, 1604.
[11], 890, [1] p.; 30cm.

English translation by W. Traheron.
Title vithin ornamental border; head-pieces;
initials.
Title-page mutilated.
Allison, p. 124, no. 16; Palau, 167361; Porqueras-
Laurenti, no. 18; Ticknor, p. 226.
Reel 107, No. 672

MEXÍA, PEDRO, 1496-1552.
[Historia imperial y cesarea. Italian].
Le Vite de gli (sic) Imperadori (sic) Romani da
Giulio Cesare fino à Massimiliano tratte per M.
Lodovico Dolce Dal Libro Spagnuolo del Signor
Pietro Messia. A queste già furono accopiate le
Vite di Ridolfo, e Matthias, descritte da Paolo
Santorio Napolitano, con tutte le Effigie di esse
imperadori dal naturale, cosi antichi, come moderni,
in particolare della Casa d'Austria. Ma in questa
vltima impressione sono state perfettionate con
l'Aggionta (sic) della Vita di Ferdinando Secondo,
Ferdinando Terzo, e la Coronatione di Leopoldo
regnante. Venetia: Presso Gio, Maria Turrini e
Gio.: Brigonci, 1664.
[47], 980, [1] p.; 22cm.

Italian translation by Lodovico Dolce.
Pagination errors throughout.
Palau, 167358; Porqueras-Laurenti, no. 8.
Reel 106, No. 671

MEXÍA, PEDRO, 1496-1552.
Silva de varia leccion. Compvesta por Pedro Mexia,
natural de Sevilla. En la qval se tratan mvchas
cosos (sic) muy agradables, y curiosas. Van Añadidas
en Esta Vltima Impresion quinta y sexta parte, y un
Paneresis de Isocrates, traducido de Latin en lengua
Castellana por el mismo Autor, con muchas sentencias
Morales. A Don Francisco De San Martin Ocina,
Cavallero de la Orden de Calatrava, del Consejo de
su Magestad, y su Secretario, Contador del Consejo
de la Santa Cruzada, y mayor de estos Reynos de
Castilla, y Leon, y Secretario de su Deputacion &c.
Madrid: por Matheo de Espinosa y Arteaga, 1673.
[13], 571, [14] p.; 21cm.

Graesse, p. 511; Palau, 167284; Porqueras-Laurenti,
no. 5.
Reel 108, No. 674

MEXÍA, PEDRO, 1496-1552.
[Silva de varia lección. Dutch].
De Verscheydē lessen Petri Messiae ... waer inne
beschreven worden de weerdichste gheschiedenissen aller
Keyseren, Coningen, ende loflycker mannen. Mitsgaders
een Register, aenwijsenden over een geglyck Capittel
den sommarischen inhoudt. Hiez zyn noch by gevoecht
seven verscheyden tsamnsprekinghen: owergheset nyt den
Fransoysche, in onse Nederduytsche tale. Amsterdam:
Voor Pieter Jiacobs. Paets; Ghedruckt by Paulus
Ravensteyen Anno 1617.
2 pts. in 1 (674, [11] p.; 163, [1] p.); 16cm.

Dutch translation by unknown.
Palau, 167339; Porqueras-Laurenti, no. 17.
Reel 110, No. 687

MEXÍA, PEDRO, 1496-1552.
[Silva de varia leccion. English].
The Foreste or collection of histories, no lesse
profitable, then pleasant ... Dooen out of French into
Englishe, by Thomas Fortescue. London: Printed by
Jhon (sic) Kyngston, for William Iones, 1571.
[6], 187, [5] l. ; 22cm.

English translation by Thomas Fortescue.
Allison, p. 125, no. 18; Pollard and Redgrave,
no. 17849; Porqueras-Laurenti, no. 20.
Reel 110, No. 683

MEXÍA, PEDRO, 1496-1552.
[Silva de varia leccion. English].
The Foreste or collection of histories, no lesse
profitable, then pleasant ... Dooen out of Frenche
into Englishe, by Thomas Fortescue. London: Printed
by John Day, 1576.
[1], 152, [4] l. ; 22cm.

Lacks title-page and prelim. leaves, and
signatures K₄ (folio 40).
Pagination errors throughout.
Allison, p. 125, no. 18.1; Palau, 167334; Pollard
and Redgrave, no. 17850; Porqueras-Laurenti, no. 22.
Reel 110, No. 684

MEXÍA, PEDRO, 1496-1552.
[Silva de varia leccion. English].
The Foreste or collection of histories, no lesse
profitable, then pleasant ... Dooen out of Frenche
into Englishe, by Thomas Fortescue. London:
Printed by John Day, 1576.
[6], 152, [4] l. ; 22cm.

Pagination errors throughout.
Allison, p. 125; no. 18.1; Palau, 167334; Pollard
and Redgrave, no. 17850; Porqueras-Laurenti, no. 21.
Reel 110, No. 685

MEXÍA, PEDRO, 1496-1552.
[Silva de varia leccion. Italian]
Selva di varia lettione ... di nvovo corretta et
aggiuntaui la quarta parte. Tradotta ... per Lucio
Mavro. Venetia: Appresso Giordano Ziletti, 1556.
[96], 879 p.; 16cm.

Italian translation by Lucio Maura.
Doublet, p. 92; Graesse. IV. p. 512; Porqueras-
Laurenti, no. 9.
Reel 108, No. 675

MEXÍA, PEDRO, 1496-1552.
[Silva de varia leccion. Italian].
Selva di varia lettione di Pietro Messia Spagnvolo,
da lvi divisa in tre parti: alle qvali s'è aggivnta
la quarta di Francesco Sansovino ... Dopo questa
haverrano in Breve i lettori vna nvova seconda Selva
non piu data in luce. Venetia: Presso Giorgio
De Cavalli, 1564.
[9], 380, [1] p.; 21cm.

Italian translation by Lucio Mauro.
With commentary notes by Girolamo Privli.
Edited by Pietro Ochieri.
Palau, 167291; Porqueras-Laurenti, no. 10;
Short-title, II, p. 389.
Reel 108, No. 676

MEXÍA, PEDRO, 1496-1552.
[Silva de varia leccion. Italian].
Selva di varia lettione di Pietro Messia, divisa in
cinqve parte ... Ampliate et di nuevo rivedute per
Francesco Sansouino. Venetia: Appresso Alessandro
Griffio, 1579.
[8], 444 l.; 16cm.

Italian translation by Mambrino da Fabriano.
Palau, 167296; Porqueras-Laurenti, no. 11.
Reel 108, No. 678

MEXÍA, PEDRO, 1496-1552.
[Silva de varia leccion. Italian].
Della selva di varia lettione di Pietro Messia.
[Venetia: Nella stamparia di Ambrosio Dei, 1615-1616.
([23], 357, [2] p.; [9], 214 p.; [12], 186, [1] p.);
16cm.

Parts 1-3 paged continuously.
Part 4 has special t.-p.: Della selva rinovata di
Pietro Messia, parte quarta ... Appresso Ambrosio, &
Bartolomeo Dei, Fratelli, 1616.
[Revised and enlarged by Mambrino Roseo da Fabriano
and Bartolomeo Dionigi da Fano].
Part 5 has special t.-p.: Della selva rinovata di
Pietro Messia, parte qvinta ... [Revised and enlarged
by Francesco Sansovino and Bartolomeo Dionigi da Fana.
Bound with the author's: Nvova seconda selva
rinovata di varia lettione ..., 1616.
Graesse, IV, p. 512; Palau, 167302; Porqueras-
Laurenti, no. 13.
Reel 109, No. 679

MEXÍA, PEDRO, 1496-1552.
[Silva de varia leccion. Italian].
Selva rinovata di varia lettione di Pietro Messia
... Di Mambrin Roseo Francesco Sansovino. Diuisa in
cinque Parti: doue si leggono historie particolari
antiche e moderne, dal principio del mondo fino a'
tempi nostri. Con l'aggionta (sic) delli (sic)
raggionamenti Filosofici in Dialogo dell' istesso avtore
curiosissimi. Con la nvova seconda selva
accrescivta da Bartolomeo Dionigi da Fano: ripiena
di cose notabili e singolari per oratori, historici,
predicatori, e ogni qualità di persone. Venetia:
Appresso A. et B. Dei, Fratelli, 1616.
5 pts. in 3 ([33], 357, [1] p.; [16], 214, [1] p.;
[13], 186, [1] p.); 23cm.

Italian translation by Alfonso de Ulloa.
Each of the five parts of the Selva rinovata...
has a special t.-p.:
Della Selva Di Varia Lettione Di Pietro Messia,
Parte Seconda [Terza, Qvarta, Qvinta].
T.-p. of the Nvova seconda selva reads: Nvova seconda
selva rinovata di varia lettione. Che segve Pietro
Messia, diuisa in quatro Parti, nelle quali si leggono
gloriosi fatti, et notabili successi di diuersi
tempi. In questa nouissima impressione ampliata et
con diligenza reuista da Bartolomeo Dionigi da Fano.
Each of the five parts of the Nvova seconda selva
rinovata... has a caption title and is paged
continuously. 277 p.
T.-p. of Ragionamenti reads: Ragionamenti dottissimi
et cvriosi del Illustre e Nobil Caualiere Pietro Messia.
Tradotti dalla lingua spagnuola nella nostra italiana
dal Sig. Alfonso Vlloa. ...
Each of the 3 parts of Ragionamenti has a half-
title page and is paged continuously. 112 p.
Colophon of the first vol. dated 1615.
Parte seconda and Parte terza have half-title with
contents, printer's device, and date: 1615.
Title vignettes (printer's device).
Palau, 167302; Porqueras-Laurenti, no. 14.
Reel 109, No. 681

MEXÍA, PEDRO, 1496-1552.
[Silva de varia leccion. Italian].
Selva rinovata di varia lettione di Pietro Messia...
di Mambrin Roseo, Francisco Sansovino. Diuisa in
cinque parti: doue si leggono historie particolari
antiche, e moderne, dal principio del mondo fino a'
tempi nostri. Aggiuntovi di nvovo alcvni raggionamenti
Filosofici in Dialogo dell'istesso Avttore
curiosissimi. Con la nuova seconda Selva, accrescivta
da Bartolomeo Dionigi da Fano, ripiena di questioni, e
dubbij singolari per oratori, historici, predicatori, e
ogni qualità di persone. Con due tauole, vna dei
capitoli, l'altra per alfabeto delle cose notabili.
Venetia: Appresso Ghirardo Imberti, 1626.
   5 pts. in 1 ([31], 311 p.; [17], 252 p.; 90 p.;
[12], 182 p.; [8], 175 p.); 22cm.

   In Italian translation.
   Each part has separate title pages and paging.
   Part 2: Nvova seconda Selva rinovata di varia
lettione, che segve Pietro Messia, diuisa in quattro
parti, nelle quali si leggono gloriosi fatti, e
notabili successi di diuersi tempi. In questa
nouissima impressione ampliata, e con diligenza
reuista da Bartolomeo Dionigi da Fano.
   Part 3: Ragionamenti dottissimi e cvriosi
dell'Illvstre, e Nobil Caualliere Pietro Messia ...
Ne i quali (sic) filosoficamente trattandosi di
diuerse materie si viene in congnitione di molte,
e varie cose non piu dette, nè scritte da altri,
Tradotti dalla lingua spagnuola nella nostra
italiana dal Signor Alfonso Vlloa.
   Part 4: Della Selva rinovata di Pietro Messia
parre (sic) quarta, aggivnta da Mambrin da Fabriano,
nella qual si narra notabili, e curiose historie delle
quattro parti del mondo ... E in particolare
dell'Italia oue si racconta cose singolari per ogni
stato, e qualità di persone. Novamente da
Bartolomeo Dionigi da Fano diligentemente ríuedute, et
ampliata.
   Part 5: Della selva rinovata di varia lettione di
Pietro Messia parte quinta aggivnta da Francesco
Sansovino.
   Palau, 167303; Porqueras-Laurenti, no. 15.
Reels 109 & 110, No. 682

MEXÍA, PEDRO, 1496-1552.
Nvova seconda selva di varia lettione, che segue.
Pietro Messia. Venetia: Presso Fabio & Agostino
Zoppini Fratelli, 1581.
   [9], 198, [2] p.; 16cm.

   Italian translation by Gieronimo Giglio.
   Pagination errors throughout.
Reel 108, No. 677

MEXÍA, PEDRO, 1496-1552.
Nvova Seconda Selva Rinovata Di Varia Lettione.
Che Segve Pietro Messia, Diuisa In quartro parti,
nelle quali si leggono gloriosi fatti e notabili
successi de' diuersi tempi. Venetia: Appresso
Ambrosio, & Bartolomeo Dei, Fratelli, 1616.
   [25], 277 p.

   Bound with the author's: Della selva di varia
lettione, 1615-1616.
   Graesse, IV, p. 512; Palau, 167302; Porqueras-
Laurenti, no. 13.
Reel 109, No. 680

MEXÍA, PEDRO, 1496-1552.
   The Rarities of the World, containing Rules and
Observations touching the Beginning of Kingdomes and
Common-Wealths, the Division of the Ages, First
written in Spanish ... afterwards translated into
French, and now into English by J. B. Gent. London:
Printed by Bernard Alsop, dwelling near the upper
Pump in Grub Street, 1651.
   [9], 134, [1] p.; 17cm.

   English translation by J. B(aildon).
   Colophon: "London, Printed by Bernard Alsop,
1650."
   Allison, p. 125, no. 20; Palau, 167337;
Porqueras-Laurenti, no. 23.
Reel 110, No. 686

MICHELI MARQUEZ, JOSÉ, 17th cent.
   Deleite Y Amargvra De Las Dos Cortes, Celestial Y
Terrena. Con La Assistencia De Los Ingenios, y
lagrímas derramadas en la Corte del Dios Momo: el
consuelo que reciben, quexas que dan a Iupiter, para
que visite las Cortes de los Planetas, Dioses,
Monarcas, Principes, Señorias, y Republicas del Orbe,
y modo de sus gouiernos. Amonestacion que les dà
Iupiter, lo que les encarga; joyas y villetes que
dexa a todos para bien gouernar. Por el Doctor don
Ioseph Micheli Marquez, Vicecancelario, Cauallero de
la Orden Constantiniana. Madrid: Por Iuan Sanchez,
1642.
   [6], 98, [2] l.; 19cm.

   Pagination errors throughout.
   HC384/3383; HC:NS4/142; Palau, 168288; Penney,
p. 359; Salva, II, 1904.
Reel 112, No. 698

MILAN. LAWS, STATUTES, etc. (Felipe IV, King of Spain,
     1606-1665)
   Ordini Reali. In Milano: Nella Reg. Duc. Corte,
per Marc' Antonio Pandolfo Malatesta Stampator Re.
Cam. Con Priuilegio, [1630?-1692]
   7 v. in 2; 30cm.

   Vol. I: 1. Ordini Diversi di Sva Maesta Cattolica.
            Tomo Primo. [n.d.], [4], 142 p.
            2. Ordini Et Lettere Reali Di Sva Maesta
            Cattolica. Tomo Secondo. [n.d.] [16], 353 p.
            3. Lettere Diverse Di Sva Maesta, Et
            Ordini Di Sva Eccellenza, Fatti In Diversi
            Tempi. Tomo Terzo, 1679. [8], 133 p.
   Vol. II: 4. Lettere Diverse Di Sva Maesta, Et
            Ordini Di Sva Eccellenza, Fatti In Diversi
            Tempi. Tomo Qvarto, 1679. [14], 228 p.
            5. Lettere Diverse Di Sva Maesta, Et
            Ordini Di Sva Eccelenza, Fatti In Diversi
            Tempi. Tomo Qvinto, 1680. [14], 314 p.
            6. Lettere Et Ordini Di Sva Maesta,
            Scritte Ai Sig.ri Governatori, et all'
            Ill.mo Magistrato Ordinario toccante
            diuerse cose di sua Hazienda, [n.d.]
            [12], 198 p.
            7. Lettere Diverse Di Sva Maesta, Et
            Ordini Di Sva Eccellenza, Fatti In Diversi
            Tempi. Tomo Settimo, 1692. [12], 110 p.
Reel 52, No. 295

MIRA DE AMESCUA, ANTONIO, fl. 1600.
El negro del meior amo. Comedia Famosa. Del Doctor
Mira De Mescua. [n.p.]: A costa de Luis de la Marca
[n.d.]
44 p.; 21cm.

Bound with: Cardona y Alagon, Antonio Folch de. El
mas heroyco silencio. Comedia famosa. Valencia, 1688.
Reel 33, No. 152

MIRANDA Y PAZ, FRANCISCO DE.
El Desengañado Philosophia Moral. Vanitas
Vanitatvm Et Omnia Vanitas. Eccles. C.1. Por D.
Francisco De Miranda Y Paz. Salmanticense Capellan
de su Mag.d en la Real Capilla de los Señores
Reyes nueuos sita en la Sta Iglesia de Toledo.
Toledo: por Francisco Caluo Impresor, 1663.
[6], 205, [4] l.; 20cm.

Engraved title-page.
Pagination errors throughout.
HC387/4746; Palau, 172279; Penney, p. 362; Pérez
Pastor, no. 567.
Reel 112, No. 699

MIRAVALL Y FLORCADELL, VICENTE DE.
Tortosa Civdad Fidelissima Y Exemplar. Motivos Qve
El Rey Nvestro Señor Don Felipe el Grande, Quarto de
Castilla, y Tercero de Aragon, ha tenido para concederla
estos Gloriosos Titulos; En premio de la Lealtad que
ha mostrado en las Alteraciones de Cataluña. O. D. C.
A la Generosa Proteccion del Señor Don Geronimo de
Villanueua, Cauallero del Orden de Calatraua, Comendador
de Santiuañez, en la de Alcantara, Del Consejo de su
Magestad en los de Guerra y Aragon, Protonotario de los
Reynos de aquella Corona, y su Secretario del Estado
de la Parte de España. Por Don Vicente de Mirauall y
Florcadell, Doctor en ambos Derechos. Arcediano Mayor
y Canonigo de la Santa Iglesia de Vich. Madrid: En
la Imprenta del Reyno, 1641.
[8], 80, [1] l.; 20cm.

Pagination errors throughout.
First Edition
Palau, 172333; Ticknor, p. 231.
Reel 112, No. 700

MIRAVETE DE BLANCAS, MARTIN.
Alegaciones Del Dotor Martin Miravete De Blancas,
Abogado Del Reyno De Aragon, en la declaracion, que
por el Fiscal de la Magestad Serenissima del Rey
nuestro Señor se pide en la Corte del Iusticia de
Aragon, sobre la nominacion de Virrey estrangero.
Omnia S. R. E. animaduersioni subiecta sunto.
Çaragoça: en casa del Prior del Pilar, por
Lorenço de Robles impresor del Reyno de Aragon, y
de la Vniuersidad, 1591.
[9], 394, [2] p.; 32cm.

Pagination errors throughout.
Reel 112, No. 701

MOLES, FADRIQUE, fl. 1631-1637.
Amistades De Principes Por Don Fadriqve Moles,
Cavallero del Orden Militar de san Iuan. A Don Carlos
Coloma, Del Consejo de Estado y Guerra del Rey
nuestro Señor, Gentilhombre de la Camara de su
Magestad, y su Mayordomo. Madrid: En la Imprenta
Real, 1637.
[4], 68 l.; 20cm.

Palau, 174250; Simón Díaz, Impresos, no. 1387.
Reel 112, No. 702

MOLES, FADRIQUE, fl. 1631-1637.
In Processv Iosephi Gviger, & Mariae Bernardae
Egizabal conivgvm. Super apprenhensione in Articulo
Proprictatis ... [n.p.-n.d.].
[1], 6p.

Caption title..
Bound with: Leon, González de. Por el Señor D.
Migvel Batista de Lanvza ... En el Processo ...
[Zaragoza. 1652].
And: Perat, Juan. Por Ivan Pallares, en la
Revocacion De Tutela que Pretende Don Francisco
Rvbalcaba.
Reel 112, No. 703

MOLINA, ANTONIO DE, d. 1619?
Exercicios Espiritvales De Las Excelencias,
Provecho, Y Necessidad De la Oracion mental,
reduzidos a dotrina, y Meditaciones: sacados de los
Santos Padres y Dotores de la Iglesia. Por
Padre don Antonio de Molina, Monge de la Cartuxa de
Miraflores. Dirigidos A Nvestro Glorioso Padre San
Bruno, fundador de nuestra sagrada Religion. Primera
Y Segvnda Parte. Burgos: por Iuan Bautista Varesio,
1622.
[13], 716, [71] p.; 20cm.

Los tratados que contiene se dizen en la hoja
siguiente.
Reel 112, No. 706

MOLINA, ANTONIO DE, d. 1619?
Instrvccion De Sacerdotes, En Qve Se les Da
Dotrina muy importante, para conocer la alteza del
sagrado oficio Sacerdotal: y para exercitarle
deuidamente. Sacada toda de los Santos Padres, y
Dotores de la Iglesia. Por Fray Antonio De Molina
Indigno Monge de la Cartuxa de Miraflores. Dirigida
Al Illvstrissimo Señor el Cardenal Capara.
Corregida y emendada por el mismo Autor, y añadida
aora nueuamente vna Tabla de la Sagrada Escritura.
Los Tratados que contiene se dizen en la hoja
siguiente. Barcelona: Por Sebastian de Cormellas,
al Call, 1637.
[24], 552, [65] p.; 20cm.

Colophon: "Con Licencia En Barcelona, Por
Sebastian de Cormellas al Call. Año de 1637."
Pagination errors throughout.
Reel 112, No. 707

MOLINA, ANTONIO DE, d. 1619?
Tractatvs De Oratione Mentali In quo docetur, vti
in ea diuersi affectus & actus interni virtutum
exercendi sint Idiomate Hispanico primùm conscriptus
auctore V. Patre D. Antonio De Molina Religioso
professo Cartusiae de Miraflores Et secundò in
Gallicum, demùmque in hunc sonum Latinum translatus,
ac obstetricante manu N.A. in lucem extractus.
Gandavi: Apud Alexandrum Sersanders, 1611.
[9], 176, [1] p.; 13cm.

Pagination errors throughout.
Reel 113, No. 708

MOLINA LAMA Y GUZMÁN, GERÓNIMO DE.
Vivir Contra La Fortvna, Escvelas Politicas De
Seneca, Para Hazer Rostro A Los Trabajos, Y Estar
Consolados Entre Las Miserias Del Tiempo. El Licenciado
Don Geronimo De Molina Lama y Guzman, Abogado en los
Reales Consejos, Alcalde mayor de la Ciudad de Murcia,
Gouernador de las armas, y Alcalde mayor de la de
Cartagena. Mvrcia: n.p., 1652.
[24], 191 l.; 20cm.

Palau, 174772; Simón Díaz, Impresos, no. 23.
Reel 113, No. 709

MOLINO, MIGUEL DEL, ed.
Repertorivm, Fororvm, Et Observantiarvm Regni
Aragonum, vnã pluribus cũ determinationibus cõsilij
iustitiae Aragonũ practicis atque cautelis eisdem
fideliter annexis. Fvervnt Etiam Additae Aliqvae Novae
Forales Dispositiones, quas isto   Signo inuenies: ac
cum maximo sumptu & labore concordantiae ad foros
nouissimè reformatos per numeros in margine descriptos:
numerum foliorum designantes. Ac etiam literam c
ibidem reperies, quae foros correctos indicabit.
Authore Michaele del Molino Iurisperito. In hac quoq;
tertia editione huius Repertorij fuerũt aliae
moderniores fororum, & eiusdem autoris apostillae ad
marginem àdditae, quae alphabetico signo demostrantur.
Quae omnia fuerunt recognita per Ioannem Michaelem
Perez à Bordalua iurisperitum, ex commissione eidem
facta per dominos Dipputatos Regni Aragonum.
Caesaravgvstae, Ex Officina Dominici à Portonarijs
S.C.R.M. Regni Aragoniae Typographi, 1585.
[6], 342 l.; 33cm.

Engraved title-page.
Two columns.
HC:NSI/757; Penney, p. 33; Sánchez, no. 638.
Reel 113, No. 710

MOLINOS, PEDRO.
Practica Ivdiciaria Del Reyno De Aragon. Compvesta
Por Pedro Molinos, Notario, y Ciudadano, que fue de
la Ciudad de Zaragoca. Y De Nvevo Añadida Por Cvriales
De La Misma Ciudad, en esta tercera, y vltima
impression, con algunos processos, y muchas mas
aduertencias que la antigua tenia, segun la pratica,
y nueuas disposiciones Forales de los años, y 1646. ...
Çaragoça: Por Diego Dormer, 1649.
[32], 436, [1] p.; 31cm.

HC:NS4/662; Jiménez Catalán, no. 546; Penney,
p. 363; Palau, 175115.
Reel 113, No. 711

MONARDES, NICOLÁS, 1512 (ca.) - 1588.
[Historia medicinal. English].
Loyfvll Nevves Ovt Of The newe founde worlde, wherein is declared the rare and singuler vertues of diuerse
and sundrie Hearbes, Trees, Oyles, Plantes, and
Stones, with their aplications, aswell for Phisicke as
Chirurgie, the saied beyng well applied bryngeth suche
present remedie for all deseases, as maie seme
altogether incredible: not withstandyng by practize
founde out, to bee true: Also the portrature of the
saied Hearbes, very aptly discribed: Englished by John
Frampton. Marchaunt. London: by Willyam Norton,
1577.
[3], 109, [2] l.; 18cm.

English translation by John Frampton.
Gothic type. Three parts:
Running titles: The Firse (sic) Parte Of This Booke
Treateth Of the thynges that are brought from the
Occidentall Indias, whiche serueth for the vse of
Medicine, and of the order that must bee kept in the

MONARDES (Cont'd)
taking of the roote called Mechoacan, wherein are
discouered greate secretes of Nature, and greate
experiences, made and compiled by Doctor Monardus,
Phisition of Seuill. Fol. I - 32.
The Seconde Part Of This Booke Is Of The Thinges
that are brought from our Occidentall Indias, which
serue for the vse of Medicine, where is treated of
the tabaco, and of the Sassafras, and of the Carto
Sancto, and of many other Hearbes and Plantes, Seedes
and Licores, that newly hath come from these partes,
of greate vertues and maruueilous effectes. Made by
the Doctor Monardvs, Phisition of Seuill. Fol. 33 - 86.
The Third Parte Of The Medicinall Historie, whiche
doth treate of the things that are brought frõ
our occidentall Indias, which doeth serue for the vse
of Medicine. Where is put many thinges Medicinall,
that hath greate secretes and vertues, Now newly
made by the saide Doctor Monardes, after that he
made the firste and seconde parte. Fol. 87 - 109.
Illustrated.
Pagination errors throughout.
Allison, p. 128, no. 26.1; Graesse, IV, p. 573;
Palau, 175497; Pollard and Redgrave, no. 18005a.
Reel 113, No. 712

MONARDES, NICOLÁS, 1512(ca.) - 1588.
[Historia medicinal. English].
Ioyfvll Newes Out of the New - found VVworlde.
Wherein are declared, the rare and singuler vertues
of diuers Herbs, Trees, Plantes, Oyles & Stones,
with their applications, aswell to the vse of Phisicke,
as of Chirurgery: which being well applyed, bring
such present remedie for all deseases, as may seeme
altogether incredible: notwithstanding by practice
found out to be true. Also the portrature of the said
Hearbs, verie aptly described: Englished by John
Frampton Marchant. Newly corrected as by conference
with the olde copies may appeare. Whereonto are added
three other bookes treating of the Bezaar stone, the
herb Escuerconera, the properties of Iron and Steele
in Medicine, and the benefit of Snow. London:
Printed by E. Allde, by the assigned of Bonham
Norton, 1596.
[3], 187, [1] l.; 18cm.

English translation by John Frampton.
Gothic type.
Title within ornamental border.
In 6 parts, continuously paged, with special title
pages.
Running titles: The First Part Of This Booke
Treateth Of The things that are brought from the
Occidentall Indias, which serue for the vse of Medicine,
and of the order that must be kept in taking the roote
called Mechoacan, wherein are discouered great secretes
of Nature, and great experiences: made and compiled by
Doctor Monardus, Phisition of Seuill. Fol. 1-32.
The Second parte Of this Booke is of the things
that are brought from our Occidentall Indias which
serue for the vse of Medicine, wherein is treated of
the Tabaco, and of the Saffaras, and of the Carlo
Sancto, and of many other hearbes & plants, seedes and
licoures, that newly are brought from those partes,
of great vertues and meruellous effectes. VVritten
by Doctor Monardus Phisition of Seuill. Fol. 33-87.
The Third Parte Of The Medicinall Historie, which
treateth of the things that are brought from our
Occidentall Indias, seruing for the vse of Medicine.
Wherein there is mention made of many things Medicinall,
that have great secretes and virtues. Nowe newly set
foorth by the sayde Doctor Monardus, after that he had
made the first and second partes. Fol. 87-110.

MONARDES (Cont'd)
A Booke which treateth of two medicines most excellent against all venome, which are the Bezaar stone, & the hearbe Escuerconera. Wherein are declared their maruellous effectes & great vertues, with the manner how to cure the sayd venom & the order which is to be vsed for to be preserued from them. Where shall be seene greate secretes in medicine and many experiences. Newly compyled by Doctor Monardus of Seuill. 1574. 1580. Fol. 111-138.
The Dialogve Of Yron, vvwhich treateth of the greatnesse thereof, and how it is the most excellent metall of all others, and the thing most necessarie for the seruice of man: and of the greate medicinall vertues which it hath. An Eccho for the Doctor Monardus Phisition of Seuill. In Seuill in the House of Alonso Escriuano. Fol. 139-163. (i.e. 172).
The Booke Which Treath Of The Snow, And Of properties & vertues thereof: And of the maner that should be vsed to make the drinke cold therwith, & of the other waies wherewith drinke is to he (sic) made cold: Whereof is shewed partly, in the latter part of the second Dialogue of Iron. With other curiosities which will giue contentment by other ancient thinges worthy to bee knowen, which in this treatise shall be declared. Written by Doctor Monardus Phisition of Seuill. 1574. Fol. 173-187 (i.e. 180).
Allison, p. 129, no. 26.3; Graesse, IV, p. 573; Palau, 175499; Pollard and Redgrave, no. 18007.
Reel 114, No. 713

MONARDES, NICOLÁS, 1512(ca.) - 1588.
[Historia medicinal. Latin].
Nicolai Monardi Hispalensis Medici praestantissimi, Libri Tres, Magna Medicinae Secreta Et Varia Experimenta continentes: Et illi quidem Hispanico sermone conscripti; nunc verò recens Latio donati à Carolo Clvsio Atrebate. Horum seriem proxima pagina indicabit. [Antverpiae, 1605].
[1], 52 p.; 35cm.

Pt. 3 Latin translation by L'Écluse Charles, 1526-1609.
IN: Caroli Clvsii Atrebatis, Aulae Caesareae queondam Familiaris, Exoticorvm Libri Decem: Quibus Animalium, Plantatum, Aromatum, aliorumáque peregrinorum Fructum historiae describuntur: Item Petri Bellonii Observationes, eodem Carlo Clusio interprete. Series totius operis pos Praefationem indicabitur. Antverpiae: Plantiniana Raphelengii, 1605.
Reel 114, No. 715

MONARDES, NICOLÁS, 1512(ca.) - 1588.
Dos Libros, El V - No Qve Trata De Todas Las Cosas que traen de nuestras Indias Occidentales, que siruen al vso de la Medicina, y el otro que trata de la Piedra Bezaar, y de la Yerua Escuerçonera. Cõpuestos por el doctor Nicoloso de Monardes Medico de Seuilla. Sevilla: En Casa De Hernando Diaz, en la calle de la Sierpe, 1569.
[148] l.; 16cm.

Leaf Hiij missing.
Antonio, Bibl. Hisp. Nova, II, p. 154; Escudero, nos. 630, 647; HC327/ 349, 1168; Heredia, I, no. 486; Medina, Bibl. Hisp. Amer, no. 207; Palau, 175485-11; Penney, p. 364; Sabin, no. 49936; Salvá, II, 2723; Thomas, p. 61.
Reel 114, No. 714

MONARDES, NICOLÁS, 1512(ca.) - 1588.
Simplicivm Medicamentorvm Ex Novo Orbe Delatorvm, Qvorvm In Medicina Vsvs Est, Historia. Hispanico sermone descripta à D. Nicolao Monardis, Hispalensi Medico; Latio deinde donata, & annotationibus, iconibúsque affabre depictis illustrata à Carolo Clvsio Atrebate. Altera Editio. Antverpiae: Christophori Plantini, Architypographi Regij, 1579.
[1], 84, [3] p.; 17cm.

Adams, I, no. 1593, II, no. 321; Doublet, p. 93, 98: Medina Bibl. Hisp-Amer., no. 258.
Reel 114, No. 716

MONCADA, PEDRO DE, 1619-1696.
Practica De La Comvnion Pvramente Espiritval. Sacada De los Santos, Concilios, Padres de la Iglesia, Doctores Escolasticos, y Maestros de espiritu. Exercicio de devocion substancial, y vtilissima. Dividida En Dos Partes, O Tratados: El primero, de todo lo que toca à su essencia, propiedades, y frutos. El segundo del exercicio que de ella puede aver quando se assiste à la Missa, de sus misterios, antiguedad, y origen de sus Ritos. Por El Padre Pedro de Moncada, Teologo, de la Compañia de Iesus, natural de Toledo. Madrid: Por Iulian de Paredes, Impressor de Libros. 1690.
[33], 294, [1] p.; 21cm.

Palau, 175739; Simon Díaz, Impresos, no. 446, Jesuitas, no. 855.
Reel 114, No. 717

MONTALVO, FRANCISCO ANTONIO DE, 17th Cent.
Noticias Fvnebres De Las Magestvosas Exeqvias, que hizo la felicissima Ciudad De Palermo, Cabeca Coronada de Sicilia. En La Mverte De Maria Lvysa De Borbon Nvestra Señora Reyna De Las Españas. De Orden Del Excelentissimo Señor Dvqve De Vzeda, Virrey, Y Capitan General deste Reyno. Execvtada Por El Ilvstre D. Lvys Riggio, Principe De Campo Florido, del habito de Santiago, Maestro Racional del Real Patrimonio. Qve Escribia El Maestro Fr. Francisco De Montalbo De La Sagrada Religion De S. Geronimo, Doctor Teologo, y Predicador de Su Magestad. Palermo: por Thomas Romolo, Impressor del S. Officio, 1689.
[7], 152, [1] p.; 31cm.

Half-title: Noticias Fvnebres De Montalbo.
Palau, 177328.
Reel 114, No. 718

MONTEMAYOR, JORGE DE, 1520? - 1561.
La Diana De Iorge De Montemayor, nueuamente corregida, y reuista Por Alonso De Vlloa. Parte Primera. Hanse añadido en esta vltima impression los verdaderos amores de Abencerrage, y la hermosa Xarifa. La infelice historia de Piramo y Tisbe. Van tanbien las Damas de Aragon, y Catalanas (sic), y algunas Castellanas, que hasta aqui no hauian sido impressas. Al Illustre Señor Don Rodrigo de Sande. Venecia: 1568.
215, [1] l.; 14cm.

Jerez, p. 76; Palau, 177949; Penney, p. 367; Short-title, II, p. 415, Sunderland, no. 8613; Thomas, p. 61; Ticknor, p. 234; Toda y Güell, Italia, no. 3388.
Reel 114, No. 719

MONTEMAYOR, JORGE DE, 1520? - 1561.
Primera Adicion De Los Siete Libros De La Diana De
George De Montemayor. Dirigida al Illustre señor
don Ioan, Castella de Vilanoua, señor de las Baronias
de Bicorb y Quesa, &c. Pamplona: Por Thomas Porrâlis,
1578.
239, [1] *l*.; 13cm.

Pagination errors throughout.
Graesse, IV, p. 585; Jerez, p. 70, 82; Palau,
177954; Pérez Goyena, no. 115; Salvá, II, 1912.
Reel 114, No. 720

MONTEMAYOR, JORGE DE, 1520? - 1561.
Los Siete Libros De La Diana De George De Monte
Mayor. Agora nueuamente añadida come se puede uer
en la tabla. Tornada a imprimir de nueuo, y a
corregir con mucha diligencia. Dirigida al muy
Illustre Señor don Iuan de Castella de Villanoua,
Señor de las Baronias de Bicorb, y Quesa. Venetia:
Appresso Giacomo Vicenci, 1585.
228 *l*.; 13cm.

Pagination errors throughout.
With this is bound his: Segvnda Parte De La Diana
De George De Monte Mayor. Por Alonso Pérez. Tornada
a imprimer de nueuo, y a corregir con mucha
diligencia..., 1585.
Adams, I, nos. 1710, 1712; Graesse, IV, p. 585;
Palau, 177958; Penney, p. 367; Salvá, II, 1914; Short-
title, II, p. 416; Thomas, p. 61.
Reel 114, No. 721

MONTEMAYOR, JORGE DE, 1520? - 1561.
Segvnda Parte De La Diana De George De Monte Mayor.
Por Alonso Perez. Dirigida al muy Illustre señor
don Berenguer de Castro, y Ceruellon, Barô de la
Laguna. señor de la casa de Castro, Vizcôde de Illa.
Anvers: En casa de Pedro Bellero, 1581.
224, [9] *l*.; 13cm.

Adams, I, no. 1711; Graesse, IV, p. 585; Jerez, p.
70; Palau, 177956; Peeters-Fontainas, II, no. 1053;
Salvá, II, 1913; Vaganay, no. 524.
Reel 115, No. 723

MONTEMAYOR, JORGE DE, 1520? - 1561.
Segvnda Parte De La Diana De George De Monte Mayor.
Por Alonso Pérez. Tornada a imprimer de nueuo, y a
corregir con mucha diligencia. Dirigida al muy
Illustre señor don Berengver de Castro, y Ceruellon,.
Baron de la Laguna, señor de la casa de Castro,
Vizconde de Illa. Venetia: Appresso Giacomo
Vincenci, 1585.
228, [5] *l*.; 13cm.

Adams, I, nos. 1710, 1712; Grasse, IV, p. 585;
Palau, 177958; Penney, p. 367; Salvá, II, 1914;
Short-title, II, p. 416; Thomas, p. 61.
Reel 115, No. 722

MONTEMAYOR, JORGE DE, 1520? - 1561.
[Los siete libros de la Diana. English]
Diana Of George Of Montemayor: Translated out of
Spanish into English by Bartholomew Yong of the Middle
Temple Gentleman. London: Printed by Edm. Bollifant,
Impensis G. B, 1598.
[9], 496, [1] p.; 27cm.

MONTEMAYOR (Cont'd)
Parts 1-3. English translation by Bartholomew Young.
Title within ornamental border.
Manuscript note on fly leaf: "This pastoral romance
is said to be the foundation of Shakespeare's Two
Gentlemen of Verona and of Pyramus and Thisbe in
Midsummer Night's Dream. It is also said to have been
partly translated by Sir Philip Sidney."
Part 2 is a translation of the Diana of Alonzo
Pérez, and part 3 is a translation of the Diana
enamorada of Gaspar Gil Polo.
Pagination errors throughout.
Allison, p. 130, no. 29; Graesse, IV, p. 586;
Pollard and Redgrave, no. 18044; Ticknor, p. 234.
Reel 115, No. 724

MONTEMAYOR, JORGE DE, 1520? - 1561.
[Los siete libros de la Diana. French]
Los Siete Libros De La Diana De George De Montemayor.
Où sous le nom de Bergers & Bergeres sont compris les
amours des plus signalez d'Espagne. Traduicts
d'Espagnol en François, & conferez és deux langues.
P. S. G. P. Et de nouueau, reueus & corrigez par le
sieur I.D. Bertranet. Paris: Pour Toussaincts du
Bray, 1611.
[4], 347, [11] *l*.; 16cm.

French translation by P.S.G. Pavillon.
Pagination errors throughout.
Doublet, p. 94; Foulché-Delbosc, Bibliographie, V,
no. 859; Gallardo, no. 3119; Jerez, p. 70; Palau,
177965; Penney, p. 368; Ticknor, p. 234.
Reel 115, No. 725

MONTEMAYOR, JORGE DE, 1520? - 1561.
[Los siete libros de la Diana. French]
Los Siete Libros De La Diana De George De Montemajor.
Où sous le nom de Bergers & Bergeres sont compris les
amours des plus signalez d'Espagne. Traduicts
d'Espagnol en François, & conferez és deux langues.
P.S.G.P. Paris: Chez Rolet Boutonné, au Palais, en la
Gallerie des Prisoniers pres la Chancellerie, 1613.
[4], 347, [10] *l*.; 17cm.

French translation by P. S. G. Pavillon.
Pagination errors throughout.
This edition lacks the verses addressed to J.D.
Bertranet and the Extraict du priuilege, both of which
are in the edition of 1611, which has also "Et de
nouueau, reueus et corrigez par le seeur I.D. Bertranet."
A very rare edition, not to be confused with those
listed by Foulché-Delbosc (Bibliographie, V., nos.
901-903), Ticknor (p. 234) and the Union Catalog
(vol. 392, p. 48) which have different title-pages.
Palau, 177966; Penney, p. 368.
Reel 115, No. 726

MORALES, AMBROSIO DE see OCAMPO, FLORIÁN DE.

MORENO PORCEL, FRANCISCO.
Retrato de Manuel Faria y Sovsa, Cauallero de
Orden Militar de Christo y de la casa Real. Contiene
vna relacion de su vida, vn catalogo de sus escritos,
y vn sumario de sus elogios, recogidos de varios
autores por d. Francisco Moreno Porcel. [Madrid,
1650]
87 [1] p.; 21cm.

Bound with: FARIA E SOUSA, Manuel de: El Gran
Iusticia de Aragõ Don Martin Batista De Lanuza. A
Dõ Miguel Batista De LaNuza Cav.º âla Orden de
Santiago del Cõsejo del Rei N.º Señor i su Protonot,
º en los Reynos de la Corona de Aragon Por Manuel
de Faria i Sousa Cav.º âla Ordẽ ã Christo i de la
Casa Real, 1650.
Reel 51, No. 287

MOSES BEN MAIMON, 1135-1204.
Canones Ethici R. Moseh Meimonidis, Hebraeorum
sapientissimi, Ex Hebraeo in Latinum versi,
uberioribusque Notis illustrati à Georgio Gentio, Ad
virum doctissimum praestantissimumque Gerebrandvm
Anslo. Amstelodami: Apud Ioh. & Cornelivm Blaev,
1640.
[21], 160, [3] p.; 20cm.

Hebrew title, Hilkoth deoth, at head of title page.
Hebrew and Latin in parallel columns.
The second tractate of the first book, Madda, of
the author's Mishneh Torah.
Includes index.
Palau, 147413.
Reel 115, No. 729

MOSES BEN MAIMON, 1135-1204.
Canones Poenitentiae Hebraicè R. Mose Aegyptio
descripti, Latinitate donati à G. N. Conatus iis, qui
leterarum Hebraicarum studiosō sunt, in primis
gratus; sed & aliis non inutilis futurus, si rectè
conjicimus. Cantabrigiae: Ex Academiae celeberrimae
Typographeo, 1631.
[7], 34 p.; 20cm.

Hebrew title at head of title page.
The fifth tractate of the first book Madda, of the
author's Mishneh Torah.
Reel 115, No. 728

MOSES BEN MAIMON, 1135-1204.
Constitvtiones De Fvndamentis Legis Rabbi Mosis F.
Maiiemon. Latinè redditae per Guilielmum Vorstivm
C. F. Additis quibusdam notulis, & Abravanelis scripto,
de Fidei Capite. Amstelodami: Apud Guiliel. & Iohannem
Blaev, 1638.
[9], 148 p.; 20cm.

Hebrew title at head of title page: Hilkhot Yesodei
ha-torah.
The first tractate of the first book, Madda, of the
author's Mishneh Torah.
Bound with: Abravanel, Isaac. Liber De Capite
Fidei, In quo continentur radices & capita vel
princípia religionis, Avtore Isaaco Abravanele ...,
1638.
Hebrew and Latin in parallel columns.
Palau, 147408.
Reel 115, No. 730

MOSES BEN MAIMON, 1135-1204.
[De idololatria liber]
R. Mosis Maimonidae De Idololatria Liber, cum
interpretatione Latina & Notis Dionysii Vossii.
Amsterdam: Apud Ioh. & Cornelivm Blaev. 1641.
[3], 174, [1] p.; 20cm.

Hebrew and Latin in parallel columns.
The fourth tractate of the first book, Madda of
the author's Mishneh Torah.
With this is Vossius, Gerardus Joannes: De Theologia
Gentili, Et Physiologia Christiana sive De Origine Ac
Progressv Idolatriae, ad veterum gesta, ac rerum
naturam, reductae; Deqve Natvrae Mirandis quibus homo
adducitur ad Deum Liber I, Et II., 1641.
Pagination errors throughout.
Palau, 147417.
Reel 116, No. 736

MOSES BEN MAIMON, 1135-1204.
[De idololatria liber]
R. Mosis Maimonidae De Idololatria Liber, cum
interpretatione Latina, & notis, Dionysii Vossii.
Amsterdami: Apud Ioh. & Cornelivm Blaev, 1642.
[13], 174, [1] p.; 20cm.

Hebrew and Latin in parallel columns.
The fourth tractate of the first book, Madda, of the
author's Mishneh Torah.
Palau, 147417.
Reel 116, No. 738

MOSES BEN MAIMON, 1135-1204.
De Jvre Pauperis Et Peregrini Apud Judaeos. Latine
vertit & notis illustravit Humphridus Prideaux, A. M.
Aedis Christi Alumnus. Oxonii: E Theatro
Sheldoniano, 1679.
[33], 168, [1], 21cm.

Text and translation, in parallel columns, of
selections from the Mishneh Torah.
Palau, 147422.
Reel 117, No. 740

MOSES BEN MAIMON, 1135-1204.
Porta Mosis Sive, Dissertationes Aliqvot à R. Mose
Maimonide, suis in varias Mishnaioth, sive textus
Talmudici partes, Commentariis praemissae, quae ad
universam fere Iundaeroum disciplinam aditum aperiunt.
Nunc primùm Arabicè prout ab ipso Autore conscriptae
sunt, & Latinè editae. Unâ cum Appendice Notarum
Miscellanea, operâ & studio Edvardi Pocokii Linqvarum
Hebraicae & Arabicae in Academia Oxoniensi Professoris...
Oxoniae: Excudebat H. Hall Academiae Typographus,
Impensis R. Davis, 1655.
([25]; 355 p.; [5], 436, [29] p.), 19cm.

Hebrew title at head of title page: Bab Musi.
Selections from the author's Kitāb al-Sirāj, in
their Judeo-Arabic original and in Latin translation.
Includes: Appendix Notarvm Miscellanea ... Non est
in Lege [S. Scriptura] vel una litera, à quâ non
dependeant montes magni, 1654.
Pagination errors throughout.
Palau, 147338.
Reel 117, No. 739

MOSES BEN MAIMON, 1135-1204.
Rabbi Mosis Majemonidis Liber מורה נבוכים Doctor
Perplexorum: Ad dubia & obscuriora Scripturae loca
rectius intelligenda veluti Clavem continens, Prout
in Praesatione, in quâ de Authoris vitâ, & Operis totius
ratione agitur, pleniùs explicatur: Primùm ab Authore in
Lingua Arabica ante C C C C L. circiter annos in
Aegypto Conscriptus: Deinde à R. Samuele Aben Tybbon
Hispano in Linguam Hebraeam, stylo Philosophico &
scholastico, adeoque difficillimo, translatus: Nunc
verò novè, ad Linaguae Hebraicae cognitionem uberiùs
propagandam, ejiuq & amplitudinem evidentius Christianorum Scholis declarandam, in Linguam Latinam perspicuè
& fideliter Conversus, à Johanne Buxtorfio, Fil.
Additi sunt Indices Locorum Scripturae, Rerum, &
Vocum Hebraicarum. Basileae: Sumptibus & impensis
Ludovici König, excudebat Jo. Jacob Genath, 1629.
[41], 532, [53] p.; 20cm.

Reel 116, No. 732

MOSES BEN MAIMON, 1135-1204.
Rabbi Mosis Majemonidis Liber[מורה נבוכים] Doctor
Perplexorum: Ad dubia & obscuriora Scripturae loca
rectius intelligenda veluti Clavem continens, Prout
in Praesatione, in quâ de Authoris vitâ, & Operis
totius ratione aqitur, pleniûs explicatur ...
Basileae: Sumptibus & impensis Ludovici König,
excudebat Jo. Jacob Genath, 1629.
[40], 532, [53] p.; 20cm.

Bound with: John the Evangelist. Epistola...
Reel 116, No. 733

MOSES BEN MAIMON, 1135-1204.
Symbolvm Fidei Ivdaeorvm Er. Mose Aegyptio.
Praecationes Eorvmdem pro defunctis, è lib. Mahzor.
Aliae, in quibus commemor ationem suorum Diuorum
Faciunt. Aliae pro his, qui despondentur & coniugātur,
è Breuiario Hebraeorum. Sexcenta Tredecim Legis
praecepta, è More Nebuchim. Interprete G. Genebrardo
Theologo Parisiensi. Parisiis: Apud Martinum
Iuuenem, via S. Ionnis Lateranensis, ad insigne
Serpentis, 1569.
[20], 66 Z.; 17cm.

In two parts. Hebrew and Latin, each with separate
title-page and foliation. Pagination and signatures
of Part II in Hebrew.
The 613 precepts are in Latin only.
Maimonides' arrangement of the 613 precepts is not
in his Moreh nebukim but in his Sefer hamizowot.
Colophon: Adiuncta est his omnibus G. Genebrardi
Theologi Parisiensis Latina conuersio. Parisis: Apud
Martinum Iuuenem, M.D.LXIX.
Reel 115, No. 727

MOSES BEN MAIMON see also VOSSIUS, GERARDUS JOANNES,
Canon of Canterbury.

MOSQUERA DE BARNUEVO, FRANCISCO, fl. 1612.
La Nvmantina De el Licen.do Don Franc.co
Mosquera De Barnueuo Natural de la dicha Ciudad.
Dirigida A La Nobilissima Ciudad de Soria I a sus
Doze Linages I Casas a ellos agregadas. [Sevilla:
Luys Estupiñan, 1612.]
[-1], 371, [30] Z.; 21cm.

Engraved title - page: Soria Pvra Cabeça De
Estremadvra.
Colophon: "Sevilla, En la Imprenta de Luys
Estupiñan en este año de M.DC.XII."
Doublet, p. 94; Escudero, no. 966; Goldsmith,
p. 121; Graesse, IV, p. 615; Jerez, p. 71; Palau,
183470; Salvá, I, 821; Ticknor, p. 243.
Reel 117, No. 741

MUNTANER, RAMÓN, b. 1265-1336.
Chronica, O Descripcio dels fets, e hazanyes del
inclyt Rey Don Iavme Primer Rey Darago, de Mallorques,
e de Muntpesller: e de molts de sos descendents Feta
Per Lo Magnifich En Ramon Muntaner, lo qual serui axi
al Inclyt Rey don Iaume, coma fos fills, e descendents:
es troba present a les coses contengudes en la present
historia. Barcelona: En casa de Iaume Cortey
Librater, 1562.
[14], 248 Z.; 28cm.

Colophon: "Laus Deo. Fonch Stampada y ab molta
deligencia reuista la present Chronica dels Reys de
Arago feta per Ramon Montaner autor de vista en la
insigne ciutat de Barcelona, per Iaume Cortey impres-
sor, en lany. M.D. LXII."
Engraved woodcut border, with Jupiter at the top,
Hercules at the left, Hispalus at the right side, and
Ibervs F. Hisp. at the bottom.
Printer's device with mottoes: Cor mouet Apta
manus. Alite foelici.
Adams, I, 1941; Graesse, IV, p. 625; Palau,
184824; Penney, p. 375; Salvá, II, 3076; Thomas,
p. 62; Ticknor, p. 245.
Reel 117, No. 742

MURCIA DE LA LLANA, FRANCISCO.
Selecta Circa Aristotelis Dialecticam Svbtilioris
Doctrinae, Qvae In Complvtensi Academia Versatvr, Miro
Qvodam ordine disposita, & in dilucidam methodum
redacta. Per Licenciatvm Franciscvm Mvrcia de la
Llana in insigni eiusdem Academiae Collegio Theologorum
Collegam. Ad D. D. Didacvm De Alarcon Sacrae Caesareae
Maiestatis Senatus meritissimum Consiliarum.
Jingolstadii: Typis Wilhelmi Ederi, 1621.
[13], 440 p.; 20cm.

Palau, 185986.
Reel 117, No. 743

MURILLO, DIEGO, 1555-1616.
Discvrsos Predicables Sobre Todos Los Evangelios
Qve Canta la Iglesia, enlas Festiuidades de Christo
Nuestro Redemptor. Compvestos Por El Padre Fray Diego
Murillo, Lector de Theologia, y Guardian del Collegio
de San Diego de Caragoça, de la Orden de nuestro
Seraphico Padre San Francisco. Dirigidos al muy
Illustre y Reuerendissimo Señor Don Fray Diego de
Yepes Obispo de Taraçona, y del Consejo del Rey
nuestro señor. Aduiertase, que los libros que no
fueren firmados de mano del Author en la primera
hoja, no los reconoce el Author por suyos.
Çaragoça: Por Angelo Tauanno, 1607.
2 pts. in 1 ([21], 555 p.; 523, [168] p.); 20cm.

Caption title of Part 2: En La Fiesta De La
Admirable Ascension De Christo Redemptor nuestro.
Colophon: "Con Licencia: En Çaragoça por Angelo
Tauano. Año M DC VII."
Pagination errors throughout.
Reels 117 & 118, No. 744

MURILLO, DIEGO, 1555-1616.
    Fvndacion Milagrosa De La Capilla Angelica Y
Apostolica De La Madre De Dios Del Pilar, Y Excellencias
De La Imperial Civdad De Caragoça. Diuidese en dos
Tratados. Compvestos Por El Padre F. Diego Murillo
Predicador General, Lector de Theologia, y Padre
perpetuo de la Prouincia de Aragon, de la Orden de
nuestro Seraphico Padre San Francisco. Dirigidos
A Los Ivrados De La Misma Ciudad, Padres de la
Republica, y Regidores della. Contienen El Viage
Del Apostol Santiago a España, el fruto que hizo en
ella, con diuersas vidas de Santos, y varias cosas de
antiguedad, confirmadas con testimonios de Authores
grauissimos, y antiquissimos, y algunos dellos
extraordinarios. Barcelona: por Sebastian Mateuad.
1615.
    2 pts. in 1 v. ([33], 285, [13] p.; 452, [25] p.);
29cm.

    Pagination errors throughout.
    Goldsmith, p. 122; Graesse, IV, p. 628;
HC384/2329; Palau 186170; Penney, p. 375; La Serna,
no. 4624.
Reel 118, No. 745

MUT, VICENTE, 1614-1687.
    Vida De La Venerable Madre Soror Isabel Cifra,
Fvndadora De La Casa De La Edvcacion De La Civdad De
Mallorca Escrita Por Don Vicente Mvt, Sargento Mayor,
Ingeniero, y Coronista del Reyno de Mallorca.
Dedicada A Los Señores Ivrados De Dicha Civdad, Y
Reyno. Mallorca: en casa la Viuda Piza, 1655.
    [13], 136, [1] p.; 20cm.

    Palau, 186762.
Reel 118, No. 746

N

NADAL, GERÓNIMO, 1507-1580.
Adnotationes Et Meditationes In Evangelia Qvae In
Sacrosancto Missae Sacrificio Toto Anno Legvntvr.
Cvm Evangeliorvm Concordantia historiae integritati
sufficienti. Accessit & Index historiam ipsam
Euangelicam in ordinem temporis vitae Christi distribuens.
Secunda editio. Auctore Hieronymo Natali. Societatis
Iesv Theologo. Antuerpiae: excudebat Martinus Nutius,
1595.
[9], 636, [5] p.; 34cm.

Bound with his Venite Ad Me Omnes Qvi Laboratis Et
Onerati Estis Et Ego Reficiam Vos. Evangelicae
Historiae Imagines Ex ordine Euangeliorum, quae toto
amo in Missae sacrificio recitantur, In ordinem
temporis vitae Christi digestae..., 1593.
Title-page and plates were designed by Marten de Vos
and Bernardino Passeri, and engraved by Antonie
Jerónimo, Adriaen Jan Wierix, Jan Collaert, and Karel
van Mallery.
Engraved title-pages.
Palau, 187146.
Reel 118, No. 747

NADAL, GERÓNIMO, 1507-1580.
Venite Ad Me Omnes Qvi Laboratis Et Onerati Estis
Et Ego Reficiam Vos. Evangelicae Historiae Imagines
Ex ordine Evangeliorum, quae toto amo in Missae
sacrificio recitantur, In ordinem temporis vitae
Christi digestae. Auctore Hieronymo Natali
Societatis Iesv Theologo Antuerpiae. Svperiorvm
Permissv, 1593.
[6], 153 p.; 34cm.

Title-page and plates were designed by Marten de
Vos and Bernardino Passeri, and engraved by Antonie
Jerónimo, Adriaen Jan Wierix, Jan Collaert, and Karel
van Mallery.
Palau, 187146 and 187147.
Reel 119, No. 748

NATIVIDAD, FR. ANTONIO DE LA see ANTONIO LA NATIVIDADE.

NATIVIDADE, ANTONIO DA.
Silva De Svfragios. Declarados, Alabados,
Encomendados, Para Comvn Prouecho de viuos, y difuntos.
Declarase el estado de las Almas; se refieren muchos
exemplos, y casos prodigiosos. Por El M. Fr. Antonio
De La Natividad; de la Orden de San Agustin, de la
Prouincia de Portugal. Tradvzidos En Lengva Castellana,
por el M. Fr. Diego de Noguera, de la misma Orden, en
la Prouincia de Castilla, Calificador de la Santa
Inquisicion. Dedicase Al Muy Ilvstre, Y Noble
Cavallero D. Iuan Luis de Berrio y Angulo, Cauallero
de la Orden de Santiago, Marques de Castellon,
señor de Baldanchuelo, Ensayador mayor y perpetuo de
la Casa de la Moneda de la Imperial Ciudad de Toledo,
Cauallerizo de la Reyna nuestra señora, y Continuo de
la Real Casa de Castilla. Con Tabla De Sermones Para
Tres Dias De Quaresma, Miercoles, Viernes, y Domingo.
Madrid: Por Bernardo Hervada, 1666.
[23], 523, [50] p.; 21cm.

Spanish translation by Fr. Diego de Noguera.
Colophon: "En Madrid. Por Bernardo de Hervada.
Año de 1666."
Reel 119, No. 749

NAVARRA Y DE LA CUEVA, PEDRO see CABREGA, PEDRO DE
NAVARRA Y DE LA, MARQUES DE.

NAVARRE (KINGDOM) -- Laws, Statutes, etc.
Fveros Del Reyno De Navarra, Desde Sv Creacion Hasta
Sv Feliz Vnion Con El De Castilla, Y Recopilacion De
Las Leyes Promvlgadas Desde Dicha Vnion Hasta El Año
1685; Recopiladas, Y Redvcidas A Lo Svstancial, Y A
Los Titvlos A Qve Corresponden, Por El Licenciado D.
Antonio Chavier Abogado de los Reales Consejos, y
Auditor General de la gente de Guerra de dicho Reyno,
sus fronteras, y comarcas. Con prologo, è indices
copiosos de Fueros, y Leyes, en que se declara su
principio, y progresso: y tabla de los vocablos mas
oscuros de dichos Fueros para su mejor inteligencia.
Pamplona: En la Imprenta de Martin Gregorio De
Zabála, Impressor deste Reyno, 1686.
([32], 232, [1] p.; [1], 646, [1] p.); 30cm.

Error in paging: no. 94-95 repeated in last group
of paging.
Ex-libris: Karl Vollmöller.
Pérez Goyena, no. 748.
Reel 119, No. 751

NAVARRO, JOSÉ, 17th CENT.
Poesia Varias De Iosef Navarro Dedicalas Al
Excelentissimo Señor Don Iaime Fernandez de Hijar,
Silva, Piños, y Cabrera, Duque, y Señor de Hijar,
Marques de Alenquer, y Conde de Belchite,
Gentilhombre de la Camara de su Magestad, &c.
Zaragoça: En la Imprenta de Migvel De Lvna,
Impressor de la Ciudad, y del Hospital R. y G. de
N. S. de Gracia, 1654.
[13], 269 p.; 20cm.

First and only edition.
Ex-libris: "D. Judas Sanz de Larrea, canonigo de
Santa Maria de Calatayud."
Jerez, p. 170; Jiménez Catalán, no. 617; Palau,
188225; Penney, p. 378.
Reel 119, No. 752

NEBRIJA, ELIO ANTONIO DE see ANTONIO DE LEBRIJA
[i.e. Elio Antonio Martínez de Cala y Jarava].

NECHONIAH BEN HA-KANAH, RABBI.
Illvstrissimo Ac Sapientissimo Domino D. Inigo De
Mendocza Comiti Tendiliae Legato Sacre Maiestatis
regis Hispaniae Paulus de Heredia salutem perpetuamqz
foelicitatem. [f. 2a:] Nevmi ae Filii Haccanae
Epistola De Secretis Ad Haccanam Filivm:. Romae:
Eucharius Silber, c. 1488.
[40] l.; 18cm.

Translation by Paulus de Heredia from Hebrew into
Latin.
Goff, P-183; Reichling, 11675.
Reel 119, No. 753

NICCOLO DE TUDESCHI, Abp. of Palermo, 1386-1445.
Lectura super quinque libros Decretalium cum
Repertorio Alphonsi Montalbo. [Basel, Johann
Amerbach, 1487-88].
4 v. ([354] l.; [264], [174] l.; [161], [268] l.;
[51], [155], [222] l.); 37cm.

Repertorium (pt. [8] undated).
British Museum Cat. (XV Cent.) III, p. 749; Goff
(Third Census) P 51 and D-176; Hain* no. 12315.
Reels 179, 180, 181 & 182, No. 1167

NICHOLAS Y SACHARLES, JUAN DE see NICOLÁS Y SACHARLES,
JUAN, psuedonym.

NICOLÁS Y SACHARLES, JUAN, PSEUD? b. c. 1570.
[Hispanus reformatus. English]
The Reformed Spaniard: To all reformed Churches,
embracing the true Faith, wheresoeuer dispersed on
the Face of the Earth: In speciall, To the most
Reuerend Arch-Bishops, Reuerend Bishops, and
Worshipfull Doctors, and Pastors, now gathered to-
gether in the venerable Synode at London, this yeare
of our Lord, 1621. Iohn de Nicholas & Sacharles,
Doctor of Physicke, wisheth health in our Lord.
First published by the Author in Latine, and now
thence faithfully Translated into English. London:
Printed for Walter Burr, 1621.
[18] l.; 18cm.

English translation by unknown.
Palau, 190516; Pollard and Redgrave, no. 18330.
Reel 119, No. 754

NICOLINI, SEBASTIÁN.
Cabeza Visible Catolica, Y Vicaria Infalible De
Cristo, En La Apostolica Catedra Romana, Continvada
Asta Nvestro Santissimo Padre, y señor Alexandro VII.
Pontifice Maximo. Epitome historial Eclesiastico.
Donde Se Aivstan Los Tiempos Mas ciertos de las
elecciones, govierno, vacantes, cismas, y los hechos
singulares de los Sucessores de San Pedro, y se
proponen brevemente Por El Dotor Sebastian Nicolini,
Canonigo de la insigne Colegial de la Ciudad de
Xativa. Que Le Dedica Al Principe De Las Eternidades
Iesv Cristo Señor nuestro, Eterno, y Summo Sacerdote.
Valencia: por Geronimo Vilagrasa, en la calle de las
Barcas, 1659.
[9], 488, [9] p.; 21cm.

Pagination irregular; numbers 251-252 repeated and
397-406 omitted.
Palau, 190487.
Reel 120, No. 755

NIEREMBERG, JUAN EUSEBIO, 1595-1658.
[Causa y remedio de los males públicos. French]
Les Veritables Cavses Des Malhevrs Presens De
L'Espagne; Tirées de l'Espagnol du P. Iean Evsebe de
Neuremberg, de la Compagnie de Iesvs. Lyon: Chez
Iean Champion, Marchand Libraire, demeurant à la
Place du Change, 1644.
[13], 250, [5] p.; 32cm.

French translation by Jean Sirmond.
Pagination errors throughout.
Palau, 190958; Foulché-Delbosc, V, no. 1401.
Reel 120, No. 756

NIEREMBERG, JUAN EUSEBIO, 1595-1658.
Contemplations Of The State of Man In This Life And
In That which is to come. Inveni portam; Spes &
Fortuna valete. By Jeremy Taylor, D.D. and late Lord
Bishop of Down and Connor. London: Printed for John
Kidgell at the Golden-Ball, near Grays-Inn Gate, in
Holborn, 1684.
[11], 303 p.; 17cm.

English adaptation by Jeremy Taylor of the English
translation by Sir Vivian Mullineaux.
Title in red and black.
Errors in paging: 241-296 omitted in numbering.
Allison, p. 133, no. 2. Not in Palau, not in Wing.
Reel 120, No. 760

NIEREMBERG, JUAN EUSEBIO, 1595-1658.
[De la afición y amor de María. French]
L'Aimable Mere De Jesus, Ov Traite' Contenant les
divers motifs qui peuvent nous inspirer du respect,
de la devotion, & de l'amour, pour la tres - sainte
Vierge. Traduit de l'Epagnol par le R. Pere D'Obeilh
de la Compagnie de Jesvs. Dedie A Madame De Maintenon
Lyon: Chez Antoine Briasson ruë Merciere au Soleil,
1688.
[9], 541, [6] p.; 15cm.

French translation by R. Père D'Obeilh.
Pagination errors throughout.
Palau, 190628.
Reel 120, No. 757

NIEREMBERG, JUAN EUSEBIO, 1595-1658.
De La Diferencia Entre Lo Temporal, Y Eterno.
Crisol De Desengaños, Con la memoria de la Eternidad,
Postrimerias humanas, y principales Misterios Diuinos.
Por El P. Ivan Evsebio Nieremberg, de la Compañia de
Iesvs. Añadido En Esta Vltima Impression, vna Inuectiua,
contra el adorno superfluo de las Galas. Dedicado Al
Muy Ilvstre Señor D. Ioseph Galaerán de Pinós, General
Titular de la Artilleria de Granada; señor de las
Baronias de Rialp, y Seró; señor del Terrós, Brianson,
y la Lladrell; Carlàn de Agramonte; señor de Tanca la
puerta; Baron de Labanca, Torach, Lluças, y Bauda;
señor de Tudela, Colldelrat, y Grallo; señor de
Vilafortun; y Baron de Barberà, &c. 1670. Barcelona:
en casa de Francisco Cormellas, Mercader por Iacinto
Andrev Impressor.
[13], 408, [41] p.; 20cm.

13th ed.
Palau, 190838.
Reel 120, No. 758

NIEREMBERG, JUAN EUSEBIO, 1595-1658.
[De La Diferencia Entre Lo Temporal, y Eterno.
English]
A Treatise Of The Difference Bbtwixt (sic) Temporal
And Eternal: Composed in Spanish By Eusebius
Nieremberg, S. J. Translated into English By Sir Vivian
Mullineaux, Knight. And since Reviewed according to
the tenth and last Spanish Edition. [n.p.] 1672.
[16], 589 p.; 18cm.

English translation by Vivian Mullineaux.
Allison, p. 133, no. 1; Palau, 190912; Wing, N. 1115.
Reel 120, No. 759

NIEREMBERG, JUAN EUSEBIO, 1595-1658.
[Dictámen de espiritu. German]
Hoffzimmer der Klugen, oder, Unterricht, wie sich
eine Person, so wohl bey Hof, oder in anders
Verrichtungen sich geschicklich verhalten soll. Aus
den Frantzöischen übersetzet durch Georg Martzi.
Franckfurth: 1692.
[9], 238, [1] p.; 15cm.

German translation by Georg Martzi.
Title in red and black. Error in paging: numbers
49-58 omitted.
A translation of one of François d'Obeilh's French
versions of the author's Dictámenes.
Reel 120, No. 761

NIEREMBERG, JUAN EUSEBIO, 1595-1658.
[Flores espirituales. English].
Flores Solitudinis. Certaine Rare and Elegant
Pieces: Viz. Two Excellent Discourses Of 1.
Temperance, and Patience; 2. Life and Death. By
I.E. Nierembergius. [Pt. 2:] The World Contemned; By
Eucherius, Bp of Lyons. [Pt. 3:] And the Life of
Paulinus, Bp of Nola. Collected in his Sicknesse and
Retirements, By Henry Vaughan. Silurist. Tantus Amor
Florum, & generandi gloria Mellis. London: Printed
for Humphrey Moseley at the Princes Armes in St. Pauls
Church-yard, 1654.
[2], 191 p.; 165 p.; 15cm.

English translation by Henry Vaughan, Silurist.
Parts II and III have separate signatures and
pagination.
Not in Allison, not in Palau.
Reel 120, No. 763

NIEREMBERG, JUAN EUSEBIO, 1595-1658.
Ioannis Evsebii Nierembergii Madritensis Ex
Societate Iesv In Academia Regia Madritensi
Physiologiae Professoris Historia Natvrae, Maxime
Peregrinae, Libris XVI Distincta. In quibus rarissima
Naturae arcana, etiam astronomica, & ignota Indiarum
animalia, quadrupedes, aues, pisces, reptilia, insecta,
zoophyta, plantae, metalla, lapides, & alia mineralia,
fluuiorumque & elementorum conditiones, etiam cum
proprietatibus medicinalibus, describuntur; nouae &
curiosissimae quaestiones disputantur, ac plura
sacrae Scripturae loca erudite enodantur. Accedunt de
miris & miraculosis Naturis in Europâ Libri duo: item
de iisdem in Terrâ Hebraeis promissâ Liber vnus.
Antverpiae: Plantiniana Balthasaris Moreti, 1635.
[9], 502, [105] p.; 37cm.

Palau, 190738.
Reel 121, No. 764

NIEREMBERG, JUAN EUSEBIO, 1595-1658.
Libro De La Vida. Iesvs Crvcificado. Impresso En
Iervsalen, en la officina del monte Caluario,
cumplidos treynta y tres años de su edad. A Costa De
La Sangre del Hijo de Dios. Adornado, Y Brevemente
dispuesto, para que se imprima en los coracones de
todos, con las meditaciones principales de la Passion,
y de los siete miembros de Christo mas atormentados.
Por el Padre Iuan Eusebio Nieremberg, de la Compañia
de Iesus. Barcelona: Por Pedro Lacaualleria, 1634.
[2], 30 *l*.; 11cm.

Palau, 190731.
Reel 121, No. 765

NIEREMBERG, JUAN EUSEBIO, 1595-1658.
Obras Christianas Del P. Juan Evsebio Nieremberg,
De La Compañia de Jesvs. Qve Contienen Lo Qve Debe
El Hombre hazer para viuir, y morir Christianamente,
temiendo á Dios, despreciando el mundo, estimando la
gracia, entendiendo la Doctrina Christiana, y
preparandose para la muerte... En Sevilla: Por
Lvqas Martin De Hermosilla, 1686.
3v. ([14], 752, [7] p.; [2], 387 *l*.; [2], 385,
[17] *l*.); 30cm.

Each volume is paged separately and has its own
title page.
Volume 2: Obras Christianas Del P. Juan Evsebio
Nieremberg ... Qve Contienen Los Tratados, que mas
ayudan al Christiano à leuantar el espiritu, y
vnirse con Dias, con vida perfecta.

NIEREMBERG (Cont'd)
Volume 3: Obras Filosoficas Del P. Juan Evsebio
Nieremberg, De La Compañia De Jesvs. Ethicas,
Politicas, y Fisicas, Que contienen lo principal de
la Filosofia Moral, Ciuil, y Natural, todo conforme à
la piedad Christiana.
Leaves 244-246, 384 of v. 3 lacking.
Palau, 190598; Salvá, II, no. 3956; Simón Díaz,
Jesuitas, no. 1093.
Reels 121 & 122, No. 766, Vols. 1-3

NIEREMBERG, JUAN EUSEBIO, 1595-1658.
Obras Y Dias. Manval De Señores Y Principes. En
Qve Se Propone Con Sv Pvreza, Y Rigor La Especvlacion,
Y Execvcion Politica, Y Particvlar De
Todas Virtvdes. Compvesto Por El Padre Ivan Eusebio
Nieremberg, de la Compañia de Iesvs. Al Exc.mo S.or
Don Gaspar De Gvzman, Conde Dvqve, Gran Canciller De
Las Indias, &c. Madrid: Por la viuda de Alonso
Martin, 1629.
[5], 220, [1] *l*.; 21cm.

Palau, 190604; Simón Díaz, Jesuitas, no. 1015:
Ticknor, p. 249.
Reel 122, No. 767

NIEREMBERG, JUAN EUSEBIO, 1595-1658.
Obras Y Dias. Manval De Señores Y Principes. En
Qve Se Propone Con Sv Pvreza, Y Rigor La Especvlacion,
Y Execvcion Politica, Economica, Y Particvlar De Todas
Virtvdes. Compvesto Por El Padre Ivan Eusebio
Nieremberg, de la Compañia de Iesvs. Revisto En Esta
Impression, Y Anadido Con Vna Centvria De Dictamenes
Prudentes, Por El Mismo Avtor. 50. Madrid: Por
Maria De Qviñones, 1641.
[17], 382, [1] p.; 21cm.

Palau, 190605; Simón Díaz, Jesuitas, no. 1016.
Reel 122, No. 768

NIEREMBERG, JUAN EUSEBIO, 1595-1658.
Vida Del Dichoso Y venerable Padre Marcelo
Francisco Matrilli, de la Compañia de Iesus, que murio
en el Iapon por la Fè de Christo, sacada de los
processos Autenticos de su vida y muerte. A Sv
Alteza Del Serenissimo Principe nuestro Señor Don
Baltasar Carlos. La dedica, y mandô à la Estampa Don
Geronimo Valle de la Cerda y Villanueua Cauallero de
la Orden de Calatraua. Madrid: Por Maria de
Quiñones, 1640.
[6], 134, [1] *l*.; 21cm.

Goldsmith, p. 123, no. 43; Palau, 190807; Salvá,
II, 3796; Simón Díaz, Jesuitas, no. 1043.
Reel 122, No. 769

NIEREMBERG, JUAN EUSEBIO, 1595-1658.
Vida Divina, Y Camino Real Para La Perfeccion Con
La Vida Del Venerable Padre Pedro Canisio de la
Compañia de Iesus. Por El Padre Ivan Eusebio Nieremberg, de la misma Compañia. Revista, Y Añadida en
esta impression por el mismo Autor. Madrid: en
la Imprenta Real, 1635.
[7], 255, [2] *l*.; 15cm.

Colophon: "En Madrid En la Imprenta Real, Año de
1635."
Palau, 190708.
Reel 122, No. 770

NIEREMBERG, JUAN EUSEBIO, 1595-1658 see also
 PALAFOX Y MENDOZA, JUAN DE. El Pastor De
 Noche Bvena...

NISENO, DIEGO, d. 1656.
 Elogio Evangelico Fvneral: En El Fallecimiento Del
Doctor Iuan Perez de Montalban, Clerigo Presbitero,
Doctor en Sacra Teologia, i Notario del Santo Tribunal
de la Inquisicion Por F. Diego Niseno, Vmilde Alumno
de la Inclita i Esclarecida Familia del Gran Basilio,
despues de Iesu Cristo i los Apostoles, Primer Padre,
i Legislador de la Monastica vida. ... En Madrid:
En la Imprenta del Reino, 1639.
 [4], 34 l.; 20cm.

 Pagination errors throughout.
 Title page mutilated causing loss of print.
 Bound with: GRANDE DE TENA, PEDRO, ed., Lagrimas
Panegricas A La Tenorana Mverte Del Gran Poeta, I
Teologo Insigne Doctor Iuan Perez de Montalban, Clerigo
Presbitero, i Notario de la Santa Inquisicion, Natural
de la Inperial Villa de Madrid... Madrid, 1639, and
QUINTANA, Francisco de, Oración panegirica ... Madrid.
En Madrid: En la Inprenta [sic] del Reino, 1639.
 Goldsmith, p. 124, no. 50; Palau, 191834; Penney,
p. 384; Salvá, I, 257.
Reel 68, No. 410

NISENO, DIEGO, d. 1656.
 El Gran Padre De Los Creyentes Abrahan. Avtor F.
Diego Niseno Monge de la Sagrada Religion del gran
Padre San Basilio: despues de Iesu Cristo, i los
Apostoles, Primer Legislador, Facilmente Principe, i
inclito Patriarca de todos los Monges. Lleva cuatro
Indices; de Libro, i Capitulos, de la sagrada Escritura,
Cosas notables, i Remisiones a los Evangelios de la
Cuaresma. Barcelona: Por Sebastian de Cormellas al
Call, 1636.
 [12], 251, [17] l.; 21cm.

 Pagination errors throughout.
 HC387/3534; Palau, 191827; Penney, p. 384.
Reel 122, No. 771

NOYDENS, BENITO REMIGIO, 1630-1685.
 Pormptvario Moral De Qvestiones Practicas Y Casos
Repentinos En La Teologia Moral, Para Examen De
Cvras, Y Confessores. Por El P. Benito Remigio
Noydens Antuerpiense Teologo, y Religioso de la sagrada
Religion de los Clerigos Regulares Menores. Los
Motivos Del Avtor, Y vtilidad de la Obra, refiere en
el Prologo. Barcelona: por Antonio Lacavalleria, 1668.
 [9], 339, [6] p.; 16cm.

 Palau, 195993.
Reel 122, No. 772

NOYDENS, BENITO REMIGIO, 1630-1685.
 Visita General Y Espiritval Colirio De Los Ivdios;
Y promtvario Catolico De Los mas principales
fundamentos de la Fe, y Religion Christiana. Por El
Padre Benito Remigio Noydens, Antuerpiense Teologo, y
Religioso de la sagrada Religion de los PP. Clerigo
Regulares Menores. Los Tratados que contiene este
Libro se verän en la hoja siguiente. Dirigido A la
Magestad de Dios Christo N. Señor. Madrid: En La
Imprenta Real, 1662.
 [16], 292 p.; 21cm.

 Goldsmith, p. 124, no. 58; Palau, 195998.
Reel 123, No. 773

NOYDENS, BENITO REMIGIO see also COVARRUBIAS HOROZCO
SEBASTIÁN DE.

NUNEZ, PEDRO, fl. 1492-1537.
 Petri Nonii Salaciensis Opera: Quae complectuntur
primùm, Dvos Libros, In Qvorvm Priore Tractantur
pulcherríma Problemata: In Altero Traduntur ex
Mathematicis disciplinis regulae & instrumenta Artis
Navigandi, quibus varia rerum Astronomicarum ...
circa coelestium corporum motus explorare possumus.
Deinde, Annotationes in Aristotelis problema Mechanicum
de Motu Navigii ex remis: Item in Georgii Pvrbachii
Planetarvm Theoricas Annotationes, quibus multa
hactenus perperam intellecta, ab alijsq̃ praeterita
exponuntur. Eivsdem, De Erratis Orontii Finoei
Liber Vnus. Postremo, De Crepvsculis Lib. I. Cvm
Libello Allacen de causis Crepusculorum. Quae
quemadmodum mole exigua videntur, ita virtute ingentia,
Lector candide, intelliges. Basileae: Per
Sebastianvm Henricpetri, 1592.
 [13], 439, [2] p.; 31cm.

 Colophon: Basileae, Per Sebastianvm Henric Petri:
Anno CIↃ IↃ XCII.
 De Erratis Orontii Finaei (pp. 312-372) has
half-title: De Erratis Orontii Finaei Delphinatis,
Qvi Pvtavit Inter Datas Dvas Lineas, Binas Medias
Proportionales Svb Continva Proportione inuenisse,
circulum quadrasse Cubum duplicasse, Multangulum
rectilineum quodcunque in circulo describendi artem
tradidisse, & longitudinis locorum differntias aliter
quàm per eclipses lunares, etiam dato quouis tempore
manifestas fecisse, Petri Nonii Salaciensis Liber Vnvs.
 De Crepvsculis (pp. 373-439) has half-title also:
De Crepvsculis Petri Nonii Salaciensis, Liber Vnvs.
Item, Allacen Arabis vetustissimi, de causis
Crepusculorum Liber vnvs, à Gerardo Cremonensi iam
olim Latinitate donatus, & per eundem Petrvm Novivm
denuõ recognitus.
 Adams, II, no. 371; Palau, 196745.
Reel 123, No. 774

NÚÑEZ, PEDRO JUAN, 1522-1602.
 Apposita M. T. Ciceronis, Collecta A Petro Ioanne
Nvnnesio Valentino, Ad Reuerendiss. & Illustriss.
D. Franciscũ à Nauarra Archiepiscopum Valentinum.
His accesserunt additiones quaedam & explicationes
Latinae dictionum Graecarũ. Valentiae: Excudebat
viduae Ioannis Mey 1556.
 ([8], 296, [1] l.; 44, [4] l.; 15cm.).

 In 2 sections, separately paged.
 Palau, 196891.
Reel 123, No. 775

NÚÑEZ, PEDRO JUAN, 1522-1602.
 Epitheta M. T. Ciceronis Collecta A. P. Ioanne.
Nvnnesio Valentino Iunior Aldvs.Manvtivs. Pavlli.
F. Aldi. N. Venetiis. 1570.
 [16], 627, [3] p.; 15cm.

 Adams, II, no. 377; Palau, 196891; Short-Title,
II, p. 475.
Reel 123, No. 776

NÚÑEZ, PEDRO JUAN, 1522-1602.
Phrynichi Epitomae Dictionvm Atticarum Libri III.
Sive Ecloga, A Petr. Io. Nunnesio Valentino integritati
restituta, Latinē conuersa, Eiusdemq̄; & Dauidis
Hoeschelij Aug. Notis, in quis & aliorum auctorum loca
partim emendantur, partim illustrantur, aucta.
Avgvstae Vindelicorvm, typis Michaēlis Mangeri. 1601.
([9], 93, [16] p.; 133, [9] p.; 20cm.)

In 2 separately paged sections.
Palau, 196912.
Reel 123, No. 777

NÚÑEZ, PEDRO JVAN see also SACRO BOSCO, JOANNES DE.

NÚÑEZ DE CASTRO, ALONSO, b. 1627 - d. about 1670.
Coronica De Los Señores Reyes De Castilla, Don
Sancho el Deseado, Don Alonso el Octauo, y Don Enrique
el Primero. En Qve Se Refiere Todo Lo Svcedido En
los Reynos de España, desde el año de mil ciento y
treinta y seis, hasta el de mil y ducientos y diez
y siete. Comprobado Con Los Historiadores De Mayor
Credito, y con diferentes instrumentos de
Priuilegios, Escrituras, Donaciones, y otras memorias
antiguas, sacadas con toda diligencia, y cuidado
de los mejores Archiuos. Dase Noticia De Diferentes
Familias, y Ilustres Varones, que florecieron en
estos años en Armas, santidad, y letras. Dedicado
Al Rey Nvestro Señor, Por mano de Don Garcia de
Avellaneda y Haro, Conde de Castrillo. Madrid:
Por Pablo de Val, 1665.
[33], 372 p.; 29cm.

Goldsmith, p. 125, no. 86; Graesse, IV, p. 702;
Knapp-Huntington, p. 253; Palau, 197146; Penney,
p. 388; Salvá, II, 3083; Simón Díaz, Impresos,
no. 2309; Ticknor, p. 251.
Reel 123, No. 778

NÚÑEZ DE CASTRO, ALONSO, b. 1627 - d.(ca.) 1670.
Libro Historico Politico. Solo Madrid Es Corte, Y
El Cortesano En Madrid. Quarta impression, con
diferentes Adiciones, dividido en quatro Libros. En
El Primero Se Discurren Las Ventajas, que Madrid, yà
en quanto Poblacion yà en quanto Corte, haze à
las demàs del Orbe. Danse individuales noticias de
todos los Consejos, y Tribunales su modo de Govierno,
y Ministros de que se componen. La Casa Real, y sus
Oficios, y de todas las rentas de su Magestad, y
Provisiones que haze, dentro, y fuera de España. Los
tres siguientes instruyen al Cortesano con Dogmas
Christianamente Politicos, para adorno del
entendimiento, aliño de la voluntad, y perfeccion de
la memoria. Dedicado Al Muy Ilvstre Señor D.
Francisco Maria Pasqval Mercader y Cervellon, quinto
Conde de Buñol y de Cervellon, Baron de Sieteaguas,
Oropesa, Macastre, Yatoba, Aiborache, y Mirabonel.
Por Don Alonso Nuñez De Castro, Coronista de su
Magestad. Barcelona: Por Vicente Suria, Impressor,
1698.
[17], 450 p.; 21cm.

Fourth edition.
Title in red and black.
Errors in paging: 352-355 omitted in numbering.
In double columns.
Goldsmith, p. 125, no. 90; HC384/1639; Palau,
197142; Penney, p. 388.
Reel 123, No. 779

NÚÑEZ DE CASTRO, ALONSO, b. 1627 - d.(ca.) 1670.
Seneca Impugnado De Seneca En Questiones Politicas,
Imorales. A Don Miguel Batista De Lanuza Cavallero del
Orden de Santiago, del Consejo del Rey N. S. y su
Prothonotario en los Reynos de la Corona de Aragon.
Por Don Alonso Nuñez de Castro Coronista General d̄ los
Reinos d̄ Castilla. Madrid: Por Pablo de Val, 1650.
[19], 82, [11] l.; 21cm.

Hc387/3544; Palau, 197136; Penney, p. 388; Simón
Díaz, Impresos, no. 21.
Reel 123, No. 780

NÚÑEZ DE CASTRO, ALONSO, b. 1627 - d.(ca.) 1670.
Vida De San Fernando El Tercero Rey De Castilla, Y
Leon. Ley Viva De Principes Perfectos. Desempeño
De Los Preceptos Mas Seberos, Con Qve Estrecharon A
Svs Principes, Svbditos, Politicos, Y Estadistas.
Por Don Alonso Nvnez De Castro, Coronista de su
Magestad. Madrid: Por la Viuda de Francisco Nieto,
1673.
[28], 210, [18] l.; 21cm.

Palau, 197147; Simón Díaz, Impresos, no. 812.
Reel 124, No. 781

NÚÑEZ DE GUZMÁN, FERNANDO, d. 1552?
In Omnia L Annaei Senecae Scripta Fernandi Pinciani
Viri grǣce latinēq̄ doctissimī, Castigationes utilis-
simae fauste occipiunt. In Lib. Primvm De Beneficiis.
IN: Opera L. Annaei Senecae Et Ad Dicendi Facvltatem,
Et Ad Bene Vivendvm utilissima, per Des. Erasmvm
Rotero & Matthaeum Fortunatum, ex fide ueterum
codicum, tum ex probatis autoribus, postremo sagici
nonnunquā diuinatione, sic emendata, ut ad genuinam
lectionem minimum desiderare possis. I Adiecta Svnt
Scholia D. Erasmi Roterdami in bonam partem operis.
Beati Rhenani in Ludum de morte Claudij Caesaris.
Rodolphi Agricolae in Declamationes aliquot
Commentarioli. Fernandi Pinciani castigationes in
uniuersum opus. Index rerum & uerborium locuples.
Basileae: 1552.
[48] l.; 29cm.
Reel 124, No. 784

NÚÑEZ DE GUZMÁN, FERNANDO, d. 1552?
Refranes, O Proverbios En Romance, Qve Nvevamente
colligiō y glossō el Comendador Hernan Nuñez,
Professor eminētissimo de Rhetorica, y Griego, en
Salamanca. Van Pvestos por la orden del A b c.
Dirigidos Al Illvstrissimo señor Marques de Mondejar,
Presidente del consejo de las Indias, &c. Van Tambien
Aqvi añadidas vnas coplas, hechas a su muerte.
Salmanca: En casa de Iuan de Canoua, 1555.
[6], 142 l.; 28cm.

First edition.
Engraved title-page.
Jerez, p. 74; Heredia, no. 3737; Palau, 197515;
Penney, p. 388; Salvá, II, 2110; Thomas, p. 63.
Reel 124, No. 782

NÚÑEZ DE GUZMÁN, FERNANDO, d. 1552?

Refranes O Proverbios En Romance, Qve Coligio, Y glossò el Comendador Hernan Nuñez, professor de Retorica, y Griego, en la Vniuersidad de Salamanca. Y La Filosofia VVlgar De Ivan De Mal Lara, en mil refranes glossados, que son todos los que hasta aora en Castellano andan impressos. Van Ivntamente Las Qvatro cartas de Blasco de Garay, hechas en refranes, para enseñar el vso dellos. Lerida: Luys Manescal, 1621.

[4], 399 l.; 21cm.

In 2 continuously paged volumes.
La Filosofía Vulgar has special title-page: La Filosofia VVlgar. De Ivan De Mal Lara, Vezino de Seuilla. A La C. R. M. Del Rey Don Filipe nuestro Señor dirigida. Primera Parte, Que Contiene Mil Refranes glossados. pp. 121-399.
Ex-libris: Thomas Gaisford.
Colophon: "En Lerida Por Luys Menescal. Año MDCXXI."
Goldsmith, p. 125, no. 97; Knapp, p. 51; Palau, 197518; Penney, p. 388; Salvá, II, 2113; Ticknor, p. 251.
Reel 124, No. 783

NÚÑEZ DE VILLAIZÁN, JUAN, fl. 1595.

Don Fernando Quarto Rey de Castilla y de Leon, &c. El qual gano a Gibraltar. Cronica del muy valeroso rey don Fernando, 4to Visnieto del sancto rey don Fernando que gano a Seuilla. Nieto del rey dõ Alonso que fue par è emperador, hizo el libro de las siete partidas y fue hijo del rey dõ Sancho el Brauo. Cuyas cronicas estan impressas. y fue padre del rey dõ Alõso Onzeno q̃ gano las Algeziras. y abuelo del rey don Pedro. Cuyas cronicas tambiẽ estan impressas. Este es el rey don Fernãdo que dizen que murio emplazado de los Caruajales. Valladolid: 1554.

78, [1] l.; 30cm.

Engraved title-page.
Imperfect: nos. 65-72 omitted in foliation. Fol. lxiv wanting.
Not in Palau's Manual ...
Reel 124, No. 785

NÚÑEZ DE TOLEDO Y GUZMÁN, FERNANDO see NÚÑEZ DE GUZMAN, FERNANDO.

O

OCAMPO, FLORIÁN DE, c. 1499 - 1555, ed.
La Coronica General De España. Que continuaua
Ambrosio de Morales natural de Cordoua, Coronista del
Rey Catholico nuestro señor don Philipe segundo deste
nombre, y cathredatico de Rhetorica en la
Vniuersidad de Alcala de Henares. Prossiguiendo (sic)
adelante de los cinco libros, que el Maestro Florian
de Ocampo Coronista del Emperador don Carlos V. dexo
escritos. Todo lo de las antiguedades de España, y
la manera del entenderlas, y aueriguarlas, va puesto
al cabo en otra obra por si. Alcala De Henares: En
casa de Iuan Iñiquez de Lequerica, 1574.
[14], 418, [22] l.; 30cm.

Engraved title-page.
Catalina, no. 495; HC:NS4/434/2; Palau, 198379;
Penney, p. 158; Thomas, p. 64.
Reel 124, No. 786

OCAMPO, FLORIÁN DE, c. 1499 - 1555, ed.
Hispania Vincit. Los Cinco Libros primeros dela
Cronica general de España, que recopila el maëstro
Florian do Campo, Cronista del Rey nuestro señor, por
mandado de su Magestad, en Camora. Medina del
Campo: por Guillermo de Millis, 1553.
336, [10] l.; 30cm.

Title in red and black (Roman letter) beneath
large woodcut coat-of-arms of the Emperor Charles V,
some chapter headings also in red and black.
Adams, II, no. 15; HC:NS4/434; Palau, 198378;
Penney, p. 158; Pérez Pastor, no. 101.
Reel 125, No. 788

OCAMPO, FLORIÁN DE, c. 1499 - 1555, ed.
Los Cinco Libros Primeros Dela Coronica general de
España, que recopilaua el maestro Floriã de Ocãpo,
coronista del Rey nuestro señor, por mandado de su
Magestad, en Camora. Alcala: En casa de Iuan
Iñiguez de Lequerica, 1578.
222, [8] l.; 30cm.

Engraved title-page.
Pagination errors throughout.
Catalina, no. 534; Penney, p. 158; Salvá, II, 3090.
Reel 125, No. 789

OCAMPO, FLORIÁN DE, c. 1499 - 1555, ed.
Los Cinco Libros Postreros De La Coronica General
De España. Que continuaua Ambrosio de Morales natural
de Cordoua, Coronista del Rey Catholico nuestro Señor
don Philipe segundo deste nombre. Prossiguiendo
adelante la restauracion de España, desde que le
començo a Ganar de los Moros, hasta el rey don Bermudo
el tercero deste nombre. De Lo Demas Qve Va Pvesto
Con la Coronica, se dara razon luego al principio.
Cordoua: por Gabriel Ramos Bejarano impressor de
libro, 1586.
[14], 350, [8] l.

HC:NS4/434/4; Palau, 198383; Penney, p. 158; Salvá,
II, 3090; Thomas, p. 64; Valdenebro, 22.
Reel 125, No. 790

OCAMPO, FLORIÁN DE, c. 1555, ed.
Los. Otros. Dos. Libros. Vndecimo. Y. Dvo Decimo.
De La Coronica. General De España. Que continuaua
Ambrosio de Morales natural de Cordoua, Coronista del
Rey Catholico nuestro señor don Philipe segundo deste
nõbre, y cathredatico de Rethorica en la Vniuersidad
de Alcala de Henares. Prossiguiendo adelante de
los cinco libros, que el Maestro Florian de Ocampo
Coronista del Emperador don Carlos V. dexo escritos.
Van juntas con esta parte de la coronica las Anti-
guedades de España, que hasta agora se han podido
escreuir. Alcala De Henares: En casa de Iuan
Yñiquez de Lequerica, 1577.
2v. ([8], 226, [5] l.; [6], 131, [2] l.); 30cm.

Vol. II of his Coronica General ... 1574.
His Antiguedades has separate title-page: Las
Antigvedades De Las Civdades De España. Que van
nombradas en la Coronica, con la aueriguacion de sus
sitios, y nõbres antiguos. Que escreuia Ambrosio de
Morales natural de Cordoua, Coronista del Rey
Catholico nuestro señor don Philipe segũdo deste
nõbre, y cathredatico de Rhetorica en la Vniuersidad
de Alcala de Henares. Con Vn Discvrso General, Donde
se enseña todo lo que a estas aueriguaciones pertenece,
para bien hazerlas y entender las antiguedades. Con
otras cosas, cuya summa va puesta luego a la quarta
hoja, [1577].
Pagination errors throughout.
Catalina, no. 521; Graesse, V, p. 4; HC:NS4/434/3;
Palau, 198381; Penney, p. 158.
Reel 125, No. 787

OLDOINI, AGOSTINO, 1612-1683 see CHACÓN, ALFONSO, 1540-
1599.

OLMO, JOSÉ VICENTE DEL, 1611-1696.
Relacion Historica Del Avto General De Fe, Qve Se
Celebro En Madrid Este Año de 1680. Con Assistencia
Del Rey N.S. Carlos II. Y De Las Magestades De La
Reina N. S. Y La Avgvstissima Reina Madre. Siendo
Inquisidor General et Excelent.ᵐᵒ Sr. D. Diego
Sarmiento de Valladares. Dedicada A La S. C. M. Del
Rey N. S. Refierense Con Cvriosa Pvntvalidad todas
las circunstancias de tan Glorioso Triunfo de la
Fe, con el Catalogo de los Señores, que se hizieron
Familiares, y el Sumario de las Sentencias de los
Reos. Vã inserta la Estampa de toda la Perspectiva
del Teatro, Plaça, y Valcones. Por Ioseph Del Olmo,
Alcayde, y Familiar del Santo Oficio, Ayuda de la
Furriela de su Magestad, y Maestro mayor del Buen
Retiro, y Villa de Madrid. Impresso por Roqve Rico
De Miranda, 1680.
[16], 308 p.; 21cm.

Pagination errors throughout.
Engraved half-title: Relacion Del Avto Gen. De La
Fee. Q. Se Celebró, En Madrid, En Presencia De Svs
Mgᵈᵉˢ El Dia 30 De Ivnio De 1670. Dedicado al Rey
N. S. Carlos Seg.ᵈᵒ Gran Monarcha de España, y del
nuevo Mundo, que Dios guarde. Por Joseph del Olmo
Ayuda de la Furriela de su Mg. Alcaide, y Familiar đ
sᵗᵒ Off.º y M.ma. đ M. marcus Orozco.
Goldsmith, p. 126, no. 18; HC:380/514; Palau,
201026; Penney, p. 392; Salvá, 3960.
Reel 125, No. 791

OÑA, PEDRO DE.
El Ignacio De Cantabria Por el Lic.do Pedro de
Oña Dirigido a la Compañia de IHS. Sevilla: Por
Francisco De Lyra, 1639.
[4], 214, [1] l.; 21cm.

Engraved title-page.
Jerez, p. 76; Escudero, no. 1542; Palau, 201624;
Penney, p. 393; Salvá I, 831.
Reel 126, No. 792

ORIGEN, Y Estado Del Colegio De Los Notarios Del Nvmero
De Çaragoça Contiene Vn Svmario De Los Privilegios,
Qve Los Serenissimos Reyes Le Concedieron.
Estatvtos Qve Le Dio La Civdad, Sentencias Ganadas,
Y Firmas Obtenidas Por El Colegio. Las Ordinaciones
Del, Y Rvbrica De Los Colegiales, y Notarios, con
sus Indices, y Nombres. Çaragoça: por Iuan Nogves,
1650.
[23], 127, [10] p.; 29cm.

Palau, 204095.
Reel 126, No. 793

ORMAZA, JOSEPH, 1617-c. 1676.
Sermon En La Assvmpcion De Maria Señora Predicador
Por El Padre Ioseph Ormaza, De la Compañía de Iesvs,
Lector De Theologia En El Colegio De La Ciudad de
Tudela. Dalo A La Estampa El Doctor Don Gonzalo Perez
Ledesma, Canonigo Dignidad de la Santa Iglesia de Leon.
Zaragoça: En el Hospital Real, y General de nuestra
Señora de Gracia, 1648.
27 p.; 21cm.

Bound with this is: Ledesma, Gonzalo Perez.
Censvra De La Eloqvencia, Para Calificar Svs Obras, Y
Señaladamente Las Del Pvlpito. Dalo A La Estampa El
Doctor Don Gonzalo Perez Ledesma, Canonigo Dignidad de
la Santa Iglesia de Leon, 1648.
Palau, 204296; Simón Díaz, Jesuitas, no. 1143.
Reel 126, No. 794

ORSINI, FULVIO, 1529-1600 see AGUSTÍN, ANTONIO, abp.
of Tarragona.

OSSUNA Y RUS, MARTÍN DE.
Memorias, Y Recuerdos De Lo Sagrado, Y Real De La
Repvblica De Dios. Dedicadas Al Serenissimo Sr. El
Señor D. Jvan De Avstria, Por El P. Fr. Martin De
Ossvna Y Rvs, del Orden de N. Señora del Carmen de
Observancia, y Colegial de S. Alberto de Seuilla.
Seuilla: por Jvan Cabeças, 1679.
2 pts. ([39], 602 p.; [3], 384, [31] p.); 20-22cm.

Part II has special title-page: Memorias Sagradas.
Segvnda Parte. Sigvese El Origen, Y Progressos De
Las Sagradas Religiones, Qve Prometimos Escrito Por
el Padre Fray Martin de Ossuna y Rus, de la Orden de
nuestra Señora del Carmen, Colegial de San Alberto, &c.
Palau, 206769.
Reel 126, No. 796

OUDIN, CÉSAR DE, d. 1625.
[Grammaire Espagnolle. English]
A Grammar Spanish And English Or A Briefe And
compendious Method, teaching to reade, write, speake,
and pronounce the Spanish Tongve. Composed In French
by Caesar Oudin, and by him the third time corrected
and augmented. Englished, and of many wants supplied,
by I.W. Who hath also translated out of Spanish the
fiue Dialogues of Iuan de Luna, Cast. which are annexed
to the Grammar. London: Printed by Iohn Haviland,
1622.
[17], 303 p.; 17cm.

OUDIN (Cont'd)
English translation by I.W. (i.e. James Wadsworth).
Juan de Luna's Dialogues ... (pp. 216-303).
Goldsmith, p. 128, no. 94; Knapp-Huntington,
p. 59; Penney, p. 400; Pollard and Redgrave, no.
18897; Palau, 207288.
Reel 127, No. 805

OUDIN, CÉSAR DE, d. 1625.
Grammaire Espagnolle, Mise Et Expliqvee En
François. Par Cesar Ovdin, Secretaire Interprete du
Roy, és langues Germanique, italienne, & Espagnolle,
& Secretaire ordinaire de Monseigneur le Prince de
Condé. Paris: Chez Marc Orry, 1610.
[16], 204 p.; 18cm.

Knapp-Huntington, p. 44; Penney, p. 400.
Reel 127, No. 802

OUDIN, CÉSAR DE, d. 1625.
Grammaire Espagnolle Expliqvee En François. Par
Cesar Ovdin, Secretaire Interprete du Roy, és langues
Germanique, Italienne, & Espagnolle. Augmentée en
ceste derniere edition, par Antoine Ovdin, Professeur
des mesmes langues. Paris: Chez Pierre Billaine,
1632.
[9], 231 p.; 18cm.

Bound with: Salazar, Ambrosio de, b. 1575? : Espeio
General De La Gramatica En Dialogos, Para Saber La
natural y perfecta pronunciacion de la langua
Castellana. ... Dirigido à la Sacra y Real Magestad
del Christianissimo Rey de Francia y de Nauarra. Por
..., 1636.
Doublet, p. 100; Knapp-Huntington, p. 45; Palau,
207274; Penney, p. 400.
Reel 127, No. 803

OUDIN, CÉSAR DE, d. 1625.
Refranes O Proverbios Castellanos Traduzidos en
lengua Francesa. Proverbes Espagnols Tradvicts En
François, par Cesar Ovdin, Secretaire Interprete
du Roy. Reueus, corrigez & augmentez en ceste
seconde edition, par le mesme. Paris: Chez Marc
Orry, ruë S. Iaques, au Lyon Rampant. 1609.
[17], 256 p.; 18cm.

Title and text in Spanish and French.
Doublet, p. 100; Graesse, V, p. 64; Knapp-
Huntington, p. 259; Palau, 207293; Penney, p. 400;
Vindel, P. Bg 474.
Reel 126, No. 797

OUDIN, CÉSAR DE, d. 1625.
Refranes O Proverbios Espagnoles Tradvzidos En
Lengva Francesa. Proverbes Espagnols Traduite en
Francois. Par Cesar Oudin, Secretaire Interprete du
Roy. Con Cartas en Refranes de Blasco de Garay.
Brvxelles: chez Rutger Velpius, & Hubert Anthoine
a l'Aigle d'or pres de la Court, 1612.
[172] l.; 15cm.

Folio K11a has special t.-p.: Cartas En Refranes
De Blasco de Garay Racionero De La Santa Iglesia De
Toledo. Brvsselas: por Roger Velpio, 1612.
La Serna, II, no. 3421 (dated: 1611); Palau,
207294; Peeters-Fontainas, I, p. 259 and II, pp.
517-18, no. 1008.
Reel 126, No. 798

OUDIN, CÉSAR DE, d. 1625.
Refranes O Proverbios Castellanos, traduzidos en
lengua Francesa. Proverbes Espagnols Traduits en
François. Par Cesar Ovdin, Secretaire Interprete
du Roy Reueus, Corrigez & augmentez en cette derniere
edition. A Paris, Chez Antoine De Sommaville,
au Palais, sur le deuxiéme Perron, allant à la
sainte-Chapelle, à l'Escu de France. M.DC.LIX (1659).

Ex-libris: George Wilbraham.
Doublet, p. 100; Palau, 207298.
No. 799: Not Available

OUDIN, CÉSAR DE, d. 1625.
Tesoro De Las Dos Lengvas Española Y Francesa.
Thresor Des Devx Langves Espagnolle Et Francoise:
Avqvel Est Continve (sic) L'Explication de toutes
les deux respectiuement l'vne par l'autre: Diuisé en
deux parties. Par Cesar Ovdin, Secretaire
Interprète du Roy és langues Germanique, Italienne
& Espagnolle, & Secretaire ordinaire de
Monseigneur le Prince de Condé. Reueu, corrigé,
augmenté, illustré, & enrichy en ceste quatriesme
Edition d'vn grand nombre de Dictions & Phrases: &
d'vn Vocabulaire des mots de jargon en langue
Espagnolle, par le mesme Autheur. Brvxelles: chez
Hubert Antoine, 1625.
2v. in 1 ([366] *l*.; [249] *l*.)

Part II has special t.-p.: Seconde Partie Dv Thresor
Des Devx Langves Francoise Et Espagnolle. En Laquelle
Est Contenue l'explication des dictions Francoises en
Espagnol, pour faciliter le moyen, à ceux qui desiront
attaindre la perfection de composer en langue Espagnolle.
In double columns.
Knapp-Huntington, p. 46; Palau, 207306-II; Penney,
p. 400; Peeters-Fontainas, II, no. 1011.
Reel 126, No. 800

OUDIN, CÉSAR DE, d. 1625.
Tesoro De Las Dos Lenguas, Española Y Francesa. De
Caesar Oudin. Añadido Conforme A Las Memorias del
Autor, con muchas Frasis (sic) y Dicciones; y con el
Vocabulario de Xerigonça, en su Orden Alfabetico. Por
Antonio Oudin, Secretario Interprete del Rey de
Francia. Nuevamente Corregido Y Aumentado de
infinidad de Omissiones, Adiciones, y Vocablos; con
sus Generos: Y con un Vocabulario de las principales
Ciudades, Villas, Reynos, Provincias, y Rios del
Mundo. Por Juan Mommarte, Impresor jurado. Bruselas:
En casa del dicho Juan Mommarte, 1660.
2v. in 1 ([274] *l*.; [234] *l*.].

Part II has special t.-p.: Seconde Partie Du Tresor
Des Deux Langues, Françoise Et Espagnolle, Par Cesar
Oudin, Interprete du Roy. Nouvellement reveu, &
augmenté de plusieurs Mots, avec leurs Genres; &
d'un Vocabulaire des principales Villes, Regions, &
Fleuves du Monde, par J. M.
In double columns.
Knapp-Huntington, p. 47; Palau, 207308; Peeters-
Fontainas, II, 1012; Penney, p. 400.
Reel 127, No. 801

OVEN, JUAN see OWEN, JOHN, b.c. 1560 - d. 1622.

OVIDIUS NASO, PUBLIUS, b. 43 B.C., d. 18 A.D.
[Heroides. Spanish]
Heroyda Ovidiana. Dido Aeneas. Con Parafrasis
Española, Y Morales Reparos Ilvstrada. Por Sebastian
de Alvarado Y Alvear, Professor de Rhetorica y letras
Humanas, Natural de Burgos. Al Ilvstrissimo, Y
Ecelentissimo Señor Don Carlos Coloma de los Consejos
de Estado y guerra de la Magestad Catholica; General
de las armas Reales en los Estados de Flandes;
Castellano de Cambray; Gouernador y Capitan general
de Cambrasi; Comendador de la Orden de Santiago. &c.
Bovrdeos: En Casa de Gvillermo Millanges, Impressor
del Rey de Francia, 1628.
[20], 333, [7] p.; 21cm.

Spanish translation by Sebastián de Alvarado y
Alvear.
Colophon: Omnia Sactae Matris Ecclesiae censurae,
& bonorum judicio, & eruditorum limae subijcio.
Goldsmith, p. 129, no. 108; Jerez, p. 118; Graesse,
V, p. 85; Palau, 207547; Penney, p. 401; Salvá, I, 835.
Reel 127, No. 806

OVIDIUS NASO, PUBLIUS, b. 43 B.C., d. 18 A.D.
[Metamorphoses. Spanish]
Las Metamorphoses, o Transformaciones del muy
excelente poeta Ouidio, repartidas en quinze libros y
traduzidas en Castellano. Anvers: En casa de Iuan
Steelsio, 1551.
[20], 236 *l*.

Spanish translation by Jorge de Bustamante.
Gallardo, no. 1507; Jerez, p. 121; Palau, 207841;
Peeters-Fontaines, II, no. 1013; Penney, p. 401.
Reel 127, No. 807

OVIDIUS NASO, PUBLIUS, b. 43 B.C., d. 18 A.D.
[Metamorphoses. Spanish]
Las Transformaciones de Ouidio: Traduzidas del verso
Latino, en tercetos, y octauas rimas, Por el Licēciado
Viana. En lēgua vulgar Castellana. Con El Comento,
Y Explicacion de las Fabulas: reduziendolas a Phil-
osophia natural, y moral, y Astrologia, e Historia.
Dirigido, Lo Vno, Y Lo Otro, a Hernando de Vega
Cotes y Fonseca, Presidente del Consejo de las
Indias. Valladolid: por Diego Fernandez de Cordoua,
1589.
2v. in 1 ([20], 179, [2] *l*.; 314, [5] *l*.) 21cm.

Spanish translation by Pedro Sánchez de Viana.
Pagination errors.
Vol. II.has separate title-page: Anotaciones Sobre
Los Qvinze libros de las Trāsformaciones de Ouidio.
Con la Mithologia de las fabulas, y otras cosas.
Por el Licenciado Pedro Sanchez de Viana. Dirigidas
A Hernando de Vega Cotes y Fonseca, Presidente del
Consejo de las Indias.
Graesse, V, p. 85; Jerez, P. 96; Palau, 207496;
Penney, p. 401, Salvá, I, no. 840; Ticknor, p. 256.
Reels 127 & 128, No. 808

OVIDIUS NASO, PUBLIUS, b. 43 B.C., d. 18 A.D.
[Metamorphoses. Spanish]
Metamorphoseos Del Excelente Poeta Ouidio Nasson.
Traduzidos en verso suelto y octaua rima: con sus
allegorias al fin de cada libro. Por el Doctor
Antonio Perez Sigler natural de Salamanca. Nueuamente
agora enmēdados, y añadido por el mismo autor vn
Diccionario Poetico copiosissimo. Dirigido a Don
Pedro Fernández de Castro, Conde de Lemos y de Andrade,
Marques de Sarria, Presidente de el Real Consejo de
Indias. Bvrgos: Por Iuan Baptista Varesio, 1609.
[22], 584, [1] l.; 13cm.

Spanish translation by Antonio Pérez Sigler.
Colophon: "Con privilegio. en Bvrgos. Por Iuan
Baptista Varesio. 1609."
Goldsmith, p. 129, no. 109; Graesse, p. 85;
Palau, 207501; Penney, p. 401; Salvá, I, no. 839.
Reel 128, No. 809

OVIEDO Y VALDÉS, GONZALO FERNANDEZ DE, 1478-1557.
[Relación sumaria de la historia natural de las
Indias. Italian]
Svmmario De La Generale Historia De L'Indie
Occidentali Cavato Da Libri Scritti Dal Signor Don
Pietro Martyre Del Consiglio Delle Indie Della Maesta
De L'Imperatore, Et Da Molte Altre Particvlari
Relationi. [In Vinegia: Del mese d'Ottobre, 1534.]
3 pts. in 1 (79, [2] l.; 66 l.; [15] l.); 20cm.

Title of Part II: Svmmario De La Natvrale Et
General Historia del' Indie occidentali, composta da
Gonzalo ferdinando del Ouiedo, altrimenti di valde
natio de la terra di Madrid ...
Title of Part III: Libro Vltimo Del Svmmario Delle
Indie Occidentali.
Colophon: "In Vinegia, Del mese d'Ottobre. MDXXXIIII".
Palau, V, 89536; Short-Title, I, p. 590; Simón
Díaz, X, 1138 (Part I only).
Reel 53, No. 304, Pts. 1-3

OWEN, JOHN, b. c. 1560 - d. 1622.
[Epigrammatum. Spanish]
Agvdezas De Jvan Oven. Tradvcidas En Metro
Castellano. Ilvstradas, Con Adiciones, Y Notas Por
Don Francisco De La Torre, Cavallero de la Orden de
Calatrava. Dedicadas A La Proteccion Del Ex.mo
Señor Don Guillermo Godolphin, Embaxador del
Serenissimo Rey de la Gran Bretaña, à su Magestad
Catholica. Madrid: Por Francisco Sanz, 1674.
2 pts. in 1 ([17], 346 p.; [16], 346, [7] p.);
21cm.

Spanish translation by Francisco de la Torre.
Part II has special title-page: Agvdezas De Ivan
Oven, Tradvcidas En Verso Castellano, Illustradas
con Adiciones, y Notas, Por Don Francisco De La Torre,
Cavallero del Abito de Calatrava. Obra Posthvma,
Qve Recogio, Saca A Lvz, y dedica à la Proteccion, y
Amparo del Señor Don Pedro Boil de Arenos, Varon-
Marquès de Boil, Varon de Borriol, Señor de Alfafar,
Y Mazanaza en el Reyno de Valencia; Don Ioseph Carlos
Garcez Boil y de la Sierra su Sobrino. Segvnda Parte,
Qve Contiene El Libro Llamado Vno, con los Disticos
Morales, y Politicos de Miguel Verino, que se traducen
proseguidamente todos en vn Romance. Madrid: Por
Antonio Gonzalez de Reyes, 1682.
Pagination Errors throughout.
Goldsmith, p. 129, no. 114; Graesse, V, p. 98;
Jerez, p. 104; Palau, 207460; Penney, p. 402; Salvá,
I, 834.
Reel 128, No. 810

P

PABLO DE SANTA MARIA, bp. see BIBLE. LATIN. 1492
VULGATE.

PACHECO Y NARVAES, LUIS, fl. 17th cent.
Libro De Las Grandezas De La Espada, En Qve Se
Declaran Mvchos Secretos del que compuso el Comendador
Geronimo de Carrança. En el qual cada vno se podrà
licionar, y deprender à solas, sin tener necessidad
de Maestro que le enseñe. Dirigido à Don Felipe. III.
Rey de las Españas, y de la mayor parte del mundo,
nuestro señor. Compuesto por D. Luys Pacheco de
Naruaez, natural de la ciudad de Baeça, y vezino en
la isla de gran Canaria, y Sargento mayor de la de
Lançarote. Madrid: los herederos de Iuan Iñiguez
de Lequerica, 1600.
[24], 319, [10] l.; 20cm.

Engraved title-page.
Pagination errors throughout.
Colophon: "En Madrid En la Imprenta del Licêciado
Varez de Castro Año De M DC."
Palau, 208246; Penney, p. 402; Pérez Pastor, no.
704; Salvá, II, 2654; Thomas, p. 66.
Reel 128, No. 811

PADILLA, LORENZO DE, 1485 - c. 1540.
El Libro Primero: De Las Antigvedades De España Qve
Escrivio Don Lorenço De Padilla, Arcediano de Ronda,
Cronista de su Magestad Cesarea: Pvblicale Don Ioseph
Pellicer de Ossau, i Tovar, Cavallero del Orden de
Santiago, Señor de la Casa de Pellicer, i de Ossua,
Cronista Mayor del Rey Nuestro Señor, i de su Consejo.
Y Le Dedica Al Excelentissimo Señor Don Manuel de
Zuñiga i Guzman. de Aça i Sotomayor Duque de Bejar,
i de Mandas, Marques de Gibraleon, i de Terranova,
Conde de Belacaçar, i de Bañares, Vizconde de la
Puebla de Alcoçer, Iusticia Mayor de Castilla,
Cavallero Cavallero del Orden del Toyson de Oro.
Valencia: 1669.
[12], 54, [1] l.; 14cm.

Graesse, V, p. 101; Palau, 208367.
Reel 128, No. 812

PADILLA Y MANRIQUE, LUISA MARIA DE, COUNTESS OF ARANDA.
Lagrimas De La Nobleza. Al Ex.mo Sr Don Antonio
Ximenez d Vrrea Conde de Aranda, Vizconde d Viota,
Sor del Vizcondado d Rueda en el Ro de Aragon y en
el de Valencia de la Tenencia de Alcalaten, Varonias
d Mislara Benilova y Cortes. Dado A La Estampa Por
El M. F. Pedro Henrique Pastor De La Orden de N. P. S.
Augustin. Çaragoza: por Pedro Lanaja, 1619.
[35], 601, [8] p.; 16cm.

Engraved title-page.
Third part only. Title-page shaved.
Colophon: "Con Licencia En Çaragoça Por Pedro Lanaja
y Lamarca, Impressor del Reyno de Aragon, y de la
Vniuersidad Año 1639."
Pagination errors throughout.
Goldsmith, p. 130, no. 24; Jiménez Catalán, no.
398; Palau, 208372; Penney, p. 403.
Reel 128, No. 813

PALACIO, PAULUS DE see PALACIOS DE SALAZAR, PAULUS.

PALACIOS DE SALAZAR, PAULUS, d. 1582.
Pavli De Palacio Granatensis, S. Th D. Et In
Inclyta Lusitanorum Conimbricensi Adacemia, S.
Scripturae Professoris, Enarrationes in Sacrosanctum
Iesu Christi Euangelium secundum Matthaeum. Omnia
Ecclesiae iudicio submissa sunto. Antverpiae: In
aedibus Viduae & haeredum Ioannis Stelsij, 1572.
[41], 986, [3] p.; 16cm.

Extremely rare. Not in Palau, not in Salvá.
Reel 129, No. 814

PALACIOS DE SALAZAR, PAULUS, d. 1582.
In Ecclesiasticvm Commentarivs Pivs Et Doctvs,
Authore Pavlo De Palacio Granatensi, D. Henrici
Lvsitaniae Regis, & S. Romanae Ecclesiae Cardinalis
Concionatore: & D. Catharinae Lusitanorum Reginae
Eleemosynario: & S. Literarum in Inclyta
Conimbricensium Academia Enarratore. Cum Indice
rerum insigniorum, & Capitum. Nunc primùm in Germania
emendatiùs editus. Coloniae Apud Geruinum
Calenium: & haeredes Iohannis Qventilij, 1593.
[25], 776 p.; 16cm.

Adams, II, no. 58; Palau, 209063.
Reel 129, No. 815

PALAFOX Y MENDOZA, JUAN DE, bp. 1600-1659.
Al Rey Nuestro Señor. Satisfacion Al Memorial De
Los Religiosos De La Compañia De Jesus De La Nueva-
España. Por La Dignidad Episcopal De La Puebla De
los Angeles Sobre La Execucion, Y Obediencia Del
Breve Apostolico de Nuestro Santissimo Padre
Innocencio X. Expedido En Su Favor A XIIII. De
Mayo de M.DC.XLVIII. Y Passado Repetidamente, Y
Mandado Executar por el Supremo Consejo de las
Indias. En El Qual Determino Su Santidad Veinte y
seis Decretos Sacramentales, y Jurisdiccionales,
importantes al bien de las Almas. Madrid: Por
Gregorio De Mata, 1652.
315 p.; 30cm.

Pagination errors throughout.
Goldsmith, p. 130, no. 42; Graesse, V, p. 104;
Laurenti-Porqueras, Impresos de Palafox, no. 2;
Palau, 209718.
Reel 129, No. 816

PALAFOX Y MENDOZA, JUAN DE, bp. 1600-1659.
Al Rey Nuestro Señor. Satisfacion Al Memorial De
Los Religiosos De La Compañia De Jesus De La Nueva-
España. Por La Dignidad Episcopal De La Puebla De
los Angeles Sobre La Execucion, Y Obediencia Del Breve
Apostolico de Nuestro Santissimo Padre Innocencio X.
Expedido En Su Favor A XIIII. De Mayo de M.DC.XLVIII.
Y Passado Repetidamente, Y Mandado Executar por el
Supremo Consejo de las Indias. En El Qual Determino
Su Santidad Veinte y seis Decretos Sacramentales, y
Jurisdiccionales, importantes al bien de las Almas.
n.p. (Mexico?) 1652.
[1], 158 l.; 27cm.

Bustamante, no. 2297; HC327/470; Laurenti-
Porqueras, Impresos de Palafox, no. 3; Palau, 209717;
Penney, p. 404.
Reel 129, No. 817

PALAFOX Y MENDOZA, JUAN DE, bp. 1600-1659.
Carta Pastoral De La Paciencia En Los Trabajos,
Y Amor A Los Enemigos. Por, El Ilvstrissimo, Y
Reverendissimo Señor D. Iuan de Palafox y Mendoza
Obispo de Osma, del Consejo de su Magestad. Madrid:
por Diego Diaz de la Carrera Impressor del Reyno,
1655.
    [8], 168, [1] l.; 15cm.

    Pagination errors throughout.
    "A la Santa escvela de Christo nuestro Señor,
de la imperial Villa de Madrid": leaves 122-168.
    Laurenti-Porqueras, Impresos de Palafox, no. 4;
Palau, 209592.
Reel 129, No. 818

PALAFOX Y MENDOZA, JUAN DE, bp. 1600-1659.
    Carta Que El' Illustrissimo, Excelentissimo, Y
Venerable Señor Don Juan De Palafox Y Mendoza, Del
Consejo De Su Magestad, Virrey de la Nueva España,
Visitador, y Legislador de todos sus Tribunales, Juez
de Residencia de tres Virreys, Arzobispo electo de
Mexico, Obispo de la Puebla de los Angeles en
aquellos Reynos, y de Osma en los de Castilla,
Escribio Al Padre Oratio Carocchi, Preposito de la
Casa Professa de la Sagrada Compañia de Jesus.
Sacada de su Original, que se halla en el Noviciado
de Carmelitas Descalzos de la Puebla de los Angeles
en la Nueva España. Madrid: Por Gregorio Rodriguez,
1646.
    288 p.; 15cm.

    Bound with the author's: [Epistola. Ad Summum
Pontificem Innocentium X.], 1650.
    Laurenti-Porqueras, Impresos de Palafox, nos. 5,
8; Palau, nos. 209675, 209689.
Reel 129, No. 819

PALAFOX Y MENDOZA, JUAN DE, bp. 1600-1659.
    Defensa Canonica Por La Dignidad Del Obispo De
La Pvebla De Los Angeles; Por Sv Ivrisdiccion
Ordinaria, I Por La Avctoridad De Svs Pvestos. En
El Pleito Qve Han Movido Los Padres De La Compañia
De Iesvs De La Dicha Civdad; Sobre No haber querido
pedirle las Licencias que deben tener, i que les
offresciò, para Predicar, i Confessar en su Obispado:
ni exhibir las antiguas, o Privilegios en contrario,
para guardarselos. Dirigida Al Rei Nvestro Señor.
[Madrid: n.p., 1648].
    240, [19] l.; 22cm.

    Brief prepared by Fernando Ortiz de Valdés.
    Colophon: "En Madrid a XVI de Iunio de
M.DC.XLVIII. Don Fernando Ortiz de Valdés."
    Laurenti-Porqueras, Impresos de Palafox, no. 12;
Palau, 209720.
Reel 130, No. 822

PALAFOX Y MENDOZA JUAN DE, bp. 1600-1659.
    [Epistola. Ad Summum Pontificem Innocentium X.
Spanish]
    Carta Segunda De Tres, Que El Venerable Señor
Don Juan De Palafox, Escribio Al Sumo Pontifice
Inocencio X. Sobre Los Dos Pleytos, Que Litigaba
con los Padres Jesuitas; sobre Diezmos, y Jurisdicion.
Sevilla: Por Francisco Lira, 1650.
    94 p.; 15cm.

    Translation by unknown.
    Bound with the author's: Carta Que El' Illustris-
simo, ... Senor Don Juan De Palafox Y Mendoza ...,
1646.
    Laurenti-Porqueras, Impresos de Palafox, nos. 5,
8; Palau, nos. 209675, 209689.
Reel 129, No. 820

PALAFOX Y MENDOZA, JUAN DE, bp. 1600-1659.
    [Epistola Ad Summum Pontificem Innocentium X.
French]
    Lettre De l'Illustrissime Iean De Palafox De
Mendoza, Euesque d'Angelopolis dans l'Amerique, &
Doyen du Conseil des Indes, Av Pape Innocent X.
Contenant diuerses plaintes de cet Euesque contre
les entreprises & les violences des Iesuites, & leur
maniere peu euangelique de prescher l'Euangile dans
les Indes Occidentales. Du 8 Ianuier 1649. Traduit
sur l'Original latin. [n.p.-n.d.] 1659.
    30 p.; 24cm.

    French translation by Robert Arnauld d'Antilly.
    First French edition of Palafox's least restrained
denunciation of the Jesuits. Other than the second
French edition and one Spanish edition, both of 1659,
there were no other printings of this letter until
after it was removed from the Index ... in 1761.
    Title page lacking.
    Caption title, 4to., marbled paper wrappers.
    HC346/181; Laurenti-Porqueras, Impresos de Palafox,
no. 34; Palau, 209688; Penney, p. 404.
Reel 129, No. 821

PALAFOX Y MENDOZA, JUAN DE, bp. 1600-1659.
    Excelencias De San Pedro, Principe De Los Apostoles
Vicario Vniversal De Iesv Christo Nvestro Bien. Qve
Ofrece Al Aprovechamiento De Las Almas, El Ilvstrissimo,
Y Reverendissimo Señor Don Ivan De Palafox Y Mendoza,
Obispo De Osma, Del Consejo De Sv Magestad. Dedicale
A Nvstro Santissimo Padre Alexandro VII. Madrid: Por
Pable de Val, 1659.
    [86], 516, [39] p.; 30cm.

    Half-title: Excelencias De S. Pedro, Principe De
Los Apostoles, Vicario Vniversal De Iesv Christo
Nvstro Señor.
    Vol. III of his Obras.
    Goldsmith, p. 131, no. 48; Graesse, V, p. 104;
Laurenti-Porqueras, Impresos de Palafox, no. 13;
Medina, Bibl. Hisp. Amer., no. 1300.
Reel 130, No. 823

PALAFOX Y MENDOZA, JUAN DE, bp. 1600-1659.
    Forma Qve Se Debe Gvardar En El Pararse, Sentarse,
Hincar Las Rodillas, Y Inclinarse; A si en las
Missas Solemnes, Feriales, y Rezadas como tambien
en las horas Canonicas, en el Coro; còforme al rito
del Ceremonial nuevo Romano, mandado imprimir, con sus
reglas por el Illustrissimo, y Reverendissimo Señor,
Don Iuan De Palafox, y mendoza Obispo de la Puebla
de los Angeles. Puebla de los Angeles: por el
Bachiller Iuan Blanco de Alcaçar, 1649.
    6 l.; 22cm.

    Modern red mottles calf bdg., gold tooled.
    Bound with his: Reglas Y Ordenanzas Del Coro Desta
Santa Iglesia Cathedral de la Puebla de los Angeles,
1649.
    Laurenti-Porqueras, Impresos de Palafox, nos. 14,
20; Medina, La imprenta en Puebla, no. 25; Palau.
209706.
Reel 130, No. 824

PALAFOX Y MENDOZA, JUAN DE, bp. 1600-1659.
    [Historia de la conquista de China. English]
    The History Of The Conquest Of China By The Tartars.
Together with an Account of Several remarkable things,
concerning the Religion, Manners, and Customes of
both Nations, but especially of the latter. First
writ in (sic) Spanish, by Señor Palafox Bishop of
Osma, and Vice - Roy of Mexico. And now rendred
English. London: Printed by W. Godbid, 1671.
    [33], 588, [5] p.; 16cm.

PALAFOX Y MENDOZA (Cont'd)
English translation by unknown.
Pagination errors throughout.
First ed. from the French version of Sieur Collé.
Allison, pp. 137-38, no. 3; Laurenti-Porqueras,
Impresos de Palafox, no. 35; Palau, 209795.
Reel 130, No. 828

PALAFOX Y MENDOZA, JUAN DE, bp. 1600-1659.
[Historia de la conquista de China. French]
Histoire De La Conqueste De La Chine Par Les Tartares.
Contenant Plusieurs Choses Remarquables, touchant la
Religion, les Moeurs, & les Coûtumes de ces deux Nations,
& principalement de la derniere. Ecrite en Espagnol
par M. De Palafox, Euesque d'Osma. Et Traduite en
Francois par le Sieur Colle. Dedié à Monseigneur
Le Davphin. Paris: Chez Antoine Bertier, 1670.
[19], 478, [1] p.; 17cm.

French translation by Sieur Collé.
Colophon: "A Paris, De l'Imprimerie de Barthelemy
Vitré M.DC.LXIX."
Doublet, p. 101; Goldsmith, p. 131, no. 49;
Laurenti-Porqueras, Impresos de Palafox, no. 33;
Palau, 209791.
Reel 130, No. 827

PALAFOX Y MENDOZA, JUAN DE, bp. 1600-1659.
Historia Real Sagrada, Lvz De Principes. Y
Svbditos. Dedicada Al Principe Nvestro Señor. Por
El Illvstrissimo, Y Reverendissimo Don Iuan de
Palafox, y Mendoça, Obispo de la Puebla de los
Angeles, del Consejo de su Magestad. En la Ciudad
de los Angeles: Por Francisco Robledo, 1643.
[42], 242, [15] l.; 28cm.

Pagination errors throughout.
Laurenti-Porqueras, Impresos de Palafox, no. 15;
Medina, La imprenta en Puebla, no. 4; Palau, 209621;
Ticknor, p. 257.
Reel 130, No. 826

PALAFOX Y MENDOZA, JUAN DE, bp. 1600-1659.
Historia Real Sagrada. Lvz De Principes, Y
Svbditos. Inivsticias Qve Intervinieron En La
Mverte De Christo Bien Nvestro. Por El Ilvstrissimo,
y Reuerendissimo señor Don Iuan de Palafox y
Mendoza, Obispo de la Puebla de los Angeles, del
Consejo de su Magestad. Vistos, corregidos, añadidos,
y enmendados por el mismo Autor, y dedicados al
Principe nuestro Señor. Madrid: Por Melchor
Alegre, 1668.
[44], 257, [11] l.; 30cm.

Vol. I of his Obras.
Laurenti-Porqueras, Impresos de Palafox, no. 1;
Medina, Bibl. Hisp. Amer., no. 1451; Palau, 209560.
Reel 131, No. 830

PALAFOX Y MENDOZA, JUAN DE, bp. 1600-1659.
Luz A Los Vivos Y Escarmiento En Los Muertos. Por
El Ilvstrissimo, Y Reverendissimo Señor Don Juan de
Palafox y Mendoza, Obispo de Osma, del Consejo del
Rey nuestro Señor. Madrid: Por Bernardo de Villa-
Diego, 1668.
[41], 380, [29] p.; 30cm.

Vol. II of his Obras.
Graesse, V, p. 104; Laurenti-Porqueras, Impresos
de Palafox, no. 1; Palau, 209560.
Reel 131, No. 831

PALAFOX Y MENDOZA, JUAN DE, bp. 1600-1659.
Memorial De Pleyto, Qve En gouierno, y Justicia
siguen el señor Fiscal, y las Iglesias Metropolitanas,
y Catedrales de las Indias Occidentales, Con Las
Religiones De S. Domingo, S. Agustin, N. S. de la
Merced, Compañia de Iesus, y las demás que tienen
haziendas de labor, y ganados en aquellos Reynos, y
Prouincias: Sobre Qve Las Dichas Religiones Pagven
diezmo de las dichas haziendas, que han adquirido,
y que en adelante adquirieren. [n.p.-n.d.] [Madrid?
ca. 1650]
[13], 794, [1] l.; 32cm.

Caption title.
In manuscript on spine: "Palafox s.re los diezms
de Indias."
Laurenti-Porqueras, Impresos de Palafox, no. 16.
Reel 131, No. 829

PALAFOX Y MENDOZA, JUAN DE, bp. 1600-1659.
[Obras... Spanish]
Tomo Qvarto De Las Obras Del Ilvstrissimo, Y
Reverendissimo Señor Don Ivan De Palafox Y Mendoza,
Obispo De Osma, Del Consejo De Sv Magestad. Madrid:
Por Maria de Quiñones, 1664.
[21], 622, [25] p.; 30cm.

Vol. IV of his Obras. Contains: Semanas espirituales.
Suavidad de la virtud. Reverencia del matrimonio.
Miserias de la vida. Peligros del agrado. Riesgos
de sacerdotes. Ejercicios de recogimiento interior.
Carta de un caballero a otra corte. Vida de la
serenísima infanta sor Margarita de la Cruz. Vida
de San Juan el limosnero, patriarca y obispo de
Alejandria. Peregrinación de Philotea.
Graesse, V, p. 104; Laurenti-Porqueras, Impresos de
Palafox, no. 1; Palau. 209560.
Volumes 1 - 3: Not Available
Reel 132, No. 832, Vol. 4

PALAFOX Y MENDOZA, JUAN DE, bp. 1600-1659.
[Obras... Spanish]
Tomo Qvinto De Las Obras Del Ilvstrissimo Y
Reverendissimo Señor Don Ivan De Palafox Y Mendoza,
Obispo De Osma, Del Consejo Del Rey Nvestro Señor.
Madrid: Por Pablo De Val, 1665.
[81], 523 p.; 30cm.

Vol. V of his Obras. Contains: Breve tratado de
la señal de la Santa Cruz. Verdades historiales de
la Religión Católica. Libro segundo. Luces de la
Fe en la Iglesia. Explicacion de los Artículos de la
Fe. De los otros cinco Artículos que están en el
Credo. Explicación de los siete Sacramentos. --
Soliloquios espirituales. Diario, y ejercicios en
que se ocupaba ... -- Diversos dictamenes espirituales,
morales, y políticos. -- Respuesta a un prelado grave,
que pidió direcciones para seguir perfectamente la
pobreza evangélica. -- Respuesta a un prebendado, que
consultó al señor Obispo acerca del gobierno espiritual
de su persona.-- Respuesta y discurso sobre las
frecuentes translaciones, que se hacen de los señores
Obispos de unas iglesias a otras. Epístola exortatoria
a los Curas, y Beneficiados del Obispado de la Puebla
de los Angeles. -- Carta Pastoral, previniendo los
ánimos a la consagración del celebre templo de la
Puebla de los Angeles. -- Ejemplos de los príncipes y
señores que favorecieron las iglesias, y del buen
suceso de suscosas. Y de los príncipes que fueron
contra ellas, y del mal suceso de las suyas. -- Carta
Pastoral. -- Carta Pastoral, conocimientos de la
divina gracia, y bondad.
Pagination errors throughout.
Graesse, V, p. 104; Laurenti-Porqueras, Impresos
de Palafox, no. 1; Palau, 209560.
Reel 132, No. 832, Vol. 5

PALAFOX Y MENDOZA, JUAN DE, bp. 1600-1659.
   [Obras... Spanish]
   Tomo Sexto De Las Obras Del Ilvstrissimo, Y
Reverendissimo Señor Don Jvan De Palafox Y Mendoza,
Obispo De Osma, Del Consejo Del Rey Nvestro Señor.
Madrid: Por Melchor Alegre, 1667.
   [13], 718, [21] p.; 30cm.

   Vol. VI of his Obras. Contains: Sucesos del año
de 38. Sitio y socorro de Fuente-Rabia, ... — El
Pastor de Nochebuena. — Preguntas que un devoto hizo
al Señor Obispo, y sus respuestas. — Carta Pastoral
de la paciencia en los trabajos, y amor a los enemigos.
— Carta Pastoral a la Santa Escuela de Christo,
fundada en la imperial villa de Madrid. — Carta
Pastoral dictamenes de curas. — Carta Pastoral a
los curas, y beneficiados del Obispado de Osma. —
Carta Pastoral de la devoción de la Virgen María, y
de su santo rosario. — Segunda Carta Pastoral a los
curas, y beneficiados del Obispado de Osma. — Carta
Pastoral a los sacerdotes, que es la trompeta de
Ezechiel. — Diario espiritual, para curas, y
sacerdotes, particularmente en lugares cortos. —
Constituciones de la congregación, y Santa Escuela
de Christo, fundada en la Ciudad de Soria. —
Epístolas a la Reina de Suecia, y otras. — Carta a
la Excelentísima Señora Marquesa de Guadaleste. —
Bocados espirituales, políticos, místicos, morales. —
Texto de la doctrina cristiana. — Ejercicios devotos,
en que se pide su favor a la Virgen, para la muerte. —
Carta Pastoral de Jesus orando en el huerto. Breve
tratado de la oración. — Meditaciones de postrime-
rias, repartidas por los días de la semana. —
Rosario del corazón. — De la naturaleza del Indio. —
Tratado de bien escribir, y de la ortografia perfecta.
— Varias poesías espirituales.
   Graesse, V, p. 104; Laurenti-Porqueras, Impresos
de Palafox, no. 1; Palau, 209560.
Reel 132, No. 832, Vol. 6

PALAFOX Y MENDOZA, JUAN DE, bp. 1600-1659.
   [Obras... Spanish]
   Tomo Septimo De Las Obras Del Ilvstrissimo, Y
Reverendissimo Señor Don Juan De Palafox Y Mendoza,
Obispado De Osma; Del Consejo Del Rey Nuestro Señor.
Madrid: Por Bernardo de Villa Diego, 1669.
   [25], 494, [35] p.; 30cm.

   Vol. VII of his Obras. Contains: Año espiritual.
Manual de estados y profesiones por ... Don Juan de
Palafox y Mendoza, ... Cartas de la seráfica, y
mística doctora Santa Teresa de Jesus, Madre y
Fundadora de la Reforma, de la Orden de nuestra
Señora del Carmen de la Primitiva Observancia. Con
notas del ... señor Don Juan de Palafox y Mendoza,
Obispo de Osma ... Recogidas por orden del reverendísimo
Padre Fray Diego de la Presentación, General de los
Carmelitas Descalzos de la Primitiva Observancia.
   Graesse, V, p. 104; Laurenti-Porqueras, Impresos
de Palafox, no. 1; Palau, 209560.
Reel 132, No. 832, Vol. 7

PALAFOX Y MENDOZA, JUAN DE, bp. 1600-1659.
   [Obras... Spanish]
   Tomo Octavo, De Las Obras De El Ilvstrissimo, Y
Reverendissimo Señor Don Ivan De Palafox Y Mendoza
Obispo De Osma, Del Conseio De El Rey Nvstro Señor.
Madrid: Por Bernardo de Villa-Diego, 1671.
   [37], 562, [39] p.; 30cm.

   Vol. VIII of Obras. Contains: Introducción
al varón de deseos. —"Primera parte del varón
de deseos. — Vida del venerable Padre San Henrique
Suson, de la Orden de Santo Domingo, ... — Memorial
al Rey Nuestro Señor, sobre la inmunidad eclesiástica.
— Historia de las guerras civiles de la China, y de

PALAFOX Y MENDOZA (Cont'd)
la conquista de aquel dilatado imperio por el
Tártaro. — Suspiros de un pastor ausente, atribulado,
y contento: ofrécelos a Dios por sus ovejas. —
Cartas a la Excelentísima Señora Doña Ana de Ligne,
Marquesa de Guadaleste.
   Graesse, V, p. 104; Laurenti-Porqueras, Impresos
de Palafox, no. 1; Palau, 209560.
Reel 132, No. 832, Vol. 8

PALAFOX Y MENDOZA, JUAN DE.
   El Pastor De Noche Bvena; Avtor El Illvstrissimo, I
Reuerendissimo Señor Don Ivan Palafox, I Mendoza,
Obispo de la Puebla de los Angeles: Del Consejo de
su Magestad en el Real de las Indias. Encaminale.
Al señor D. Francisco Antonio de Alarcon, Cavallero
del Orden de Santiago i Presidente de Hazienda. El
Licenciado Lvis Mvñoz. Van añadidas al fin vnas
consideraciones, i remedios para conseruar la amistad
de Dios, del P. Eusebio Nieremberg. Valencia: Por
Claudio Macè, junto al Colegio del Patriarca, 1646.
   [23], 94, [4] l.; 15cm.

   Some index pages missing.
   Pagination errors throughout.
   Pages missing.
   Palau, 209631; Ticknor, p. 249.
Reel 120, No. 762

PALAFOX Y MENDOZA, JUAN DE, bp. 1600-1659.
   Peregrinacion De Philotea Al Santo Templo Y Monte
De La Crvz Del Illvstrissimo, Y Reverendissimo Señor
Don Ivan de Palafox y Mendoza, del Consejo de su
Magestad. Obispo de Osma, &c. A la mas casta
Asvsena; Al mas fino Eliotropo; A la mas temprana flor
de Almendro; Esposo Maria, y Padre Putatibo de Iesvs
San Ioseph. Barcelona: en casa Cormellas, por Layme
Cays, 1683.
   [25], 215, [2] p.; 21cm.

   HC346/182; Laurenti-Porqueras, Impresos de Palafox,
no. 19; Palau, 209764; Penney, p. 404.
Reel 133, No. 833

PALAFOX Y MENDOZA, JUAN DE, bp. 1600-1659.
   Reglas Y Ordenanzas Del Coro Desta Santa Iglesia
Cathedral de la Puebla de los Angeles. Puebla de los
Angeles: por el Bachiller Iuan Blanco de Alcacar,
1649.
   12 l.; 22cm.

   Bound with the author's: Forma Qve Se Debe Gvardar
en El Pararse, Sentarse, Hincar Las Rodillas, Y
Inclinarse..., 1649.
   Laurenti-Porqueras, Impresos de Palafox, nos. 14,
20; Medina, La imprenta en Puebla, no. 25; Palau,
209706.
Reel 130, No. 825

PALAFOX Y MENDOZA, JUAN DE, bp. 1600-1659.
   Semana Santa Inivsticias Qve Intervinieron En La
Mverte De Christo Nvestro Redemptor. Al Eminentissimo,
Y Reuerendissimo Señor, Don Baltasar de Moscoso y
Sandoual, Cardenal de la Santa Iglesia Romana, Obispo
de Iaen, del Consejo de Estado de su Magestad. Por El
Illvstrissimo, Y Reverendissimo Señor, Don Iuan de
Palafox y Mendoça. Obispo de la Puebla de los
Angeles, Y Visitador general de la Nueva España,
y del Consejo de su Magestad. Mexico: por Francisco
Robledo, Impressor del Secreto del Santo Oficio, 1644.
   [8], 235, [2] l.; 21cm.

   Goldsmith, p. 131; no. 56; Laurenti-Porqueras,
Impresos de Palafox, no. 20; Medina, La imprenta en
México, no. 584; Palau, 209683.
Reel 133, No. 834

PALAFOX Y MENDOZA, JUAN DE, bp. 1600-1659.
Sitio y socorro de Fventerabia y svcesos del año
de mil y seiscientos y treinta y ocho. Escritos de
orden de Sv Magestad. Madrid: en la Imprenta de
Cat.ª del barrio, [1639].
[5], 450 p.; 21cm.

Pagination errors throughout.
Laurenti-Porqueras, Impresos de Palafox, no. 22;
Medina, Bibl. Hisp. - Amer., no. 998; Palau, 209570.
Reel 133, No. 835

PALAFOX Y MENDOZA, JUAN DE, bp. 1600-1659.
Varon de deseos, en qve se declaran las tres vias
de la vida espiritval. Purgatiua, Illuminatiua, y
Vnitiua. Dedicado a la Reyna Nvestra Señora y
ofrecido al aprovechamiento espiritual de las almas
deuotas. Por el Illvstrissimo, y Reverendissimo Don
Iuan de Palafox, y Mendoca, Obispo de la Puebla de
los Angeles. Madrid: En la Imprenta Real, 1652.
[39], 422, [65] p.; 20cm.

Pagination errors throughout.
Goldsmith, p. 131, no. 58; Laurenti-Porqueras,
Impresos de Palafox, no. 23; Medina, Bibl. Hisp.-
Amer., no. 1177; Palau, 209615.
Reel 133, No. 836

PALAFOX Y MENDOZA, JUAN DE, bp. 1600-1659.
Vida de S. Ivan el Limosnero, Patriarca, y Obispo
de Alexandria. Escrita por el Ilvstrissimo, y
Reuerendissimo Señor Don Iuan de Palafox y Mendoza,
Obispo de la Puebla de los Angeles, del Consejo de
su Magestad, y del Supremo de Aragon. Al
aproueçhamiento de las almas de su cargo. Y vna carta
consolatoria a sus subditos, de la resignacion en los
trabajos. Dedicada al Excelentissimo Señor Duque de
Medina-Celi, y de Alcalà, Marques de Tarifa, y
Cogolludo, Capitan General del Mar Oceano, Costas
y Exercitos del Andaluzia. Madrid: Por Domingo
Garcia y Morràs, 1650.
[15], 150, [3] Z.; 22cm.

1st edition.
Laurenti-Porqueras, Impresos de Palafox, no. 24;
Medina, Bibl. Hisp.-Amer., no. 1149; Palau, 209709;
Simón Díaz, Impresos, no. 877.
Reel 133, No. 837

PALAFOX Y MENDOZA, JUAN DE, bp. 1600-1659.
Vida interior del Excelentissimo Señor Don Juan de
Palafox y Mendoza, Obispo antes de la Puebla de los
Angeles, Virrey, y Capitan General de la Nueva-
España. Visitador de tres Virreyes de ella; Arzobispo
electo de Mexico, de el Consejo Supremo de Aragon.
La qval vida el mismo señor Obispo dexò escrita.
Bruselas: por Francisco Foppens, 1682.
[13], 220, [3] p.; 20cm.

Possibly spurious. Cf. manuscript note on prelim.
leaf.
Laurenti-Porqueras, Impresos de Palafox, no. 25;
Medina, Bibl. Hisp.-Amer., no. 1733; Palau, 209799;
Peeters-Fontainas, Bibliographie, II, no. 1032;
Sabin, no. 58303.
Reel 133, No. 838

PALAFOX Y MENDOZA, JUAN DE, bp. 1600-1659.
Vida interior del Excelentissimo Señor Don Juan de
Palafox y Mendoza, Obispo antes de la Puebla de los
Angeles, Virrey, y Capitan General de la Nueva-
España. Visitador de tres Virreyes de ella; Arzobispo
electo de Mexico, de el Consejo Supremo de Aragon.
La qval vida el mismo señor Obispo dexò escrita.
Barcelona: Por Antonio Ferrer, 1687.
[9], 327 p.; 20cm.

PALAFOX Y MENDOZA (Cont'd)
Laurenti-Porqueras, Impresos de Palafox, no. 26;
Medina, Bibl. Hisp.-Amer., no. 1804; Palau, 209800.
Reel 133, No. 839

PALAFOX Y MENDOZA, JUAN DE, bp. 1600-1659.
Vida interior del Ilvstrissimo, y Venerable Señor
D. Juan de Palafox y Mendoza, del consejo de Su
Magestad, y su Consejero en los Supremos de Guerra,
Indias, y Aragon, Obispo de la Puebla de los Angeles,
Arçobispo electo de Mexico, Virrey, Presidente,
Governador, y Capitan General de la Nueva-España,
Visitador de todos sus Tribunales, Juez de residencia
de tres Virreyes, y Obispo de la Santa Iglesia de
Osma. Copiada fielmente por la qve el mismo escrivio
contitulo (sic) de Confessiones, y Confusiones, que
Original se conserva oy en el Archivo del Convento de
S. Hermenegildo de Madrid de la Esclarecida Religion
de Carmelitas Descalços. Sevilla: por Lvcas Martin,
1691.
[65], 465, [34] p.; 21cm.

Escudero, no. 1872; Laurenti-Porqueras, Impresos de
Palafox, no. 28; Medina, Bibl.Hisp.-Amer., no. 1875;
Palau, 209802.
Reel 133, No. 840

PALAFOX Y MENDOZA, JUAN DE, bp. 1600-1659.
Vida interior del Ilvstrissimo, y Venerable Señor
D. Juan de Palafox y Mendoza, del consejo de Su
Magestad, y su Consejero en los Supremos de Guerra,
Indias, y Aragon, Obispo de la Puebla de los Angeles,
Arçobispo electo de Mexico, Virrey, Presidente,
Governador, y Capitan General de la Nueva-España,
Visitador de todos sus Tribunales, Juez de residencia
de tres Virreyes, y Obispo de la Santa Iglesia de
Osma. Copiada fielmente por la qve el mismo escrivio
contitulo (sic) de Confessiones, y Confusiones, que
Original se conserva oy en el Archivo del Convento
de S. Hermenegildo de Madrid de la Esclarecida
Religion de Carmelitas Descalços. Sevilla: L. Martin,
1691.
[61], 583 p.; 21cm.

Laurenti-Porqueras, Impresos de Palafox, no. 27;
Palau, 209801.
Reel 134, No. 841

PALET, JUAN see PALLET, JEAN.

PALLET, JEAN.
Diccionario Muy Copioso De La lengua Española y
Françesa. En El Qval Son Declaradas todas las
palabras Castellanas y Françesas, con sus proprias
y naturales significaciones sacadas de muchos y muy
excelentes Autores antiguos y modernos. Por el
Doctor Ioan Palet Medico. Brvxelles: Chez Rvtger
Velpivs, 1606.
2 pts. (207 Z.; 160 Z.); 17cm.

Part II has special t.-p.: Dictionaire Tres-Ample
De La Langve Espagnole & Francoise. [1607]
Doublet, p. 102; Heredia, no. 5076; La Serna, II,
2730; Palau, 210184; Peeters-Fontainas, II, no. 1034;
Salvá, II, 2372; Viñaza, no. 724.
Reel 134, No. 842, Part 1 & 2

PALMERÍN DE OLIVIA.
Palmerin D'Oliva. The First Part. Shewing The Mirrovr Of Nobilitie, the Map of Honour, Anatomie of rare Fortunes, Heroicall presidents of Love, wonder of Chivalrie, and the most accomplished Knight in all perfection. Presenting to Noble minds, their Courtly desire, to Gentiles their expectations, and to the inferiour sort, how to imitate their Vertues: Handled with modestie to shun offence, yet delightfull for Recreation. Written in Spanish, Italian, and French: and from them turned into English, by A. M. one of the Messengers of his Majesties Chamber. Patere & Abstine. London: Printed for B. Alsop and T. Favvcet, 1637.
2 pts. ([174] l.; [186] l); 21cm.

English translation by Anthony Munday.
2 pts.
Part II has special t.-p.: Palmerin D'oliva. The Second Part: Of The Honovrable Historie Of Palmerin D'Oliva. Continuing his rare fortunes, Knightly deeds of Chiualry, happy successe in love, and how he was crowned Emperour of Constantinople. Herein is likewise concluded the variable troubles of the Prince Trineus, and faire Agriola the Kings daughter of England: with their fortunate.Marriage.
Imperfect: lacks all after signatures Aa8
Allison, p. 138, no. 4.4; Graesse, V, p. 113; Palau, 210494; Pollard and Redgrave, no. 19160.
Reel 135, No. 848

PALMERÍN DE OLIVA.
L'Histoire De Palmerin D'Olive, Filz Dv Roy Florendos de Macedone, & de la belle Griane, fille de Remicius Empereur de Constantinople: discours plaisant & de singuliere recreation, traduit jadis par vn Auteur incertain de Castillan en Francoys, mis en lumiere & en son entier, selon nostre vulgaire, par Ian Maugin, dit le petit Angeuin. Reueu & emendé par le mesme Auteur. Probe Et Tacite. Anvers: Chez Ian Waesberghe, 1572.
[8], 223, [1] l.; 19cm.

French translation by Jean Maugin.
Author unknown, possibly a carpenter's daughter at Burgos.
Text printed in double columns.
Doublet, p. 102; Graesse, V, p. 113; Foulché-Delbosc, V, no. 370; Palau, 210479.
Reel 135, No. 846

PALMERÍN DE OLIVA.
Historia Di Palmerin D'Oliva. Il Qval Per Sve Prodezze fu soblimato all'Imperio Greco. Venetia: Appresso Domenico Farri, 1573.
324 l.; 16cm.

Italian translation by unknown.
Pagination errors throughout.
Graesse, V, p. 113; Palau, 210489; Toda y Güell, Italia, III, no. 3719.
Reel 135, No. 847

PALMERIN OF ENGLAND.
The First Part Of The No Lesse Rare, Then Excellent and stately History, of the Famous and fortunate Prince Palmerin of England. Declaring The Birth of him, and Prince Florian du Desart his Brother, in the Forrest of Great Britaine: The course of their Lives afterward in pursuing Knightly Adventures and performing incomparable deeds of Chivalry. Wherein Gentlemen may find choise of sweet Inventions, and Gentlewomen be satisfied in Courtly expectations. Translated out

PALMERIN OF ENGLAND (Cont'd)
of French, by A. M. one of the Messengers of her Majesties Chamber. Patere aut abstine. London: Printed by Ber: Alsop and Tho: Favvcot, 1639.
2v. ([216] l.; [223] l.); 19cm.

English translation by Anthony Munday.
Gothic type.
The Epistle dedicatory to both parts signed: A. Munday.
Munday's translation of a French version of the Portuguese romance: Cronica de Palmerim de Inglaterra (better known as Palmerín de Inglaterra) by probably Francisco de Moraes.
Vol. II has special title page: The Second Part Of The No Lesse Rare, Then Excellent and stately History, of the famous and fortunate Prince Palmerin of England, and Florian Dv Desart his Brother. Containing Their Knightly deeds of Chivalrie, successe in their Loves pursuite, and other admirable Fortunes. ...
Book-plates: Ex Mvsaeo Hvthii.
Allison, p. 132, no. 32.3; Palau, 210465; Pollard and Redgrave, no. 19164.
Reel 134, No. 844

PALMERIN OF ENGLAND.
The Famous History of the Noble and Valiant Prince Palmerin of England: The First Part Declaring His Birth, and Prince Florian du Desart his Brother, in the Forrest of Great Brittain. London: Printed by R. I. for SS., 1664.
2v. (218] l.; [208]); 19cm.

Vol. II has special title-page.
Allison, p. 132, no. 32.4; Palau, 210465; Wing H. 3794-5.
Reel 135, No. 845

PALMERIN OF ENGLAND.
Di Palmerino D'Inghilterra Figliuolo del Rè Don Duardo, Libro Secondo: Nelquale si raccontano di molte sue prodezze, & di Floriano dal Deserto suo fratello, con alcuni gloriosi fatti del Prencipe (sic) Florendo, figliuolo di Primaleone. Tradotto di Spagnuolo in Italiano. Venetia: Appresso Lucio Spineda, 1609.
[4], 298, [1] l.; 15cm.

Italian translation by unknown.
Book 2.
Book 1, not available.
Palau, 210463.
Reel 134, No.843, Book 2

PALMERIN OF ENGLAND.
Di Palmerino D'Inghilterra, Figliuolo del Rè Don Duardo, & di Floriano dal Deserto suo fratello, Libro Terzo: Nelquale si trattano insieme le valorose imprese di Primaleone secondo, & di molti altri giouani Cauallieri, con molte strane auenture, mirabili successi, e Stratageme (sic) non mai più intese. Tradotto di Spagnuolo in lingua Italiana. Venetia: Appresso Lucio Spineda, 1609.
[8], 299, [1] l.; 15cm.

Italian translation by unknown.
Book 3.
Palau, 210463.
Reel 134, No. 843, Book 3

PALMIRENO, JUAN LORENZO, 1514-1580?
Phrases Circeronis obscvriores In Hispanicam
Lingvam Conversae A Lavrentio Palmyreno. Item
Eivsdem Hypotyposes clarissimorum virorum ad
extemporalem dicendi Facultatem Vtilissimae. Eivsdem
Oratio Post reditum in Academia Valentina Mense
Augusto. Valentiae: Petri à Huete, 1572.
55, [1] l.
Bound in the author's: Vocabvlario Del Hvmanista...,
1569.
Palau, 210545, Penney, p. 406; Salvá, II, 2734.
Reel 135, No. 850

PALMIRENO, JUAN LORENZO, 1514-1580?
Vocabvlario Del Hvmanista, compuesto por Lorenço
Palmreno (sic): donde se trata de aues, peces,
quadrupedos, con sus vocablos de caçar, y pescar,
veruas, metales, monedas, piedras preciosas, gomas,
drogas, olores, y otras cosas que el estudioso en
letras humanas ha menester: Dirigido Al Illustrissimo
y Reuerendissimo señor don Ioan de Ribera Patriarcha
de Antiochia, y Arçobispo de Valencia &c. Hay tambien
vn vocabulario de antiguallas para entender a
Ciceron, Cesar, y Virgilio. Valentiae: Ex typographia
Petri à Huete, 1569.
2 pts. ([74] l.; 128 p.); 15cm.

Pagination errors throughout.
Part II has special t.p.: Segvnda Parte Del
Vocabvlario del Humanista de Lorenço Palmyreno, que
trata de las Monedas, Metales, y Piedras Preciosas.
Declaranse muchos passos de la sagrada Escriptura en
lo que toca a siclos, y talentos, y asses, &c.
Bound with the Author's: Phrases Ciceronis
Obscvriores In Hispanicam Lingvam Conversae A Lavrentio
Palmyreno. Item Eivsdem Hypotyposes clarissimorum
virorum ad extemporalem dicendi facultatem vtilissimae.
Eivsdem Oratio Post reditum in Academia Valentina Mense
Augusto..., 1572.
Palau, 210545; Penney, p. 406; Salvá, II, 2734.
Reel 135, No. 849

PALMIRENO, JUAN LORENZO, 1514-1580?
Vocabvlario Del Hvmanista de Lorenço Palmireno.
Añadieronse en esta segunda impression, Pons caesaris.
Selecta animalia, Stromata. &c. Barcelona: Impresso
en casa de Pedro Malo, 1575.
[166] l.; 16cm.

Graesse, V, p. 116; Palau, 210547; Salvá, II, 2735;
Thomas, p. 67.
Reel 135, No. 851

PAPEL al Conde Duque sobre la baja de la moneda. -
Decreto de remisión al Consejo de Castilla con
otro en que pormenor daba la noticia del estado
de las cosas de la Monarchia. - Copia de consulta
que la Cámara dio el 11 de Octubre de 1623. -
Copia de consulta que el Conde Duque hizo a S. M.
en el año 1621, excusándose de recibir unos escritos
que le presentó el Obispo de Catania. - Consulta
que el Conde Duque hizo a S. M. el año 1627 en
razon de cómo y cuándo se han de nombrar los
tributos a los vasallos cuanto deben y cómo se
ha de distribuir. - Receta para agua de canela
que inventó un Bachiller de Amor. - Receta de
chocolate que se ha de servir despues del agua
de canela compuesta por un Indio esclavo de Amor.
48 manuscript l.

Bound with: HERRERA Y SOTOMAYOR, JACINTO DE, fl.
1644. Iornada que su Magestad hizo a la Andalvzia.
[Madrid: En la Imprenta Real, 1624].
Palau, 114276 (List only printed folios 1-6).
Reel 77, No. 484.26

PARKE, ROBERT (translator) see GONZÁLEZ DE MENDOZA,
JUAN, bp. 1550-1620.

PASQUAL Y ORBANEJA, GABRIEL.
Vida De San Indalecio, Y Almeria Ilustrada en su
antiguedad, origen, y grandeza. Tesoro Escondido De
La Perla Mas Hermosa. Historial Discurso de su primer
Obispo y Prelado Apostol de Andalucia S. Indalecio.
Progresos De Su Milagrosa Vida, Y Predicacion gloriosa;
luzes eclipsadas en su muerte, y sepultura, que
sirvieron de Aurora al descubrimiento, y translacion
gloriosa de su Santissimo cuerpo al Reyno de Aragon.
Primera, Segunda, Y Tercera Parte. Noticias recogidas
de diversos fragmentos, que han estado retirados en el
silencio. En obligacion de promessa (que favorecido
en vna enfermedad) al Santo hizo la pluma devota De El
Doctor Don Gabriel Pasqual Y Orbaneja, Calificador de
el Santo Oficio de la Inquisicion, Cathedratico de
Prima de Theologia, que fue en la Vniversidad de
Ossuna, despues Magistral de Pulpito, Vicario de la
Iglesia de Velez Malaga, Arcipreste y Prior Dignidades
en la Santa Iglesia Cathedral de Almeria, y Dean, que
fue de ella, electo Obispo de la Iglesia, y Ciudad de
Ariano en el Reyno de Napoles, que renuncio.
Almeria: por Antonio Lopez Hidalgo, 1699.
3 pts. ([37], 182 p.; [4], 292 p.; [4], 168 p.);
29cm.

Each part has special t.-p.: Part II: Almeria
Ilustrada, Parte II. De Nuestro Historial discurso en
la Ilustracion de Almeria. Contiene La Predicacion. Y
Martyrio, Con los demás sucessos de el glorioso Apostol
de la Betica S. Indalecio, Primer Obispo, Y Prelado
de la Santa, y Apostolica Iglesia Vrcitana, ō Almeriense.
Noticias De Sus Seis Compañeros San Cecilio, San
Tesifon, San Torquato, San Eufrasio, San Hiscio, y
San Segundo, Discipulos del Apostol Santiago, vnico
Patron de las Españas. Con Las Memorias De Los
Breviarios, Martyrologios antiguos, y reglas historiales
para su mayor inteligencia. Siglo Primero De La Ley
de Gracia.
Part III: Parte Tercera De Nuestro Historial
discurso en la ilustracion de Almeria. En Que Se
Manifiesta el milagroso hallazgo de el santo cuerpo
de nuestro Apostol de la Betica, S. Indalecio, primero
Obispo de Vrci, ō Almeria. Translacion De Sus
Gloriosas Reliquias, y las de su Discipulo, Santiago,
segūdo Obispo de la misma Ciudad, al Real Monasterio
de San Juan de la Peña en las Montañas de Xaca, Reyno
de Aragon. Refierese La Insigne reliquia de nuestro
Apostol, que en la ausencia de su santissimo cuerpo
goza para su consuelo la Santa Iglesia de Almeria.
Con Noticias De Las demás, â que se dá sagrado culto
en diversas Iglesias de España. Con Otras Antiguedades,
Que ilustran, y ennoblecen dicha Santa, y Apostolica
Iglesia.
HC387/1990; Palau, 214324; Penney, p. 409; Salvá,
II, 3110.
Reel 136, No. 852, Part 1-3

PAULUS DE SANCTA MARIA (PABLO DE SANTA MARIA, bp.),
see Bible. Latin. 1492. Vulgate.

PEDRAZA, JUAN DE, fl. 1530.
Svmma de casos de Conciencia. Agora nueuaměte
compuesta, por el Doctor Fray Iuan de Pedraza, en dos
breues Volumines muy necessaria a Ecclesiasticos, y
Seculares, y a Confesores, y penitentes. Alcala de
Henares: en casa de Sebastian Martinez, 1568.
[6], 162 l.; 16cm.

Several errors in foliation. Irregularity in
signatures: leaf a3 (privilege dated 1568) bound
between A2 and A3 (privilege dated 1567); leaf D2
signed C2.
Palau, 216084.
Reel 137, No. 854

PEDRAZA, JUAN DE, fl. 1530.
  Svmma De Casos De Consciencia nueuamente compuesto
por el doctor Fray Ioan de Pedraza, en dos breues
volumines, muy necessaria a ecclesiasticos, y seglares,
a confesores, y penitentes. Añadio se vna Christiana
instituciõ de como se deua oyr missa. Mas vn tratado
de memorias para que no caygan en algunos descuydos
los confessores. Barcelona: Enla casa dela compañia,
1571.
  2 pts. (128 ℓ.; 50 ℓ.) 15cm.

  Running title of part II: Svmma De Casos De
consciencia. Agora nueuamente compuesta por el doctor
Fray Ioan de Pedraza, en dos breues volumines: muy
necessaria a ecclesiasticos, y seglares, a confessores,
y penitentes, &c. Y una instruction (sic) y doctrina
Christiana de como todo Christiano deue oyr missa.
Segun el miestro (sic) Fray Bartolome de miranda lo
predico delante el Rey de Inglaterra y Principe de
España.
  Colophon: "En Barcelona en la emprenta de Pablo
Contey y Pedro Malo 1571."
  Palau, 216094.
  Reel 137, No. 855

PEDRO DE ALCÁNTARA, SAINT, 1499-1562.
  [Tratado de la oración y meditación. English]
  A Golden Treatise Of Mentall Praier, With diuerse
spirituall rules and directions, no lesse profitable
then necessaire for all sortes of people. First
composed by the venerable and blessed Father, Fr. Peter
De Alcantara, of the Seraphicall Order of S. Francis.
Beatified the 18. of Aprill. 1622. Translated into
English by G. VV. To vvvhich is prefixed a briefe
relation of the life, and death of the same Father
vvritten by G. VV. of the same Order and obseruance.
Brvxelles: By the Widowe of Hvbert Antone, called
Velpius, 1632.
  [83], 176 p.; 15cm.

  English translation by Giles Willoughby.
  Reel 137, No. 856

PELIGER, JUAN VICENTE.
  Primera Y Segvnda Parte Del Estilo Y Metodo de
escrivir cartas missivas, y responder, como conviene
a ellas en qualquier genero de conceptos, negocios, y
ocasiones, conforme a la nueva prematica de Castilla.
Cõpuesto, y traçado por Iuan Vicente Peliger, natural
dela insigne y leal ciudad de Valēcia de Aragõ.
Agora en esta vltima Impression corregido, y enmendado.
Sevilla: por Simon Faxardo, 1627.
  ([8], 99 ℓ.; [5], 85, [1] ℓ.); 15cm.

  Pagination errors throughout.
  Error in foliation: leaves 89-104 (1st group)
numb. 83-99.
  First edition (1599) has title: Formulario y estilo
curioso de escribir.
  Palau, 216535.
  Reel 137, No. 857

PELLICER DE OSSAU Y TOVAR, JOSÉ, 1602-1679.
  Alma De La Gloria De España: Eternidad, Magestad,
Felicidad, Y Esperanza Svya, En Las Reales Bodas.
Epitalamio D. O. C. Al Rey Nvestro Señor. Por Don
Ioseph Pellicer De Tovar, Señor de la Cassa de Pellicer,
y de Ossav. Cronista Mayor de Su Magestad, y de su
Consejo. Madrid: Por Gregorio Rodrigvez, 1650.
  [6], 52 ℓ.; 21cm.

  Gallardo, no. 3372; Goldsmith, p. 133, no. 127;
Jerez, p. 79; Palau, 21660; Penney, p. 412; Ticknor,
p. 263.
  Reel 137, No. 858

PELLICER DE OSSAU Y TOVAR, JOSÉ, 1602-1679.
  Aparato A la Monarchia Antigva De Las Españas, En
Los Tres Tiempos Del Mvndo, El Adelon, El Mithico, Y
El Historico. Primera Parte D. O. C. Al Rey Nvestro
Señor Don Carlos Segvndo, Catolico Monarca Svyo: Por
Don Ioseph Pellicer De Ossav Y Tovar, Cavallero Del
Orden De Sant-Iago, Señor De Las Casas De Pellicer, Y
De Ossav, Cronista Mayor, Y Del Consejo De Sv Magestad.
Valençia: Por Benito Macè, 1673.
  [24], 339, [2] p.; 21cm.

  Pagination errors throughout.
  Palau, 216828.
  Reel 137, No. 859

PELLICER DE OSSAU Y TOVAR, JOSÉ, 1602-1679.
  Argenis, Por Don Ioseph Pellicer De Salas Y Tovar.
A Don Antonio De Negro, Noble De la Serenissima
Republica de Genoua. Madrid: Por Luis Sanchez, 1626.
  [6], 454, [1] ℓ.; 21cm.

  Colophon: "En Madrid Por Luys Sanchez, Año
M.DC.XXVI."
  A translation of John Barclay's Argenis.
  Morante, 496; Palau, 216693; Penney, p. 51.
  Reel 137, No. 860

PELLICER DE OSSAU Y TOVAR, JOSÉ, 1602-1679.
  [De Praestenda Lege Regia, in Catalonia Principatu,
Brevis Dissertatio 1641. Spanish]
  Idea Del Principado De Cataluña. Recopilacion De
Sus Monumentos Antiguos, Y Modernos, Y Examen De
Sus Privilegios. Dedicada Al Rey Nuestro Señor, Por
Don Ioseph Pellizer De Tobar, Coronista Mayor De
Su Magestad. Amberes: Por Geronymo Berdus, 1653.
  [25], 578, 3 p.; 16cm.

  Spanish translation by the author.
  Pagination errors throughout.
  Palau, 216733; Peeters-Fontainas, II, no. 1047.
  Reel 138, No. 864

PELLICER DE OSSAU Y TOVAR, JOSÉ, 1602-1679.
  Epitalamio En Las Bodas De Los Excelentissimos
Señores Don Gaspar Ivan Alfonso Perez De Gvzman El
Bveno, Y Doña Antonia De Haro, Condes De Niebla.
Dedvcido De Los Antigvos Griegos, Y Latinos. Por,
Don Ioseph Pellizer De Ossav Y Tovar, Cavallero Del
Orden De Santi-Iago, Señor De La Casa De Pellizer Y
De Ossav, Cronista Mayor De Sv Magestad, Y De Sv
Conseio. [s.n.:s.ℓ.], 1658.
  52 ℓ.; 20cm.

  Imperfect: all after leaf 52 wanting.
  Palau, 216782.
  Reel 138, No. 861

PELLICER DE OSSAU Y TOVAR, JOSÉ, 1602-1679.
  El Fenix Y Sv Historia Natvral, Escrita En veinte
y dos Exercitaciones, Diatribes, o Capitulos. Al
Señor Don Lvis Mendez de Haro Gentil-Hombre de la
Camara de su Magestad. Por don Ioseph Pellicer de
Salas y Tobar, Señor de la casa de Pellicer, Cronista
de los Reynos de Castiila (sic). Madrid: en la
Imprenta del Reyno, 1630.
  [20], 24, 260, [17] ℓ.; 15cm.

  Pagination errors throughout.
  Colophon: "En Madrid, En la Imprenta del Reino
Año CIƆIƆC XXX."
  Goldsmith, p. 133, no. 131; Palau, 216699; Penney,
p. 412; Salvá, I, 856; Ticknor, p. 263.
  Reel 138, No. 862

PELLICER DE OSSAU Y TOVAR, JOSÉ, 1602-1679.
Informe Del Origen, Antigvedad, Calidad, I Svcession De La Excelentissima Casa De Sarmiento De Villamayor, Y Las Vnidas A Ella Por Casamiento: Escrito A Instancia Del Excelentissimo Señor Don Felipe Baltasar De Gante, Cavallero Del Orden Del Toyson De Oro. Principe, I Conde De Isinghien, Gentilhombre De La Camara De Sv Magestad I Sv Governador, I Capitan General Del Dvcado De Gveldres. Por Don Ioseph Pellizer De Ossav I Tovar, Cavallero del Orden de Sant-Iago, Señor de la Casa de Pellizer, i de Ossav, Cronista Mayor de su Magestad, i de su Consejo. Madrid: n.p., 1663.
120 *l*.; 21cm.

Doublet, p. 103; Palau, 216801; Salvá, II, 3588.
Reel 138, No. 865

PELLICER DE OSSAU Y TOVAR, JOSÉ, 1602-1679.
Ivstificacion De La Grandeça, Y Cobertvra De Primera Clase, En La Casa, Y Persona De Don Fernando De Zvñiga, Noveno Conde De Miranda, Grande Antigvo De Castilla, Qvinto Dvqve De Peñaranda, Con Segunda Grandeça, Sexto Marqves De La Bañeça Decimo Vizconde de Val-Duerna, Señor De Las Qvatro Casas De Rica-Ombria, En Castilla, i Leon, De Aca, Avellaneda, Fuente-Almexir, i Bacan, Y Poseedor De Sus Estados, Solares, i Patronazgos. Escrita à Su Instancia, Por Don Ioseph Pellicer De Ossav, Y Tovar, Cavallero del Orden de Sant-Iago, Cronista Mayor que Fue De La Magestad Catolica del Rey Nuestro Señor Don Felipe Qvarto, Y Que de Presente lo Es Del Rey Nuestro Señor, Don Carlos Segvndo. Madrid: Por Diego Diaz De La Carrera, 1668.
[2], 144, [1] *l*.; 30cm.

Goldsmith, p. 133, no. 134; Palau, 216806.
Reel 138, No. 866

PELLICER DE OSSAU Y TOVAR, JOSÉ, 1602-1679.
Lecciones solemnes a las obras de don Lvis de Gongora y Argote, Pindaro Andalvz, Principe de los Poëtas Liricos de España. Escrivialas don Ioseph Pellicer Salas y Tovar, Señor de la Casa de Pellicer, Y Chronista de los Reinos de Castilla. Dedicadas Al Serenissimo Señor Cardenal Infante don Fernando de Austria. Madrid: En la Imprenta del Reino, 1630.
[51] p., 836 col., [50] col.; 22cm.

Half-title: De don Ioseph Pellicer de Salas y Tovar Lecciones solemnes a las obras de don Lvis de Gongora y Argote, capellan de Sv Magestad, racionero de la Sta Iglesia de Cordova.
Critical commentary of Gongora's Polifemo, Soledades, Panegirico and Tisbe.
Pagination errors throughout.
Goldsmith, p. 133, no. 135; Jerez, p. 79; Millé, 282; Palau, 216700; Penney, p. 412; Ticknor, p. 156.
Reel 138, No. 867

PELLICER DE OSSAU Y TOVAR, JOSÉ, 1602-1679.
Maximo, Obispo De La Santa Iglesia De Zaragoza, En España. Distingvido De Marco, Levita, I Monge Del Sagrado Monasterio Del Cassino, En Italia. Apendice Al Aparato De La Monarchia Antigva De Las Españas. Qve Escrive Don Ioseph Pellicer De Ossav I Tovar, Cavallero de la Orden de Sant-Iago, Señor De La Casa De Pellicer, I De Ossav, Del Consejo de su Magestad, i su Cronista Mayor de España. Valencia: Por Benito Mace, Iunto al Insigne Colegio del Señor Patriarcha, 1671.
3 pts. ([27], 76 *l*.; [20] *l*.; 112 *l*.); 21cm.

PELLICER DE OSSAU Y TOVAR (Cont'd)
Part II has special title-page: Maximo Obispo De La Santa Iglesia De Zaragoza, En España, Distingvido De Marco, Levita, Y Monge Del Sagrado Monasterio Del Casino, En Italia: Segvnda Parte; Qve Escrive Don Ioseph Pellicer De Ossav Y Tovar; Cavallero Del Orden De Sant Iago, Señor De La Casa De Pelicer, Y De Ossav, Del Consejo De Sv Magestad, Sv Chronista Mayor De España. Gentil-Hombre Barlet Servant de su Real Boca i Casa.
Part III has special title-page: Maximo Obispo De Zaragoza En España, Distingvido De Marco Levita. Monge Del Casino (sic) En Italia: Libro Tercero. Por Don Ioseph Pellicer De Ossav Y Tovar, Cavallero Del Orden De Sant-Iago.
Pagination errors throughout.
Bustamante, nos. 3200-3201; HC398/619; Palau, 216821; Penney, p. 412; Simón Díaz, Impresos, no. 1030.
Reel 138, No. 868

PELLICER, DE OSSAU Y TOVAR, JOSÉ, 1602-1679.
Memorial De La Calidad, I Servicios De La Casa De Don Sancho Abarca De Herrera Nvñez De Gvzman, Y Lvna: Cavallero Noble Del Reyno De Aragon: Noveno Señor De Las Baronias. De Garci-Pollera, Y Navasa, Señor De Las Villas, Y Lvgares De La Rosa, Azin, Vergosa, Sede, Y Santa Maria, De Igvazar, Y Sv Honor, Capitan De Las Compañias De Ambas Gvardias De Pie, Y De A Cavallo De Sv Magestad, En Aqvel Reyno; Señor En El, Del Mayorazgo De Herrera, Y De Otro Deste Apellido En Toledo, Y Ocaña. A La Reyna Nvestra Señora. Madrid: Por Francisco Sanz, 1674.
38 *l*.; 24cm.

Bears the engraved signature and seal of Don Joseph Pellicer de Tovar.
Palau, 216833; Penney, p. 349.
Reel 138, No. 869

PELLICER DE OSSAU Y TOVAR, JOSÉ, 1602-1679.
Poblacion, y lengva primitiva de España, recopilada del aparato a sv monarchia antigva en los tres tiempos, el Adelon, el Mithico, y el Historico, qve escrivia Don Ioseph Pellicer de Ossay y Tovar. Valencia: Benito Macè, 1672.
52 *l*.; 21cm.

Lacks first four pages and title-page.
Goldsmith, p. 133, no. 139; Palau, 216827; Salvá, II, 3114.
Reel 138, No. 870

PELLICER DE OSSAU Y TOVAR, JOSÉ, 1602-1679.
El Seyano Germanico Alberto VVenceslao, Evsebio De Vvolstein, Duque de Mekelburg, De Fridland, de Glogovv, i de Saghen, Principe de Vvandalia, i del S. R. Imperio, señor de RostocK, i Vvismar, Cavallero del Orden del Toyson de Oro, Generalissimo del Imperio Romano, Traiciones que dispuso, rebelion que formò, levantamiento que meditava, Contra la Magestad Imperial, i Augustissima Casa, con la justificacion de su muerte. Sacada de los mas fieles, i verdaderos originales. Por Don Ioseph Pellicer De Tovar, i Abarca, señor de la casa de Pellicer, Coronista de las Coronas de Castilla, i Leon, i del Reyno de Aragon, &c. Dedicado A la grande, i esclaracida proteccion del Eminentissimo Señor Don Gaspar De Boria, I De Velasco, Principe de la Iglesia, Cardenal, Arçobispo, Obispo, Protector, Embajador, Virrey, Presidente, i Consejero de Estado. Barcelona: por Pedro Lacavalleria, 1639.
[28], 74, [1] *l*.; 16cm.

Pagination errors throughout.
Heredia, no. 3243; Jerez, p. 83; Palau, 216723; Penney, p. 413.
Reel 138, No. 863

PELLICER DE OSSAU Y TOVAR, JOSÉ, 1602-1679.
Svcession De Los Reynos De Portvgal Y El Algarbe,
Fevdos Antigvos De La Corona De Castilla: Dados en
Dote A Doña Teresa Y Don Enrique de Borgoña, Tiran-
izados la primera vez por Don Iuan Maestre de Auis;
Conmouidos luego por Don Antonio Prior de Ocrato:
Incorporados despues en la Monarquia de España, Por
derecho de Sangre, y otros Ocho diuersos Titulos, que
Justificaron la Vnion en la Real Persona Del Rey Don
Felipe Segundo el Prudente. Posseidos pacificamente
En el Reynado de su Hijo Don Felipe Tercero, el
Piadoso, Y vltimamente Sublevados Por los Complices
en el Leuantamiento de Don Iuan de Bragança,
Vsurpando la Voz, y Titulo de Rey y quebrantando La
Fè Deuida, Omenage Hecho, y Iuramento Prestado A
su Legitimo, Verdadero, Natural, y Soberano Señor.
Don Felipe Qvarto El Grande, Rey Catolico de Entrambas
Españas, Monarca Potentissimo en Ambos Mundos.
En Logroño: Por Pedro de Mon Gaston Fox, 1641.
4, 18 l.; 21cm.

Goldsmith, p. 133, no. 140; Palau, 216730.
Reel 138, No. 871

PEÑA, JUAN ANTONIO DE LA, fl. 1623-1638.
[Relación y juego de cañas que la Magestad
Católica - hizo a los veynte y uno de Agosto, 1623.
deste presente año. English]
A Relation Of The Royall Festiuities, and Juego de
Cañas [A Turnament of Darting with Reedes after the
manner of Spaine] made by the King of Spaine at Madrid,
the 21 of August this present yeere, 1623. To Honour
the Espousall Treaties of the Illustrious Prince of
Wales, with the Lady Infanta Maria of Austria. Before
the departure of the Prince from his Court towards
the Sea-side, to take shipping for his returne into
England. Composed by Doctor Iuan Antonio de la Pena,
natife of Madrid, and faithfully translated out of the
Spanish printed Copie. London: Printed for Henry
Seyle, 1623.
[5], 22 p.; 19cm.

English translation by unknown.
Bound with: A Trve Relation and Iovrnall, Of The
Manner Of The Arrivall, and Magnificent Entertainment,
giuen to the High and Mighty Prince Charles, Prince of
Great Britaine, by the King of Spaine in his Court at
Madrid, 1623.
Two Royall Entertainments, Lately Given To the Most
Illvstriovs Prince Charles, Prince of Great Britaine, by
the High and Mighty Philip the fourth King of Spaine,
&c. At the Feast of Easter and Pentecost, 1623.
A Continuation Of a former Relation Concerning The
Entertainment giuen to the Prince His Highnesse by the
King of Spaine in his Court at Madrid, 1623.
The Ioyfull Returne, Of The Most Illvstrious Prince,
Charles, Prince of great Brittaine, from the Court of
Spaine. Together, With a Relation of his Magnificent
Entertainment in Madrid, and on his way to St. Anderas,
by the King of Spaine. The Royall and Princely Gifts
interchangeably giuen, 1623.
The Popes Letter To the Prince: In Latine, Spanish,
and English. Done according to the Latine and Spanish
Coppies Printed at Madrid. A Iesuites Oration to the
Prince, in Latine and English, 1623.
Signatures: A-F⁴
Allison, p. 139, no. 6; Graesse, p. 190; Palau,
217386; Pollard and Redgrave, no. 19594.
Reel 138, No. 872

PERAT, JUAN.
Por Ivan Pallares, en la Revocacion de Tvtela Qve
Pretende Don Francisco Rvbalcaba.
6 p.

PERAT (Cont'd)
Bound in: Moles, Fadrique. In Processv Iesiphi
Gviger ...
Caption title.
Reel 112, No. 705

PEREA, JEROME DE, 1597-1670.
Vida, Y Elogio De Doña Catalina De Mendoza,
Fundadora del Colegio de la Compañia de Iesus de
Alcalâ de Henares. Escrita Por El Padre Geronimo De
Perea de la misma Compañia de Iesvs. Dedicala A
La Excelent.ᵐᵃ Señora Doña Isabel de Sandoual,
Duquesa de Ossuna, Condesa de Vreña. Madrid: En la
Imprenta Real, 1653.
[6], 95, [1] l.; 21cm.

Pagination errors throughout.
Palau, 218279; Simón Díaz, Jesuitas, no. 1244.
Reel 139, No. 876

PEREIRA, BENITO, 1535 (ca.) - 1610.
De Magia. De Observatione Somniorvm, Et De
Divinatione Astrologica, Libri Tres. Adversvs
Fallaces, Et Svperstitiosas Artes. Auctore Benedicto
Pererio Valentino Societatis Iesv. Accesservnt Indices
Dvo. Primus est Capitum, & Disputationum. Alter
Rerum Verborumque copiosus. Coloniae Agrippinae: Apud
Ioannem Gymnicum sub Monocerore, 1598.
[6], 236, [6] p.; 17cm.

Reel 139, No. 877

PÉREZ, ALONSO see MONTEMAYOR, JORGE, Segvnda Parte de
la Diana...

PÉREZ, ANTONIO, 1534-1611.
Ant. Perezii Ad Comitem Essexivm, singularem
Angliae Magnatem, & ad Alios Epistolarvm. Centuria
vna. Parisiis, s.n., [1600].
66 l.

Bound in the author's: Cartas...
Graesse, p. 200; Palau, 219042, 219045, 219051;
Paul, Catalogue, nos. 589, 597; Penney, p. 416;
Salvá, II, 2376.
Reel 139, No. 880

PÉREZ, ANTONIO, 1534-1611
Antonii Perezii Ad Comitem Essexivm Singvlarem
Angliae Magnatem, &c. ad Alios. Epistolarvm Centuria
una. Dum Castè Lucem. [s.l.:s.n., 16--?]
64, [1] p.

Bound in his: Relaciones ..., 1624.
Reel 140, No. 891

PÉREZ, Antonio, 1534-1611.
Aphorismos De Las Cartas Espanolas, (sic) Y
Latinas De Ant. Perez. Paris: s.n., [ca. 1598].
40, 7 l.

A second part, separately paged (7 l.), has caption
title: El Cvrioso a la Piedad.
Bound in the author's: Cartas...
Graesse, p. 200; Palau, 219042, 219045, 219051;
Paul, Catalogue, nos. 589, 597; Penney, p. 416;
Salvá, II, 2376.
Reel 139, No. 881

PÉREZ, ANTONIO, 1534-1611.
Aphorismos De Las Cartas Espannolas, Y Latinas De
Ant. Perez. In Spe. [s.l.:s.n., 16--?]
32 p.

Bound in: Relaciones ..., 1624.
Reel 140, No. 893

PÉREZ, ANTONIO, 1534-1611.
Aphorismos Del Libro De Las Relaciones de Antonio
Perez. Monstrvm Fortunae. [s.l.:s.n., 16--?]
36 p.

Bound in his: Relaciones ..., 1624.
Reel 140, No. 892

PÉREZ, ANTONIO, 1534-1611.
Aphorismos De Las Segvndas Cartas De Ant. Perez
Inuidiae scopus, Inuidorum scopulus. [s.l.:s.n.,
16--?]
46 p.

Bound in his: Relaciones ..., 1624.
Reel 140, No. 894

PÉREZ, ANTONIO, 1534-1611.
Cartas de Antonio Perez Secretario De Estado, Que
Fve Del Rey Catholico Don Phelippe II. de este nombre.
Para Diversas Personas despues de su salida de España.
[s.l.:s.n., 16--?].

Bound in his: Relaciones..., 1624.
Reel 140, No. 888

PÉREZ, ANTONIO , 1534-1611.
Cartas De Antonio Perez A. Donna Ioanna Coello Sv
Mvger Y A Sus Hijos. Escriptas las mas dellas no para
embiarse, particularmenti las primeras, porque oun
estaua en prision, sino por entretenimiento en la
soledad de su destierro. [s.l.:s.n., 16--]
45 p.

Bound in his: Relaciones..., 1624.
Reel 140, No. 890

PÉREZ, ANTONIO, 1534-1611.
Cartas De Antonio Perez A Dona (sic) Ioanna Coello
su muger, y à sus Hijos. Escriptas las mas dellas no
para embiarse particularmente las primeras, porque aun
estaua en prision, sino por entretenimiento en las
soledad de su destierro. [s.l., s.n.]
19 l.

Bound in the author's: Cartas...
Graesse, p. 200; Palau, 219042, 219045, 219051;
Paul, Catalogue, nos. 589, 597; Penney, p. 416;
Salvá, II, 2376.
Reel 139, No. 879

PÉREZ, ANTONIO, 1534-1611.
Cartas De Antonio Perez Secretario De Estado que
fue del Rey Catholico Don Phelippe II. de este nombre.
Para diuersas personas despues de su salida de España.
147, 12 l.; 17cm.

A second part, separately paged (12 l.) has caption
title: Gil De Mesa a Todos.
Reel 139, No. 878

PÉREZ, ANTONIO, 1534-1611.
Las Obras Y Relaciones De Ant. Perez Secretario De
Estado, Qve Fve del Rey de España Don Phelippe II
deste nombre. Illvstrat, Dvm Vexat. Geneva: Por
Iuan de la Plance, 1631.
[18], 1126 p.; 16cm.

Pagination errors throughout.
Salvá, II, 2374; Ticknor, p. 264.
Reel 139, No. 882

PÉREZ, ANTONIO, 1534-1611.
Las Obras Y Relaciones De Ant. Perez Secretario De
Estado, Qve Fve del Rey de España Don Phelippe II.
deste nombre. Illvstrat, Dvm Vexat. M.DC. Geneva:
Por Ivan di Tornes, 1644.
[33], 1126 p.; 16cm.

Palau, 219025.
Reel 139, No. 883

PÉREZ, ANTONIO, 1534-1611.
Las Obras Y Relaciones De Antonio Perez Secretario
de Estado que fue del Rey de España, Don Phelippe,
Secondo deste nombre Illvstrat Dvm Vexat. Ginevra:
Appresso Samvel De Tovrnes, 1676.
2v. ([39], 1126 p.; 16cm.)

Paged continuously.
Palau, 219030.
Reel 140, No. 884

PÉREZ, ANTONIO, 1534-1611.
Pedaços De Historia, ô Relaçiones, assy llamádas
por sus Auctores los Peregrinos. Retrato Al Vivo Del
Natvral De La Fortvna. La Primera Relaçion contiene
el discurso de las Prisiones, y Auenturas de Antonio
Perez, Aquel Secretario de Estado del Rey Catholico
Don Phelippe II deste nombre, desde su primera
prision, hasta su salida de los Reynos de España.
Otra relaçion de lo Succedido en Caragoça de Aragon
à 24. de Septiembre del año de 1591. por la Libertad
de Antonio Perez, y de sus Fueros, y Iusticia.
Contienen de mas estas Relaciones, la Razon, y Verdad
del Hecho, y del Derecho del Rey, y Reyno de Aragon,
y dé aquella miserable confusion del Poder, y de la
Iusticia. De mas de esto, El Memorial, que Antonio
Perez hizo del Hecho de su causa, para presentar en
el Iuyzio del Tribunal de Iusticia (que llaman de
Aragon) donde respondió llamado à el de su Rey, como
Parte. Leon: [s.n.,15--.] [London, Richard Field,
1594].
[9], 389, [18]; 19cm.

Adams, II, no. 670; Graesse, p. 200; Palau,
219033; Paul, Catalogue, no. 680; Penney, p.416;
Salvá, II, 2379; Ticknor, p. 2379; Ungerer
(Printing of Spanish Books in Elizabethan England),
p. 195, no. 6.
Reel 140, No. 885

PÉREZ, ANTONIO, 1534-1611.
Relaciones De Antonio Perez Secretario De Estado,
Qve fue, del Rey de España Don Phelippe II. deste
nombre. Paris: (s.n.), 1598.
[14], 222, [29] l.; 19 l.; 17cm.

A second part, separately paged (19 l.), has
caption title: Antonio Perez a los Cvriosos.
Illustration and verses entitled In Emblema Titij
nostri poena appear on 2nd leaf of last group of
leaves; the verses alone on verso of the 14th prelim.
leaf.

PÉREZ (Cont'd)
Errors in numb. of leaves: 169-220 numb. 167-218;
221-222 are numb. as pages 219-222.
Imperfect: leaf 180 (i.e. 182) missing.
El memorial, qve Ant. Perez presentō del hecho de
su causa en el juyzio del tribunal del Justicia (que
llaman de Aragon: leaves 168-217 (i.e. 219).
Adams, II, no. 673; Thomas, p. 68.
Reel 140, No. 886

PÉREZ, ANTONIO, 1534-1611.
Relaciones De Antonio Perez Secretario De Estado,
Qve fue del Rey de España Don Phelippe II. deste
nombre Illvstrat, Dvm Vexat. Segun la Copia Imprimida
Paris: (s.n.), 1624.
[24], 163 p.; 23cm.

Bound with 7 items by the same author, each with its
own pagination and title-page:
- Cartas De Antonio Perez Secretario de Estado, Qve
Fve Del Rey Catholico Don Phelippe II. de este nombre.
Para Diversas Personas despues de su salida de España.
154 p.
- Segvndas Cartas De Antonio Perez. Famā
meliore, quām Fortunâ. Mas los Aphorismos dellas,
sacados por el Cvrioso que sacō los de las Primeras.
171 p.
- Segvndas Cartas De Ant. Perez Notvm Pericvlis Nomen.
Para doña Ioanna Coello su Muger, y para algunos de sus
Hijos. P. 173-187 (cont.), [4] p.
- Cartas De Antonio Perez A Donna Ioanna Coello Sv
Mvger, Y A sus Hijos. Escriptas las mas dellas no para
embiarse, particularmente las primeras, porque aun
estaua en prision, sino por entretenimiento en la
soledad de su destierro. 45 p.
- Antonii Perezii Ad Comitem Essexivm Singvlarem
Angliae Magnatem, &c. ad Alios. Epistolarvm Centuria
vna. Dum Castē Lucem. 64, [1] p.
- Aphorismos Del Libro De Las Relaçiones De Antonio
Perez. Monstrvm Fortunae. 36 p.
- Aphorismos De Las Cartas Espannolas, Y Latinas De
Ant. Perez. In Spe. 32 p.
- Aphorismos De Las Segvndas Cartas De Ant. Perez.
Inuidiae scopus, Inuidorum scopulus. 46 p.
HC: NS4/443/4; Palau, 219038; Penney, p. 416.
Reel 140, No. 887

PÉREZ, ANTONIO, 1534-1611.
Segvndas Cartas De Antonio Perez. Famā meliore,
quām Fortunā Mas los Aphorismos dellas, sacados por el
Cvrioso que sacō los de las primeras. [s.l.:s.n.,
16--?]
187, [4] p.

Bound in his: Relaciones ..., 1624.
On page [173], another t.-p.: Segvndas Cartas...
Notvm Pericvlis Nomen. Para doña Ioanna Coello su
Muger, y para algunos de sus Hijos.
Reel 140, No. 889

PÉREZ, DIEGO, fl. 1574 see CASTILLE, Laws, Statutes, etc.

PÉREZ, GONZALO, 16th cent. (translator) see HOMER.

PÉREZ DE AYALA, MARTÍN, abp. of Valentia, 1504-1566.
De Divinis Apostolicis Atqve Ecclesiasticis
Traditionibus, deque authoritate ac ut earum
sacrosancta, adsertiones ceu libri decē. In quibus
fere uniuersa Ecclesiae antiquitas, circa dogmata
Apostolica, orthodoxae elucidatur. Authore R. P.
Domino Martino Peresio, Aiala, Guidixiensium Episcopo,
ac S. Theologiae Professore. Venetiis: Ad Signvm Spei,
1551.
[8], 336 l.; 16cm.

PÉREZ (Cont'd)
Pagination errors throughout.
Palau, 219670.
Reel 140, No. 895

PÉREZ DE AYALA, MARTÍN, abp. of Valentia, 1504-1566.
Martini Peresii Aiala, Episcopi Gvidixiensis, De
Vera Ratione Christianismi, Instructio. Coloniae:
Apud Iasparem Gennepaeum, 1554.
[82] l.; 13cm.

Bound with: Colymata Sive Impedimenta Christianae
Vitae, Qvibvs Hodie Mvlto Maxima Christifidelium pars
praepeditur, quo minus ad Euangelicae integritatis
apicem perueniat, 1554. 85 unnumbered.
Bound with: Loci Commvnes Et Conclvsiones Catholicae,
ex diui Augustini dictis. Quibus ostenduntur
Lutheranorum mendacia, 1554. [72].
Reel 141, No. 896

PÉREZ DE HITA, GINÉS, 1544?-1619?
Historia De Las Gverras Civiles De Granada. Paris:
En la tienda de Iago Cotinet, en la caille de San
Victor, al cabo de San Dionis, 1660.
[4], 686 p.; 16cm.

Doublet, p. 104; Palau, 221169; Penney, p. 418;
Salvá, II, 1926.
Reel 141, No. 899

PÉREZ DE HITA, GINÉS, 1544?-1619?
[Historia De Las Gverras Civiles De Granada. French]
Histoire Des Guerres Civiles De Grenade, Traduite
d'Espagnol en François. Premiere Partie. Paris:
Chez la Veuve Loüis Billaine, 1683.
3 pts. in 1 ([17], 223 p.; [4], 244 p.; [4]; 171,
[3] p.); 15cm.

French translation by Mlle. de La Roche-Guilhem,
d. ca. 1710.
Part II has special t.-p.: Histoire Des Guerres
Civiles De Grenade, Traduite d'Espagnol en François.
Seconde Partie.
Part III has special t.-p.: Histoire Des Guerres
Civiles De Grenade, Traduite d'Espagnol en François.
Troisiéme Partie.
Dedication signed by the translator: Mlle. de La
Roche Guilhem.
Doublet, p. 104.
Reel 141, No. 900

PÉREZ DE LARA, ALFONSO, fl. 1608-1629.
Compendio De Las Tres Gracias De La Santa Cruzada,
Subsidio, y Escusado, que su Santidad concede a la
Sacra Catolica Real Magestad del Rey Don Felipe III.
nuestro señor, para gastos de la guerra contra infieles,
y la pratica dellas, assi en el Consejo, como en los
Iuzgados de los Subdelegados. Recopilado De Mandado
Del Señor Martin de Cordoua, Prior y señor de Iunquera,
del Consejo de su Magestad, y Comissario general de
la Santa Cruzada. Por El Licenciado Alonso Perez De
Lara del Consejo de Su Mag.d Primero Alcalde del
crimen en la Real Chancilleria de Lima, y aora Fiscal
en su Real Audiencia de Galicia. Madrid: En la
Imprenta Real, 1610.
2 pts. ([21], 338 p.; 146, [21] p.); 29cm.

Errors in pagination: p. 53-58 (2nd group) omitted;
pages 187, 218, 237 misnumbered 185, 821, 207; blank
leaf inserted after p. 146 (3rd group).
HC346/184; Palau, 221236; Penney, p. 419; Pérez
Pastor, no. 1110.
Reel 141, No. 901

PÉREZ DE MONTALBÁN, JUAN, 1602-1638.
Amor, Privanca, Y Castigo Tragedia. Del Doctor
Ivan Perez de Montaluan. Representòla Andres de la
Bega. [s.l.:s.n.]
21 ℓ.

Bound in his: Svcessos Y Prodigios De Amor ...,
1633.
Lacks title-page.
Reel 142, No. 906

PÉREZ DE MONTALBÁN, JUAN, 1602-1638.
Comedia Famosa, El Divino Nazareno Sanson. Del
Doctor Juan Perez De Montalvan [s.l.:s.n.]
[19] ℓ.

Bound in his: Svcessos Y Prodigios De Amor ...,
1633.
Lacks title-page.
Reel 142, No. 907

PÉREZ DE MONTALBÁN, JUAN, 1602-1638.
Comedia Famosa El Principe Prodigioso. Del
Doctor Iuan Perez de Montalvan. [s.l.:s.n.]
[20] ℓ.

Bound in his: Svcessos Y Prodigios De Amor ...,
1633.
Lacks title-page.
Reel 142, No. 908

PÉREZ DE MONTALBÁN, JUAN, 1602-1638.
Don Florisel De Niqvea. Comedia Famosa Del Doctor
Ivan Perez De Montaluan. [s.l.:s.n.]
p. 281-328.

Bound in his: Svcessos Y Prodigios De Amor ...,
1633.
Lacks title-page.
Reel 142, No. 908

PÉREZ DE MONTALBÁN, JUAN, 1602-1638.
Don Florisel De Niqvea. Comedia Famosa. Del Dotor
Ivan Perez De Montalvan. [Madrid?]: a costa de Luys de
la Marca, n.d.
40 p.
Reel 33, No. 155

PÉREZ DE MONTALBÁN, JUAN 1602-1638.
Fama Posthuma Y Elogios Panegiricos A La Vida Y
Muerte Del Doctor Frey Lope đ Vega Por El Doctor Juan
Perez de Montalvan natural de Madrid. Madrid: Ymprenta
del reyno, 1636.
[8], 231, [1]; 20 cm.

Pagination errors throughout.
Imperfect: lacks title-page. Contains 178 poems in
praise of Lope de Vega, 1 letter and 1 anonymous play.
Gallardo, III, no. 3454; Graesse, p. 582; Palau,
221664; Simón Díaz, Impresos, no. 1819.
Colophon: "En Madrid En la Imprenta del Reyno Año
1636."
Reel 141, No. 903

PÉREZ DE MONTALBÁN, JUAN, 1602-1638.
Orfeo En Lengva Castellana. A La Decima Mvsa. Por
El Licenciada Iuan Perez de Montaluan, natural de
Madrid. Barcelona: En casa de Pedro Lacavalleria,
1640.
[6], 32 ℓ.

In his work: Svcessos Y Prodigios De Amor.
Heredia, no. 6104; Palau, 221607; Penney, p. 419.
Reel 142, No. 911

PÉREZ DE MONTALBÁN, JUAN 1602-1638.
Para Todos Exemplos Morales, Hvmanos, Y Divinos. En
Qve Se Traten Diversas Ciencias, Materias, y Facultades.
Repartidos En Los Siete Dias De La Semana. Dirigido
Al Doctor Don Diego De La Cveva Y Salazar, Cura propio
de la Parroquial de San Gines de la Villa de Madrid, y
Examinador Synodal del Arcobispado de Toledo, Colegial
del Insigne de Theologos de la Vniuersidad de Alcalà.
Y Con Algvnas Adiciones Nvevas En esta nona impression.
Por El Doctor Ivan Perez De Montalvan, Natural de
Madrid, y Notario del Santo Oficio de la Inquisicion.
70 o. Alcalà: por María Fernandez, 1661.
[17], 548 p.; 21cm.

Bourland, p. 147; Jerez, p. 153; Palau, 221655;
Penney, p. 419.
Reel 141, No. 904

PÉREZ DE MONTALBÁN, JUAN, 1602-1638.
Svcessos, Y Prodigios De Amor. En Ocho Novelas
Exemplares. Por El Doctor Ivan Perez De Montalvan,
natural de la villa de Madrid, y Notario del Santo
Oficio de la Inquisicion. Dirigidas a diuersas
personas. Sexta impression. 42. Seuilla: Por Andres
Grande, 1633.
[4], 164 ℓ.; 21cm.

Bound with the author's:
- Amor, Privanca, Y Castigo Tragedia. Del Doctor
Ivan Perez de Montaluan. Representòla Andres de la
Bega. 21 ℓ.
- Comedia Famosa, El Divino Nazareno Sanson. Del
Doctor Juan Perez de Montalvan. [19] ℓ.
- Don Florisel De Niqvea. Comedia Famosa Del Doctor
Ivan Perez de Montaluan. p. 281-328.
- Comedia Famosa El Principe Prodigioso. Del Doctor
Iuan Perez de Montalvan. [20] ℓ.
Bourland, p. 131-32; Escudero, no. 1476; Graesse,
IV, p. 582; Heredia, no. 6105; Jerez, p. 80; Palau,
221605; Penney, p. 419.
Reel 142, No. 905

PÉREZ DE MONTALBÁN, JUAN, 1602-1638.
Svcessos Y Prodigios De Amor. En Ocho Novelas
Exemplares. Añadido En Esta Vltima Impression el
Orfeo a la Decima Musa. Por El Licenciado Ivan Perez
de Montaluan, natural de Madrid. Dirigidas adiuersas
personas. Barcelona: por Pedro Lacavalleria, 1640.
[4], 190 ℓ.; 16cm.

His Orfeo has separate title-page and foliation:
Orfeo En Lengva Castellana. A La Decima Mvsa. Por El
Licenciado Iuan Perez de Montaluan, natural de Madrid.
Heredia, no. 6104; Palau, 221607; Penney, p. 419.
Reel 142, No. 910

PÉREZ DE MONTALBÁN, JUAN, 1602-1638.
[Sucesos y prodigios de Amor. English]
Aurora Ismenia And The Prince By Don Juan Perez De
Montalvan. Oronta The Cyprian Virgin: By Sign.ʳ
Girolamo Preti. Tout vient a poinct qui peut attendre.
Translated by Thomas Stanley Esq; The Second Edition,
with Additions. London: Printed by W. Wilson, 1650.
2 pts. (87 p.; 14, [8] p.); 16cm.

English translation by Thomas Stanley, Esq.
The Oronta The Cyprian Virgin: By Sig.ʳ Girolamo
Preti has separate title-page and signatures.
Reel 141, No. 902

PÉREZ DE MONTALBÁN, JUAN, 1602-1638.
   Teagenes y Clariquea. Del Dotor Ivan Perez De Montalvan.
[Madrid: Ioseph Fernandez De Bvendia, n.d.
   48 p.; 21cm.

   Bound with: Cardona y Alagon, Antonio Folch de. El
mas heroyco silencio. Comedia Famosa. Valencia, 1688.
Reel 33, No. 153

PÉREZ DE MONTALBÁN, JUAN, 1602-1638.
   Vida Y Purgatorio De S. Patricio, Arzobispo, y
Primado de Hibernia. Escrita Por El Doctor Juan Perez
de Montalván, natural de la Villa de Madrid, y Notario
de la Santa Inquisicion. Barcelona: por Pablo Campins,
1657.
   [4], 178 p.; 15cm.

   Half-title: Vida Y Purgatorio De S. Patricio.
   A pirated edition.
   Palau, 221636.
Reel 142, No. 912

PÉREZ DE MOYA, JUAN, d. 1596.
   Comparaciones. O Similes Para Los Vicios Y Virtudes,
muy vtil y necessario para Predicadores y otras personas
curiosas. Ordenado por el Bachiller Iuan Perez de
Moya, natural de Santisteuan del Puerto. Dirigido al
muy Illustre Señor Matheo Vazquez, de lecca, del
cōsejo de su M. y susecretario: (sic) de la Sancta
general Inquisicion. Alcala: de Henares en casa de
Hernan Ramirez, 1586.
   222 l.; 15cm.

   Palau, 221740.
Reel 142, No. 913

PÉREZ DE MOYA, JUAN, d. 1596.
   Tratado De Mathematicas En Qve Se Contienen Cosas
De Arithmetica, Geometria, Cosmographia, y Philosophia
natural. Con otras varias materias, necessarias a
todas artes Liberales, y Mechanicas. Puestas por la
orden q̃ a la buelta de la hoja veras. Ordenado por
el Bachiller Iuan Perez de Moya, natural de Sant
Esteuan del Puerto. Dirigido A La S. C. R. M. De
Don Phelipe Rey de España nuestro señor. Alcala: Por
Iuan Gracian, 1573.
   [16], 752, [20] p.; 29cm.

   Adams, II, no. 689; Graesse, IV, p. 619; Palau,
221702; Thomas, p. 69.
Reel 142, No. 914

PÉREZ DE OLIVA, FERNÁN, b. 1494-1533 ca.
   Las Obas (sic) Del Maestro Fernan Perez De Oliva
Natvral De Cordoua: Rector que fue de la
Vniuersidad de Salamanca, y Cathedratico de
Theologia en ella. Con otras cosas que van añadidas,
como se dara razon luego al principio. Dirigidas Al
Illustrissimo Señor el Cardenal de Toledo don Gaspar
de Quiroga. Cordoua: por Gabriel Ramos Bejarano,
1586.
   [23], 283 l.; 21cm.

   Pagination errors throughout.
   Colophon: "Acobose de imprimir este libro de las
obras del Maestro Fernan Perez de Oliua y lo demas, en
la muy noble ciudad de Cordoua, en casa de Gabriel Ramos
Bejarano impressor de libros. A costa de Francisco
Roberto mercader de libros. En el mes de Deziembre
del año de M.D. L. XXXV."
   Title-page trimmed at bottom.
   Adams, II, no. 690; Graesse, V, p. 201; Palau,
221828; Penney, p. 420; Salvá, I, 1354; Thomas, p. 69;
Valdenebro, 23.
Reel 142, No. 915

PÉREZ DE VALDIVIA, DIEGO, 1510-1589.
   Aviso De Gente Recogida, Y En Especial De La Dedicada
Al Servicio De Dios, En El Qval Se Dan Consejos, Y
Remedios Contra Los Peligros, y tentaciones, que en
el Camino del Cielo se suelen ofrecer, y se dā orden
de vida para qualquier estado de persona en todos los
tiempos del año. Compvesto Por El mvy Reverendo Doctor
Diego Perez, Catedratico de Escritura en la Vniuersidad
de Barcelona. Dedicado A Lvis De Avila Y Toledo,
Criado De La Catholica Magestad de Carlos Segundo
nuestro Señor, y Sargento de la Guarda Vieja Española.
Madrid: En la Imprenta del Reyno, 1678.
   [28], 448, [35] p.; 20cm.

   Pagination errors throughout.
   Palau, 222591.
Reel 143, No. 916

PÉREZ DE VALDIVIA, DIEGO, 1510-1589.
   Docvmentos Salvdables Para Las Almas Piadosas Qve
Con Espirity, Y Sentimiento quieren exercitar las obras,
y exercicios que Iesu Christo nuestro Señor y la santa
Iglesia Catholica Romana enfeña. Coligidos de la
doctrina delos santos por el muy reuerendo Padre Diego
Perez doctor en sancta Theologia, y predicador del
Euangelio, y cathedratico de santa Escritura enla
vniuersidad de Barcelona. Dirigido al muy Illustre
y Reuerendissimo Señor don Ioan Dymas Loris Obispo de
Barcelona, y del consejo de su Magestad. Lo contenido
en este libro boluiendo esta hoja lo veran. Barcelona:
en casa de Pedro Malo Año de Christo, 1588.
   2v. in 1 ([12], 347, [11] l.; [8], 51, [3] l.); 16cm.

   Vol. II has title: Docvmentos Particvlares, Para
La Vida Heremitica: entre los quales ay muchas doctrinas
que para todo estado de hombres Christianos son vtiles.
Coligidos delos sanctos y de experiencias, por el
Padre Diego Perez doctor en sancta Theologia y
cathedratico de Scriptura en la vniuersidad de
Barcelona...
   Palau, 222606.
Reel 143, No. 917

PÉREZ DE VALENCIA, JAIME, 1408-1490.
   D. Iacobi Parem De Valentia Christopolitani Episcopi.
Doctissimae Et Plane Divinae Explanationes In
Centvmqvinqvaginta Psalmos Dauidicos. In Cantica
officialia, seu ferialia, & euangelica, quae in
ecclesiasticis officiis decantantur. In Canticum
Sanctorum Ambrosii, & Augustini. Item Tractatus
sanè quàm argutus Quaestionum quinque cum earum
subtilissimis resolutionibus contra Iudaeos Christianae
fidei aduersarios. Vna Cvm excellentissima
Expalantione In Cantica Canticorvm. Adiecta nuperrimè
in Simbolum Diui Atanasii Episcopi aurea expositione.
Omnia nunc demum ad vetustorum exemplarium fidem
accurratissimè recognita, & emendata. Addito Dyplice
Indice. Altero Psalmorum & Canticorum. Altero
singularium rerum & verborum toto opere memorabilium
locupletissimo. Venetijs: Excudebat Bartholomaeus
Rubinus, 1568.
   [33], 1019, [2] p.; 22cm.

   Palau, 222642.
Reel 143, No. 918

PÉREZ DEL BARRIO ANGULO, GABRIEL.
   Direccion De Secretarios De Señores, Y Las Materias,
Cvydados, Y Obligaciones Qve les tocan, con las
virtudes de que se han de preciar, estilo, y orden
del despacho y expediente, manejo de papeles de ministros, formularios de cartas, prouisiones de oficios,
y vn compendio en razon de acrecentar estado, y
hazienda, oficio de Contador, y otras curiosidades que

PÉREZ DEL BARRIO ANGULO (Cont'd)
se declaran en la primera hoja. Por Gabriel Perez del
Barrio Angulo, Secretario del Marques de los Velez, y
Alcayde de la Fortaleza de su villa de Librilla.
Dirigido al Marques de Cañete don Iuan Andrea Hurtado
de Mendoca. Madrid: Por Alonso Martin de Balboa, 1613.
[16], 246 l.; 21cm.

Pagination errors throughout.
Colophon: "En Madrid Por Alonso Martin de Balboa.
Año de M.DC.XIII." First edition.
Palau, 219805; Pérez Pastor, no. 1243; Penney, p. 421.
Reel 143, No. 919

PÉREZ DEL BARRIO ANGULO, GABRIEL.
Secretario Y Consegero De Señores Y Ministros:
Cargos, Materias, Cvydados, Obligaciones y curioso
Agricultor de quanto el Gouierno, y la Pluma piden para
cumplir con ellas: El indice las toca, y estan
ilustradas con sentencias, conceptos, y curiosidades,
no tocadas. Al Ilvstrissimo Don Ivan Chvmazero De
Sotomayor y Carrillo, Presidente de Castilla, &c.
Por Gabriel Perez Del Barrio Angylo, Alcayde de la villa
de Librilla, por el Excelentissimo Marques de los
Velez, y Ayo del inmediato Marques de Flores de Auila
su primo. 87. o. Madrid: Por Francisco Garcia de
Arroyo, Impressor del Reyno, 1645.
[12], 338, [1] l.; 20cm.

Pagination errors throughout.
Palau, 219809.
Reel 143, No. 920

PÉREZ DEL CASTILLO, BALTASAR.
El Estado En Qve Dios Llama A Cada Vno; Del Maestro
Baltasar Perez del Castillo, Canonigo dela sancta
yglesia, e (sic) natural de Burgos. Dirigido al muy
illustre Señor don Hieronymo Manrique, del cōsejo dela
sancta y general Inquisiciō de España y Arcediano de
Carmona. ET AVRA. Salamanca: por los herederos de
Mathias Gast, 1578.
[8], 94, [3] l.; 22cm.

Colophon: "En Salamanca Por los herederos de Mathias
Gast 1578."
Palau, 220020.
Reel 144, No. 921

PÉREZ DEL CASTILLO, BALTASAR (translator) see also
DU CHOUL, GUILLAUME.

PERPIÑA, PEDRO JUAN, 1530-1566.
Petri Ioannis Perpiniani E Societate Iesv Orationes
Qvinqve. His adiunctae sunt M. Ant. Mureti I.C. &
Ciuis Rom. II Ioann. Baptistae Rasarij I. E quibus
elonquentiae praesertim studiosi multam vtilitatem
percipient, & Ciceronem rectè imitandi viam ac rationem
cognoscent. Excudebat Sebaldvs Mayer. 1572.
72 l.; 16cm.

Palau, 223591.
Reel 144, No. 922

PERPIÑA, PEDRO JUAN, 1530-1566.
R. P. Petri Ioannis Perpiniani Valentini, Societatis
Iesv Presbyteri. Orationes Dvodeviginti. Editio
Nova: Cui accesserunt Orationes quinquae, à totidem
eiusdem Societatis Presbyteris Romae pridem dicta;
nunc primùm Galliae excusae. A naeuis omnia, quibus
hactenus abundarunt, qua potuit diligentiâ, fidelissmè
vindicata. Lvgdvni: Apud Antonivm Sovbron, 1622.
[16], 748, [4] p.; 12cm.

Reel 144, No. 923

PERPIÑA, PEDRO JUAN, 1530-1566.
Petri Joannis Perpiniani Soc. Jesu. Aliquot Epistolae.
Ubi, Praeter Caetera, de attis rhetoricae locis
communibus, ac de juventute Grecis Latinisque literis
erudienda agitur. Proferre in lucem coeperat ex eadem
Societate. Franciscus Vavassor. Parisiis: Apud Viduam
Claudii Thiboust, Et Petrum Esclassan, Juratum Bibliop.
Vniversit. ordin. viâ D. Joan. Later. è regione
Collegij Regij, 1683.
[8], 192 p.; 16cm.

Palau, 223624.
Reel 144, No. 924

PERSIUS FLACCUS, AULUS.
Commentaria Aelii Antonii Nebrissensis Grammatici,
In Sex A. Persii Satyras. Parisiis: Ex Officina
Roberti Stephani E Regione Scholae Decretorvm, 1527.
2 pts. (77, [1] l.; [14] l.); 16cm.

Part II has special t.-p.: A. Persii Flacci
Satyrae Sex.
Colophon: Excudebat In Sva Officina Robertvs
Stephanus, Anno Redemptionis Nostrae Millesimo,
Qvingentessimo, Septimo Et Vicesimo, Qvinto Calen.
Ivnii.
Palau, 223854.
Reel 144, No. 925

PETRARCA, FRANCESCO, 1304-1374.
[Canzoniere. Spanish]
De Los Sonetos, Canciones. Mandriales Y Sextinas
del gran Poeta y Orador Francisco Petrarca,
Tradvzidos De Toscano Por Salusque Lusitano, Parte
Primera. Con Breves Svmarios, ō Argumentos en todos
los Sonetos y Canciones que declaran la intencion
del autor. Compvestos Por El Mismo. Con Dos Tablas,
Vna Castellana, y la otra Toscana y Castellana.
Venecia: En casa de Nicolao Beuilaqua, 1567.
[17], 164, [5] p.; 21cm.

Spanish translation by Selomoh Usque, pseudonym
for Salamon ben Abraham.
Adams, II, no. 842; Gallardo, no. 3799; Graesse,
V, p. 232; Jerez, p. 95; Palau, 224264; Penney, p.
423; Short-Title, II, p. 559; Thomas, p. 70.
Reel 144, No. 926

PETRARCA, FRANCESCO, 1304-1374.
[Canzoniere. Spanish]
Sonetos Y Canciones Del Poeta Francisco Petrarcha,
que traduzia Henrique Garces de lengua Thoscana en
Castellana. Dirigido A Philippo Segundo deste nōbre,
Manarcha (sic) primero de las Españas, è Indias
Oriental, y Occidental. Madrid: Impresso en casa
de Guillermo Droy, 1591.
[14], 178 l.; 21cm.

Spanish translation by Enrique Garces.
Adams, II, no. 843; Graesse, V, p. 232; Salvá,
I, 873; Thomas, p. 70.
Reel 144, No. 927

PETRARCA, FRANCESCO. 1304-1374.
[I Trionfi. Spanish]
Los Trivmphos De Francisco Petrarcha, ahora
nueuamente traduzidos en Lengua Castellana, en la
medida, y numero de versos, que tienen en el Toscano,
y con nueua glosa. Dirigidos al illustrissimo Señor
don Ioan de la Cerda, Duque de Medinaceli, Marques de
cogolludo, Conde del gran puerto de sancta Maria:
Señor de las villas de Deça y Enciso, &c.. Medina:
del Campo por Guillermo de Millis, 1555.
[10], 189, [4] l.; 21cm.

Spanish translation by Hernando del Hozes.
Graesse, V, p. 232; Palau, 224258; Penney, p. 423;
Salvá, I, 877; Ticknor, p. 272.
Reel 144, No. 928

PHILIP, king of Spain see FELIPE.

PIMENTEL, DOMINGO and CHUMACERO Y CARRILLO, JUAN.
Memorial De Sv Magestad Catolica Que dieron a
nuestro muy Santo Padre Vrbano Papa VIII. D. Fray
Domingo Pimentel Obispo de Cordoua, y D. Iuan
Chumaçero, y Carrillo de su Consejo, y Camara, en la
embajada, à que vinieron el año de 633. incluso en el,
otro, que presentaron los Reynos de Castilla juntos
en Cortes el año antecediente, sobre diferentes
agrauios, que reciben en las expediciones de Roma, de
que piden reformacion, fol. I. Respuesta, que entregò
Monseñor Maraldi Secretario de Breues de orden de su
Santidad, en satisfaccion a los Capitulos referidos,
fol. 4 I. Replica, que entregaron los mismos a su
Santidad, respondiẽdo al descargo, que se propuso
en cada vno de los Capitulos, fol. 55. [n.p.-n.d.].
[3], 160 p.; 29cm.

Pagination errors throughout.
Palau, 67968; Salvá, II, 3659.
Reel 144, No. 929

PINTO DE VITORIA, JUAN, d. 1631.
Vida Del Venerable Siervo De Dios N.P.M.F. Ivan
Sanz del Orden de nuestra Señora del Carmen. Escrita
por el P. Presentado Fr. Iuan Pinto de Vitoria Letor
de Theologia en el Carmen de Valencia. Con el Sermõ
que predicõ nuestro muy R.P. Prouincial el Maestro
Fr. Esteuan de Thous, siendo Prior de dicho Conuento.:
A Doña Maria de Corella, y de Mendoca, Condessa de
la Puebla. Valencia: en casa de Iuan Chrysostomo
Garriz, 1612.
[17], 298 p.; 15cm.

Includes the author's: Vida Del Principe Sacro
De Macedonia Don Pedro Cernouichio, aliàs Fr. Angelo
Cernouichio, Religioso professo, y Sacerdote de la
Orden de nuestra Señora del Carmen. A doña Guiomar
de Corella, y Cardenas, Condessa de Cocentayna, y de
la Puebla. pp. 299-348, [5] p.
Reel 144, No. 930

PINU, JOSEPHUS A.
Carmen Continens Narrationem Non Qvidem Historicam
Sed Confictam admonendae adolescentiae causa, ut
cogitet, & distinctionem ordinum diuinitus factam
esse, & unicuiq; elaborandum esse, ut virtute suam
personam tueatur. Huic additum est aliud,
comprehendens res aliquas insignes laudatissimorum
Caesarum Germanorum, & simul indicationem temporis,
quo Maximilianus legitimis Electorum suffragijs
Caesar electus est, Scriptum ad eundem. Avthore
Iosepho A Piny Poeta Coronato. [n.p.-n.d.].
8 l.; 15cm.

Last poem dated 1564.
Reel 144, No. 931

PLINIUS SECUNDUS, CAIUS.
[Naturalis Historiae. Spanish]
Tradvcion De Los Libros De Caio Plinio Segvndo, De
La Historia Natvral De Los Animales. Hecha Por El
Licenciado Geronimo De Huerta, Medico y Filosofo. Y
Anotada Por El Mesmo Con Anotaciones curiosas: en las
quales pone los nombres, la forma, la naturaleza, la
templanca, las costumbres y propiedades de todos los
Animales, Pescados, Aues, y Insectos, y el prouecho,
ò daño que pueden causar à los hombres: y los
Geroglificos que tuuieron dellos los Antiguos: con
otras muchas cosas curiosas. Primera Parte. Dirigida
Al Rey Don Felipe. III. Nvestro Señor, Rey de las
Españas, è Indias. Madrid: Por Luys Sanchez, 1599.
[10], 314 l.; 21cm.

Spanish translation by Geronimo de Herta. Bks.7-8].
Pagination errors throughout.
Graesse, V, p. 344; Palau, 229066; Penney, p. 431;
Pérez Pastor, no. 645; Thomas, p. 71.
Reel 145, No. 933

PLINIUS SECUNDUS, CAIUS.
[Naturalis Historiae. Spanish]
Libro Nono, De Caio Plinio Segvndo, De La Historia
Natvral de los pescados del mar, de lagos, estanques,
y rios. Hecha Por El Licenciado Geronimo de Huerta,
Medico y Filosofo. Dirigida Al Rey Don Felipe III.
Rey de las Españas, e Indias. Madrid: En casa de
Pedro Madrigal, 1603.
[4], 156, [8] l.; 21cm.

Spanish translation by Geronimo de Huerta.
Goldsmith, p. 141, no. 428; Graesse, V, p. 344;
Palau, 229068; Penney, p. 431; Pérez Pastor, no. 848;
Salvá, II, 2739.
Reel 144, No. 932

PLUTARCH.
[Moralia. Spanish]
Morales de Plutarco Traduzidos de lengua Griega
en Castellana. Los titulos de las obras que en morales
se contienen se veran enla plana siguiente. Alcala:
por Juan de Brocar, 1548.
[3], 201 l.; 30cm.

Spanish translation by Diego Gracián.
Lacks seven preliminary leaves and 3 leaves at end.
Adams, II, no. 1646; Catalina, no. 224; Graesse,
V, p. 372; Palau, 229182; Penney, p. 431; Salvá, II,
3981.
Reel 145, No. 934

PLUTARCH.
[Vitae illvstrium vivorum graecorum et romanorvm.
Spanish]
Las Vidas De Los Ilvstres Y Excelentes Varones
Griegos y Romanos, escritas primero en lengua Griega
por el graue Philosopho y verdadero historiador
Plutarcho de Cheronea, y agora nueuamente traduzidas
en Castellano Por Juan Castro de Salinas.
Imprimieronse en la Imperial Ciudad de Colonia, y
vendense en Anvers: en casa de Arnoldo Bircman, 1562.
2 pts. ([2], 320 l.; 71, [3] l.; 27 (?) cm.)

Spanish translation by Juan Castro de Salinas
pseud. for Francisco Enzinas.
Colophon: "Acabose De Imprimir las vidas de los
ilustres & excelentes Varones Griegos y Romanos
pareadas en la ciudad Imperial de Colonia, à costas
de los Herederos de Arnoldo Bircman. Año M.D.LXII."
Adams, II, no. 1629; Graesse, V, p. 372; La Serna,
IV, no. 6396; Morante, Cat., no. 6682; Palau, 229115;
Peeters-Fontainas, II, no. 1066.
Reel 145, No. 935

POELMANN, THEODOR, 1510?-1607?
Aviani Aesopicarvm Fabvlarvm Liber. A Theod.
Pvlmanno Cranebvrgio Ex Membranis In Lvcem Editvs.
Antverpiae: Ex officina Christophori Plantini, 1585.
29, [2] p.; 13cm.

Bound in: Del Rio, Martin Antoine. Ad Cl. Clavdiani
V. C. Opera..., 1585.
Reel 153, No. 1012

POELMANN, THEODOR, 1510?-1607?
Aviani Aesopicarvm Fabvlarvm Liber, A Theod.
Pvlmanno Cranebvrgio Ex Membranis In Lvcem Editvs.
Antverpiae: Ex officina Plantiniana, Apud Ioannem
Moretum, 1607.
29, [2] p.; 13cm.

Bound in: Del Rio, Martin Antoine. Ad Cl.
Clavdiani V.C. Opera...1607.
Reel 153, No. 1015

POELMANN, THEODOR, 1510?-1607?
Cl. Clavdianvs, Theod. Pvlmanni Craneburgii
Diligentia, & fide summa, è vetustis codicibus
restitutus. Antverpiae: Ex officina Christophori
Plantini, 1571.
353, [6] p.; 13cm.

Bound in Del Rio, Martin Antoine. Ad. Cl. Clavdiani
V.C. Opera..., 1572.
Reel 153, No. 1009

POELMANN, THEODOR, 1510?-1607?
Cl. Clavdianvs, Theod. Pvlmanni Cranburgii Diligentia,
& fide summa, è vetustis codicibus restitutus.
Anterpiae: Ex officina Christophori Plantini, 1585.
351 p.; 13cm.

Bound in: Del Rio, Martin Antoine. Ad Cl.
Clavdiani V. C. Opera..., 1585.
Reel 153, No. 1011

POELMAN, THEODOR, 1510?-1607?
Cl. Clavdianvs, Theod. Pvlmanni Cranebvrgii
Diligentia, & fide summa, è vetustis codicibus
restitutus. Vnà cum M. Ant. Del-rio Notis.
Antverpiae: Ex officina Plantiniana, Apud Ioannem
Moretum, 1607.
351 p.; 13cm.

Bound in: Del Rio, Martin Antoine. Ad Cl. Clavdiani
V.C. Opera...1607.
Reel 153, No. 1014

POLANCO, JUAN ALFONSO.
Breve Directorivm Ad Confessarii Et Confitentis
munus ritè obeundum concinnatum. Per M. Ioannem
Polancum Theologum Societatis Iesv. Et ab eodem
multis in locis recognitum. Maceratae: Apud
Sebastianum Martellinum, 1576.
173, [6] p.; 17cm.

Colophon: Maceratae, Apud Sebastianum Martellinum
M D L X X V I.
Palau, 230173.
Reel 145, No. 936

POLO, GASPAR GIL, 1516?-1591?
[Los cinco libros de la Diana enamorada. Latin]
Casp. Barthi Erotodidascalus, Sive Nemoralium
Libri V. Ad Hispanicvm Gasperis Gilli, Poli.
Cum Figuris Aeneis. Anoviae: Typis Wechelianis,
Apud Danielem & Davidem Aubrios, & Clementem
Schleichium, 1625.
[15], 315 p.: ill.; 18cm.

Latin translation by Casparus Barthius.
Illus. title-page, engraved; head - pieces;
initials.
Bound in vellum.
Palau, 102088; Penney, p. 229; Simón Díaz, X,
no. 5316.
Reel 58, No. 349

POLO DE MEDINA, SALVADOR JACINTO, 1603-1676.
Obras En Prossa, (sic) Y Verso, De Salvador Iacinto
Polo De Medina, Natvral de la Ciudad de Murcia.
Recogidas Por Vn aficionado suyo. Dedicadas A La
Soberana Reyna De Cielo, Y Tierra, Santissima Señora
nuestra, Concebida en gracia en el primer instante de
su animacion. Amen. Zaragoça: por Diego Dormer, 1670.
[8], 311 p.; 21cm.

Colophon: "Con Licencia, En Zaragoça, por Diego
Dormer, Impressor de la ciudad, y su real hospital.
Año 1670."
Goldsmith, p. 142, no. 440; Jiménez Catalán, no.
802; Knapp-Huntington, p. 268; Palau, 230512; Penney,
p. 432; Salvá, II, 1941.
Reel 145, No. 937

PONCE DE LEÓN, BASILIO, 1569-1629.
Celeberrimae Academiae Salmanticensis De Tenenda
Et Docenda Doctrina SS. Avgvstini Et Thomae Aqvinatis
Ivdicivm, Statvto, Ivramento Qve Solemni firmatum et
contra impugnates propugnatum. Per Sapientissimum
Magistrum F. Basilivm Pontivm Legionensem Ordinis
Sancti Augustini Cathedraticum Salmanticensem.
Editio Qvarta. Post vnam Hispanam, alteram Romanam
& Duacensem tertiam. Parisiis: Sumptibus Simeonis
Piget, 1657.
[2], 36 p.; 37cm.

Bound with: Medicis, Girolamo de: Svmmae
Theologiae S. Thomae Aqvinatis Doctoris Angelici
Formalis Explicatio. Qvo Omnia Argvmenta, Et
Rationes, quae in singulis Articulis tractantur, non
modica claritate formantur, & explicantur,
Argumentorumque Responsiones explicatae ad ipsorum
partes aptè accommodantur... Part 1 and 2.
Reel 145, No. 938

PONCE DE LEÓN, GONZALO, b. 1530.
Scholastica Assertio Pro Disciplina Ecclesiastica.
Qua demostratur Henrici Borbonij Biarmensis ad Galliae
Regnum perpetua inhabilitas, sacrae Scripturae verbis,
Conciliorum decretis, Maximorum Pontificum
constitutionibus, sanctorum Patrum sentetijs,
Historiarum monumentis, Auctorum testimonijs, Iure
communi, Pontificio, & Caesareo comprobata. Auctore
D. Consalvo Ponce De Leon Hispalensi I.V.D. Archidiacono
Talauerensi in Ecclesia Toletana. Adiectae sunt
Bullae Pontificiae, quae in hac causa hactenus prodiere.
Romae: Ex Typographia Gabiana, 1593.
[9], 184 p.; 18cm.

Doublet, p. 106; Palau, 230979.
Reel 146, No. 940

PRIMALEON OF GREECE.
Le Troisiesme Livre De Primaleon De Grece, Fils
De Palmerin d'Oliue, Empereur de Constantinople.
Auquel les faits heroiques mariages & merueilleuses
amours d'eceluy, sont tant bien deduites & exprimes,
que le Lecteur, outre le prefit, n'en peut recueillir
sinon plaisir & contentement. Traduit d'Espagnol en
François. Lyon: Chez Pierre Riguad, 1609.
426, [11] p.; 12cm.

French translation by unknown.
Palau, 237221.
Reel 146, No. 941

PRUDENTIUS CLEMENS, AURELIUS, 348-ca. 410.
Aurelii Prudentii Clementis, Viri Consvlaris, Opera:
Commentarijs Aelij Antonij Nebrissensis, atq Ioannis
Sichardi scholijs Illustrata. [Antverpiae: Typis Aegid.
Diesth, 1546].
262, [2] l.; 16cm.

English title-page.
Colophon: Finis Impressvm Antverpiae, Anno humanae
salutis. 1546. Typis Aegid. Diesth.
The dedication, by Joannes Sichard, is dated: anno
M.D.XXXXVII. mense martio.
On verso of title-page: Librorvm, qvi in hoc opere
habentur, singulorum catalogus. Psychomachia,
Cathemerinon, Persitephanon, Apotheosis, Hamartigenia,
Contra Symmachom ... libri duo, Enchiridion Noui &
Veteris Testamenti.
Includes "Avrelii Prvdentii vita per Aldvm Romanvm"
(leaves 4-6) and "Symmachi Relatio ad Valentinianum"
(leaves 227-229).
Adams, II, no. 2183; Graesse, V, p. 467; Palau,
239824.
Reel 146, No. 942

PUENTE, LUIS DE LA, 1554-1624.
[Meditaciones de los principales misterios. Latin]
Meditationes Praecipvis Fidei Nostrae Mysteriis,
Vitae Ac Passionis D. N. Iesv Christi, Et B.V. Mariae,
Sanctorumq; & Euangeliorum toto anno occurrentium,
Cvm Orationis Mentalis Circa E adem (sic) Praxi.
Avtore R. P. Lvdovico De Ponto Vallis-Oletano Hispanicè
editae, & in duos Tomos diuisae. Interprete R. P.
Melchiore Trevinnio, Vtroqve Societatis Iesv Religioso.
Hac Editione Actae Svmmariis Sev Synopsi singularum
Meditationum. Coloniae Agrippinae: Apud Ioannem
Kinchivm sub Monocerote, 1619.
([17], 148 p.; 687 p.; 21cm.)

Latin translation by Melchor Treviño.
Errors in pagination: p. 66-104 (first group)
numbered 510-516, 117-148; p. 193-208 (second group)
numbered 199 - 214; other misprints.
Reel 146, No. 943

PULGAR, HERNANDO, DEL, 1436-ca. 1492.
Habes In Hoc Volvmine Amice Lector. Aelii Antonii
Nebrissensis Rervm A Fernando & Elisabe Hispaniarū
foelicissimis Regibus gestar Decades duas. Necnō
belli Nauariensis libros duos. Annexa insuper
Archiepi Roderici Chronica, alijsq historijs antehac
non excussis. [Granada: Apvd Inclytam Granqtam,
1545].
3 pts. ([8], 86 l.; [4], 122 l.; [2], 77, [1] l.);
33cm.

Part II has special t.-p.: Reverendissimi Ac
Illvstrissimi Domini Domini Roderici Toletanae
Dioecisis Archiepiscopi rerum in Hispania gestarum
Chronicon Libri nouem nuperrime excussi. Adiecta insuper Ostrogothorum,
Hugnorum, Vandalorum caeterorumq historia. Necnon
Genealogia Regum Hispanorum Reuerēdi patris Domini
Alphōsi de Carthagena Episcopi Burgensis.
Part III has special t.-p.: Episcopi Gervndensis
Paralipomenon Hispaniae Libri Decem Antehac Non
Excvssi.
Engraved title-pages.
Pagination errors throughout.
Palau, 242126.
Reels 146 & 147, No. 944

PULMANN, THEODORE see POELMANN, THEODOR.

Q

QUESTIERS, CATHARINA, 1631-1669.
Casimier, Of Gedempte Hoogmoet. Bly-Spel. Gerijmt
door Catharina Questiers. Gespeelt op d'Amsterdamse
Schoubrugh. T'Amsterdam: Voor Gerard Smit, 1656.
33 *l*.; 20cm.

Plays and poems by Joost van den Vondel and others.
Purports to be a translation of a comedia by Félix
Lope de Vega Carpio.
Reel 147, No. 945

QUEVEDO Y HOYOS, ANTONIO DE.
Libro De Indicios Y Tormentos; Qve Contiene Toda
La Practica Criminal, Y Modo de Sustanciar el processo
indicatiuamente, hasta descubrir el delito y
delinquente, y ponerle en estado de condenarle, ò
absoluerle. Al Señor D. Ivan Chvmacero Sotomayor,
Cauallero del Orden de Santiago, del Supremo Consejo
y Camara del mui catolico y mayor Monarca Felipe
Qvarto, Rei de las Españas y Nueuo-mundo. Por El
Licenciado D. Antonio De Qvevedo Y Hoyos, Abocado De
Los Reales Consejos y Corte, natural de la villa de
Reinosa, en las Montañas de Castilla-Vieja. Madrid:
En la Imprenta de Francisco Martinez, 1632.
[12], 100, [9] *l*.; 21cm.

Palau, 243555.
Reel 147, No. 946

QUEVEDO Y VILLEGAS, FRANCISCO GOMEZ DE, 1580-1645.
La Caida Para Levantarse. El Ciego Para Dar Vista.
El Montante De La Iglesia. En La Vida De San Pablo
Apostol Escriue Don Francisco de Queuedo Villegas.
Obra Teologa, Etica, y Politica. Al Señor D.
Francisco De de (sic) Faro Conde de Odemira, del
Consejo de S. Magestad, y Veedor de su Real hazienda
&c. Lisboa: Por Pablo CraesbeecK, 1648.
[13], 126 *l*.; 14cm.

Half-title: La caida Para Levantarse El Ciego
Para Dar Vista El Montante De La Iglesia en la Vida
de S. Pablo Apostolo (sic) escriue D. Francisco De
Qvevedo Al Señor D. Francisco De Faro Conde de
Odemira, del consejo de S. Magestad y Veedor de su
Real hazienda &c.
Leaves 52-56 are bound in the following order:
52, 54, 56, 55. Some misprints in the foliation.
Jerez, p. 86; Nepomuceno, no. 1387; Palau,
244312; Penney, p. 445.
Reel 147, No. 947

QUEVEDO Y VILLEGAS, FRANCISCO GOMEZ DE, 1580-1645.
Carta Al Serenissimo, Mvy Alto, Y myv Poderoso Lvis
XIII. Rey Christianissimo De Francia. Escrivela A Sv
Magestad Christianissima Don Francisco De Qvevedo
Villegas, Cauallero del Habito de San Iacobo, y Señor
de la Villa de la Torre de Iuan Abad. En Razon De Las
Nefandas acciones, y sacrilegios execrables que
cometio contra el derecho diuino, y humano en la
Villa de Tillimon en Flandes Mos de Xatillon Vgonote,
con el exercito descomulgado de Frances Hereges. En
Caragoca: En el Hospital Real y General de Nuestra
Señora de Gracia, Acosta de Pedro Escuer Mercader de
Libros, 1935 [1635].
50 p.; 21cm.

Bound in: Céspedes y Meneses, Gonzalo de: Francia
Engañada. Francia Respondida ... Empresso en Caller,
Año 1635.
Palau, 244297.
Reel 41, No. 218

QUEVEDO Y VILLEGAS, FRANCISCO GOMEZ DE, 1580-1645.
Epicteto Y Phocilides en Español Con Consonantes.
Con el Origen de los Estoïcos, y su defensa contra
Plutarco y la defensa de Epicuro, contra la comun
opinion. [s.l.:s.n., 16--?]
93 p.

Lacks title page.
Caption title.
Bound in the author's: Obras..., 1660.
Reel 148, No. 960

QUEVEDO Y VILLEGAS, FRANCISCO GOMEZ DE, 1580-1645.
Epicteto y Phocilides En Español Con Consonantes.
Con el Origen de los Estoïcos y su defensa contra
Plutarco, y la comun opinion. [s.l.:s.n.]
86, [18] p.; 23cm.

Bound in the author's: Obras..., 1670.
Reel 149, No. 963

QUEVEDO Y VILLEGAS, FRANCISCO GOMEZ DE, 1580-1645.
Epicteto, Y Phocilides En Español Con Consonantes.
Con el Origen de los Estoïs, y su defensa contra
Plutarco, y la defensa de Epicuro, contra la comun
opinion. A Don Juan de Herrera su amigo, Cavallero
del Abito de Santiago, Cavallerizo del Excelentissimo
Señor Conde Duque, y Capitan Cavallos. [s.l.:s.n.],
16--?
86, [20] p.

The fourth volume of the author's Obras...
On Spine: Obras de Qvevedo. IIII.
Bound in the author's: Las Tres Ultimas Musas
Castellanas De Don Francisco De Quevedo Villegas, 1671.
Reel 152, No. 988

QUEVEDO Y VILLEGAS, FRANCISCO GOMEZ DE, 1580-1645.
La Fortvna Con Seso I La Hora De Todos, Fantasia
Moral. Avtor Rifroscrancor Viveque Vasgel Duacense.
Traduzido de Latin en Español Por Don Estevan Plvvianes
del Padron, Natural de la Villa de Cueva Pilona. A
Don Vincencio Ivan De Lastanosa. Zaragoça: por los
herederos de Pedro Lanaja, i Lamarca, 1650.
[8], 220 p.; 16cm.

First edition.
Graesse, p. 524; Jerez, p. 86; Jiménez Catalán,
563; Palau, 244353; Penney, p. 446; Salvá, II, 1946;
Ticknor, p. 293.
Reel 147, No. 948

QUEVEDO Y VILLEGAS, FRANCISCO GOMEZ DE, 1580-1645.
La Fortvna con Seso, I La Hora De Todos Fantasia
Moral Avtor Nisroscrancod Diveque Vasgello Duacense.
Traduzido de Latin en Español ... Corregida, i
enmendada en esta Segunda Impression. A Don
Vincencio Ivan De Lastanosa. Zaragoça: por los
Herederos de Pedro Lanaja, i Lamarca, 1650.
[8], 220 p.; 16cm.

Palau, 244354; Salva, II, 1947.
Reel 147, No. 949

QUEVEDO Y VILLEGAS, FRANCISCO GOMEZ DE, 1580-1645.
Historia De La Vida Del Bvscon, LLamado Don Pablos;
Exemplo de Vagamundos, y espejo de Tacaños. Por Don
Francisco de Queuedo Villegas, Cauallero del Orden de
Santiago, y señor de la Villa de Iuan Abad.
Añadieronse en essa vltima Impression otros tratados
del mismo Autor, que aunque parecen gracioses (sic)
tienen muchas cosas vtiles, y prouechosas para la
vida como se vera en la oja siguiente. Rvan: A costa
de Carlos Osmont, en calle del Palacio, 1629.
[9], 164, [2] p.; 16cm.

Bound with the author's: A) Sveños, Y Discvrsos De
Verdades, Descvbridoras De Abusos, Vicios, y Engaños,
en todos los Officios, y Estados del Mundo..., 1629.
B) El Perro, y la Calentvra.
Graesse, p. 524; Laurenti, no. 1651; Palau, 243862;
Penney, p. 446; Salvá, II, 1949.
Reel 147, No. 952

QUEVEDO Y VILLEGAS, FRANCISCO GOMEZ DE, 1580-1645.
The Life And Adventures Of Buscon The Witty Spaniard.
Put into English by a Person of Honour. To which is
added, The Provident Knight. By Don Francisco de
Quevedo, A Spanish Cavalier. The Second Edition.
London: Printed for Henry Herringman, 1670.
247 p.; 17cm.

English translation by John Davies of Kidwelly.
Includes: The Provident Knight, Or, Sir Parsimoniovs
Thrift. By Don Francisco de Quevedo, A Spanish Cavalier.
Allison, p. 152, no. 3.1; Graesse, p. 524; Laurenti,
no. 1797; Palau, 243999; Wing. Q 191a.
Reel 147, No. 955

QUEVEDO Y VILLEGAS, FRANCISCO GOMEZ DE, 1580-1645.
La Hora. Escriviola Nvestro Gran Español Don
Francisco De Qvevedo. Con Este Titvlo. La Fortvna
Con Seso Y la Hora de Todos, Phantasia Moral. Avtor
Rifroscrancot Viveque Vasgel Duacense. [pseud.]
Traduzido de Latin, en Español. Por Don Estevan
Plvvianes del Padron, natural de la Villa de Cuerva-
Pilona. Dedicado Al Excelentissimo Señor, Marques de
Mortara, &c. Zaragoça: por Iuan de Ybar, 1651.
[9], 220 p.; 16cm.

Colophon: "Con Licencia, En Zaragoça, por Juan de
Ybar, año, 1651."
Palau, 244335.
Reel 147, No. 950

QUEVEDO Y VILLEGAS, FRANCISCO GOMEZ DE, 1580-1645.
[La Hora] Fortune In Her Wits, Or, The Hour of all
Men. Written In Spanish by the most Ingenious Don
Francisco de Quivedo (sic) Villegas, Author of the
Visions of Hell. Translated into English By Capt.
John Stevens. London: Printed for R. Sare at Gray's -
Inn Gate, F. Saunders in the New - Exchange, and Tho.
Bennet, in St. Paul's Church-Yard, 1697.
[17], 131 p.; 19cm.

English translation by Capt. John Stevens.
Allison, p. 152, no. 5; Graesse, p. 524; Palau,
244357; Wing, W. 188.
Reel 147, No. 951

QUEVEDO Y VILLEGAS, FRANCISCO GOMEZ DE, 1580-1645.
Ivgvetes De La Niñez, y trauessuras de el Ingenio.
De Don Francisco de Queuedo Villegas, Cauallero de la
Orden de Santiago. Corregidas De Los Descvidos de
los trasladadores, y añadidas muchas cosas que

QUEVEDO Y VILLEGAS (Cont'd)
faltauan, conforme a sus originales, despues del nueuo
Catalogo. Sevilla: Por Andres Grande, 1634.
[8], 168, [1] l.; 16cm.

Escudero, no. 1485; Jerez, p. 86; Palau, 244284;
Penney, p. 446.
Reel 147, No. 956

QUEVEDO Y VILLEGAS, FRANCISCO GOMEZ DE, 1580-1645.
Ivgvetes De La Niñez, Y Travessvras de el Ingenio.
De Don Francisco De Queuedo Villegas, Cauallero de la
Orden de Santiago. Corregidas De Los Descvidos De
los trasladadores y añadidas muchas cosas que
faltauan, conforme à sus originales, despues del
nueuo Catalogo. Barcelona: por Pedro Lacavalleria,
1635.
[8], 140 l.; 16cm.

Bound with the author's: Politica De Dios, Govierno
De Christo, Tirania De Satanas ... 1629.
Boix, 291; Graesse, p. 523; Jerez, p. 86; Palau,
244285; Penney, p. 446 (Politica...: Palau, 243817;
Crosby, Sources, p. 108-09.
Reel 148, No. 957

QUEVEDO Y VILLEGAS, FRANCISCO GOMEZ DE, 1580-1645.
Obras De Don Francisco De Quevedo Villegas,
Cavallero de la Orden de Santiago, Señor de la Villa
de la Torre de Juan-Abad. Dedicadas A su Excellencia
el Marques de Caracena &c. Governador, y Capitan
general de los Payses Baxos, y Borgoña. Brusselas,
Por Francisco Foppens, 1660.
3v.([6], 692, [1] p.; [5], 584 p.; [5], 492,
[19] p.); 22cm.

Imperfect; p. 424-582 (i.e. 426-584). pagination
errors.
Vol. III has special t.-p.: Poësia De Don Francisco
De Quevedo Villegas, Cavallero de la Orden de Santiago,
Señor de la Villa de la Torre de Juan-Abad. Dedicadas
Al Excelent[mo] Señor Don Luis De Benavides, Carillo, Y
Toledo, &c. Marques De Caracena, &c. Governador Y
Capitan General De Los Payses Baxos, &c.
Vols. II and III have imprint date 1661.
Bound with this is his: Epicteto, Y Phocilides.
93 p.
Heredia, no. 6399; La Serna, II, no. 3480; Palau,
243574; Peeters-Fontainas, II, 1088; Vindel, no. 2338.
Reel 148, No. 959

QUEVEDO Y VILLEGAS, FRANCISCO GOMEZ DE, 1580-1645.
Obras De Don Francisco De Quevedo Villegas,
Cauallero de la Orden de Santiago, Señor de la Villa
de la Torre de Juan-Abad. Dedicadas Al Excellentissimo
Señor Don Luis De Benavides, Carillo, y Toledo &c. ...
Segunda Parte. Brusselas: De la Emprenta de
Francisco Foppens, 1670.
2v.([4], 582 p.; [5], 488 p.); 23cm.

Vol. III has separate title-page: Poësias De Don
Francisco De Quevedo Villegas... Tercera Parte ...
Bound with the author's: Las Tres Ultimàs Musas
Castellanas De Don Francisco De Quevedo Villegas,
Cauallero de la Orden de Santiago...1671.
And with his: Epicteto y Phocilides.
A reprint of the 1661 edition. Some editions have
a different title-page, printer's device and pre-
liminary foliation.
H C: NS4/167; Palau, 243575; Peeters-Fontainas,
II, no. 1089; Ticknor, p. 292.
Vol. l unavailable.
Reel 148, No. 961

QUEVEDO Y VILLEGAS, FRANCISCO GOMEZ DE, 1580-1645.
Obras De Don Francisco De Quevedo Villegas,
Cavallero de la Orden de Santiago, Señor de la Villa
de la Torre de Juan-Abad. Divididas En Tres Tomos.
Nueva Impression corregida y ilustrada con muchas
Estampas muy donosas y apropriadas à la materia.
Amberes: Por Henrico Y Cornelio Verdussen, 1699.
3v.([12], 542, [2] p.; [6], 472 p.; [6], 592,
[14] p.); 23cm.

Engraved title-page, plates, ports. Title preceded
by a frontis, as the 1660 edition, except the
printer's address: En Amberes Por Henrico Y Cornelio
Verdvssen Mercaderes De Libros. Año M.D. CX.CIX
(1699).
Vols. II and III have separate title pages.
This edition does not contain Las tres ultimas Musas.
HC:NS4/164; Palau, 243580; Penney, p. 446; Peeters-
Fontainas, II, no. 1090.
Reel 149, No. 964

QUEVEDO Y VILLEGAS, FRANCISCO GOMEZ DE, 1580-1645.
[Obras De Don Francisco De Quevedo Villegas. French.]
Les Oevvres De Dom Francisco de Quevedo, chevalier
Espagnol ... Traduction nouuelle. Paris: Chez
Iacqves Le Gras, 1664.
2v. (335, [12] p.; [2], 416 p.); 16cm.

Plagiarism of La Geneste's translation, which was
first published in Rouen in 1645.
Vol. I lacks title-page.
Vol. II has separate title-page: Les Oevvres De
Qvevedo Traduction nouuelle. Tome Seconde.
Palau, 243706; Foulché-Delbosc, V, no. 1616.
Reel 149, No. 965

QUEVEDO Y VILLEGAS, FRANCISCO GOMEZ DE, 1580-1645.
[Obras De Don Francisco De Quevedo Villegas. French.]
Les Oeuvres De Don Francisco De Quevedo Villegas,
Chevalier Espagnol. Premiere Partie Contenante le
Coureur de Nuit ou l'Avanturier Nocturne, l'Avanturier
Buscon, & les Lettres du Chevalier de l'Epargne.
Nouvelle Traduction de l'Espagnol en François par le
Sr. Raclots Parisien, &c. enrichie de Figures en taille
douce. Brusselles: Chez Josse De Grieck, 1699.
2v. ([3], 528, [13] p.; [3], 420 p.); 16cm.

La Geneste's translation.
Vol. II has separate half-title and title-page.
Les Oeuvres De Don Francisco de Quevedo Villegas.
Chevalier Espagnol. Seconde Partie. Contenante les
sept Visions: de l'Algouazil Demoniaque, de la Mort,
du Jugement Final, des Foux Amoureux, du Monde en
son Interieur, de l'Enfer, & de l'Enfer Reformé.
Nouvelle Traduction de l'Espagnol en François par le
Sr. Raclots Parisien, & enrichie de Figures en taille
douce.
Palau, 243713.
Reel 149, No. 966

QUEVEDO Y VILLEGAS, FRANCISCO GOMEZ DE, 1580-1645.
Parte Primera De Las Obras En Prosa De Don Francisco
De Qvevedo Villegas, Cavallero de la Orden de Santiago,
señor de la Torre de Iuan Abad. Dedicadas A Don
Alonso Carnero, Cauallero de el Orden de Santiago,
Señor de la Villa de Chapineria, Regidor perpetuo
de la Ciudad de Avila, de el Consejo de su Magestad,
y su Secretario de Estado, &c. Corregida, Y Enmendada
En Esta vltima impression. Madrid: Por Antonio
Gonçalez de Reyes, 1687.
[8], 608 p.; 21cm.

Palau, 243579.
Reel 150, No. 967

QUEVEDO Y VILLEGAS, FRANCISCO GOMEZ DE, 1580-1645.
El Parnasso Español, Monte En Dos Cvmbres Dividido
Con Las Nveve Mvsas Castellanas. Donde Se Contienen
Poesias de D. Francisco de Quevedo Villegas, Cauallero
de la Orden de Santiago, y señor de la Villa de la
Torre de Iuan Abad. Al Señor Salvador Correa De
Saa, y Benauides, Gouernador, y Capitan General de
los Reynos de Angola, del Consejo de Guerra de S.
Magest. &c. Ilvstradas Por Don Ioseph Antonio
Gonzalez de Salas, Cauallero de la Orden de Calatraua,
y señor de la antigua casa de los Gonzalez de Vadiella.
Lisboa: En la Imprenta de Pablo Craesbeck, 1652.
[12], 500, [15] p.; 21cm.

Graesse, p. 523; Jerez p. 85; Palau, 244332;
Penney, p. 446.
Reel 150, No. 968

QUEVEDO Y VILLEGAS, FRANCISCO GOMEZ DE, 1580-1645.
El Parnaso Español, Y Mvsas Castellanas, de Don
Francisco de Queuedo Villegas, Caballero de la Orden
de Santiago, Señor de la Villa de la Torre de Iuan
Abad. Corregidas, I Enmendades de nuevo en esta
impression, por el Doctor Amuso Cultifragio, Academico
ocioso de Lobaina. Madrid: Por Melchor Sanchez, 1668.
[8], 502, [17] p.; 21cm.

Jerez, p. 85; Palau, 244334; Penney, p. 446;
Salvá, I, 1366.
Reel 150, No. 969

QUEVEDO Y VILLEGAS, FRANCISCO GOMEZ DE, 1580-1645.
El Perro. Y La Calentvra. [s.l.:s.n., 16--?]
35 p.

Caption title only.
Bound in the author's: Historia De La Vida Del
Buscon..., 1629.
Reel 147, No. 954

QUEVEDO Y VILLEGAS, FRANCISCO GOMEZ DE, 1580-1645.
Politica De Dios. Govierno De Christo: Tyranie De
Satanas. Escriuelo con las plumas de los
Euangelistas, Don Francisco de Queuedo Villegas,
Cauallero del Orden de Santiago, y señor de la Villa
de Iuan Abad. Al Conde Duque, gran Canciller, mi
señor, Don Gaspar de Guzman, Conde de Oliuares,
Sumilier de Corps, y Cauallerizo mayor de su Magestad.
Zaragoça: Por Pedro Verges, 1626.
[10], 81, [1] l.; 15cm.

Second edition. Ex-libris: Liechtensteinianis.
Colophon: "Con licencia, en Çaragoça: Por Pedro
Verges. Año 1626."
Errors in foliation: 26 (i.e. 20), 51 (i.e. 50);
53 (i.e. 52), 69 (i.e. 6), 74 (i.e. 7), 81 (i.e. 8).
Crosby, Sources, p. 99-100; Jiménez Catalán,
p. 153-54.
Reel 150, No. 970

QUEVEDO Y VILLEGAS, FRANCISCO GOMEZ DE, 1580-1645.
Politica De Dios, Govierno De Christo, Tirania De
Satanas. Escriuelo con las plumas de los
Evangelistas, don Francisco de Quevedo Villegas,
Cauallero del Orden de Santiago, y señor de la villa
de Iuan Abad. Al Conde Duque, gran Canciller, mi señor,
don Gaspar de Guzman, Conde de Oliuares, Sumilier de
Corps, y Cauallerizo mayor de su Magestad.
Barcelona: Por Pedro Lacavalleria, 1629.
[9], 64, [3] l.; 16cm.

Bound with the author's: Ivgvetes De La Niñez..,
1635.
Palau, 243817; Crosby, Sources, pp. 108-109.
Reel 148, No. 958

QUEVEDO Y VILLEGAS, FRANCISCO GOMEZ DE, 1580-1645.
Politica De Dios, Govierno De Christo. Avtor Don
Francisco De Queuedo Villegas Cauallero del Orden de
Santiago, señor de la villa de la Torre de Iuan Abad.
A Don Gaspar De Gvzman Conde Duque, gran Canciller mi
señor. Lleva Añadidos Tres Capitulos que le faltauan,
y algunas planas, y renglones, y va restituido a
la verdad de su original. Paulo I. Cor. 3.
Vnusquisque autem videat quomodo super aedificet
fundamentum enim aliud nemo potest ponere praeter id
quod positum est, quod est Christvs Iesvs. Ioan. cap.
13. Exemplum enim dedi vobis, vt quē admodū, ego feci
vobis, ita & vos faciatis. Lisboa: Por Mathias
Rodrigues, 1630.
[13], 90, [2] l.; 16cm.

Folio 90ᵛ "A quien lee," signed by the author.
Errors in foliation: 3 (i.e. 4), 14 (i.e. 15),
16 (i.e. 61), 42 (i.e. 24), 44-88 (i.e. 46-90),
80 (i.e. 79), 81 (i.e. 80), 82 (i.e. 81).
Crosby, Sources, p. 109-110; Palau, 243819.
Reel 150, No. 971

QUEVEDO Y VILLEGAS, FRANCISCO GOMEZ DE, 1580-1645.
Politica De Dios, Govierno de Christo: Tirania de
Satanas. Escriuelo con las plumas de los Euangelistas,
Don Francisco de Queuedo Villegas, Cauallero del Orden
de Santiago, y señor de la Villa de Ioan (sic) Abad.
Al Conde Duque, gran Canciller, mi señor, Don Gaspar
de Guzman, Conde de Oliuares, Sumilier de Corps, y
Cauallerizo mayor de su Magestad. Añadidos a este
Tratado. I. La Historia del Buscon. 2. Los
sueños. 3. Discurso de todos los dañados, y malos.
4. Cuento de Cuentos. Pamplona: Por Carlos de
Labàyen, 1631.
[14], 397, [5] l.; 15cm.

Includes: A) Historia De La Vida Del Bvscon
Llamado Don Pablos; Exemplo de Vagamundos, y espejo
de Tacaños. Por Don Francisco de Queuedo Villegas,
Cauallero del Orden de Santiago, y señor de la Villa
de Iuan Abad. A Don Fray Iuan Augustin de Funes,
Cauallero de la Sagrada Religion de San Iuan Bautista
de Ierusalem, en la Castellania de Amposta, del Reyno
de Aragon.
B) Sveños, Y Discvrsos De Verdades Descvbridoras
De Abvsos, Vicios, y Engaños, en todos los Oficios,
y Estados del Mundo. Por Don Francisco de Queuedo
Villegas Cauallero del Orden de Santiago y Señor de
Iuan Abad. Corregidos y emendados en esta impression,
y añadida la casa de los Locos de Amor.
C) El Peor Scondriio De La Mverte. Discvrso De
Todos Los dañados y malos. Para Qve Vnos No Lo sean,
y otros lo dexen de ser. Avtor Don Francisco de
Queuedo Villegas, Cauallero del Orden de Santiago, y
señor de la Villa de Iuan Abad.
Crosby, Sources, p. 110-111; Doublet, p. 108;
Palau, 243820; Pérez-Goyena, I, p. 263; Salvá, 1951.
Reel 150, No. 972

QUEVEDO Y VILLEGAS, FRANCISCO GOMEZ DE, 1580-1645.
Politica De Dios, I Govierno De Xpō, Sacada De La
Sagrada Escritura Para Acierto De Rey I Reino En
Svs Acciones: Por Don Francisco De Quevedo Villegas,
Cauallero de la Orden de Santiago, Senor de la Torre
de Ioan Abad. Madrid: (s.n.), 1655.
[41], 362 p.; 20cm.

Half-title: Politica De Dios, Y Govierno De Christo
Nvestro Señor.
Errors in pagination: 168, 169 (i.e. 169, 170),
278 (i.e. 277).
Crosby, Sources, p. 117-118; Palau, 243823.
Reel 150, No. 973

QUEVEDO Y VILLEGAS, FRANCISCO GOMEZ DE, 1580-1645.
Politica De Dios, Y Govierno De Christo, Sacada De
La Sagrada Escritvra Para acierto de Rey, y Reyno en
sus acciones. Al Señor Don Sancho De Villegas
Velasco de la Vega y Zeualllos, Señor, y Pariente
mayor de la Casa, y Linage de Villegas, del Consejo de
su Magestad, y Alcalde de su Casa, y Corte, &c. Por
D. Francisco De Qvevedo Villegas Cauallero de la
Orden de Santiago, Señor de la Torre de Iuan Abad.
Madrid: En La Imprenta Real, 1666.
[48], 347, [5] p.; 20cm.

Half-Title: Politica De Dios. Y Govierno De
Christo Nvestro Señor.
Errors in foliation and pagination: 1. 20 (i.e.
24), p. 29 (i.e. 26), 31 (i.e. 13), 79 (i.e. 76),
107 (i.e. 113), 187 (i.e. 18), 191 (i.e. 161).
Numerous other errors in pagination.
Crosby, Política, p. 560; Palau, 243825.
Reel 150, No. 974

QUEVEDO Y VILLEGAS, FRANCISCO GOMEZ DE, 1580-1645.
Primera Parte De La Vida De Marco Brvto. Escriuiola
por el Texto de Plutarco, ponderada con discursos,
Don Francisco De Qvevedo Villegas, Cauallero de la
Orden de Santiago, señor de la Villa de la Torre de
Iuan Abad. Dedicada Al Exelentᵐᵒ Señor Duque del
Infantado. Segvnda Impression. Madrid: Por Diego
Diaz De La Carrera, 1645.
[16], 128, [1] l.; 17cm.

Half title: Marco Bruto Escrivele por el Texto
de Plvtarco D. Fr.ᶜᵒ de Queuedo. Villegas Cau. ᵒ del
Abito de Santiago, y S.ᵒʳ de la Torre de Joan Abad.
Palau, 244314; Penney, p. 447; Sancha, p. 108.
Reel 152, No. 989

QUEVEDO Y VILLEGAS, FRANCISCO GOMEZ DE, 1580-1645.
Providencia De Dios, Padecida De Los Qve La Niegan,
Y Gozada De Los Qve La Confiessan. Doctrina
Estudiada En Los Gvsanos, y Persecvciones De Job.
Obra Postvma De Don Francisco De Qvevedo Villegas,
Cavallero del Orden de San-Tiago, Señor de la Villa
de la Torre de Iuan Abad. Dedicada Al Mvy Ilvstre
Señor Don Jvan Lvis Lopez, del Consejo de su Magestad,
y su Regente en el Sacro, y Supremo de los Reynos de
la Corona de Aragon. Zaragoça: Por Pasqval Bveno,
1700.
[12], 75 p.; 21cm.

Palau, 244361.
Reel 151, No. 975

QUEVEDO Y VILLEGAS, FRANCISCO GOMEZ, DE, 1580-1645.
Sveños, Y Discvrsos De Verdades Descvbridoras De
Abvsos, Vicios, y Engaños, en todos los Oficios, y
Estados del Mundo. Por Don Francisco de Queuedo
Villegas, Cauallero del Orden de Santiago, y Señor de
Iuan Abad. Corregidos y emendados en esta impression,
y añadida la casa de los Locos de Amor. Valencia: Por
Iuan Bautista Marçal, 1628.
[8], 124, [1] p.; 16cm.

Palau, 244036.
Reel 151, No. 976

QUEVEDO Y VILLEGAS, FRANCISCO GOMEZ DE, 1580-1645.
Sveños y Discursos De Verdades, Descvbridoras De
Abusos, Vicios, y Engaños, en todos los Officios, y
Estados del Mundo. Por Don Francisco de Quevedo
Villegas, Cauallero de la Orden de Santiago, y Señor
de Iuan Abad. Corregidos y enmendados en esta vltima
Impression Rvan: A costa de Carlos Osmoni, 1629.
[4], 196 p.

Bound in the author's: Historia De La Vida Del
Buscon..., 1629.
Reel 147, No. 953

QUEVEDO Y VILLEGAS, FRANCISCO GOMEZ DE, 1580-1645.
Sueños Y Discvrsos O Desvelos Soñolientos De
verdades soñadas descubridoras de Abusos, Vicios, y
engaños en todos los Oficios, y Estados del Mundo.
Por D. Francisco de Quevedo Villegas, Cavallero del
Orden de Santiago, Señor de la Villa de Juan Abad.
Perpiñan: en Casa de Cornelli Reynier, 1679.
[2], 235 p.; 16cm.

Graesse, p. 524; Palau, 244050.
Reel 151, No. 977

QUEVEDO Y VILLEGAS, FRANCISCO GOMEZ DE, 1580-1645.
[Sveños Y Discvrsos. English]
The Visions Of Dom Francisco de Quevedo Villegas,
Knight of the Order of St. James. Made English by
R. L. London: Printed for H. Herringman, 1667.
[7], 344 p.; 17cm.

English translation by Roger L'Estrange.
Allison, p. 153; Knapp-Huntington, p. 271; Palau,
244176; Penney, p. 447; Pepys, vol. 3, p. 145; Wing
Q. 196.
Reel 151, No. 980

QUEVEDO Y VILLEGAS, FRANCISCO GOMEZ DE, 1580-1645.
[Sveños Y Discvrsos. English]
The Visions Of Dom Francisco de Quevedo Villegas,
Knight of the Order Of St. James. Made English by
R. L. The Third Edition Corrected. London: Printed
for H. Herringman, 1668.
[7], 344 p.; 17cm.

English translation by Roger L'Estrange.
Allison, p. 153, no. 7.2; Wing Q. 197.
Reel 151, No. 981

QUEVEDO Y VILLEGAS, FRANCISCO GOMEZ DE, 1580-1645.
[Sveños Y Discvrsos. English]
The Visions Of Dom Francisco De Quevedo Villegas,
Knight of the Order Of St. James. Written Originally
in Spanish, now made English by J. Dodington, Esquire,
The True Edition. Licensed according to Order.
London: for John Playfere, 1668.
[5], 225 p.; 17cm.

English translation by J. Dodington, Esq.
Allison, p. 153, no. 7.1; Wing Q.196b.
Reel 151, No. 982

QUEVEDO Y VILLEGAS, FRANCISCO GOMEZ DE, 1580-1645.
[Sveños Y Discvrsos. English]
The Visions Of Dom Francisco de Quevedo Villegas,
Knight of the Order Of St. James. Made English by
R. L. The Sixth Edition Corrected. London: Printed
for H. Herringman, 1678.
[7], 344 p.; 17cm.

English translation by Sir Roger L'Estrange.
Allison, p. 153, no. 7.5; Palau, 244180; Wing Q. 200.
Reel 151, No. 983

QUEVEDO Y VILLEGAS, FRANCISCO GOMEZ, DE. 1580-1645.
[Sveños Y Discvrsos. English]
The Visions Of Dom Francisco De Quevedo Vellegas
(sic): The Second Part Containing many Strange And
Wonderful Remarques. Being Divided into several Parts,
or Visions: Very Pleasant and Profitable for all
Considerate Persons. London: Printed by T. Haly,
1682.
[5], 288 p.; 17cm.

English translation by Sir Roger L'Estrange.
Error in pagination: 287 (i.e. 257).
Allison, p. 153, no. 7.6; Palau, 244181; Wing
Q. 200a.
Reel 151, No. 984

QUEVEDO Y VILLEGAS, FRANCISCO GOMEZ DE, 1580-1645.
[Sveños Y Discvrsos. English]
The Visions Of Dom Francisco de Quevedo Villegas,
Knight of the Order Of St. James. Made English by
Sir Roger L'Estrange. The Eighth Edition Corrected.
London: Printed for Richard Sare, 1696.
[8], 344 p.; 19cm.

English translation by Sir Roger L'Estrange.
Allison, p. 153, no. 7.8; Knapp-Huntington, p. 271;
Palau, 244184; Penney, p. 447; Wing Q. 202.
Reel 151, No. 985

QUEVEDO Y VILLEGAS, FRANCISCO GOMEZ DE, 1580-1645.
[Sveños Y Discvrsos. French]
Les Visions De Don Francisco De Queuedo Villegas,
Cheualier de l'Ordre S. Iacques, & Seigneur de Iuan-
Abad. Traduites d'Espagnol. Par le Sieur De La
Geneste. Paris: Chez Pierre Billaine, 1633.
[8], 462 p.; 17cm.

French translation by Sieur de la Geneste.
Pagination errors throughout.
Foulché-Delbosc, V, no. 1254; Palau, 244095.
Reel 151, No. 978

QUEVEDO Y VILLEGAS, FRANCISCO GOMEZ DE, 1580-1645.
[Sveños Y Discvrsos. French]
Les Visions De Dom Francisco De Qvevedo Villegas
Cheualier de l'Ordre S. Iacques, & Seigneur de Iuan-
Abad. Traduites d'Espagnol. Par le Sieur De La
Geneste. Paris: Chez Pierre Billaine, 1634.
[17], 461, [1]; 17cm.

French translation by Sieur de la Geneste.
Pagination errors throughout.
Foulché-Delbosc, V, no. 1264.
Reel 151, No. 979

QUEVEDO Y VILLEGAS, FRANCISCO GOMEZ DE, 1580-1645.
[Sveños Y Discvrsos. Italian]
Estratto De' Sogni Di D. Francesco Qvevedo.
Trasportati dal Francese per Innocentio Maranaviti.
Dedicato Al Sig. Givseppe Ganassa. Sign. mio
Collendiss. Venetia: Per Gasparo Coradici, 1670.
[4], 140 p.; 18cm.

Italian translation by Innocenzo Maranaviti.
Reel 151, No. 986

QUEVEDO Y VILLEGAS, FRANCISCO GOMEZ DE, 1580-1645.
La Tres Ultimas Musas Castellanas De Don Francisco De Quevedo Villegas, Cavallero de la Orden de Santiago, Señor de la Villa de la Torre de Juan-Abad. Sacadas de la Libreria de Don Pedro Aldrete Quevedo y Villegas, Colegial del Mayor del Arcobispo de la Universidad de Salamanca, Señor de la Villa de la Torre de Juan-Abad. [s.l.:s.n.], 1671.
[12], 200, [5] p.; 23cm.

Bound in the author's: Obras..., 1670.
Reel 149, No. 962

QUEVEDO Y VILLEGAS, FRANCISCO GOMEZ DE, 1580-1645.
Las Tres Ultimas Musas Castellanas De Don Francisco De Quevedo Villegas, Cavallero de la Orden de Santiago, Señor de la Villa de la Torre de Juan-Abad. Sacadas de la Libreria de Don Pedro Aldrete Quevedo y Villegas, Colegial del Mayor del Arcobispo de la Universidad de Salamanca, Señor de la Villa de la Torre de Juan-Abad. (s.l.:s.n.), 1671.
[6], 200, [4] p.; 24cm.

Bound with his: Epicteto, Y Phocilides En Español Con Consonantes. Con el Origen de los Estoicos, y su defensa contra Plutarco, y la defensa de Epicuro, contra la comun opinion.
Palau, 244336.
Reel 152, No. 987

QUEVEDO Y VILLEGAS, FRANCISCO GOMEZ DE, 1580-1645
[Opere. Spanish translation by Francisco Gómez de Quevedo Villegas] see MALVESSI, VIRGILIO, marchese, 1599-1654.

QUINTANA, FRANCISCO DE, fl. 1626.
Oracion Panegirica; O Sermon Fvnebre. Honores Extremos del Doctor Iuan Perez de Montalban. Cvidado Afectvoso de su intimo Amigo, el Doctor Francisco de Quintana, Rector del Hospital de la Concepcion, vulgarmente la Latina. [n.p.-n.d.]
14 l.; 20cm.

Title page and introduction wanting.
Bound with: GRANDE DE TENA, PEDRO: Lagrimas Panegiricas A La Tenprana Mverte Del Gran Poeta, I Teologo Insigne Doctor Iuan Perez de Montalban, ... En Madrid: En la Imprenta del Reino, 1639.
Gallardo, no. 2404; Goldsmith, p. 78, no. 339; Penney, p. 242; Salvá, I, 257; Ticknor, p. 162.
Reel 68, No. 411

QUINTANADUEÑAS, ANTONIO DE see FELIPE IV, King of Spain, 1605-1665.

QUINTERO, JACINTO, fl. 1639.
Discvrsos Evangelicos De Qvaresma. Para Svs Tres Principales Dias, Domingos, Miercoles, y Viernes. Predicolos El P. Iacinto Qvintero de los Clerigos Reglares Menores. Antes Lector de Teologia en su Colegio de san Carlos de la Vniuersidad de Salamanca. Aora Assistente Prouincial de la Prouincia de España. 71. Segunda Impression. Madrid: Por Pablo De Val, 1653.
[13], 526, [30] p.; 21cm.

Imperfect: p. 469-476, 481-484, and 493-496 wanting.
Error in paging: p. 256 incorrectly numbered 536.
Reel 152, No. 990

QUIROS, FRANCISCO BERNARDO DE, see BERNARDO DE QUIROS, FRANCISCO.

R

RADES Y ANDRADA, FRANCISCO DE, 16th cent, (fl. 1572).
Chronica De Las tres Ordenes y Cauallerias de
Sanctiago, Calatraua y Alcantara: en la qual se trata
de su origen y successo, y notables hechos en armas
de los Maestres y Caualleros de ellas: y de muchos
Señores de Titulo y otros Nobles que descienden de los
Maestres: y de muchos otros Linages de España.
Compuesta por el Licenciado Frey Francisco de Rades
y Andrada Capellan de su Magestad, de la Orden de
Calatraua. Toledo: en casa de Iuan de Ayala, 1572.
3 pts. in 1 ([12], 73 *l.*; 85 *l.*; 55 *l.*); 30cm.

Engraved title-page.
Cosens, no. 3613; Palau, 246034; Penney, p. 449;
Pérez Pastor, Toledo, no. 332; Salvá, II, 1664.
Reel 152, No. 991

RAJAS, PABLO ALBINIANO DE, 1584-1667.
In Obitv Philippi Tertii Hispaniarvm Regis Catholici
Ad Caesaravgvstanos Oratio. Dixit Pavlvs Albinianvs
De Rajas Societatis Iesv Theologus. Ad Clarissimvm
Virvm D. Mart. Babtistam De Lanvza Ivstitiae In
Aragonia Svmmvm Praesidem. Caesaraugustae, Apud
Ioannem à Lanaja & Quartanet Anno 1621.
[2], 32 p.; 21cm.

Bound in the author's: Lagrimas De Caragoea En La
Mverte De Filipo..., 1621.
Jerez, p. 87; Jiménez Catalán, no. 207; Palau,
246433-II; Penney, p. 450; Salvá, I, no. 337; Simón
Díaz, Jesuitas, no. 1397.
Reel 152, No. 993

RAJAS, PABLO ALBINIANO DE, 1584-1667.
Lagrimas De Caragoca En La Mverte De Filipo. Rey
II. De Aragon Deste Apellido. Y Exeqvias. Que, con
aparato Real à su memoria celebrò Recogiolas El P.
Paulo de Rajas de la Compañia De Iesvs Mandandolo a
la misma Ciudad[Albinianus incidebat] Caragoca: Por
Juan de Lenaja, y Quartanet, 1621.
[11], 261 p.; 21cm.

Engraved title-page.
Bound with his: In Obitv Philippi Tertii
Hispaniarvm Regis Catholici Ad Caesaravgvstanos Oratio.
Dixit Pavlvs Albinianvs De Rajas Societatis Iesv
Theologus. Ad Clarissimvm Virvm D. Mart. Babtistam
De Lanvza Ivstitiae..., 1621.
Jerez, p. 87; Jiménez Catalán, no. 207; Palau,
246433-II; Penney, p. 450; Salvá, I, no. 337; Simón
Díaz, Jesuitas, no. 1397.
Reel 152, No. 992

REFLEXIÓN al voto del Marqués de Fresno sobre la
sucesión a estos reinos de la Francia.
25 manuscript *l.*

Bound with: HERRERA Y SOTOMAYOR, JACINTO DE, fl.
1644. Iornada que su Magestad hizo a la Andalvzia.
[Madrid: En la Imprenta Real, 1624].
Palau, 114276 (List only printed folios 1-6).
Reel 77, No. 484.15

REGOLE Bellissime D'Amore In Modo Di Dialogo Di M.
Giovanni Boccaccio. Interlocvtori. Il Signor
Alcibiade, & Filaterio giouane. Tradotte Di Latino
in volgare, da M. Angelo Ambrosini. Opera Degna,
E Bella. Doue s'insegna che cosa sia amore. Qual
siano i nobili effetti, & saporiti frutti di quello.
Qual siano le persone che non sono buone all'amore.
In che modo s'aquisti. Come s'accresca. Come si
possi mantenere. Come mancha (sic). Con altre
bellissime regole d'amore. Cvm Gratia, E Privilegio.
[n.p., n.d.]
31 *l.*; 16cm.

Reel 54, No. 316

RELACIÓN del temblor, y terromoto qve Dios Nuestro Señor
fue seruido de embair à la Ciudad del Cuzco à 31.
de Março este año passado de 1650. Iueues a las
dos de la tarde, con particulares misericordias
suyas, como se experimentaron en el tiempo de su
mayor ruina. Dase cuenta de las asperissimas
penitencias publicas, que las Religiones hazian
por las calles, en procesion, mouiendo à
edificacion al mas endurecido pecho. Madrid: por
Iulian de Paredes, 1651.
[4] p.; 30cm.

Colophon: Con licencia. En Madrid, por Iulian
de Paredes, impressor de libros, Año 1651. Vendese
en su casa, en la calle de la Concepcion Geronima.
Lacks title-page.
Gallardo, Ensayo, vol. I, no. 587; Medina, Bibl.
Hisp. Amer., no. 1162; Palau, 258365; Sabin, no. 18214.
Reel 152, No. 1001

RELACIÓN Svmaria Cierta, Y Verdadera, Del Processo
Actitado en la Corte del señor Iusticia de Aragon:
a instancia de la Magestad del Rey don Phelipe
nuestro señor, contra los Diputados, y Vniuersidad
del Reyno de Aragon, acerca del poder y facultad que
su Magestad tiene en el dicho Reyno de Aragon de
nombrar Lugarteniente general suyo, natural, o
estrangero: como mas de su Real seruicio sea, y le
pareciere mas conueniente para el bien publico,
vtilidad, y buen gouierno del dicho Reyno de Aragon,
&c. Caragoca: por Lorenço de Robles Impressor del
Reyno de Aragon, 1590.
[2], 132 p.; 33cm.

Pagination errors throughout.
Palau, 257246.
Reel 152, No. 994

RELACIÓN verdadera de la batalla de Kempen, entre el
exercito del Conde de Guebrian Capitan del Rey
Christianissimo, y el Exercito de Lamboy Capitan
General del Emperador, a los 17. de Enero de 1642.
Valencia: (s.n.), 1642.
[2] *l.*; 21cm.

Lacks title-page.
Reel 152, No. 997

RELACIÓN verdadera de la grande batalla, que huvo
entre Franceses y Españoles, sobre el socorro de
Perpiñan, a los 29. de Enero de 1642. Pamplona:
s.n. 1642.

Lacks title-page.
Reel 152, No. 998

RELACIÓN Verdadera De La Nveva, Y Señalada Victoria que
han tenido las Armas Imperiales, y Polacas sobre la
Ciudad, y Fortaleza de Strigonia, con la toma del
importante Fuerte de Barkam. Traducido de Italiano
en nuestro Idioma Castellano. [s.l.:s.n.),
c. 1683-1684.
[4] l.; 20cm.

Reel 152, No. 1003

RELACIÓN verdadera de las fiestas que se hizieron a
las velaciones del Rey Nuestro Señor, que Dios guarde,
en la Villa de Naualcarnero, en que se declara, y
da cuenta de los Señores que le assistieron, libreas,
y gala que sacaron, y otras diferentes cosas, que con
toda verdad se leerán en este pliego. Madrid: Por
Iuan Sanchez, 1649.
[2] l.; 30cm.

Lacks title-page.
Palau, 258355.
Reel 152, No. 1000

RELACIÓN Verdadera De Todo Lo Qve Ha Passado en Perpiñan,
el tiempo que estuuieron cercados, que fue desde
21. de Abril de 1642. hasta 9 de Setiembre de dicho
año, en el qual dia se rindio a los Mariscales de
Scomberg, y al de la Mesleraya en nombre del Rey
Christianissimo Luys XIII. nuestro Rey y señor
(que Dios guarde) y de algunas cosas particulares,
mas para causar admiracion, que para ser crehidas,
que han sucedido en dicho cerco. Escrita, y
apuntada puntualmente por vn natural de la misma
Villa de Perpiñan, que estuuo presente a todo.
Barcelona: en la Emprenta de Iayme Romeu, delante
Santiago, 1642.
[4] l.; 21cm.

Palau, 258253.
Reel 152, No. 999

RELACIÓN Verdadera, del acompañamiento y Baptismo, de
la serenissima Princesa, Margarita, Maria, Catalina.
Madrid: Por Diego Flamenco, 1623.
[2] l.; 33cm.

Lacks title-page.
Palau, 257711.
Reel 152, No. 995

RELACIÓN Verdadera Del Viage, Seqvito, Y Entrada, Qve
Hizo En Londres el Excelentissimo señor Principe de
Ligni, de Amblice, y del Sacro Imperio, Cavallero
del Insigne Orden del Tuson de Oro, Capitan General
de la Caualleria de los Estados de Flandes, Em-
baxador extraordinario al Serenissimo Carlos Segundo,
Rey de la gran Bretaña, por la Magestad del Rey
Don Felipe Quarto nuestro Señor (que Dios guarde)
para darle la norabuena de la possession de sus
Reynos, en que al presente se halla. Refiese
Assimesmo La Resolvcion que el Rey de la Gran
Bretaña tomò, de mandar hazer justicia de 28.
personas, que fueron Iuezes, y solicitaron la
muerte del Rey Carlos Primero, su padre, y otras
cosas particulares sucedidas en aquellos Reynos.
Este año de 1660. Sevilla: por Iuan Gomez de
Blas, 1660.
[4] l.; 20cm.

Montoto, no. 172; Palau, 258594.
Reel 152, No. 1002

RELACIÓN Verdadera, y puntual Del Sitio, Y Conqvista
De La Fortaleza De Brem. Que se rindiò à las
Armas de S. M. Cath: Y A Sv Capitan General El
Exc.^mo Señor Marqves De Leganes Sabado 27. de Marzo
de 1638. Milan: por Iuan Baptista Malatesta,
Empressor Regio, y Cameral, 1638.
[18] p.; 33cm.

[Archivio Cavagna Sangiuliani (Sezione seconda),
vol. 571].
Palau, 258120.
Reel 152, No. 996

REPRESENTACIÓN del infeliz estado de la Monarchia de
España y medio de que pende su repaso se trata
de que conviene elegir para la sucesión al Duque
de Anjou.
9 manuscript l.
Bound with: HERRERA Y SOTOMAYOR, JACINTO DE, fl.
1644. Iornada que su Magestad hizo a la Andalvzia.
[Madrid: En la Imprenta Real, 1624].
Palau, 114276 (List only printed folios 1-6).
Reel 77, No. 484.12

RESPUESTA Al Manifiesto De Francia. Con Licencia.
Madrid: En la Imprenta de Francisco Martinez,
Año 1635.
54 p.; 21cm.

Bound in: CÉSPEDES Y MENESES, Gonzalo de: Francia
Engañada. Francia Respondida ... Empresso en Caller,
Año 1635.
Pages lacking [?] at beginning of text.
Simón Díaz, VIII, 4004.
Reel 41, No. 219

RESPUESTA De Vn Vassallo De Sv Magestad, De los
Estados de Flandes, a los manifiestos del Rey
de Francia. Tradvcida De Frances. Por don Martin
Goblet, natural de Madrid. Con Licencia. Por los
herederos de la viuda de Pedro de Madrigal, Año
1635. A costa de Pedro Coello mercader de libros.
Pp. 53-63.; 21cm.

Continues pagination of previously bound work.
Bound in: CÉSPEDES Y MENESES, Gonzalo de: Francia
Engañada. Francia Respondida ... Empresso en Caller,
Año 1635.
Palau, 262681; Simón Díaz, VIII, 4004.
Reel 41, No. 223

RESPUESTA que en gentilhombre español retirado de
la Corte a un Ministro del Consejo de Estado sobre
la sucesión de la Monarchía de España traducida
de la lengua portuguesa en que se hace presente
las conveniencias y razones que hay para elegir
al Rey de Portugal.
20 manuscript l.
Bound with: HERRERA Y SOTOMAYOR, JACINTO DE, fl.
1644. Iornada que su Magestad hizo a la Andalvzia.
[Madrid: En la Imprenta Real, 1624].
Palau, 114276 (List only printed folios 1-6).
Reel 77, No. 484.10

REVOCACIÓN que el Rey N. S. D. Carlos II que esta
gloria hizo el 2 de Octubre de 1700 al Decreto
que dio al Conde de Oropesa el 8 de Septiembre
de 1638.
4 manuscript l.
Bound with: HERRERA Y SOTOMAYOR, JACINTO DE, fl.
1644. Iornada que su Magestad hizo a la Andalvzia.
[Madrid: En la Imprenta Real, 1624].
Palau, 114276 (List only printed folios 1-6).
Reel 77, No. 484.16

RIBERA, FRANCISCO DE, S.J. 1537-1591.
Francisci Riberae Villa - Castinensis, Presbyteri Societatis Iesv. Doctorisque Theologi. In sacram Beati Ioannis Apostoli, & Euangelistae Apocalypsin Commentarij. Cum quinque Indicibus, quorum Primus continet quaestiones Scripturae, Secundus regulas, qui sunt in limine operis, Tertius eiusdem Scripturae locos explicatos, Quartus rerum, atque verborum, Quintus Euangeliorum totius anni in vsum Concionatorum. His Adivncti Svnt, Quinque libri de Templo, & de iis quae ad Templum pertinent. Ad multorum locorum, tam Apocalypsis, quàm reliquorum librorum intelligentiam cum primis vtiles. Lvgdvni: Ex Officina Ivntarvm, 1593.
[17], 447, [40] p.; 23cm.

Bound with his: Francisci Riberae Villa-Castinensis, Presbyteri Societatis Iesv. Doctorisque Theologi. De Templo, & de iis quae ad Templum pertinent, libri quinque. Ad Sacrae scripturae intelligentiam ita necessarij, vt vix in ea paginam integram legas, in qua tibi vsui non sint.
Adams, II, no. 478; Simón Díaz, Jesuitas, no. 1428.
Reel 152, No. 1004

RIBERA, FRANCISCO DE, S.J. 1537-1591.
Francisci Riberae Villa-Castinensis, Presbyteri Societatis Iesv. Doctorisque Theologi. De Templo, & de iis quae ad Templum pertinent, libri quinque. Ad Sacrae scripturae intelligentiam ita necessarij, vt vix in ea paginam integram legas, in qua tibi vsui non sint. Cum quinque copiosis Indicibus: Primus est capitum singulorum librorum, secundus quaestionum Scripturae, qui ante primum librum sunt, Tertius locorum, Quartus rerum, atque verborum, Quintus Euangeliorum totius anni in vsum Concionatorum. Lvgdvni: Ex Officina Ivntarvm, 1593.
[9], 320, [43] p.; 23cm.

Latin text in italics; commentary in roman type. Dedicatory epistle of Jean Baptiste Regnauld, editor.
In manuscript on title-page: Michaelis Pauli, & Fratū Mon. Ben.
Bound in the author's: Francisci Riberae Villa-Castinensis,...
Reel 152, No. 1005

RIBERA, FRANCISCO DE, 1537-1591.
[Vida de Santa Teresa. Italian.]
La Vita Della B. Madre Teresa Di Giesv, Fondatrice De Gli Scalzi Carmelitani. Composta dal Reuerendo Padre Francesco Riuiera della Compagnia di Giesv, e Trasportata dalla Spagnuolanella lingua Italiana dal Signor Cosimo Gaci, Canonico di San Lorenzo in Damaso. Venetia: Ad instanza di Giulio Burchioni, 1603.
[25], 334 p.; 21cm.

Italian translation by Cosimo Gaci.
Palau, 266841.
Reel 153, No. 1006

RIFER DE BROCALDINO, SANEDRIO.
El Porqve De Todas Las Cosas. Le Escrive El Doctor Sanedrio Rifer de Brocaldino. Y Le Consagra Al Tesorero Don Diego Lopez de la Flor, Regidor de Alcalà de Henares. Madrid: Por Andres Garcia de la Iglesia, 1668.
[8], 85 l.; 15cm.

Pagination errors throughout.
Palau, 267951.
Reel 153, No. 1007

RIO, MARTIN ANTONIO DEL, S.J. see DEL RIO, MARTIN ANTOINE.

RIPOLL, JUAN.
Dialogo De Consvelo Por La Expvlsion De Los Moriscos De España. Compvesto Y Ordenado por Iuan Ripol, Ciudadano Caragoca, y Escriuano de Mandamiento de su Magestad, en el Reyno de Aragon. Repartido en neue Paragraphos. En Pamplona: por Nicolas de Assiayn, Impressor del Reyno de Nauarra, 1613.
[1], 23 l; 21 cm.

Bound with: GUADALAJARA Y JAVIER, MARCOS DE: Memorable Expvlsion Y Ivstissimo Destierro de los Moriscos de España. Nvevamente Compvesta Y Ordenada por F. Marco de Guadalajara y Xauier, Religioso y general Historiador de la Orden de nuestra Señora del Carmen Obseruante en la Prouincia de Aragon. Pamplona, 1613.
Doublet, p. 112; Goldsmith, p. 151, no. 125; Jerez, p, 49; Penney, p. 245; Pérez Goyena, no. 286; Salvá, II, 2972; Ticknor, p. 163.
Reel 68, No. 416

RIUS, ANTONIO, S.J. 1645-1716.
Festivos Y Magestvosos Cvltos, Qve La Nobilissima, Y Muy illustre Ciudad de Barcelona en 23. y 30 de Octubre 1686. Dedicò à su Inclita Hija, Patrona, Virgen, y Protomartyr Santa Eulalia, motivados en la Extension del Rezo proprio de la Santa, que obtuvo para toda España de la Santidad de nuestro Beatissimo Padre Innocencio XI. con Decreto despachado en Roma en 32 de Agosto 1686. Siendo Conselleres Los Muy Illustres Señores Ioseph Melteli, Ciudadano honrado de Barcelona, Don Domingo de Vardier, Doctor Miguel Matali, Ioseph Duran, Raphael Roca, y Ioseph Refart. Barcelona: en casa Cormellas, por Iayme Cays, 1686.
139 p.; 21cm.

Title-page repaired and part of title supplied.
Reel 156, No. 1025

RIVADENEIRA, PEDRO DE, S.J. 1527-1611.
Bibliotheca Scriptorvm Societatis Iesv, Post excusum Anno M.DC. VIII. Catalogum R. P. Petri Ribadeneirae Societatis Eivsdem Theologi; Nunc hoc nouo apparatu librorum ad annum reparatae salutis M.DC.XLII. editorum concinnata, & illustrium virorum elogiis adornata, A Philippo Alegambe Brvxellensi Ex Eadem Societate Iesv. Accedit Catalogus Religiosorum Societatis Iesu, que hactenus pro Catholicâ fide & pietate in variis mundi plagis interempti sunt. Antverpiae: Apud Ioannem Mevrsivm, 1643.
[25], 576, [1] p.; 32cm.

Doublet, p. 113; Palau, 266561; Simón Díaz, Jesuitas, no. 1571.
Reel 156, No. 1026

RIVADENEIRA, PEDRO DE, 1527-1611.
Obras Del Padre Pedro De Ribadeneyra de la Compañia de Iesus, agora de nueuo reuistas y acrecentadas. Lo Qve Se Contiene En Esta postrera impression se vera en la hoja siguiente. Madrid: en la imprenta de Luis Sanchez, 1605.
[12], 965, [4] p.; 31cm.

In two parts, continuously paged.
Part II has separate title-page: Segvnda Parte De Las Obras Del P. Pedro De Ribadeneyra de la Compañia de Iesus. Historia Ecclesiastica del scisma del Reyno de Inglaterra. En La Qval Se Tratan Algvnas De las cosas mas notables que han sucedido en aquel Reyno, tocantes a nuestra santa Religion. Recogida De Diversos Y Graves Autores; por el mismo padre.
Pagination errors throughout.
Palau, 266196; Salvá, II, 3501; Simón Díaz, Jesuitas, no. 1495.
Reel 157, No. 1028

RIVADENEIRA, PEDRO DE, 1527-1611.
Tratado De La Religion Y Virtvdes Qve Deve tener el
Principe Christiano, para gouernar y conferuar sus
Estados. Contra lo que Nicolas Machiavelo y los Polit-
icos deste tiempo enseñan. Escrito Por El P. Pedro
de Ribadeneyra de la Compañia de Iesvs. Dirigido al
Principe de Espana D. Felipe nuestro Señor. Anveres:
En La Emprenta Plantiniana, 1597.
437,[10] p.; 15cm.

Colophon: "En Anveres, En La Emprenta Plantiniana,
Cerca Ivan Moreto. M.D.XCVII."
Palau, 266334; Peeters-Fontainas, II, no. 1123;
Simón Díaz, Jesuitas, no. 1527.
Reel 157, No. 1029

RIVADENEIRA, PEDRO DE, 1527-1611.
[Tratado de la tribulación y desartre...Latin.]
R. P. Petri Ribadeneirae, Societatis Iesv Presbyteri,
De Tribvlationibvs huius seculi Libri Duo. In Qvibvs
De Omnibvs humanae vitae miserijs, ac calamitatibus
agitur: veraque, ad salutares ex ijs, animae fructus
colligendos, remedia suggeruntur. Coloniae: Apud
Conradum Butgenium, 1604.
[13], 410 p.; 13cm.

Latin translation.
Colophon: Typis Joannis Christophori, 1604.
Pagination errors throughout.
Palau, 266303.
Reel 156, No. 1027

RIVADENEIRA, PEDRO DE, 1527-1611.
Vita Ignatii Loiolae Qvi Religionem Clericorum
Societatis Iesv instituit. A Petro Ribadeneira
sacerdote Societatis eiusdem pridem conscripta, &
nunc denuò recognita & locupletata. Madriti: Apud
viduam Alphonsi Gomezij Regij Typographi, 1586.
[12], 347, [14] ℓ.; 15cm.

Error in foliation: leaf 170 numb. 152.
Dedicatory epistle signed: Iuan Vazquez.
Palau, 266203; Perez Pastor, Madrid, I no. 247;
Simón Díaz, Jesuitas, no. 1567.
Reel 157, No. 1030

RIVADENEIRA, PEDRO DE, 1527-1611.
Vita B. P. Ignatii Qui Religionem Clericorum
Societatis Iesv instituit, Nuper à R. P. Petro
Ribadeneira eiusdem Societatis Hispanicè conscripta,
Etab eodem rebus memorabilibus illustrisque miraculis
ita locupletata, vt alia ab illa priore quam ante
aliquot annos in lucem edidit videri possit; A P.
Gaspare Qvartemont eiusdem Societatis latiné conuersa.
Ipris Flandrorvm: Apud Franciscvm Bellettvm, 1612.
[13], 199, [2] p.; 13cm.

Pagination errors throughout.
Reel 157, No. 1031

RIVADENEIRA, PEDRO DE, 1527-1611.
Vida Del P. Ignacio De Loyola, fundador de la
Religion de la Compañia de Iesus. Escripta (sic) en
Latin por el padre Pedro de Ribadeneyra de la misma
Compañia, y aora nueuamente traduzida en Romance, y
añadida por el mismo Autor. Dirigida al Illustriss.
y Reuerendiss. señor don Gaspar de Quiroga, Cardenal y
Arcobispo de Toledo, Inquisidor general, &c. Madrid:
Por Alonso Gomez Impressor de su Magestad, 1583.
[12], 304, [9] ℓ.; 21cm.

Spanish translation by the author.
Palau, 266222, Pérez Pastor, Madrid, I, no. 191:
Simón Díaz, Jesuitas, no. 1498.
Reel 157, No. 1032

RIVADENEIRA, PEDRO DE, 1527-1611.
Vita Del P. S. Ignatio Loiola, Fondatore Della
Religione della Compagnia di Giesv. Canonizato dalla
Santità di N. S. Papa Gregorio XV. alli 12. di Marzo
1622. Descritta già 20 anni sono in lingua Spagnuola
del P. Pietro Ribadeneyra. Et hora di nuouo trasportata
nella nostra Italiana da yna persona diuota a comune
vtilità ad instanza di Gio. Battista Bidelli libraro
di questa Città. Dedicata All' Illustriss. &
Excellentiss. Sig. Il Sig. Dvca Di Feria Gouernatore
de lo Stato di Milano per Sua Maestà Cattolica, &c.
Milano: Per Gio. Battista Bidelli, 1622.
[4], 113 p.; 17cm.

Italian translation by José Boero?
Palau, 266243.
Reel 157, No. 1033

ROA, MARTIN DE, 1561-1637.
Martini De Roa Cordvbensis Ex Societate Iesv
Singvlarivm Locorvm, Ac Rervm Libri V. Quibus insuper
duo alij eiusdem Auctoris libri adiuncti sunt. De Die
Natali Sacro, Et Profano, vnus: Alter Singularium item
locorum Liber VI. In quibus cum ex sacris, tum ex
humanis literis, multa ex Gentium, Hebraeorumque
moribus explicantur. Nunc sedulo emendati, & locis
sanctae Sripturae, qui deerant, aucti. Ad D. Petrvm
Fernandez de Corduba, Marchionem de Priego, &c.
Lvgdvni: Svmptibvs Horatii Cardon, 1604.
2 pts. ([33], 460, [81] p.; [17], 204, [33] p.);
16cm.

Part II has separate title-page: Martini De Roa
Cordvbensis Ex Societate Iesv De Die Natali Sacro, Et
Profano, Liber Vnvs. Singvlarivm Item Locorvm.
Liber VI. AD. D Ioannem Baptistam Centuriornem,
Marchionem Astapae.
Palau, 270576.
Reel 158, No. 1034, 2 Parts

ROA, MARTIN DE, 1561-1637.
Martini De Roa Cordvbensis, Ex Societate Iesv,
Theologi, & sacrae Paginae Magistri, Singvlarivm S.
Scriptvrae. Pars II. In qua cum ex sacris, tum ex
humanis multa ex Gentium, Hebraeorumque moribus
explicantur. Lvgdvni: Sump. Iacobi, & Petri Prost,
1634.
[25], 655, [90] p.; 16cm.

Part II only, part I unavailable.
Palau, 270577.
Reel 158, No. 1035

RODERICUS SANCTIUS see SÁNCHEZ DE AREVALO, RODRIGO.

RODOLPHUS, GERARDUS.
De Litteris Canonicis, Videlicet Formatis, Pacificis,
Commendatitiis, Ac Dimissoriis, Qvibvs In Ecclesia
Primitiua Sancti Patres ex generaliu Conciliorum
decretis, in sacrosancta Nicaena synodo prius
excogitatis, vsi sunt. Qvarvm Explicatione Non solum
intima vetustatis penetralia reserantur in rebus
ecclesiasticis, sed & Iuonis, Burchardi, & Gratiani
decreta, Conciliorum tomi, & aliorum ecclesiasticorum
tam recentium quàm veterum atque prophanorum scripta
ab innumeris mendis repurgata, pristino suo
nitorirestituuntur. Gerardo Rodolpho Graviensi
Avctore. Coloniae: Apud Geruinum Calenium, &
haeredes Ioannis Quentelij, 1582.
[17], 95 p.; 17cm.

Bound in: Sánchez De Las Brozas, Francisco. De
Avtoribvs Interpretandis ..., 1582.
Adams, II, no. 654.
Reel 166, No. 1082

RODRIGUES LOBO, FRANCISCO, 17th cent.
La Lornada Qve La Magestad Catholica Del Rey Don
Phelippe III. De Las Hespañas hizo a su Reyno de
Portugal; y el Triumpho, y pompa con que le recibio
la insigne Ciudad de Lisboa el año de 1619. Compvesta
En Varios Romances por Francisco Rodriguez Lobo.
Lisboa: Por Pedro Crasbeeck Impressor del Rey, 1623.
[2], 92, [1] l.; 20cm.

Alenda, no. 695; Gallardo, IV, no. 3676; Goldsmith,
p. 152; Jerez, p. 89; Palau, 274235; Penney, p. 475;
Salvá, I, 358; Simón Díaz, Impresos, no. 2673.
Reel 158, No. 1037

RODRÍGUEZ, ALONSO, 1526-1616.
[Exercicios de perfección y virtudes cristianas.
English]
The Practice Of Christian Perfection Written in
Spanish by R^d. Father Alphonsus Rodriguez of the
Society of Jesus. Translated into English out of the
French Copy of Mr. Regnier Des-Marais, of the Royal
Academy of Paris. The First Part. London: Printed by
Thomas Hales, 1697.
3 pts. ([37], 616 p.; [23], 548 p.; [15], 464 p.);
22cm.

English translation by John Warner.
Part II has separate title-page: The Practice Of
Christian Perfection Written in Spanish by R^d. Father
Alphonsus Rodriguez of the Society of Jesus. Trans-
lated into English out of the French Copy of Mr. Regnier
Des-Marais. of the Royal Academy of Paris. The Second
Part, 1698.
Part III has separate title-page: The Practice Of
Christian Perfection Written in Spanish by R^d. Father
Alphonsus Rodriguez of the Society of Jesus. Trans-
lated into English out of the French Copy of Mr.
Regnier Des-Marais, of the Royal Academy of Paris.
The Third Part, 1699.
Allison, p. 158, no. 14; Graesse, p. 145; Wing R.
1772.
Reel 158, No. 106, 3 Parts

ROJAS, ALONSO DE see ROXAS, ALONSO DE, 1588-1653.

ROJAS, FERNANDO DE, d. 1541.
[La Celestina. English]
The Spanish Bawd Represented In Celestina: Or, The
Tragicke-Comedy of Calisto and Melibea. Wherein is
contained, besides the pleasantnesse and sweetnesse of
the stile, many Philosophicall Sentences, and profitable
Instructions necessary for the younger sort: Shewing
the deceits and subtilties housed in the bosomes of
false seruants, and Cunny-catching Bawds. London:
Printed by J. B., 1631.
[15], 202 p.; 21cm.

English translation by Jame Mabbe.
Pagination errors throughout.
Allison, p. 159, no. 16; Palau, 51213; Penney,
p. 122; Pollard and Redgrave, no. 4911; Ticknor, p. 70.
Reel 159, No. 1042

ROJAS, FERNANDO DE, d. 1541.
[La Celestina. Italian]
Celestina. Tragicomedia De Calisto Et Melibea
Nvovamente Tradotta De lingua Castigliana in Italiano
idioma. Aggiontoui di nuouo tutto quello che fin al
giorno presente li mancaua. Dapoi ogni oltra
impressione nouissimamente corretta, distinta, ordinata,
et in piu cōmoda forma redotta, adornata lequal cose
nelle altre impressione non si troua. [Venice:
Stampata per Pietro de Nicolini da Sabio, 1535.]
112 l.; 15cm.

ROJAS (Cont'd)
Italian translation by Alfonso de Ordoñez.
Colophon: "Finisse la Trigicomedia intitolata
Calisto & Melibea, tradotta de lingua spagnola in
italiano idioma nouamente coretta, stampata per
Pietro de Nicolini da Sabio M. D. X X X V."
Pagination errors throughout.
Graesse, p. 98; Palau, 51193; Short-title, III,
p. 36.
Reel 159, No. 1040

ROJAS, FERNANDO DE, d. 1541.
[La Celestina. Italian]
Celestina. Tragicomedia De Calisto Et Melibea
Nvovamente Tradotta de lingua Castigliana in Italiano
idioma. Dapoi ogni altra impressione nouissimamente
corretta, distinta, ordinata, & in piu commoda forma
ridotta. Adornata di tutte le sue figure a ogni atto
corrispondenti lequal cose nelle altre impressione non
si truoua. [Venice: Stampata per Giouann' antonio e
Pietro de Nicolini da Sabio, 1541.]
112 l.; 15cm.

Italian translation by Alfonso de Ordoñez.
Colophon: "Finisse la Trigicomedia intitolata
Calisto & Melibea, tradotta de lingua spagnola in
Italiano idioma nouamente coretta, stampata per
Giouann' antonio e Pietro de Nicolini da Sabio M.D.XLI.
Del mese di Mazzo (sic)."
Pagination errors throughout.
Graesse, p. 98; Palau, 51194; Short-title, III,
p. 36; Ticknor, p. 70.
Reel 159, No. 1041

ROJAS, FERNANDO DE, d. 1541.
[La Celestina. Italian]
Celestina Tragicomedia De Calisto Et Melibea
Novamente Tradocta de lingua castigliana in Italiano
idioma. Aggiontoui di nuouo tutto quello che fin al
giorno presente li manchaua. Dapoi ogni altra impressione nouissimamēte correcta, distincta ordenada,
& in piu commoda forma reducta, adornada, lequal cose
nelle altre impressione non si troua. Vinegia: per
Gregorio de Gregori Nel, 1625.
119, [1] l.; 16cm.

Italian translation by Alfonso de Ordoñez.
Colophon: "Stampata in Vinegia per Gregorio de
Gregori Nel anno del signor. M.D.XXV. Nel mese de
Nouēbre."
Pagination errors throughout.
Heredia, no. 2303; Palau, 51191; Ticknor, p. 70.
Reel 159, No. 1039

ROJAS ZORILLA, FRANCISCO DE, 1607-1684.
La gran comedia de los aspides de Cleopatra ...
Valencia: en casa Luis la Marca, [n.d.]
47 p.; 21cm.

Bound with: Cardona Y Alagón, Antonio Folch de, 1623-
1694. El mas herovco silencio. Comedia famosa. Valencia,
1688.
Reel 33, No. 151

ROMANCE Nuevo De La Mverte, y testamento de la Reyna
de España Doña Luysa. [s.l.:s.n.]
2 l.; 21cm.

Colophon: "En Barcelona: oir Vicēte Suria à la
calle de la Paja año 1689. Vendese a la mesma
Imprenta."
Palau, 276819.
Reel 159, No. 1043

ROXAS, ALONSO DE, 1588-1653.
Al Rey Nvestro Señor Por La Provincia De La Compañia
De Iesvs De la Nueva España. En Satisfacion De Vn
Libro De El Visitador Obispo D. Iuan de Palafox y
Mendoza. Pvblicado En Nombre De El Dean, Y Cabildo
De Sy Iglesia Catedral De La Pvebla De Los Angeles.
[México? 1650?]
278 p.; 20cm.

[Palafox y Mendoza; a collection, vol. 23]
Memorial signed: Alonso de Roxas, procurador
general de la Provincia de la Compañia de Iesus de
Nueva España.
Running title: Memorial al rey n. s. Apendiz al
Memorial: p. 242-78.
HC325/660; Laurenti-Porqueras, Impresos de Palafox,
no. 2; Leclerc, no. 1257; Palau, 275714; Simon Díaz,
Jesuitas, no. 1681.
Reel 159, No. 1038

RUBIO, ANTONIO, 1548-1615.
Logica Mexicana siue Commentarii in vniversam
Aristotelis Logicam. Autore R. P. Antonio Rvbio
Rodensi, Societatis Iesu Theologo, & Professore in
Regia Mexicanorum Academia. Cum duplici indice,
quorum vnus quaestiones in hac parte discussas,
alteres consideratione dignas refert. Pars Prior.
Quae quid contineat vide versa pagina. Cum priuilegio
S. Coes. Maiest. & Superiorum permissu. Coloniae
Agrippinae: Sumptibus Arnoldi Mylii Birckmanni, 1605.
3 pts. (1256 cols. [12] p.; 792 cols; 210 cols.;
[11] p.); 23cm.

Second part has separate t.-p.: Logicae Mexicanae,
siue Commentariorvm In Vniversam Aristotelis Logicam.
Autore R. P. Antonio Rvbio Rodensi, Societatis Iesu
Theologo, & Professore in Regia Mexicanorum Academia.
Pars Posterior. Cum priuilegio S. Caes. Maiest. &
Superiorum permissu.
Third part has caption title: Generalis Dispvtatio
De Habitibvs, Sev Virtvtibvs intellectvalibus ad
partem Posterioristicam spectantibus.
Vol. I imperfect: title-page and 2nd prelim leaf
wanting.
Medina, Bibl. Hisp. Amer, II, no. 505; Palau,
280352.
Reel 159, No. 1044

RUBIO, ANTONIO, 1548-1615.
Logica Mexicana R. P. Antonii Rvvio Rodensis,
Doctoris Theologi, Societatis Iesv. Hocest Commentarii
Breviores Et maxime perspicui in Vniuersam Aristotelis
Dialecticam: Vna cum dubiis & Quaestionibus hac
tempestate agitari solitis. Nvnc Primvm In Gallia
Editi, cum Capitum, Dubiorum, Questionum & rerum
notabilium, quae in iis continentur, Indice. Parisiis:
Apud Ioannes Petit, 1615.
[21], 738, [13] p.; 17cm.

Pagination errors throughout.
Medina, Bibl. His.-Amer., no. 629; Palau, 280355.
Reel 159, No. 1045

RUBIO, ANTONIO, 1548-1615.
R. P. Antonii Rvvio Rodensis, Doctoris Theologi
Societatis Iesu, S. Theologiae Professoris, Commentarii
In Libros Aristotelis Stagiritae Philosophorum Principis
de Anima: vna cum dubijs & quaestionibus hac tempestate
in scholis agitari solitis. Nvnc Primvm In Germania
Editi, Cvm Dvplici Indice, quorum vnus discussas omnes
quaestiones, alterres omnes notabiles complectitur.
Ad D. D. Ildephonsum De la Mota, Episcopum
Tlaxcalensem, Regiumque Consiliarum. Permissv
Svperiorvm. Coloniae Agrippinae: Apud Ioannem Crithium
sub signo Galli, 1613.
[9], 542, [21] p.; 21cm.

RUBIO (Cont'd)
Colophon: Coloniae Agrippinae Excudebat Petrus à
Brachel Anno. M.D. CXIIII.
Pagination errors throughout.
Palau, 280378.
Reel 160, No. 1046

RUBIO, ANTONIO, 1548-1615.
R. P. Antonii Rvvio Rodensis, Doctoris Theologi,
Societatis Iesu, S. Theologiae Professoris, Commentarii
In Libros Aristotelis Stagiritae, Philosophorum
Principis. De Anima Vna Cvm Dvbiis Et Quaestionibvs
In scholis hac tempestate agitari solitis, Cvm Dvplici
Indice, Vno Capitvm, Altero rerum notabilium. Permissv
Svperiorvm. Coloniae Agrippinae: Apud Ioannem
Crithium sub signo Galli, 1644.
[7], 512, [19] p.; 20cm.

Double columns. Book-plate of the Library of the
Society for promoting Christian knowledge.
Reel 160, No. 1047

RUBIO, ANTONIO, 1548-1615.
R. P. Antonii Rvvio Rodensis, Doctoria Theologi,
Societatis Iesv, Commentarii In Vniversam Aristotelis
Dialecticam: vna cvm dubiis & quaestionibus hac
tempestate agitari solitis. Nvnc Primvm In Germania
Editi, Cvm Capitum, Dubiorum, Quaestionum, & rerum
notabilium, quae in iis contenentur, Indice. Permissv
Svperiorvm. Coloniae Agrippinae: Apud Ioannem Crithium,
1621.
[11], 530, [13] p.; 21cm.

In double columns.
Ex-libris: W. H. Hadow. MCMII. Coll. Vicorn. Oxon.;
stamp of H. A. Pottinger, Worcester College, Oxford,
on verso of title-page.
Pagination errors throughout.
Palau, 280381.
Reel 160, No. 1048

RUBIO, ANTONIO, 1548-1615.
R. P. Antonii Rvvio Rodensis, Doctoris Theologi,
Societatis Iesu, Commentarii In Vniversam Aristotelis
Dialecticam: una cum dubiis & quastionibus hac
tempestate agitari solitis. Nvnc Denvo In Germania
Editi, Cum Capitum, Dubiorum, Quaestionum, & Rerum
notabilium, quae in iis continentur, Indice. Permissv
Svperiorvm. Londini: Typis Tho. Harper, Impensis
Rich. Whitaker, 1641.
[9], 530, [13] p.; 21cm.

Palau, 280350.
Reel 160, No. 1049

Rvdimenta Lingve Persice. Authore Ludovico De
Dieu ... Lvgdvni Batavorvm, 1639.
[8], 95 p.; 21cm.

Bound with: Javier, Jerónimo. Historia Christi
Persice Conscripta ..., 1639.
Reel 83, No. 533A

S

SAAVEDRA FAJARDO, DIEGO DE, 1584-1648.
Corona Gothica Castellana Y Avstriaca. Politicamente
illustrada Por Don Diego Saavedra Faxardo, Cavallero
De La Orden De Santiago, del Consejo de su Magestad en
el Supremo de las Indias, y su Plenipotenciario para
la paz vniuersal. Dedicada A Don Geronimo Serra Marin,
Hijo Primogenito De Don Ivan Bavtista Serra Conde de
Villaalegre en Castilla, Marques de Mornes, Correo
mayor de su Magestad en el Estado de Milan, &c.
Madrid: Por Andres Garcia de la Iglesia, 1658.
[21], 556, [37] p.; 21cm.

Pagination errors throughout.
Doublet, p. 116; Graesse, p. 200; Goldsmith, p. 158,
no. 6; Palau, 283498.
Reel 160, No. 1050

SAAVEDRA FAJARDO, DIEGO DE, 1584-1648.
Idea De Vn Principe Politico Christiano. Representada
en cien Empresas. Dedicada. Al Principe De Las
Españas Nvestro Señor Por Don Diego Saavedra Fajardo del
Consejo de su Magestad en el Supremo de las Indias, i
su Embajador extraordinario en Mantua i Esguizaron i
Residente en Alemania. Monaco: En la emprenta de
Nicolao Enrico, 1640.
[17], 711, [5] p.; 24cm.

Engraved title-page.
Pagination errors throughout.
Goldsmith, p. 158, no. 7; Graesse, p. 200; Palau,
283441.
Reel 160, No. 1051

SAAVEDRA FAJARDO, DIEGO DE, 1584-1648.
Idea De Vn Principe Politico Christiano Rapresentada
en cien empresas Dedicada Al Principe De Las Españas
Nvestro Señor Por Don Diego de Saauedra Faxardo
Cauallero del Orden de S. Iago, del Consejo de su
Mag.^d en el supremo de las Indias, i su Embajador
Plenipotenciario en los Treze Cantones, en la Dieta
Imperial de Ratisbona por el Circulo, i Casa de Borgona,
i en el Congreso de Munster para la Paz General.
Monaco, A 1 de Marzo, 1640. Milan, A 20 de Abril, 1642.
[21], 752 p.; 24cm.

Engraved title-page: Hoc Opvs.
Goldsmith, p. 158, no. 8; Palau, 283442; Toda y
Güell, Italia, 4508.
Reel 161, No. 1052

SAAVEDRA FAJARDO, DIEGO DE, 1584-1648.
Idea De Vn Principe Politico Christiano, Representada
En Cien Empressas. Va Enmendada En Esta Tercera
Impression de todos los hierros que avia en las otras.
Dedicada Al Principe De Las Españas Nvestro Señor.
Por Don Diego de Saavedra Faxardo, Cavallero del Orden
de Santiago, del Consejo de Su Magestad en el Supremo
de las Indias, y su Embaxador Plenipotenciario en los
treze Cantones, en la Dieta Imperial de Ratisbona, por
el circulo, y casa de Borgoña, y en el Congresso de
Munster para la paz General. Valencia: por Geronimo
Vilagrasa, 1655.
[17], 694 p.; 21cm.

Goldsmith, p. 158, no. 9; Graesse, p. 200; Palau
283445.
Reel 161, No. 1053

SAAVEDRA, FAJARDO, DIEGO DE, 1584-1648.
Idea De Vn Principe Politico Christiano, Representada
En Cien Empressas. Dedicadas Al Señor Licenciado Don
Ivan De Giles Pretel, Abogado Primario, Celebre, y
Eruditissimo de los Reales Consejos en esta Corte,
Consultor del Santo Oficio, Assessor de la Sacra
Assemblea de la Religion de San Iuan, y de la Capitania
General de la Artilleria de España. Por Don Diego
Saavedra Faxardo, Cavallero del Orden de Santiago, del
Consejo de su Magestad en el de Indias, y su Embaxador
Plenipotenciario para la paz general. Madrid: por
Andres Garcia de la Iglesia y a su costa, 1666.
[17], 692, [3] p.; 21cm.

Pagination errors throughout.
Palau, 283456.
Reel 161, No. 1054

SAAVEDRA FAJARDO, DIEGO DE, 1584-1648.
[Idea De Vn Principe Politico-Christiano. English]
The Royal Politician Represented In One Hundred
Emblems. Written in Spanish by Don Diego Saavedra
Faxardo, Knight of the Order of St. Jago, Plenipoten-
tiary Ambassador To the Cantons of Switzerland, At
the Imperial Diet at Ratisbon, At the Famous Treaty of
Mvnster, And of the Supreme Council of State for both
the Indies. With a large Preface, containing an
Account of the Author, his Works, and the Usefulness
thereof. Done into English from the Original. By
Sir J. A. Astry. Vol. I. London: Printed for Matt.
Gylliflower And Luke Meredith, 1700.
2v. ([21], 376 p.; [5], 384, [1] p.); 19cm.

English translation by Sir James Astry.
Vol. II has separate title-page.
Frontispiece of vol. I (portrait of William, duke
of Gloucester) is duplicated in vol. II.
Allison, p. 160; Graesse, p. 200; Palau, 283484;
Ticknor, p. 315; Wing S. 211.
Reel 162, No. 1058

SAAVEDRA FAJARDO, DIEGO DE, 1584-1648.
[Idea De Vn Principe Politico-Christiano. Latin]
Idea Principis Christiano-Politici 101 Sijmbolis
expressa A. Didaco Saavedra Faxardo. Amstelodami:
Apud Ioh. Ianssonium Iuniorem, 1651.
[25], 831, [4] p.; 14cm.

Latin translation.
Engraved title-page.
Graesse, p. 200; Palau, 283479.
Reel 161, No. 1055

SAAVEDRA FAJARDO, DIEGO DE, 1584-1648.
[Idea De Vn Principe Politico-Christiano. Latin]
Idea Principis Christiano-Politici 101 Sijmbolis
expressa A. Didaco Saavedra Faxardo Equite &c.
Amstelodami: Apud Joannem Jacobi Fil: Schipper, 1659.
[25], 831, [4] p.; 13cm.

Latin translation.
Engraved title-page.
Graesse, p. 200; Knapp-Huntington, p. 283; Palau,
283483; Penney, p. 486; Ticknor, p. 315.
Reel 162, No. 1056

SAAVEDRA FAJARDO, DIEGO DE, 1584-1648.
[Idea De Vn Principe Politico-Christiano. Latin]
Idea Principis Christiano-Politici Symbolis C I.
expressa. á Didaco Saavedra Faxardo, Equite, &c.
Ab inummeris priorum editionum mendis expurgata.
Parisiis: Apud Fridericvm Leonardvm, 1660.
599, [6] p.; 14cm.

Latin translation.
Engraved title-page.
Graesse, p. 200; Palau, 283485.
Reel 162, No. 1057

SABUCO DE NANTES, OLIVA,(supposed author)see SABUCO Y
ALVAREZ, MIGUEL.

SABUCO Y ALVAREZ, MIGUEL, fl. 1590.
Nveva Filosofia De La Natvraleza del hõbre, no
conocida ni alcancada de los grandes filosofos antiguos:
la qual mejora la vida y salud humana. Compuesta por
doña Oliua Sabuco. Esta segunda impression ya
enmendada, y añadidas algunas cosas curiosas, y vna
Tabla. Madrid: por P. Madrigal, 1588.
[8], 368, [6] l.; 15cm.

First published in 1587.
Authorship of Oliva Sabuco questioned; now recognized
to be the work of her father, Miguel Sabuco y Alvarez.
Graesse, p. 203; HC398/1938; Palau, 283885; Penney,
p. 487; Salvä, II, 2747.
Reel 162, No. 1059

SACRO BOSCO, JOANNES DE, fl. 1230.
[Sphaera mundi]
Vberrimum sphere mundi cõmetũ intersertis etiã
questionibus dñi Petri de aliaco. [Paris: Gug
Marchant for Jean Petet, Feb. 1498]
[100] l.: ill.; 27cm.

The commentary is by Petrus Cirvellus.
Includes woodcuts: 3 illus., title-page border,
diagrams.
Goff, J. 418; Klebs, no. 874.25; Proctor, no. 8015;
Reichling, nos. 14120-5363.
Reel 162, No. 1060

SACRO BOSCO, JOANNES DE, fl. 1230 [i.e. John Holywood]
Sphera mundi. In laudem vberrimi huius nouic
cõmentarij Petri Ciruelli Darocensis in astronomicum
Sphere mundi opusculũ Petrus de lerma Burgensis ad
lectorẽ ... Paris: Jean Petit, 1515.
76 l.; 27cm.

Title page missing.
First leaf missing. Various errors in numbering of
leaves.
Colophon: Impressum est hoc opusculum Anno dominice
natiutitais. 1515. in mẽse Augusti Parisius, impensis
Johannis Petit.
Reel 162, No. 1061

SACRO BOSCO, JOANNES DE, fl. 1230 [i.e. John Holywood]
Sphaera Ioannis De Sacro Bosco Emendata. Eliae
Vineti Santonis scholia in eandem Sphaeram, ab ipso
authore restituta. Adiunximus huic libro compendium
in Sphaeram, per Pierium Valerianum Bellunensem, Et,
Petri Nonii Salaciencis Demonstrationem eorum, quae
in extremo capite de Climatibus Sacroboscius scribit
de inaequali Climatum latitudine, eodem Vineto
interprete. Lvtetiae: Apud Gulielmum Cauellat, 1558.
102, [2] l.; 17cm.

Graesse, [date only], p. 210.
Reel 162, No. 1062

SACRO BOSCO, JOANNES DE, fl. 1230 [i.e. John Holywood]
Sphaera Ioannis De Sacro Bosco Emendata. Eliae
Vineti Santonis scholia in eandẽ Sphaerã, ab ipso
authore restituta. Quibus nunc accessere scholia
Heronis. Adiunximus huic libro compendium in Sphaerum
per Pierum Valerianum Bellunensem, Et Petri Nonii
Salaciensis Demonstrationem eorum, quae in extremo
capite de climatibus Sacroboscius scribit de inaequali
climatũ latitudine, eodem Vineto interprete. Coloniae:
Apud Gosuinum Cholinum, 1591.
[12], 80, [5] l.; 16cm.

Errors in foliation: leaves 73-92 numbered 64-84.
Exactly the same as the 1594 edition.
Reel 162, No. 1063

SALAMANCA, ALEJO DE.
F. Alexii Salamancae Zamorensis, Ordinis Minorvm,
Regvlar. obseruantiae, prouinciae D. Iacobi, De
republica Christi Dialogi tres: Quibus primõ suum
quisque Legislatorem obseruet: deinde Leges pro
virili seruet: postremõ quàm absolutissimus Ciuis
(erroribus quorundam interim, ac haeribus explosis)
euadat. His passim inspersa sunt prophanae literaturae
quaedã haud prosus indigna lectu. Opvs Examinatvm
Per D. Inqviss. Haereticae prauitatis, nec antehac
typis excusum: Sed & quod plus praestabit in recessu,
quàm in fronte promittit. S.C.C.M. Dedicatum opus,
cun eiusdem Caesaris priuilegio in decennium.
Lvgdvni: Apud Sebastianum Barptolemaei Honorati,
1556.
[47], 301, [2] p.; 16cm.

Adams, II, no. 92; Palau, 285930.
Reel 162, No. 1064

SALAMANCA. UNIVERSIDAD see PONCE DE LEÓN, BASILIO,
1569-1629.

SALAMON BEN ABRAHAM (translator) see PETRARCA, FRANCESCO.

SALAZAR, AMBROSIO DE, b. 1575?
Espeio General De La Gramatica En Dialogos, Para
Saber La natural y perfecta pronunciacion de la lengua
Castellana. ... Dirigido à la Sacra y Real Magestad
del Christianissimo Rey de Francia y de Nauarra. Por
Ambrosio De Salazar. A Roven : Iacqves Cailloüe, 1636.
[7], 506 p.

Bound in: Oudin, César de. Grammaire Espagnolle
Expliqvee En Francois, 1632.
Reel 127, No. 804

SALAZAR, FERNANDO DE, ed. see BENTIVOGLIO, ANTONIO
GALEAZZO.

SALAZAR DE MENDOZA, PEDRO, d. 1629.
Cronica de el Gran Cardenal de España, Don Pedro
Goncalez de Mendoca, Arcobispo de la muy santa Iglesia
Primada de las Españas: Patriarcha de Alejandria
Canciller mayor de los Reynos de Castilla, y de
Toledo. Al Dvqve de el Infantado, Don Rodrigo Diaz
de Vibar, de Mendoca, de la Vega, y de Luna, Conde del
Cid. Por el Doctor Pedro de Salazar, y Mendoca,
Canonigo Penitenciario, de la mesma muy santa Iglesia.
Toledo: En la Emprenta de doña Maria Ortiz de Sarauia,
1625.
[3], 479 p.; 27cm.

Imperfect: title-page wanting, replaced by hand-
written title-page; p. 63-66 wanting; many errors in
numbering of pages.
In double columns.
Goldsmith, p. 161, no. 97; Knapp-Huntington, p. 289;
Palau, 286873; Penney, p. 492; Pérez Pastor, no. 523;
Salvá, II, 3509; Ticknor, p. 318.
Reel 163, No. 1065

SALAZAR DE MENDOZA, PEDRO.
Historia De Los Svccessos De La Gverra. Che (sic)
La Magestad Del Invitissimo Don Carlos Quinto
Emperador de los Romanos, y Rey de España, y Alemaña,
hizo contra los Principes, y Ciudades rebeldes de
Alemaña, y del fin que tuuo. Compuesta por Pedro de
Salazar uizino de la uilla de Madrid. Dirigida Al
Serenissimo Señor Don Felipe Principe de España
con todas las particularidades ansi en lo que toca
a la Historia. como a la descrition (sic) de toda a
quella Tierra. Napoles: Juan Pablo Suganappo,
1548.
[4], 96 l.; 29cm.

Short-Title, III, p. 105.
Reel 163, No. 1067

SALAZAR DE MENDOZA, PEDRO, d. 1129.
Origen De Las Dignidades Seglares De Castilla Y
Leon Con Relacion Summaria de los Reyes de estos
Reynos de sus actiones; casamientos: hijos:muertes:
sepulturas. De Los Qve Las Han Creado y tenido y de
muchas Ricos Homes. confirmadores de priuilegios
&ª. Para El Principe De España don Filipe nuestro
señor. Por El Doctor Salazar de Mendoca. [Toledo:
Por Diego Rodriguez de Valdiuielso, 1618].
[4], 189, [1]; 30cm.

Engraved title-page.
Pagination errors throughout.
Doublet, p. 117; Goldsmith, p. 161, no. 99;
Knapp-Huntington, p. 284; Palau, 286867; Penny,
p. 492; Pérez Pastor, no. 497; Salvá, II 3602; Ticknor,
p. 318.
Reel 163, No. 1066

SALAZAR DE MENDOZA, PEDRO, d. 1629.
Origen De Las Dignidades Seglares De Castila, (sic)
Y Leon. Con Relacion Svmaria De Los Reyes De estos Reynos,
de sus acciones, casamientos, hijos, muertes, sepulturas.
De Los Qve Las Han Creado, y tenido, y de muchos Ricos
Homes, Confirmadores de Priuilegios, &c. Con vn Resumen
al fin de las mercedes que su Magestad ha hecho de
Marqueses, y Condes, desde el año de 1621. hasta fin del
de 1656. Para El Principe De España Don Felipe nuestro
Señor. Por El Doctor Salazar De Mendoza. Madrid: en la
Imprenta Real, 1657.
[4], 189, [3] l.; 30cm.

Bound with: CARRILLO, ALONSO. Origen De La Dignidad
De Grande De Castilla Preeminencias De Qve Goza En los
Actos publicos, y Palacio de los Reyes de España. Madrid:
Imprenta Real, 1657.
Reel 33, No. 159

SALAZAR MARDONES, CRISTÓBAL.
Ilvstracion Y Defensa De La Fabvla De Piramo Y
Tisbe, Compvesta Por D. Lvis De Gongora y Argote,
Capellan de su Magestad, y Racionero de la Santa
Yglesia de Cordoua. Escriuialas Christoual de
Salazar Mardones, criado de su Magestad, y Oficial mas
antiguo de la Secretaria del Reyno de Sicilia.
Dedicadas A D. Francisco de los Cobos y Luna, Conde
de Ricla, Gentil hombre de la Camara de su Magestad,
y Primogenito del Marques de Camarasa. Madrid: En
la Imprenta Real, 1636.
[10], 192, [1] l.; 23cm.

Guzmán & Reyes, 9; Jerez, p. 94; Palau, 286861;
Penney, p. 235; Ticknor, p. 318.
Reel 163, No. 1068

SALAZAR Y CASTRO, LUIS DE, 1658-1734.
Advertencias Historicas, Sobre Las Obras De
Algvnos Doctos Escritores Modernos, Donde Con Las
Chronicas, Y Con Las Escritvras, Solicita Sv Mejor
Inteligencia D. Lvis De Salazar Y Castro, Cavallero
De La Orden De Calatrava, Y Chronista Del Rey N.S.
Madrid: Por Matheo De Llanos y Gvzman, 1688.
[21], 384 p.; 23cm.

Gallardo, no. 3780; HC384/719; Palau, 286800;
Penney, p. 493.
Reel 163, No. 1069

SALAZAR Y TORRES, AGUSTIN DE, 1642-1675.
Cythara De Apolo, Varias Poesias, Divinas, Y
Humanas, Que Escrivio Don Agustin De Salazar Y Torres;
Y Saca A Luz D. Juan De Vera Tasis Y Villarroel, Su
Mayor Amigo. Dedicadas A Don Ysidoro De Burgos
Mantilla y Barcena, &c. Primera Parte. Madrid:
Por Antonio Gonçalez de Reyes, 1694.
2v. ([49], 305, [7] p.; [4], 424 p.); 23cm.

Vol. II has separate title-page: Cythara De Apolo,
Loas, Y Comedias Diferentes, Que Escriviò Don
Agustin De Salazar Y Torres, Y Saca A Luz, D. Juan
De Vera Tasis Y Villarroel, Su Mayor Amigo. Dedicadas
A Don Isidoro De Burgos, Mantilla y Barcena, &c.
Segunda Parte.
Graesse, p. 230; Jerez, p. 94; Palau, 286928;
Penney, p. 493; Salvá, I, 1404; Ticknor, p. 318.
Reel 163, No. 1070

SALINAS, MIGUEL, d. 1577.
Rhetorica en lengua Castellana en la qual se pone
muy en breue lo necessario para saber bien hablar y
escreuir: y conocer quienhabla y escriue bien. Una
manera para poner por exercicio las reglas de la
Rhetorica. Un tratado de los auisos en que consite
la breuedad y abundancia. Otro tratado de la
forma q̃ se deue tener en leer los autores: y sacar
dellos lo mejor pa [sic] poder se dello aprouechar
quãdo fuere menester todo en lengua Castellana:
cõpuesto por vn frayle de la orden de sant Hieronymo.
(s.l.:s.n.), 1541.
[4], 117 l.; 21cm.

Engraved title-page.
Colophon: "Fue impressa esta presente obra y
nueua inuenciõ de Rhetorica en romãce a loor y
alabança de nr̃o señor Jesu Christo, y de su
gloriosissima m̃adre en la muy noble villa y
florentissima vniuersidad d Alcala de Henares en
casa de Joã de Brocar, a ocho dias del mes de
Febrero: del año M.D.xli."
Graesse, p. 233; Palau, 287547; Salvá, II, 2401.
Reel 163, No. 1071

SALÓN, MIGUEL BARTOMOLÉ, 1539-1621.
   Vida Y Milagros Del Ilvstrissimo, y gloriosissimo
Padre de los Pobres Santo Tomas de Villanueva,
Arcobispo de Valencia, del Orden de N.P.S. Agustin,
Prouincial de la Prouincia de Castilla, y Andaluzia,
y Colegial mayor del insgne Colegio de S. Ildefonso de
Alcalà. Escrita Por El M.R.P.M. Fr. Migvel Salon, de
la mesma Orden, Cathedratico de Visperas de Theologia
de la Vniuersidad de Valencia. Impressa nueuamente
Por El P. Fr. Benito De Aste Examinador Synodal del
Arcobispado de Toledo, con vn Sermon añadido
al fin sobre las principales virtudes de la vida del
Santo. Dedicase Al Excelentissimo Señor D. Christoual
Crespi de Valdaura, Vicecanciller de los Reynos de la
Corona de Aragon, Presidente de su Supremo Consejo,
y de la Iunta del Gouierno Vniuersal de España.
Madrid: En la Imprenta Real, 1670.
   [25], 573, [8] p.; 21cm.

   "Nota" bound at the end, 19 p.
   Palau, 287922.
Reel 163, No. 1072

SAN JUAN CLIMACO see JOANNES CLIMACUS, Saint.

SAN PEDRO, DIEGO DE, fl. 1500.
   [Carcel de amor. Italian]
   Carcer d'amore traduto [sic] dal magnifico miser
Lelio de Manfredi Ferrarese: de Idioma Spagnolo in
lingua materna. Nouamente Stampato. (s.l.:s.n.),
n.d.
   48 l.; 16cm.

   Italian translation by Lelio Mandredi.
   Bound with: Achilles, Tatius: Amorosi Ragionamenti.
Dialogo, Nel Qvale Si Racconta Vn Compassionevole
Amore di Dve Amanti ..., 1546.
   Graesse, p. 258; Palau, vol. XVIII, p. 209.
Reel 164, No. 1073

SAN PEDRO, DIEGO DE, fl. 1500.
   [Carcel De Amor. Spanish.]
   Carcel De Amor. La Prison D'Amovr. En deux
langages, Espagnol & Francois, pour ceux qui voudront
apprendre l'vn par l'autre. Paris: Pour Galiot
Corrozet, 1595.
   377 p.; 12cm.

   Vignette: In Corde Prvdentis Reqviescit Sapientia.
   Palau, XVIII, p. 208. See also Foulché-Delbosc,
V, no. 652.
Reel 164, No. 1075

SÁNCHEZ, GASPAR, 1554-1628.
   Gasparis Sanctii Centvmpvteolani, E Societate
Iesv Theologi, In Collegio Complvtensi sacrarum
literarum Interpretis, In Qvatvor Libros Regvm, &
duos Paralipomenon, Commentarii. Nvnc Primvm
Prodevnt. Indicibus cūm Locorum Scripturae, Regularum,
& Prouerbialium; tum rerum memorabilium illustrati.
Lvgdvni: Svmpt. Iacobi Cardon Et Petri Cavellati, 1623.
   [11] p.; [12], 1692, [72] col.; 36cm.

   Engraved title-page. Jesuit device: IHS.
   Dedication to Cardenal Agustín Spinola.
   Palau, 294151.
Reel 164, No. 1076

SÁNCHEZ, TOMÁS, 1550-1610.
   R. Patris Thomae Sanchez Cordvbensis, E' Societate
Iesv, De Sancto Matrimonii Sacramento Dispvtationvm
Tomi Tres. Posterior & accuratior Editio, Superiorum
auctoritate recognita, sparsisque hinc inde mendis,
quae in priori exciderant, expurgata; vberrimis
praeterea Indicibus, altero Disputationum, altero
rerum scitu digniorum ditata. Complectitur hic Tomus
libros VI. quorum I. agit de Sponsalibus. II. de
Essentia, & Consensu Matrimonij in genere. III. de
Consensu clandestino. IV. de Consensu coacto. V. de
Consensu conditionato. VI. de Donationibus inter
coniuges, sponsalitia Largitate, & Arrhis. Tomvs
Primvs. Lvgdvni: Sumptibus societatis Typographorum,
1621.
   3v. in 1 ([21], 500 p.; 403 p.; 408, [62] p.);
36cm.

   Vol. II has separate t.-p.: R. Patris Th. Sanchez
Cordvbensis, E' Societate Iesv, De Sancto Matrimonii
Sacramento Dispvtationvm Tomus Secundus: In quo etiam
continetur liber septimus, qui de Impedimentis
Matrimonij agit.
   Vol. III has separate t.-p.: R. Patris Th. Sanchez
Cordvbensis, E' Societate Iesv, De Sancto Matrimonii
Sacramento Dispvtationvm Tomus Tertius. In hos
tertio Tomo continentur, liber VIII. qui est de
Dispensationibus: & IX. qui de debito coniugali: ac
demm X. qui de diuortio agit, cum indice rerum
locupletissimo. [Indices).
   Palau, 294477; Simón Díaz Jesuitas, no. 1756.
Reel 165, No. 1077

SÁNCHEZ, TOMÁS, 1550-1610.
   Dispvtationvm De S.^{to} Matrimonii Sacramento,
Avthore Thoma Sanchez Cordubensi è Societate Iesv,
Libri Decem In Tres Tomos Distribvti. I.Tom. de
Sponsalibus, Essentia, & consensu Matr. in genere,
Consensu Clandestino, Consensu Coacto, Consensu
Conditionato Donat. inter Coniug. & Spons. &c. II.
Tom. de Impedimentis Matrimonij. III. Tom. de
Dispensationibus, Debito Coniugali, Diuortio. Cvm
Triplici Indice Dispvtationvm: Iure Pontificio, &
Caesareo: & rerum omnium refertissimo. Svperiorvm
Permissv. Venetiis: Apvd Ivntas, 1625.
   3v. ([65], 551 p.; [61], 402 p.; 425 p.); 31cm.

   Vol. II has separate title-page: Dispvtationvm De
S.^{to} Matrimonii Sacramento, Avthore Thoma Sanchez
Cordvbensi è Societate Iesv, Tomvs Secvndvs, In Qvo
Continetvr Liber Septimvs, Qui de impedimentis
Matrimonij agit. Cvm Triplici Indice Dispvtationvm:
Iure Pontificio, & Caesareo: & rerum omnium
refertissimo.
   Vol. III has separate title-page: Dispvtationvm
De S.^{to} Matrimonii Sacramento, Avthore Thoma Sanchez
Cordvbensi è Societate Iesv, Tomvs Tertivs, In Qvo
Continentvr Libri Octavvs, Qui de Dispensationibus:
Nonvs, Qui de Debito coniugali: Decimvs, Qui de
Diuortio agit. Cvm Triplici Indice Dispvtationvm:
Iure Pontificio, & Caesareo: & rerum omnium
refertissimo.
   Title of vol. I in red and black.
   Pagination errors throughout.
   Palau, 294480.
Reel 166, No. 1078

SÁNCHEZ DE AREVALO, RODRIGO, bp. of Zamora, 1404-1470.
   Speculum vite humane In quo discutiuntur cōmoda &
incommoda: dulcia & amara: solatia & miserie: prospera
& adversa: laudes & pericula omnium Statuum. Auctor
Nobilissimi huius libri fuit dñs Rodericus Epus
Zamoreñ. Castellanus. & Referendarius Pape Pauli.
II. In Theologia: vtroqz Jure & omnibus alijs bonis
litteris Doctissimus. Summus Christiane Religionis
cultos & defensor: Feruētissimsqz & Cōstantissimus

SÁNCHEZ DE AREVALO (Cont'd)
salutis alarum Zelator. Venetiis: per Lazarum de
Soardis, 1513.
58, [1] l.; 23cm.

Colophon: Impressum Venetijs per Lazarum de Soardis
Die. 19. Ianuarij. 1513. Qui a Senatu Venetorum
obtinuit que nullus imprimere seu imprimi facere aude
at eorum in territorio sub mulcta vt suis in gratijs
patet.
Adams, II, no. 648; Palau, 272031.
Reel 166, No. 1079

SÁNCHEZ DE LAS BROZAS, FRANCISCO, 1523-1601.
De Avtoribvs Interpretandis, Sive De Exercitatione,
Francisci Sanctii Brocensis in inclyta Salmanticensi
Academia Rhetorices professoris. Antverpiae: Ex
officina Christophori Plantini, Architypographi Regij,
1582.
28, [1] p.; 17cm.

Bound with: A) Lipsius, Justus: Electorvm Liber
I. In Qvo, praeter censuras, varij prisci ritus, 1580.
B) Rodolphus, Gerardus. De Litteris Canonicis,
Videlicet Formatis, Pacificis, Commendatitiis, Ac
Dimissoriis, Qvibvs In Ecclesia Primitiua Sancti
Patres ex generaliu Conciliorum decretis, in sacrosancta
Nicaena synodo prius excogitatis, vsi sunt.., 1582.
C) Busbecq, Ogier Ghislain de, Itinera
Constantinopolitanvm Et Amasianvm Ab Augerio Gislenio
Busbequio ad Solimannum Turcarum Imperatorem C. M.
Oratore confecta. Eiusdem Bvsbeqvii de re militari
contra Turcam instituenda consilium.
Adams, I, no. 3330.
Reel 166, No. 1080

SÁNCHEZ DE LAS BROZAS, FRANCISCO, 1523-1601.
Francisci Sanctii Minerva, Sive De Causis Latinae
linguae Commentarius, cui accedunt animadversiones &
notae. Gasperis Scioppii & longe uberiores Jacobi
Perizonii. Editio Altera, Priori Emendatior.
Franequerae: Apud Leonardum Strickium, Bibliopolam,
1693.
[11], 650, 52, [21] p.; 16cm.

Engraved Half-title: Francisci Sanctii Minerva cum
Animadversionibus Casp. Scjoppjj et Ja. Perizonjj.
Franeqverae, Apud Leonardum Strickium A° CIƆIƆCLXXXXIV.
Appended after p. 650: Francisci Sanctii Brocensis
Grammatica Latina.
Palau, 294877.
Reel 166, No. 1084

SÁNCHEZ DE LAS BROZAS, FRANCISCO.
Paradoxa Francisci Sanctii Brocensis In Inclyta
Salmanticensi Academia Primarii Rhetorices. Graecaeqve
Lingvae Doctoris. Antverpiae: Ex officina Christophori
Plantini, Architypographi Regij, 1582.
95, [1] p.; 17cm.

Bound with:
A) Gulielmus, Janus: Iani Gvlielmii Verisimilivm
Libri Tres. Antverpiae: Ex officina Christophori
Plantini, 1582. [16], 108, [3] p.
B) Sánchez de las Brozas, Francisco: De Avtoribvs
Interpretandis, Sive De Exercitatione, Francisci
Sanctii Brocensis in inclyta Salmanticensi Academia
Rhetorices professoris. Antverpiae: Ex officina
Christophori Plantini, Architypographi Regij, 1582.
28, [1] p.
C) Augurello, Giovanni Aurelio: Ioannis Avrelii
Avgvrelli P. Ariminensis Chrysopoeiae Libri III. Et
Geronticon Liber I. Antverpiae: Ex officina
Christophori Plantini, 1582. 99 p.
Adams, I, no. 2155 (Ioannis Avrelli Avgvrelli only);
Palau, 294869 (Paradoxa Francisci Sanctii Brocensis
only).
Reel 166, No. 1085

SÁNCHEZ DE VIANA, PEDRO (translator) see OVIDIUS NASO,
PUBLIUS, Las Transformaciones ..., 1589.

SANDOVAL, PRUDENCIO DE, bp. of Pamplona, ca. 1560-1620.
Chronica Del Inclito Emperador De España, Don Alonso
VII. deste nombre Rey de Castilla y Leon, hijo de don
Ramon de Borgoña, y de doña Hurraca, Reyna propietaria
de Castilla. Sacada De Vn Libro Muy Antigvo escrito
de mano con letras de los Godos, por relacion de
los mismos que lo vieron, y de muchas escrituras y
priuilegios originales del mesmo Emperador, y otros.
Por F. Prvdencio De Sandoval, Predicador de la Orden
de S. Benito. Dirigida A Don Francisco Gomez de
Sandoval y Roxas Duque de Lerma, Marques de Denia, Ced,
y Ampudia, del Consejo de Estado del Rey don Felipe
III. nuestro Señor, y su Cauallerico mayor, y Sumiller
de Corps, Comendador Mayor de Castilla, y Alcavde del
Castillo de Burgos y de la casa Real de Tordesillas.
Madrid: Por Luis Sanchez, 1600.
[25], 491 p.; 30 cm.

"Las casa de quien se trata en este libro: " p.
185-491. Missing pages 459-460.
Pagination errors throughout.
Adams, II, no. 308; Graesse, p. 263; Knapp-Huntington,
p. 289; Palau, 297139; Penney, p. 499; Pérez Pastor, no.
718; Ticknor, p. 322.
Reel 167, No. 1088

SANDOVAL, PRUDENCIO DE, bp. of Pamplona, ca. 1560-1620.
Historia De La Vida Y Hechos Del Emperador Carlos
V. Max. Fortissimo. Rey Catholico De España Y De Las
Indias, Islas, y tierra firme del Mar Oceano. Al
Catholico Rey Don Felipe III. deste nombre nuestro
Señor. Por el Maestro Don Fray Prvdencio De Sandoval
su Coronista, Obispo de Pamplona. Primera Parte.
Tratanse en esta primera parte los hechos desde el
Año 1500. hasta el de 1528. Pamplona: En casa de
Bartholome Paris mercader Librero, 1634 [i.e.1614?]
2v. ([29], 895, [30] p.; [5], 898, [15] p.); 32cm.

Vol. 2 t.-p. also reads: Tratanse En Esta Segvnda
Parte Los Hechos Desde El Año 1528. hasta el de 1557.
en que el Emperador se fue al Cielo ..., 1614.
Goldsmith, p. 164, no. 206; Palau, XIX, p. 383;
Penney, p. 499; Pérez Goyena, no. 457.
Reels 167 & 168, No. 1089, Vol. 1 & 2

SANDOVAL, PRUDENCIO DE, bp. of Pamplona, ca. 1560-1620.
La Historia Del Imperador Carlos Qvinto, Maximo
Fortissimo Rey De Las Españas. Qve Escrivio En Treinta
Y Tres Libros El M.D. Fr. Prvdencio De Sandoval,
Chronista del Señor Rey D. Felipe III. despues Obispo
de Pamplona. Abreuiados, y añadidos con diuersas, y
curiosas noticias, pertenecientes a esta Historia. Por
Don Ioseph Martinez De La Pvente. Y Dedicados Al Mvy
Alto, Mvy Poderoso, Y Mvy Catolico Señor Don Carlos II
Rey De Las Españas, Y Del Nvevo Mvndo, De Las Indias,
Islas, Y Tierra-Firme del mar Occeano, y demàs
adjacentes, Archiduque de Austria, Duque de Borgoña,
de Brauante, y Milan. Conde de Abspurg, de Flandes,
y de Tirol, &c. En Manos Del Excelentissimo Señor
D. Ivan Francisco De La Cerda Aragon Folch de Cardona
Enriquez de Ribera y Sandoual, Duque de Medina Celi,
de Sogorve, de Cardona, de Alcala, y de Lerma, Marques
de Denia, Adelantado Mayor de Castilla, Condestable de
Aragõ &c. Cauallero de la Insigne Orden del Toyson de
Oro, Sumiller de Corps del Rey N. S. y Capitan General
del mar Occeano, Costas, y Exercitos de Andalucia.
Madrid: Por Ioseph Fernandez de Buendia, 1675.
[29], 518 p.; 21cm.

Goldsmith, p. 164, no. 209; Palau, 297149; Salvá,
II, 3034.
Reel 168, No. 1090

SANDOVAL, PRUDENCIO DE, bp. of Pamplona, ca. 1560-1620.
[Historia de la vida y hechos del Emperador Carlos V. English]
  The Civil Wars Of Spain, In the beginning of the Reign of Charls the 5^t, Emperor of Germanie, and King of that nation. Written originally in the Spanish-tongue, by Prudencio de Sandoval, Doctor of Divinitie, and Abbat of the Monasterie of St Isidro el Real, in Valladolid, of the Order of St Bennet, Historiographer Roial to Philip the Third; never yet Translated, now put into English by Captain J.W. London: Printed by William Du Gard, 1652.
  [9], 387 p.; 28cm.

  English translation by James Wadsworth the Younger.
  Title vignette (device formerly used by Robert Young. MacKerrow no. 405).
  Allison, p. 162, no. 7; Palau, 297153; Wing S. 664.
Reel 168, No. 1091

SANTA CRUZ DE DUEÑA, MELCHOR DE, fl. 1574.
  Floresta Española, De Apoteghmas o Sentencias, sabia y graciosamente dichas de algunos Españoles Colegidas Por Melchior De Santa Cruz, de Dueñas, vezino de la Ciudad de Toledo. La Floresta Spagnola, Ov Le Plaisant Bocage, Contenant plusieurs comptes [sic], gosseries, brocards, cassades, & graues sentences de personnes de tous estats. Brvxelles: Par Rutger Velpius, & Hubert Anthoine, à l'Aigle d'or pres de la Court, 1614.
  [2], 509, [1] p.; 16cm.

  Translation by Pissevin or Pissivin.
  Doublet, p. 119; Heredia, no. 6272; Palau, 297948; Peeter-Fontainas, II, no. 1171; Salvá, II, 2163.
Reel 169, No. 1092

SANTORO, JUAN BASILIO.
  Prado Espiritval Recopilado De Antigvos, Clarissimos, Y Santos Doctores, Por El Doctor Iuan Basilio Sanctoro. Dirigido Al Illvstrissimo Señor Don Iuan Bautista de Azevedo, Patriarca de las Indias, Obispo de Valladolid, del Consejo de su Magestad, Inquisidor Apostolico General contra la heretica prauedad y apostasia en sus Reynos, y Señorios, &. Aora Nvevamente Añadido De Mvchas y diuersas Flores de Santos, por el mismo Autor. Primera Y Segvnda Parte. Lerida: Por Luys Manescal mercader de Libros, 1619.
  2 pts. ([16], 169, [1] l.; [4], 213, [11] l.); 30cm.

  Part II has a separate title-page and pagination.
  Imperfect: title-page and 3 following leaves mutilated and repaired, with some loss of text; the outer columns of the last 2 leaves of the Table at the end have been cut away; 3rd and 4th leaves from the end are mutilated and repaired, with some loss of text.
  Palau, 300506.
Reel 169, No. 1093

SANTOS, FRANCISCO, fl. 1663.
  Descripcion Del Real Monasterio De S. Lorenzo Del Escorial, Vnica Maravilla Del Mvndo, Fabrica Del Prvdentissimo Rey Filipo Segvndo. Coronada Por El Catholico Rey Filipo Qvarto El Grande, Con La Magestvosa Obra Del Pantheon, Y Translacion De Los Cverpos Reales, Reedificada Por Nvestro Rey, Y Señor Carlos II. Despves Del Incendio. Dedicada A Sy Magestad Catholica: Por El Padre Fr. Francisco De Los Santos, Professo De La Misma Real Casa, Lector que fue de Sagrada Escritura, y Rector en su Ilustre

SANTOS (Cont'd)
Colegio, Prior de los Monasterios de Bornos, y Benauente, Visitador General de Castilla, y Leon, y actualmente Historiador General de la Orden de San Geronimo. Madrid: En la Imprenta de Bernardo de Villa Diego, Impressor de su Magestad, 1681.
  [6], 163, [5] l.; 30cm.

  Pagination errors throughout.
  Doublet, p. 120; HC:NS4/265; Palau, 300552; Penney, p. 505; Salvá, II, 2592.
Reel 169, No. 1096

SANTOS, FRANCISCO, fl. 1663.
  El Sastre Del Campillo. Su Autor Francisco Santos, Criado de su Magestad, y natural de Madrid. Madrid: Por Lorenço Garcia, 1685.
  [4], 140, [1] l.; 15cm.

  Pagination errors, 27-31 omitted in numbering.
  Goldsmith, p. 166, no. 249; Palau, 300580; Penney, p. 505; Salvá, II, 1981.
Reel 169, No. 1094

SANTOS, FRANCISCO, fl. 1663.
  Las Tarascas De Madrid, Y Tribvnal Espantoso. Passos Del Hombre perdido, y relacion del espiritu malo. Dedicado A D. Manvel Balvin Y Verriz, Official de Estado en el de Guerra, y Oficial Mayor de Cruzada. Sv Avtor Francisco Santos, Criado del Rey Nuestro Señor. Valencia: Por Francisco Antonio de Burgos, 1694.
  [31], 317, [2] p.; 15cm.

  Pagination errors throughout.
  Goldsmith, p. 166, no. 251; Jerez, p. 97; Palau, 300568; Penney, p. 505; Ticknor, p. 324.
Reel 169, No. 1095

SARAGOSSA.
  [Laws, etc.]
  Recopilacion De Los Estatvtos De La Civdad De Zaragoza. Por Los Señores Ivrados, Capitol, y Consejo, con poder de Concello general. Confirmados, y decretados el primero de Deziembre de 1635. Zaragoça: en el Hospital Real, y General de Nuestra Señora de Gracia, [1636?]
  [4], 312, [8] p.; 28cm.

  Colophon: "Acabose Esta Obra Siendo Ivrados los muy Ilustres señores Doctor Don Geronimo Lopez, Doctor Don Geronimo Ardid, Doctor Don Miguel Castellod, Doctor Don Iuan Francisco Romeu, y Don Manuel de Pasamar."
  HC:S4/712; Penney, p. 612; Palau, 252473.
Reel 202, No. 1297

SARAGOSSA.
  [Laws, etc.]
  Ordinaciones De La Imperial Civdad De Zaragoza, Dadas Por La Magestad Catolica Del Señor Rei Felipe Tercero En Aragon, Año M.DC.LVIII. Çaragoça: En la Imprenta de Migvel De Lvna, Impressor de la Ciudad, 1659.
  [10], 208, [9] p.; 28cm.

  Palau, 203409.
Reel 202, No. 1295

SARAGOSSA.
[Laws, etc.]
Ordinaciones De La Imperial Civdad De Zaragoza;
Concedidas Por La Catolica, Sacra, Y Real Magestad
Del Señor Rey D. Carlos Segvndo, Y Sv Madre La Señora
Reyna Doña Mariana De Avstria, su Tutora, Curadora, y
Governadora vniversal de todos sus Reinos, y Monarquia,
en veinte y tres dias del mes de Deziembre del año 1669.
Zaragoça: En la Imprenta de los Herederos de Diego
Dormer, Impressores de la Ciudad, 1675.
[32], 218, [10] l.; 28cm.

Palau, 203410.
Reel 202, No. 1296

SARMIENTO DE MENDOZA, MANUEL.
Milicia Evangelica, Para Contrastar La Idolatria de
los Gētiles, conquistar almas, derribar la humana
prudencia, desterrar la auaricia de ministros. De
D. Manuel Sarmiento de Mendoca, Maestro y publico
professor de la S. Teologia, y dos vezes Rector de la
Vniuersidad de Salamanca, Canonigo Magistral de la
S. Iglesia de Seuilla. Al Excelentissimo señor Cõde
Duque, &c. Madrid: Por Iuan Gõçalez, 1628.
[8], 147, [1] l.; 16cm.

Vignette: El cuchillo le da el fruto.
Palau, 302397.
Reel 169, No. 1097

SAYAS RABANERA Y ORTUBIA, FRANCISCO DIEGO DE, d. 1680.
Anales De Aragon Desde El Año De MDXXV. Del
Nacimiento De Nvestro Redemptor Hasta El De MDXXV
Escrivialos Don Fran.co Diego De Savas Rabanera Y
Ortvbia Chronista Del Rey N.o S.r Y El Mayor Del
Reyno De Aragon. Inclita Facta Docent. [Zaragoza:
Por Los Herederos De P.o La Naia Impresores Del Reyno,
1666].
[39], 840, [57] p.; 30cm.

Engraved title-page.
Imperfect: p. 807-8 and 813-14 wanting.
Pagination errors throughout.
One of the works supplementary to Zurita's Anales,
following that of Leonardo y Argensola.
The "Censura" of Don José Pellicer d Ossua y
Tovar is dated January 8, 1667, and the dedications,
February 24, 1667.
Errors in binding: p. 327-28 follow p. 329030 and
331-32 follow 333-34.
Goldsmith, p. 167, no. 290; Jeménez Catalán, no.
754; HC:NS4/464; Palau, 303368; Penney, p. 507; Salvá,
I, 549; Ticknor, p. 325.
Reel 169, No. 1098

SCOTT, THOMAS, 1580?-1626.
Vox Popvli. Or Newes From Spayne, translated
according to the Spanish coppie. Which may serve to
forewarn both England and the United Provinces how
farre to trust to Spanish pretences. [s.l.:s.n.], 1620.
28 p.; 18cm.

Bound with the author's: The Second Part Of Vox
Popvli, or Gondomar appearing in the likenes of
Matchiauell in a Spanish Parliament, wherein are
discouered his treacherous & subtile Practises To the
ruine as well of England as the Netherlandes Faithfully
Translated out of the Spanish Coppie by a well-willer
to England and Holland. The second edition.
Church, 380A; HC:398/751; Palau, 303696; Penney,
p. 510.
Reel 170, No. 1099

SCOTT, THOMAS, 1580?-1626.
The Second Part of Vox Popvli, or, Gondomar appearing in the likeness of Matchiauell in a Spanish
Parliament, wherein are discouered his treacherous &
subtile Practises To the ruine as well of England as
the Netherlandes Faithfully translated out of the
Spanish Coppie by a well-willer to England and Holland.
The second edition. Goricom: by Ashuerus Jans, 1624.
[7], 60 p.

Reel 170, No. 1100

SENECA, LUCIUS ANNAEUS.
[De Benefici. Spanish]
Espeio De Bienechores Y Agradecidos: Qve contiene
Los siete Libros De Beneficios de Lucio Aneo Seneca,
insigne Filosofo moral: agora de nueuo traduzidos de
Latin en Castellano por Fray Gaspar Ruyz Montiano,
de la Orden de San Benito. Tiene Notados Y Declarados
Por El Mesmo Traductor algunos de los lugares mas
difficiles. (sic) Y al cabo del libro tiene quatro
Tablas de nueua inuencion, muy prouechosas para todo
genero de personas especialmente, para Predicadores,
y para Cortesanos que lo quieren parecer en sus
cartas y conuersaciones. Dirigido A Don Ivan De
Mendoza Duque del Infantado. Barcelona: en casa
Sebastian de Cormellas al Call, 1606.
[37], 479, [2] p.; 21cm.

Spanish translation by Gaspar Ruiz Montiano.
Colophon: "Impresso en Barcelona, en la Emprenta de
Sebastian de Cormellas. Año. M.DC.VI."
Palau, 308117.
Reel 170, No. 1103

SENECA, LUCIUS ANNAEUS.
[De Benefici. Spanish]
Los Libros de beneficijs De Lucio Aeneo Seneca.
A Aebucio Liberal. Traducidos por el Li.do P.o
Fernandez Nauarrete Canonigo de San Etiago Cousultor
del S.to off.o Cappellan y S.rio de sus Mag.des y de
Camara del S. Car.l Infante. Dedicados a su Alt.a
Madrid: En la Emprenta del Reyno, 1629.
[5], 224 l.; 21cm.

Spanish translation by Pedro Fernández Navarrete.
Engraved title-page.
Pagination errors throughout.
Palau, 308118.
Reel 170, No. 1104

SENECA, LUCIUS ANNAEUS.
[Epistolae. Spanish]
Epistolas de Seneca en Romance: nueuamẽte impressas
y corregidas y emendadas. [Alcala de Henares: en
casa de Miguel de Eguia, 1529].
73, [3] l.; 26cm.

Spanish translation by unknown.
Engraved title-page, with several vignettes.
Colophon: "En la vniversidad Alcala d'Henares en
casa de Miguel de Eguia a xv. d'Enero. M.D.XXIX -
anos."
Errors in foliation: 8 (i.e. 12).
Graesse, p. 354; Palau, 308016; Salvá, II, 4005.
Reel 170, No. 1102

SENECA, LUCIUS ANNAEUS.
[Variorum. Spanish]
Libros De Lucio Anneo Seneca, En Qve tracta. I.
Dela vida bienauenturada. II. Delas siete artes
liberales. III. Delos preceptos y doctrinas.
IIII. Dela prouidencia de Dios. V. Dela misma
prouidencia de Dios. Traduzidos en Castellano, por
mandado del muy alto principe, el rey don Iuan de
Castilla de Leon el segundo. Anvers: En casa de
Iuan Steelsio, 1551.
[8], 196, [12] ℓ.; 16cm.

Spanish translation by unknown.
Pagination errors: 9-16 omitted in page numbering.
Adams, II, no. 895; Graesse, p. 354; La Serna, II,
1465; Palau, 307671; Peeters-Fontainas, II, 1184.
Reel 170, No. 1101

SENECA, LUCIUS ANNAEUS see also NÚÑEZ DE GUZMÁN,
FERNANDO: DEL RIO, MARTIN ANTOINE.

SENNERT, ANDREAS, 1606-1689 see Bible. N.T. 1 John.
Syriac. 1652.

SEPULVEDA, JUAN GINES DE, 1490-1573.
Ioannis Genesii Sepvlvedae Cordvbensis Sacrosanctae
Theologiae Doctoris, Caroli V. Imperatoris, Historici.
Opera, quae reperiri potuerunt Omnia. Quorum elenchum
vide lector pagina quinta. Nvnc Primvm Singvlari
Stvdio in Hispania, Italia, & Gallia ad publicam
vtilitatem conquisita, & iam simul in lucem edita.
Adiectus est copiosus rerum memorabilium index.
Agrippinae: In Officina Birckmannica, sumptibus
Arnoldi Mylij, 1602.
[13], 634, [17] p.; 20cm.

Pagination errors throughout.
Palau, 309311.
Reel 170, No. 1105

SERNA, ALONSO DE LA.
Sermon. En Las Onras Qve El Cabildo De La Santa
Iglesia de Sevilla celebró al Ilustrissimo señor
don Pedro de Castro y Quiñones su Arcobispo, en siete
de Enero de 1624. Por el Maestro don Alonso de la
Serna, Racionero de la misma Iglesia, Consultor del
Santo Oficio, y Administrador del hospital del Cardenal.
A don Pedro Giron de Ribera, Marques de Alcala,
señor de las villas de Lobon, Chuzena, y el Alpicar,
de la Orden de Santiago de la Espada, &c. Sevilla:
por Francisco de Lyra, 1624.
12 p.; 19cm.

Palau, 309696; Penney, p. 514.
Reel 170, No. 1106

SESSE, JOSEPE DE, d. 1629.
Inhibitionvm Et Magistratvs Ivstitiae Aragonvm
Tractatvs. In Qvo De Inhibitionibvs, Et Execytione
Privilegiata, & guarentigia facienda, ac eadem in vim
exceptionum, seu iurisfirmae retardanda agitur:
variaque iuris resoluciones practicae cum todidem
decissionibus; nec non consuetudines Regni Aragonum ad
iuris terminos redacta tradunctur, & explanatur.
Avtore Iosepho De Sese I.V.D. Olim In Ilerdensi, Et
Caesaraugustano Gymnasio Iuris Canonici publico
interprete, deinde Iustitiae Aragonum Locumtenente, nunc

SESSE (Cont'd)
vero Regijeiusdem Regni Senatus Consiliario, ac aulae
causarum criminalium Decano. Illvstrissimo Ac
Admodvm Illvstribvs D. D Don Didaco Fernandez Cabrera
& de Bouadilla Comiti de Chinchona, ac praesidi Don
Monserrato Guardiola, Don Ioanni Sabater Didaco
Clauero, Don Iosepho Bañatos, Martino Monter de la
Cueua, Don Philipo Tallada, Saluatori Fontanet, Sacri
supremi Senatus inclytae Corona Regni Aragonum
Senatoribus dicatum opus. Barcinonae: Ex Typographia
Gabrielis Graells, & Geraldi Dotil, 1608.
[25], 806, [104], [4], 43 p.; 28cm.

Included at end: Svmmarivm Eorvm ... and
Responsvm In Syndicatv.
Palau, 311100; Penney, p. 515.
Reel 170, No. 1107

SESSÉ Y PIÑOL, JOSÉ DE see SESSE, JOSEPPE DE.

SHIRLY, JAMES, 1596-1666.
The Yovng Admirall. As It Was Presented By her
Majesties Servants, at the private house in Drury Lane.
Written by James Shirly. London: Printed by Tho.
Cotes, for Andrew Crooke and William Cooke, 1637.
[74] p.; 19cm.

Plot taken from Lope de Vega's Don Lope de Cardona.
Reel 170, No. 1108

SIMANCAS, JACOBUS, bp. of Zamora, d. 1583.
Iacobi Simancae Pacensis Episcopi. De Catholicis
Institvtionibvs Liber, Ad praecauendas & extirpandas
haereses admodum necessarius, tertio nunc editus.
Romae: In Aedibus Populi Romani Anno Iubilaei, 1575.
[32], 522, [1] p.; 23cm.

Adams, II, no. 1145; Palau, 314059.
Reel 171, No. 1109

SIMANCAS, JACOBUS, bp. of Zamora, d. 1583.
De Repvblica Libri IX. Opus collectum ex omnibus,
qui de ea optime scripserunt, auctoribus. Per R. D.
Iacobvm Simancam, Pacensem Episcopvm. Cum duplici
Indice, & Priuilegijs. Venetiis: apud Bologninum
Zalterium, 1569.
[17], 303, [1] p.; 23cm.

Printer's device: venetia.
Pagination errors throughout.
Bound with: Barbaranus, Julius: Officinae Ivlii
Barbarani Tomi Tres: Promptvarivm Rervm Electarvm, In
re praesertim Romana. Index Titvlorvm Omnivm. 1569.
Adams, II, no. 1147; Palau, 314065.
Reel 171, No. 1110

SOAREZ, CYPRIANO, 1524-1593.
De Arte Rhetorica Libri Tres. Ex Aristotele,
Cicerone & Quinctiliano praecipuè deprompti. Avctore
Cypriano Soario Sacerdote Societatis Iesv. Coloniae:
Apud Maternum Cholinum, 1570.
193, [15] p.; 16cm.

Bound with Caesarius, Joannes: Rhetorica Ioannis
Caesarii, ... 1565.
Adams, I, no. 102 (Rhetorica ... only).
Reel 173, No. 1138

SOARES DE ALARCÃO, JOÃO, 1580-1618.
La Iffanta (sic) Coronada, Por El Rey Don Pedro,
Doña Ines De Castro. En Octava Rima, Por Don Ivan
Soares de Alarcõ, Alcalde Mayor de Torres Vedras, y
Maestre sala de su Magestad. Lisboa: Por Pedro
CrasbeecK, 1606.
[8], 87, [1] l.; 23cm.

Title-page within ornamental border.
Pagination error: 61-64 omitted in page numbering.
Palau, 315405; Penney, p. 522.
Reel 171, No. 1112

SOAREZ DE ALARCÓN, JUAN see SOARES DE ALARCÃO, JOÃO.

SOLÍS Y RIVADENEYRA, ANTONIO DE, 1610-1686.
Comedias De Don Antonio De Solis, Secretario Del
Rey N. Señor, Oficial de Estado, y su Cronista, &c.
Dedicadas A Miguel Rodriguez, Escriuano de la Real
Casa del papel Sellado, &c. 50. ps. Madrid: Por
Melchor Alvarez, 1681.
[9], 382, [1] p.; 21cm.

Colophon: "Con Licencia. En Madrid en la Officina
de Melchor Alvarez. Año de 1681."
Contains: 1. Triunfos de amor y fortuna: 2. Loa;
3. Euridice y Orfeo; 4. El amor al uso; 5. Al alcanzar
del secreto. 6. Las amazonas; 7. El doctor Carlino;
8. Un bobo hace ciento; 9. La gitanilla; 10. Amparar
al enemigo.
Goldsmith, p. 170, no. 407; Palau, 318547.
Reel 171, No. 1113

SOLIS Y RIVADENEYRA, ANTONIO DE, 1610-1686.
Historia De La Conqvista De Mexico, Poblacion, Y
Progressos De La America Septentrional, Conocida Por
El Nombre De Nveva España. Escriviala Don Antonio De
Solis Secretario De Sv Magestad, Y Sv Chronista Mayor
de las Indias, Dedicase Al Illvstrissimo Señor Don
Gvillen De Rocafvll Y Rocaberti, Por La Gracia De Dios
Vizconde de Rocaberti, Conde de Peralada, y de Albatera,
&c. Barcelona: En la Imprenta de Ioseph Llopis
Impressor de Libros, 1691.
[21], 548, [15] p.; 29cm.

Half-title: Historia De La Nveva España: Por Don
Antonio De Solis.
Title printed in red and black.
Describes the voyages of Grijalva and Cortés,
and the overland Spanish assault on the Aztec capital.
Second edition.
Printer's device: En Lupus In Fabula.
Pagination errors throughout.
Goldsmith, p. 170, no. 414; Medina, Bibl. Hisp-Amer.,
III, no. 1880; Palau, 318603; Penney, p. 523; Sabin,
no. 86447.
Reel 171, No. 1114

SOLÍS Y RIVADENEYRA, ANTONIO DE, 1610-1686.
Varias Poesias, Sagradas, Y Profanas, Qve Dexò
Escritas (Avnove No Juntas, Ni Retocadas) Don Antonio
De Solis Y Ribadeneyra, Oficial de la Secretaria de
Estado, y Secretario de su Magestad, y su Chronista
Mayor de las Indias. Recogidas, Y Dadas A Lvz Por
Don Jvan De Goveneche. Dedicadas A La Excelentissima
Señora Doña Josepha Alvarez de Toledo y Portugal Tellez
Giron, Hija de los Excelentissimos Señores Condes de
Oropesa. Madrid: En la Imprenta de Antonio Roman,
1692.
[44], 328 p.; 23cm.

SOLÍS Y RIVADENEYRA (Cont'd)
First edition.
Goldsmith, p. 171, no. 418; Graesse, p. 432;
Jerez, p. 99; Palau, 318550; Penney, p. 523; Salvá,
I, no. 1421; Ticknor, p. 336.
Reel 171, No. 1115

SOLÓRZANO PEREIRA, JUAN DE, 1575-1655.
D. Ioannis De Solorzano Pereira I.V.D. Ex Eqvestri
Militia Divi Iacobi, Et In Regiis Svpremis Castellae,
Et Indiarvm Consiliis Antiqvissimi, Et Iam Emeriti
Senatoris. Emblemata Centvm, Regio Politica. Aeneis
Laminis Affabre Caelata. Vividisqve, Et Limatis
carminibus explicita, & singularibus commentarijs
affatim illustrata. Qvibvs, Qvicqvid Ad Regvm
Institvtionem, Et Rectam Reip. Administrationem
conducere, & pertinere videtur, summu studio disseritur.
Opys Vel Ipsa Varietate, Et Vtilitate Rerum, &
Materiarum, quas continet (sic) expetendum, & omnium
Facultatum Professoribus summopere necessarium. Cùm
quadruplici Indice Absolutissimo. Primo, uniusciusque
Emblematis mentem complectente. Altero loca Sacrae
Scripturae. Tertio, Leges, & Canones, qae (sic)
citantur, & illustrantur, designante. Et quartò,
copiosissimam rerum omnium, & sententiarum farraginem,
qua in toto opere continentur, ubertim Lectoribus
effundente. [In Typographia Domin, Garciae. Morras,
Matriti, 1653].
[41], 844, [87] p.; 31cm.

HC:NS4/211; Medina, Bibl. Hisp.-Amer., III, no.
1200; Palau, 318996; Penney, p. 523.
Reel 172, No. 1116

SOLSONA, FRANCISCO, 16th cent.
Stylvs Capibreviandi, Cvm Qvodam Vtili Clavsvlarum
tractatu per Franciscum Solsona Notarium publicum
Barcinone in lucem editus. Qvibvs Accesservnt Alii
tractatus, quorum omnium ordinem ac numerum altera pagina
indicabit. Barcinone: Sebastiani à Cormellas, 1594.
157, [7] l.; 15cm.

Last 4 leaves repaired.
Colophon: "Con Licencia Estampat en Barcelona en
casa Sebastian de Cormellas al Call. Any, 1594."
Pagination errors throughout.
Palau, 319015.
Reel 172, No. 1117

SOTO, ANDRES.
Captivi Temporis Redemptio. Libellvs Ordinvm
Omnivm Hominibvs Omnibus vtilissimus: in quo Temporis
pretium, vtque viculis eripiendum fit, declaratur: Per
Reverendiss. P. F. Andraeam Soto, Ordinis Francisci
Reformatorum prouinciae Conceptionis. Ephes. V.
Redimentes tempus quoniam dies mali sunt. Coloniae:
Apud Ioannem Crithium, 1611.
137, [4] p.; 13cm.

Reel 172, No. 1118

SOTO, DOMINGO DE, FRAY, 1494-1560.
Relectio F. Dominici Soto Segobiensis Theologi
Ordinis Predicatorum, Caesareae Maiestati Caroli V.
à sacris Confessionibus. De Ratione Tegendi, Et
Detegendi Secretvm. Brixiae: Apvd Petrvm Mariam
Marchetvm, 1582.
[25], 376 p.; 16cm.

Colophon: Brixiae, apud Iacobus, & Polyoretum de
Turlinis.
Adams, II, no. 1499; Palau, 320080.
Reel 172, No. 1119

SOTO, HERNANDO DE, 1500 (ca.)-1542, supposed author.
[Relacam verdadeira. English.]
  The Worthye And Famovs History, Of The Travailes,
Discouery, & Conquest, of that great Continent of
Terra Florida, being liuely Paraleld, with that of
our now Inhabited Virginia. As also The Comodities of
the said Country, With diuers excellent and rich mynes,
of Golde, Siluer, and other Mettals, &c. which cannot
but giue vs a great and exceeding hope of our Virginia,
being so neere of one Continent. Accomplished and
effected, by that worthy Generall and Captaine, Don
Ferdinaudo (sic) de Soto, and six hundreth Spaniards
his followers. London: Printed for Mathew Lownes, 1611.
  [9], 180 p.; 18cm.

  English translation by Richard Hakluyt.
  Second edition.
  Allison, p. 169, no. 21.1; Pollard and Redgrave,
no. 22939.
Reel 172, No. 1120

SOTO, PEDRO DE, d. 1563.
  Compendivm Doctrinae Catholicae, In Vsvm Plebis
Christianae rectè instituendae: ex libris institutionis
Christianae R. P. F. Petri de Soto, Dominicani Theologi,
Confessoris Caesareae Maiest. collectu, additis cuiqz
loco aptis precatiunculis: & adiuncta breui
explicatione Ecclesiastici cultus, maximè sacrae
Missae: & nunc denuo ab eadē Authore ampliori
explicatione locupletatum, ut sequens indicat pagina.
Iussu, & authoritate Reuerendissimi Domini Othonis,
Cardinalis & Epis. Aug. editū. Sinite paruulos uenire
ad me. Matth. 19. [Morguntia?: Excudebat F. Behem?] 1554.
  [12], 115 l.; 16cm.

  NUC - Mogvntia [Excudebat F. Behem]
  Adams, II, no. 1507; Palau, 320310.
Reel 172, No. 1121

SOTO, PEDRO DE, d. 1563.
  Compendivm Doctrinae Catholicae, in vsum plebis
Christianae rectè instituendae, à R. P. F. Petro de
Soto, Dominicano Theologo, Confessore Caes. Maiest.
collectum. Additis cuiqz loco aptis precatiunculis:
& adiuncta breui explicatione sacrae Missae: nunc
denuò ab eodem Autore ampliori explicatione locupletatum.
Accessit In Hac editione Paruus Catechismus
Catholicorum, authore D. Petro Canisio. Iussu &
Authoritate Reuerendiss. Domini Othonis, Card. & epis.
Augusta. editum. [Dilingae: Excudebat Sebaldus Meyer,
1564.]
  [16], 208 l.; 18cm.

  Bookplate: Josef Becker.
Reel 172, No. 1122

SOTO, PEDRO DE, d. 1563
  Institvtionis Christianae Libri Tres Priores: Ivssv
Reverendissimi Domini. D. Othonis Cardinalis & Episcopi
Augustani a doctis Theologis lecti & probati, ac
illius authoritate editi. Avthore R. P. D. Petro De
Soto, dominicano, Theologo, & confessore Caesareae
Magestatis. Avgvstae Vindelicorvm: imprimebat
Valentinus Othmar, 1548.
  [4], 117, [1] l.; 23cm.

  Pagination errors throughout.
  Adams, II, no. 1508; Palau, 320299.
Reel 172, No. 1123

SPAIN.
  [Laws, etc. 1527]
  Las leyes del estilo. E declaraciones sobre las
leyes del fuero. [Burgos: J. de Junta, 1527].
  xxx, [1] l.; 29cm.

  Caption: "Aqui comiençan las leyes del estilo:
que por otra manera se llaman declaracion delas leyes
del fuero."
  Black letters.
  Title surmounted by vignette (Coat of arms of Spain)
with legend: Leyes del estilo, within ornamental
border.
  Palau, 235263.
Reel 172, No. 1125

SPAIN.
  [Laws, etc. 1552].
  La prematica que su magestad ha mādado hazer este
año de. M.D.Lij. de la pena que han de auer los ladrones
y rufianes y vagamundos y para que sean castigados los
holgazanes ansi hombres como mugeres y los esclauos
de qualquier edad que sean que fueren presos. Venden
se en casa de Salzedo Librero en Alcala de Henares:
[Joan de Brocar, 1552.]
  [4] l.; 28cm.

  Engraved title-page.
  Colophon: "Fue impressa en Alcala de Henares. En
casa de Joan de Brocar defūto que sancta gloria aya.
A diez y nueve dias del mes de diziembre del año
de mil y quinientos y cincuenta y dos."
  Palau, 235124.
Reel 172, No. 1126

SPAIN.
  [Laws, etc. 1570]
  Philippi II. Regis Catholici Edictvm De Librorum
prohibitorvm Catalogo obseruando. Antverpiae: Ex
officina Christophori Plantini M.D.LXX (1570)
  8 l. 120 p.; 16cm.

  Adams, II, no. 1013; Palau, 87262; Peeters-Fontainas,
I, no. 620.
No. 1127: Not Available

SPAIN.
  [Laws, etc. 1590.]
  Prematica En que se prohibe el arredarse los oficios
de Escriuanos de Camara, Y procuradorias, Recetorias,
y Escriuanias del Numero. Y que à los tales oficios
no sean admitidos al vso dellos, sino constare tener
de propia hazienda y patrimonio la tercia parte del
valor dellos. Madrid: Por Pedro Madrigal, 1590.
  [4] l.; 29cm.

  Palau, 235240.
Reel 172, No. 1128

SPAIN.
  [Laws, etc., 1594.]
  Prematica para que lo dispuesto por las leyes
contra los que jugaren, dados, bueltos, y carteta: se
entienda y execute, contra los que jugaren los juegos
que dizen del bolillo y trompico, palo o instrumento
que tengan encuentros, o hazares, o reparos, y los
tuuieren, vendieren, o hizieren, y dieren casa y
tableros para los jugar (sic). Madrid: Por Tomas de
Iunta, 1594.
  [4] l.; 29cm.

  Palau, 235263.
Reel 172, No. 1129

SPAIN.
[Laws, etc., 1594]
Prematicas que han salido este año de nouenta y quatro, publicadas en diez y nueue dias de Enero del dicho año: demas de las quales se mandan guardar otras que estauan hechas hasta agora, y se acrecientan las penas a los transgressores, y se da la orden que se ha de tener para la execucion y obseruancia dellas. Madrid: por Pedro Madrigal, 1594.
[44] l.; 28cm.

Contains:
A) Prematica En que se da nueua orden en el examẽ de los Medicos, y cirujanos, y boticarios: demas de lo que por otra esta proueydo, 1593. [5] l.
B) Prematica en que se manda guardar la de los tratamientos y cortesias, y se acrecientan las penas contra los transgressores de lo en ella, y en esta contenido: y que se proceda de oficio no auiendo denunciador, o no prosiguiendo la causa: y la justicia que no lo hiziere y tuuiere cuidado de executarlo, pague de sus bienes las penas que auian de pagar los condenados, y sea suspendido de oficio por dos años, 1594. [6] l.
C) Prematica En que se manda guardar lo proueido por el capitulo de Cortes, en que se prohibio andar coches cõ menos de quatro cauallos, y que se entienda y estienda lo por el prohibido en carricoches, y carros largos, y otros qualesquiera, 1594. [4] l.
D) Prematica En que se manda guardar lo prouido por vn capitulo de las Cortes, del año de ochenta y seis: en que se prohibio que los hombres no puedan traer en los cuellos, ni en puños, guarnicion alguna, ni almidon, ni gomas, ni filetes: sino sola la lechugilla de olanda. ò lienço, con vna, ò dos vaynillas, y se declara q̃ sean de vn dozauo de vara de medir, y q̃ las vaynillas y filetes no sean de color sino blancas: y se acrecientan las penas contra los que excedieren, 1594. [4] l.
E) Prematica En que se prohibe hazer y vender bufetes, escritorios, arquillas, braseros, chapines, mesas, contadores, y otras cosas guarnecidas de plata batida releuada, estampada, tallada, y llana, y que las pierda quien las hiziere, o vendiere, o comprare, 1594. [2] l.
F) Prematica En que se manda guardar la en que se dio la forma en la labor de las sedas, y se declara el peso que ha de tener cada vara, 1594. [4] l.

G) Prematica En Qve Se Manda Gvardar La de los vestidos y trajes, con las declaraciones que en ella se refieren: y se declara que los hombres puedan traer los vestidos que tuuieren hechos contra las dichas leyes, por todo el año de nouenta y quatro, y las mugeres por el de nouenta y cinco, 1594. [4] l.
H) Prematica Para Qve Lo Dispvesto Por Las Leyes contra los que jugaren dados, bueltos, y carteta, se entienda y execute contra los que jugaren los juegos que dizen del bolillo y trompico, palo, o instrumento que tengan encuentros, o azares, o reparos, y los tuuieren, vendieren, o hizieren, y dieren casa y tableros para los jugar. (sic), 1594. [4] l.
I) Prematica en que se pone el precio que por cada mula de alquiler ha de lleuar cada vn dia, y por meses, y que el retorno se dexe libremente a las personas que las alquilaren, 1594. [4] l.
J) Prematica En Qve Se Manda Gvardar Las hechas, so las penas en ellas contenidas, y las que mas en cada vna dellas, y adiciones y declaraciones nueuas se ponen y declaran: y que auiendo denunciador, y no prosiguiendo las causas, se proceda de oficio, y no se puedan moderar las penas: y los que visitaren las carceles, se informen del cuydado que ha auido por las justicias, de la guarda y execucion dellas, y para cada vn año se nombre vno del Consejo, y de las dichas Chancillerias y Audiencias, que tẽga particular cuydado del cumplimiento y execucion dellas, y de informar al que presidiere, y à los acuerdos, 1594. [5] l.

SPAIN (Cont'd)
HC 398/ 1651/6-9; Palau, 235256; Penney, p. 535; Pérez Pastor, no. 454.
Reel 172, No. 1130

SPAIN.
[Laws, etc., 1600.]
[Señor ... de la administracion y aumento de la Real Hazienda ... he recopilado todos los medios de consideracion, que han llegado a mi noticia ... Madrid 19 Sept. 1600.]
[2], 78 l.; 29cm.

Title-page wanting.
Reel 173, No. 1131

SPAIN.
[Laws, etc., 1610.]
Prematica En Qve Se Mandan guardar las leyes, que ponen penas a los que en las Catedras que se proueyeren en las Vniuersidades de Salamanca, Valladolid, y Alcala, hizieren sobornos, ò otros malos tratos, y se añaden penas mas graues. Madrid: Por Iuan de la Cuesta, 1610.
[4] l.; 29cm.

Palau, 235369.
Reel 173, No. 1132

SPAIN.
[Laws, etc., 1611].
Pragmatica De Tratamientos, y cortesias, y se acrecientan las penas contra los transgressores de lo en ella contenido. Madrid: Por Iuan de la Cuesta, 1611.
[7] l.; 29cm.

Goldsmith, p. 175, no. 560; Palau, 253395.
Reel 173, No. 1133

SPAIN.
[Laws, etc., 1611.]
Pragmatica En Que Se Da La Forma, cerca de las personas que se prohibe andar en coches, y los que pueden andar en ellos, y como se ayan de hazer, y que sean de quatro cauallos. Madrid: Por Iuan de la Cuesta, 1611.
[5] l.; 29cm.

Goldsmith, p. 175, no. 561; Palau, 235397.
Reel 173, No. 1134

SPAIN.
[Laws, etc., 1633.]
Prematica Sobre Las Cosas Tocantes a la conseruacion y aumento de la cria del ganado, y arredamientos de las dehessas donde pastan. Madrid: por Iuan Gonçalez, 1633.
[6] l.; 29cm.

Palau, 235456.
Reel 173, No. 1135

SPAIN.
[Laws, etc., 1691.]
Pragmatica Qve Sv Magestad Manda publicar, para que se guarde, execute, y observe la que se publicò el año de 1684. sobre la reformacion en el Excesso de Trages, Coches, y otras cosas en esta contenidas. Madrid: Por Julian de Paredes, Impressor de Libros, 1691.
[5] l.; 29cm.

Palau, 235539.
Reel 173, No. 1136

SPAIN.
    [Laws, etc., 1691]
    Pragmatica Que Sv Magestad Manda publicar, para que
se guarde, execute, y observe la que se publicò el
año de 1684. Sobre la reformacion en el excesso de
Trages, Coches, y otras cosas en esta contenidas.
Sevilla: Por Juan Francisco de Blas, 1691.
    4 l.; 29cm.

    Escudero, no. 1877; Goldsmith, p. 181, no. 741;
Palau, 235540; Penney, p. 539.
Reel 173, No. 1137

SPAIN. SOVEREIGNS, etc. see Name of Sovereign, (ALFONSO,
    FELIPE).

SPAIN. TREATIES, ETC. (CHARLES II) see HERRARA Y
    SOTOMAYOR, JACINTO DE: Iornada que su Magestad hizo
    a la ANDALVZIA (#5).

SUÁREZ, CIPRIANO, S.J. see SOAREZ, CYPRIANO.

SUÁREZ, FRANCISCO, 1548-1617.
    Defensio Fidei Catholicae, Et Apostolicae Aduersus
Anglicanae sectae errores, Cvm Responsione Ad Apologiam
Pro Ivramento Fidelitatis, & Praefationem monitoriam
Serenissimi Iacobia Angliae Regis. Authore F. D.
Francisco Svario Granatensis è Societate Iesv Sacrae
Theologiae in celebri Conimbricensi Academia Primario
Professore. Ad Serenissimos Totivs Christiani Orbis
Catholicos Reges, ac Principes. Conimbricae: Apud
Didacum Gomez de Loureyro Academiae Typographum, 1613.
    [17], 780, [27] p.; 28cm.

    Goldsmith, p. 187, no. 950; Palau, 323555.
Reel 173, No. 1140

SUÁREZ, FRANCISCO, 1548-1617.
    R. P. Francisci Svarez, Granatensis, E Societate
Iesv Doctoris Theologi, Et In Conimbricensi Academia
Sacrarum Literarum Primarij Professoris. Defensio
Fidei Catholicae Et Apostolicae Adversvs Anglicanae
Sectae Errores. Cvm Responsione Ad Apologiam Pro
Ivramento Fide - delitatis, & Praefationem monitoriam
Serenissimi Iacobi Magnae Britanniae Regis. Ad
Serenissimos Totivs Christiani Orbis Catholicos Reges
Et Principes. Mogvntiae: Sumptibus Hermanni Mylii
Birckmanni. Excudebat Balthasar Lippius, 1619.
    [13], 448, [15] p.; 36cm.

    Palau, 323557.
Reel 173, No. 1141

SUÁREZ, FRANCISCO, 1548-1617.
    Francisci Svarez, E Societate Iesv. Metaphysicarvm
Dispvtationvm, In quibus, & naturalis Theologìa
ordinatè traditur, & Quaestiones ad omnes duodecim
Aristotelis libros pertinentes, accuratè disputantur,
Tomi Dvo. Cum quinque Indicibus: quorum prior
Disputationes, & Sectiones vtriusque Tomi complectitur.
Secundus breuem Aristotelici textus expositionem
continet, & loca, vbi Quaestiones ad textum pertinentes
hoc in opere disputantur, designat. Tertius est rerum
praecipuarum in vtroque Tomo contentarum. Quartus
est Philosophicus. Quintus verò Theologicus. Summa
recenter cura, prae cunctis alijs hucusque impressis,
à mendis omnibus expurgati. Cvm Licentia Svperiorvm.
Venetiis: Apud Petrum Mariam Bertanvm, 1619.
    2 vols. ([107], 602 p.; 662 p.); 36cm.

SUÁREZ (Cont'd)
    Part II has separate title-page: J. Tomvs Posterior.
Summa recenter cura, prae cunctis alijs huncusque
impressis, à mendis omnibus expurgatus.
    Pagination errors throughout.
    Palau, 323488.
Reel 174, No. 1142

SUÁREZ, FRANCISCO, 1548-1617.
    Doct. Francisci Svarez Granatensis, Ex Societate
Iesv Tractatus Theologicus, De Vera Intelligentia
Avxilii Efficacis, eisque Concordia, cum libero arbitrio.
Opvs Posthvmvm, Ad stabiliendas definitiones Fidei,
à S.D.N. Innocentio X. contra Iansenium eiusque
Partiarios, editas, accommodatum. Prodit Nvnc Primvm.
Lvgdvni: Sumpt. Philip. Borde, Laur. Arnaud, & Cl.
Riguad, 1655.
    [9], 414, (i.e. 408), [11] p.; 36cm.

    Pagination errors throughout.
    Palau, 323603.
Reel 175, No. 1143

SUÁREZ, FRANCISCO, 1548-1617.
    Doctoris Francisci Svarez Granatensis De Societate
Iesv In Celebri Conimbricensi Academia Theologica
facultatis Primarij professoris. Varia Opvscvla
Theologica. 1. De Concursu, motione & auxilio Dei.
Lib. III. 2. De Scientia Dei futurorum contingentium.
Lib. II. 3. De Auxilio efficaci. Breuis resolutio.
4. De Libertate diuinae voluntatis. Relectio prior.
5. De Reuiuiscentia meritorum. Relectio altera. 6.
De Iustitia Dei. Disputatio. Matriti: Apud Ioannem
Flandrum, 1599.
    [13], 574, [19] p.; 30cm.

    Pages missing at end of item.
    Adams, II, no. 2008; Palau, 323504.
Reel 175, No. 1144

SUÁREZ, FRANCISCO, 1548-1617.
    Editio vltra praecedentes exquisita, & à mendis
repurgata. Cum Indice gemino, vno locorum sacrae
Scripturae, altero rerum. Lvgdvni: Sumptibus Horatij
Cardon, 1611.
    [17], 816, [31] p.; 24cm.

    Palau, 323507.
Reel 175, No. 1145

SUÁREZ, RODRIGO see JUAREZ, RODRIGO.

SUÁREZ DE ALARCÓN, Antonio, Count of Torresvedras.
    Relaciones Genealogicas De La Casa De Los Marqveses
De Trocifal, Condes De Torresvedras, Sv Varonia
Zevallos De Alarcon, Y Por La Casa, Y Primer Apellido
Svarez, Escriviolas Don Antonio Svarez De Alarcon
primogenito de esta casa; Ofrecelas Al Rey Catolico
Don Felipe IV. El Grande N. S. Madrid: Por Diego
Diaz De La Carrera Impressor del Reyno, 1656.
    [13], 435, 135 p.; 29cm.

    Goldsmith, p. 187, no. 956; HC 346/1389; Palau,
323797; Penney, p. 546; Salvá, II, 3604; Simón Díaz,
Impresos, no. 3423.
Reel 176, No. 1147

SUÁREZ DE FIGUEROA, CHRISTOBAL, fl. 1613.
    La Constante Amarilis, De Christoval Suarez de
Figueroa, En Qvatre Discovrs, Traduite d'Espagnol en
Francois par N. L. Parisien. Lyon: Par Clavde
Morillon Imprimeur de M. De Montpensier, 1614.
    [17], 565, [18] p.; 17cm.

    French translation by Nicolas Lancelot.
    Engraved title-page.
    Jerez, p. 100; Palau, 323902; Penney, p. 546;
Salvá, II, 2003; Vaganay, no. 883.
Reel 176, No. 1148

SUÁREZ DE FIGUEROA, CHRISTOBAL, fl. 1613.
    España Defendida Poema Heroico De D. Christoval
Svarez De Figveroa Avditor de exercito y Prouincia
q fue por su Magestad. En esta quinta Impresion por
su Autor reconocido y de las erratas enmendado.
Napoles: Por Egidio Longo Regio Impresor, 1644.
    [9], 499 p.; 20cm.

    Engraved title-page.
    Palau, vol. 22, p. 244; Penney, p. 546; Salvá, I, 986.
Reel 176, No. 1149

SUÁREZ DE FIGUEROA, CHRISTOBAL, fl. 1613.
    El Passagero Advertencias Vtilissimas A La Vida
Hvmana. Por El Doctor Christoval Suarez de Figueroa.
A La Excellentissima Republica de Luca. 45. Barcelona:
Por Geronimo Margarit, 1618.
    [6], 371 l.; 15cm.

    Pagination errors throughout.
    Lower edge of title-page repaired with loss of some
words in imprint.
    Gallardo, no. 3987; Goldsmith, p. 187, no. 963;
Palau, 323914; Penney, p. 546; Salvá, II, 2004.
Reel 176, No. 1150

SUÁREZ DE FIGUEROA, CHRISTOBAL, fl. 1613.
    Plaza Vniversal De Todas Ciencias Y Artes, Parte
Tradvcida De Toscano, y parte compuesta Por El Doctor
Christoval Suarez de Figueroa. A Don Duarte, Marques
de Frechilla, y Villarramiel, Marques de Malagon,
Señor de las villas de Paracuellos, y Hernancauallero,
Comendador de Villanueua de la Serena. Madrid: Por
Luis Sanchez, 1615.
    [8], 368, [1] l.; 22cm.

    A translation from Tommaso Garzoni: La Piazza
Universale. Spanish translation with additions by
Christobal Suárez de Figueroa.
    Pagination errors throughout.
    Goldsmith, p. 187, no. 964; Palau, 323908; Penney,
p. 546; Salvá, II, 2426.
Reel 176, No. 1151

SUÁREZ DE MENDOZA Y FIGUEROA, ENRIQUE.
    Evstorgio Y Clorilene Historia Moscovica. Por
Don Enriqve Svarez De Mendoza Y Figveroa. Al
Excelentissimo Señor Don Iayme De Silva, Yxar, Sarmiento,
Pinòs, y Cabrera, Cerda, y Villaldrando, Conde de
Salinas, Duque, y Señor de Yxar, Marques de Alenquer,
Conde de Ribadeo, de Belchite, de Aliaga, de Balfagona,
Vizconde de Canet, y Ylla, Señor de las Varonias de
la Portella, Peramola, Grions, Alcaliz, y Estacho,
Conde de Guimeran, Vizconde de Evol, y Alqueforadat,
Señor de las Varonias de Albero, y Vicien, y de la
Villa de Frescano en el Reyno de Aragon, Señor de la
Villa de Villarrubia de los Ojos de Guadiana,
Gentilhombre de la Camara de su Magestad, y su Gran
Camarlengo de la Corona de Aragon. 41. Çaragoça:
por Ivan de Ybar, 1665.
    [25], 152, [1] l.; 20cm.

    Jerez, p. 100; Jiménez Catalán, 745; Palau, 323999;
Penney, p. 546; Salvá, II, 2007.
Reel 176, No. 1152

T

TACITUS, PUBLIUS CORNELIUS.
   [Opera. Spanish]
   Las Obras De C. Cornelio Tacito, Traducidas de
Latin en Castellano por Emanvel Sveyro, natural de la
ciudad de Anuers. Dirigidas à Su Alteza Serenissima.
Anvers: En casa de los Herederos de Pedro Bellero,
1613.
   [9], 1050, [15] p.; 21cm.

   Spanish translation by Emanuel Sueyro.
   Pagination errors throughout.
   La Serna, III, no. 4210; Palau, 326435; Peeters-
Fontainas, II, no. 1251.
Reel 177, No. 1153

TACITUS, PUBLIUS CORNELIUS.
   [Opera. Spanish]
   Las Obras De C. Cornelio Tacito. Traduzidas de
Latin en Castellano por Emanuel Sueyro, natural de la
ciudad de Anvers. Dirigidas al serenissimo Principe
Alberto ... Madrid: Por la viuda de Alonso Martin,
1614.
   2 pts. ([9], 383 p.; 294, [33] p.); 21cm.

   Palau, 326436.
Reel 177, No. 1154

TACITUS, PUBLIUS CORNELIUS.
   [Opera. Spanish]
   Tacito Español Ilvstrado Con Aforismos, por Don
Baltasar Alamos de Barientos. Dirigido A Don Francisco
Gomez de Sandoual y Rojas Duque de Lerma Marques de
Denia &c. Madrid: por Luis Sãchez, 1614.
   [29], 1003, [156] p.; 30cm.

   Spanish translation by Baltasar Alamos de Barrientos.
   Engraved title page.
   Ex-libris: Prince of Liechtenstein.
   Pagination errors throughout.
   Missing pages.
   Doublet, p. 125; Goldsmith, p. 189, no. 2; Palau,
326438; Penney, p. 548, Pérez Pastor, no. 1307;
Salvá, II, 2793.
Reel 177, No. 1155

TACITUS, PUBLIUS CORNELIUS see also ALAMOS DE BARRIENTOS,
   BALTASAR.

TAMAYO DE VARGAS, TOMÁS, 1587-1641.
   Diego García De Paredes i Relacion Breve De Sv
Tiempo Al Rei Catholico N.S. Don Phelippe IV. Por Don
Thomas Tamaio de Vargas. Madrid: Luis Sanchez, 1621.
   [12], 141, [1] l.; 21cm.

   Engraved title-page.
   Colophon: "En Madrid. Por Luis Sanchez. Año
de M.DC.XXI."
   Goldsmith, p. 188, no. 13; Jerez, p. 106; Palau,
327110; Penney, p. 549; Pérez Pastor, no. 1793;
Salvá, II, 3519.
Reel 177, No. 1156

TAMAYO DE VARGAS, TOMÁS, 1587-1641.
   Flavio Lvcio Dextro Caballero Español De Barcelona
Prefecto Pretorio De Oriente Governador De Toledo Por
los Años del Sor de CCCC. Defendido Por Don Thomas
Tamaio de Vargas Al L.^do Don Francisco Fernandez
Bertran Abbad Maior de la Sta Igl.^a Coll. de Oliuares
Protonotario Apostolico &c. Madrid: Por Pedro
Tazo, 1624.
   2 pts. ([12], 108 l.; [4], 146, [9] l.); 21cm.

   Half-title: Novedades Antigvas de España. Por
Don Thomas Tamaio De Vargas.
   Engraved title-page.
   Part II has special t.-p.: Antigvedad De La Religion
Christiana ...
   A defense of the authenticity of the fragments
attributed to Flavius Lucius Dexter and others, but
actually by Jerónimo Román de la Higuera.
   Goldsmith, p. 188, no. 15; Graesse, p. 24; Palau,
327111; Penney, p. 549; Pérez Pastor, no. 2128;
Salvá, II, 3194.
Reel 178, No. 1157

TAMAYO DE VARGAS, TOMÁS, 1587-1641.
   Historia General De España Del P. D. Iuan de
Mariana. Defendida Por El Doctor Don Thomas Tamaio
De Vargas. Contra Las Advertencias de Pedro Mantuano,
Al Illustriss. Don Bernardo de Sandoual i Rojas
Cardenal, Arcobispo de Toledo, Primado de las Españas,
Inquisidor General, Chanciller maior de Castilla, &c.
Toledo: por Diego Rodriguez, 1616.
   [24], 341, [55] p.; 21cm.

   Goldsmith, p. 188, no. 16; Graesse, p. 24; HC327/557;
Palau, 327108; Penney, p. 549; Pérez Pastor, no. 487;
Salvá, II, 3195.
Reel 178, No. 1158

TARAFA, FRANCISCO, fl. 1550.
   Francisci Taraphae Barcinonen. De origine, ac
rebus gestis Regum Hispaniae liber, multarum rerum
cognitione refertus. Antverpiae: In Aedibus Ioannis
Steelsij, 1553.
   201, [24] p.; 16cm.

   Portrait: Franciscvs Tarapha Canonicvs Barchinonen-
sis.
   Adams, II, no. 131; Bartlett, no. 184; HC336/329;
Palau, 327552; Penney, p. 550.
Reel 178, No. 1159

TARSIA, PAOLO ANTONIO DI.
   Tvmvltos De La Civdad Y Reyno De Napoles En El
Año De 1647. Por Don Pablo Antonio De Tarsia, Doctor
En Sagrada Theologia, y Abad de San Antonio, Patronato
de su Casa, en la Ciudad de Conversano. Leon De
Francia: A costa de Clavdio Bvrgea, Mercader de
Libros, 1670.
   [11], 195, [28] p.; 24cm.

   Pagination errors throughout.
   Goldsmith, p. 189, no. 32; HC398/354; Palau, 328075;
Penney, p. 551; Vaganay, no. 1151.
Reel 178, No. 1160

TARSIS, JUAN DE, CONDE DE VILLAMEDIANA see VILLAMEDIANA,
   JUAN DE TARSIS Y PERALTA, CONDE DE.

TAYLOR, JEREMY, bp. of Down and Connor (1613-1667),
   (translator) see NIEREMBERG, JUAN EUSEBIO: De La
   Diferencia Entre Lo Temporal y Eterno, 1684.

TEDESCHI, NICCOLÒ see NICCOLÒ DÉ TUDESCHI.

TEIXEIRA, JOSÉ, 1543-1620.
Rervm Ab Henrici Borbonii Franciae Protoprincipis Majoribus gestarum, Epitome. Ejusdémque Henrici Genealogiae Explicatio, A Divo Ludovico per Borbonios, atque ab Imbaldo Trimollio ad utrumque dicti Henrici parentem repetitae. [Printer's device]. Parisiis: Apud Leodegarivm Delaz, via Iacobaea, sub Sole aureo, 1598.
2 pts. in 1 (237, [2] p.; 62 p.); 15cm.

2nd edition.
Palau, 328884.
Reel 182, No. 1169

TEIXEIRA, JOSÉ, (1543-1620).
[Rerum ab Henrici Condaei. French]
Explication De La Genealogie De Treshavlt Et Trespvissant Henry Prince de Conde, Premier Prince du Conde, Premier Prince du Sang de France: Descendant en ligne legitime masculine de S. Louys, par les premiers Comte & Duc de Bourbon: & d'Imbavld Seigneur de la Trimoville, jusques aux pere & mere dudict Prince Henri. Recueillie en Latin par R. P. F. Ios. Tex. Portugais, de l'Ordre des Freres Predicateurs, Maistre en saincte Theologie. Et mise en Francois par I. D. M. Paris: En la boutique de Plantin, ruê S. Iacques, à l'enseigne du Compas, 1596.
[17], 88, [9] p.; 16cm.

French translation from Latin by Jean de Montlyard.
Graesse, p. 47.
Reel 182, No. 1168

TEIXEIRA, JOSÉ, 1543-1620.
Stemmata Franciae, Item Navarrae Regvm, A prima utriusque gentis origine usque ad Christianissimum Franciae & Navarrae Regem Henricvm Magnvm Avgvstvm. Authore R. P. F. Iosepho Texera Ord. Praedicatorum, Sacrae Theol. Magistro. Lvgdvni Batavorvm: Apud Ioannem Maire, 1619.
[18], 192 p.; 21cm.

Palau, 328867.
Reel 182, No. 1171

TEIXEIRA, JOSÉ, 1543-1620.
[Tratado paranetico. English]
The Spanish Pilgrime: Or, An Admirable Discovery of a Romish Catholicke. Shewing how necessary and important it is, for the Protestant Kings, Princes, and Potentates of Europe, to make warre vpon the King of Spaines owne countrey: Also where, and by what meanes, his Dominions may be inuaded and easily ruinated; as the English heretofore going into Spaine, did constraine the Kings of Castile to demand peace in all humility, and what great losse it hath beene, and still is to all Christendome, for default of putting the same in execution. Wherein hee makes apparant (sic) by good and euident reasons, infallible arguments, most true and certaine Histories, and notable examples, the right way, and true meanes to resist the violence of the Spanish King, to breake the course of his designes, to beate downe his pride, and to ruinate his puissance. London: Printed by B. A., 1625.
[13], 136 p.; 18cm.

TEIXEIRA (Cont'd)
English translation from French by J. D. Dralymont (pseud. of Jean de Montlyard.
Pages 126-127, 129-130 omitted in numbering.
"A work usually ascribed to José Texeira, but is doubtful whether he was really the author".
Allison, p. 191; Knapp-Huntington, p. 297; Palau, 328879; Penney, p. 552; Pollard and Redgrave, no. 23863.
Reel 182, No. 1170

TEJEDA, FERNANDO, fl. 1620-1633.
Miracles vnmasked. A Treatise Prouing that Miracles are not infallible signes of the true and Orthodoxe Faith: That Popish Miracles are either counterfeit or diuellish. Euidently confirmed by authorities of holy Scripture, of antient (sic) Doctors, of graue and learned Spanish Authors, by weighty reasons, manifest examples, and most true Histories which haue happened in Spaine, and appeare in Bookes there Printed. By Ferdinando Texeda, Batchelar in Diuinity. London: Printed by T. S. for Edward Blackamore, 1625.
31 p.; 20cm.

"The bookes out of which this treatise of gathered": 3rd preliminary leaf. The Spanish original of this treatise was probably never published.
Allison, p. 174, no. 9; Pollard and Redgrave, no. 23921.
Reel 182, No. 1172

TÉLLEZ, GABRIEL, 1570?-1648.
Deleytar Aprovechando. Por El Maestro Tirso De Molina. A La Excelentissima Señora Doña Maria de los Remedios y la Cueua, Condesa de Fuensalida, y Virreyna de Nauarra. Madrid: Por Iuan Garcia Infaçon, 1677.
[6], 338 l.; 20cm.

Pagination errors throughout.
Colophon has date of first edition, 1635.
Numerous errors and inconsistencies in paging.
Graesse, p. 569; Jerez, p. 138; Palau, 329484; Penney, p. 553; Salvá, I, 1445; Ticknor, p. 369.
Reel 182, No. 1173

TERENTIUS AFER, PUBLIUS.
[Comedies. Spanish]
Las Seis Comedias De Terencio, Escritas En Latin Y Traduzidas en vulgar Castellano por Pedro Simon Abril professor de letras humanas y philosophia, natural de Alcaraz. Dedicadas al muy alto y muy poderoso señor Don Hernando De Avstria principe de las Españas. Çaragoça: en casa de Iuan Soler, Impressor de libros, 1577.
[8], 396 l.; 16cm.

Spanish translation by Pedro Simón Abril.
Colophon: Caesaraugustae apud Ioannem Soler et viduam Ioannis a Villanova. Idibus Quintilis. M.D.L.XXVII. Expensis ac sumptibus Petri a Molinos civis Caesaraugustani. Francisci Simonis bibliopolae.
Title-page mutilated.
Pagination errors; pages 395, 396 missing.
Graesse, p. 65; Jerez, p. 1; Palau, 330364; Sánchez, no. 533; Thomas, p. 92.
Reel 183, No. 1174

TERENTIUS AFER, PUBLIUS.
Las Seys Comedias De Terentio Conforme ala (sic)
edicion del Faerno, Impressas en Latin, y traduzidas
en Castellano por Pedro Simon Abril natural de Alcaraz.
Dedicadas Al Muy Alto y muy poderoso señor don Hernando
de Austria Principe de las Españas. Alcala: Por Iuan
Gracian, 1583.
[8], 344, [1] l.; 15cm.

Latin and Spanish on opposite pages.
Colophon: "Impresso en Alcala de Henares por Iua
Graciã. Año 1583."
Parchment binding; leather thongs.
Adams, II, no. 378; Catalina, no. 584; Jerez,
p. 117; Palau, 330365; Penney p. 554; Thomas, p. 92.
Reel 183, No. 1175

TERESA, SAINT, 1515-1582.
Cartas De Santa Teresa De Jesus, Madre Y Fvndadora
De la Reforma de la Orden de Nuestra Señora del Carmen,
de la primitiva Observancia: Con Notas del Excelentissimo
y Reverendissimo Don Juan De Palafox Y Mendoza, Obispo
de Osma, del Consejo de su Magestad. Recogidas por
orden del Reverendissimo Padre Fray Diego De La
Presentacion. General que fue de los Carmelitas
Descalcos de la primitiva Observancia. Tomo I. Y II.
De Las Cartas. Brusselas: Por Francisco Foppens,
1674.
2v. ([17], 268, [16] p.; [8], 242, [11] p.); 33cm.

Part II - p. 236-237 omitted in numbering.
Graesse, p. 129; Palau, 299208; Peeters-Fontainas,
II, no. 1265.
Reel 183, No. 1177

TERESA, SAINT, 1515-1582.
Las Obras De La S. Madre Teresa De Iesvs Fvndadora
De La Reformacion De Las Descalcas Y Descalcos De N.
Señora Del Carmen. Edicion Segunda. Primera Parte
Qve Contiene Sv Vida. [Segvnda Parte. Qve Contiene
El Govierno Espiritval Del Alma.] [Tercera Parte.
Qve Contiene Svs Fundaciones Y Visitas Religiosas.]
Anveres: En La Emprenta Plantiniana De Balthasar
Moreto, 1649.
3v. ([41], 489 p.; 620 p.; 351, [86] p.); 21cm.

Doublet, p. 126; Graesse, p. 129, Palau, XIX, p.
456; Peeters-Fontainas, II, no. 1259; Penney, p. 555.
Reels 183 & 184, No. 1178

TERESA, SAINT, 1515-1582.
Las Obras De La S. Madre Teresa De Iesvs Fundadora
De La Reformacion De Las Descalcas Y Descalcos De N.
Señora Del Carmen. Edicion Segunda. Quarta Parte Que
Contiene Svs Cartas, con las Notas de Don Ioan De
Palafox Y Mendoza, Obispo de Osma. Anvers: En La
Emprenta Plantiniana De Blathasar Moreto, 1661.
[49], 578, [35] p.; 21cm.

Engraved title-page.
Second title-page: Cartas De La Santa Madre
Teresa De Iesvs, Con Notas del Excelentissimo y
Reverendissimo Don Ivan De Palafox Y Mendoza, Obispo
de Osma, del Consejo de su Magestad. Recogidas por
Orden del Reverendissimo Padre Fray Diego De La

TERESA (Cont'd)
Presentacion, General de los Carmelitas Descalcos de
la primitiva Observancia: y por èl dedicados à la
Magestad del Rey Don Felipe El Quarto, Nuestro Señor.
Palau, XIX, p. 456; Peeters-Fontainas, II, no.
1264; Penney, p. 555; Vaganay, no. 1130.
Reel 184, No. 1179

TERESA, SAINT, 1515-1582.
Obras De La Gloriosa Madre Santa Teresa De Jesus,
Fundadora De La Reforma De La Orden De Nuestra Señora
Del Carmen, De La Primitiva Observancia. Dedicadas
à la Magestad Catolica de la Reyna Nuestra Señora,
Doña Maria-Ana De Austria, &c. Brusselas: Por
Francisco Foppens, 1675.
[27], 612, [29] p.; 34cm.

Graesse, p. 129; Palau, 298523; Peeters-Fontainas,
II, no. 1261.
Reel 184, No. 1180

TERESA, SAINT, 1515-1582.
[Vida de Santa Teresa. English]
The Flaming Hart Of The Life Of The Gloriovs S.
Teresa, Foundresse of the Reformation, of the Order
of the All-Immaculate Virgin-Mother, our B. Lady, of
Mount-Carmel. This History of her Life, vvas vvritten
by the Saint her selfe, in Spanish; and is nevvly
novv, Translated into English, in the yeare of our
Lord God, 1642. Aut mori, aut pati. Either to dye,
or els to suffer. Antwerpe: Printed by Iohannes
Mevrsivs, 1642.
[73], 660, [11] p.; 16cm.

English version by Tobias Mathew, S.J.
Allison, p. 172, no. 6; Palau, 298989; Wing, T. 753.
Reel 184, No. 1181

TERESA, SAINT see also RIBERA, FRANCISCO DE: Vida de
Santa Teresa.

TERRASSA, PEDRO see TERRASSE, PETRUS.

TERRASSE, PETRUS, d. 1511.
[Oratio de diuina providencia]
Oratio de diuĩa prouidẽtia in capella pape corã
sanctissimo dño nr̃o Sixto papa. iiij. l sacerrimo.
R. Car. senatu habita a venerando sacre theologie
baccalario formato fratre Petro Terrasse sacri ordinis
Carmelitarum dominica. iiij. quadragesime. anno a
Natiuitate domini. Mccccxxxiiij. [Rome: Stephan
Plannck, after 9 March, 1483].
[6] l.; 20cm.

Lacks a title-page.
Graesse, vol. 7, p. 69; Hain, 15369; Proctor, no.
3806.
Reel 183, No. 1176

TEXEIRA, JOSÉ see TEIXEIRA, JOSÉ.

THERESA OF JESUS, Teresa Sánchez de Cepeda y Ahumada,
Saint see TERESA, SAINT.

THOMAS AQUINAS, SAINT, 1225?-1274.
[Commentum in libros Ethicorum Aristotelis]
Egregii Doctoris Sancti Thome De Aqvino In Libros Polithicorvm Ar. [istotelis] Comentvm Foeliciter Incipit. Barcelona: Peter Brun and Nicolaus Spindeler, 19 December 1478.
208 *l*.; 31cm.

Leonardus Brunus Aretinus, translator. Joannes Ferrarius, editor.
Colophon: Petro bruno & Nicholao spindeler germanae gentis: qui sūma cum industria huiuscemodi impressionem apud Barchinonaz urbez clarissimam. xviiii. mensis Decembris anno salutis christiane Millesimo Quadrīgentesimo Septuagesimo octauo comulatissime absoluerunt: cōmeritas laudes de tanto beneficio ī rempublicam habere non obliuiscatur.
Lacks title-page.
Caption title follows uniform titles.
In double columns.
Goff. T-250 (with error in date of publication [i.e. 18 Dec. 1478]); Hain, 1514b; Palau, 300334.
Reel 184, No. 1182

THOMAS AQUINAS, SAINT, 1225?-1274.
[Commentum in libros Ethicorum Aristotelis]
Tratado Del Govierno De Los Principes, Del Angelico Doctor Santo Tomas de Aquino. Tradvcido En Nvestra Lengva Castellana por don Alonso Ordoñez das Syjas y Tobar, señor de Sampayo, &c. Al Excelentissimo Señor Don Gaspar de Guzman, Conde de Oliuares, Sumiller de Corps, y Cauallerizo mayor de su Magestad, y de su Consejo de Estado y Guerra, Alcayde perpetuo de los Reales Alcacares de Seuilla, y gran Canciller de las Indias. Madrid: Por Iuan Gonçalez, 1625.
[6], 112, [4] *l*.; 21cm.

Spanish translation by Alonso Ordoñez das Seyjas y Tovar.
Palau, 300356.
Reel 184, No. 1183

TIRSO DE MOLINA see TÉLLEZ, GABRIEL.

TORDO Viscaino.
27 manuscript *l*.
Bound with: HERRERA Y SOTOMAYOR, JACINTO DE, fl. 1644. Iornada que su Magestad hizo a la Andalvzia. [Madrid: En la Imprenta Real, 1624].
Palau, 114276 (List only printed folios 1-6).
Reel 77, No. 484.30

TORQUEMADA, ANTONIO DE, 16th cent.
[Jardín de Flores. English]
The Spanish Mandeuile of Miracles. Or The Garden of curious Flowers. VVherin are handled sundry points of Humanity, Philosophy, Diuinitie, and Geography, beautified with many strange and pleasant Histories. First written in Spanish, by Anthonio De Torquemeda, and out of that tongue translated into English. It was dedicated by the Author, to the Right honourable and reuerent Prelate, Don Diego Sarmento de soto Maior, Bishop of Astorga. &c. It is deuided into six Treatises, composed in manner of a Dialogue, as in the next page shall appeare. London: Printed by I.R. for Edmund Matts, 1600.
[5], 158, [3] *l*.; 19cm.

English translation by Ferdinand Walker.
Imperfect: title-page mutilated.
Allison, p. 174, no. 12; Graesse, p. 174; Palau, 334927; Pollard and Redgrave, no. 24135.
Reel 184, No. 1184

TORQUEMADA, JUAN DE, CARDINAL, 1388-1468.
[De efficacia aque benedictae]
Incipit tractatus de efficacia aque benedicte per venerandū magistrum Iohannem de turre cremata sacre theologie pfessorem ordinis predicato. tempore concilij basiliensis cōpilat⁹ contra petrū anglicum heretico defensorem in bohemia. Augsburg: Anton Sorg, ca. 1475.
[8] *l*.

Colophon: Hec sunt reuerendissime pater, dñe que vester humilis capellanus Iohes de turri cremata ad ppleuma p magistrū petrum anglicum ppositum vestre dñatōni celeriter annotaui. que vestre reuerendissime paternitatis linee: correctōni cum omni reuerētis presento.
Capital spaces, with guide-letters. Initial-strokes, and underlines supplied in red.
Lacks title-page.
Caption title follows uniform title.
Goff, T-508; Hain* 15739; Proctor, 1664.
Reel 185, No. 1185

TORQUEMADA, JUAN DE, CARDINAL, 1388-1468.
[De efficacia aquae benedictae]
Incipit tractatus de efficacia aque benedicte per venerandū magistrum Iohannem de turre cremata sacre theologie pfessorem ordinis predicato. tempore concilij basiliensis cōpilat⁹ contra petrū anglicum heretico defensorem in bohemia. [Augsburg: Anton Sorg, about 1476?]
[8] *l*.

Colophon: Hec sunt reuerendissime pater, dñe que vester humilis capellanus Iohes de turri cremata ad ppleuma p magistrū petrum anglicum ppositum vestre dñatōni celeriter annotaui. que vestre reuerendissime paternitatis linee: correctōni cum omni reuerētia presento.
Lacks title-page.
Caption title follows uniform title.
Goff, T-509; Copinger, 15738*; Proctor, no. 1663.
Reel 185, No. 1186

TORQUEMADA, JUAN DE, CARDINAL, 1388-1468.
[Expositio Psalterii]
Beatissimo patri : clementissimo domino Pio secundo potifici maximo Iohes de Turrecremata sabines episcop⁹: sancte Romane ecclie cardinalis ... Psalmus primus in quo describitur processus in beatitudinem... [Strassburg: (Printer of the 1481 'Legenda Aurea') April 23, 1482].
[124] *l*.

Lacks title-page.
Colophon: Reueredissimi cardinalis: tituli sancti Sixti domini Iohannis d' Turrecremata: expositio breuis et vtilis super toto psalterio Argentine impressa. Anno domini. Mcccclxxxii. nono Kal! Mai feliciter est consummata, 123ᵇ - 124ᵃ [Index of Psalms].
Goff, T-527; Hain, 15703; Proctor, no. 414.
Reel 185, No. 1187

TORQUEMADA, JUAN DE, CARDINAL, 1388-1468.
[Expositio super toto Psalterio]
Beatissimo patri: clementissimo dño Pio secundo Pontifici maximo Johānes de Turrecremata Sabinēsis Episcopus Sancte Romane Ecclesie Cardinalis Sancti Sixti Vulgariter nuncupatus post humilem recōmendationem ad pedum oscula beatorum. [Zaragoza: Paul Hurus and Juan Blanco, ca. 1482].
[177] *l*.; 30cm.

TORQUEMADA (Cont'd)
Lacks title-page.
A variant of Hain, 15704, without place and date.
Bound in contemporary brown half morocco and oak boards,
traces of clasps.
The text of this rare edition is identical with the
edition dated November 12, 1482 (Zaragoza, Paul Hurus
and Juan Blanco), and contains the same typographical
characteristics. Fol. aij is adorned with an
ornamental border made up of flowers, birds, and a
snail. This border is perhaps the first to have
appeared in Spanish incunabulae. The punctuation
marks are not to be found in any other production
during this period. Finally the words, "(Be)atus vir
qui no abit" on aiiij recto, "Iare fremuerunt" on
aiiij verso, "(Do)mine cur multiplicati sunt qui" on
av recto, and "Im inuocarem" on av verso are absolutely
different from the types of the text, and appear to
be engraved on wood. This is not true of the capitals,
which are the same as those in the text.
Goff, T-529; Haebler, no. 651; Stillwell, T-477.
Reel 185, No. 1188

TORQUEMADA, JUAN DE, CARDINAL, 1388-1468.
Expositio In psalterium Reuerondissimi. B. Ioānis
Yspani de Turre Cremata. [Venice: Lazarus de Soardis,
1513].
124 l.; 16cm.

Engraved title-page.
Colophon: Venetijs per Lazarum de Soardis q.
obtinuit a dominio Veneto quod nullus possit imprimere
nec imprimi facere in eorum dominio sub pena ut patet
in suis privilegiis die XXVII, Aprilis, M.CCCCXIII.
Adams, II, no. 1173 (date only); Palau, 334973.
Reel 185, No. 1189

TORQUEMADA, JUAN DE, CARDINAL, 1388-1468.
[Meditationes seu Contemplationes Deuotissimae]
Incipiūt cōtemplacōes deuotissime per
reuerendissimū dominū dm̄m Iohānem de turrecremata
cardinalē quonda sancti Sixti edite ato in
parietibus circuitus Marie mineruenedū literarū
caracteribus veeciam vmaginum signris ornatissime
descripte ato depicte. [Cologne: Printer of
Albertus Magnus. De virtutibus (Johannes Solidi,
ca. 1474].
[15] l.

Lacks title-page.
Caption title follows uniform title.
Goff, T-537; Copinger, no. 15721; Palau, 334939;
Stillweel, T-485.
Reel 185, No. 1190

TORQUEMADA, JUAN DE, CARDINAL, 1388-1468.
[Quaestiones Euangeliorum de Tempore sanctis [and]
Flos theologiae]
Tabula questionū Incipit tabula ōstionū. In prima
dominica aduēt dñi⁹ est euangeliū ... [Basel:
Johann Amerbach, not after 1484].
[350] l.

Colophon: Explicit materia aurea enucleata flos
theologie nuncupata. applicabilis ad sermones per totum
annū tazde tempre q3 de sanctis cu registro thematum.
et tabula abcdaria omnium materiarū in libro presenti
contentarum.
Lacks title-page.
Caption title follows uniform title.

TORQUEMADA (Cont'd)
A copy with wide margins and including the portion
entitled Flos theologiae as described by Hain (*15714).
It should be noted that several copies e.g. British
Museum (IB.37283), the Bodlein copy, and those at
Berlin and Besançon, have either the Questiones
Euangeliorum.. or the Flos theologiae, not both
together.
Goff, T-553; Copinger, no. 15714; Proctor, no.
7566; Stillwell, T-501.
Reel 185, No. 1192

TORQUEMADA, JUAN DE, CARDINAL, 1388-1468.
Quaestiones euangeliorum tam de tempore quā de
sanctis Iohānis de turre cremata cardinalis.
[Strassburg: Printer of the 1483 Jordanus de Quedlin-
burg (Georg Husner), ca. 1485].
[291] l.

Colophon: Finiunt questiōes euangeliorū tam de
tempore q̄ de sanctis domini Iohannis de turrecremata
Cardinalis feliciter.
Goff, T-554; Copinger, no. 15713*; Proctor, no. 634;
Stillwell, T-502.
Reel 185, No. 1191

TORQUEMADA, JUAN DE, CARDINAL, 1388-1468.
[Summa de ecclesia contra impugnatores potestatis
summi pontificis]
Incipiunt Capitula huius Primi Libri. [Rome:
Eucharius Silber, April 27, 1489].
[216] l.

Lacks title-page.
Caption title follows uniform title.
Colophon: Hec Summa Reuerendissimi patris dñi
domini Io. de Turrecremata Sancte Romane ecclesie
tituli Sancte Marie in Transtiberim presbyteri
Cardinalis Sancti Sixti vulgariter nuncupati: contra
Ecclesie apostoli Petri aduersarios intitulata:
ac per Euchariū Silber al's Franck natione Alemanum
maximo cū ingenio ac maturitate Rome impressa ab Anno
nostre salutis .M. cccc. lxxxix. Indictione .vij Die
✝o Lune. xxvij. mensis Aprilis Pontificatus
Sanctissimi in xp̄o patris dñi nostri domini
Innocentij pape Octaui Anno Quinto: finit feliciter.
Goff, T-555; Copinger, no. 15730; Palau, 33500;
Stillwell, T-503.
Reel 185, No. 1193

TORQUEMADA, JUAN DE, CARDINAL, 1388-1468.
[Summa de ecclesia contra impugnatores potestatis
summi pontificis et auctoritate Papali ex sententiis
Sancti Thomae]
Sūme de ecclesia domini Ioannis de Turrecremata:
cardinalis sancti Sixti vulgo nuncupati repertoriū seu
tabula alphabetica. [Lyon: Johannes Trechsel, I &
II) Sept. 20, 1496].
[8] l.

Lacks title-page.
Caption title follows uniform title.
Second Colophon: Expliciunt flores sententiaru beati
Thome de aquino de auctoritate summi pōtificis collecti
per magistrum Iohannē de turrecremata in concilio
basilieñ. Anno domini. Millesimo quadringentesi-
motrigesimoseptimo: ordinis fratrū p̄dicato sacri
apostolici palatij magistrū. Impressi aūt Lugduni p
Magistru Iohannem Trechsel. Anno. M.CCCC.XCVI.die
vero.XX. mensis Septembris. Deo gratias.
Goff, T-556; Copinger, no. 157232* (incl. Hain,
no. 1422*); Proctor, no. 8608.
Reel 185, No. 1194

TORQUEMADA, JUAN DE, CARDINAL, 1388-1468.
Tractatvs De Veritate Conceptionis Beatissime
virginis, pro facienda relatione coram patribus
Concilii Basilee Anno Dñi M.CCCC.XXXVII. Mense Iulio.
De Mandato Sedis Apostolicae Legatorum, eidem sacro
Concilio presidentium Compilatus. Per Reverendvm
Patrem Fratrem, Ioannem de Turecremata, sacre Theologiae
professorem ordinis Predicatorum, tunc sacri apostolici
Palatii Magistrum. Postea Illustrissimum &
Reuerendissimum. S.R. Ecclesie Cardinalem Episcopum
Portuensem, nunc primo impressus. Romae: Apvd
Antonivm Blandvm Asulanum, 1547.
[10], 276, [17] l.; 21cm.

Pagination errors throughout.
Palau, 335025.
Reel 186, No. 1195

TORRE, FRANCISCO DE LA see TORRE Y SEVIL, FRANCISCO DE LA.

TORRE Y SEVIL, FRANCISCO DE LA, 17th cent.
Entretenimiento De Las Mvsas, En Esta Baraxa
Nveva De Versos. Dividida En Qvatro Manjares, De
Asvntos Sacros, Heroicos, Liricos, Y Bvrlescos.
Compvesta Por Feniso De La Torre, Natvral De Tortosa.
Ofrecida A La Proteccion De Don Geronimo de la
Torre, Cavallero Noble, Varon de San Iuan Castillo,
señor de Almudafor, y Meslofa, y Regidor del Hospital
Real y General, de nuestra Señora de Gracia, en el
Reino de Aragon. Çaragoça: Por Iuan de Ybar, 1654.
[17], 160 p.; 21cm.

Graesse, p. 175.
Reel 186, No. 1196

TORRES, JERÓNIMO, 1527-1611, ed.
Confessio Avgvstiniana In Libros Qvatvor Distribvta,
Et Certis Capitivs Locorvm Theologicorvm, qui sunt
hodie scitu dignissimi, comprehensa: nunc primum ex
omnibus B. Avrelii Avgvstini libris in vnum opus bona
fide ac studio singulari redacta per D. Hieronymvm
Torrensem, Societatis Iesv Theologum, & Academiae
Dilinganae Professorem. Habes hîc Christiane Lector
eius fidei, doctrinae ac Religionis confessionem, quam
Catholici supra mille & ducentos annos, id est, inde
ab aetate D. Augustini vbiq gentium sequuntur, vnum
idemó cum Augustino sentientes & prositentes.
Accessit Geminvs Et Copiosvs Index: prior Capitum &
Argumentorum, quae in hisce libris ordine tractantur:
posterior earum rerum, quae in opere toto praecipuĕ
sunt obseruandae. Dilingae: apud Sebaldvm Mayer,
1567.
[32], 330, [24] l.; 20cm.

Pagination errors throughout.
[Augustinus, Aurelius, Saint, bp. of Hippe]
Palau, 336509.
Reel 186, No. 1197

TORRES, JUAN DE, 1547-1599.
Philosophia Moral De Principes, Para Sv Bvena
Crianca y gouierno: y para personas de todos estados.
Compvesta Por El Padre Iuan de Torres, de la Compañia
de Iesvs. Dirigida A Don Gomez Davila. Marques de
Velada, del Consejo de Estado: Ayo y Mayordomo mayor
del Principe nuestro señor. Tratanse enella varias
materias muy vtiles para Predicadores. Bvrgos: Por
Philippe de Iunta y Iuan Baptista Varesio, 1596.
[40], 953, [76] p.; 27cm.

Imperfect: numerous errors in paging.
Pages 24-26 (and in index) missing.
Adams, II, no. 832; Graesse, p. 176; Palau,
336553; Simon Díaz, Jesuitas, no. 1884.
Reel 186, No. 1198

TORRES, JUAN DE, 1547-1599.
Philosophia Moral De Principes, Para Sv Bvena
Crianca y gouierno: y para personas de todos estados.
Compvesta Por El Padre Iuan de Torres, de la Compañia
de Iesvs. Dirigida A Don Gomez Davila, Marques de
Velada, del Consejo de Estado: Ayo y Mayordomo mayor
del Principe nuestro señor. Tratense enella varias
materias muy vtiles para Predicadores. Lisboa:
Impresso por Pedro Crasbeeck, 1602.
[33], 786, [75] p.; 28cm.

Palau, 336556; Simón Diaz, Jesuitas, no. 1887.
Reel 186, No. 1199

TRATADO de paz entre esta corona y la de Francia
ajustado por el Exe^mo· Sr. D. Luis Mendez de Haro
y Guzman, ... Conde de Olivares ... y por el Sr.
Cardenal Julio Mazarini. Madrid: Domingo Garcia
Morras, 1660.
32 printed l.
Bound with: HERRERA Y SOTOMAYOR, JACINTO DE, fl.
1644. Iornada que su Magestad hizo a la Andalvzia.
[Madrid: En la Imprenta Real, 1624].
Palau, 114276 (List only printed folios 1-6).
Reel 77, No. 484.5

TRATADO de repartación de la Monarchia de España
entre el Rey Cristianissimo y el Rey de Inglaterra
y Estados Generales de Holanda.
6 manuscript l.
Bound with: HERRERA Y SOTOMAYOR, JACINTO DE, fl.
1644. Iornada que su Magestad hizo a la Andalvzia.
[Madrid: En la Imprenta Real, 1624].
Palau, 114276 (List only printed folios 1-6).
Reel 77, No. 484.13

TRUJILLO, TOMÁS DE.
Libro Llamado Reprobacion de trajes, y abuso de
Juramentos. Con vn tratado de lymosnas. Cōpuesto
por el muy Reuerendo padre fray Thomas de Trugillo,
Presentado en S. Theologia: de la orden de nuestra
Señora de la merced. Dirigido a la Sacra, Catholica,
Real Magestad del Rey don Philippe segundo, nuestro
señor. [Navarre: s.n.], 1563.
[16], 230, [10] ℓ.; 15cm.

Engraved title-page.
Colophon: "Fue impressa la presente obra con licencia
Real, en el Reyno de Nauarra: veynte y quatro dias
del mes de Abril. Del año de mil y quinientos y
sesenta y tres años."
Palau, 341779; Pérez Goyena, no. 71.
Reel 187, No. 1200

A TRVE Relation and Iovrnall, Of the Manner of the
Arrivall, and Magnificent Entertainment, given to
the High and Mighty Prince Charles, Prince of Great
Britaine, by the King of Spaine in his Court at
Madrid. Published by Authority. London: Printed
by Iohn Haviland for William Barret, 1623.
[3], 35p.

Bound in: Peña, Juan Antonio de la. [Relación
y juego de cañas que la Magestad Católica- ...]
Allison, p. 139, no. 6; Graesse, p. 190; Palau,
217386; Pollard and Redgrave, no. 19594.
Reel 138, No. 873

TUDESCHIS, NICOLAUS DE see NICCOLÒ DE TUDESCHI, Abp.of
Palermo.

TWO Royall Entertainments, Lately Given To The Most
Illvstriovs Prince Charles, Prince of Great
Britaine, by the High and Mighty Philip the fourth
King of Spaine, &c. At the Feast of Easter and
Pentecost. Translated out of the Spanish originals.
Printed at Madrid. London: Printed for Nathaniel
Butter, 1623.
[3], 37p.

Bound in: Peña, Juan Antonio de la. [Relación
y juego de cañas que la Magestad Católica-...]
Allison, p. 139, no. 6; Graesse, p. 190; Palau,
217386; Pollard and Redgrave, no. 19594.
Reel 138, No. 874

U

ULENHART, NICLAS (translator) see LAZARILLO DE TORMES, 1617.

ULLOA, ALFONSO DE, d. ca. 1580.
Historia Dell'Impresa Di Tripoli Di Barbaria. Della presa del Pegnon di Velez Della Gomera in Africa, fatte per comandamento del Serenissimo Re Catolico. Et il successo della potentissima Armata Turchesca, venuta sopra l'Isola di Malta, l'anno M D L X V. Nuouamente mandata in luce de Alfonso Vlloa. Alla quale sono state aggiunte dal medesimo le cose fatte in Vngheria l'anno M D L X V I. da Sultan Solimano, con la narratione della morte di esso sotto Seghetto, & la creatione di Selim suo figliuolo. La descrittione dell'Isola di Malta. Il disegno dell'Isola delle Zerbe, e del forte, fattoui da Christiani, & la sua descrittione, & altre cose notabili. Venetia: Appresso gli heredi di Marchiò Sessa, 1569.
[3], 87, [1] l.; 24cm.

Palau, 343403; Short-title, III, p. 332.
Reel 187, No. 1201

ULLOA, ALFONSO DE, d. ca. 1580.
Vita Del Potentissimo, E Christianias. Imperatore Ferdinando Primo. Descritta dal Sig. Alfonso Vlloa. Nella Qvale Vengono Comprese, e trattate con bellissimo ordine le guerre di Europa co i fatti de' Principi Christiani. Cominciando dall'anno M D X X. fino al M D L X I I I I. Doue si dicono molte cose non mai piu intese, nè dette da altri nelle Historie. Et è scritta col medesimo stile della Vita di Carlo V. perche l'Autore di questa opera compose ancora quella. Con Priuilegio del Sommo Pontifice, della Maesta Cesarea, del Re Catolico, della Signoria di Venetia, e di altri Principi per anni XX. All'Invittissimo Imperatore Massimiliano Secondo. Venetia: Appresso Camillo, & Francesco Franceschini Fratelli, 1565.
[33], 451, [5] p.; 20cm.

Pagination errors throughout.
Palau, 343406; Short-title, III, p. 333.
Reel 187, No. 1202

ULLOA, ALFONSO DE, d. ca. 1580.
Vita Del Valorosissimo E Gran Capitano Don Ferrante Gonzaga, Principe Di Molfetta, &c. Descritta Dal Signor Alfonso Vlloa. Nella quale oltre i suoi fatti, & di molti altri Principi & Capitani si descriuono le guerre d'Italia, & d'altri paesi: Comminciando dall'Anno M.D. XXV. doue il Guicciardini finisce le sue Historie, fino al M.D.LVII. Venetia: Appresso Nicolò Beuilacqua, 1563.
[5], 187, [1] l.; 20cm.

Adams, II, no. 46; Graesse, p. 224; Palau, 343405; Short-title, III, p. 333.
Reel 187, No. 1204

ULLOA, ALFONSO DE, d. ca. 1580.
Vita Dell'Invittissimo, E Sacratissimo Imperator Carlo V. Descritta Dal Signor Alfonso Vlloa. Con l'aggiunta di molte cose vtili all'Historia, che nelle altre impressioni mancauano. Nella quale si comprendono le cose piu notabili, occorse al suo tēpo: incominciando dall'anno M.D. insino al MDLX. Di nuouo ristampata, & con molta diligenza ricorretta. Con vna copiosissima Tauola delle cose principali, che nell'opera si contengono. Al Potentissimo, & Christianissimo Re Filippo, Secōdo Rè di Spagna, &c. Venetia: Appresso gli Heredi di Francesco Rampazetto. Ad Instanza di Lorenzo Pichi, 1581.
341, (i.e. 344), [9] l.; 21cm.

Pagination errors throughout.
Palau, 343396; Short-title, III, p. 333.
Reel 187, No. 1203

ULLOA, ALFONSO DE see also BANDELLO, MATTEO.

ULLOA, ALFONSO DE (translator) see also BUETER, PEDRO ANTONIO; COVARRUBIAS, PEDRO DE; FUENTES, ALFONSO DE: Le Sei Giornate ...; MEXIA, PEDRO: Historia imperial Y Cesara, Silva de varia leccion; URREA, JERONIMO DE JIMÉNEZ; ZARATE, AGUSTIN DE.

ULLOA Y PEREIRA, LUIS DE, 1584-1674.
Obras De Don Lvis De Vlloa Pereira. Prosas, Y Versos. Añadidas En Esta Vltima Impression Recogidas, Y Dadas A La Estampa Por D. Ivan Antonio De Vlloa Pereira su hijo, Regidor, y Alguacil Mayor de la Ciudad de Toro, con primera voz, y voto en su Ayuntamiento. Dedicados Al Serenissimo Señor Don Ivan De Avstria. Madrid: Por Francisco Sanz, En la Imprenta del Reyno, 1674.
[17], 386 p.; 21cm.

Pagination errors throughout.
Gallardo, no. 4112; Graesse, p. 224; Jerez, p. 107; Palau, 343507; Penney, p. 571; Salvá, I, 1012; Ticknor, p. 381.
Reel 187, No. 1205

ULLOA Y PEREIRA, LUIS DE, 1584-1674.
Versos Qve Escrivio D. Lvis De Vlloa Pereira, Sacados De Algvnos De Svs Borradores. Dirigidos A La Alteza Del Señor Don Iuan de Austria. Madrid: Por Diego Diaz, 1659.
[8], 215, [5] l.; 21cm.

Includes: Defensa De Libros Fabvlosos, Y Poesias Honestas, Y De Las Comedias Qve Ha introducido el vso, en la forma que oy se representan en España, Con Extremos Diferentes de las antiguas, Acvsadas, Y Condenadas por santos, y autores graues. Por D. Lvis de Vlloa. l. 190-215, 6 l. Paged continuously with the first work.
Pagination errors throughout.
Goldsmith, p. 194, no. 6; Palau, 343506; Salvá, I, 1011; Simón Díaz, Impresos, no. 1778.
Reel 187, No. 1206

URREA, JERÓNIMO DE JIMÉNEZ DE, fl. 1550.
[Diálogo de la verdadera honra militar. Italian]
Dialogo Del Vero Honore Militare, Nel qvale Si Diffiniscono tutte le querele, che possono occorrere fra l'uno e l'altr'huomo. Con molti notabili esempij d'antichi, & moderni. Composto Dall'Illvstre Sig. Don Geronimo di Vrrea Vicerè di Puglia, & del consiglio di sua Maestà Catolica. Et nuouamente tradotto di lingua Spagnuola Da Alfonso Vlloa. Venetia: Appresso Gli Heredi Di Marchio Sessa, 1569.
[20], 191 l.; 16cm.

Italian translation by Alfonso de Ulloa.
Pagination errors throughout.
Graesse, p. 229; Short-title, III, p. 408.
Reel 187, No. 1207

URREA, MIGUEL DE (translator) see VITRUVIUS POLLIO.

USQUE, SELOMOH [SALAMON BEN ABRAHAM (translator)] see PETRARCA, FRANCESCO.

V

VALBUENA, BERNARDO DE, bp. of Puerto Rico, 1568-1627.
El Bernardo, o Victoria de Roncesvalles Poema heroyco Del Doctor Don Bernardo de Balbuena. Obra toda texida de vna admirable variedad de cosas Antiguedades de España, Casas, y linages nobles della, Costumbres de gentes Geograficas Descripciones delas mas floridas Partes Del mundo, Fabricas de edificios y Suntuosos Palacios, Iardines, Cacas y frescuras, Transformaciones, y Encantamentos De nueuo y Peregrino Artificio Ilenos De sentencias, y moralidades. Madrid: Por Diego Flamenco, 1624.
[8], 290 l; 21cm.

Title vignette.
Leaves printed on both sides.
Gallardo II, 1296; Goldsmith, no. 18; Palau 23340; Penney p. 49; Pérez Pastor 2049; Salvá 1529; Simón Díaz, VI, 2288.
Reel 20, No. 92

VALDÉS, JUAN DE, d. 1541.
[Ciento y diez considersciones. English]
The Hundred And Ten Considerations Of Signior Iohn Valdesso: Treating Of Those things which are most profitable, most necessary, and most perfect in our Christian Profession. Written In Spanish. Brought out of Italy by Vegerius, and first set forth in Italian at Basel by Caelius Secundus Curio, Anno 1550. Afterward translated into French, and Printed at Lions 1563. and again at Paris 1565. And now translated out of the Italian Copy into English, with notes. Whereunto is added an Epistle of the Authors, or a Preface to his Divine Commentary upon the Romans. I Cor. 2. Howbeit we speak wisdome amongst them that are perfect, yet not the wisdome of this world. Oxford: Printed by Leonard Lichfield, Printer to the Vniversity, 1638.
[33], 311, [12] p.; 16cm.

English translation by Nicholas Ferrar.
Translated by N. Ferrar from the Italian edition of C.S. Curione which is entitled: Le cento a dieci divine considerazioni.
Allison, p. 177, no. 3; Knapp-Huntington, p. 323; Palau, 347559; Penney, p. 574; Pollard and Redgrave, no. 24571.
Reel 187, No. 1208

VALDÉS, JUAN DE, d. 1541.
[Ciento y diez consideraciones. English]
Divine Considerations Treating Of those things which are most profitable, most necessary, and most perfect in our Christian Profession. By John Valdesso. I. Cor. 2.6. Howbeit we speak wisdome amongst them that are perfect; yet not the wisdome of this world. Cambridge: Printed for E. D. by Roger Daniel, Printer to the University, 1646.
[23], 437, [18] p.; 16cm.

This is Nicholas Ferrer's translation revised.
Allison, p. 178, no. 3.1; Palau, vol. 25, p. 15; Wing V. 22.
Reel 188, No. 1209

VALDÉS, RODRIGO DE, 1609-1682.
Poema Heroyco Hispano-Latino Panegvrico De La Fvndacion, Y Grandezas de la muy Noble, y Leal Ciudad de Lima. Obra Postvma Del M.R.P.M. Rodrigo De Valdes, de la Compañia De Jesvs, Cathedratico de Prima jubilado, y Prefecto Regente de Estudios en el Colegio Maximo de San Pablo. Sacale A La Lvz El Doct. D. Francisco Garabito de Leon y Messia, Cura-Rector de la Iglesia Metropolitana de Lima, Visitador, y Examinador General en su Arcobispado, &c. Sobrino, y Primo-hermano del Autor. Dedicale Al Rey nuestro Señor D. Carlos Segvndo, Rey de las Españas, Emperador de las Indias, &c. Madrid: en la Imprenta de Antonio Roman, 1687.
[112], 184, [8] p.; 20cm.

Gallardo, no. 4133; Palau, 347681; Penney, p. 574; Salvá, I, 1014.
Reel 188, No. 1210

VALERA, CIPRIANO DE, 1532?-1625.
[Dos tratados: del Papa, de la misa. English]
Two Treatises: The first, Of The Lives Of The Popes, And Their Doctrine. The second, Of The Masse: The One and the other collected of that, which the Doctors, and ancient Councels, and the sacred Scripture do teach. Also A Swarme of false Miracles, wherewith Marie de la Visitacion, Prioresse of the Annuntiada of Lisbon, deceiued very many: and how she was discouered, and condemned. Reuelation 17. I. Come, and I will shew thee the condemnation of the great Whore, which sitteth vpon many waters. And vers. 15. The waters which thou sawest, where the Whore sitteth, are people, and multitudes, and nations, and tongues. The second edition in Spanish augmented by the Author himselfe, M. Cyprian Valera, and translated into English by Iohn Golburne. 1600. London: by Iohn Harison, 1600.
[10], 445, [2] p.; 21cm.

English translation by John Goldbourne.
Pagination errors throughout.
Allsion, p. 178, no. 4; Knapp-Huntington, p. 325; Palau, 348572; Pollard and Redgrave, 24581.
Reel 188, No. 1211

VALERA, DIEGO DE, b. ca. 1412-d. ca. 1483.
[Cronica de España]
La siguiente coronica vlustrissima prīcesa es partida en quatro partes principales ... [Sevilla: Printed by Alonso del Puerto Alone [for] Michael Dachauer and Garcia del Castello, 1482].
[185] l.

Lacks title-page.
Caption title follows the uniform title.
First Colophon: Fue acabada esta copilacion enla villa del puerto de santa maria bispera de san iuā de iunio del año del señor de mill y quatrocientos y ochenta y vn años sevendo el abreuiador della en hedad de sesenta y nueue años ...
Epilogue and Second Colophon: Muchas cosas son illustrissima princesa que me persuaden asi alguna cosa por ingenio o trabaio de estudio fallar se pueda a nuestros cōtenporaneos y aun alos que venirse esperan por modo de breuedad. la qual es amiga de todo sano entendimiento la comuniquemos ... [Sevilla: 1482] [185] l.
Goff, V-13; Copinger, no. 15766; Haebler, no. 654; Madsen, no. 4052; Escudero, no. 8; Palau, 348586; Proctor, no. 9519A; Salvá, II, 3204; Simón Díaz, III, no. 6481; Thomas, p. 96.
Reel 188, No. 1212

VALERIUS MAXIMUS.
[Liber factorum et dictorum memorabilium. Spanish]
Los Nveve Libros De Los Exemplos. Y Virtvdes
Morales De Valerio Maximo, Tradvzidos, Y Comentados
En Lengva Castellana. Por Diego Lopez, Maestro De
Latinidad, Y Letras Humans en la muy noble, y antigua
ciudad de Merida. Madrid: En la Imprenta Real, (n.d.)
[4], 170 l.; 21cm.

Spanish translation and commentary by Diego López.
Half-title: Exemplos, Y Virtvdes Morales De Valerio
Maximo.
Title of vol. II: Comento Sobre Los Nveve Libros
De Los Exemplos, Y Virtvdes Morales De Valerio Maximo.
En Qve Se Explican Historias, Antigvedades, Y el sentido
de lugares dificultosos, que tiene el Autor; y
assimismo de muchos Oradores, y Poetas. Por Diego
Lopez, Maestro de Latinidad, y letras humanas, en la
muy noble, y antigua ciudad de Merida. Madrid: Por
Bernardo de Villa Diego, 1672. 158, [6] l.
Pagination errors throughout.
Palau, 348870.
Reel 188, No. 1213

VALLE ANTIGORIO -- Laws, statutes, etc.
Statvta, Et Privilegia Valliis Antigorii Excell.^mo
Principi D.D. Don Ioanni Thomae Enriqvez De Cabrera,
Et Toledo Comiti De Melgar Ex Proceribus Regij
Cubiculi S.R. Cath. Maiest., eiusque Gubernatori, &
Capitaneo Generali Status Mediolani Dicata. Nouisque
additionibus sub quacunque Statutorum rubrica Egregii
I.C.D. Don Francisci De Villegas Y Contardi Dictae
Vallis Antigorij Praetoris anni 1684., & 1685. Ac
priuilegijs denuo publicae dictae Vallis vtilitati
cum Statutis ad posteros etiam noua impressione
restauratis. Genevae: ex Typographia Basilij
Cattanei, 1685.
[12], 5-248, [6] p.; 29cm.

Published in the same year at Milan.
Reel 188, No. 1214

VALLÉS, PEDRO DE, fl. 1550.
Historia Del Fortissimo, Y Prudentissimo Capitan
Don Hernando de Aualos Marques de Pescara, con los
hechos memorables de otros siete excelētissimos
Capitanes del Emperador Don Carlos V. Rey de España,
que fueron en su tiempo, es a saber, el Prospero
Coluna, el Duq de Borbon, Don Carlos Lanoy, Don Hugo
de Moncada, Philiberto Principe de Orange, Antonio
de Leyua, y el Marques del Guasto, Recopilada por
el Maestro Valles con vna adicion hecha por Diego de
Fuentes, dōde se trata la presa de Africa y assi mismo
la conquista de Sena con otras azañas particulares.
Anvers: En casa de Philippo Nutio, 1570.
[8], 355, [1], 71 l.; 16cm.

The addition by Diego de Fuentes is paged separately
and has its own title page: Conqvista De Africa Donde
Se Hallaran agora nueuamente recopiladas por Diego
de Fuentes muchas y muy notables hazañas de
particulares caualleros. Dirigida al Illustrissimo
señor don Iuan Ximenez de Vrrea Conde de Aranda y
Vizconde de Viota. &c. mi señor.
Adams, II, no. 213; Heredia, no. 3165; Morante, no.
9710; Peeters-Fontainas, II, 1337; Penney, p. 579;
Salvá, II, 3526; Thomas, p. 96; Vindel, no. 3077 and
1067.
Reel 188, No. 1215

VAREN DE SOTO, BASILIO (translator) see BENTIVOGLIO,
GUIDO, CARDINAL, 1579-1644.

VARRO, MARCUS TERENTIUS see AGUSTÍN, ANTONIO,
abp. of Tarragona.

VÁZQUEZ, AGUSTÍN, S.J. 1615-1676.
Exortacion Espiritval Del Licenciado D. Simon Marcos
De Nestares, Vicario General De La Armada Real de
España, y Exercito de el Mar Oceano, Administrador
general del Hospital Real de la dicha Armada; A Los
Capellanes Mayores y Menores de los Tercios, y
Nauios, Con Insercion De Algvnos Pareceres de
Theologos, y Juristas, cerca de la potestad de la
Vicaria general, y sus Capellanes, para el recurso
del Prelado, y mayor acierto del vso de las facultades,
y privilegios, que gozan en virtud de Bulas
Apostolicas. Cadiz: (s.n.), 1674.
260, [1] p.; 20cm.

Colophon: Conclusum anno 1675.
Pages 209-216 are duplicated in this copy.
Palau, 353616.
Reel 188, No. 1216

VEGA CARPIO, LOPE FELIX DE, 1562-1635.
Arcadia, Prosas, Y Versos De Lope De Vega Carpio,
del Abito de S. Iuan. Con Vna Exposicion De los
nombres historicos, y Poeticos. Al Excelentissimo
señor Don Iuan Tellez Giron Quarto Duque de Ossuna.
Madrid: Por Gregorio Rodriguez, 1645.
[8], 181 (i.e. 283), [33] l.; 15cm.

Pagination errors throughout.
Jerez, p. 110; Palau, 356307; Penney, p. 584.
Reel 190, No. 1228

VEGA CARPIO, LOPE FELIX DE, 1562-1635.
La Circe con otras Rimas y Prosas De Lope de Vega
Carpio. [Madrid]: En casa de la Biuda de Alonso
Martin a costa de Alonso Pérez, 1624.
[4], 233, [4] l.; 21cm.

First edition.
Lacks title-page.
Pages missing at end, (l.234-263?].
Palau, 356455; Penney, p. 584; Pérez Pastor, III,
no. 2137; Salvá, I, 1028; Simón Díaz, Impresos, no.
2046; Sunderland, no. 12830; Ticknor, p. 392.
Reel 189, No. 1217

VEGA CARPIO, LOPE FELIX DE, 1562-1635.
Comedia famosa, Dineros son calidad De Lope de Vega
Carpio [n.p.-n.d.] Vendese en casa de Luis la Marca,
Mercader de Libros, en la Placa de la Seo.
34 p.; 16cm.

Bound with Cardona y Alagon, Antonio Folch de: El Mas
herovco Silencio. Comedia famosa. Valencia, 1688.
Reel 33, No. 154

VEGA CARPIO, LOPE FELIX DE, 1562-1635.
[Corona Tragica. Vida Y Muerte De La Serentissima
Reyna De Escocia Maria Estvarda A Nvestro SS. Padre
Vrbano VIII P.M. Por Lope Felix De Vega Carpio.
Procurador Fiscal de la Camara Apostolica, Capellan
de San Segundo en la Santa Iglesia de Avila. Madrid:
por la viuda de Luis Sanchez, 1627].
[6], 127, [1] l.; 21cm.

Lacks title-page.
Pages (unnumbered) missing.
Pagination errors throughout.
Goldsmith, p. 201, no. 276; Graesse, p. 269;
Jerez, p. 111; Palau, 356473; Penney, p. 585; Salvá,
I, no. 1029.
Reel 189, No. 1219

VEGA CARPIO, LOPE FELIX DE, 1562-1635.
La Dorotea Accion En Prosa. De Frey Lope Felix De
Vega Carpio, Del Habito De San Ivan. A Ramon Dorda
Y Sala, Escriuano de Mandamiento y Camara de su
Magestad en su sacro Supremo y Real Consejo de la
Corona de Aragon, y oficial mayor de la Secretaria
de Cataluña. [Exi de Theatro Cato, Adhibe mentem
Cicero]. Madrid: En la Imprenta Real, 1654.
[8], 222, [1] l.; 15cm.

Pagination errors throughout.
Jerez, p. 111; Palau, 356482; Penney, p. 585;
Salvá, I, 1475.
Reel 189, No. 1220

VEGA CARPIO, LOPE FELIX DE, 1562-1635.
Isidro. Poema Castellano De Lope De Vega Carpio.
Secretario del Marques de Sarria. En Que se Escrive
La Vida del bienauenturado Isidor, Labrador de
Madrid, y su Patron diuino Dirigida A La Mvy Insigne
Villa de Madrid. Madrid: En casa de Pedro Madrigal,
1602.
[12], 255 l.; 15cm.

Title-page, 1st and 7th l. wanting. Also last 9
leaves wanting.
Goldsmith, p. 201, no. 281; Palau, 356319; Penney,
p. 586; Pérez Pastor, no. 827.
Reel 190, No. 1223

VEGA CARPIO, LOPE FELIX DE, 1562-1635.
S. Isidro. Poema Castellano. Por Frey Lope Felix
de Vega Carpio, del Abito de san Iuan. En Qve Se
Escrive La vida del bien auenturado san Isidro,
Labrador de Madrid, y su Patron diuino. Dirigida A
La Mvy Insigne Villa de Madrid. Madrid: En la
Imprenta del Reyno. A costa de Alonso Perez
mercader de libros, 1638.
[8], 207, [9] l.; 15cm.

Colophon: "En Madrid En la imprenta del Reyno,
año de 1638."
Jerez, p. 110; Morante, no. 9886; Palau, 356323;
Penney, p. 586.
Reel 190. No. 1224

VEGA CARPIO, LOPE FELIX DE, 1562-1635.
Iervsalen Conqvistada, Epopeya Tragica. De Lope
Felis De Vega Carpio Familiar del Santo Oficio de la
Inquisicion. A La Magestad De Felipe Hermenegildo
Primero deste nombre, y Tercero del primero. Legant
prius, & postea descpiciant, ne videantur non ex
iudicio, sed ex odij praesumptione ignorata damnare.
Hiero. in praefactione Isay. ad Paul. & Euit.
Madrid: En la imprenta de Iuan de la Cuesta, 1609.
[16], 536 l.; 20cm.

First edition.
Goldsmith, p. 201, no. 279; Graesse, p. 269;
Jerez, p. 110; Penney, p. 586; Pérez Pastor, Madrid,
no. 1073; Salvá, I, 1034.
Reel 189, No. 1221

VEGA CARPIO, LOPE FELIX DE, 1562-1635.
Iervsalen Conqvistada, Epopeya Tragica. De Lope
Felis De Vega Carpio Familiar del S. Oficio de la
Inquisicion. A La Magestad De Felipe Hermenegildo
Primero deste nombre, y Tercero del primero ...
Barcelona: [Gabriel Graells y Giraldo Dotil, 1609].
[16], 536 l.; 16cm.

VEGA CARPIO (Cont'd)
Colophon: Soli Deo Honor & Gloria. "En
Barcelona, En la Emprenta de Gabriel Graells y Giraldo
Dotil. Any 1609."
Pagination errors throughout.
Goldsmith, p. 201, no. 278; Graesse, p. 269;
Jerez, p. 110; Penney, p. 596; Palau, 356353; Salvá,
I, 1035.
Reel 189, No. 1222

VEGA CARPIO, LOPE FELIX DE, 1562-1635.
Ivsta Poetica, Y Alabanzas Ivstas Que hizo la
Insigne Villa de Madrid al bienauenturado San Isidro
en las Fiestas de su Beatificacion, recopiladas por
Lope de Vega Carpio. Dirigidas A La Misma Insigne
Villa. Madrid: por la viuda de Alonso Martin, 1620.
[8], 140 l.; 21cm.

Vignette: Labrè, cultiuè, cogi, Con Piedad, con
Fè, con Zelo. Tierras, Virtudes, y Cielo.
Goldsmith, p. 201, no. 273; Graesse, p. 270;
Jerez, p. 110; Palau, 356421; Penney, p. 586; Pérez
Pastor, no. 1706; Salvá, I, 408; Ticknor, p. 393.
Reel 190, No. 1225

VEGA CARPIO, LOPE FELIX DE, 1562-1635.
Lavrel De Apolo, Con Otras Rimas. Al Excel.mo
Señor Don Ivan Alfonso Enriqvez De Cabrera, Almirante
de Castilla. Por Lope Felix De Vega Carpio, del Abito
de San Iuan [Summa felicitas inuidere nemini.]
Madrid: Por Iuan Gonçalez, 1630.
[8], 129 (i.e. 125), [1] l.; 20cm.

Includes "La selva sin amor" (fol. 103-115),
"Al qvadro, y retrato de Sv Magestad que hizo Pedro
Pablo de Rubens" (fol. 116-17), "Epistola a Don
Michael de Solis" (fol. 118-123), "Sonetos."
Imperfect: leaf [8] wanting; leaves [1] - [3]
mutilated, with some loss of text; remnants of title-
page mounted.
Colophon: "En Madrid. Por Iuan Gonçalez, año
1630."
Goldsmith, p. 201, no. 263; Jerez, p. 111; Palau,
356475; Penney, p. 586; Salvá, I, 1478; Simón
Díaz, Impresos, no. 1755; Ticknor, p. 393.
Reel 190, No. 1226

VEGA CARPIO, LOPE FELIX DE, 1562-1635.
Pastores de Belen, prosas y versos divinos ...
[Nicolas de Pamplona : Assiayn, 1612].
[3], [6], 334 l.; 13cm.

Lacks title-page and fol. A1, 23, 82, 86, 329-331,
334-335.
Palau, 356370.
Reel 190, No. 1227

VEGA CARPIO, LOPE FELIX DE, 1562-1635.
Rimas De Lope De Vega Carpio. Aora De Nvevo
añadidas. Con El Nvevo Arte de hazer Comedias deste
tiempo. Madrid: Por la viuda de Alonso Martin, 1621.
[16], 208 l.; 12cm.

PI-page 134 omitted in pagination.
Pagination errors throughout.
Cosens, no. 4671; Palau, 356339; Penney, p. 587;
Pérez Pastor, no. 1804.
Reel 190, No. 1229

VEGA CARPIO, LOPE FELIX DE, 1562-1635.
Rimas Hvmanas Y Divinas, Del Licenciado Tome De
Bvrgillos, No Sacadas De Blibiotecas (sic) Ningvna,
(que en Castellano se llama Libreria) sino de papeles
de amigos y borradores suyos. Al Excelentissimo
Señor Dvque de Sessa, Gran Almirante de Napoles.
Por Frey Lope Felix De Vega Carpio ... Madrid:
en la Imprenta del Reyno, 1634.
[5], 160 l.; 21cm.

Half-title: Rimas Y Gatomachia De Burguillos Por
Lope de Vega Carpio.
Lacks title-page and ¶2 (first leaf is ¶3).
Pages missing.
Jerez, p. 111; Palau, 356512; Penney, p. 587;
Salvá, I, 492; Simón Díaz, Impresos, no. 1759.
Reel 190, No. 1230

VEGA CARPIO, LOPE FELIX DE, 1562-1635.
Rimas Hvmanas Y Divinas, Del Licenciado Tome De
Bvrgvillos. No Sacadas De Biblioteca ninguna (que
en Castellano se llama Libreria) sino de papeles de
amigos, y borradores suyos Al Excelentissimo Señor
Duque de Sessa, Gran Almirante de Napoles, &c. Por
Frey Lope Felix De Vega Carpio, del Abito de San Iuan.
Madrid: En la Imprenta Real, 1674.
[8], 160 l.; 20cm.

Jerez, p. 111; Palau, 356513; Penney, p. 587;
Salvá, I, 493.
Reel 190, No. 1231

VEGA CARPIO, LOPE FELIX DE, 1562-1635.
Rimas. Sacras. Primera Parte De Lope De Vega
Carpio Clerigo Presbytero. Con cien octauas a la
vida de la Magdalena. Dirigidas Al Padre Fray
Martin de san Cirilo Religioso Descalco de N.
Señora del Carmen. Con priuilegio de castilla, y
Aragon: Por la Viuda de Alõso Martin, 1614.
[12], 188, [6] l.; 16cm.

Jerez, p. 110; Penney, p. 587; Pérez Pastor, no.
1310; Salvá, I, 1038.
Reel 191, No. 1232

VEGA CARPIO, LOPE FELIX DE, 1562-1635.
Segvnda Parte De Las Comedias De Lope De Vega
Carpio, Que contiene otras doze, cuyos nombres van
en la hoja segunda. Dirigidas a doña Casilda de Gauna
Varona, muger de don Alonso Velez de Gueuara, Alcalde
mayor de la ciudad de Burgos. Amberes: en casa de la
biuda y herederos de Pedro Bellero, 1611.
[6], 669 (i.e. 645), [1] p.; 16cm.

Colophon: Antverpiae, Excudebat Andreas Bacz, 1611.
The twelve plays are: La fuerza lastimosa; La
ocasion perdida; El gallardo catalan; El mayorazgo
dudoso; La condesa Matilde; Los Benavídes; Los
comendadores de Córdova; La bella malmaridada; Los
tres diamantes; La quinta de Florencia; El padrino
desposado; Ferias de Madrid.
Pagination errors throughout.
Goldsmith, p. 199, no. 131; Heredia, no. 2368;
Jerez, p. 111; Palau, 355269; Peeters-Fontainas, II,
no. 1346; Penney, p. 585; Salvá, I, 1469.
Reel 189, No. 1218

VEGA CARPIO, LOPE FELIX DE, 1562-1635.
Trivnfo De La Fee, En Los Reynos Del Iapon, Por
los años de 1614. y 1615. Al Ilvstrissimo y
Reuerendissimo señor el Cardenal de Sandoual, Dean
de Toledo. Por Lope De Vega Carpio, Procurador fiscal
de la Camara Apostolica en el Arcobispado de Toledo.
Madrid: Por la viuda de Alonso Martin, 1618.
[8], 104, [9] l.; 17cm.

VEGA CARPIO (Cont'd)
Colophon: "En Madrid, Por la viuda de Alonso Martin
de Balboa."
Jerez, p. 156; Palau, 356408; Penney, p. 588;
Pérez Pastor, no. 1579; Simón Díaz, Impresos, no. 1188.
Reel 191, No. 1233

VEGA CARPIO, LOPE FELIX DE see also QUESTIERS,
CATHARINA, 1631-1669; SHIRLEY, JAMES, 1596-1666.

VELASCO DE GOUVÊA, FRANCISCO.
Perfidia De Alemania, Y De Castilla, En La Prision,
Entrega, accusacion, y processo, Del Serenissimo
Infante De Portvgal Don Dvarte. Fidelidad De Los
Portvgveses, En La Acclamacion De Sv legitimo Rey,
el muy Alto, y muy Poderoso Don Ivan, Qvarto Deste
Nombre, Nuestro Señor. Padre De La Patria, Restaurador
de la libertad. Contra Los pretensos derechos de
la Corona Castellana. Respondese A lo que errada,
fatua, y escandalosamente quiso escriuir Don Nicolàs
Fernandes de Castro, Senador de Milan, y en Salamanca
Cathedratico de la Cathedra pequeña de Codigo. Obra
Que fundó sobre las doctrinas Canonicas, Legales,
Theologicas, Filosoficas, y Polyticas, el Doctor
Francisco Velasco de Gouuea: Cathedratico Iubilado en
Canones en la Vniuersidad de Coimbra, Arcediano de
Villanueua de Cerbera en la Primaz Iglesia de Braga,
Senador de Agrauios del supremo Tribunal de Iusticia
en Portugal. Lisboa: En la Emprenta Craesbeekiana,
1652.
[13], 390, [29] l.; 29cm.

Small folio, half crimson morocco. Title in red and
black; Roman letter; double columns. Engraved
frontispiece with portrait and arms of Joao IV.
Goldsmith, p. 203, no. 327; HC384/302; Heredia, no.
7674; Palau, 357269; Penney, p. 589.
Reel 191, No. 1234

VÉLEZ DE GUEVARA Y DUEÑAS, LUIS, 1579-1644.
El Diablo Coivelo. Novela De La Otra Vida Tradvzida
A Esta por Luys Velez de Gueuara. Barcelona: En la
Emprenta administrada por Sebastian de Cormellas
Mercader, 1646.
[4], 67 l.; 15cm.

Jerez, p. 112; Penney, p. 590.
Reel 191, No. 1235

VERGIL see VIRGILIUS MARO, PUBLIUS.

VERRIUS FLACCUS, MARCUS see AGUSTÍN, ANTONIO, abp. of
Tarragona.

VILLAMEDIANA, JUAN DE TARSIS Y PERALTA, CONDE DE,
1580-1622.
Obras De Don Ivan De Tarsis Conde De Villamediana,
Y Correo Mayor De Sv Magestad. Recogidas Por El
Licenciado Dionisio Hipolito de los Valles. Al
Excelentissimo Señor Conde de Lemos, &c. Çaragoça: por
Iuan de Lanaja y Quartanet Impresor del Reino de
Aragon, y de la Vniuersidad, 1629.
[9], 403, [2] p.; 20cm.

Vignette: Poëtae nobis duces sapientiae.
Graesse, p. 317; Jerez, p. 103; Jimenez Catalán,
no. 287; Penney, p. 551; Salvá, I, 1495; Ticknor, p.
403.
Reel 178, No. 1161

VILLAMEDIANA, JUAN DE TARSIS Y PERALTA, CONDE DE, 1580-1622.
Obras De Don Ivan De Tarsis Conde De Villamediana, Y Correo Mayor De Sv Magestad. Recogidas Por El Licenciado Dionisio Hipolito de los Valles. Al Excelentissimo Señor Conde de Lemos, &c. Zaragoça: por Iuan de Lanaja y Quartanet, Impressor del Reino de Aragon, y de la Vniuersidad, 1634.
[9], 332 p.; 20cm.

The second very rare edition.
Pagination errors throughout.
Reel 178, No. 1162

VILLAMEDIANA, JUAN DE TARSIS Y PERALTA, CONDE DE, 1580-1622.
Obras De D. Ivan De Tarsis, Conde De Villamediana, Y Correo Mayor De Sv Magestad. Recogidas Por El Licenciado Dionisio Hipolito De Los Valles. Dedicadas A Don Francisco De Villa-Nueua Texeda, Cauallero de la Orden de Santiago. 58. Madrid: Por Diego Diaz de la Carrera, 1634.
[17], 432 p.; 21cm.

Hole in title-page where date was given.
Graesse, p. 317; Knapp, p. 67; Penney, p. 551; Ticknor, p. 403.
Reel 178, No. 1163

VILLAMEDIANA, JUAN DE TARSIS Y PERALTA, CONDE DE, 1580-1622.
Obras De Don Ivan De Tarsis Conde De Villamediana, Y Correo Mayor De Sv Magestad. Recogidas por el Licenciado Dionisio Hipolito de los Valles. A D. Henriqve De Zvñiga y Avila. Conde de Brantevilla, Mayordomo de su Magestad, de la Orden y Cavalleria de Calatrava, hijo primogenito del Excelentissimo señor Marques de Mirabel. Añadido en esta segunda Impression. 58. Madrid: Por Maria de Quiñones, 1635.
[18], 437, [1] p.; 20cm.

First title-page with royal coat of arms.
Colophon: "Con Licencia. En Madrid Por Maria de Quiñones. Año M.DC.XXXV."
Numerous errors in pagination: 33 (i.e. 39); 35 (i.e. 37); 262 (i.e. 162); 320 (i.e. 310); 370 (i.e. 366); 371 (i.e. 367); and signatures H^3 (i.e. G^3).
Heredia, no. 5675; Jerez, p. 103; Penney, p. 551; Salvá, I, 1496.
Reel 178, No. 1164

VILLAMEDIANA, JUAN DE TARSIS Y PERALTA, CONDE DE, 1580-1622.
Obras De Don Ivan De Tarsis Conde De Villamediana, Y Correo Mayor De Sv Magestad. Recogidas por el Licenciado Dionisio Hipolito de los Valles. 58. A Don Francisco De Villanueva Y Texeda, Cavallero de la Orden de Santiago. Madrid: Por Diego Diaz de la Carrera, 1643.
[17], 437, [2] p.; 20cm.

Pagination errors throughout.
Missing pages 433, 434.
Gallardo, no. 4018; Jerez, p. 103; Penney, p. 551.
Reel 179, No. 1165

VILLAMEDIANA, JUAN DE TARSIS Y PERALTA, CONDE DE, 1580-1622.
Obras De Don Ivan De Tarsis Conde De Villamediana, Y Correo Mayor De Sv Magestad. Recogidas Por El Licenciado Dionisio Hipolito de los Valles. Al Excellentissimo Señor Conde de Lemos, &c. Barcelona: Por Antonio Lacaualleria, 1648.
[4], 284, [1] l.; 15cm.

Gallardo, no. 4019; Heredia, no. 5676; Jerez, p. 103; Penney, p. 551.
Reel 179, No. 1166

VILLEGAS, ESTEBÁN MANUEL DE.
Las Amatorias De Don Estevan Manvel de Villegas. Con La Tradvcion de Horacio, Anacreonte, y otros Poetas. Dedicado A La Magestad Catolica de Felipe Tercero. Naxera: por Iuan de Mongaston, 1620.
[4], 160, [1] l.; 21cm.

Bound with the author's: Las Eroticas De Don Estevan Manvel De Villegas. Qve Contienen. Las Elegias. lib. I. Los Edylios, iib (sic) II. Los Sopetos lib. III. Las Latinas, lib. IIII. Dedicadas A Don Pedro Fernandez De Castro Conde De Lemos. Segvnda Parte.
Printer's device: Rompe y luze.
Pagination errors throughout.
Gallardo, nos. 4325-26; Graesse, p. 321; Jerez, p. 114; Penney, p. 601; Salvá, I, 1064; Ticknor, p. 404.
Reel 191, No. 1236

VILLEGAS, ESTEBÁN MANUEL DE.
Las Eroticas De Don Estevan Manvel De Villegas. Qve Contienen. Les Elegias. lib. I. Los Edylios, iib (sic) II. Los Sonetos lib. III. Las Latinas, lib. IIII. Dedicadas A Don Pedro Fernandez De Castro Conde De Lemos. Segvnda Parte. Najera: por Iuan de Mongaston, 1617.
87 l.; 21cm.

Bound in the author's: Las Amatorias ..., 1620.
Reel 191, No. 1237

VILLEGAS SELVAGO, ALONSO DE, b. 1534 - d. after 1602.
Flos Sanctorvm y Historia general, de la vida y hechos de Iesu Christo, Dios y señor nuestro, y de todos los Santos de que reza y haze fiesta la Iglesia catolica, conforme al Breuiario Romano, reformado por el decreto del Santo Concilio Tridentino: junto cõ las vidas de los santos propios de España, y de otros Extrauagantes. Quitadas algunas cosos aprocrifas e inciertas. Y añadidas muchas figuras y autoridades de la sagrada Escritura, traydas a proposito de las historias de los santos. Y muchas anotaciones curiosas, y considera-raciones prouechosas. Colegido todo de autores graues y aprouados. Dirigido al Rey Don Felipe Nvestro Señor, Segvndo desta nombre. por el Maestro Alonso de Villegas. Capellã en la capilla mocarabe de la Santa yglesia de Toledo, y natural de la misma ciudad. En esta vltima impression van añadidas algunes cosas, y puestas otras en mejor estilo, por el mismo autor. Toledo: por la viuda de Iuan Rodriguez, 1591.
2 pts. ([10], 432 l.; 128 l.; 36cm.)

Imperfect: Lacks title-page and final pages.
Pérez Pastor, Toledo, no. 401.
Reel 191, No. 1238

VILLEGAS Y CONTARDI, FRANCESCO DE see VALLE ANTIGORIO — Laws, statutes, etc.

VIRGILIUS MARO, PUBLIUS, b. 70 B.C. d. 19 B.C.
[Aeneid. Spanish]
La Eneida De Virgilio, Principe De Los Poetas
Latinos traduzida en octaua rima, y verso Castellano:
ahora en esta vltima impression reformada, y limada
con mucho estudio, y cuydado, de tal manera, que se
puede dezir nueua traduccion. Dirigida A La S.C.R.M.
Del Rey Don Phelippe segundo deste nombre, nuestro
señor. Ha se añadido en esta octaua impression lo
siguiente. Las dos Eglogas de Virgilio, Primera, y
Quarta. El libro tredecimo de Mapheo Veggio Poeta
Laudense, intitulado, Supplemento (sic) de la
Eneida de Virgilio. Vna tabla, que contiene la
declaraciõ de los nombres proprios. y vocablos, y
lugares difficultosos, esparzidos por toda la Obra.
Svstine, Et Abstine. Lisboa: Impressa en casa de
Vicente Aluarez, 1614.
[12], 482, [41] l.; 15cm.

Spanish translation by Gregorio Hernández Velasco.
Goldsmith, p. 210, no. 583; Jerez, p. 50; La
Serna, no. 2950; Penney, p. 602.
Reel 192, No. 1239

VIRGILIUS MARO, PUBLIUS, b. 70 B.C. d. 19 B.C.
[Ecclogae. Spanish]
Las Eclogas Y Georgicas De Virgilio, y Rimas, y el
Pompeyo tragedia. De Christoval de Mesa. A Don
Alonso Fernandez de Cordoua, y Figueroa Marques de
Priego, y Montaluan, señor de la Casa de Aguilar, y
Castroelrio, y Villefranca. Madrid: Por Iuan de la
Cuesta, 1618.
[8], 191, [1] l.; 15cm.

Spanish translation by Cristobal de Mesa.
Colophon: "En Madrid. Por Iuan de la Cuesta.
Año M.DC.XVIII."
Pagination errors throughout.
Gallardo, no. 3060; Graesse, p. 356; Jerez, p. 68;
Penney, p. 602; Pérez Pastor, no. 1554; Simón Díaz,
Impresos, no. 2057.
Reel 194, No. 1241

VIRGILIUS MARO, PUBLIUS, b. 70 B.C. d. 19 B.C.
[Opera. Spanish]
Las Obras De Pvblio Virgilio Maron. Tradvzido En
Prosa Castellana. Por Diego Lopez, Natvral De La
Villa De Valencia, Orden de Alcantara, y Preceptor en
la Villa de Olmedo. Con Comento, Y Anotaciones.
Donde se declaran las Historias, y Fabulas, y el
sentido de los Versos dificultosos que tiene el Poeta.
Al Señor D. Francisco De Bovrnonvila De Perapertvssa
Vilademany, y de Cruillas: Visconde de Ioch: Vervessor
de Viledemany: Noble de Cruilles: Baron de Rabollet, de
Rodès, y Rupidera; de Rupit, y Fornils: Señor de las
Villas de Taradell, Santa Coloma de Farnès, y de los
Lugares de Viladrau, Castañet, y Lasparra: Baron por
indiviso de Gelida, &c. Cavallero de la Orden de
San-Hiago, Capitan de Coracas de las Guardias de su
Excelencia, el Excelentissimo Señor Duque de Bovrnovila
su Tio, Virrey Capitan General del Principado de
Cathaluña, y del Exercito de su Magestad. Barcelona:
En la Imprenta de Antonio Ferrer, Y Baltasar Ferrer
Libreros, 1679.
[8], 548, [4] p.; 21cm.

Spanish translation by Diego López, with commentary
and notes.
HC387/984; Penney, p. 602.
Reel 194, No. 1242

VIRGILIUS MARO, PUBLIUS, b. 70 B.C. d. 19 B.C.
P. Virgilii Maronis Bvcolica Et Georgica Argumentis,
Explicationibus, Notis illustrata, Avctore Io.
Lvdovico De La Cerda Toletano, Societatis Iesv, in
Curia Philippi Regis Hispaniae Primario Eloquentiae
Professore. Editio cùm accurata, tum locupletata,
& Indicibvs necessariis insignita. Lvgdvni: Sumptibus
Horatij Cardon, 1619.
3 v.([48], 516, [15] p.; [48], 759, [24] p.; [12],
784, [111] p.; 35cm.

Engraved title-page.
Vol. II has separate t.-p.: P. Virgilii Maronis
Priores Sex Libri Aeneidos Argvmentis, Explicationibvs
Notis Illvstrati, Auctore Ioanne Ludouico de la Cerda
Toletano Societatis Iesv, in curia Philippi Regis
Hispaniae Primario Eloquentiae Professore, Editio quae
non ante lucem vidit Cum indicibus necessariis.
Vol. III has separate t.-p.: Virgilii Maronis
Posteriores Sex Libri Aeneidos Argvmentis,
Explicationibvs Notis Illvstrati, Auctore Ioanne
Ludouico de la Cerda Toletano Societatis Iesv, in
curia Philippe Regis Hispaniae Primario Eloquentiae
Professore, Editio quae non anté lucem vidit. Accessit
ad calcem Index Erythraei ad facilorem vocum
disquisitionem.
The third volume is designated as "Tertia pars" in
the "Ivdicivm regii censoris," dated Matrit. M.DC.XVII.
"Index Erythraei Virgiliano operi cvivsslibet
impressionis ab Antonio Mario Basso Cremonensi ac-
comodatus"; [83] p. at end of vol. III.
Pagination errors throughout.
Reels 192 & 193, No. 1240

VITRIÁN Y PUJADAS, JUAN, 1570-1646 (translator) see
COMINES, PHILIPPE DE, SIEUR D'ARGENTON, 1445-1509.

VITRUVIUS POLLIO, MARCUS.
[De Architectura. Spanish]
M. Vitrvvio Pollion De Architectvra, Dividido En
diez libros, traduzidos de Latin en Castellano por
Miguel de Vrrea Architecto, y sacado en su perfectiõ
por Iuan Gracian impressor vezino de Alcala. Dirigido
A La S. C.R.M. Del Rey Don Phelippe Segundo deste
nombre nuestro Señor. Alcala: de Henares por Iuan
Gracian, 1582.
178 (i.e. 138), [9] l.; 30cm.

First Spanish translation by Miguel de Urrea.
Errors in paging: leaves 121-138 numbered 161-176.
Adams, II, no. 919.
Reel 194, No. 1243

VITRY, PHILIPPE DE, bp. of Meaux, d. 1362 see GUEVARA,
ANTONIO DE, d. 1545?

VITTORI, GIROLAMO, fl. 1609.
Tesoro De Las Tres Lengvas Española, Francesa, Y
Italiana. Thresor Des Trois Langves, Espagnole,
Francoise, Et Italienne. Auquel est contenue l'
explication de toutes les trois respectiuement l'vne
par l'autre: Diuise en trois parties. Le tout
recuilli des plus celebres Auteurs que iusques ici
ont escrit aux trois langues, Espagnolle, Francoise,
& Italienne, par Hierosme Victor Bolonnois. Derniere
edition reueu & augmentee en plusieurs endroits.
Geneve: De L'Imprimerie de Iaqves Crespin, 1644.
3 pts. in 1 (570 p.; 420 p.; 504 p.); 24cm.

VITTORI (Cont'd)
Title of pt. II: Seconde Partie Dv Thresor Des
Trois Langves, Francoise, Italienne Et Espagnolle.
En laguelle est contenuë l'explication des dictions
Francoises en Italien & Espagnol, pour faciliter le
moyen à ceuz qui desirent atteindre la perfection de
composer en la langue Italienne & Espagnole.
Title of pt. III: Terza Parte Del Tesoro Delle
Tre Lingve, Italiana, Francese, e Spagnuola. Dove
Sono Le Voci Italiane dichiarate in Francese e
Spagnuolo, per aiutar chi desidera nelle tre sudette
ligue perfettamente comporre. Hora Nvovamente Posta
In luce, cauata da diuersi Autori e Lessicografi,
massime del Vocabolaro della Crvsca.
Errors in paging: part I, p. 465-480 numbered 365-
378; part II, p. 125-128 repeated; part III, p. 473-
480 omitted.
Errors in binding: part III, p. 229-236 bound in
the following order: 231-232, 229-230, 236-235, 233-
234.
Penney, p. 604.
Reel 194, No. 1244

VITUS AMERBACH.
Commentaria Viti Amerbachii in Ciceronis tres
libros de Officijs. Liber Ad Lectorem. Non tantum
tibi nunc lector me trado legendum, Trado sed ut
nostri censor & esse queas: Sic tamen, ut lector
maneas, censorq́; nec ultra, Quàm decet officium,
progrediare tuum. Este procul, quibus est odium
uenale, fauorq́; Pectoraq́; Illyrica sunt nigrior
apice. Hos uolo, quos ficum, Quiq; scapham possunt dicere uelle scapham. Quod si non illos
potero uitare, paratum Nepenthes norint semper
adesse mihi. Antverpiae : excudedum curabat
Antonius Goinus, 1539.
125 p.

Bound in: Vives, Juan Luis: Lingvae Latinae
Exercitatio, 1544.
Adams, I, no. 959
Reel 197, No. 1271

VIVES, JUAN LUIS, 1492-1540.
Ioannis Lvdovici Vivis Valentini, Ad Veram Sapientiam
Introdvctio: Libellus doctus & elegans, ab alijs
eius opusculis separatus. Eivsdem Satellitium
animi, siue symbola, Principum institutioni potissimum
destinata. Adiecimvs. Isocratis Oratoris disertissimi
orationem ad Nicoclem, de regno administrando, per
Ottomarum Luscinium è Graeco in sermonem Latinum
traductam. Coloniae Agrippinae: Apud Ioannem Gymnicum
sub Monocerote, 1578.
[71] l.; 11cm.

Reel 194, No. 1245

VIVES, JUAN LUIS, 1492-1540.
Ioannis Lodovici Vivis Valentini, Ad Sapientiam
introductio: Enchiridion repurgandis saeculi bujus
vitiis accommodatissimum. Aberdoniae: Excudebat
Eduardus Rabanus, Impensis Davidis Melvil, 1623.
[142] p.; 11cm.

Reel 194, No. 1246

VIVES, JUAN LUIS, 1492-1540.
Ioan. Lvd. Vivis Introdvctio ad veram sapientiam.
Eiusdem Preculae quaedam & Meditationes piae itemq́
Satellitium animi, siue Heroica symbola plusquam
ducenta. Libellus prorsus aureolus, atq educationi
primae aetatis, si quis alius, cum primis appositus,
iterum iam editus. Helmaestadii: (s.n.), 1630.
[16], 224 p.; 11cm.

Reel 194, No. 1247

VIVES, JUAN LUIS, 1492-1540.
Joannis Lodovici Vivis, Valentini. Ad Sapientiam
Introductio. Satellitium Aliaque eiusdem. Quorum
series ante Praefationem & Autoris Vitam exhibetur.
Lvgdvni Batavorvm: Apud Davidem Lopez de Haro, 1644.
166 p.; 13cm.

Pagination errors throughout.
Reel 194, No. 1248

VIVES, JUAN LUIS, 1492-1540.
[Ad sapientiam introductio. English]
Introdvction to wisedome. Banket of sapience.
Preceptes of Agapetus. [London: Thom. Berthelet,
1550].
[112], 86, [28] l.; 11cm.

English translation by Richard Morysome.
Colophon: "Imprinted At London in Fletestrete,
(sic) in the hous(sic) of Tho. Berthelet. Cum
priuilegio ad imprimendum solum. Anno dñi. 1550."
Pagination errors throughout.
Pollard and Redgrave, no. 24849.
Reel 194, No. 1249

VIVES, JUAN LUIS, 1492-1540.
Ioannis Lodovici Vivis Valentini, De Concordia &
discordia in humano genere ad Carolum V. Caesarem,
Libri Quattuor. De Pacificatione, Lib. Vnus. Q.misera
esset vita Christianorum sub Turca. Lib. vnus.
[Antuerpiae]: Michael Hillenius excudebat, [1529].
3 pts. in 1 ([216] l.; [44] l.; [16] l.; 16cm.

Engraved title-page.
Part II has title-page: Ioannis Lodovici Vivis De
Pacificatione Liber Vnus.
Part III has title-page: Ioannis Lodovici Vivis
De Conditione Vitae Christianorum sub Turca.
Adams, II, no. 945.
Reel 195, No. 1250

VIVES, JUAN LUIS, 1492-1540.
Wannenher Ordung menschlicher beywonung, Erschaffung
der speiss, anfang der Stätt, allerley handthierũg,
aussteylũg der gũter, Vrsprung der Mintz, wie die
Metall in die welt kommen, Von Schũl vnnd lermeistern.
Wie man sol gũts thũn mit radtschlag, fleiss, arbeit,
vndersichtung, gelt. Das grosser Herrn macht auff den
vnderthonen fuget, Von warem Gemeinem nutz, Wie mann
der Bertlerey weren, vnd der Armũt in Repub. bey zeit sol
zũ hilff kummen. Von zucht armer leũt kinder. Von
dem Meinen vnd Deinen, dadurch alle vnrũg in der welt
entstadt. Das Christenthumb sey in wolthat. Vnd
wie vil vñ auff was weiss einem veden seye gũts
zũthũn. Wie die Oberkeiten yeder statt vnd Pollicey
dem verarmen yrer burger begegnen. Von Spitälen,
Weysenheũsern, Von gemeinem almũsen gegen armen
gefangnen im krieg, verbrenten, schiffbrũchigen,
Zangkfrawen bey eren zubehalten, Christen vom Tũrkē
zu entledigen, Vom letsten willē der stiffter, so mit
soll geendert, sunder gehalten werdē. Alles nutzlich
zũ lesen fũr frumme Oberheit und liebe Vnderthonen.
Johannes Ludoicus Vives. [Strassburg: 1534].
[60] l.; 21cm.

German translation from Latin by C. Hedio.
Graesse, vol. VII, p. 380; Palau, vol. VII
(Barcelona 1st ed. 1926), p. 216.
Reel 195, No. 1251

VIVES, JUAN LUIS, 1492-1540.
De Conscribendis Epistolis Ioannis Lvdovici Viuis
Valentini Libellus. uere aureus. Des. Erasmi Roterodami
Compendiū postremo iam ab eodem recognitum. Conradi
Celtis Methodus. Christophori Hegendrophini Methodus.
Omnia Nvnc Demvm Longè quàm antea & emendatius excusa,
& Indice rerum in hisce memorabilium locupletissimo
aucta. Basileae: [Per B. Lasium & T. Platterum, 1536].
85, [9] l.; 16cm.

Bound with: Macropedius, Georgius: Epistolarvm
Artificiose conscribendarum Methodvs ..., 1582.
Numerous errors in pagination.
Reel 195, No. 1252

VIVES, JUAN LUIS, 1492-1540.
De Conscribendis Epistolis, Ioannis Lvdovici Vivis
Valentini Libellus uerè aureus. D. Erasmi Roterodami
Compendium, postremô ab eodem recognitum. Conradi
Celtis Methodus. Christophori Hegendorphini Methodus.
Omnia studiosè excusa, ac indice aucta. Coloniae:
Excudebat Petrus Horst, 1579.
149, [14] p.; 16cm.

Error in paging: nos. 113-116 omitted: other errors
also.
Reel 195, No. 1254

VIVES, JUAN LUIS, 1492-1540.
Ioannis Lodovici Vivis Valentini De Disciplinis
Libri XX. Antverpiae: Michael Hillenivs In Rapo,
1531.
3 tomes in 2 pts. bound in 1 v. ([4], 140 (i.e.
160) l.; 78 l.); 30cm.

Tome 1: De Corruptis Artibus Liber Primus [-Septimus].
Tome 2: De Tradendis Disciplinis Sev De Institvtione
Christiana Liber Primvs.
Tome 3: De Prima Philosophia siue de intimo naturae
opificio Liber primus. [- octavus].
Doublet, p. 135.
Reel 195, No. 1255

VIVES, JUAN LUIS, 1492-1540.
Ioannis Lvdovici Viuis Valentini, de Disciplinis
Libri XX. in tres Tomos distincti, quorum ordinem
uersa pagella indicabit. Cum indice nouo, eoq
accuratissimo. Coloniae: Apud Ioannem Gymnicum, 1536.
[32], 654 p.; 16cm.

Engraved title-page.
Bound with: Agrippa von Nettesheim; Henrici Cornelii
Agrippae Ab Nettesheim De in certitudine ..., 1536.
Adam, II, no. 947; Doublet, p. 135.
Reel 195, No. 1256

VIVES, JUAN LUIS, 1492-1540.
Ioannis Lvdovici Vivis Valentini, De Disciplinis
Libri XX. in tres Tomos distincti, quorum ordinem
versa pagella indicabit. Cum indice copiosissimo.
Lvgdvni: Apud Ioannem Frelonium, 1551.
[41], 613, [1] p.; 18cm.

Errors in paging: p. 94, 202, and 203 wrongly number-
ed 76, 203, and 189 respectively.
In manuscript inside front cover: Sum ex libris
Anthonij Longuni J.V.D.
Colophon: Lvgdvni, Excudebat Ioannes Frellonius.
[Line] 1551.
Doublet, p. 135.
Reel 195, No. 1258

VIVES, JUAN LUIS, 1492-1540.
Ioannis Ludovici Vivis, Valentini, De Disciplinis
Libri XII: septem de Corruptis Artibus; quinque de
tradendis Disciplinis. Cum indice copioso. Lugduni
Batavorum: Ex Officina Joan Maire, 1636.
[12], 693, [16] p.; 14cm.

Doublet, p. 135.
Reel 196, No. 1259

VIVES, JUAN LUIS, 1492-1540.
Ioannis Lodovici Vivis Valentini Declamationes
Sex. Syllanae Qvinqve. Sexta, qua respondet Parieti
palmato Quintiliani. Eivsdem Ioan. Lodo. Vivis De
praesenti statu Europae, & bello Turcico diuersa
opuscula. Item. Isocratis Orationes Dvae,
Areopagitica & Nicocles, eodem Ioan. Lodo. Vive
Interprete. Omnia per ipsum autorem nunc demum &
aucta, & recognita. Adiecto etiam rerum & uerborum
Indice diligentissimo. Basileae: [Robert Winter,
1538].
[12], 315, [37] p.; 21cm.

Colophon: Basileae in officina Roberti Winter, anno
M.D.XXXVIII. mense Martio.
Adams, II, no. 962.
Reel 196, No. 1260

VIVES, JUAN LUIS, 1492-1540.
Ioannis Lodovici Vivis Valentini de Institutione
foeminae Christiane ad Inclytam D. Catharinam Hispanam,
Angliae Reginam, Libri tres. Ab autore ipso recogniti,
aucti, & reconcinnati. Vnâ cura rerum & uerborum
diligentissimo Indice. Basileae: [Robert Winter],
1538.
[56], 318, [2] p.; 17cm.

Colophon: Basilea, per Robertvm Winter, mense
avgusto, anno M.D. XXXVIII.
On fly-leaf: "Dedié à Catharine d'Aragon, première
femme de Hen. VIII."
Pagination errors throughout.
Reel 196, No. 1261

VIVES, JUAN LUIS, 1492-1540.
A Verie Fruitfull and pleasant booke: called the
Instruction of a Christian Woman. Made first in
Latin, by the right famous Clearke M. Levves Vives,
and translated out of Latin into English, by Richard
Hyrde. London: Printed by Iohn Danter, 1592.
[7], 209] l.; 14cm.

English translation by Richard Hyrde.
Reel 196, No. 1262

VIVES, JUAN LUIS, 1492-1540.
Ioannis Lodovici Vivis Valentini, De Officio Mariti,
Liber doctissimus, lectuꝗ utilissimus, ab ipso autore
multis in locis nunc primum auctus & recognitus.
Vnâ cum rerum ac uerborum diligentissimo Indice.
Basileae: [Roberti Winter, 1538].
[40], 155, [5] p.; 14cm.

Colophon: Basileae in Officina Roberti VVinter, Anno
Domini M.D.XXXVIII. Mense Martio.
Title-page mutilated, bottom clipped out and repaired.
Reel 196, No. 1263

VIVES, JUAN LUIS, 1492-1540.
Ioannis Lvdovici Vivis Valentini De Officio Mariti
Liber Vnus. De Institvtione Foeminae Christianae Libri
tres. De Ingenvorvm Adolescentum ac Puellarum
Institutione Libri duo. Omnes ab Autore ipso recogniti,
aucti ac reconcinnati, unã cum rerum ac uerborum
locupletissimo Indice. Basileae: [Roberti Winter,
1540].
[16], 614, [74] p.; 14cm.

Colophon: Basileae In Officina Roberti VVinter Anno
M.D.XXXX. mense Septembri.
Pagination errors throughout.
Adams, II, no. 954.
Reel 196, No. 1264

VIVES, JUAN LUIS, 1492-1540.
De Ratione Stvdii Pverilis Epistole due Ioan.
Lvdovici Vivis, quibus absolutissimam ingenuorum
adolescentium ac puellarum institutionem, doctissima
breuitate complectitur. Eivsdem Ad ueram
Sapientiam introductio. Item. Satellitium animi,
siue Symbola, ad omnem totius uitae, maxime Principum
institutionem, mire conducentia. Libellus uere
aureus, & oui non solum uersetur omnium manibus, sed
edificatur etiam, dignissimus. Lipsiae: [Michaelem
Blum Mensae Aprilis, 1538].
145, [30] p.; 14cm.
Reel 196, No. 1265
Colophon: Excvsvm Per Michaelem Blum Mensae Aprilis.
Anno M.D.XXXVIII.
Reel 196, No. 1265

VIVES, JUAN LUIS, 1492-1540.
Ioannis Lodovici Vivis Valentini, Excitationes animi
In Deum. Praeparatio animi ad orandum. Commentarius
in oratione Dominicam. Preces & meditationes
quottidianae. Preces & meditationes generales.
Eivsdem Ad ueram Sapientiam introductio. Satellitium
animi, siue Symbola, Principum institutioni
potissimum destinata. Ex postrema recognitione autoris.
Basileae: [Robert Winter, 1540].
540 (i.e. 504) p.; 11cm.

Colophon: Basileae, In Officina Roberti VVinter
Mense Septembri Anno M.D.XXXX.
Reel 196, No. 1266

VIVES, JUAN LUIS, 1492-1540.
Ioannis Lodovici Vivis Valentini, Excitationes animi
in Deum. Praeparatio animi ad orandum. Commentarius
in orationem Dominicon. Preces & meditationes
quotidianae. Preces & meditationes generales.
Eivsdem Ad ueram Sapientiam introductio. Satellitium
animi, siue Symbola, Principum institutioni potissimum
destinata. Basilea: [Ioannis Oporini, 1548].
410, [9] p.; 11cm.

Colophon: Basileae, Ex officina Ioannis Oporini.
Anno M.D.XLVIII. Mense Augusto.
Reel 196, No. 1267

VIVES, JUAN LUIS, 1492-1540.
Ioannis Lodovici Vivis Valentini, Excitationes animi
in Deum. Praeparatio animi ad orandum. Commentarius
in orationem Dominicã. Preces & meditationes
quotidianae. Preces & meditationes generales. Eisdem
Ad veram Sapiẽtiam introductio. Satellitium animi,
siue Symbola, Principum institutioni potissimum
destinata. * Ex postreme recognitione Authoris.
Lṽdvni: Apud Theobaldum Paganum, 1550.
339, [1] p.; 11cm.

Reel 196, No. 1268

VIVES, JUAN LUIS, 1492-1540.
Lingvae Latinae Exercitatio, Ioan. Lodo Viuis
Valentini Libellus ualde doctus & elegans, nunco
denuo in lucem ẽditus. Coloniae: excudebat Ioan.
Gymnicus, 1544.
[54] ℓ.; 15cm.

Bound with A): Baptista Mantuanus: Bap. Mantuani
Carmelitae Theologi Adolescentia seu Bucolica, breuibus
Iodoci Badij commentariis illustrata, 1546.
B). Vitus Amerbach: Commentaria Viti Amerbachii in
Ciceronis tres libros de Officijs. Liber Ad Lectorem,
1539.
Reel 197, No. 1269

VIVES, JUAN LUIS, 1492-1540.
Ioannis Ludovici Vivis Valentini Colloquia, siue
Linguae Latinae exercitatio. Accessit & uocum aliquot
difficilioru explicatio, & rerum uerborumq; memorabilium
diligentiss. Index. Basileae: Per Ioan. Oporinum.
[n.d. 1560?].
168, [24] p.; 16cm.

Reel 197, No. 1272

VIVES, JUAN LUIS, 1492-1540.
Lingvae Latinae Exercitatio, Ioanne Lodovico Vive
Avtore. Disce puer linguae, quae sunt abstrusa
Latinae, Hic liber, aut nullus, quae dabit apta tibi.
Habet & musca splenem. Antverpiae: Excudebat Ioannes
Lõeus, 1561.
144 p.; 16cm.

Adams, II, no. 968.
Reel 197, No. 1273

VIVES, JUAN LUIS, 1492-1540.
Ioannis Lodouici Viuis Valentini, Linguae Latinae
Exercitatio. Annotationes praeterea in singula
Colloquia, doctissimi viri Petri Mottae
Complutensis, in Hispanae iuuentutis gratiam adiecimus
Cum Indice Latinohispanico vocum difficiliorum ab
Ioanne Ramires compilato. Antverpiae: In aedib.
Viduae & Haeredum Ioan. Stelsii, 1567.
162, [12] p.; 16cm.

Bound in old vellum with leather clasps.
Reel 197, No. 1274

VIVES, JUAN LUIS, 1492-1540.
Flores Italici, Ac Latini Idiomatis, E' Viridario
Exercitationis Ioannis Lvdovici Viuis excerpti, Et
Ab Horatio Tvscanella Italicè interpretati. Nunc
primũm in gratiam studiosorum omnium: sed praecipue
Exterarum Nationum, impressi, & in lucem editi.
Venetijs: ex Officina Velgrisiana, 1570.
[10], 293 p.; 16cm.

Reel 197, No. 1275

VIVES, JUAN LUIS, 1492-1540.
Colloqvia, Sive Exercitatio Latinae Linguae,
Iohannis Lvdovici Vivis Valentini. Ioan. Thomae
Freigii notis, ex praestantissimis quibusq autoribus
desumtis, illustrata. Adiectum habes etiam in fine
Indicem triplicem, & quidem locupletissimum, quorum
primus res & verba: alter nomina Auctorum, qui in
his notis continentur & citantur: ultimus dialogorum
argumenta vel brevissimas summas complectitur.
Noribergae: [excudebat Paulus Kauffmann, 1582].
302, [33] p.; 16cm.

Title-page mutilated.
Adams, II, no. 969.
Reel 197, No. 1276

VIVES, JUAN LUIS, 1492-1540.
Prima Loqvendi Latine Exercitatio Ad Propriorvm
Et Idoneorvm Vocabvlorvm Copiam comparandam secundum
ordinem rerum earum, quae in quotidiano versantur vsu
olim Per Ioannem Lvdovicvm Vivem Conscripta & in
dialogos aliquot distincta. Nunc denuò dilingenter
examinata atq; ad frequentatam in Gymnasio Montano
instituendi rationem accommodata. Coloniae
Agrippinae: Apud Gosuinum Cholinum, 1594.
147, [5] p.; 16cm.

"Gvalthervs Xylander professoribus inferiorum
classium": 5 p. at end.
Reel 197, No. 1277

VIVES, JUAN LUIS, 1492-1540.
Lingvae Latinae Exercitatio, Ioanne Lodovico Vive
Avctore. Disce puer linguae, quae sunt abstrusa
latinae. Hic liber, aut nullus, quae dabit apta tibi.
Londini: Excusum pro Societate Stationariorum, 1628.
[55] l.; 11cm.

Vignette representing the tree of knowledge.
Pollard and Redgraves, no. 24853a.
Reel 197, No. 1278

VIVES, JUAN LUIS, 1492-1540.
Colloqvia, Sive Exercitatio Latinae Linguae.
Joannis Ludovici Vivis Valentini: Notis, ex T. Fregio
& Martinio aliisque Autoribus desumptis, illustrata.
Goudae: Apud Franciscum, Hoolm, 1662.
[4], 246, [10] p.; 14cm.

Reel 197, No. 1279

VIVES, JUAN LUIS, 1492-1540.
Les Dialogves De Ian Loys Vives, Tradvits De Latin
En Francoys. Pour l'exercice des deux langues. Par B.
Iamyn. A Monseignevr Charles De Lorraine. Ausquelz
est adioustée l'explication Francoise des motz latins
plus rares & moins vsages. Par Gilles de Housteuile.
Auec ample declaration & traduction des passages grecz
en Latin par P. de la Motte. Paris: Pour Gabriel
Buon, au clos Bruneau, à l'enseigne S. Claude, 1564.
152, [41] l.; 11cm.

French translation by Benjamin Jamin.
Latin and French.
Reel 197, No. 1280

VIVES, JUAN LUIS, 1492-1540.
Les Dialogves De Ian Loys Vives, Tradvits De Latin
En langues. Pour l'exercice des deux langues. Par B.
Iamyn. A Monseignevr Charles De Lorraine. Ausquelz
est adioustée l'explication Francoise des motz latins
plus rares & moins vsages. Par Gilles de Housteuile.
Auec ample declaration & traduction des passages grecz
en Latin par P. de la Motte. Paris: Pour Gabriel
Buon, au clos Bruneau, à l'enseigne S. Claude, 1571.
152, [41] l.; 11cm.

French translation by Benjamin Jamin.
Latin and French.
Reel 197, No. 1281

VIVES, JUAN LUIS, 1492-1540.
Les Dialogves De Ian Loys Vives, Tradvits De Latin
En Francoys. Pour l'exercice des deux langues. Par B.
Iamyn. A Monseignevr Charles De Lorraine. Ausquelz
est adioustée l'explication Francoise des motz latins
plus rares & moins vsages. Par Gilles de Housteuile.
Auec ample declaration & traduction des passages grecz
en Latin par P. de la Motte. Paris, Pour Gabriel Bvon,
au clos Bruneau, à l'enseigne S. Claude, 1588.
199, [56] l.; 11cm.

French translation by Benjamin Jamin.
Latin and French.
Reel 197, No. 1282

VIVES, JUAN LUIS, 1492-1540.
Opvscvla Aliqvot Vere Catholica, Ac Imprimis
erudita, Ioannis Lodouici Viuis Valentini, accurate
impressa. Introdvctio ad Sapientiam. Satellitivm
siue Symbola. De Ratione Studij puerilia Epistolae
II. Argentorati: apud Petrum Schoeffer, [1524].
[100] l.; 14cm.

Reel 197, No. 1283

VIVES, JUAN LUIS, 1492-1540.
Io. Lodovici Vivis Valentini Opera, In Dvos Distincta
Tomos: Qvibvs Omnes Ipsivs Lvcvbrationes, quoquot
unquam in lucem editas uoluit, complectuntur: praeter
Commentarios in Augustinum De ciuitate Dei, quorum
desiderio si quis afficiatur, apud Frobenium inueniet.
Quae uerò singulis tomis contineantur, in utriusq
sectionis primo ternione indicatur. Adiunctus est
his omnibus Index uberrimus. Basileae: [Nicolavm
Episcopivm, 1555].
2 v. in 1 ([64], 687 p.; 978 (i.e. 977), [3] p.);
36cm.

Vol. II has separate title-page: Secvndvs Tomvs
Io. Lodovici Vivis Valentini Opervm, Qvo Qvae Com-
plectantvr, Versa facie cognoscere licet.
Colophon: Basileae, apvd Nicolavm Episcopivm
ivniorem, anno salutis humana MDLV mense augusto.
Edited by Uldrichus Coccius.
Adams, II, no. 935.
Reel 198, No. 1284

VIVES, JUAN LUIS see also AUGUSTINUS, AURELIUS;
CERVANTES DE SALAZAR, FRANCISCO; ERASMUS, DESIDERIUS.

Vivir Contra La Fortuna see MOLINA LAMA Y GUZMÁN,
    GERONIMO DE.

VOSSIUS, GERARDUS JOANNES, 1577-1649.
    De Theologia Gentili, Et Physiologia Christiana sive
De Origine Ac Progressv Idolatriae, ad veterum gesta,
ac rerum naturam, reductae; Deqve Natvrae Mirandis
quibus homo adducitur ad Deum Liber I, Et II.
Amsterdami: Apud Ioh. et Cornelivm Blaev, 1641.
    [3], 734, [39] p.; 20cm.

    Bound in: Moses ben Maimon. R. Mosis Maimonidae
De Idololatria Liber..., 1641.
    Pagination errors throughout.
    Palau, 147417.
Reel 116, No. 737

VOSSIUS, GERARDUS JOANNES, CANON OF CANTERBURY,
    1577-1649.
    Opera in sex tomos divisa. Quorum series post
praefationem exhibetur. Amstelodami: Ex typographia
P. & J. Blaev, prostant apud Janssonio-Waesbergios,
Henricum Viduam T. Boom & R. Goethals, 1701.
    6 v.

    In this copy vols. 2-6 have special title-pages
with dates 1695, 1697, 1699, 1700 and 1701 respectively.
    Vol. 5 Contains: R. Mosis Maimonidae De Idololatria
Liber, cum interpretatione Latina, & Notis, Dionysii
Vossii. [Printer's device: Indefessus Agendo].
Reels 199, 200 & 201, No. 1285

VOTO del Marques de Fresno sobre la sucession de la
    Monarchia de España.
    13 manuscript *l.*
    Bound with: HERRERA Y SOTOMAYOR, JACINTO DE, fl.
1644. Iornada que su Magestad hizo a la Andalvzia.
[Madrid: En la Imprenta Real, 1624].
    Palau, 114276 (List only printed folios 1-6).
Reel 77, No. 484.14

W

WALDSEEMÜLLER, MARTIN, 1470?-1522?
Cosmographie introductio: cum quibusdam Geometrie ac
Astronomie principijs ad eam rem necessarijs. Insuper
quattuor Americi Vespucij nauigationes. Uniuersalis
Cosmographie descriptio tam in solido q̄ plano eis
etiam insertis que Ptholomeo ignota a nuperis
reperta sunt. Cum deus astra regat et terre climata
Cesar Nec tellus, nec eis sydera maius habent. [Apud
Argentoracus: Joannes Grüninger, 1509].
[34] l.; 21cm.

Colophon: Preisit apud Argentoracus hocopus Ingenisus
vir Joannes grüniger. Anno post natū saluatorē supia
sequimillesimū Nono. Joanne Adelpho Mulicho
Argentineñ Castigatore.
Gothic type. Text in single columns, 37 lines to
a full page.
One folded diagram, unsigned, attached to signature
D¹.
First published in 1507 at St. Dié. This is the
edition said to have been used by Navarrete for the
Spanish version of his Colección.
Church 32; Graesse, p. 280; Penney, p. 606.
Reel 201, No. 1286

WALDSEEMÜLLER, MARTIN, 1470?-1522?
Elementale Cosmographicum, quo totius & Astronomiae
& Geographiae rudimenta, certissimis breuissimis q̄ue
docentur apodixbus. Recens castigatum & emendatum,
figurisque & annotationibus opportuniss. illustratum.
Adiunximus huic libro Cosmographiae introductionē cum
quibusdam Geometriae ac Astronomiae principiis ad eam
rem necessariis. Parisiis: Apud Gulielmum Cauellat,
in pingui Gallina, 1551.
2 pts. (35 l.; 38 l.); 16cm.

Title-page of 2nd part reads: Cosmographiae Introductio Cum Qvibvsdam Geometriae ac Astronomiae
principiis adeam rem nessariis, 1551.
Reel 201, No. 1287

WEIDNER, JOHAN LEONHARD.
Hispanicae Dominationis Arcana per I. L. W. Lugd.
Batavor. Apud Abraham Commelinum et D. Lopez de
Haio, 1653.
[4], 208 p.; 14cm.

Engraved title-page.
Reel 201, No. 1288

WINGFIELD, ANTHONY, (possible author). A True Coppie see
ESSEX, ROBERT DEVEREUX, earl of.

WIT, FREDERIK DE.
Atlas major sin Platea Vitulina sub Signo de Witte
Pascaert. Amstedodami: apud Fredericum de Wit,
[ca. 1671].
[52] l.; 55 x 34cm.

Reel 201, No. 1289

WIT, FREDERIK DE.
Atlas. Tot Amsterdam: bij Fredirick de Wit in de
Calvertstraet bij den Dam inde Witte Paskaert,
[ca. 1688].
[103] l.

Imperfect: maps no. 35, 72, 76-77 wanting.
Two maps are numbered 61, and two other 64.
In addition to the maps of Wit, the Atlas contains
maps by Allard, Blaeu, De Henares, Gerritz Hondius,
Janssen Labanna, Sholtano á Sterringa, Thuilier, N.
Visscher.
Map no. 59 is dated 1660; no. 38, 1671; no. 73,
1688; no. 69, 1662.
HC339/74; Penney, p. 608.
Reel 201, No. 1290

XYZ

XAVIER, HIERONYMUS see JAVIER, JERÓNIMO.

XIMENEZ DE CISNEROS, FRANCISCO, Cardinal (JIMÉNEZ DE
    CISNEROS, FRANCISCO, Cardinal) see Bible. Polyglot.
    1514-1517.

XIMÉNEZ PATÓN, BARTOLOMÉ see JIMÉNEZ PATÓN, BARTOLOMÉ.

ZAPATA, LUIS DE.
    Carlo Famoso De don Luys Capata, a la C.R.M. Del
Rey Don Phelippe Segvndo Nvestro Señor. A Gloria Y
Honrra (sic) De nuestro Señor, so protection y
correction de la sancta madre Yglesia. Valencia: en
casa de Ioan Mey, 1566.
    [4], 289, [1] l.; 20cm.

    Jerez, p. 117; Penney, p. 611; Salvá, I, no. 1087.
Reel 202, No. 1294

ZARAGOZA [LAWS, ETC.] see SARAGOSSA [LAWS, ETC.]

ZARAGOZA DE HEREDIA, MIGUEL ANGEL, bp. of Teano, d. 1623.
    Escvela De La Perfeta Y Verdadera Sabidvria. Donde
Se Mvestra La obligacion que todos tenemos de seguir
perfectamente a Dios, y de la que cada vno tiene en
su estado. Por El Doctor Don Miguel Zaragoca de
Heredia, Dean de Alicante, y Abad mitrado en Sicilia.
Dirigido Al Excelentissimo señor Duque, Marques de
Denia. Madrid: Por Alonso Martin de Balboa, 1612.
    [26], 524, [84] p.; 18cm.

Reel 202, No. 1298

ZÁRATE, AGUSTÍN DE, b. 1514.
    [Historia del descubrimiento y conquista de las
provincias del Peru. Italian]
    Le Historie Del Sig. Agostino Di Zárate Contatore
Et Consigliero (sic) Dell'Imperatore Carlo V. Dello
Scoprimento Et Conqvista Del Perv', nelle quali si
ha piena & particolar relatione delle cose successe
in quelle bande, dal principio fino alla pacificatione
delle Prouincie, si in quel che tocca allo scoprimento,
come al sucesso delle guerre ciuili occorse fra gli
Spagnuoli & Capitani, che lo conquistarono. Nvovamente
di Lingva Castigliana Tradotte dal S. Alfonso Vlloa.
Vinegia: Appresso Gabriel Giolito De' Ferrari, 1563.
    [16], 294 p.; 21cm.

    Italian translation by Alfonso de Ulloa.
    Bartlett, no. 246; Penney, p. 612; Short-Title, III,
p. 416.
Reel 202, No. 1299

ZAVALETA, JUAN DE, b. 1625.
    Errores Celebrados De La Antigvedad. Sv Avtor Don
Jvan De Zavaleta. Lisboa: Na Officina de Domingos
Carneyro, 1665.
    [4], 154, [4] p.; 15cm.

    Imperfect; upper corners of the first 17 pages torn
away and repaired, with some loss of text.
    Penney, p. 610.
Reel 201, No. 1291

ZAVALETA, JUAN DE, b. 1625.
    Obras En Prosa De Don Ivan De Zavaleta. Coronista
Del Rey Nvestro Señor, Por El Mismo Añadidas. Y Por
El Dedicadas. Al Ilvstrissimo Señor Conde De
Villavmbrosa. Del Consejo Svpremo De Castilla en su
Real Camara. Y Presidente Del Real Consejo De
Hazienda, y sus Tribunales. Madrid: Por Andres
Garcia de la Iglesia, 1667.
    [8], 490 p.; 20cm.

Reel 201, No. 1292

ZAVALETA, JUAN DE, b. 1625.
    Obras En Prosa De D. Ivan De Zavaleta, Coronista
Del Rey Nvestro Señor. Por êl mismo añadidas.
Segvnda Impression. Dedicadas Al Señor D. Alonso
Marqvez De Prado, Colegial mayor de el insigne Colegio
del Arcobispo, Catedratico de Digasto viejo de la
Vniuersidad de Salamanca, Oydor de la Real Chancilleria
de Valladolid, del Consejo de Hazienda, Fiscal del
Consejo Real de Castilla, y Oydor del mismo Consejo,
Cauallero del Orden de Alcantara, &c. Madrid: Por
Ioseph Fernandez de Buendia, 1672.
    [8], 546 p.; 20cm.

    Pagination errors throughout.
Reel 201, No. 1293

ZURITA Y CASTRO, GERÓNIMO, 1512-1580.
    Anales De La Corona De Aragon. Compvestos Por
Geronymo Cvrita, Chronista de dicho Reyno. Tomo
Primero. Va Añadida, De Nvevo, En Esta Impresion, En
El Vltimo tomo, vna Apologia de Ambrosio de Morales,
con vn parecer del Doctor Iuan Paez de Castro, todo en
defensa destos Anales. Çaragoça: en el Colegio de S.
Vicente Ferrer, por Lorenço de Robles, Impressor del
mismo Reyno, 1610.
    7 v. ([12], 454 l.; [8], 458 l.; [12], 326 l.; [8],
371 l.; [8], 351 l.; [8], 407, [3], 31 l.; [8],
747 l.); 21cm.

    Each volume has a separate title-page:
    Vol. 2: Los Cinco Libros Postreros De La Primera
Parte De Los Anales De La Corona De Aragon. Compuestos
por Geronymo Curita Chronista de dicho Reyno. Tomo
Segvndo.
    Vol. 3: Los Cinco Libros Primeros De La Segvnda
Parte De Los Anales De La Corona De Aragon. Compuestos
por Geronymo Curita Chronista de dicho Reyno. Tomo
Tercero.
    Vol. 4: Los Cinco Libros Postreros De La Segvnda
Parte De Los Anales De La Corona De Aragon. Compuestos
por Geronymo Curita Chronista de dicho Reyno. Tomo
Qvarto.

ZURITA Y CASTRO (Cont'd)
    Vol. 5: Historia Del Rey Don Hernando El Catholico
De Las Empresas, Y Ligas De Italia. Compvesta Por
Geronymo Curita Chronista del Reyno de Aragon. Tomo
Qvinto.
    Vol. 6: Los Cinco Libros Postreros De La Historia
Del Rey Don Hernando El Catholico. De las empresas, y
ligas de Italia. Compvestos Por Geronymo Cvrita
Chronista del Reyno de Aragon. Tomo Sexto.
    Vol. 7: Indice De Las Cosas Mas Notables, Qve
Se Hallan En Las Qvatro Partes de los Annales, y las
dos de la Istoria de Goernimo Curita, Cronista del
Reyno de Aragon. Dirigido A Los Illvstrissimos
Señores Diputados del.
    Pagination errors throughout.
    Missing pages 446-447 in vol. 1.
    Salvá, II, 3231.
Reels 203 & 204, No. 1301

ZURITA Y CASTRO, GERÓNIMO, 1512-1580.
    Indices Rervm Ab Aragoniae Regibvs Gestarvm Ab
Initiis Regni Ad Annvm MCDX. A Hieronymo Svrita
Tribvs Libris Parati Et Expositi. Rob. Viscardi
Calabriae Ducis, & Rogerii eius fratris Calabriae, &
Siciliae Ducis Principum Normannorvm, & eorum fratrum
rerum in Campania, Apulia, Bruttijs, Calabris, & in
Sicilia gestarum Libri V. auctore Gavfredo Malaterra
Rogerij ipsius hortatu. Rogerii Siciliae Regis rerum
gestarum, quibus Siciliae regnum in Campania, Calabris,
Bruttijs, & Apulia vsque ad ecclesiasticae ditionis
fines constituit: Libri IV. Auctore Alexandro Coenibij
S. Saluatoris Vallis Celesinae Abbate: qui & hortatione
Mathildis eiusdem Rogerij sororis eam historiam
conscripsit. Genealogia Rob. Viscardi, & eorum
Principum, qui Siciliae regnum adepti sunt: ex Ptolemaei
Lvcensis Chronicis decerpta: qua Dyrrhachinae domus
Principum propagines certa, & constanti complexione
appinguntur. Caesaravgvstae: Ex officina Dominici a
Portonarijs de Vrsinis, S. C. M. & Regni Aragoniae
Typographi, 1578.
    [4], 407, [4] p.; 29cm.

    Part II. t.-p. reads: Roberti Viscardi Calabriae
Dvcis, Et Rogerii Eivs Fratris Calabriae, Et Siciliae
Dvcis Principvm Normannorum, & eorum fratrum rerum
in Campania, Apulia, Bruttijs, Calabris, & in Sicilia
gestarum Libri IV. Auctore Gaufredo Malaterra monacho
Rogerij ipsius horratu ... Caesaravgvstae: Ex officina
Dominici a Portonarijs de Vrsinis, S.C.M. & Regni
Aragoniae Typographi, 1578.
    155 p.

    Bookplate: Del P. Onofre de S.ta. Ana, Escolapio.
    HC:NS4/494; Penney, p. 614; Salvá, III, 3232;
Sánchez, no. 549.
Reel 202, No. 1300

INDEX OF PRINTERS

A., B. - London
1625 Teixeira, Jose. *The Spanish Pilgrime*
(*Reel 182, No. 1170*)

Aertssens, Henri - Antwerp
1617 Agustin, Antonio. *Antiqvitatvm*
(*Reel 4, No. 18*)
1653 Agustin, Antonio. *Antiqvitatvm*
(*Reel 4, No. 19*)

Alberti, Olivier - Venice
1600 Casas, Cristobal de las. *Vocabulario*
(*Reel 36, No. 181*)

Albinus, Joannes - Mainz
1603 Del Rio, Martin Antoine. *Disqvititionvm*
(*Reels 153 & 154, No. 1018*)

Alegre, Melchor - Madrid
1668 Argaiz, Gregorio de. *Corona Real*
(*Reel 17, No. 75*)
1668 Palafox y Mendoza, Juan de. *Historia Real*
(*Reel 131, No. 830*)

Allde, Edward - London
1598 Luis de Granada. *Devotion [Libro De La Oracion Y Meditacion]*
(*Reel 67, No. 403*)
1623 Almansa y Mendoza, Andres de. *The Ioyfull Returne*
(*Reel 10, No. 48*)
1623 Pena, Juan Antonio de la. *[Relacion Y Juego De Canas]*
(*Reel 138, No. 872*)

Allot, Robert - Oxford
1633 Aleman, Mateo. *The Rogve [W. Turner for R. Allot]*
(*Reel 8, No. 42*)
1634 Aleman, Mateo. *The Rogve To which is added, the Tragi-Comedy [R.B. for R. Allot]*
(*Reel 8, No. 42*)

Alsop, Bernard - London
1619 Guevara, Antonio de. *[The Diall of princes [Relox De Principes. Eng.]*
(*Reel 73, No. 451*)
1651 Mexia, Pedro. *[The Rarities of the World*
(*Reel 110, No. 686*)

Alsop, Bernard and Fawcett, T. - London
1637 Palmerin de Oliva. *Palmerin D'Oliva (pts. 1-2)*
(*Reel 135, No. 848*)
1639 Palmerin of England. *Palmerin of England (pts. 1-2)*
(*Reel 134, No. 844*)

Alvarez, Melchor - Madrid
  1681 Solis y Rivadeneyra, Antonio de. *Comedias De Don Antonio De Solis*
        (Reel 171, No. 1113)
  1691 Castillo Mantilla y Cossio, Gabriel de. *Laverintho Poetico*
        (Reel 38, No. 194)

Alvarez, Vicente - Lisboa
  1614 Virgilius Maro, Publius. *[Aeneid] La Eneida De Virgilio*
        (Reel 192, No. 1239)

Amerbach, Johann - Basel
  1484 Torquemada, Juan de. *Quaestiones Euangeliorum*
        (Reel 185, No. 1192)
  1487 Tedeschi, Niccolo de. *Decretalium Cum Repertorio*
        (Reels 179-182, No. 1167)

Amoros, Carles - Barcelona
  1543 Boscan Almogaver, Juan. *Las Obras*
        (Reel 27, No. 130)
  1554 Boscan Almogaver, Juan. *Las Obras*
        (Reel 27, No. 131)

Angelieri, Giorgio - Venice
  1581 Luis de Granada. *Memoriale Della Vita Christiana, 2 pts.*
        (Reel 64, No. 387)

Antonio De Lebrija (i.e. Elio Antonio Martinez de Cala y Jarava - Lebrija (Granada)
  1577 Antonio de Lebrija. *Sapientvm Dicta*
        (Reel 16, No. 68)

Aperger, Andrea - Augsburg
  1617 Lazarillo de Tormes.
        (Reel 88, No. 567)
  1618 Winckelfelder, Isaac. *Historien*
        (Reel 88, No. 567)

Ashuerus, Jans. - Goricum (?)
  1624 Scott, Thomas. *Vox Popvli (pt. 2)*
        (Reel 170, No. 1100)

Assiayn, Nicolas de - Pamplona
  1612 Vega Carpio, Lope Felix de. *Pastores De Belen*
        (Reel 190, No. 1227)
  1613 Guadalajara y Javier, Marcos de. *Memorable Expvlsion*
        (Reel 68, No. 415)
  1613 Ripoll, Juan. *Dialogo De Consvelo*
        (Reel 68, No. 416)
  1620 Castillo, Francisco del. *Migaias Caydas*
        (Reel 38, No. 192)

Audeley, John - London
  1566 Guevara, Antonio de. *[Libro Aureo. English] The Golden Boke*
        (Reel 71, No. 434)

Ayala, Juan de - Toledo
    1572 Rades y Andrada, Francisco de. *Chronica De Las Tres Ordenes*
          (Reel 152, No. 991)

Ayala, Lorenzo de - Madrid
    1598 Herrera y Tordesillas, Antonio de. *Historia De Antonio De Herrera*
          (Reel 77, No. 485)

B., R. - see Allot, Robert
          (Reel 77, No. 485)

Baba, Andrea - Venice
    1625 Cervantes Saavedra, Miguel de. *[El Ingenioso Hidalgo Don Quijote De La Mancha] Dell'ingegnoso ... Don Chisciotte*
          (Reel 40, No. 210)

Barezzi, Barezzo - Venice
    1629 Cervantes Saavedra, Miguel de. *[Novelas Ejemplores] Il Novelliere*
          (Reel 40, No. 209)

Barnes, Joseph - Oxford
    1586 Corro, Antonio de]. *Reglas Gramaticales*
          (Reel 45, No. 243)

Basa, Bernardo - Venice
    1596 Acosta, Jose de. *Historia Naturale*
          (Reel 2, No. 7)

Basa, Domenico - Rome
    1583 Agustin, Antonio. *De Legibus*
          (Reel 3, No. 17)

Bedmar, Lucas de - Madrid
    1671 Gonzalex de Rosende, A. *Vida I Virtvdes Del Ill. mo*
          (Reel 61, No. 366)
    1698 Catholic Church. Diocese of Caracas, Venezuela. *Constituciones*
          (Reel 39, No. 201)

Behem, Franciscus - Mainz
    1554 Soto, Pedro de. *Compendivm Doctrinae Catholicae*
          (Reel 172, No. 1121)

Bell, A. (Rhodes, H. and Castle, E.) - London
    1700 Carlos Ii, King of Spain. *Last Will*
          (Reel 33, No. 156)

Bellere, Jean - Antwerp
    1554 Gomara, Francisco Lopez de. *La Historia General ... De Las Indias 2 vols.*
          (Reel 91, No. 587)

Bellere, Pierre (Heirs of) - Antwerp
  1581 Gomara, Francisco Lopez de. *Segvnda Parte De La Diana*
        (Reel 115, No. 723)
  1613 Tacitus, Publius Cornelius. *[Opera Spanish] Las Obras*
        (Reel 177, No. 1153)

Bellettvm, Francisco - Flandrorvm
  1612 Rivadeneira, Pedro. *Vita B. R. Ignatii Qui Religionem*
        (Reel 157, No. 1031)

Beraud, Jean - Lyons
  1582 Amadis de Gaula. *Le Dixneviesme Livre*
        (Reel 12, No. 50, Bk. 19)

Berevvout, Joannes - Dordrecht
  1619 Agustin, Antonio. *Varro, Marcus Terentius*
        (Reel 4, No. 20)

Beros, Luis - Murcia
  1617 Cascales, Francisco de. *Tablas Poeticas*
        (Reel 36, No. 183)
  1621 Cascales, Francisco de. *Al Bven Genio*
        (Reel 36, No. 184)

Bertano, Antonio - Venice
  1587 Casas, Cristobal de las. *Vocabulario*
        (Reel 36, No. 180)

Bertano, Pietro Maria - Venice
  1619 Suarez, Francisco. *Metaphysicarvm Dispvtationvm (2 vols.)*
        (Reel 174, No. 1142)

Berthelet, Thomas - London
  1536 Guevara, Antonio de. *[Libro Aureo. English] The Golden Boke*
        (Reel 70, No. 431)
  1546 Guevara, Antonio de. *[Libro Aureo. English] The Golden Boke*
        (Reel 70, No. 432)
  1550 Vives, Juan Luis. *[Ad Sapientiam Introductio. English]*
        Introduction to Wisedome
        (Reel 194, No. 1249)

Bertier, Antoine - Paris
  1670 Palafox y Mendoza, Juan de. *[Historia De La Conquista De China.*
        French] Histoire De La Conqueste De La Chine
        (Reel 130, No. 827)

Bevilacqua, Giovanni B. - Turin
  1593 Isidorus, Saint. *Sententiarvm Libri III*
        (Reel 82, No. 521)
  1593 Isidorus, Saint. *Chronicon D. Isidori*
        (Reel 82, No. 521)

Bevilacqua, Nicolo - Venice

1563 Ulloa, Alfonso de. *Vita Del Valorosissimo*
(Reel 187, No. 1204)

1567 Petrarca, Francesco. [Canzoniere, Spanish] *De Los Sonetos*
(Reel 144, No. 926)

Bidelli, Gio. Battista - Milan

1622 Rivadeniera, Pedro de. *Vita Del P. S. Ignatio Loiola*
(Reel 157, No. 1033)

Billaine, Jacob - Paris

1651 Maldonado, Juan de. *Theologi Commentarii*
(Reel 98, No. 624)

Billaine, Louis (Widow of) - Paris

1661 Castillo Solorzano, Alonso de. [La Garduna de Seville. French]
(Reel 38, No. 196)

1683 Perez de Hita, Gines. [Historia De Las Guerras. French]
Histoire Des Guerres (pts. 1-3)
(Reel 141, No. 900)

Billaine, Pierre - Paris

1619 Del Rio, Martin Antoine. *Syntagmatis Tragoediae (vol. 2)*
(Reel 156, No. 1024)

1620 Del Rio, Martin Antoine. *Syntagmatis Tragici Pars Vltima
(vol. 3)*
(Reel 156, No. 1024)

1620 Del Rio, Martin Antoine. *Syntagma Tragoediae (vol. 1)*
(Reel 156, No. 1024)

1632 Oudin, Cesar de. *Grammaire Espagnolle*
(Reel 127, No. 803)

1633 Quevedo y Villegas, Francisco Gomez de. [Svenos Y Discvrsos.
French] *Les Visions*
(Reel 151, No. 978)

1634 Quevedo y Villegas, Francisco Gomez de. [Svenos Y Discvrsos. French]
Les Visions
(Reel 151, No. 979)

Bindoni, A., and Pasini, M. - Venice

1550 Guevara, Antonio de. [Libro Avreo. Italian] *Vita, gesti, costvmi*
(Reel 71, No. 440)

1551 Guevara, Antonio de. [Libro Avreo. Italian] *Vita, gesti, costvmi*
(Reel 71, No. 441)

Birckmann, Arnold - Antwerp

1553 Livius, Titus. [Ex XIII T. Livii Decadibus. Spanish]
Todas Las Decadas
(Reels 90-91, No. 583)

Birckmann, Arnold - Cologne

1562 Plutarch. *Vitae Illvstrium*
(Reel 145, No. 935)

Birckmann, Arnold Mylius (In Officina Birckmannica) - Cologne (Agrippina)
  1582 Luis de Granada. *Ecclesiasticae Rhetoricae*
        (Reel 64, No. 391)
  1596 Acosta, Jose. *De Natvra Novi*
        (Reel 1, No. 6)
  1602 Sepulveda, Juan Gines de. *Opera*
        (Reel 170, No. 1105)
  1605 Rubio, Antonio. *Logica Mexicana (pts. 1-2)*
        (Reel 159, No. 1044)

Birckmann, Herman Mylius - Cologne
  1619 Suarez, Francisco. *Defensio Fidei*
        (Feel 173, No. 1141)

Blado, Antonio (d'Asola) - Rome
  1547 Torquemada, Juan de. *Tractatvs De Veritate*
        (Reel 186, No. 1195)

Blaeu, Johannem - Amsterdam
  1659 Gracian y Morales, BaHaser. *Oracvlo Manval*
        (Reel 62, No. 377)
  1659 Gracian y Morales, BaHaser. *El Heroe*
        (Reel 63, No. 384)

Blaeu, Johannem and Cornelium - Amsterdam
  1641 Moses ben Maimon. *De Idololatria*
        (Reel 116, No. 736)
  1642 Moses ben Maimon. *De Idololatria*
        (Reel 116, No. 738)

Blaeu, Johannem and Guiliel - Amsterdam
  1638 Abravanel, Isaac. *Liber De Capite Fidei*
        (Reel 115, No. 731)
  1638 Moses ben Maimon. *Constitvtiones*
        (Reel 115, No. 730)
  1640 Moses ben Maimon. *Canones Ethici*
        (Reel 115, No. 729)

Blaeu, P. & J. - Amsterdam
  1641 Vossius, Gerardus Joannes. *Theologia Gentili*
        (Reel 116, No. 737)

Blanco de Alcazar, Juan - Puebla de los Angeles
  1649 Palafox y Mendoza, Juan de. *Forma Qve Se Debe Gvardar*
        (Reel 130, No. 824)
  1649 Palafox y Mendoza, Juan de. *Reglas Y Ordenanzas*
        (Reel 130, No. 825)

Blare, J. (and Deacon, J.) - London
  1694 Amadis de Gaula. *The most excellent*
        (Reel 14, No. 53)

Blas, Juan Francisco de - Seville
  1691 Spain -- Laws, etc, 1691. *Pragmatica Qve Sv Magestad Manda Publicar*
        (Reel 173, No. 1137)

Blount, Edward - London
  1622 Aleman, Mateo. *The Rogve*
        (Reel 7, No. 39)
  1623 Aleman, Mateo. *The Rogve*
        (Reel 8, No. 40)

Blum, Michael - Leipzig
  1534 Isidorus, Saint. *De Officis*
        (Reel 82, No. 526)
  1538 Vives, Juan Louis de. *De Ratione Stvdii Pverilis*
        (Reel 196, No. 1265)

Blavius, Joannes - Lisbon (Olyssippone)
  1564 Fonseca, Pedro de. *Institvtionvm Dialecticarvm*
        (Reel 55, No. 330)

Boissat, Horacio (and Remus, George) - Lyons
  1661 Davila, Juan Bautista. *Passion del Hombre-Dios*
        (Reel 46, No. 250)

Bollifant, Edmond -- London
  1598 Montemayor, Jorge de. *[Los Siete Libros de la Diane. English] Diana*
        (Reel 115, No. 724)

Bonardo, Cornelio - Salamanca
  1586 Leon, Luis Ponce de. *La Perfecta Casada*
        (Reel 88, No. 569)

Bonelli, Michele - Venice
  1575 Antonio de Lebrija. *Vocabvlarivm Vtriusqve Ivris*
        (Reel 16, No. 69)

Bonellis, Manfredus (De Monteferrato) - Venice
  ca. 1495 Escobar, Andres de. *Interrogationes*
        (Reel 48, No. 268)

Bonfans, Nicolas - Paris
  1577 Amadis de Gaula. *Le Qvatorziesme Livre*
        (Reel 11, No. 50, bk. 14)

Bonhomme, Mathias M. - Lyons
  1549 Alciati, Andrea. *Los Emblemas*
        (Reel 6, No. 29)

Bonis, Novello de - Naples
  1680 Marcos da Lisboa. *[Chronicas de los Frayles Menores. Italian] Croniche Degli Ordini (vols. 1-4)*
        (Reel 100, No. 637)

Bordazar, Jaime - Valencia
1688 Cardona y Alagon, Antonio Folch de. *El Mas Herovco Silencio*
(Reel 33, No. 149)

Borde, Philippe - Lyons
1655 Suarez, Francisco. *De Vera Intelligentia*
(Reel 175, No. 1143)

Bordoni, Girolamo - Milan
1608 Cervantes Saavedra, Miguel de. *Relatione*
(Reel 40, No. 208)
1611 Mantuano, Pedro. *Advertencias*
(Reel 99, No. 631)

Bornat, Claudio - Barcelona
1560 March Mosen, Ausias. *Les Obres*
(Reel 99, No. 635)

Boudot, Martin & Jean (Widow of) - Paris
1684 Gracian y Morales, BaHasar. *[Oraculo Manual. French] L'Homme De Cour*
(Reel 62, No. 378)
1685 Gracian y Morales, BaHasar. *[Oraculo Manual. French] L'Homme De Cour*
(Reel 62, No. 379)

Bourgeat, Claude - Lyons
1659 Izquierdo, Sebastian. *Pharvs Scientiarvm*
(Reel 82, No. 527)

Boutonne, Rolet - Paris
1613 Montemayor, Jorge de. *Los Siete Libros De La Diana*
(Reel 115, No. 726)

Bray, Toussaincts - Paris
1611 Montemayor, Jorge de. *Los Siete Libros De La Diana*
(Reel 115, No. 725)

Briasson, Antoine - Lyons
1688 Nieremberg, Juan Eusebio. *L'Aimable Mere De Jesus*
(Reel 120, No. 757)

Brocar, Arnaldo Guillermo de - Alcala de Henares (Compluti)
1514-1517 Bible. *Polyglot*
(Reels 22-24, No. 112)

Brocar, Juan de - Alcala de Henares (Compluti)
1541 Salinas, Miguel. *Rhetorica en Lengua Castellana*
(Reel 163, No. 1071)
1546 Cervantes de Salazar, Francisco. *Obras*
(Reel 40, No. 207)
1548 Plutarch. *[Moralia. Spanish] Morales de Plutarco*
(Reel 145, No. 934)
1552 Spain -- Laws, etc. *La Prematica Que Su Magestad Ha Madado Hazer*
(Reel 172, No. 1126)
1553 Cordoba, Antonio de. *Libellvs de Detractione*
(Reel 45, No. 240)

Brome, Henry (by T.N. for H. Brome) - London
1681   Gracian y Morales, Baltasar.   *[El Criticon. English] The Critick*
        (Reel 62, No. 376)

Brun, Peter, and Spindeler, Nicolaus - Barcelona
1478   Thomas Aquinas, Saint.   *Commentum In Libros Ethicorum Aristotelis*
        (Reel 184, No. 1182)

Brunet, Augustin - Paris
1699   Gracian y Morales, Baltasar.   *[El Criticon. French] L'Homme Detrompe*
        (Reel 62, No. 374)

Bueno, Pasqual - Zaragoza
1696   Fleichier, Esprit.   *[Histoire du Cardinal Ximenez. Spanish]*
        Historia Del El Senor Cardenal
        (Reel 54, No. 312)
1700   Quevedo y Villegas, Francisco Gomez de.   *Providencia De Dios*
        (Reel 151, No. 975)

Buon, Gabriel - Paris
1564   Vives, Juan Luis.   *Les Dialogves*
        (Reel 197, No. 1280)
1571   Vives, Juan Luis.   *Les Dialogves*
        (Reel 197, No. 1281
1588   Vives, Juan Luis.   *Les Dialogves*
        (Reel 197, No. 1283)

Burchioni, Guilio - Venice
1603   Ribera, Francisco de.   *La Vita Della B. Madre Teresa*
        (Reel 153, No. 1006)

Burgea, Claudio - Lyons
1670   Tarsia, Paolo Antonio di.   *Tvmvltos De La Civdad Y Revno De Napoles*
        (Reel 178, No. 1160)

Burgos, Francisco Antonio de - Valencia
1694   Santos, Francisco.   *Las Tarascas De Madrid*
        (Reel 169, No. 1095)

Butgenius, Conrad - Cologne
1604   Rivadeneira, Pedro de.   *[Tratado de la Tribulacion y desastre...*
        Latin] De Tribvlationibvs
        (Reel 156, No. 1027)

Butter, Nathaniel - London
1623   Gregorius XV, Pope.   *The Popes Letter*
        (Reel 68, No. 413)
1623

Bynneman, Henry - London
1575   Guevara, Antonio de.   *[Epistolas Familiares. English] The Familiar*
        Epistles
        (Reel 70, No. 425)

Cabarte, Pedro - Zaragoza
    1624   Aragon. Laws, statutes, etc. *Fveros Y Observancias*
          (Reel 16, No. 74A)
    1624   Aragon. Laws, statutes, etc. *Fveros Del Reyno De Aragon*
          (Reel 16, No. 74, B & C)
    1624   Aragon. Laws, statutes, etc. *Fveros, Y Actos*
          (Reel 16, No. 74D)
    1624   Aragon. Laws, statutes, etc. *Fori, Qvibvs*
          (Reel 16, No. 74F)
    1625   Aldovera y Monsalve, Jeronime de. *Discursos*
          (Reel 6, No. 31)
    1627   Aragon. Laws, statutes, etc. *Fveros, Y Actos*
          (Reel 16, No. 746)
    1647   Aragon. Laws, statutes, etc. *Fveros Y Actos*
          (Reel 16, No. 74H)

Cabezas, Juan - Seville
    1679   Ossuna y Rus, Martin de. *Memorias, Y Recuerdos (pts. 1-2)*
          (Reel 126, No. 796)

Cailloue, Jacques - Rouen
    1636   Salazar, Ambrosio de. *Espeio General*
          (Reel 127, No. 804)

Calenius, Gervinus, & heirs of Quentel, Johannis - Cologne
    1593   Placios de Salazar, Paulus. *In Ecclesiasticvm Commentarivs*
          (Reel 129, No. 815)

Calvo, Francisco - Toledo
    1663   Miranda y Paz, Francisco de. *El Desenganado*
          (Reel 112, No. 699)

Campins, Pablo - Barcelona
    1657   Perez de Montalban, Juan. *Vida Y Purgatorio*
          (Reel 142, No. 912)

Canova, Juan de - Salamanca
    1555   Nunez de Guzman, Fernando. *Refranes*
          (Reel 124, No. 782)

Canto, Francisco del - Medina Del Campo
    1552   Juan Bautista de Vinones. *Espejo De La Conciencia*
          (Reel 85, No. 545)
    1590   Juan de los Angeles, Fray. *Trivmphos Del Amor De Dios*
          (Reel 86, No. 546)

Cardon, Horace - Lyons
- 1604 Roa, Martin de. *De Die Natali Sacro, 2 pts.*
  (Reel 158, No. 1034)
- 1607 Maldonado, Juan de. *Theologi, Commentarii*
  (Reel 97, No. 623)
- 1608 Del Rio, Martin Antoine. *Commentarivs*
  (Reel 153, No. 1017)
- 1609 Medrano, Diego de. *De Consensv Connvbiali*
  (Reel 105, No. 663)
- 1611 Suarez, Francisco. *Varia Opvscula*
  (Reel 175, No. 1145)
- 1612 Del Rio, Martin Antoine. *Disqvisitionvm*
  (Reel 154, No. 1020)
- 1612 Virgilius Maro Publius. *Priores Sex Libri Aenei, vol. 2*
  (Reel 193, No. 1240)
- 1614 Del Rio, Martin Antoine. *Adagialia*
  (Reel 153, No. 1016)
- 1617 Virgilius Maro Publius. *Posteriores Sex Libri Aeneidos, vol. 3*
  (Reel 193, No. 1240)
- 1619 Virgilius Maro Publius. *Bvcolica Et Georgica, vol. 1*
  (Reel 192, No. 1240)

Cardon, Jacob, and Cavellati, Pierre - Lyons
- 1623 Sanchez, Gaspar. *Gasparis Sanctii Centvmpvteolani*
  (Reel 164, No. 1076)

Carneyro, Domingos - Lisboa
- 1665 Zavaleta, Juan de. *Errores Celebrados*
  (Reel 201, No. 1291)

Casa de la Compania - Barcelona
- 1571 Pedraza, Juan de. *Svmma De Casos De Consciencia (pts. 1-2)*
  (Reel 137, No. 855)

Cormellas, (Casa de). - Barcelona
- 1683 Palafox y Mendoza, Juan de. *Pereginacon De Philotea*
  (Reel 133, No. 833)
- 1686 Rius, Antonio. *Festivos Y Magestvosos Cvltos*
  (Reel 156, No. 1025)

Castle, E. (Rhodes, H. and Bell, A.) - London
- 1700 Carlos II, King of Spain. *Last will*
  (Reel 33, No. 156)

Cattani, Basilio - Geneva
- 1685 Valle Antigorio -- Laws, statutes, etc. *Statvta, Et Privilegia*
  (Reel 188, No. 1214)

Cavalli, Giorgio de - Venice
- 1564 Mexia, Pedro. *[Silva de Varia Leccion. Italian] Selva Di Varia Lettione*
  (Reel 108, No. 676)

Cavalli, Giorgio de - Venice
1564 Mexia, Pedro. *[Silva de Varia Leccion. Italian] Selva Di Varia Lettione*
(*Reel 108, No. 676*)

Cavellat, Guillaume - Paris
1551 Waldseemuller, Martin. *Elementale Cosmographicum*
(*Reel 201, No. 1287*)
1558 Sacro Bosco, Joannes de. *Sphaera Ioannis De Sacro Bosco Emendata*
(*Reel 162, No. 1062*)

Cavellati, Pierre (see Cardon, Jacob)

Cays, Jaime (see Cormellas, Casa de)

Cea Tesa, Francisco - Salamanca
1611 Bathe, William. *Ianva Lingvarvm*
(*Reel 21, No. 104*)

Centrat, Jaime - Barcelona
1603 Marquez, Juan. *Los Dos Estados*
(*Reel 103, No. 653*)

Champion, Jean - Lyons
1644 Nieremberg, Juan Eusebio. *[Causa y Remedio...French] Les Veritables Cavs.*
(*Reel 120, No. 756*)

Cholinus, Gosuinus - Cologne
1591 Sacro Bosco, Joannes de. *Sphaera Ioannis De Sacro Bosco Emendata*
(*Reel 162, No. 1063*)
1594 Vives, Juan L. *Prima Loqvendi Latine*
(*Reel 197, No. 1277*)
1605 Fonseca, Pedro de. *Institvtionvm Dialecticarvm*
(*Reel 55, No. 334*)

Cholinus, Maternus - Cologne
1570 Soarez, Cypriano. *De Arte Rhetorica Libri Tres*
(*Reel 173, No. 1138*
1586 Fonseca, Pedro de. *Institvtionvm Dialecticarvm*
(*Reel 55, No. 331*)

Cloquemin, Louis - Lyons
1581 Amadis de Gaula. *Le Vingtiesme Et Penvltime livre*
(*Reel 12, No. 50, Bk. 20*)
1581 Amadis de Gaula. *Le Vingt Vniesme Et Dernier livre*
(*Reel 12, No. 50, Bk. 21*)

Clouzier, Gervais - Paris
1670 Garcilaso de la Vega, El Inca. *[La Florida del Inca. French]*
Histoire De La Floride (vos. 1-2)
(Reel 57, No. 346)

Coci, George - Zaragoza
1510 Cassianus, Joannes. *Collationes Patru, ... et Speculum*
(Reel 36, No. 186)
1543 Guevara, Antonio de. *Epistolas Familiares (Bk. I)*
(Reel 69, No. 420)

Coello, Pedro - Madrid
1655 Quevedo y Villegas, Francisco Gomez de. *Politica De Dios*
(Reel 150, No. 973)

Collombat, Jacques - Paris
1696 Gracian y Morales, Baltasar. *[El Criticon. French]* L'Homme Detrompe
(Reel 62, No. 375)

Colonia, Arnold - Leipzig
1493 Isidorus, Saint. *De Summo Bono Libri*
(Reel 82, No. 523)

Colonia, Paulus de, (et Socii) - Seville
1491 Lull, Ramon. *De Conceptione*
(Reel 95, No. 616)

Comin da Trino - Venice
1549 Guevara, Antonio de. *Vita, Gesti, Costumi*
(Reel 71, No. 439)

Commelin, Abraham - Lyons
1653 Weidner, Johan Leonhard. *Hispanicae Dominationis*
(Reel 201, No. 1288)

Coppenius, Aegidius (Diesthemius) - Antwerp
1546 Prudentius Clemens, Aurelius. *Opera*
(Reel 146, No. 942)

Coradici, Gasparo - Venice
1670 Quevedo y Villegas, Francisco Gomez de. *[Suenox Y Discursos. Italian]*
Estratto De' Sogni
(Reel 151, No. 986)

Cormellas, Casa de - Barcelona
1697 Berart, Serapio de. *Manisfestacion*
(Reel 22, No. 108)

Cormellas, Francisco - Barcelona
    1670 Nieremberg, Juan Eusebio. *De La Diferencia Entre Lo Temporal, Y Eterno*
        (*Reel 120, No. 758*)

Cormellas, Sebastian de - Barcelona
    1594 Solsona, Francisco. *Stylvs Capibreviandi*
        (*Reel 172, No. 1117*)
    1606 Seneca, Lucius Annaeus. *[De Benefici. Spanish] Espeio De Bienechores*
        (*Reel 170, No. 1103*)
    1617 Juan de Santa Maria. *Tratado De Repvblica*
        (*Reel 86, No. 547*)
    1619 Juan de la Cruz. *Obras Espiritvales*
        (*Reel 84, No. 539*)
    1628 Garibay y Zamalloa, Esteban. *Compendio Historical (vols. 1-4)*
        (*Reel 58, No. 348*)
    1634 Cespedes y Meneses, Gonzalo de. *De La Historia De D. Felipe El IIII*
        (*Reel 41, No. 216*)
    1636 Nieremberg, Juan Eusebio. *El Gran Padre*
        (*Reel 122, No. 771*)
    1637 Molina, Antonio de. *Instrvccion De Sacerdotes*
        (*Reel 112, No. 707*)
    1646 Velez de Guevara y Duenas, Luis. *El Diablo Coivelo*
        (*Reel 191, No. 1235*)

Cornetti, Giacomo - Venice
    1592 Acosta, Cristobal de. *Tratado*
        (*Reel 1, No. 4*)

Correa de Montenegro, F. (Widow of) - Madrid
    1622 Lopez de Haro, Alonso. *Nobiliario Genealogico (pt. 2)*
        (*Reel 92, No. 589*)

Corrozet, Galiot - Paris
    1595 San Pedro, Diego de. *Carcel De Amor*
        (*Reel 164, No. 1075*)

Cortey, Jaume - Barcelona
    1562 Muntaner, Ramon. *Chronica*
        (*Reel 117, No. 742*)

Costilla, Jorge - Valencia
    1512 Lull, Ramon. *Logica Nova*
        (*Reel 95, No. 615*)

Cotes, Thomas, (for Crooke, Andrew & William) - London
    1637 Shirly, James. *The Yovng Admirall*
        (*Reel 170, No. 1108*)

Cotinet, Jacques - Paris
- 1660 Perez de Hita, Gines. *Historia De Las Gverras Civiles*
  (Reel 141, No. 899)

Craesbeeck, Paulo - Lisboa
- 1648 Malvezzi, Virgilio. *[Opere. Spanish] Las Obras*
  (Reel 98, No. 627)
- 1648 Quevedo y Villegas, Francisco Gomez de. *La Caida Para Levantarse*
  (Reel 147, No. 947)
- 1652 Quevedo y Villegas, Francisco Gomez de. *El Parnasso Espanol*
  (Reel 150, No. 968)
- 1653 Doze Comedias.
  (Reel 47, No. 261)

Craesbeeck, Pedro - Lisboa
- 1597 Index Librorum Prohibitorum. *Index Librorvm*
  (Reel 80, No. 512)
- 1602 Torres, Juan de. *Philosophia Moral*
  (Reel 186, No. 1199)
- 1605 Garcilaso de la Vega, El Inca. *La Florida Del Ynca*
  (Reel 57, No. 345)
- 1606 Soarez de Alarao, Joao. *La Iffanta Coronada*
  (Reel 171, No. 1112)
- 1623 Rodrigues Lobo, Francisco. *La Iornada Qve La Magestad Catholica*
  (Reel 158, No. 1037)
- 1631 Cespedes y Meneses, Gonzalo de. *De La Historia De D. Felipe IIII*
  (Reel 41, No. 215)

Craesbeeck de Mello, Antonio - Lisboa
- 1674 Faria E Sousa, Manuel de. *Asia Portuguesa*
  (Reel 50, No. 284, vol. 2)
- 1674 Faria E Sousa, Manuel de. *Noches Claras*
  (Reel 51, No. 288)
- 1675 Faria E Sousa, Manuel de. *Asia Portuguesa (vol. III)*
  (Reel 50, No. 284, vol. 3)
- 1676 Mello, Francisco Manuel de. *Epanaphoras De Varia Historia*
  (Reel 110, No. 690)
- 1678 Faria E Sousa, M. de. *Evropa Portuguesa*
  (Reels 50 & 51, No. 285, vol. 1)
- 1679 Faria E Sousa, M. de. *Evropa Portuguesa*
  (Reels 50 & 51, No. 285, vol. 2)
- 1680 Faria E Sousa, M. de. *Evropa Portuguesa*
  (Reels 50 & 51, No. 285, vol. 3)
- 1681 Faria E Sousa, M. de. *Africa Portvguesa*
  (Reel 50, No. 283)

Craesbeekiana, Emprenta - Lisboa
- 1652 Velasco de Gouvea, Francisco. *Perfidia De Alemania*
  (Reel 191, No. 1234)

Crespin, Jacques - Geneva
    1644   Vittori, Girolamo. *Tesoro De Las Tres Lenguas*
            (Reel 194, No. 1244)

Crisostomo Garriz, Juan - Valencia
    1612   Pinto de Vitoria, Juan. *Vida Del Venerable Siervo De Dios*
            (Reel 144, No. 930)

Crithium, Joannes - Cologne
    1611   Soto, Andres. *Captivi Temporis Redemptio*
            (Reel 172, No. 1118)
    1613   Rubio, Antonio. *Commentarii In Libros Aristotelis*
            (Reel 160, No. 1046)
    1621   Rubio, Antonio. *Commentarii In Vniversam Aristotelis*
            (Reel 160, No. 1048)
    1644   Rubio, Antonio. *Commentarii In Libros Aristotelis*
            (Reel 160, No. 1047)

Crooke, Andrew (see Cotes, Thomas)

Cuesta, Juan de la - Segovia
    1588   Horozco y Covarrubias, Juan de. *Tratado De La Verdadera*
            (Reel 78, No. 495)
    1598   Horozco y Covarrubias, Juan de. *Emblemas Morales*
            (Reel 78, No. 492)

Cuesta, Juan de la - Madrid
    1606   Diaz Rengifo, Juan. *Arte Poetica*
            (Reel 47, No. 257)
    1606   Garcia de Cespedes, Andres. *Regimiento De Navegacion*
            (Reel 56, No. 342)
    1609   Vega Carpio, Lope Felix de. *Iervsalen Conqvistada*
            (Reel 189, No. 1221)
    1610   Hurtado de Mendoza, Diego. *Obras*
            (Reel 80, No. 507)
    1610   Spain. Laws, etc., 1610. *Prematica En Qve Se Mandan Guardar Las Leyes*
            (Reel 173, No. 1132)
    1611   Spain. Laws, etc., 1611. *Pragmatica De Tratamientos*
            (Reel 173, No. 1133)
    1611   Spain. Laws, etc., 1633. *Pragmatica En Qve Se Da La Forma*
            (Reel 173, No. 1134)
    1611   Carrillo y Sotomayor, Luis. *Obras*
            (Reel 34, No. 165)
    1612   Epictetus. *Dotrina Del Estoico*
            (Reel 48, No. 264)
    1612   Joannes Climacus, Saint. *[Scala Paradisi. Spanish] Libro ...*
            Llamado La Escala Espiritval
            (Reel 84, No. 536)

Cuesta, Juan de la - Madrid (cont'd)
  1614 Augustinus, Aurelius, Saint. *La Ciudad de Dios*
        (*Reel 18, No. 82*)
  1617 Hieronymus, Saint. *[Epistolae. Spanish] Epistolas Selectas*
        (*Reel 77, No. 487*)
  1618 Virgilius Maro, Publius. *Eccologae*
        (*Reel 194, No. 1241*)

Cuesta, Pedro de la - Baeza
  1614 Jiminez Paton, Bartolome. *Epitóme*
        (*Reel 83, No. 534*)
  1615 Barros, Alonso de. *Provebios (sic)*
        (*Reel 21, No. 101*)
  1621 Jiminez Paton, Bartolome. *Mercvrivs Trimegistvs*
        (*Reel 83, No. 535*)

Curteti, Francisco - Zaragoza
  1563 Trujillo, Tomas de. *Libro Llámado Reprobacion de Trajes*
        (*Reel 187, No. 1200*)

Da Costa, Juan - Lisboa
  1667 Gongora y Argote, Luis de. *Obras*
        (*Reel 60, No. 357*)

Daniel, Roger (for E.D.) - Cambridge
  1646 Valdex, Juan de. *[Ciento y Diez Consideraciones. English]*
        Divine Considerations
        (*Reel 188, No. 1209*)

Danter, John - London
  1592 Vives, Juan Luis. *Instruction of a Christian Woman*
        (*Reel 196, No. 1262*)

Darby, J. (for D. Brown) - London
  1699 Casas, Bartolome de las. *Voyages and Discoveries*
        (*Reel 35, No. 176*)

Davis, R. - Oxford
  1655 Moses ben Maimon. *Porta Mosis Sive*
        (*Reel 117, No. 739*)

Day, John - London
  1576 Mexia, Pedro. *[Silva de Varia Leccion. English] The Forest (2 copies)*
        (*Reel 110, Nos. 684 & 685*)

Deacon, J. (and Blare, J.) - London
  1694 Amadis de Gaula. *The Most excellent*
        (*Reel 14, No. 53*)

De Grieck, Josse - Bruxelles
  1699 Quevedo y Villegas, Francisco Gomez de. *[Obras. French]*
      Les Oeuvres (vols. 1-2)
      (Reel 149, No. 966)

Dei, Ambrosio and Bartolomeo - Venice
  1615 Mexia, Pedro. *[Silva de Varia Leccion. Italian] Della selva di*
      varia lettione (pts. 1-3)
      (Reel 109, No. 679)
  1616 Mexia, Pedro. *[Silva de Varia Leccion. Italian] Della selva di*
      varia lettione (pts. 4-5)
      (Reel 109, No. 681)

Delaz, Leodegarius - Paris
  1598 Teixeira, Jose. *Rervm Ab Henrici Borbonii*
      (Reel 182, No. 1169)

De La Mare, Jean - Rouen
  1632 Aleman, Mateo. *Le Gvevx Ov La Vie*
      (Reel 7, No. 38, pt. 1)
  1633 Aleman, Mateo. *Le Volevr Ov La Vie*
      (Reel 7, No. 38, pt. 2)

Delgado, Juan - Madrid
  1625 Jauregui y Aguilar, Juan de. *Apologia*
      (Reel 83, No. 528)

De Luna, Miguel - Zaragoza
  1654 Navarro, Jose. *Poesia Varias*
      (Reel 119, No. 752)

Deversini, Blasi, and Masotti, Zanobii - Rome
  1651 Hernandez, Francisco. *Nova Plantarvm*
      (Reel 76, No. 481)

De Zetter, Jacob - Amsterdam
  1665 Linda, Lucas de. *Descriptio Orbis*
      (Reel 90, No. 580)

Diaz, Diego - Madrid
  1659 Ulloa y Pereira, Luis de. *Versos*
      (Reel 187, No. 1206)

Diaz, Fernando - Seville
  1584 Collenuccio, Pandolfo. *[Del Compendio dell'Istoria. Spanish]*
      Historia Del Reyno De Napoles
      (Reel 44, No. 235)

Diaz, Hernando - Seville
1569   Monardes, Nicolas. *Dos Libros*
        (*Reel 114, No. 714*)
1570   Mexia, Pedro. *Dialogos Eruditos*
        (*Reel 105, No. 664*)
1571   Mercado, Thomas de. *Svmma De Tratos*
        (*Reel 111, No. 697*)

Diaz, Manuel - Coimbra
1657   Guevara, Antonio de. *Libro Llamado Menosprecio*
        (*Reel 73, No. 455*)
1657   Guevara, Antonio de. *Libro Llamado Aviso de Privados*
        (*Reel 73, No. 456*)
1657   Guevara, Antonio de. *Libro de los Inventores*
        (*Reel 73, No. 457*)

Diaz de la Carrera, Diego - Madrid
1634   Villamediana, Juan de Tarsis y Peralta, Conde de. *Obras*
        (*Reel 178, No. 1163*)
1641   Lopez de Vega, Antonio. *Heraclito I Democrito*
        (*Reel 92, No. 592*)
1642   Juvenalis Decimus, Junius. *Satiras*
        (*Reel 86, No. 550*)
1643   Villamediana, Juan de Tarsis y Peralta, Conde de. *Obras*
        (*Reel 179, No. 1165*)
1645   Gongora y Argote, Luis de. *Las Obras (vol. 2)*
        (*Reel 59, No. 355*)
1645   Quevedo y Villegas, Francisco Gomez de. *Marco Bruto*
        (*Reel 152, No. 989*)
1648   Borja, Francisco de. *Las Obras En Verso*
        (*Reel 27, No. 126*)
1650   Faria E Sousa, M. de. *En Gran Iusticia de Arago*
        (*Reel 51, No. 286*)
1653   Boccalini, Triano. *Aviso del Parnaso (pt. I)*
        (*Reel 26, No. 125*)
1655   Palafox y Mendoza, Juan de. *Carta Pastoral*
        (*Reel 129, No. 818*)
1656   Suarez de Alarcon, Antonio. *Relaciones Genealogicas*
        (*Reel 176, No. 1147*)
1657   Martinez de Grimaldo, Jose. *Fvndacion, Y Fiestas*
        (*Reel 104, No. 657*)
1668   Pellicer de Ossau y Tovar, Jose. *Ivstificacion De La Grandeca*
        (*Reel 138, No. 866*)

Diaz, Huerta, D. - Madrid
1667   Index Librorum Prohibitorum
        (*Reel 81, No. 513*)

Didier, Francois - Lyons
1578 Amadis de Gaula. *Le Seiziesme Livre*
(*Reel 11, No. 50, Bk. 16*)

Diesthemius, Aegidius (see Coppenius, Aegidius)

Dolet, E. - Lyons
1543 Guevara, Antonio de. *[Menosprecio De Corte y Alabanza De Aldea. French] Dv'mespris de la covrt*
(*Reel 74, No. 465*)

Dorico, Valerio (and Luigi) - Rome
1555 Gomara, Francisco Lopez de. *[Historia De Mexico. Italian]*
(*Reel 91, No. 588*)

Dormer, Diego - Zaragoza
1641 Blancas y Tomas, Geronimo de. *Coronaciones De Los Serenissmos Reyes*
(*Reel 26, No. 119*)
1641 Blancas y Tomas, Geronimo de. *Modo De Proceder*
(*Reel 26, No. 118*)
1641 Martel, Jeronimo. *Forma De Celebrar*
(*Reel 26, No. 120*)
1649 Molinos, Pedro. *Practica Ivdiciaria*
(*Reel 113, No. 711*)

Dormer, Diego (Heirs of) - Zaragoza
1670 Polo de Medina, Salvador Jacinto. *Obras*
(*Reel 145, No. 937*)
1675 Saragossa -- Laws, etc. *Ordinaciones*
(*Reel 202, No. 1296*)
1680 Blancas y Tomas, Geronimo de. *[Ad Reqùm Aragonùm. Spanish] Inscriptiones Latinas* (*Reel 25, No. 117*)
1680 Andres de Uztarroz, Juan Francisco. *Progressos*
(*Reel 14, No. 58*)
1683 Dormer, Diego Jose. *Discvrsos*
(*Reel 47, No. 260*)

Dotil, Francisco - Barcelona
1611 Marques de Careaga, Gutierre. *Desengano De Fortvna*
(*Reel 103, No. 650*)

Dotil, Giraldo (see Nogues, Rafael)

Droy (Drouy), Guillermo - Madrid
1591 Camoes, Luis de. *Los Lvsiadas*
(*Reel 31, No. 145*)
1591 Petrarca, Francesco. *[Canzionere. Spanish] Los Sonetos Y Canciones*
(*Reel 144, No. 927*)

Du Bray, Joannem - Paris
    1663 Agustin, Antonio. *Fámiliae Rómanae*
          (Reel 5, No. 23)

Du Gard, William - London
    1652 Sandoval, Prudencio de. *[Historia de la Vida ... English]*
          The Civil Wars Of Spain
          (Reel 168, No. 1091)

Duplastre, Antonio - Madrid
    1639 Camoes, Luis de. *Los Lvsiadas (vol. 2)*
          (Reel 31, No. 146)

Du Val, Dionvsius (Denis) - Paris
    1586 Augustinus, Aurelius, Saint. *De Civitate Dei*
          (Reel 18, No. 80)

Eguia, Miguel de - Alcala de Henares (Compluti)
    1526 Alfonso, De Zamora (also known as Alphonsus, of Zamora)
          Grámmatice Hebraice
          (Reel 10, No. 47)
    1529 Seneca, Lucius Annaeus. *Epistolas de Seneca*
          (Reel 170, No. 1102)
    1536 Appianus (of Alexandria, Gr.) *[De Bellis Civilibus Rómanórum.*
          Spanish] Historia
          (Reel 16, No. 73)

Eld, George - London
    1610 Augustinus, Aurelius, Saint. *Of the Citie of God*
          (Reel 19, No. 83)

Elzevier, B. and A - Paris
    1645 Fernandez Villa Real, Manuel. *[Politico Cristianísmo. French]*
          Le Politique
          (Reel 53, No. 305)

Elzevier, Louis & Daniel - Amsterdam
    1656 Fernandez, Marcus, Garnier, Philippe, Donati, L. *Dialogues En*
          Quatre Langues
          (Reel 53, No. 302)

Enrico, Nicolao - Monaco
    1640 Saavedra Fajardo, Diego de. *Idea De Vn Principe Christiano*
          (Reel 160, No. 1051)

Episcopius, Nicolaus (junior) - Basel
    1555 Vives, Juan Luis. *Valentini Opera*
          (Reel 198, No. 1284)

Escribano, Alonso - Seville
    1570 Casas, Cristobal de las. *Vocabulario*
          (Reel 35, No. 177)

Espinosa y Arteaga, Matheo - Madrid
    1668 Guevara, Antonio de. *Epistolas Familiares*
          (Reel 69, No. 422)
    1669 Guevara, Antonio de. *Vidas De Los Diez Emperadores Romanos*
          (Reel 75, No. 477)
    1673 Mexia, Pedro. *Silva De Varia Leccion*
          (Reel 108, No. 674)

Estupinan, Luis - Seville
    1612 Mosquera de Barnuevo, Francisco. *La Numantina*
          (Reel 117, No. 741)

Faber, Franciscus - Lyons
    1590 Del Rio, Martin Antoine. *Ex Miscellaneorum Scriptoribus (pts. 1-2)*
          (Reel 155, No. 1022)

Fajardo, Simon - Seville
    1627 Peliger, Juan Vicente. *Estilo Y Metodo De Escrir Cartas*
          (Reel 137, No. 857)

Farri, Domenico - Venice
    1567 Fuentes, Alonso de. *Le Sei Giornate*
          (Reel 56, No. 339)
    1573 Palmerin de Oliva. *Historia Di Palmerin*
          (Reel 135, No. 847)

Fawcett, T. (see Alsop, B. and ...)

Fei, Andrea - Rome
    1625 Agustin, Antonio. *Dialoghi*
          (Reel 4, No. 22)

Fernandez, Juan - Salamanca
    1581 Estella, Diego de. *Pimera Parte Del Libro De La Vanidad (pts. 1 & 3)*
          (Reel 49, No. 278)

Fernandez, Maria - Alcala de Henares (Compluti)
    1651 Lopez de Zarate, Francisco. *Obras Varias*
          (Reel 93, No. 593)
    1661 Perez de Montalban, Juan. *Para Todos Exemplos Morales*
          (Reel 141, No. 904)

Fernandez de Buendia, Joseph - Madrid
    1672 Zaveleta, Juan de. *Obras En Prosa*
          (Reel 201, No. 1293)
    1675 Sandoval, Prudencio de. *La Historia Del Imperador Carlos Qvinto*
          (Reel 168, No. 1090)
    1680 Ferrer de Valdecebro, Andres. *El Templo De La Fama*
          (Reel 53, No. 311)

Fernandez de Cordoba, Alonso y Diego - Valladolid
    1570 Azpilcueta, Martin de. *Manval de Confessores*
         (Reel 19, No. 87)

Fernandez de Cordoba, Diego - Valladolid
    1588 Lopez de Tovar, Gregorio. *Leyes De Las Siete Partidas*
         (Reel 92, No. 591)
    1589 Ovidius Naso, Publius. *Las Transformaciones* *(2 vols.)*
         (Reel 127 & 128, No. 1808)

Ferrer, Antonio (and Co.) - Barcelona
    1687 Palafox y Mendoza, Juan de. *Vida Interior*
         (Reel 133, No. 839)

Ferrer, Antonio and Balthasar - Barcelona
    1679 Virgilius Marso, Publius. *Las Obras*
         (Reel 194, No. 1242)
    1686 Francois de Sales, Saint. *[Lettres. Spanish]* *Cartas (pts. 1-2)*
         (Reels 55 & 56, No. 336)

Field, Richard - London
    1594 Perez, Antonio. *Pedacos de Historia*
         (Reel 140, No. 885)
    1614 Luis de Granada. *A Paradise of Prayers*
         (Reel 68, No. 408)

Fingel, Wilhelm J. - Wittenberg
    1652 Bible N.T.I John. Syriac. *Epistola D. Johannis*
         (Reel 116, No. 734)

Figuero, Rafael - Barcelona
    1697 Mallorca, Francisco de. *El Sol De La Iglesia*
         (Reel 98, No. 625)

Flamenco, Diego - Madrid
    1623 Relacion. *Verdadera*
         (Reel 152, No. 995)
    1624 Valbuena, Bernardo de. *El Bernardo*
         (Reel 20, No. 92)

Flandrum, Joannem - Madrid
         Suarez, Francisco. *Varia Opvscvla.*
         (Reel 175, No. 1144)

Flesher, J. - London
    1652 Fonseca, Cristobal de. *[Tratado Del Amor De Dios. English]*
         A Discourse of Holy Love
         (Reel 54, No. 328)

Flesher, Miles - London

1685 Gracian y Morales, Baltasar. *[Oraculo Manual. English]* *The Courtiers Manual*
(*Reel 63, No. 381*)

1688 Garcilaso de la Vega, El Inca. *[Commentarios Reales. English]* *The Royal Commentaries*
(*Reel 57, No. 347*)

Foppens, Francisco - Bruxelles

1659 Gongora y Argote, Luis de. *Obras*
(*Reel 60, No. 356*)

1660 Quevedo y Villegas, Francisco Gomez de. *Obras (vol. 1)*
(*Reel 148, No. 959*)

1661 Quevedo y Villegas, Francisco Gomez de. *Obras (vol. 2)*
(*Reel 148, No. 959*)

1661 Quevedo y Villegas, Francisco Gomez de. *Poësias (vol. 3)*
(*Reel 148, No. 959*)

1670 Quevedo y Villegas, Francisco Gomez de. *Poësias*
(*Reel 148, No. 961*)

1670 Quevedo y Villegas, Francisco Gomez de. *Epicteto, Y Phocilides*
(*Reel 149, No. 963*)

1670 Quevedo y Villegas, Francisco Gomez de. *Obras (vol. 2)*
(*Reel 148, No. 961*)

1674 Teresa, Saint. *Cartas De Santa Teresa*
(*Reel 183, No. 1177*)

1675 Teresa, Saint. *Obras De*
(*Reel 184, No. 1180*)

1677 Faria E Sousa, Manuel de. *Epitome de Las Historias Portvgvesas*
(*Reel 52, No. 291*)

1680 Borja, Juan de. *Empresas Morales*
(*Reel 27, No. 129*)

1682 Palafox y Mendoza, Juan de. *Vida Interior*
(*Reel 133, No. 838*)

1689 Euclides. *[Elements of Geometry. Spanish]* *Elementos Geometricos*
(*Reel 50, No. 282*)

Foquel, Guillelmo - Salamanca

1586 Leon, Luis Ponce de. *De Los Nombres De Christo*
(*Reel 88, No. 570*)

1587 Leon, Luis Ponce de. *La Perfecta Casada*
(*Reel 88, No. 569*)

Frambotti, Paolo - Patauij

1661 Alciati, Andrea. *Emblemata*
(*Reel 5, No. 28*)

Franceschini, Camillo - Venice

1556 Bandello, Matteo. *Novelle (vol. 1)*
(*Reel 20, No. 94*)

Franceschini, Camillo & Francesco - Venice
1565   Ulloa, Alfonso de. *Vita Del Potentissimo*
      (Reel 187, No. 1202)

Frellaeus, Frellon, Joannes - Lyons
1551   Vives, Juan Luis. *De Disciplinis Libri XX*
      (Reel 195, No. 1258)

Froschouer, Johann - Augsburg
1508   Escobar, Andres de. *Modus confitendi*
      (Reel 48, No. 272)

Gabiana, Typographia - Rome
1593   Ponce de Leon, Gonzalo. *Scholastica Assertio*
      (Reel 146, No. 940)

Gafaro, Jacomo - Pamplona
1639-40   Malvezzi, Virgilio. *La Libra*
      (Reel 98, No. 626)

Gamonetus, Philippe - Geneva
1664   Escobar del Corro, Juan. *Tractatvs Bipartitvs De Pvritate*
      (Reel 48, No. 274)

Garcia, Francisco - Madrid
1648   Lopez de Zarate, Francisco. *Poema Heroico*
      (Reel 93, No. 594)

Garcia, Juan - Alcala de Henares (Compluti)
1626   Ferrer Maldonado, Lorenzo. *Imagen Del Mvndo*
      (Reel 53, No. 309)

Garcia, Lorenzo - Madrid
1684   Jauregui y Aguilar, Juan. *La Farsalia*
      (Reel 83, No. 530)
1685   Santos, Francisco. *El Sastre Del Campillo*
      (Reel 169, No. 1094)

Garcia de Arroyo, Francisco - Madrid
1645   Perez del Barrio Angulo, Gabriel. *Secretario y Consegero*
      (Reel 143, No. 920)

Garcia de la Iglesia, Andres - Madrid
1658   Saavedra Fajardo, Diego de. *Corona Gothica Castellana*
      (Reel 160, No. 1050)
1666   Saavedra Fajardo, Diego de. *Idea de Vn Principe Politico Christiano*
      (Reel 161, No. 1054)
1667   Zavaleta, Juan de. *Obras En Prosa*
      (Reel 201, No. 1292)

Garcia de la Iglesia, Andres - Madrid (cont'd)
  1668 Rifer de Bracaldino, Sanedrio. *El Porqve De Todos Las Cosas*
       (Reel 153, No. 1007)
  1669 Mariana, Juan de. *Historia General De Espana (vol. 1-2)*
       (Reel 102, No. 648)
  1670 Diamante, Juan Bautista. *Comedias*
       (Reel 47, No. 255)

Garcia Infazon, Juan - Madrid
  1677 Tellez, Gabriel. *Deleytar Aprovechando*
       (Reel 182, No. 1173)
  1681 Antonio de Lebrija. *Diccionario De Romance (pt. 2)*
       (Reel 15, No. 65)
  1690 Cruz, Juan Ines de la. *Poemas*
       (Reel 46, No. 248)
  1690 Calderon de la Barca, Pedro. *Avtos Sacramentales*
       (Reel 31, No. 141)
  1692 Castrillo, Hernando. *Historia y Magia*
       (Reel 39, No. 197)
  1699 Antonio de Lebrija. *Dictionarivm*
       (Reel 15, No. 65)

Garcia Morras, Domingo - Madrid
  1650 Palafox y Mendoza, Juan de. *Vida de S. Ivan*
       (Reel 133, No. 837)
  1653 Solorzano Pereira, Juan de. *Emblemata Centvm*
       (Reel 172, No. 1116)
  1660 Spain. Treaties, etc. *Tratado De Paz*
       (Reel 77, No. 484.5)

Gargano, Juan B. - Naples
  1613 Cerone, Pietro. *El Melopeo y Maestro*
       (Reel 39, No. 205)

Gast, Mathias (Heirs of) - Salamanca
  1578 Perez del Castillo, Baltasar. *El Estado En Qve Dios Llama A Cada Vno*
       (Reel 144, No. 921)
  1583 Luis de Granada. *De La Introdvction Del Symbolo De La Fe (vols. 1-3)*
       (Reel 66, No. 400)
  1585 Leon, Luis Ponce de. *De Los Nombres De Christo*
       (Reel 88, No. 568)

Gennepaeus, Jaspar - Cologne
  1554 Perez de Ayala, Martin. *De Vera Ratione Christianismi*
       (Reel 141, No. 896)

Giglio, P.G. - Venice
  1559 Guevara, Antonio de. *[Aviso de Privados ... Italian] Aviso De Favoriti*
       (Reel 73, No. 460)

Ginammi, Marco - Venice
    1630 Casas, Bartolome de las. *Breuissima relacion*
          (Reel 35, No. 172)
    1643 Casas, Bartolome de las. *Breuissima relacion*
          (Reel 35, No. 171)
    1645 Casas, Bartolome de las. *Conqvista Dell'Indie*
          (Reel 35, No. 170)

Giolito De' Ferrari, Gabriel - Venice
    1543 Flores, Juan de. *[Historia de Aurelio...Italian] Historia Di Avrelio*
          (Reel 54, No. 322)
    1546 [Odyssey. Spanish]. *Amorosi Raggionamenti (see Flores, Juan de)*
          (Reel 54, No. 314)
    1553 Homer. *La Vlyxea de Homero*
          (Reel 77, No. 488)
    1556 Beuter, Pedro Antonio. *Cronica*
          (Reel 22, No. 111)
    1557 Guevara, Antonio de. *[Libro Aureo. Italian] Vita, gesti, costvmi*
          (Reel 71, No. 442)
    1558 Mexia, Pedro. *[Historia Imperial ... Italian] Le Vite di tvtti gl'imperadori (sic)*
          (Reel 106, No. 669)
    1563 Zarate, Agustin de. *[Historia Del Descubrimiento ... Italian] Le Historie*
          (Reel 202, No. 1299)

Girault, A. - Paris
    1538 Guevara, Antonio de. *[Libro Aureo. French] Liure Aore De Marc Aurele*
          (Reel 71, No. 435)

Ghemart, Adrian - Valladolid
    1570 Azpilcueta, Manuel de. *Addiciones (sic) del Manual de Confessores*
          (Reel 19, No. 88)

Giuliani, Giovanni Antonio - Venice
    1615 Guevara, Antonio de. *[Libro Aureo. Italian] Vita, gesti, costvmi*
          (Reel 72, No. 445)

Giunta, Bernardo - Venice
    1581 Guevara, Antonio de. *[Aviso de Privados...Italian] Aviso de favoriti*
          (Reel 73, No. 461)

Giunta, Philip de and Varesio, Juan Baptista - Burgos
    1593 Cid (El) Campeador. *Cid Ruy Diez Campeador*
          (Reel 44, No. 234)

Giunta Press - Venice
    1620 Alamos de Barrientos, Baltasar. *[Opera. Italian] Opere*
          (Reel 5, No. 24)
    1625 Sanchez, Tomas. *Dispvtationvm De S. to Matrimonii (vols. 1-3)*
          (Reel 166, No. 1078)
    1652 Del Rio, Martin Antoine. *Disqvisitionvm*
          (Reel 155, No. 1021)

Godbid, W. - London
    1671 Palafox y Mendoza, Juan de. *[Historia de la Conquista...Eng.]*
              The History of The Conquest of China
              (Reel 130, No. 828)

Goin, Antonius - Antwerp
    1539 Vitus Amerbach. *Commentaria Viti Amerbachii in Ciceronis Tres Libros*
              (Reel 197, No. 1271)

Gomez, Alonso - Madrid
    1583 Rivadeneira, Pedro de. *Vida Del P. Ignacio De Loyola*
              (Reel 157, No. 1032)

Gomez, Alfonso (Widow of) - Madrid
    1586 Rivadeneira, Pedro de. *Vita Ignatii Loiolae*
              (Reel 157, No. 1030)

Gomez de Blas, Juan - Seville
    1660 Relacion. *Verdadera Del Viage*
              (Reel 152, No. 1002)
    1666 Breve. *Relacion Del Horroroso Incendio*
              (Reel 28, No. 135)

Gomez de Lorenzo, Jaime - Coimbra
    1613 Suarez, Francisco. *Defensio Fidei*
              (Reel 173, No. 1140)

Gonzalez, Juan - Madrid
    1624 Jauregui y Aguilar, Juan de. *Discvrso Poetico*
              (Reel 83, No. 529)
    1624 Jauregui y Aguilar, Juan de. *Orfeo*
              (Reel 83, No. 531)
    1625 Thomas Aquinas, Saint. *[Commentum...] Tratado Del Goviemo*
              (Reel 184, No. 1183)
    1627 Bocangel y Unzuleta, Gabriel. *Rimas y Prosas*
              (Reel 26, No. 123)
    1628 Sarmiento de Mendoza, Manuel. *Milicia Evangelica*
              (Reel 169, No. 1097)
    1629 Gongora y Argote, Luis de. *El Polifemo*
              (Reel 60, No. 361)
    1630 Vega Carpio, Lope Felix de. *Lavrel De Apolo*
              (Reel 190, No. 1226)
    1633 Spain. Laws, etc., 1633. *Prematica Sobre Las Cosas Tocantes a la Conseruacion*
              (Reel 173, No. 1135)

Gonzalez de Reyes, Antonio - Madrid
    1675 Escalona y Agüero, Gaspar de. *Gazophilativm Regivm*
              (Reel 48, No. 266)
    1678 Martinez de la Puente, Jose. *Epitome De La Cronica Del Rey Don Ivan*
              (Reel 104, No. 658)

Gonzalez de Reyes, Antonio - Madrid (cont'd)
    1682 Owen, John. *Agvdezas De Ivan Oven (pt. 2)*
            (Reel 128, No. 810)
    1687 Quevedo y Villegas, Francisco Gomez de. *Parte Primera De Las Obras*
            (Reel 150, No. 967)
    1694 Salazar y Torres, Agustin de. *Cythara De Apolo (vols. 1-2)*
            (Reel 163, No. 1070)

Gorbin, Aegidius - Paris
    1578 Lull, Ramon. *Ars Brevis*
            (Reel 94, No. 604)
    1578 Lull, Ramon. *Liber de Articuli Fidei*
            (Reel 94, No. 605)
    1578 Lull, Ramon. *[Ars Cabbalistica] or Opusculum .. de Auditu Cabbalistico*
            (Reel 94, No. 606)

Gracian, Juan - Alcala de Henares (Compluti)
    1573 Perez de Moya, Juan. *Tratado de Mathematicas*
            (Reel 142, No. 914)
    1576 Medina, Pedro de. *Libro De La Verdad*
            (Reel 104, No. 662)
    1580 Camoes, Luis de. *Los Lvsiadas*
            (Reel 31, No. 144)
    1582 Vitruvius Pollio, Marcus. *De Architectvra*
            (Reel 194, No. 1243)
    1583 Terentius, Publius afer. *Las Seys Comedias*
            (Reel 183, No. 1175)

Graells, Gabriel (also see Nogues, Rafael) - Barcelona
    1608 Sesse, Josepe de. *Inhibitionvm Et Magistratatvs Ivstiatiae*
            (Reel 170, No. 1107)

Grande, Andres - Seville
    1633 Perez de Montalban, Juan. *Svcessos, Y Prodigios De Amor.*
            (Reel 142, No. 905)
    1634 Quevedo y Villegas, Francisco Gomez de. *Ivgvetes De La Ninez*
            (Reel 148, No. 956)

Grapheus, Jean - Antwerp
    1539 Guevara, Antonio de. *Libro Avreo*
            (Reel 70, No. 429)

Gregori, Gregorio de - Venice
    1625 Rojas, Fernando de. *Celestina*
            (Reel 159, No. 1039)

Gregorio de Zabala, Martin - Pamplona
    1686 Navarre (Kingdom). *Fveros Del Reyno*
            (Reel 119, No. 751)

Gross, Henning - Leipzig
  1615 Guevara, Antonio de. *Horologium Principum*
       (Reel 73, No. 454)
  1619 Guevara, Antonio de. *Cortegiano*
       (Reel 73, No. 462)
  1619 Guevara, Antonio de. *Zwey Schöne Tractätlein*
       (Reel 74, No. 463)

Grüninger, Johann - Strassburg
  1492 Bible. Latin. 1492. *Vulgate*
       (Reel 136 & 137, No. 853)
  1509 Waldseemüller, Martin. *Cosmographie Introductio*
       (Reel 201, No. 1286)

Gryphius, Sebastian - Lyons
  1544 Agustin, Antonio. *Amendationum*
       (Reel 3, No. 13)

Guasp, Gabriel - Mallorca
  1635 Cases, Gabriel. *Interrogatori*
       (Reel 36, No. 185)

Guerra, Domenico & Giovanni Battista - Venice
  1572 Guevara, Antonio de. *[Libro Aureo.] Vita, Gesti, Costvmi*
       (Reel 72, No. 444)

Guzman, Bernardino de - Toledo
  1617 Lopez Madera, Gregorio. *Excellencias De Sa Ivan Baptista*
       (Reel 93, No. 598)

Guzman, Tomas - Toledo
  1599 Mariana, Juan de. *De Ponderibvs Et Mensuris*
       (Reel 101, No. 638)

Gymnicus I, Joannes - Cologne
  1536 Vives, Juan Luis. *De Disciplinis Libri XX*
       (Reel 195, No. 1256)
  1536 Aggripa von Nettesheim, Henrich Cornelius. *De Incertitudine & Vanitate Scientiarum*
       (Reel 195, No. 1257)
  1544 Vives, Juan Luis. *Lingvae Latinae Exercitatio*
       (Reel 197, No. 1269)
  1578 Vives, Juan Luis. *Ad Veram Sapientiam*
       (Reel 194, No. 1245)

Gymnicus II, Joannes - Cologne
  1598 Pereira, Benito. *De Magia*
       (Reel 139, No. 877)

Hagembach, Pedro - Toledo
1504 Aug. 28 Catholic Church. *Aurea Expositio*
(Reel 39, No. 200)

Hainrichs, Niclas - Augsburg
1617 Lazarillo de Tormes.
(Reel 88, No. 567)

Hales, Thomas - London
1697-1699 Rodriguez, Alonso. *[Exercicios de perfeccion ...]* *The Practice Of Christian Perfection (pts. 1-3)*
(Reel 158, No. 1036)

Hallervord, Johannis - Rostock
1638 Fabricius, Johann. *Specimen Arabicum*
(Reel 87, No. 560)

Haly, T. - London
1682 Quevedo y Villegas, Francisco Gomez. *[Suenos y Discursos. English] The Visions*
(Reel 151, No. 984)

Hamman, Johannes - Venice
1492, Oct. 31 Alfonso X, el Sabio. *Tabulae Astronomicae*
(Reel 10, No. 46)

Harison, John - London
1600 Valera, Cipriano de. *[Dos Tratados ...] Two Treatises*
(Reel 188, No. 1211)

Hasrey, John - Antwerp
1614 Andrete, Bernardo J. *Varias Antigvedades*

Haviland, John - London
1622 Oudin, Cesar de. *[Grammaire Espagnolle.] A Grammar Spanish and English*
(Reel 138, No. 875)
1623 *A trve Relation and Iovrnall*
(Reel 138, No. 873)
1623 *A continvation Of a former Relation*
(Reel 138, No. 875)

Henricpetri, Sebastian - Basle
1592 Nunez, Pedro. *Opera*
(Reel 123, No. 774)

Henricum, Nicolau - Munich
1599 Guevara, Antonio de. *Lustgarten vnd Weckvhr*
(Reel 73, No. 450)
1605 Cerda, Juan Luis de la. *Paedia Religiosorum*
(Reel 39, No. 203)

Herringman, Henry (Printed for) - London
    1667   Quevedo y Villegas, Francisco Gomez de. *[Suenos y Discursos]*
            The Visions
            (Reel 151, No. 980)
    1668   Quevedo y Villegas, Francisco Gomez de. *[Suenos y Discursos]*
            The Visions
            (Reel 151, No. 981)
    1670   Quevedo y Villegas, Francisco Gomez de. *The Life and Adventures*
            of Buscon
            (Reel 147, No. 955)
    1678   Quevedo y Villegas, Francisco Gomez de. *[Suenos y Discursos]*
            The Visions
            (Reel 151, No. 983)

Hervada, Beranardo - Madrid
    1666   Antonio da Natividade. *Silva*
            (Reel 119, No. 749)

Hillenius, Michael - Antwerp
    1529   Vives, Juan Luis. *De Concordia & discordia in humano genere (pts. 1-3)*
            (Reel 195, No. 1250)
    1531   Vives, Juan Luis. *De Disciplinis Libri XX (bks. 1-3)*
            (Reel 195, No. 1255)

Hodgkin, Thomas - London
    1687   Cervantes Saavedra, Miguel de. *The History Of ... Don Quixote*
            (Reel 40, No. 212)

Hodgkinsonne, Richard - London
    1652   Cervantes Saavedra, Miguel de. *The History Of ... Don Quixote*
            (Reel 40, No. 211)
    1655   Lazarillo de Tormes. *Lazarillo, Or The Excellent History (pts. 1-2)*
            (Reel 88, No. 566)
            (see Lazarillo de Tormes). *The Pursuit Of The History*
            (Reel 88, No. 566)

Honoratus, Sebastianus Bartholomaeus - Lyons
    1556   Salamanca, Alejo de. *De Republica Christi*
            (Reel 162, No. 1064)
    1570   Agustinus, Aurelius, Saint. *De Civitate Dei. Libri XXII*
            (Reel 18, No. 79)

Hoolm, Franciscus - Gouda
    1662   Vives, Juan Luis. *Colloquia Sive Exercitatio Latinae Linguae*
            (Reel 197, No. 1279)

Horst, Petrus - Cologne
    1579   Vives, Juan Luis. *De Conscribendis Epistolis*
            (Reel 195, No. 1254)

Hospital Real - Zaragoza
    1634 Leonardo y Argensola, Lupercio and Bartolome. *Rimas*
        (Reel 89, No. 578)
    1635 Quevedo y Villegas, Francisco Gomez de. *Carta Al Serenissimo*
        (Reel 41, No. 218)
    [1636?] Saragossa -- Laws, etc. *Recopilacion De Los Estatvtos*
        (Reel 202, No. 1297)
    1638 Andres de Uztarroz, Juan Francisco. *Defensa*
        (Reel 14, No. 55)
    1648 Ormaza, Joseph. *Sermon En La Assvmpcion*
        (Reel 126, No. 794)
    1648 Ledesma, Gonzalo Perez. *Censvra De La Eloqvencia*
        (Reel 126, NO. 795)

Hubert, Antone - Bruxelles
    1624-1625 Oudin, Cesar de. *Tesoro De Las Dos Lengvas (2 pts.)*
        (Reel 126, No. 800)

Huete, Pedro - Valencia
    1569 Palmireno, Juan Lorenzo. *Vocabvlario Del Hvmanista (pts. 1-2)*
        (Reel 135, No. 849)
    1572 Palmireno, Juan Lorenzo. *Phrases Ciceronis*
        (Reel 135, No. 850)

Huete, Pedro (Widow of) - Valencia
    1584 Gomez Miedes, Bernardino. *La Historia*
        (Reel 59, No. 352)

Hupfuff, Mathias - Strassburg
    1507 Escobar, Andres de. *Modus Confitendi*
        (Reel 48, No. 271)

Hurus, Paul, and Blanco, Juan - Zaragoza
    1482 Torquemada, Juan de. *Expositio Psalterii*
        (Reel 185, No. 1188)

Husner, Georg - Strassburg
    [1485] Torquemada, Juan de. *Quaestiones Cuangeliorum Tam de Tempore*
        (Reel 185, No. 1191)

Iacobi, Lorenzo - Amsterdam
    1602 Bible. Spanish. 1602. *Valera*
        (Reel 24, No. 113)

Imberti, Domenico - Venice
    1605 Castaniza, Juan de. *Historia*
        (Reel 37, No. 187)

Imberti, Ghirardo - Venice
    1626   Mexia, Pedro. *Selva rinovata di varia lettione (pts. 1-5)*
            (Reels 109 & 110, No. 682)

Imprenta del Reyno - Madrid
    1629   Seneca, Lucius Annaeus. *[De Benefici. Spanish] Los Libros de beneficijs*
            (Reel 170, No. 1104)
    1630   Pellicer de Ossau y Tovar, Jose. *El Fenix Y Sv Historia*
            (Reel 138, No. 862)
    1630   Pellicer de Ossau y Tovar, Jose. *Lecciones Solemnes*
            (Reel 138, No. 867)
    1632   Diaz del Castillo, Bernal. *Historia*
            (Reel 47, No. 256)
    1633   Gongora y Argote, Luis de. *Todas Las Obras*
            (Reel 60, No. 358)
    1634   Gongora y Argote, Luis de. *Todas Las Obras*
            (Reel 60, No. 359)
    1634   Vega Carpio, Lope Felix de. *Rimas Hvmanas Y Divinas*
            (Reel 190, No. 1230)
    1636   Perez de Montalban, Juan. *Fama Posthuma*
            (Reel 141, No. 903)
    1636   Salazar Mardones, Cristobal. *Ilvstracion Y Defensa De La Fabvla*
            (Reel 163, No. 1068)
    1638   Lanuza, Miguel Batista. *Vida De La Bendita Madre Isabel*
            (Reel 87, No. 558)
    1638   Vega Carpio, Lope Felix de. *S. Isidro. Poema Castellano*
            (Reel 190, No. 1224)
    1639   Grande de Tena, Pedro. *Lagrimas Panegircas*
            (Reel 68, No. 409)
    1639   Nieremberg, Juan E. *Elogio Evangelico*
            (Reel 68, No. 410)
    1641   Laynez, Joseph. *Libro Nvevo El Privado Christiano*
            (Reel 87, No. 555)
    1657   Carrillo, Alonso. *Origen De La Dignidad*
            (Reel 33, No. 158)
    1657   Salazar de Mendoza, Pedro. *Historia De Los Svccessos*
            (Reel 33, No. 159)
    1678   Perez de Valdivia, Diego. *Aviso De Gente*
            (Reel 143, No. 916)

Imprenta Real - Madrid
    1604   Lipsius, Justus. *Las Politicas O Doctrina Ciuil*
            (Reel 90, No. 582)
    1610   Perez de Lara, Alfonso. *Compendio De Las Tres Gracias*
            (Reel 141, No. 901)
    1612   Herrera y Tordesillas, Anatonio de. *Tratado, Relacion Y Discvrso*
            (Reel 77, No. 486)
    1613   Mantuano, Pedro. *Advertencias*
            (Reel 99, No. 632)
    1624   Herrera y Sotomayor, Jacinto de. *Iornada que su Magestad*
            (Reel 77, No. 484)
    1626   Fernandez Navarrete, Pedro. *Conservacion De Monarqvias*
            (Reel 53, No. 306)

Imprenta Real - Madrid (cont'd)

1635 Nieremberg, Juan Eusebio. *Vida Divina*
(*Reel 122, No. 770*)

1636 Gongora y Argote, L. de. *Soledades (vols. 1-2)*
(*Reel 59, No. 355*)

1637 Moles, Fadrique. *Amistades De Principes*
(*Reel 112, No. 702*)

1652 Palafox y Mendoza, Juan de. *Varon de Deseos*
(*Reel 133, No. 836*)

1653 Perea, Jerome de. *Vida, Y Elogio De Dona Catalina*
(*Reel 139, No. 876*)

1654 Gongora y Argote, Luis de. *Todas Las Obras*
(*Reel 60, No. 360*)

1654 Manero, Pedro. *Vida De La Serenissima*
(*Reel 98, No. 628*)

1654 Vega Carpio, Lope Felix de. *La Dorotea*
(*Reel 189, No. 1220*)

[n.d.] Valerius Maximus. *Exemplos, Y Virtvdes*
(*Reel 188, No. 1213*)

1656 Castillo, Antonio del. *El Devoto Peregrino*
(*Reel 37, No. 191*)

1657 Carrillo, Alonso. *Origen de la Dignidad de Grande de Castilla*
(*Reel 33, No. 158*)

1662 Noydens, Benito Remigio. *Visita General Y Espiritval*
(*Reel 123, No. 773*)

1666 Quevedo y Villegas, Francisco Gomez de. *Politica De Dios*
(*Reel 150, No. 974*)

1670 Salon, Miguel Bartomoie. *Vida Y Milagros Del Ilvstrissimo...*
(*Reel 163, No. 1072*)

1672 Luis de Granada. *Simbolo De La Fe*
(*Reel 66, No. 399*)

1674 Gonzalez Vaquero, Miguel. *La Mvger Fverte*
(*Reel 61, No. 368*)

1674 Vega Carpio, Lope Felix de. *Rimas Hvmanas Y Divinas*
(*Reel 190, No. 1231*)

Iniguez, Juan (de Lequerica) - Alcala de Henares (Compluti)

1574 Ocampo, Florian de. *La Coronica General*
(*Reel 124, No. 786*)

1575 Ocampo, Florian de. *Las Antigvedades (vol. 1)*
(*Reel 125, No. 1787*)

1577 Ocampo, Florian de. *Los Otros Dos Libros De La Coronica General (vol. 2)*
(*Reel 125, No. 787*)

1578 Ocampo, Florian de. *Los Cinco Libros Primeros De la Coronica*
(*Reel 125, No. 789*)

1582 Huelga Cipriano de la. *Commentaria In Librvm Beati Iob*
(*Reel 80, No. 506*)

1589 Guzman, Juan de. *Rhetorica*
(*Reel 75, No. 480*)

1593 Medina, Bartolome de. *Breve Instruccion*
(*Reel 104, NO. 660*)

Iniguez, Juan (Heirs of) - Madrid
  1600   Pacheco y Navaes, Luis.   *Libro De Las Grandezas*
          (Reel 128, No. 811)

Islip, Adam - London
  1594   Huarte de San Juan, Juan.   *The Examination of Mens Wits*
          (Reel 79, No. 500)
  1596   Huarte de San Juan, Juan.   *The Examination of Mens Wits*
          (Reel 79, No. 501)
  1604   Huarte de San Juan, Juan.   *The Examination of Mens Wits*
          (Reel 79, No. 502)
  1616   Huarte de San Juan, Juan.   *The Examination of Mens Wits*
          (Reel 79, No. 503)
  1629   Fonseca, Cristobal de.   *Devovt Contemplations*
          (Reel 54, No. 327)

Ivntarum, (Officina) - Lyons
  1593   Ribera, Francisco de.   *In Sacram Beati ... Apocalypsin*
          (Reel 152, No. 1004)
  1593   Ribera, Francisco de.   *De Templo, & de iis quae ad Templum*
          (Reel 152, No. 1005)

Janson, Jonsson, Joannes - Amsterdam
  1623   Agustin Antonio.   *Opera Omnia*
          (Reel 4, No. 21)
  1651   Saavedra Fajardo, Diego de.   *Idea Principis Christiano-Politici*
          (Reel 161, No. 1055)
  1659   Saavedra Fajardo, Diego de.   *Idea Principis Christiano-Politici*
          (Reel 162, NO. 1056)

Jansz, Broer - Amsterdam
  1624   Acosta, Jose de.   *Historie Naturael*
          (Reel 2, No. 12)

Johnson, Thomas (for Fran. Kirkman) - London
  1671   Fernandez, Jeronimo.   *The Honour of Chivalry*
          (Reel 53, No. 299)

Junta, Felipe de - Borgos
  1588   Lucanus, Marcus Annaeus.   *Lvcano Tradvzido De Verso*
          (Reel 94, No. 602)

Junta, Felipe de, and Varesio, Juan B. - Burgos
  1596   Torres, Juan de.   *Philosophia Moral*
          (Reel 186, No. 1198)

Junta, Juan de - Burgos
  1527   Spain. Laws, etc. *Leyes del Estilo*
          (Reel 172, No. 1125)

Junta, Lucas - Salamanca
  1582 Leon, Luis Ponce de. *In Cantica Canticorum (vols. 1-2)*
        (Reel 89, No. 574)

Junta, Tomas de - Madrid
  1594 Spain. Laws, etc. *Prematica Para que los Dispuesto por las Leyes ...*
        (Reel 172, No. 1129)
  1622 Lavanha, Joao Baptista. *Viage De La Catholica Real Magestad*
        (Reel 87, No. 561)

Juvenis, Martinus - Paris
  1569 Moses ben Maimon. *Symbolvm Fidei Ivdaeorvm*
        (Reel 115, No. 727)

Kauffman,, Paulus - Nuremberg
  1582 Vives, Juan L. *Exercitatio Latinae Linguae*
        (Reel 197, No. 1276)

Kempffern, Matthaeo - Frankfurt
  1644 Guevara, Antonio de. *Opera Politica Et Historica*
        (Reels 74 & 75, No. 472)

Kinchius, Joannes - Cologne
  1619 Puente, Luis de la. *Meditationes Praecipvis Fidei*
        (Reel 146, No. 943)

König, Jacob - Mainz
  1606 Del Rio, Martin Antonio. *Disquisitionum (vols. 1-3)*
        (Reel 154, No. 1019)

König, Ludwig - Basle
  1629 Moses ben Maimon. *Rabbi Mosis ... Liber*
        (Reel 116, NO. 733)

Kromayer, Gottfried A. - Mainz
  1687 Gracian y Morales, B. *L'Homme de Cour*
        (Reel 62, No. 380)

Kyngston, John - London
  1571 Mexia, Pedro. *The Forest*
        (Reel 110, No. 683)

La Barrera, Alonso de - Seville
  1580 Garcilaso de la Vega. *Obras*
        (Reel 56, No. 344)

Labayen, Carlos de - Pamplona
  1631 Quevedo y Villegas, F. G. de. *Politica De Dios*
        (Reel 150, No. 972)
  1631 Quevedo y Villegas, F. G. de. *Historia De La Vida Del Byscon*
        (Reel 150, No. 972)
  1631 Quevedo y Villegas, F. G. de. *Svenos, Y Discvrsos*
        (Reel 150, No. 972)
  1631 Quevedo y Villegas, F. G. de. *El Peor Scondriio*
        (Reel 150, No. 972)

Lacavalleria, Antonio de - Barcelona

    1648 Villamediana, Juan de Tarsis y Peralta, Conde de. *Obras*
         (*Reel 179, No. 1166*)

    1664 Gracian y Morales, B. *Tres Partes De El Criticon*
         (*Reel 62, No. 373*)

    1699 Horatius Flaccus, Q. *Obras*
         (*Reel 78, No. 491*)

Lacavalleria, Pedro de - Barcelona

    1629 Quevedo y Villegas, F. G. de. *Politica De Dios*
         (*Reel 148, No. 958*)

    1634 Nieremerg, Juan E. *Libro De La Vida*
         (*Reel 121, No. 765*)

    1635 Quevedo y Villegas, F. G. de. *Ivgvetes De La Ninez*
         (*Reel 148, No. 957*)

    1639 Pellicer de Ossau y Tovar, J. *El Seyano Germanico*
         (*Reel 138, No. 863*)

    1640 Perez de Montalban, J. *Svcessos y Prodigios De Amor*
         (*Reel 142, No. 910*)

    1640 Perez de Montalban, J. *Orfeo*
         (*Reel 142, No. 910*)

    1642 Lacavalleria, Pedro de. *Dictionario Castellano*
         (*Reel 86, No. 553*)

    1668 Noydens, Benito R. *Promptvario Moral*
         (*Reel 122, No. 772*)

Lanaja y Lamarca, Pedro - Zaragoza

    1619 Padilla y Manrique, Luisa M. de. *Lagrimas De La Nobleza*
         (*Reel 128, No. 813*)

    1650 Quevedo y Villegas, F. G. de. *La Fortvna Con Seso*
         (*Reel 147, No. 949*)

    1666 Sayas Rabanera y Ortubia F. de. *Anales De Aragon*
         (*Reel 169, No. 1098*)

Lanaja y Quartanet, Juan - Zaragoza

    1610 Zurita y Castro, J. *Los Cinco Libros Postreros (vol. II)*
         (*Reels 203 & 204, No. 1301*)

    1610 Zurita y Castro, J. *Los Cinco Libros Primeros (vol. III)*
         (*Reels 203 & 204, No. 1301*)

    1610 Zurita y Castro, J. *Los Cinco Libros Postreros (vols. IV and VI)*
         (*Reels 203 & 204, No. 1301*)

    1621 Leonardo de Argensola, L. *Declaracion Svmaria De La Historia de Aragon*
         (*Reel 152, No. 992*)

    1621 Rajas, Pablo Albiniano de. *Lagrimas De Caragoca*
         (*Reel 152, No. 992*)

    1622 Cespedes y Meneses, G. de. *Historia apologetica*
         (*Reel 41, No. 213*)

    1629 Tarsis, Juan de. *Obras*
         (*Reel 178, No. 1161*)

    1630 Leonardo de Argensola, B. *Los Anales De Aragon*
         (*Reel 89, No. 576*)

    1634 Villamediana, Juan e Tarsis y Peralta, Conde de. *Obras*
         (*Reel 178, No. 1162*)

L'Angelier, Arnoul, Arnold - Paris
 1547 Flores, Juan. *L'Historia di Aurelio*
 (*Reel 54, No. 323*)

Larumbe, Juan de - Zaragoza
 1623 Cespedes y Meneses, G. de. *Historias peregrinas*
 (*Reel 41, No. 214*)
 1640 Boccalini. T. *Discvrsos politicos*
 (*Reel 26, No. 124*)

Lasius, Balthasar, & Platter, Thomas - Basle
 1536 Vives, Juan L. *De Conscribendis Epistolis*
 (*Reel 195, No. 1252*)

Lasso, Cristobal, & Garcia, Francisco - Medina del Campo
 1603 Huarte de San Juan, Juan. *Examen De Ingenios*
 (*Reel 79, No. 496*)

Lasso, Pedro - Salamanca
 1578 Guevara, Antonio de. *Epistolas Familiares (pt. II)*
 (*Reel 69, No. 421*)
 1581 Castiglione, B. *El Cortesano*
 (*Reel 37, No. 189*)

Latorre, Diego - Zaragoza
 1623 Felices de Caceres, J. B. *El Cavallero De Avila*
 (*Reel 52, No. 292*)

Leake, William - London
 1653 Lazarillo de Tormes. *Lazarillo, Or the Excellent History (pts. 1-2)*
 (*Reel 88, No. 565*)

Le Gras, Jacques - Paris
 1664 Quevedo y Villegas, F. G. de. *Les Oevvres*
 (*Reel 74, No. 466*)

Leon, Juan de - Seville
 1590 Acosta, Jose. *Historia natural*
 (*Reel 1, No. 5*)

Lichfield, Leonard - Oxford
 1638 Valdes, Juan de. *The Hundred And Ten Considerations*
 (*Reel 187, No. 1208*)

Lippius, Balthasar - Mainz
 1605 Mariana, Juan de. *De Rege Et Regis*
 (*Reel 101, No. 639*)
 1605 Mariana, Juan de. *De Ponderibvs Et Mensvris*
 (*Reel 101, No. 639*)
 1605 Mariana, Juan de. *Hispani E. Societate Iesu Historiae*
 (*Reel 102, No. 644*)

Llanos y Guzman, Mateo de - Madrid
    1668 Salazar y Castro, L. de. *Advertencias Historicas*
        (*Reel 163, No. 1069*)

Llopis, Jose - Barcelona
    1691 Solis y Rivadeneyra, A. *Historia De La Nveva Espana*
        (*Reel 171, No. 1114*)
    1693 Juana Ines de la Cruz *Segundo tomo de las obras*
        (*Reel 46, No. 249*)

Locarni, Pietro M. - Milan
    1608 Cervantes Saavedra, M. de. *Relatione*
        (*Reel 40, No. 208*)

Loe, Jean - Antwerp
    1561 Vives, Juan L. *Lingvae Latinae. Exercitatio*
        (*Reel 197, No. 1273*)

Longhi, Giuseppe - Bologna
    1674 Linda, Lucas de. *Le Relationi Et Descrittioni*
        (*Reel 90, No. 581*)

Longo, Egidio - Naples
    1644 Suarez de Figueroa, C. *Espana Defendida*
        (*Reel 176, No. 1149*)

Lope, Lopez de Haro, David - Lyon
    1644 Vives, Juan L. *Ad Sapientiam Introductio*
        (*Reel 194, No. 1248*)
    1653 Weidner, Johan L. *Hispanicae Dominationis*
        (*Reel 201, No. 1288*)

Lopez Hidalgo, Antonio - Almeria
    1699 Pasqual y Orbaneja, G. *Vida De San Indalecio*
        (*Reel 136, No. 852*)
    1699 Pasqual y Orbaneja, G. *Almeria Ilustrada*
        (*Reel 136, No. 852*)
    1699 Pasqual y Orbaneja, G. *Ilustracion de Almeria*
        (*Reel 136, No. 852*)

Lorenzini, Francesco (da Turino) - Venice
    1560 Amadis de Gaula. *Splandiano, E Le Sve Prodezze*
        (*Reel 13, No. 51*)
    1563 Flores, Juan de *Lettere Amorose*
        (*Reel 54, No. 313*)

Loriente, Tomas - Barcelona
    1696 Ferrer de Valdecebro, A. *Goviemo General*
        (*Reel 53, No. 310*)
    1699 Constituciones *Reglas*
        (*Reel 45, No. 237*)

Lorme, Louis de - Amsterdam
    1698 Casas, Bartolome de las. *Relations des Voyages*
        (*Reel 35, No. 174*)

Lownes, Mathew - London
1604 Mexia, Pedro. *The Historie of all the Romane emperors*
(*Reel 107, No. 672*)
1611 Soto, Hernando de. *The Worthye And Famovs History*
(*Reel 172, No. 1120*)
1623 Mexia, Pedro. *The Imperiall historie*
(*Reel 107, No. 673*)

L'Oyselet, George - Rouen
1584 Luis de Granada. *Of Prayer, and Meditation*
(*Reel 67, No. 402*)
1599 Luis de Granada. *A Memoriall of a Christian Life*
(*Reel 64, No. 389*)

Lucius, Jacob - Helmstadt
1630 Vives, Juan L. *Introdvctio ad veram Sapientiam*
(*Reel 194, No. 1247*)

Luna, Miguel de - Zaragoza
1659 Saragossa. Laws, statutes, etc. *Ordinaciones*
(*Reel 202, No. 1295*)

Lyra, Manuel de - Lisboa
1584 Estella, Diego de. *Tercera Parte Del Libro De La Vanidad*
(*Reel 49, No. 279*)

Lyra Varreto, Francisco de - Seville
1618 Jauregui y Aguilar, Juan. de. *Rimas*
(*Reel 83, No. 532*)
1624 Serna, Alonso de la. *Sermon*
(*Reel 170, No. 1106*)
1639 Ona, Pedro de. *El Ignacio De Cantabria*
(*Reel 126, No. 792*)
1650 Palafox y Mendoza, J. de. *Carta Segunda De Tres*
(*Reel 129, No. 820*)

Mace, Benito - Valencia
1671 Pellicer de Ossau y Tovar, J. *Maximo Obispo De La Santa Iglesia*
(*Reel 138, No. 868*)
1672 Pellicer de Ossau y Tovar, J. *Poblacion, y lengva*
(*Reel 138, No. 870*)
1673 Pellicer de Ossau y Tovar, J. *Aparato A la Monarchia*
(*Reel 137, No. 859*)
1675 Pellicer de Ossau y Tovar, J. *Maximo Obispo De La Santa Iglesia (pt. 2)*
(*Reel 138, No. 868*)

Mace, Claudio - Valencia
1646 Nieremberg, Juan E. *El Pastor De Noche*
(*Reel 120, No. 762*)

Madrigal, Pedro (Heirs of) - Madrid

1588 Sabucco y Alvarez, M. *Nveva Filosofia De La Natvraleza*
(Reel 162, No. 1059)

1589 Cicero, Marcus T. *Las Epistolas*
(Reel 44, No. 232)

1590 Spain. Laws, statutes, etc. *Prematica En que se prohibe el arredarse*
(Reel 172, No. 1128)

1592 Mendoza, Bernardino de. *Comentarios*
(Reel 111, No. 695)

1593 Spain. Laws, statutes, etc. *Prematica En que se da nueua orden*
(Reel 172, No. 1130)

1594 Spain. Laws, statutes, etc. *Prematicas que han salido este ano*
(Reel 172, No. 1130)

1594 Spain. Laws, statutes, etc. *Prematica En que se manda guardar*
(Reel 172, No. 1130)

1594 Spain. Laws, statutues, etc. *Prematica En que se prohibe hazer y yender bufetes*
(Reel 172, No. 1130)

1594 Spain. Laws, statutues, etc. *Prematica En Qve Se Manda Gvardar La de Los vestidos*
(Reel 172, No. 1130)

1594 Spain. Laws, statutues, etc. *Prematica en que se pone el precio*
(Reel 172, No. 1130)

1594 Spain. Laws, statutes, etc. *Prematica En Qve Se Manda Gvardar Las hechas*
(Reel 172, No. 1130)

1600 Gutierrez de Los Rios, G. *Noticia general*
(Reel 75, No. 479)

1602 Vega Carpio, L. F. de. *Isidro. Poema Castellano*
(Reel 190, No. 1223)

1603 Plinius Secundus, C. *Historia Natvral*
(Reel 144, No. 932)

1635 Declaracion de Sv Alteza
(Reel 41, No. 220)

1635 Respuesta de Vn Vasallo
(Reel 41, No. 223)

Maietti, Roberto - Venice

1598 Azpilcueta, M. de. *Compendivm omnivm opervm*
(Reel 20, No. 91)

Maire, Jean - Lyon

1619 Teixeira, Jose. *Stemmata Franciae*
(Reel 182, No. 1171)

1636 Vives, Juan L. *De Disciplinis Libri XII*
(Reel 196, No. 1259)

Malatesta, Giovan Battista - Milan
      1638 Relacion Verdadera, y Puntual
            (Reel 152, No. 996)

Malatesta, Marc'Antonio Pandolfo - Milan
      1630 Felipe IV. *Ordini Reali*
            (Reel 52, No. 295)
      1679 Felipe IV. *Lettere Diverse*
            (Reel 52, No. 295)
      1680 Felipe IV. *Lettere Diverse*
            (Reel 52, No. 295)
      1692 Felipe IV. *Lettere Diverse*
            (Reel 52, No. 295)

Malo, Pablo - Barcelona
      1592 Camos, Marco A. de. *Microcosmia*
            (Reel 32, No. 147)

Malo, Pedro - Barcelona
      1575 Palmireno, Juan L. *Vocabvlario Del Hymanista*
            (Reel 135, No. 851)
      1588 Perez de Valdiviva, D. *Docvmentos Salvdables*
            (Reel 143, No. 917)
      1588 Perez de Valdivia, D. *Docvmentos Particvlares*
            (Reel 143, No. 917)

Manescal, Luis - Lerida
      1619 Santoro, Juan B. *Prado Espiritval*
            (Reel 169, No. 1093)
      1621 Nunez de Guzman, F. *Refranes*
            (Reel 124, No. 783)
      1621 Nunez de Guzman, F. *La Filosofia Vulgar*
            (Reel 124, No. 783)

Manger, Michael - Augsburg
      1601 Nunez, Pedro J. *Phrynici Epitomae Dictionvm*
            (Reel 123, No. 777)

Manuzio, Aldo (Sons of) - Venice
      1545 Abrabanel, Leon. *Dialoghi di amore*
            (Reel 1, No. 1)
      1546 Guevara, Antonio de. *Vita, gesti, costvmi*
            (Reel 71, No. 438)
      1549 Abrabanel, Leon. *Dialoghi di amore*
            (Reel 1, No. 2)
      1552 Abrabanel, Leon. *Dialoghi di amore*
            (Reel 1, No. 3)

Manuzio, Aldo (the younger) - Venice
      1570 Nunez, Pedro J. *Ciceronis Collecta*
            (Reel 123, No. 776)
      1586 Huarte de San Juan, Juan. *Essame De Gl 'Lngegni*
            (Reel 79, No. 498)
      1590 Huarte de San Juan, Juan. *Essame De Gl 'Ingegni*
            (No. 499 not available)

Manuzio, Paolo (Aldine Press) - Rome
    1563 Diaz de Vargas F. *Francisci Vargas*
          (Reel 47, No. 259)

Marca, Luis la - Valencia
    (n.d.) Rojas Zorilla, F. de. *La gran comedia de los aspides*
          (Reel 33, No. 151)

Marchand, Guy - Paris
    1494 Isidorus, Saint. *Synonyma De Homine Et Ratione*
          (Reel 82, No. 524)
    1498 Sacro Bosco, Joannes de. *Sphaera mundi*
          (Reel 162, No. 1060)

Marchetti, Pietro M. - Brescia
    1582 Soto, Domingo de. *Relectio F. De Ratione Tegendi, Et Detegendi*
          (Reel 172, No.1119)

Marcial, Juan B. - Valencia
    1626 Gomez, V. *Goviermo De Principes*
          (Reel 58, No. 351)
    1628 Quevedo y Villegas, F. G. de. *Svenos, Y Discvrsos*
          (Reel 151, No. 976)

Mareschall, Joannes - Lyon
    1586 Index Librorum Prohibitorum. *Index Expvrgatorivs*
          (Reel 80, No. 511)

Margarit, Jeronimo - Barcelona
    1612 Guevara, Antonio de. *Aviso de privados*
          (Reel 73, No. 458)
    1618 Ferrer, P. Juan Gaspar. *Tratado De Las Comedias*
          (Reel 53, No. 307)
    1618 Suarez de Figueroa, C. *El Passagero*
          (Reel 176, No. 1150)

Marshe, Thomas - London
    1557 Guevara, Antonio de. *The golden Boke*
          (Reel 71, No. 433)

Martellinus, Sebastian - Macerata
    1576 Polanco, Juan A. *Breve Directorivm Ad Confessarii*
          (Reel 145, No. 936)

Martin, Ildefonso (Widow of) - Madrid
    1619 Bravo, Bartolome. *Thexavrvs verborvm*
          (Reel 28, No. 134)

Martin, Lucas - Sevilla
    1691 Palafox y mendoza, J. de. *Vida interior*
          (Reel 133, No. 840)

Martin de Balboa, Alonso - Madrid

    1607 Manzanares, Jeronimo P. de. *Estilo y Formvlario*
           (Reel 99, No. 575)

    1609 Leonardo de Argensola, B. *Conqvista de las Islas Malvcas*
           (Reel 89, No 575)

    1610-17 Castella Ferrer y Luzon, M. *Historia del apostol*
             (Reel 37, No. 188)

    1612 Zaragoza de Heredia, Miguel A. *Escvela De La Perfeta y Verdadera Sabidvria*
           (Reel 202, No. 1298)

    1613 Perez Del Barrio Angulo, G. *Direccion De Secretarios*
           (Reel 143, No. 919)

Martin de Balboa, Alonso (Window of) - Madrid

    1614 Tacitus Publius, C. *Las Obras*
           (Reel 177, No. 1154)

    1614 Vega Carpio, L.F. de. *Rimas Sacras*
           (Reel 191, No. 1232)

    1618 Vega Carpio, L.F. de. *Trivnfo De La Fee, En Los Reynos Del Iapon*
           (Reel 191, No. 1233)

    1619 Lopez de Zarate, F. *Varias Poesias*
           (Reel 93, No. 595)

    1620 Vega Carpio, L.F. de. *Ivsta Poetica*
           (Reel 190, No. 1225)

    1621 Caesar Caius, J. *Los comentarios*
           (Reel 29, No. 139)

    1621 Vega Carpio, L.F. de. *Rimas De Lope De Vega*
           (Reel 190, No. 1229)

    1622 Lopez de Andrade, D. *Tratados*
           (Reel 91, No. 585)

    1624 Vega Carpio, L.F. de. *La Circe*
           (Reel 189, No. 1217)

    1628 Diaz Rengifo, J. *Arte Poetica*
           (Reel 47, No. 258)

    1629 Nieremberg, Juan E. *Obras y Dias*
           (Reel 122, No. 767)

Martin de Hermosilla, Lucas - Seville

    1686 Braones, Alonso M. de. *Epitome*
           (Reel 28, No. 133)

    1686 Nieremberg, Juan E. *Obras Christianas (vols. I-II)*
           (Reels 121 & 122, No. 766)

    1686 Nieremberg, Juan E. *Obras Filosoficas*
           (Reels 121 & 122, No. 766)

Martinez, Francisco - Madrid

    1628 Faria E Sousa, M. de. *Epitome De Las Historias*
           (Reel 51, No. 289)

    1630 Gonzalez Davila, Gil. *Compendio Historico*
           (Reel 60, No. 362)

1632 Quevedo y hoyos, A. de. *Libro De Indicios*
(*Reel 147, No. 946*)
1633 Gonzalez de Salas, J. *Nueva Idea De La Tragedia*
(*Reel 61, No. 367*)
1635 Respuesta Al Manifiesto
(*Reel 41, No. 219*)
1636 Garcia de Zurita, A. *Discvrso De Las Missas*
(*Reel 56, No. 343*)
1638 Gonzalez Davila, Gil. *Historia de la vida y hechos*
(*Reel 60, No. 363*)
1642 Basta, Giorgio. *Govierno della cavalleria*
(*Reel 21, No. 103*)
1634 Benavente y benavides, C. *Advertencias*
(*Reel 21, No. 105*)
1643 Bentivoglio, Guido. *Gverra de Flandes*
(*Reel 22, No. 107*)

Martinez, Sebastian - Valladolid
1546 Guevara, Antonio de. *Mōte caluario*
(*Reel 75, No. 476*)
1550 Guevara, Antonio de. *Oratorio de religiosos*
(*Reel 75, No. 475*)
1555 March Mosen, A. *Las Obras*
(*Reel 99, No. 634*)
1568 Pedraza, Juan de. *Svmma de casos de Conciencia*
(*Reel 137, No. 854*)

Martinez de Amileta, A. - Vergara?
1632 Martinez de Amileta, Andres. *Discvrsos Politicos*
(*Reel 104, No. 656*)

Mascardo, Giacomo - Rome
1612 Fonseca, Damian. *Ivsta Expvlsion*
(*Reel 55, No. 329*)
1616 Chacon, Alfonso. *Historia*
(*Reel 41, No. 224*)

Matevat, Jaime - Barcelona
1641 Memorial Qve Se Presento Al Rey Catolico
(*Reel 111, No. 691*)

Methevad, Sebastian - Barcelona
1611 Manescal, Onofre. *Apologetica Dispvta*
(*Reel 99, No. 629*)
1611 Manescal, Onofre. *Tres Tratados*
(*Reel 99, No. 630*)
1615 Murillo, Diego. *Evndacion Milagrosa*
(*Reel 118, No. 745*)

Mathevad, Sebastian (Heirs of) - Barcelona
1685 Marcillo, Manuel. *Crisi De Catalvna*
(*Reel 100, No. 636*)

Maurry, Laurence _ Rouen
    1626   Enriquez, Gomez, A.   *Sanson Nazareno*
          (Reel 48, No. 263)

Mayer, Sebald - Diligen
    1564   Soto, Pedro de.   *Compendivm Doctrinae Catholicae*
          (Reel 172, No. 1122)
    1567   Torres, Jeronimo.   *Confessio Avgvstiniana*
          (Reel 186, No. 1197)
    1572   Perpina, Pedro J.   *Orationes Ovinqve*
          (Reel 144, No. 922)

Mearne, S. - London
    1670   Barba, Alvaro A.   *Art of Mettals*
          (Reel 21, No. 98)

Meerbeque, Jean de - Bruxelles
    1625   Carnero, Antonio.   *Historia*
          (Reel 33, No. 157)
    1625   Davila Padilla, A.   *Historia*
          (Reel 46, No. 251)

Meietus, Paulus - Padua
    1592   Mercado, Luis de.   *De Pvlsibvs*
          (Reel 111, No. 696)

Melchor, Alegre - Madrid
    1667   Palafox y Mendoza, J. de.   *Obras (vol. VI)*
          (Reel 132, No. 832, Vo. 6)

Melvil, David - Aberdeen
    1623   Vives, Juan L.   *Ad Sapientiam introductio*
          (Reel 194, No. 1246)

Mena, Hugo de - Granada
    1568   Giovio, Paolo.   *Elogios O Vidas*
          (Reel 58, No. 349)

Mena, Sebastian de - Granada
    1599   Horatius Flaccus, Q.   *Obras*
          (Reel 78, No. 490)
    1601   Lopez Madera, G.   *Discvrsos De La Certidvmbre*
          (Reel 93, No. 598)
    1596   Maldonado, Juan de.   *Theologi Commentarii (vol. I)*
          (Reel 96, No. 622)
    1597   Maldonado, Juan de.   *Theologi Commentariorvm (vol. II)*
          (Reel 96, No. 622)

Mestre, Francisco - Valencia
    1692   Jose De Jesus.   *Cielos De Fiesta*
          (Reel 85, No. 544)

Meursius, Jean - Antwerp
  1642 Teresa, Saint. *The Flaming Hart*
        (Reel 184, No. 1181)
  1643 Commines, Phillippe de. *Las Memorias*
        (Reel 45, No. 236)
  1643 Commines, Phillippe de. *Las Memorias Tomo Segvndo*
        (Reel 45, No. 236)
  1643 Rivadeneira, Pedro. *Bibliotheca Scriptorvm*
        (Reel 156, No. 1026)
  1659 Antonio, Nicolas. *De Exilio*
        (Reel 14, No. 59)

Mey, Felipe - Valencia
  1617 Madariaga, Juan de. *Del Senado*
        (Reel 95, No. 619)
  1618 Bleda, Jaime. *Coronica de los moros*
        (Reel 26, No. 122)

Mey, Juan (Widow of) - Valencia
  1556 Nunez, Pedro J. *Apposita. M.T. Ciceronis, Collecta*
        (Reel 123, No. 775)
  1566 Zapata, Luis de. *Carlo Famoso*
        (Reel 202, No. 1294)

Mey, Pedro P. - Valencia
  1604-9 Escriva, P. F. *Discvrsos*
          (Reel 49, No. 275)
  1621   Aristotle. *Historia general*
          (Reel 17, No. 78)

Michael, Claude - Tournon
  1597 Fonseca, Pedro de. *Institvtionvm Dialecticarvm*
        (Reel 55, No. 333)

Michel, Estienne - Lyon
  1578? Amadis de Gaula. *Le Dixseptieme Livre*
         (Reel 12, No. 50)

Millanges, Guillaume - Bordeaux
  1628 Ovidius Naso, P. *Heroyda Ovidiana*
        (Reel 127, No. 807)

Millis, Guillermo do - Medina del Campo
  1553 Ocampo, Florian de. *Hispanic Vincit*
        (Reel 125, No. 788)
  1555 Petrarca, Francesco. *Los Trivmphos*
        (Reel 144, No. 928)

Miloco, Benedetto - Venice
  1682 Mendo, Andres. *Epitome Opinionvm*
        (Reel 111, No. 693)

Miloco, Pietro - Venice
  1662 Casas Cristobal de las. *Vocabulario*
        (Reel 36, No. 182)

Molo, Roberto (Heirs of) - Naples
    1657 Carrillo Laso de la Vega, A. *Sagrada Eratos, y Medtaciones*
           (Reel 34, No. 164)

Mommart, Jean - Bruxelles
    1660 Oudin, Cesar de. *Tesoro De Las Dos Lenguas*
           (Reel 127, No. 801)

Mongaston, Juan de - Najera
    1617 Villegas, Esteban M. de. *Las Eroticas*
           (Reel 191, No. 1237)
    1620 Villegas, Esteban M. de. *Las Amatorias*
           (Reel 191, No. 1236)

Mon Gaston Fox, Pedro - Logrono
    1641 Pellicer de Ossau y Tovar, J. *Svcession De Los Reynos*
           (Reel 138, No. 871)

Morel, Federic - Paris
    1579 Mexia, Pedro *Discovrs des septs sages*
           (Reel 105, No. 665)

Moreto, Balthasas - Antwerp
    1649 Teresa, Saint. *Las Obras*
           (Reels 183 & 184, No. 1178)
    1661 Teresa, Saint. *Las Obras*
           (Reels 184, No. 1179)

Moretti, Nicolo - Venice
    1592 Fonseca, Pedro de. *Institvtionvm Dialecticarvm*
           (Reel 55, No. 332)

Morillon, Claude - Lyon
    1614 Suarez de Figueroa, C. *La Constante Amarilis*
           (Reel 176, No. 1148)

Newberrie, Ralph - London
    1577 Guevara, Antonio de. *The Familiar Epistles*
           (Reel 70, No. 426)
    1577 Guevara, Antonio de. *A Chronicle*
           (Reel 75, No. 478)
    1584 Guevara, Antonio de. *The Familiar Epistles*
           (Reel 70, No. 427)

Nicolini, Pietro (da Sabio) - Venice
    1535 Rojas, Fernando de. *Celestina*
           (Reel 159, No. 1040)
    1541 Rojas, Fernando, de. *Celestina*
           (Reel 159, No. 1041)

Nieto, Francisco (Widow of) - Madrid
    1673 Nunez de Castro, A. *Vida De San Fernando*
           (Reel 124, No. 781)

Nogues, Juan - Huesca
    1644 Andres de Uztarroz, J. F. *Monvmento*
          (Reel 14, No. 56)
    1646 Gracian y Morales, B. *El Politico*
          (Reel 62, No. 371)
    1650 Origen, y estado Del Colegio
          (Reel 126, No. 793)

Nogues, Rafael (A Costade) - Barcelona
    1609 Vega Carpio, Lope Felix de. *Iervsalen Conqvistada*
          (Reel 189, No. 1222)

Noort, Juan de - Madrid
    1643 Benavente y Benavides, C. *Advertencias*
          (Reel 21, No. 105)

Norton, William - London
    1577 Monardes Alfaro, Nicolas. *Ioyfvll Nevves*
          (Reel 113, No. 712)

Nutio, Phillippe - Antwerp
    1570 Valles, Pedro de. *Historia Del Fortissimo, y Prudentissimo*
          (Reel 188, No. 1215)
    1586 Justinus, Marcus Junianus. *De La Historia*
          (Reel 86, No. 549)
    1604 Guevara, Antonio de. *Libro Aureo*
          (Reel 70, No. 430)

Okes, Nicholas - London
    1619 Amadis de Gaula. (bks 1-4) *The Ancient*
          (Reel 13 & 14, No. 52)

Oporino, Jean - Basle
    1547 Mexia, Pedro. *Historia imperial*
          (Reel 105, No. 666)
    1548 Vives, Juan L. *Excitationes animi in Deum*
          (Reel 196, No. 1267)
    1560? Vives, Juan L. *Lingua Latinae exercitatio*
          (Reel 197, No. 1272)

Orry, Marc - Paris
    1598 Acosta, Jose de. *Histoire natvrelle*
          (Reel 2, No. 8)
    1609 Oudin, Cesar de. *Refranes O Proverbios*
          (Reel 126, No. 797)
    1610 Oudin, Cesar de. *Grammaire Espagnolle*
          (Reel 127, No. 802)

Ortega, Marcos de - Segovia
    1592 Horozco y Covarrubias, J. de. *Paradoxas Christianas*
          (Reel 78, No. 494)

Ortiz de Saravia, Maria - Toledo
    1625 Salazar de Mendoza, P. *Cronica de el Gran Cardenal*
          (Reel 163, No. 1065)

Ortiz de Valdes, Fernando - Madrid
    1648 Palafox y Mendoza, J. de. *Defensa Canonica*
          (Reel 130, No. 822)

Osmont, Carlos - Rouen
    1629 Quevedo y Villegas, F. G. de. *Historia De La Vida Del Buscon*
          (Reel 147, No. 955)
    1629 Quevedo y Villegas, F. G. de. *Svenos, y Discvrsos*
          (Reel 147, No. 953)

Otmar, Valentine - Augsburg
    1548 Soto, Predro de. *Institvtionis Christianae Libri Tres*
          (Reel 172, No. 1123)

Paganus, Theobald - Lyon
    1550 Vives, Juan L. *Excitationes (sic) animi in Praeparatio animi
          ad orandum*
          (Reel 196, No. 1268)

Paredes, Julian de - Madrid
    1626 Consejo Real de las Indias. Spain. *Ordenanzas*
          (Reel 172, No. 1124)
    1651 Relacion Del Temblor
          (Reel 152, No. 1001)
    1666 Gonzalez de Rosende, A. *Vida I Virtvdes Del Illmo I Exc.^{mo}
          Senor D. Ivan De Palafox*
          (Reel 119, No. 750)
    1669 Cabrega, Pedro de Nauarra y de la. P. *Logros De La Monarqvia*
          (Reel 119, No. 750)
    1690 Moncada, Pedro de. *Practica De La Comvnion*
          (Reel 114, No. 717)
    1691 Spain. Laws, statutes, etc. *Pragmatica Qve Sv Magestad Mando
          publicar*
          (Reel 173, No. 1136)
    1692 Lancina, Juan A. de. *Historia De Las Reboluciones (sic)*
          (Reel 87, No. 557)
    1694 Juan de la Cruz. *Obras (vols. I-II)*
          (Reel 85, No. 543)

Paris, Bartolome - Pamplona
    1614 Sandoval, Prudencio de. *Tratanse En Esta Segvnda Parte Los Hechos
          Desde El Ano 1528 hasta el de 1527*
          (Reels 167 & 168, No. 1089)
    1634 Sandoval, Prudencio de. *Historia De La Vida y Hechos Del Emperador*
          (Reel 167 & 168, No. 1089)

Parvus, Audoenus - Paris
    1549 Antonio de Lebrija. *Lexicon Ivris Civillis*
          (Reel 16, No. 67)

Passinger, Thomas - London
    1683 Fernandez, Jeronimo. *The Honour of Chivalry (pts. I-II)*
    (Reel 53, No. 300)

Pegen, Andreas - Glatz
    1685 Arias, Francisco. *Thesaurus*
    (Reel 17, No. 77)

Pele, Guillaume - Paris
    1635 Luis de Granada. *Rhetoricae Ecclesisticae*
    (Reel 65, No. 392)

Perna, Petrus - Basle
    1577 Isidorus, Saint. *Originum libri viginti*
    (Reel 82, No. 521)

Petit, Jean - Paris
    1509 Isidorus, Saint. *Etymologiarum libri XX*
        (Reel 81, No. 518)
    1515 Sacro Bosco, Joannes de. *Sphera mundi*
        (Reel 162, No. 1061
    1520 Isidorus, Saint. *Etymologiarum libri XX*
        (Reel 82, No. 519)

Petit, Jean (Heirs of) - Paris
    1615 Rubio, Antonio. *Logica Mexicana*
    (Reel 159, No. 1045)

Pietrasanta, Plinio - Venice
    1577 Fuentes, Alfonso de. *Somma Della Natvral Filosofia*
    (Reel 56, No. 338)

Piget, Simeon - Paris
    1657 Medicis, Girolamo de. *Svmmae Theologiae*
        (Reels 145 & 146, No. 939)
    1657 Ponce de Leon, B. *Celeberrimae Academiae*
        (Reel 145, No. 938)

Pillehotte, A. - Lyon
    1620 Bustamante de la Camara, J. *De reptilibvs*
    (Reel 28, No. 136)

Piza, Typ. (Widow) - Mallorca
    1655 Mut, Vicente. *Vida De La Veneralbe*
    (Reel 118, No. 746)

Plance, Jean de la - Geneva
    1631 Perez, Antonio. *Las Obras y Relaciones*
    (Reel 139, No. 882)

Plannck, Stephanus - Rome

    March 9, 1483 Terrassa, Pedro. *Oratio de diuia prouidentia*
        (*Reel 183, No. 1176*)

    1488-91 Isidorus, Saint. *Opusculum de Temporibus*
        (*Reel 82, No. 522*)

    1492 Bentivoglio, Antonio G. *Oratio ad Alexandrum*
        (*Reel 21, No. 106*)

Plantin, Boutique de - Paris

    1596 Teixeira, Jose. *Explication De La Genealogie*
        (*Reel 182, No. 1168*)

Plantin, Christopher - Antwerp

    1557 Cicero, Marcus T. *Orationes*
        (*Reel 44, No. 233*)

    1570 Index Librorum Prohibitorum. *Liborum prohibitorum*
        (*Reel 80, No. 510*)

    1570 Spain. Laws, statutes, etc. *Philippi II. De Librorum prohiabitorum*
        (*No. 1127 not available*)

    1572 Del Rio Martin Antoine. *Ad Cl. Clavdiani V.C. Opera*
        (*Reel 153, No. 1008*

    1572 Granada, Luis de. *Contemptvs Mvndi*
        (*Reel 65, No. 393*)

    1572 Granada, Luis de. *Memorial De La vida Christiana*
        (*Reel 64, No. 386*)

    1572 Granada, Luis, de. *Oraciones y Exercicios De deuocion*
        (*Reel 64, No. 386*)

    1575 Azpilcueta, Martin de. *Enchiridion*
        (*Reel 20, No. 90*)

    1579 Monardes Alfaro, Nicolas. *Simplicivm*
        (*Reel 114, No. 716*)

    1582 Sanchez de las Brozas, F. *De Avtoribvs*
        (*Reel 166, No. 1080*)

    1582 Sanchez de las Brozas, F. *Paradoxa*
        (*Reel 166, No. 1085*)

    1583 Granada, Luis de. *Concionvm De Tempore (vol. IV*
        (*Reel 66, No. 397*)

    1585 Del Rio, Martin Antoine. *Ad Cl. Clavdiani V. C. Opera*
        (*Reel 153, No. 1010*)

    1587 Luis de Granada. *Concionvm De Tempore (vol. II)*
        (*Reel 65, No. 395*)

    1587 Luis de Granada. *Qvinqve Conciones De Poenitentia*
        (*Reel 65, No. 395*)

    1588 Luis de Granada. *Concionvm De Tempore (vol. I)*
        (*Reel 65, No. 394*)

    1588 Luis de Granada. *Conciones De Praecipvis (vol. II)*
        (*Reel 66, No. 398*)

    1600 Luis de Granada. *Conciones Qvae De Praecipvis*
        (*Reel 66, No. 398*)

Plantiniana (Offic.), Plantin, Balthasar - Antwerp
    1634 Bivero, Pedro de. *Sacrvm Sanctvarivm*
          (Reel 25, No. 114)
    1634 Bivero, Pedro de. *Sacrvm Oratorivm*
          (Reel 25, No. 115)
    1635 Nieremberg, Juan E. *Historia Natvrae*
          (Reel 121, No. 764)
    1654 Borja, F. de. *Las Obras en verso*
          (Reel 27, No. 127)

Plantiniana (Offic.) Widow and Joannem Mortetum - Antwerp
    1593 Del Rio, Martin Antoine. *Syntagma Tragoediae Latinae (vol. I-III)*
          (Reel 155 & 156, No. 1023)
    1597 Rivadeneira, Pedro. *Tratado De La Religion*
          (Reel 157, No. 1029)
    1607 Del Rio, Martin Antoine. *Ad. Cl. Clavdiani V. C. Opera*
          (Reel 153, No. 1013)

Plantiniana (Offic.) apud C. Raphelengium - Antwerp
    1605 Monardes Alfaro, Nicolas. *Magna Medicinae Secreta*
          (Reel 114, No. 715)

Playfere, John - London
    1668 Quevedo y Villegas, F. G. de. *The Visions*
          (Reel 151, No. 982)

Poma, A. de - Madrid
    1630 Juan de la Cruz, Saint. *Obras*
          (Reel 84, No. 541)

Ponte, Giovanni B. Da - Milan
    (?) Alburquerque, Beltran de Cuevas. *Maiorazgo*
          (Reel 5, No. 26)

Populi Romani, In Aedibus - Rome
    1575 Simancas, Diego. *De Catholicis Institvtionibvs*
          (Reel 171, No. 1109)

Porralis, Thomas - Pamplona
    1578 Montemayor, Jorge de. *Los Siete Libros De La Diana*
          (Reel 114, No. 720)
    1591 Lopez de Ayala, P. *P. Coronica*
          (Reel 91, No. 586)

Portonariis, Andrea de - Salamanca
    1550 Aphthonius, Sophistes. *Proygmmasmata*
          (Reel 16, No. 71)
    1556 Aphthonius, Sophistes. *Progymmasmata*
          (Reel 16, No. 72)

Portonariis, Francisco de (da Trino) - Venice
1556 Guevara, Antonio de. *Libro aureo*
(Reel 72, No. 446)
1575 Guevara, Antonio de. *Libro aureo*
(Reel 72, No. 447)

Portonariis de Ursinis, Domenico - Venice
1578 Zurita y Castro, J. *Indices Rervm Ab Aragoniae (vols. I-II)*
(Reel 202, No. 1300)
1578 Zurita y Castro, J. *Roberti Viscardi Calabriae Dvcis (Vol. III)*
(Reel 202, No. 1300)

Portonariis y Ursino, Domingo de - Zaragoza
1585 Molino, Miguel Del. *Repertorvivm Fororvm*
(Reel 113, No. 710)

Pralard, Andre - Paris
1697 Casas, Bartolome de las. *La decouverte des Indes*
(Reel 35, No. 173)

Printer of the 1481 'Legenda Aurea' - Strassburg
1482 Torquemada, Juan de. *Expositio Psalterii*
(Reel 185, No. 1187)

Pro, Bartholemy - Montluel
1576 Amadis de Gaula. *Le Tresiesme Livre*
(Reel 11, No. 50)

Prost, Jacob and Pierre - Lyon
1634 Relacion Verdadera de la Batalla De Kempen
(Reel 152, No. 997)

Puerto Alone, Alonso del - Seville
1482 Valera Diego de. *Cronica de Espana*
(Reel 45, No. 242)

Quentel, Arnold - Colognue
1596 Luis de Granada. *Paradisvs Precvm*
(Reel 68, No. 407)
1598 Luis de Granada. *Memoriale Christianae Vitae*
(Reel 64, No. 388)

Quentel, Joannis, & Gervinus (Heirs of) - Cologne
1588 Luis de Granada. *Flores ... spiritualibus*
(Reel 67, No. 404)
1588 Luis de Granada. *Introdvctionis Ad Symbolym Fidei*
(Reel 67, No. 401)
1590 Luis de Granada. *Dvx Peccatorvm (pts. I-II)*
(Reel 67, No. 405)

Quinones, Maria de - Madrid
1635 Villa Mediana, Juan de Tarsis y Peralta, Conde de. *Obras*
(Reel 178, No. 1164)
1640 Nieremberg, Juan E. *Vida Del Dichoso*
(Reel 122, No. 769)
1641 Nieremberg, Juan E. *Obras y Dias*
(Reel 122, No. 768)
1641 Nieremberg, Juan E. *Vna Centvria De Dictamenes*
(Reel 122, No. 768)
1664 Palafox y Mendoza, Juan de. *Obras (vol. IV)*
(Reel 132, No. 832)

R., I. - London
1600 Torquemada, Antonio de. *The Spanish Mandeuile of Miracles*
(Reel 184, No. 1184)

Rabut, Rene - Granada
1592 Luna, Miguel. *La Verdadera Hystoria*
(Reel 95, No. 618)

Ramirez, Antonia (Widow) - Salamanca
1603 Leon, Luis Ponce de. *De Los Nombres De Christo*
(Reel 88, No. 571)
1603 Leon, Luis Ponce de. *La Perfecta Casada*
(Reel 88, No. 569)
1627 Correas, Gonzalo. *Trilingve De Tres Artes*
(Reel 45, No. 241)

Ramirez, Hernan - Alcala de Henares (Compluti)
1584 Fernandez de Cordoba, G. *Chronica Del Gran Capitan*
(Reel 53, No. 303)
1586 Perez de Moya, J. *Comparaciones O Similes*
(Reel 142, No. 913)

Rampazetto, Francesco - Venice
1564 Guevara, Antonio de. *Vita, gesti, costvmi*
(Reel 71, No. 443)

Rampazetto, Francesco (Heirs of) - Venice
1581 Ulloa, Alfonso de. *Vita Dell' Invittissimo*
(Reel 187, No. 1203)

Ramos Bejarano, Gabriel - Cordoba
1586 Ocampo, Florian de. *Los Cinco Libros Postreros De La Coronica General*
(Reel 125, No. 790)
1586 Perez de Oliva, F. *Las Obas (sic)*
(Reel 142, No. 915)

Ramos Bejarano, Gabriel - Seville
1619 Herrera Fernando de. *Versos*
(Reel 76, No. 483)

Ravenstein, Jean de - Amsterdam
    1672   Huarte de San Juan, Juan.   *L'Examen Des Esprits*
           (Reel 79, No. 505)

Ravenstein, N. - Amsterdam
    1638   Cohen de Lara, David.   *Vocabvlorvm Rabbinicorvm*
           (Reel 87, No. 559)

Ravenstein, Paul - Amsterdam
    1617   Mexia, Pedro.   *De Verscheyde lessen Petri Messiae*
           (Reel 110, No. 687)

Real y General Hospital - Zaragoza
    1651   Borja, F. de.   *Poema heroico*
           (Reel 27, No. 128)

Regia, Typographia - see Flandrum, Ioannem

Rene, Juan - Malaga
    1600   Marmol Carvajal, L. Del.   *Historia Del Rebelion y Castigo*
           (Reel 103, No. 649)

Reynier, Cornell - Perpinan
    1679   Quevedo y Villegas, F. G. de.   *Suenos y Discvrsos*
           (Reel 151, No. 977)

Rhodes, H. - London
    1700   Carlos II, King of Spain.   *Last will*
           (Reel 33, No. 156)

Ribbium, Joannem - Batavia
    1680   Florus, Lucius A.   *L. Annaeus Florus*
           (Reel 54, No. 326)

Ribero, Riberio, Antonio - Lisboa
    1576   Estella, Diego de.   *Primera Parte De La Vanidad*
           (Reel 49, No. 277)
    1576   Estella, Diego de.   *Segvnda Parte Del Libro De La Vanidad*
           (Reel 49, No. 277)
    1576   Luis de Granada.   *Ecclesiasticae Rhetoricae*
           (Reel 64, No. 390)

Rico de Miranda, Roque - Madrid
    1680   Olmo, Jose Del.   *Relacion Del Avto Gen. De La Fee*
           (Reel 125, No. 791)

Rigaud, Benoist - Lyon
    1578   Amadis de Gaula.   *Le Qvinziesme Livre*
           (Reel 11, No. 50)
    1592   Guevara, Antonio de.   *L'horloge des princes*
           (Reel 72m No. 449)
    1615   Amadis de Gaula.   *Le Vingt Et Troisisme Livre*
           (Reel 13, No. 50)

Rigaud, Pierre - Lyon
    1609   Primaleon of Greece. *Le Troisiesme Livre*
           (Reel 146, No. 941)

Roberts, James - London
    1598   Luis de Granada. *The Synners Gvyde*
           (Reel 67, No. 406)
    1598   Luis de Granada. *The Seconde Booke of the Sinners Guyde*
           (Reel 67, No. 406)

Robinot, Gilles - Paris
    1598   Perez, Antonio. *Relaciones De Antonio Perez*
           (Reel 140, No. 886)
    1615   Amadis de Gaula. *Le Vingt Et Devxiesme Livre*
           (Reel 13, No. 40)
    1615   Amadis de Gaula.   *Le Vingt et Qvatriene et Dernier Livre*
           (Reel 13, No. 50)

Robledo, Francisco - Ciudad de los Angeles (Puebla de los Angeles)
    1643   Palafox y Mendoza, J. de. *Historia Sagrada*
           (Reel 130, No. 826)
    1644   Palafox y Mendoza, J. de. *Semana Santa*
           (Reel 133, No. 834)

Robledo, Francisco - Mexico City
    1646   Blazquez Mayoralgo, J. *Perfecta racon*
           (Reel 26, No. 121)

Robles, Laurentius & Didacus (brothers) - Zaragoza
    1588   Blancas y Tomas, G. de. *Aragonesivm rervm*
           (Reel 25, No. 116)

Robles, Lorenzo de - Zaragoza
    1590   Felipe II. *Relacion Svmaria*
           (Reel 52, No. 293)
    1590   Relacion Svmaria Cierta
           (Reel 152, No. 994)
    1591   Miravete de Blancas, M. *Alegaciones Del Dotor Martin Miravete*
           (Reel 112, No. 701)
    1610   Zurita y castro, J. *Anales De La Corona de Aragon (vol. I)*
           (Reels 203 & 204, No. 1301)
    1610   Zurita y Castro, J. *Historia Del Rey Don Hernando El Catholico*
           (Reels 203 & 204, No. 1301)

Rodriguez, Alonso - Zaragoza
    1604   Zurita y Castro, Geronimo. *Indice De Las Cosas Mas Notables (vol 7)*
           (Reel 204, No. 1301)

Rodriguez, Diego - Toledo
    1616   Tamayo de Vargas, T. *Historia General*
           (Reel 178, No. 1158
    1623   Cevallos, Geronimo de. *Arte Real*
           (Reel 39, No. 202)

Rodriguez, Gregorio - Madrid
   1645   Vega Carpio, L.F. de. *Arcadia*
          (Reel 190, No. 1228)
   1646   Palafox y Mendoza, J. de. *Cartqa Que El 'Illustrissimo*
          (Reel 129, No. 819)
   1649   Juan de la Cruz. *Obras*
          (Reel 85, No. 542)
   1650   Pellicer de Ossau y Tovar, J. *Alma De La Gloria*
          (Reel 137, No. 858)

Rodriguez, Juan - Toledo
   1591   Villegas Selvago, A. de. *Flos Sanctorvm*
          (Reel 191, No. 1238)

Rodriguez, Mathias - Lisboa
   1630   Quevedo y Villegas, F. G. de. *Politica De Dios*
          (Reel 150, No. 971)

Rodriguez, Pedro - Toledo
   1592   Mariana, Juan de. *Historiae De Rebvs Hispaniae Libri XX*
          (Reel 101, No. 643)

Rodriguez Gamarra, Alonso - Seville
   1613   Alburquerque, Diego de. *Sermon*
          (Reel 5, No. 27)

Roigny, Jean - Paris
   1534   Castro, Alfonso de. *Aduersus omnes hereses Lib. XIII*
          (Reel 39, No. 198)

Roman, Antonio - Madrid
   1687   Valdes, Rodrigo de. *Poema Heroyco Hispano-Latino*
          (Reel 188, No. 1210)
   1692   Solis y Ravadeneyra, A. de. *Varias Poesias*
          (Reel 171, No. 1115)

Romeu, Jaime - Barcelona
   1640   Castillo Solorzano, Alonso de. *Los alivios de Casandra*
          (Reel 38, No. 195)
   1642   Relacion Verdadera de Todo Lo Qve Ha Passado En Perpinan
          (Reel 152, No. 999)

Romolo, Tommaso - Palermo
   1689   Montalvo, Francisco A. de. *Noticias Fvnebres*
          (Reel 114, No. 718)

Rossi, G. B. - Pavia
   1618   Daza, Antonio. *Historia, Vita, Miracoli*
          (Reel 47, No. 252)

Rouille, Guillaume - Lyon
1549 Alciati, Andrea. *Los emblemas*
(Reel 6, No. 29)
1569 Medina, Pedro de. *L'Art De Navigver*
(Reel 104, No. 661)
1579 Du Choul, Guillaume. *Los discvrsos*
(Reel 48, No. 262)

Rubeis, Filippo and Antonio - Rome
1677 Chacon, Alfonso. *Vitae, Et Res Gestae (vols. I-II)*
(Reel 43, No. 226)

Rubino, Bartolomeo - Venice
1568 Perez de Valencia, J. *Divinae Explanationes*
(Reel 143, No. 918)

Ruelle, Jean - Paris
1569 Guevara, Antonio de. *L'horloge des princes*
(Reel 72, No. 448)
1570 Guevara, Antonio de. *Les epistres*
(Reel 69, No. 424)

Ruiz Murga, M. - Madrid
1698 Juan de la Anunciacion. *La Inocencia vindicada*
(Reel 16, No. 70)

S., T. - London
1625 Tejeda, Fernando. *Miracles vnmasked*
(Reel 182, No. 1172)

Sanchez, Carlos - Madrid
1644-46 Boverio, Zaccaria. *Las chronicas*
(Reel 28, No. 133)

Sanchez, Juan - Madrid
1642 Micheli Marquez, J. *Deleite y Amargvra*
(Reel 112, No. 698)
1649 Relacion Veradera
(Reel 152, No. 1000)

Sanchez, Luis - Madrid
1599 Plinius Secundus, C. *Historia Natvral*
(Reel 145, No. 933)
1600 Lopez de, Montoya, Pedro *De Concordia Sacrarvm (pts. 1-2)*
(Reel 92, No. 590)
1600 Sandoval, Prudencio de. *Chronica Del Inclito*
(Reel 167, No. 1088)
1605 Espinosa, Pedro. *Flores De Poetas Ilvstres*
(Reel 49, No. 276)
1605 Lopez Pinciano, A. *El Pelayo*
(Reel 93, No. 599)
1605 Rivadeneira, Pedro. *Obras*
(Reel 157, No. 1028)

1608 Bermudez de Pedraza, F. *Antigvedad*
(*Reel 22, No. 109*)

1610 Covarrubias Orozcco, S. de. *Emblemas Morales*
(*Reel 45, No. 246*)

1610 Covarrubias Orozcco, S. de. *Tesoro de La Lengva*
(*Reel 6, No. 34*)

1611 Cabrera de Cordoba, L. *De Historia*
(*Reel 28, No. 137*)

1611 Carrillo y Sotomayor, L. *Obras*
(*Reel 34, No. 166*)

1614 Tacitus Publius, C. *Tacito Espanol*
(*Reel 177, No. 1155*)

1615 Suarez de Figueroa, C. *Plaza Vniversal*
(*Reel 176, No. 1151*)

1619 Cabrera de Cordoba, L. *Felipe Segvndo*
(*Reel 29, No. 138*)

1620 Bermudez de Pedraza, F. *El Secretario*
(*Reel 22, No. 110*)

1621 Tamayo de Vargas, T. *Diego Garcia De Paredes*
(*Reel 177, No. 1156*)

1622 Lopez de Haro, A. *Nobiliario Genealogico*
(*Reels 91 & 92, No. 589*)

1623 Lanario y Aragon, F. *Las Gverras de Flandes*
(*Reel 87, No. 556*)

1624 Maldonado, Alonso. *Chronica Vniuersal*
(*Reel 96, No. 621*)

1625 Lopez Madera, G. *Excelencias De La Monarqvia*
(*Reel 93, No. 597*)

1626 Pellicer de Ossau y Tovar, J. *Argenis*
(*Reel 137, No. 860*)

1627 Gongora y Argote, L. de. *Obras En Verso*
(*Reel 59, No. 354*)

1627 Vega Carpio, L. F. de. *Corona Tragica*
(*Reel 189, No. 1219*)

1674 Covarrubias Orozco, S. de. *Del Origen y Principio De La Lengva*
(*Reel 6, No.34*

Sanchez, Melchor - Madrid

1655 Mexia, Pedro. *Historia imperial*
(*Reel 105, No. 668*)

1666 Albornoz, Diego F de. *Cartilla*
(*Reel 5, No. 25*)

1668 Quevedo y Villegas, F. G. de. *El Parnaso*
(*Reel 150, No. 969*)

1673 Covarrubias Orozco, S. de. *Parte Segunda del Tesoro de la lengva*
(*Reel 6, No. 34*)

1674 Covarrubias Orozco, D. de. *Parte Primera del Tesoro de la lengva*
(*Reel 6, No. 34*)

Sanchez Crespo, J. - Alcala de Henares (Compluti)

1604 Alfaro, Gregorio de. *Govierno*
(*Reel 8, No. 44*)

Sanchez Ezpeleta, A. (Widow of) - Alcala de Henares (Compluti)
    1618   Juan de la Cruz. *Obras Espiritvales*
           (Reel 84, No. 538)

Sanctandreana, In Offic. - Rome
    1590   Chacon, Pedro. *De Triclinio*
           (Reel 43, No. 227)

Sanctandreanus, Petrus - Heidelberg
    1593   Agustin Antonio. *Quae extant*
           (Reel 3, No. 16)

Sanz, Francisco - Madrid
    1671   Banos de Velasco y Azevedo, J. *El Sabio en la pobreza*
           (Reel 20, No. 95)
    1672   Banos de Velasco y Azevedo, J. *El hijo de David*
           (Reel 21, No. 96)
    1674   Banos de Velasco y Azevedo, J. *Al Ayo, y Maestro*
           (Reel 21, No. 97)
    1674   Owen, John. *Agvdezas De Jvan Oven*
           (Reel 128, No. 810)
    1674   Pellicer de Ossau y Tovar, J. *Memorial de La Calidad*
           (Reel 138, No. 869)
    1674   Ulloa y Pereira, Luis de. *Obras De Don Lvis De Vlloa Pereira*
           (Reel 187, No. 1205)
    1682   Calderon de la Barca, Pedro. *Verdadera Qvinta Parte*
           (Reel 30, No. 140, pt. 5)
    1683   Calderon de la Barca, Pedro. *Sexta Parte De Comedias*
           (Reel 30, No. 140, pt. 6)
    1683   Calderon de la Barca, Pedro. *Septima Parte De Comedias*
           (Reel 30, No. 140, pt. 7)
    1684   Calderon de la Barca, Pedro. *Octava Parte De Comedias*
           (Reel 30, No. 140, pt. 8)
    1685   Calderon de la Barca, Pedro. *Primera Parte De Comedias*
           (Reel 31, No. 140, pt. 1(B)
    1685   Calderon de la Barca, Pedro. *Primera Parte De Comedias*
           (Reel 29, No. 140, pt. 1(A)
    1686   Calderon de la Barca, Pedro. *Parte Segunda De Comedias*
           (Reel 29, No. 140, pt. 2)
    1687   Calderon de la Barca, Pedro. *Tercera Parte De Comedias*
           (Reel 29, No. 140, pt.3)
    1698   Calderon de la Barca, Pedro. *Novena Parte De Comedias*
           (Reel 30, No. 140, pt. 9)

Saunders, F. - London
    1697   Guevara, Antonio de. *Spanish letters*
           (Reel 70, No. 428)

Schoeffer, Peter - Strassburg
    1524   Vives, Juan L. *Opvscvla Aliqvot Vere Catholica*
           (Reel 197, No. 1283)

Schoenwetter, G. - Frankfurt am Main
    1654 Caramuel y Lobkowitz, J. de. *Praecursor Logicus*
        (*Reel 32, No. 148*)

Schurerianis, Aedb. - Strassburg
    1513 Flores, Pedro. *Petri Flores Hispani*
        (*Reel 54, No. 325*)

Secer, Johan - Hagenau
    1529 Isidorus, Saint. *De Fide Catholica*
        (*Reel 113, No. 525*)

Sersanders, Alexander - Ghent
    1611 Molina, Antonio de. *Tractatus De Oratione*
        (*Reel 113, No. 708*)

Sertenas, Vincent - Paris
    1555 Amadis de Gaula. *Le Septiesme Livre*
        (*Reel 10, No. 50*)
    1555 Amadis de Gaula. *Le Hvtiesme Livre*
        (*Reel 10, No. 50*)

Sessa, Marchio (Heirs of) - Venice
    1569 Ulloa, Alfonso. *Historia Dell 'Impresa Di Tripoli*
        (*Reel 187, No. 1201*)
    1569 Urrea, Jeronimo de Jimenez de. *Dialogo Del Vero Honore*
        (*Reel 187, No. 1202*)

Syle, Henry - London
    1623 Pena, Juan A. de la. *A Relation of the Royall Festiuities*
        (*Reel 138, No. 872*)

Silber, Eucharius - Rome
    1485 Lull, Ramon. *Ars brevis*
        (*Reel 94, No. 603*)
    1485 Lull, Ramon. *Oamia artos*
        (*Reel 94, No. 608*)
    1488 Nechoniah ben Ha_Kanah. *Illvstrissimo Ac Sapientissimo*
        (*Reel 119, No. 752*)
    ca. 1489 Torquemada, Juan de. *Summa de ecclesia contra impugnatores*
          (*Reel 185, No. 1193*)
    1490-95 Escobar, Andres de. *Interrogationes*
          (*Reel 48, No. 269*)
    1500 Escobar, Andres de. *Modus confitendi*
        (*Reel 48, No. 270*)

Silva, Manuel da - Lisboa
    1646 Gracian y Morales, B. *El Heroe*
        (*Reel 63, No. 383*)
    1647 Mello, Francisco M. de. *El Mayor Pequeno*
        (*Reel 110, No. 689*)

Silvius, Gulielmus - Antwerp
  1572 Amadis de Gaula. *Le trezieme livre*
        (Reel 11, No. 50)
  1573 Amadis de Gaula. *L'onziesme [e le dovziesme livre [s]]*
        (Reel 11, No. 50)

Sims, Val. - Dondon
  1604 Acosta Jose de. *The Natural and Moral*
        (Reel 2, No. 10)

Sittart, Arnold - Paris
  1584 Verrius Flaccus, M. *Quae extant. (see Agustin, Antonio)*
        (Reel 3, No. 15)

Smit, Gerard - Amsterdam
  1656 Questiers, Catharina. *Casimier, of Gedempte Hoogmoet*
        (Reel 147, No. 945)

Scardis, Lazarus de - Venice
  1513 Sanchez de Arevalo, R. *Speculum vite*
        (Reel 166, No. 1079)
  1513 Torquemada, Juan de. *Expositio In psalterium*
        (Reel 185, No. 1189)

Soler, Juan - Zaragoza
  1577 Terentius, Publius afer. *Las Seis Comedias*
        (Reel 183, No. 1174)

Solidi, Johannes - Cologne
  1474 Torquemada, Juan de. *Meditationes seu Contemplationes*
        (Reel 185, No. 1190)

Sommaville, Antoine de - Paris
  1659 Oudin, Cesar de. *Refranes O Proverbios*
        (Reel 799 not available)

Sonnius, Michael - Paris
  1580 Isidorus, Saint. *Opera Omnia*
        (Reel 81, No. 515)
  1601 Isidorus, Saint. *Opera Omnia*
        (Reel 81, No. 516)

Sorg, Anton - Augsburg
  ca. 1475 Torquemada, Juan de. *De efficacia aquae benedictae*
            (Reel 185, No. 1185)
  ca. 1476 Torquemada, Juan de. *De efficacia aquae benedictae*
            (Reel 185, No. 1186)

Soubron, Antoine - Lyon
  1622 Perpina, Pedro J. *Orationes Dvodevigenti*
        (Reel 144, No. 923)

Spei, Ad Signvm - Venice
    1551 Perez de Ayala, M. *De Divinis Apostolicis*
         (Reel 140, No. 895)

Spindeler, Nicolaus (see Brun, Peter)

Spineda, Lucio - Venice
    1609 Palmerin of England. *Di Palmerino D'Inghilterra (Book 2 & 3)*
         (Reel 134, No. 843)

Steelsius, Jean - Antwerp
    1542 Justinus, Marcus J. *De La Historia*
         (Reel 86, No. 548)
    1546 Mantuanus, Baptista. *Adolescentia seu Bucolica (see Vives, Juan L.)*
    1549 Avila y Zuniga, L. de. *Comentario*
         (Reel 19, No. 86)
    1549 Cicero, Marcus T. *Officios Dela Amicicia*
         (Reel 44, No. 231)
    1551 Ovidius Naso, P. *Las Metamorphoses*
         (Reel 127, No. 807)
    1551 Seneca, Lucius A. *Libros De Lucio Anneo Seneca*
         (Reel 170, No. 1101)
    1553 Antonio de Lebrija. *Dictionarvm Ex Hispaniensi*
         (Reel 15, No. 63)
    1553 Tarafa, Francisco. *De origine, ac rebus gestis Regum Hispaniae*
         (Reel 178, No. 1159)
    1554 Lopez de Gomara, F. *Historia General De Las Indias*
         (Reel 91, No. 587)
    1556 Flores, Juan. *Histoire De Avrelio*
         (Reel 54, No. 324)
    1556 Homer. *La Vlyxea De Homero*
         (Reel 77, No. 489)
    1557 Alvarez, Francisco. *Historia. Etopia (En casa I. Latio)*
         (Reel 10, No. 49)

Steelsius, Jean (Widow and heirs of) - Antwerp
    1567 Vives, Juan L. *Linguae Latinae Exercitatio*
         (Reel 197, No. 1274)
    1570 Antonio de Lebrija. *Dictionarivm Latinohispanicvm*
         (Reel 15, No. 64)
    1570 Antonio de Lebrija. *Dictionarivm Ex Hispaniensi*
         (Reel 15, No. 64)
    1570 Antonio de Lebrija. *Dictionarivm Propriorvm Nominvm*
         (Reel 15, No. 64)
    1572 Palacios de Salazar, P. *Pavli De Palacio Granatensis, S. Th. D.*
         (Reel 129, No. 814)

Stephanus I., Robertus - Paris
    1527 Persius Flaccus, A. *Commentaria*
         (Reel 144, No. 925)

Stoer, Jacob - Geneva
    1622   Augustinus, A., Saint. *De ciuitate Dei libri XXII*
          (Reel 18, No. 81)

Strick, Leonard - Franeker
    1693   Sanchez de las Brozas, F. *Minerva cum Animadversionibus*
          (Reel 166, No. 1084)

Suganappo, Juan Pablo - Naples
    1584   Salazar de Mendoza, P. *Historia De Los Svccessos De La Gverra*
          (Reel 163, No. 1067)

Sumptibus Societatis Typographorum - Lyon
    1621   Sanchez, Tomas. *De Sancto Matrimonii Sacramento*
          (Reel 165, No. 1077)

Suria, Vicente - Barcelona
    1689   Romance Nuevo de la Mverte
          (Reel 159, No. 1043)
    1689   Nunez de Castro, A. *Lisbro Historico*
          (Reel 123, No. 779)

Swalle, Abel, and Childe, Tim - London
    1694   Gracian y Morales, B. *The Courtiers Oracle*
          (Reel 63, No. 382)

Tacuino, Giovanni (da Trino) - Venice
    1507   Lull, Ramon. *Liber proverbiorum*
          (Reel 94, No. 607)

Tayanno, Angelo - Zaragoza
    1602   Carrillo, Martin. *Apologia De La Bvlla*
          (Reel 33, No. 161)
    1602   Carrillo, Martin. *Explicacion De La Bvlla*
          (Reel 33, No. 160)
    1603   Aleman, Mateo. *Gvzman de Alfarache*
          (Reel 7, No. 36)
    1622   Carrillo, Martin. *Annales (sic) y memorias*
          (Reel 33, No. 162)
    1634   Carrillo, Martin. *Anales cronologicos*
          (Reel 34, No. 163)

Tazo, Pedro - Madrid
    1624   Tamayo de Vargas, T. *Flavio Lvcio Dextro*
          (Reel 178, No. 1157)

Terranova y Neyla, Ildefonsus a - Salamanca
    1582   Martinez, Martin. *Libri Decem Hypotyposeon*
          (Reel 104, No. 655)

Thiboust, Claude (Widow of) - Paris
    1683   Perpina, Pedro J. *Aliquot Epistolae*
          (Reel 144, No. 924)

Tinassi, Niccolo A. - Rome
    1672 Antonio, Nicolas. *Bibliotheca Hispana*
        (Reel 14 & 15, No. 60)

Tinghius, Q. Philip - Lyon
    1585 Luis de Granada. *Concionvm De Tempore (vol. III)*
        (Reel 65, No. 396)

Torubia, Antonio - Granada
    1690 Certamen Poetico
        (Reel 40, No. 206)

Tottil, R., and Marshe, Thomas - London
    1568 Guevara, Antonio de. *The diall of princes*
        (Reel 73, No. 453)

Tournes, Jean de - Geneva
    1550 Guevara, Antonio de. *Liure dore de Marc Aurele*
        (Reel 71, No. 436)
    1551 Guevara, Antonio de. *Libro llamado Menosprecio*
        (Reel 74, No. 464)
    1598 Casa, Giovanni Della. *Le Galatee*
        (Reel 35, No. 168)
    1609 Casa, Giovanni Della. *Le Galatee*
        (Reel 35, No. 169)
    1644 Perez, Antonio. *Las Obras*
        (Reel 139, No. 883)

Tournes, Samuel de - Geneva
    1697 Perez, Antonio. *Las Obras*
        (Reel 140, No. 884)

Tramezino, Michele - Venice
    1544 Guevara, Antonio de. *Aviso de favoriti*
        (Reel 73, No. 459)

Trechsel, Johannes - Lyon
    1496 Torquemada, Juan de. *Summa de ecclesia contra impugnatores*
        (Reel 85, No. 1194)

Trognesius, Cesar - J. - Antwerp
    1640 Husel, Johan Van. *Den grooten Dictionaris*
        (Reel 68, No. 414)
    1646 Husel, Johan Van. *Den grooten Dictionaris*
        (Reel 80, No. 509)

Trujillo, Sebastian - Sevilla
    1564 Mexia, Pedro. *Historia imperial*
        (Reel 105, No. 667)

Tulliety, Nicolas - Lyon
    1607 Labastida, Hernando de. *Antidotto (sic)*
        (Reel 86, No. 552)

Turner, William (for R. Allot) - Oxford
    1630 Aleman, Mateo. *The Rogve (pts. I-II)*
          (Reel 8, No. 41)

Turrini, Maria - Venice
    1664 Mexia, Pedro. *Le Vite de gli Imperadori (sic)*
          (Reel 106, No. 671)

Typis Universitatis (Carolo-Ferdinandea) - Prague
    1674 Loyola, Ignacio de, Saint. *Exercitia Spiritualia*
          (Reel 94, No. 600)

Val, Pablo de - Madrid
    1650 Nunez de Castro, A. *Seneca Impugnado*
          (Reel 123, No. 780)
    1653 Quevedo y Villegas, F. G. de. *Discvrsos Evangelicos*

    1658 Gracian y Morales, B. *El Criticon*
          (Reel 62, No. 372)
    1659 Palafox y Mendoza, J. de. *Exelencias*
          (Reel 130, No. 823)
    1664 Gracian y Morales, B. *Obras (vols. I-II)*
          (Reels 61 & 62, No. 370)
    1665 Nunez de Castro, A. *Coronica De Los Senores Reyes*
          (Reel 123, No. 778)
    1665 Palafox y Mendoza, J. de. *Obras (vol. V)*
          (Reel 132, No. 832)

Valgrisi, Vincenzo - Venice
    1544 Guevara, Antonio de. *Vita, gesti, costvmi*
          (Reel 71, No. 437)
    1561 Covarrubias, Pedro de. *Rimedio De' Givocatori*
          (Reel 45, No. 245)
    1561 Mexia, Pedro. *Vite di tutti gli Imperadori (sic)*
          (Reel 106, No. 670)
    1565 Guevara, Antonio de. *Libro primo [quarto] delle lettere*
          (Reel 69, No. 423)

Valgrisiana, Offic. - Venice
    1570 Vives, Juan L. *Flores Italici*
          (Reel 197, No. 1275)

Varesio, Juan Bautista (see also Juanta, Felipe de) - Burgos
    1609 Ovidius Naso, P. *Metamorphoseos*
          (Reel 128, No. 809)
    1622 Molina, Antonio de. *Exercicios Expiritvales*
          (Reel 112, No. 706)

Vaticana, Typographia - Rome
    1608 Chacon, Pedro. *De Ponderibus. De Mensuris*
          (Reel 44, No. 229)

Vazquez, Antonio - Alcala de Henares (Compluti)
    1634   Marquez, Juan. *El Governador Christiano*
            (Reel 103, No. 651)
    1642   Ballesteros y Saavedra, F. de. *Vida de San Carlos*
            (Reel 20, No. 93)

Velpius, Antoine (Widow of Hubert) - Bruxelles
    1632   Pedro de Alcantara, Saint. *A Golden Treatise*
            (Reel 137, No. 856)

Velpius, Roger - Bruxelles
    1606   Pallet, Jean. *Diccionario ... De La lengua Espanola (pt. I)*
            (Reel 134, No. 842)
    1607   Pallet, Jean. *Dictionaire ... De Langve Francoise (pt. II)*
            (Reel 134, No. 842)

Velpius, Roger, and Velpius, Hubert Antoine - Bruxelles
    1611   Vega Carpio, L. F. de. *Segvnda Parte De Las Comedias*
            (Reel 189, No. 1218)
    1612   Oudin Cesar de. *Refranes, O Proverbios*
            (Reel 126, No. 798)
    1612   Oudin Cesar de. *Cartas En Refranes*
            (Reel 126, No. 798)
    1612   Oudin Cesar de. *Dialogo Entre El Amor y vn Cavallero*

    1614   Santa Cruz de Duena, M. de. *Floresta Espanola*
            (Reel 169, No. 1092)

Verdussen, Henri and Corneille - Antwerp
    1694   Guarini, Giovanni B. *El Pastor Fido*
            (Reel 68, No. 417)
    1699   Quevedo y Villegas, F. G. de. *Obras (vols. I-III)*
            (Reel 149, No. 964)

Verdussen, Jerome III, and Jean-Baptiste I - Antwerp
    1653   Pellicer de Ossau y Tovar, J. *Idea Del Principado*

    1674   Barrios, Miguel de. *Las Poesias*
            (Reel 21, No. 100
    1681   Aleman, Mateo. *Gyzman de Alfarache*
            (Reel 7, No. 37)

Veret, Juan - Pamplona
    1642   Relacion Verdadera
            (Reel 152, No. 998)

Verges, Agustin - Zaragoza
    1676   Lumbier, Raymundo. *Josephina Carmelitana*
            (Reel 95, No. 617)

Verges, Pedro - Zaragoza
    1626   Quevedo y Villegas, F. G. de. *Politica De Dios*
            (Reel 150, No. 970)

Viano, Bernardino de (de Lexona, Vercellese) - Venice
    1546   Achilles, Tatius. *Amorosi Raggionamenti (see Flores, Juan de)*
            (Reel 164, No. 1074)

Vilagrassa, Jeronimo - Valencia
    1655   Saavedra Fajardo, D. de. *Idea De Vn Principe*
            (Reel 161, No. 1053)
    1659   Nicolini, Sebastian. *Cabeza Visible Catolica*
            (Reel 120, No. 755)
    1670   Alciati, Andrea. *Los emblemas*
            (Reel 6, No. 30)

Villa Diego, Bernardo de. - Madrid
    1668   Palafox y Mendoza, J. de. *Luz A Los Vivos*
            (Reel 131, No. 831)
    1669   Palafox y Mendoza, J. de. *Obras (vol. VII)*
            (Reel 132, No. 832)
    1671   Palafox y Mendoza, J. de. *Obras (vol. VIII)*
            (Reel 132, No. 832)
    1672   Valerius, Maximus. *Comento Sobre Los Nveve Libros*
            (Reel 188, No. 1213)
    1681   Santos, Francisco de Los. *Descripcion Del Real Monasterio De S.*
        Lorenzo
            (Reel 169, No. 1096)

Villaquiran, Juan de - Valladolid
    1539   Guevara, Antonio de. *Epistolas familiares*
            (Reel 68, No. 419)
    1539   Guevara, Antonio de. *Las obras*
            (Reel 74, No. 467)
    1545   Guevara, Antonio de. *Oratorio de religiosos*
            (Reel 74, No. 471)
    1545   Guevara, Antonio de. *Libro llamado Menosprecio*
            (Reel 74, No. 471)
    1545   Guevara, Antonio de. *Libro llamado auiso*
            (Reel 74, No. 471)
    1545   Guevara, Antonio de. *Libro de los inuentores*
            (Reel 74, No. 471)
    1546   Guevara, Antonio de. *Oratorio de religiosos*
            (Reel 75, No. 474)

Villela, Francisco - Lisboa
    1670   Faria e Sousa, M. de. *Epitome De Las Historias (vol. II)*
            (Reel 51, No. 290)
    1673   Faria e Sousa, M. de. *Epitome De Las Historias (vol. I)*
            (Reel 51, No. 290)

Villery, Jacques - Paris
    1690   Luis de Granada. *Les Oeuvres*
            (Reel 63, No. 385)

Vincenti, Giacomo - Venice
    1585 Montemayor, Jorge de. *Los Siete Libros De La Diana*
          (Reel 114, No. 721)
    1585 Montemayor, Jorge de. *Segvnda Parte De La Diana*
          (Reel 115, No. 722)

Vina, Giraldo de la - Lisboa
    1627 Hurtado de Mendoza, D. *Gverra De Granada*
          (Reel 80, No. 508)

Viola, Niccolo - Tortona
    1620 Marquez, Juan. *Origine Delli Frati Eremitani*
          (Reel 104, No. 654)

Vullietto, Carlo - Rome
    1606 Andrete, Bernardo J. *Del Origen, Y Principio*

Waesberge, Jean - Antwerp
    1572 Palmerin de Oliva. *L'Histoire De Palmerin*
          (Reel 135, No. 846)

Walter, Wilhelm - Heidelberg
    1664 Casas, Bartolome de las. *Regionvm Indicarum*
          (Reel 35, No. 175)

Waylande, J - London
    1557 Guevara, Antonio de. *The diall of princes*
          (Reel 73, No. 452)

Wechel, Andreas, Marnius, Claud and Aubry Joannes (Heirs of) - Frankfurt am Main
    1611 Mariana, Juan de. *De Rege Et Regis*
          (Reel 101, No. 641)
    1611 Mariana, Juan de. *De Ponderibvs Et Mensvris*
          (Reel 101, No. 641)

Wechel, Christian - Paris
    1531 Aphthonius, Sophistes. *Progymasmata. Praelvdia*

Welchelianis, Typis - Hannover
    1625 Gil Polo, Gaspar. *Erotodidascalus*
          (Reel 58, No. 349)

Wellens, Johannes - Franeker Frisiorum
    1673 Grau, Abraham de. *Specimina philosophiae*
          (Reel 68, No. 412)

Wetstenium Henricum - Amsterdam
    1689 Chacon, Pedro. *De Triclinio*
          (Reel 43, No. 228)

Whitaker, Richard - London
    1641 Rubio, Antonio. *Commentarii In Vniversam Aristotelis*
         (Reel 160, No. 1049)

Wilson, W. - London
    1650 Perez de Montalban, J. *Aurora Ismenia*
         (Reel 141, No. 902

Windet, John - London
    1608 Estella, Diego de. *A Methode Vnto Mortification*
         (Reel 50, No. 281)

Winter, Robert - Basle
    1538 Vives, Juan L. *Declamationes Sex Syllanae Qvinqve*
         (Reel 196, No. 1260)
    1538 Vives, Juan L. *Institutione foeminae Christiane*
         (Reel 196, No. 1261)
    1540 Vives, Juan L. *De Officio Mariti*
         (Reel 196, No. 1264)
    1540 Vives, Juan L. *Exitationes animi In Deum*
         (Reel 196, No. 1266)

Withagius, Joannes - Antwerp
    1582 Macropedio, Georgio. *Epistolorvm Artificiose (see Vives, Juan L.*
         De Conscribendis Epistolis ... Basileae, 1536.
         (Reel 195, No. 1253)

Wit, Frederick de - Amsterdam
    ca. 1671 Wit, Frederik de. *Atlas major*
         (Reel 201, No. 1289)
    ca. 1688 Wit, Frederik de. *Atlas*
         (Reel 201, No. 1290)

Wolfe, John - London
    1588 Gonzalez Davila, Gil. *The Historie of the great*
         (Reel 61, No. 364)
    1590 Corro, Antonio de. *The Spanish Grammar*
         (Reel 45, No. 244)

Woodcock, Thomas - London
    1589 Essex, Robert Devereux. *A Trve Coppie*
         (Reel 47, No. 254)

Ybar, Juan de - Zaragoza
    1651 Quevedo y Villegas F. G. de. *La Hora*
         (Reel 147, No. 950)
    1654 Torre, Francisco de La. *Entretenimiento De Las Mvsas*
         (Reel 186, No. 1196)
    1665 Suarez de Mendoza y Figueroa, E. *Evstorgio y Clorilene*
         (Reel 176, No. 1152)

Zainer, Gunther - Augsburg
    1472   Isidorus, Saint. *Etymologiae*
           (Reel 81, No. 517)

Zainer, Johann - Ulm
    ca. 1490   Escobar, Andres de. *Casus Papales*
           (Reel 48, No. 267)

Zalterius, Bologninus - Venice
    1569   Simancas, Diego. *De Repvblica*
           (Reel 171, No. 1110)

Zanfretti, Paulo - Venice
    1582   Casas Cristobal de las. *Vocabulario*
           (Reel 36, No. 179)

Zangrius, Petrus (Tiletanus) - Louvain
    1560   Madrid, Alonso de. *Libellvs Avreu De vera Deo*
           (Reel 96, No. 620)

Zenaro, Damian - Venice
    1576   Casa, Cristobal de las. *Vocabulario*
           (Reel 35, No. 178)
    1589   Castillo, Hernando de. *Dell 'Historia Generale*
           (Reel 38, No. 193)

Zetzner, Lazarus - Strassburg
    1598   Lull, Ramon. *Opera*
           (Reel 94, No. 612)
    1599   Furio Ceriol, F. *Specvli Avlicarvm*
           (Reel 56, No. 340)

Zetzner, Lazarus (Heirs of) - Strassburg
    1651   Lull, Ramon. *Opera*
           (Reel 95, No. 613)

Ziletti, Giordano - Venice
    1556   Mexia, Pedro. *Selva di varia lettione*
           (Reel 108, No. 675)
    1560   Verrius Flaccus, M. *Quae extant.* *(see Agustin, Antonio)*
           (Reel 3, No. 14)

Zoppini, Fabio and Agostino - Venice
    1581   Mexia, Pedro. *Nvova seconda selva di varia lettione*
           (Reel 108, No. 677)

REEL AND LOCATION NUMBERS

REEL	NUMBERS	REEL	NUMBERS
1	1 - 6	16	67 - 74
2	7 - 12	17	75 - 78
3	13 - 17	18	79 - 82
4	18 - 22	19	83 - 89
5	23 - 28	20	90 - 95
6	29 - 34	21	96 - 106
7	35 - 39	22	107 - 112 v.1
8	40 - 44	23	112 v.2 - 112 v.4
9	45 v.1 - 45 v. 2	24	112 v.5 - 113
10	45 v.3 - 50 Bk.8	25	114 - 117
11	50 Bk.11 - 50 Bk.16B	26	118 - 125 v.1
12	50 Bk.17 - 50 Bk.21	27	125 v.2 - 131
13	50 Bk.22 - 52 Bk.1	28	132 - 137
14	52 Bk.2 - 60 v.1	29	138 - 140 pt.3
15	60 v.2 - 66	30	140 pt.4 - 140 pt.9

254

REEL	NUMBERS	REEL	NUMBERS
31	140 pt.1B - 146 v.2	51	285 v.2 - 290
32	146 v.3 - 148	52	291 - 297
33	149 - 162	53	298 - 311
34	163 - 167	54	312 - 328
35	168 - 178	55	329 - 336 pt.1
36	179 - 186	56	336 pt.2 - 344
37	187 - 191	57	345 - 348 v.1
38	192 - 196	58	348 v.2 - 351
39	197 - 205	59	352 - 355
40	206 - 212	60	356 - 363
41	213 - 224	61	364 - 370 v.1
42	225	62	370 v.2 - 380
43	226 - 228	63	381 - 385
44	229 - 235	64	386 - 391
45	236 - 246	65	392 - 396
46	247 - 251	66	397 - 400
47	252 - 261	67	401 - 406
48	262 - 274	68	407 - 419
49	275 - 279	69	420 - 424
50	280 - 285 v.1	70	425 - 432

REEL	NUMBERS	REEL	NUMBERS
71	433 - 443	91	583 pt.3 - 589 pt.1
72	444 - 449	92	589 pt.2 - 592
73	450 - 462	93	593 - 599
74	463 - 472 pt.2	94	600 - 612
75	472 pt.3 - 480	95	613 - 619
76	481 - 483	96	620 - 622
77	484 - 489	97	623
78	490 - 495	98	624 - 628
79	496 - 505	99	629 - 635
80	506 - 513	100	636 - 637
81	514 - 518	101	638 - 643
82	519 - 527	102	644 - 648 v.1
83	528 - 535	103	648 v.2 - 653
84	536 - 541	104	654 - 662
85	542 - 545	105	663 - 668
86	546 - 554	106	669 - 671
87	555 - 564	107	672 - 673
88	565 - 573	108	674 - 678
89	574 - 579	109	679 - 682 pt.3
90	580 - 583 pt.2	110	682 pt.4 - 690

REEL	NUMBERS	REEL	NUMBERS
111	691 - 697	131	829 - 831
112	698 - 707	132	832 v.4 - 832 v.8
113	708 - 712	133	833 - 840
114	713 - 721	134	841 - 844
115	722 - 731	135	845 - 851
116	732 - 738	136	852 - 853 v.3
117	739 - 744 pt.1	137	853 v.4 - 860
118	744 pt.2 - 747	138	861 - 875
119	748 - 754	139	876 - 883
120	755 - 763	140	884 - 895
121	764 - 766 v.2	141	896 - 904
122	766 v.3 - 772	142	905 - 915
123	773 - 780	143	916 - 920
124	781 - 786	144	921 - 932
125	787 - 791	145	933 - 939 pt.1
126	792 - 800	146	939 pt.2 - 944 pt.1
127	801 - 808 v.1	147	944 pt.2 - 956
128	808 v.2 - 813	148	957 - 961
129	814 - 821	149	962 - 966
130	822 - 828	150	967 - 974

REEL	NUMBERS	REEL	NUMBERS
151	975 - 986	171	1109 - 1115
152	987 - 1005	172	1116 - 1130
153	1006 - 1018 v.2	173	1131 - 1142
154	1018 v.3 - 1020	174	1142 v.1 - 1142 v.2
155	1021 - 1023 v.2	175	1143 - 1146
156	1023 v.3 - 1027	176	1147 - 1152
157	1028 pt.1 - 1033	177	1153 - 1156
158	1034 - 1037	178	1157 - 1164
159	1038 - 1045	179	1165 - 1167 v.1
160	1046 - 1051	180	1167 v.2
161	1052 - 1055	181	1167 v.3
162	1056 - 1064	182	1167 v.4 - 1173
163	1065 - 1072	183	1174 - 1178 v.2
164	1073 - 1076	184	1178 v.3 - 1184
165	1077 v.1 - 1077 v.3	185	1185 - 1194
166	1078 - 1086	186	1195 - 1199
167	1087 - 1089 v.1	187	1200 - 1208
168	1089 v.2 - 1091	188	1209 - 1216
169	1092 - 1098	189	1217 - 1222
170	1099 - 1108	190	1223 - 1231

REEL	NUMBERS
191	1232 - 1238
192	1239 - 1240 v.1
193	1240 v.2 - 1240 v.3
194	1241 - 1249
195	1250 - 1258
196	1259 - 1268
197	1269 - 1283
198	1284 v.1 - 1284 v.2
199	1285 v.1-3
200	1285 v.4-5
201	1285 v.6 - 1293
202	1294 - 1300
203	1301 v.1 - 1301 v.4
204	1301 v.5 - 1301 v.7